Library of
Davidson College

Epigrams from the Anthologia Latina

Epigrams from the
ANTHOLOGIA LATINA

Text, translation and commentary

N.M. Kay

Duckworth

First published in 2006 by
Gerald Duckworth & Co. Ltd.
90-93 Cowcross Street, London EC1M 6BF
Tel: 020 7490 7300
Fax: 020 7490 0080
inquiries@duckworth-publishers.co.uk
www.ducknet.co.uk

© 2006 by N.M. Kay

All rights reserved. No part of this publication
may be reproduced, stored in a retrieval system, or
transmitted, in any form or by any means, electronic,
mechanical, photocopying, recording or otherwise,
without the prior permission of the publisher.

A catalogue record for this book is available
from the British Library

ISBN 0 7156 3406 2

Typeset by Ray Davies
Printed and bound in Great Britain by
CPI Bath

Contents

Preface	vii
Introduction	1
Select Bibliography	27
Concordance Between Editions	35

ANTHOLOGIA LATINA

Text	39
Commentary	65
Index of Names and Places	377
Index of Authors and Works	379
Index of Latin Words	381
General Index	385

Preface

I became intrigued by the shorter poems of the *Anthologia Latina* in the course of work on the epigrams of Martial and Ausonius. Since, at least comparatively speaking, little has been written about them, they seemed a good subject for closer investigation. Admittedly they carried a reputation of the lowest of the low as literature, but at least it was easy to alight upon a suitable and continuous section for study. *AL* 78 is an introductory poem to something, and it has long been suggested that it introduces the ensuing sequence of short poems in the Codex Salmasianus which continues until *AL* 188, a sequence of just the right length for an edition and commentary. In my own view at any rate, I have been fortunate in this choice: the epigrams are of much higher quality than I expected, they are varied in content and language, and nearly all of them raise issues which adequately repay examination. They have not bored me, and they still do not; I will be pleased if I have done them justice in this book.

Three friends, Jim Adams, Peter Howell and Michael Reeve, have criticised the whole of the work in draft, and it is the third lengthy publication of mine for which they have generously undertaken this task. I am immensely indebted to them: as with my two previous commentaries, almost every page of this one has benefited significantly from their comments and advice. This has gone far beyond the removal of errors and imprecise language; they have often suggested more convincing solutions to awkward problems, and they have often posed new or more pertinent questions (the selection and formulation of which is the main challenge for a commentator). I emphasise their contribution here, because in what follows I have usually made no acknowledgement of it, except where textual emendation is concerned; my inadequate excuse can only be that this reduces the length of an already long book. Remaining errors are of course my responsibility: 'si placet commune est, si displicet nostrum'. In addition I am grateful to Richard Miles for advance sight of an article of his which is due to appear in *Antiquité tardive*.

This is also the third occasion on which Deborah Blake and Ray Davies of Duckworth have seen a commentary of mine through to publication; the very nature of such books, festooned with italics, brackets, inverted commas, references, quotations, abbreviations and a variety of languages, must make them troublesome beyond the normal. That I have never been aware of that is due to their professional efficiency and helpfulness, for which I thank them.

Most unfortunately two recent books by L. Zurli appeared too late for me to acknowledge or refer to them in this work. They are 'Apographa Salmasiana: Sulla trasmissione di *"Anthologia Salmasiana"* tra sei e settecento', *Spudasmata* 96.2004, and 'Unius poetae sylloge: Verso un' edizione di *Anthologia Latina* cc 90-197 Riese^2 = 78-188 Shackleton Bailey', *Spudasmata* 105.2005.

London N.M.K.
September 2005

1

Introduction

(A) Are *AL* 78-188 a collection written by a single author?

Rudolf Peiper (*RhM* 31.1876.183 f.) suggested that the prefatory poem 90R (78 in Shackleton Bailey's edition: for the numeration of *AL* in this commentary see p. 25) stands as the preface to 90-197R (78-188), and the unity of this sequence of epigrams as a collection has been upheld subsequently, with no seriously dissenting voices: e.g. Riese in his app. crit. to 90R '*Praefatio pertinet ad c. 90-197, ni fallor*'; Shackleton Bailey in his app. crit. to 78 '*Haec ad cc. 79-188, unius poetae opus, pertinere videntur*'; W. Schetter, *Gnomon* 58.1986.300 f.; and there are some further references at Lausberg, *Einzeldistichon*, 611 n. 23. This raises two questions: (a) whether 78-188 are a collection, and (b), if so, in what sense they are a collection. The extremes of the spectrum are, on the one hand, a sequence of epigrams which are largely unrelated to each other and are not the work of a single author or the product of one time and place, and, on the other, a book of epigrams in the Martialian sense, arranged by their author as a *libellus* essentially in the form and sequence in which they appear in the Codex Salmasianus (on which see pp. 13 f. and 16 f.) and thereby in modern editions of the *AL*. Other possibilities lie between these extremes: for instance the collection might be the work of a single poet which he did not issue in book form, but the various components of which were gathered by someone after his death (this would be akin to the likely genesis of the collection of Ausonius' epigrams, on which see my commentary pp. 11 f.; 142; 296 f.), or the collection might contain the work of a small number of authors, collected together by someone because they originated from much the same time and place. The following points are relevant to these issues:

(1) The prefatory poem 78, in which the reader is told that 'hoc opus' includes the author's juvenilia ('parvula quod lusit, sensit quod iunior aetas'), and is invited to excerpt for his reading 'quod placeat', is a typical epigrammatic programme piece (see 78 intro.), and of itself implies that it was originally followed by a collection of epigrams which are the work of a single author and were intended to be read as a book. Whether what

now follows it is the essence of that book may be another matter, but it is a reasonable hypothesis to put to the test.

(2) The arrangement and taxonomy of the material in the Codex Salmasianus is succinctly described by R.G. Tarrant (*Texts and Transmission*, 10) in these words: 'the principle of affiliation is either that of form (e.g. Virgilian centos make up items 7-18[R]) or of common authorship (e.g. 287-375[R] are poems of Luxorius); some components retain their original preface (19, 20, 286, 287[R])'. Another collection by a single author is the *Aenigmata* of Symphosius (281), a work which consists of a 'praefatio' followed by a series of one hundred three-line riddles in verse. This practice of selection helps the hypothesis that 78 is the preface to what follows, and that it introduces a collection of epigrams transferred essentially en bloc to the Codex Salmasianus. There is additional supporting evidence: the scribe of the Salmasianus annotated his ms., inter alia, with references to 'Libri' which in some way comprised it. They are of differing length, and unfortunately the annotations are sometimes omitted; but Riese's reconstruction of the sequence (for which see further p. 17) plausibly assigns the whole of 'Liber XIV' to the present collection, which is another reason to regard it as a unity.

(3) There is however no epigram which indicates or suggests the closure of a book, and therefore 188 is an arbitrary and unconfirmed terminus to the collection. It is chosen because it is the last poem in the sequence beginning with 78 which is reasonably short and epigrammatic in character (189 is the 89-line '*Verba Achillis in Parthenone*'). However, the Luxorius sequence also does not have a poem to indicate closure (it ends at 370), and neither do Symphosius' *Aenigmata*. It is unlikely that a collection of pieces issued as a book by their author would have lacked a closure poem or sequence of poems, but it is less unlikely that the compiler of a florilegium like the Codex Salmasianus would have omitted it or them, simply because his anthology had not ended at that point.

(4) The length of the suggested book, with over a hundred epigrams comprising over 650 lines in total, is plausible for a collection; thus each of Martial's books I-XII contains around a hundred epigrams, and Book IV, for example, has 669 lines (see Grewing's commentary on Mart. VI, p. 24 n. 32); Luxorius, in the sequence beginning at *AL* 282, offers nearly ninety epigrams with a total of over 750 lines.

(5) The suggested book has a variety of types of epigram, metre and length which makes for a balanced collection as a whole: there are a good number of epideictic or descriptive pieces, both on objects (83-4 and 175 (candles and lamps); 90 (a sedan); 122-4 (apples); 125 (a *gillo*); 128 (a celestial globe?); 139 (a painting); 141-3 (decorated silver); 147 (a portrait

Introduction

of Vergil); 158-60 (citrons); 161-3 (statues); 165-6 (a stuffed goose); 182-5 (a game of *tabula*)), and on animals or persons (93 (an ant); 95 (a goose); 96 (a cuttlefish); 97-8 (a eunuch); 100 (a pantomime); 101 (a funambulist); 102-03 (a citharode); 104 (pyrrhic dancers); 121 (a cockerel); 176-8 (goats); and 186-7 (an elephant)); there are skoptic or satirical pieces (85 (a schoolmaster); 92 (a miller); 116 (a *leno maritus*); 117 (a pimp); 118 (a homosexual); 119 (a woman named Caballina); 120 (a poet); 126-7 (a man with a hernia); 137-8 (a lawyer with a penchant for bestiality); 145 (a wife-beaten warrior); 148 (a doctor's pupil); 172-3 (a black man); and 180-1 (a dwarf)); there are inscriptional pieces on baths and bathing (99; 108-14; 164; and 168-9), and epigrams about other buildings (89 and 115); there are epigrams on mythological themes, some of which are ecphrastic in describing works of art (86-8; 91; 94; 107; 130-36; 140; 150-57; 161-3; 167; 170; 174; and 179); and there is an assortment of other genres (80 and 82 (*tituli* from churches); 81 (an epitaph); 105-6 (praises of seasons and months); 144 (a historical piece about Mucius Scaevola); 146 (a sympotic piece); 149 (a *historiola*); 171 (the picaresque death of a cat); and 188 (an allegorical interpretation of the circus and chariot-racing)). For the fairly limited variety of metres used see p. 22, though the analysis shows that such variety as there is is distributed throughout the collection; and for the variation in length, from sixteen single-distich epigrams through the range to two pieces of twenty lines or more (106; 188), see the statistical analysis and comparison with Luxorius' collection at Lausberg, *Einzeldistichon*, 474 f. Although such variety does not prove the existence of a unified collection, it can reasonably be adduced to support it.

(6) There is some evidence of the deliberate placing together of epigrams in the suggested book: thus 80-4 have specifically Christian or Church themes; there are extended sequences of pieces on mythological topics (86-8; 130-6; 150-7), on bathing establishments (108-14), on the performing arts (100-4), on the nymph Galatea (140-3), on apples (122-4), on citrons (158-60), on goats and vines (176-8), and on the game of *tabula* (182-5); there are complementary pairs of epigrams (97-8 (a eunuch); 126-7 (man with a hernia); 137-8 (bestiality and the lawyer); 165-6 (a stuffed goose); 168-9 (Vita's baths); 172-3 (a black man); 180-1 (Bumbulus the dwarf); 186-7 (an elephant); and possibly 92-3 (aspects of the grain harvest)). On the other hand variety is maintained with sequences being split up by interposed, unrelated pieces (e.g. the lone mythological epigrams which occur at intervals throughout the collection: 91; 94; 107; 140; 167; 170; 174; 179). Again there is nothing in this which is conclusive (such as, for example, a definite cycle of skoptic epigrams which punctuate a book in the manner of Martial's on the freedman Zoilus (see my intro. to Mart. 11.12)), but the fact that it affords the architecture for an attractively varied collection weighs with other factors to support the existence of such a collection.

(7) There are some favourite modes of expression and favourite words which occur throughout the collection, which are not simply the result of frequent subjects such as bathing establishments, and which suggest that the pen of a single author might be responsible: thus, for example, there is a fascination with objects which can be described as enclosing other objects within them (see 90.1 n.) and with items which have a dual function or bestow dual benefits (108.5 n.); objects are often praised in a way which is tantamount to marketing or advertising (90 intro.); there is a marked tendency to avoid repetition of nouns by the use of synonyms, not always successfully (81.5 n.); some words are frequently used, such as e.g. *proprius* in the sense *tuus / suus* (120.4 n.), *sacer* (138.2 n.), *sollers* (168.1 n.), *varius* (169.4 n.) and *pignus* in the sense 'child' (91.4 n.); and there is a fondness for the prefix '*dis-*' (130.2 n.).

(8) A theory which has been advanced about the inscriptional epigrams in the collection (especially the 'bath' epigrams detailed in (5) above, but also e.g. 80-2) and which would tell against unity of authorship of the collection, though not necessarily against the existence of the collection as an entity, is that these poems were written down from actual inscriptions in situ and then found their way into this sequence (thus e.g. E. Courtney, *Hermathena* 129.1980.37 f.). However, it is equally possible that they could have been written for inscription and were also issued as part of a published book by their author (compare, for example, the similar sequence of inscriptional bath poems at *AL* 201-5, which is attributed by the Codex Salmasianus to its author, 'Felix, vir clarissimus'). If the evidence overall suggests that 78-188 constitute a collection, it seems improbable that an author would insert epigrams he had culled from inscriptions randomly amongst his own work.

(9) The mixture of Christian and pagan elements in the collection also merits discussion. In fact the Christian element is not strong, being confined almost exclusively to 80-4; the question whether these appositely follow the prefatory piece advertising light verse is discussed at 80 intro. Similarly, the long poem which is the last in the collection, an allegorical interpretation of the circus in pagan terms, might be thought a strange note on which to end it, but it is argued above that the end epigram(s) of the collection may be missing (see 3). However, the cohabitation of Christian and pagan elements in the collection is not a major concern: Ausonius is only one author who provides a good precedent (see my commentary on the Epigrams, p. 24).

(10) Although there is and can be no definite proof that the epigrams were all written in much the same place at much the same time, there is no evidence to the contrary, and such evidence as there is ties in with a date of around AD 500 or later and a North African location (e.g. Carthage):

Introduction

these issues are considered in detail immediately below. Again, taken in conjunction with the other factors, this tends to support the hypothesis that the sequence 78-188 belongs together as a collection.

The conclusion I draw from the above is that 78-188 almost certainly do constitute an epigram collection and that it is likely to have been written and arranged by a single author; in essence it was a *libellus* like a book of Martial. It is not complete as it has been transmitted, but it may be defective only in a small way (e.g. in the absence of a conclusion to the collection as a whole, and in the absence of those epigrams which superscriptions show to be missing (114 and 129)). This general conclusion is hereafter assumed throughout the commentary, though it is further tested at relevant points; I refer throughout to the work by the neutral term 'collection'.

(B) The date of composition and place of origin of the collection

The above analysis points towards the conclusion that 78-188 form a collection of epigrams and are probably the work of a single author, but the hypothesis needs to be further tested or corroborated by evidence relating to the date of composition and place of origin of the poems. W. Schetter (*Gnomon* 58.1986.300 f.) has suggested a date of the early sixth century with Vandal North Africa as the place of origin, and I use this as a starting hypothesis for the analysis below. The following points are relevant:

(1) There is little local detail in the epigrams, but what there is either does not contradict or supports a likely North African genesis. The town of Vita, in modern Tunisia, is mentioned at 138.3 (see note), the bad poet of 120 is said in its superscription to be from the tribe of the Arzyges, who inhabited modern southern Tunisia (see note ad loc.), and the black man of 172-3 is of the Garamantes, a tribe which lived in modern southern Libya (see 173.1 n.); the lacklustre warrior of 145 aspires to kinship with Barbatus and Varitinna, the latter of whom may be a divinity of native North African origin (see 145.1 and 2 nn.); Cumae is said to be an ocean journey away from the location of the baths in 110; the play on the title 'comes utriusque militiae' at 117.12 would have had particular resonance for a North African audience (see note); and in 172 intro. it is tentatively suggested that the 'Aegyptius' of the epigram may be identified with the 'Aegyptius' of *AL* 288 Luxorius.

(2) There is even less reference or allusion to contemporary historical events attested elsewhere, though that is not surprising in a collection of epigrams. However, 89 is an interesting piece which apparently describes

the re-use of stones from a ransacked temple of Venus to form part of a city's walls; this ties in well with what is known about the repair of the walls of Carthage, built only in 425 and repaired later in the fifth century or early in the sixth, possibly as late as 533-4 (see 89 intro.). There is unfortunately in the collection no mention of or allusion to the Vandal kings of North Africa, as there is in Luxorius (Hilderic at 194.1) or Felix (Thrasamund at 201.7, 202.3 etc.) or Florentinus (Thrasamund at 371.2); however, this need only signify (for example) that the poet of the present collection was not patronised by royalty, or that the relevant pieces have not survived as part of the collection (there is also no sign of a literary dedicatee for the collection, such as Luxorius' Faustus at 282.3), or that the collection post-dates the Vandal period (see p. 7).

(3) Some of the concerns and pre-occupations of everyday life which are evidenced by the epigrams tie in well with what is known of Vandal North Africa (which is not to say that they would be inappropriate elsewhere): for example, 99 features praise of land reclamation and the putting to good use of land in urban contexts, which is a theme shared by other Vandal poets in the *AL* such as Luxorius (see 99.3 n.); bathing and baths are a prominent theme of the collection, and this Roman legacy remained a strong favourite under the Vandals (see 99 intro.); high-class bathing establishments are referred to as 'baiae', a usage probably limited to North Africa (see 99.1 n.); and the circus and chariot-racing retained their popularity in Vandal North Africa (see 188 intro.).

(4) The evidence of literary influence on or by the epigrams in the collection, although it is limited, is supportive of a date of composition around AD 500 or later and a North African provenance (to be useful as such evidence only the interaction with late authors is relevant). For example:
  (i) 99 seems to display knowledge of *AL* 201 Felix, and to be structurally based upon it (see 99 intro.). *AL* 201 can be securely dated to late Vandal North Africa because it refers to Thrasamund, who ruled from 496 to 523. So if the interrelationship is correctly detected, 99 must date to that reign or later.
  (ii) 171 shares an unusual subject with *AL* 370 Luxorius, that of a cat killed by eating prey too large for it, and it is likely that one author influenced the other, particularly since they both use the rare noun *cattus* for 'cat' and the noun *sorex* in the rare meaning 'mouse'. It is more likely that Luxorius was the model, because his piece is much briefer and less thoroughly worked (Luxorius is connected with the rule of Hilderic (523-30)). Other possible interactions with Luxorius are between 120 and *AL* 311 (which are both attacks on a bad poet and, significantly, both in the lesser asclepiad metre, the only occasion in this collection when a metre other than elegiac distich, dactylic hexameter or hendecasyllable is employed); and between 78 and Luxorius' prefatory pieces, where there

Introduction

is similarity of themes (see 78 intro.). In these cases the precedence is impossible to establish, but if Luxorius was the model for 171, he may have been in these too.

(iii) There appear to be at least three close verbal similarities with the poems of Dracontius (whose floruit, since he is known to have been imprisoned by Gunthamund, was around 490: D.F. Bright (*C&M* 50.1999.193 f.) offers a tentative chronology of his works). These are 91.3 'mater vivo viduata marito' and Drac. *Orest.* 431 'incolumi viduata marito'; 91.6 and Drac. *Rom.* 10.530 f. (see 91.6 n.); and 187.6 'humanis veniunt usibus apta suis' and Drac. *Laud. Dei* 1.580 'usibus humanis data sunt haec cuncta venire'. Again it is difficult to establish precedence, but there is no reason why Dracontius cannot be the model (though note the remarks of E. Courtney (*Hermathena* 129.1980.42 f.; *CPh* 79.1984.309 f.) on the relationship between Dracontius and the poets of the *AL*; he suggests, for example, that 91 is the model for Dracontius' echoes).

(5) The evidence of metre (see p. 23) also supports a date of composition in late Antiquity.

In summary, all the above tests at least do not contradict the hypothesis that the collection belongs to the Vandal Africa of the sixth century, and some evidence positively supports it (it can equally be argued that no time or place suits better). It might even be conceivable that it belongs to the early days of the post-Vandalic period, though such a theory would have to be accommodated to the questions over the genesis of the Codex Salmasianus and the political, linguistic and cultural landscape of the area after Belisarius' reconquest (see p. 11 f.). Whether the author was a Vandal (though he certainly displays no knowledge of the Vandal language), a Romano-African descended from the pre-Vandalic population, a Latin-speaking immigrant to Africa, or even from some other background is not possible to determine, but in what follows in this introduction the distinctly Roman and Latin character of Vandal-African life and culture will be emphasised, a cultural milieu strongly evidenced by the author of this collection.

(C) Vandal Africa: the historical and literary context

The Vandals invaded North Africa after they were driven out of Spain by the armies of the western empire in 429; they worked their way across North Africa from west to east over the following decade until they took and occupied Carthage in 439, when it became their capital. They were governed by a succession of kings: Geiseric (428-77); Huneric, Geiseric's eldest son (477-84); Gunthamund, Geiseric's grandson (484-96); Thrasamund, Geiseric's grandson (496-523); Hilderic, Geiseric's grandson (523-30); and Gelamir, Geiseric's great-grandson (530-3). In

533 their kingdom was invaded by the army of the eastern empire under Justinian's general Belisarius, and occupation of and rule over North Africa passed to the Byzantines (for a general treatment of the period see J.H.W.G. Liebeschuetz, 'Gens into Regnum: The Vandals', in *Regna and Gentes: The Relationship between Late Antique and Early Medieval Peoples and Kingdoms in the Transformation of the Roman World*, ed. H.W. Goetz, J. Jarnut and W. Pohl, Leiden 2003, 55 f.).

A key point for the understanding of the present collection of epigrams as a product of the period of Vandal rule is the contact with the Roman empire, both west and east, which was part and parcel of the Vandal occupation of North Africa. It is true that there were frequent military clashes, especially under the rule of Geiseric: the Vandals at various times took and occupied Sicily, Sardinia and Corsica, and they sacked Rome in 455; then in the latter part of the fifth century they in turn became weakened by the insurgency of native North African peoples until their final defeat by Belisarius. But their century-long dominance of North Africa was equally underpinned by more peaceful contacts: this shows itself not only in the treaties which maintained a sometimes fragile peace (with the west in 435, 442 and 472, and with the east in 476), but also in dynastic intermarriage (Huneric married Eudocia, daughter of Valentinian III, around 456 (Proc. *Bell. Vand.* 1.5.6), and Thrasamund married Amalafrida, the sister of Theoderic the Ostrogothic ruler of Italy, around 500 (ibid. 1.8.11)), and personal friendships (Procopius stresses the closeness between Huneric and Justinian for example (*Bell. Vand.* 1.9.5); Huneric had been a hostage in the 440s at the court of Valentinian III (ibid. 1.4.13 f.); and Thrasamund was close to Anastasius (ibid. 1.8.14)). Even the honorific titles of the aristocracy under Vandal rule mirrored those of the Roman west (see Vict. Vit. 3.3 f.; *CAH* 14.554 f.): for instance Flavius Felix is a 'vir clarissimus' (*AL* 201, 248), as is Coronatus (214; 218; 220), and Luxorius is a 'vir clarissimus et spectabilis' (282). Moreover, although the Vandals naturally appropriated some of the best lands and estates for themselves, and a part of the old Roman aristocracy emigrated (Proc. *Bell. Vand.* 1.5.11 f.; Vict. Vit. 1.12 f.), plenty of it seems to have remained behind to continue a life which in many respects would have been similar to that it lived before; certainly the outward trappings of baths, circuses, hunting and gambling remained and were enthusiastically taken up by the Vandals (see intros to 99, 182-5 and 188). Silver coinage affords a particularly interesting example: some coins, probably issued in the second half of the fifth century, were minted in the name of Honorius, an emperor who had been dead for at least twenty-five years, and they also bore the legend 'Urbs Roma'; the precise reasons for this are unclear, but one obvious and intentional impact is to emphasise the tie to Rome (see C. Morrisson and J.H. Schwartz, 'Vandal silver coinage in the name of Honorius', *American Numismatic Society Museum Notes* 27.1982.149 f.; esp. 175 f.; C. Morrisson, *AntTard* 11.2003.69 f.). The official language

Introduction

and literary culture of Vandal Africa remained Latin, as is shown by the extant literature, by inscriptional evidence, and also by the Tablettes Albertini, legal documents of the late fifth century inscribed on wooden tablets, which detail the sale of land and other commercial transactions of an estate on the fringe of the Vandal kingdom, and which are written in Latin, feature persons with largely Latinate names, and are based on Roman law (see C. Courtois, C. Leschi, C. Perrat and C. Saumagne, *Tablettes Albertini: Actes privés de l'époque Vandale*, Paris 1952; Pischel, *Kulturgeschichte*, 75 f.; H. Wessel, 'Das Recht der Tablettes Albertini', *Freiburger Rechtsgeschichtliche Abhandlungen*, N.F. 40, Berlin 2003; J.P. Conant in Merrills, *Vandals*, 199 f.). Some amusing anecdotal evidence given by Victor of Vita (2.55) can also be adduced, in which he describes an incident where the Vandalic and Arian bishop Cyrila was obliged to take part in a debate with Catholics and, since he was bound to lose (implies Victor), mendaciously announced he did not know Latin: 'Cyrila dixit: nescio latine. Nostri episcopi dixerunt: semper te latine esse locutum manifesto novimus ...' (see also Courtois, *Les Vandales*, 221 f.). Religion was however a deep and significant source of friction between the Vandals and the established population, in that the Vandals were Arians and from time to time persecuted the Catholics, who had been dominant in North Africa before them. This was especially so under Geiseric and Huneric, and provides the subject of Victor of Vita's complaints in his *History of the Vandal Persecution* (similarly Isidore, in his *Historia Gothorum, Wandalorum, Sueborum* 74 f. (*MGH AA* 11.2 p. 296 f.)); under Hilderic, however, this persecution abated, and he was regarded as a peaceful leader (Proc. *Bell. Vand.* 1.9.1).

Thus in many respects, and the more so the longer they stayed in North Africa, the Vandals were Romanophiles, and it is in this climate, particularly under the later kings, that there was a thriving literary culture, to which it is argued that the present collection belongs (there is a general treatment by F. Bertini, *Autori latini sotto la dominazione vandalica*, Genoa 1974). As regards poetry, the earliest securely datable example of Latin literature from the Vandal period is a short piece by one Cato extolling a land reclamation scheme of Huneric (*AL* 382); Florentinus (371) and Flavius Felix (201-5; 248) eulogised the works of Thrasamund; Luxorius, the best-represented poet of the period who is named in the *AL*, wrote under Hilderic (194; 282-370); and Coronatus (214; 218; 220) is probably to be identified as also the author of a fragmentary work on grammar addressed to Luxorius (which can most easily be accessed at Rosenblum, *Luxorius*, 259 f.). There are many other poets in the part of the *AL* which derives from the Codex Salmasianus, often represented by a single short work, who are not known from elsewhere, are not securely datable, and cannot be assigned to the Vandalic period with certainty, but it is possible that some, if not most, of them should be (e.g. Avitus (16); Bonosus (274); Calbulus (373); Lindinus (15); Modestinus (267);

Octavianus (7); Petrus (375); Ponnanus (268); Regianus (264 f.); Reposianus (247: his *Concubitus Martis et Veneris* is remarkable in attracting dates from the second to sixth centuries; see *HLL* 247 f.; and E. Courtney, *CPh* 79.1984.309 f., arguing for a Vandalic date, contemporary with Dracontius; Symphosius (281); Tuccianus (271 f.); and Vincentius (273)). The one significant poet whose works do not owe their survival to the mss behind the *AL* is Dracontius, who was imprisoned by Gunthamund, and wrote both secular verse (the *Romulea* and the tragedy *Orestes*) and Christian (the *Satisfactio* and *De Laudibus Dei*); his work was probably known to the poet of the present collection (see p. 7 above). It is also possible that the anonymous *Aegritudo Perdicae*, known only from ms. British Library, Harley 3685, is a work of Vandal Africa (see Bright, *Epic*, 222 f.).

In addition there is a considerable extant body of prose literature dating from this period, much of it ecclesiastical in nature (it should be noted that some of its Catholic authors would have been writing when in exile from North Africa, often in Constantinople: see B. Croke, *Count Marcellinus and His Chronicle*, Oxford 2001, 87 f.). Augustine had died as the Vandals were besieging Hippo in 430, and a life of him was written by Possidius, bishop of Calama, before he was driven out of his see by the Vandals in 437 and not heard of again (see H.T. Weiskotten, *Sancti Augustini Vita Scripta a Possidio Episcopo*, Princeton 1919). Christian writing by Antoninus Honoratus of Constantine, exiled by Geiseric in the 430s, (*PL* 50.567 f.), Vigilius of Thapsa, floruit c. 480, (*PL* 62.93 f.) and St. Eugenius, Bishop of Carthage from 480 to 505, (*PL* 58.767 f.) also survives, as do some anonymous texts (*Florilegia Biblica Africana Saec. V*, ed. B. Schwank et al., *CCSL* 90.1961). Victor of Vita's history has already been mentioned and, since it concentrates on events under Huneric and later, it must belong to the closing years of the fifth century (see C. Courtois, *Victor de Vita et son oeuvre*, Algiers 1954). Many works by Fulgentius of Ruspe, bishop and saint (467-532), are extant (ed. J. Fraipont, *CCSL* 91 / 91A.1968); but he is probably not to be identified with Fulgentius, author of allegorical *mythologiae* and an allegorical interpretation of the *Aeneid*, who, it has recently been argued on the strength of an apparent allusion by him to Corippus (*Myth*. 1.24 line 2 and *Cor. Joh.* 8.279), worked in post-Vandal Africa (see G. Hays in Merrills, *Vandals*, 101 f.; also *Neue Pauly* 4.699 f.). And Ferrandus, who wrote an important life of St. Fulgentius (*PL* 65.117 f.), belongs to the end of the Vandalic period and beyond, since he died about 546-7. Of authors of non-ecclesiastical prose, Cassius Felix wrote his *De Medicina* in 447 (see 148 intro.); Martianus Capella probably wrote in Carthage around the 470s, though his date is disputed and he may even be pre-Vandalic (see D. Shanzer, *A Philosophical and Literary Commentary on Martianus Capella's De Nuptiis Philologiae et Mercurii Book I*, Berkeley and Los Angeles 1986, 5 f.; B. Baldwin, *MLatJb* 23.1988.309 f.; and, arguing for the earlier date, A. Cameron, *CPh* 81.1986.320 f.); and the grammarian Priscian (fl. 500) was born in Mauretania though he spent most of his working life in Constantinople.

One conclusion to be drawn from this brief survey is that it places most literary activity in the years of Vandal rule after Geiseric and Huneric, essentially from the 480s to the end in 533; this ties in well with the other evidence relating to the date and place of the present collection (see p. 5 f.). It should however be borne in mind, as is prima facie likely and has already been adumbrated above, that literary activity in Latin did not cease on the day the Vandals were ousted from North Africa by the Byzantines. The most illustrious example of this continuation is Flavius Cresconius Corippus, whose eight-book epic poem *Johannis*, describing the defeat of the Mauri by the *magister militum* John Troglita in 546-8, was composed around 550 and was recited by its author before the leading citizens of Carthage (*praef.* 1 f.); his later poem *In laudem Justini* was written in Constantinople around 565 in honour of Justinian's successor Justin II (see Averil Cameron, *Changing Cultures*, Paper VII, 12 f.; Paper IX, passim). The other extant Latin writing of this period is largely ecclesiastical prose and is concentrated in the two or three decades after the Vandal defeat, much of it being generated during the Three Chapters dispute, which centred on the Christological arguments between Monophysites and Chalcedonians over the divine / human nature of Christ, though it really had as much to do with the balance between the authority of the emperor and the church in religious affairs. It was the central issue of the Fifth Ecumenical Council of the Church held in Constantinople in 553, and the African bishops were opposed to what they viewed as the pro-Monophysite position of Justinian, who was unsuccessfully attempting to reconcile the two camps. These bishops would have been brought up in North Africa under the Vandals as Latin speakers as well as writers. They include Verecundus of Iunca (or Iunci), who died in 552, and wrote both a 212-line hexameter poem entitled *De satisfactione paenitentiae*, and a prose commentary on the Biblical *Cantica* (ed. R. Demeulenaere, *CCSL* 93.1976); Victor of Tunnuna, who wrote a prose chronicle containing brief annual entries, the years 444-567 being extant (ed. C. Cardelle de Hartmann, *CCSL* 173A.2001); Facundus of Hermiane, who around 550 wrote a twelve-book *Pro defensione trium capitulorum ad Iustinianum* and an *Epistula fidei catholicae in defensione trium capitulorum* (ed. J.-M. Clément and R. Vander Plaetse, *CCSL* 90A.1974); Primasius of Hadrumetum, who wrote, inter alia, a commentary on Revelation (ed. A.W. Adams, *CCSL* 92.1985); Pontianus, of see unknown, who wrote a short letter to Justinian concerning the Three Chapters controversy (*PL* 67.995 f.); Junillus, who was the author of an introduction to the Bible entitled *Instituta regularia divinae legis*, written around 542, after he had emigrated to Constantinople (ed. with useful introduction and bibliography by M. Maas, *Exegesis and Empire in the Early Byzantine Mediterranean*, Tübingen 2003); and Liberatus of Carthage, who wrote in the 560s a *Breviarium* explaining the principles of Monophysites and Nestorians (*PL* 68.963 f.), which was compiled from material translated from Greek into Latin to make it available to his African colleagues (ibid., 969). Funerary inscriptions also continued to be written in Latin (for these see Averil Cameron, *Changing Cultures*, Paper X, 155 n. 6). This Latin literary activity in the decades immediately after the Byzantine reconquest is significant for the dating of the composition of the present collection as well as for the dating of the assembly of the anthology of the Codex Salmasianus (see p. 17), since it demonstrates that 533-4 need not be a terminus ante quem for either on grounds of language and culture; as might be expected, the Byzantine reconquest did not put an immediate stop to writing in Latin in North Africa, and it took some decades for Greek to become dominant as the literary language (see Averil Cameron, *Changing Cultures*, Paper VIII, 179 f.).

It is worth briefly examining the cultural and literary context of the present collection in wider terms. Carthage had long been renowned for its schools and centres of learning (cf. Salv. *De Gub. Dei* 7.68: 'illic enim omnia officiorum publicorum instrumenta, illic artium liberalium scholae, illic philosophorum officinae, cuncta denique vel linguarum gymnasia vel morum ...'). According to Florentinus (*AL* 371.32) it was a reputation which continued under the Vandals: 'Carthago studiis, Carthago ornata magistris'. Whether and how well Greek was taught is an interesting question; it seems probable that the language was not widely read, although it would be wrong to assume complete ignorance of it. The evidence is scanty, but there is some: medical writers of the period certainly knew Greek (see 148 intro.); in his life of Fulgentius (*PL* 65.119) Ferrandus says that the saint was raised in Thelepte, where at his mother's request he learned Greek literature prior to Latin; if Martianus Capella belongs to Vandal Africa his work provides clear evidence of his knowledge of Greek (though see the somewhat sceptical comments of P. Courcelle, *Late Latin Writers and their Greek Sources*, trans. H.E. Wedeck, Cambridge Mass. 1969, 221 f.); and contact between the Vandal court and the Eastern empire, which is likely must have involved exchanges in Greek at some levels, has been remarked above (p. 8). However that may be, there is no evidence of any meaningful knowledge of Greek on the part of the author of the present collection; the humour on the etymology of the name Hippocrates at 148.6, and possibly also of the name Bumbulus at 180.2, would hardly require it, and the epigrammatic tradition in which he writes is essentially Latin. His literary pedigree is demonstrably Latin, and, not surprisingly, Vergil is the main influence: 147, about a portrait of Vergil, affords his only explicit reference to any literary figure, and his epigrams often verbally imitate, echo or allude to Vergil's poetry (for certain or probable instances see the notes at 88 intro.; 88.5; 94.3; 95.1; 99.9; 106.11; 158.1; 159.1; 159.4; 163.3; 164.1; 176.1; 177.3; and for

Introduction

possible instances see the notes at 84.4; 87.1; 89.4; 91.5; 93 intro.; 103.8; 120.9; 137.7; 173.3). He quotes a line of Martial (see 116.10 n.; possibly also a phrase at 137.4), and his scoptic pieces, as well as those which describe material objects, are in a direct line of descent from him (see esp. 122 intro.); he also has verbal reminiscences of Catullus (148.6 n.) Horace (120 intro.) and Juvenal (168.5-6 n.; 171.5 n.; and see also 97.5-6 n.), and probable ones of Ennius (151 intro.), Lucretius (87 intro.; 106.5 n.), Ovid (94 intro.) and Seneca (154.2 n.). He also seems to allude to the work of some contemporary Latin writers, and they may allude to his (see p. 6 f. above).

(D) The manuscripts and the transmission of the text

There are four main mss which form the basis of the text of the present collection of epigrams because of the quantity of material they include; there are also a handful of subsidiary mss containing only one or a few epigrams each. I discuss the major ones first, which are all florilegia:

(1) The Codex Salmasianus (A) is the most important because of the number of epigrams it contains (on it see esp. M. Spallone, 'Il Par. Lat. 10318 (Salmasiano). Dal manoscritto altomedievale ad una raccolta enciclopedica tardo-antica', *IMU* 25.1982.1 f.; *Texts and Transmission*, 9 f.; Riese, xii f.; and, for a reduced facsimile reproduction of part of it, H. Omont, *Anthologie de poètes dite de Saumaise*, Paris 1903). It alone has the whole collection, and it is the sole witness to seventy-three of the one hundred and eleven pieces which comprise it (78-84; 88-9; 91; 93-9; 103-4; 108-15; 117; 126-30; 132-3; 135-40; 143; 146-8; 150-69; 175; 179-81; 183-6: three of these numbers represent allegedly missing pieces (79; 114 and 129)). This ms. was written in uncials around AD 800, its place of origin probably being central Italy (see B. Bischoff, *Settimane di studio del centro italiano di studi sull' alto medioevo*, 22, Spoleto 1975, 1.83; M. Spallone, op. cit. 36 f.). Its whereabouts between the date of writing and 1615 are unknown, but in 1615 it was given by Jean Lacurne, bailli of Arnai le Duc, to Claude de Saumaise, from whom it takes its usual name. De Saumaise granted other scholars, such as N. Heinsius and P. Scriverius, the use of it, and their conjectures and comments are quoted as appropriate in this commentary (they are most easily, and for the most part, to be found in Burman's edition, on which see p. 21). On de Saumaise's death in 1653 the ms. passed to his son, and when he in turn died in 1661 it passed to J.B. Lantin of Dijon, in which city it remained until its transfer to the Bibliothèque Nationale in Paris around 1750; it was initially catalogued as 685 Suppl. Lat., and is now Paris lat. 10318.

The Salmasianus is incomplete both at the beginning and the end, and originally consisted of at least thirty-one fascicles, mostly quaternions, of which the first eleven are missing, the extant portion beginning with the one labelled 'XII'; this implies about 176 lost pages. It begins, in the middle of a Vergilian cento, with the 188 pages which form a considerable part of the collection today known as *Anthologia Latina* (thus 6-374 occupy pp. 1-188, with 207 misplaced at pp. 211-2; 375-7 and 378-83 are located at pp. 192-3 and 273-4 respectively). The main verse sequence ends at p. 188 with the colophon 'EPIGRAMATON EXPLI(CIT) FELICITER', and there follows a selection of prose works, which are numbered I to XVIII by the scribe (for a catalogue and description of them see Spallone, op. cit. 21 f.); this prose and poetry split, with the colophon, suggests that the 176 pages missing at the beginning may have contained verse material similar to that remaining, which would represent a total loss of about 5,000 lines.

The state of the text preserved in A cannot be said to be good; there are omissions and errors in plenty (see e.g. 108.8 n.; 183.5 n.), and corruption is sometimes demonstrably deep (e.g. 116.6 f.); however, no other ms. is significantly better overall when texts overlap. Several hands have made corrections or conjectures to A over the years, beginning with the scribe who wrote it and a contemporary or near-contemporary of his, and including Claude de Saumaise and at least two further hands dating to after the re-emergence of the ms. in 1615; Spallone comments that amendments are sometimes attributed by editors to de Saumaise which are not his (see her full treatment at op. cit. 51 f., and also *AAHG* 37.1984.251).

Various apographs of A were made in the years after 1615, and conjectures from these will be cited in the text and commentary which follow. The earliest is Juretus' of pre-1626, now Paris lat. 17904; the most significant is the so-called Schedae Divionenses (Sched.), now part of Heidelberg HS. 46, a copy of an apograph of A made by an unknown scholar between 1661 and 1756, and often preferred to A itself by Burman in his edition; and Heinsius' copy of A (supplemented by Burman), which forms another part of Heidelberg HS. 46, contains his conjectures and suggestions (see L. Zurli, *GIF* 54.2002.133 f., correcting some misconceptions about provenance and authorship).

(2) The second of the four main mss (B) is Paris lat. 8071, which was written in the ninth century (probably the third quarter) in central France, and was once owned by Jacques de Thou, whence its usual name of the Codex Thuaneus (on it see Riese, xxxiv f.; *Texts and Transmission*, 10; and, for date and provenance, B. Bischoff, *Studien und Mitteilungen zur Geschichte des Benediktiner-Ordens*, 92.1981.176; and Bischoff cited by L. Zurli, *RFIC* 129.2001.55 with n. 1). It contains about eighty epigrams now in the *AL*, most of which are also in A (though 385-7 are not), and most of which are also in the same order as that of A. Of the present collection it contains, in order, 85; 87; 90; 100-2; 105-7; [191, the *Pervigilium Veneris*]; 116; 118-25; 134; 141; 145; 149; 170-4; 182; and 187-8. Three displaced epigrams (92, 131 and 142) are located after 246. It is evident from texts such as [Ovid] *Hal.* and Gratt. *Cyn.*, which B preserves in common with

Introduction

the now fragmentary ms. Vienna 277 (s. viii ex., French), that it is a close relative of that ms., and it is a reasonable assumption that it was also a close relative as regards the epigrams in question, which are not extant in Vienna 277. The relationship is often held to be that B is a copy of Vienna 277 (e.g. *Texts and Transmission*, loc. cit.), but O. Zwierlein has argued on the basis of their excerpts from Seneca's tragedies that they are rather siblings (*Prolegomena zu einer kritischen Ausgabe der Tragödien Senecas*, Wiesbaden 1984, 15 f.). B often has errors in common with A (in the present collection 116 is a good example, where the ending of a line is erroneously repeated in consecutive hexameters at lines 5 and 7, and both mss make a similar mess of the beginning of line 6), and it preserves few good readings by itself (though 188.12 'docent' is an instance). It is thus a reasonable inference that A and B are not far removed from a common ancestor.

(3) The third main ms. (W) is Vienna 9401*, which was written c. 1501-3 by Jacopo Sannazaro (on it see *Texts and Transmission*, 10 f.); it is closely allied to B in that it contains virtually the same collection of epigrams (it omits 187) in the same order (there is a useful collation by C. Schenkl at WS 1.1879.59 f., supplemented by L. Zurli, *GIF* 50.1998.211 f.). That it was not however copied from B has been shown by a comparison of their texts of the *Pervigilium Veneris* (E. Valgiglio, 'Sulla tradizione manoscritta del Pervigilium Veneris', *BPEC* 15.1967.115 f.; W, for example, has line 40, which is absent from B). Since Sannazaro was also the discoverer of Vienna 277 it is a plausible inference that W is a copy of it, made when it was complete, and it is a valuable witness because of the number of good readings it alone preserves (e.g., from the present collection, 116.1 Graecule; 118.2 pruriat; 171.9 peremptae; 173.5 atramentatum (?); 174.6 Scyria; 182.4 is; 188.16 quot; it is however possible that some of these could be conjectures by Sannazaro).

(4) The final ms. of the four (V) is Leiden Voss. Lat. Q. 86, dating to the mid-ninth century, and of central French provenance (on it see K.A. de Meyier, *Codices Vossiani Latini II*, Leiden 1975, 197 f.; L. Zurli, *Anthologia Vossiana*, Rome 2001, vii f.); as well as containing the corpus of Senecan and Petronian epigrams and some others which are not in A or B (392-477), it has thirty-nine pieces which are in A, only two of which (144 and 265) are not also in B. Of the present collection it offers, in order, 85; 105-6; 122; 149; 172; 187; [...] 92; 144; [...] 125; 145; 121; 171; [...] 101 and 134 (the bracketed gaps in the sequence contain: sixteen further AL pieces after 187, two after 144, and Mart. 3.75 after 171; the remaining six AL pieces are embedded in some excerpts from Martial). It is a possibility, in respect of this material, that V, like W, may descend from the missing portion of Vienna 277 (thus Tarrant, *Texts and Transmission*, 12), though its radically different ordering of material from that of W suggests a

different parent (as is argued by Courtney, *Hermathena* 129.1980.47 f.). The picture is further complicated by the fact that the scribe of B, at least as regards the excerpts from Martial, seems to have had sight of V and to have had a deliberate policy of adding to its material (see L. Zurli, *RFIC* 129.2001.51 f.), which may suggest that his source was a fuller anthology than that available to the scribe of V.

It is clear from the above that the precise interrelationship between B, V, W and the missing part of Vienna 277 is uncertain, and that A drew on a much wider range of material than any of them. However, a common ancestor of all four major mss is probably not far removed from them, as is intimated by the frequent occasions on which editors emend their common text (from the present collection, and bearing in mind that a common text exists for barely a third of it, note e.g. 106.21 nomine bestie (ABVW) / vomere vertit (Sannazarius); 116.7 derisit retia quidam (ABW), erroneously repeated from 116.5; 173.4 labra (ABW) / larva (Baehrens); 188.3 duodecim annis genas (ABW) / duodenigenas (Heinsius); 188.14 adit (ABW) / adest (Riese); there are further probable examples at 90.2; 100.9; 101.2 and 3; 105.3; 106.1, 10, 11 and 13; 118.1 and 4; 120.9; 122.3; 123.1; 131.2; 182.3; 187.4; and 188.2 and 9; although there is room for dispute over individual items in such a list, the general import is evident). This is a tentative stemma for the four major mss (x, y and z are postulated):

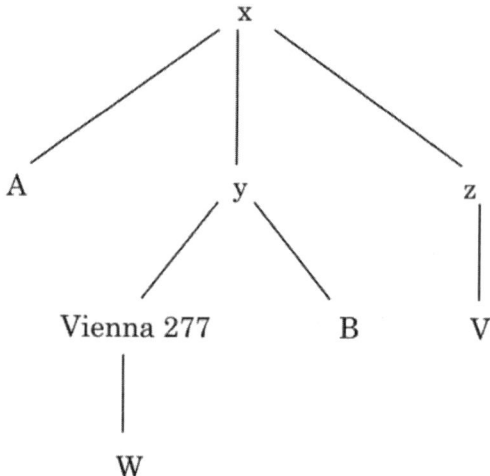

The stemma raises questions about the period of transmission before the appearance of the present collection in A, its earliest extant witness. If ABVW had a common ancestor (x in the diagram) from which A derives and excerpts were made by the parents of BVW (y and z), and if, as is argued above (p. 5 f.), the present collection was written around 500-50, x must date from between about 550 and 750. Although it is not

Introduction

possible to say with certainty what it contained, there are some clues in the way in which the AL portion of A has been annotated by the scribe. He provides two different 'checks' on the material presented: the first is an observation at irregular intervals of the number of poems which appear before the next such observation (thus before 7 he writes 'sunt vero versi CLXXII', and 172 superscriptions follow from there to 191; at 191 is stated 'sunt vero versus XXII', and 22 superscriptions follow until 213 (and it is significant that 207 is absent from A's sequence); at 214 is written 'ursus XXIII', and again 23 superscriptions follow before 248, where 'sunt versus XXXII' gives the number of superscriptions leading to Symphosius' *Aenigmata* at 281; the *Aenigmata* are followed by the final such reference, 'sunt ur' LXXXVII', which precedes the epigrams of Luxorius (282-370), and they have that number of superscriptions). It seems reasonably clear that these annotations relate to the contents of A itself, and not to any external source, because the number of superscriptions is exact, whilst one epigram at least is out of sequence (207), and the superscriptions themselves suggest there are other missing epigrams which also are not included in the count (see my intros to 113-14 and 129-30). This implies that the scribe was making a running total of the pieces he had written in A. But the other type of annotation of this kind which punctuates the whole *AL* collection appears not to relate to the contents of A, but to things outside it. These annotations refer to 'Libri', and they are obviously not complete; those that are extant refer to 'Books' as follows (mostly with an 'incipit', but on one occasion (XVI) with an 'explicit'): VIII (at 8), X (at 69), XI (at 70), XII (at 71), XIII (at 72), XVI (at 191), XX (at 214), and XXI (at 224). Riese (pp. xxi-ii) constructed from this a plausible and generally accepted sequence of twenty-four 'Libri' for A's entire AL section, including the portion now missing from the beginning (he allocates 72-9SB to Liber XIII, 78-188 to XIV, and 189 to XV, which is of relevance in considering the unity of the present collection: see p. 2). Since this sequence of annotations is not complete, and since the Libri it details are of extremely variable length (e.g. the fifteen-line 'De tabula' constitutes the whole of Book XI, whilst seven Libri constitute the more than 220 extant and missing pages of the ms. before 8SB), it is likely that the scribe has copied these annotations of 'Libri' from his source, which might be identified as x, the common ancestor of ABVW. The implication is that at some time an anthology (which might have been x itself) was made from these individual 'Libri', whatever they were and whatever the principle of excerption, but whether that anthology dates from the years immediately following the reconquest of Vandal Africa (i.e. shortly after the last datable poems in the extant portion of the *AL* section), or was made on the European mainland between say 550 and 750, remains open to debate. Although it is often stated (e.g. Riese pp. xxiv f.) that the North African flavour of the *AL* poetry in ABVW suggests compilation in the sixth century in North Africa, nearly half of what A contained appears to be missing and its existing contents are by no means exclusively North African; so compilation at a later date and in another place is possible. I may as well add here that any hunt to identify a compiler of an ancient *AL* (which has garnered candidates such as the sixteen-year-old Octavianus mentioned in the annotation before *AL* 7 (Baehrens, *PLM* 4.3 f.), and Luxorius or a pupil of his (Riese, p. xxv)), is futile.

I end this section with a short catalogue of significant mss other than the major four which have pieces from the present collection:

(a) Leipzig Rep. I. 4°. 74 (L), dated to s. ix, which contains 86 (see also 149 intro.);
(b) Paris lat. 8069 (C), dated to s. x/xi, which contains 149 and 168.5-6;
(c) Berlin Diezianus B. Sant. 66 (D), dated to s. ix, which has 176-8 (see further 176 intro.);
(d) Paris lat. 9344 (P), dated to s. xi, containing only 171; and
(e) a handful of others, which contain only 149, and are discussed in the commentary thereon.

Mention should also be made of *AL* 147, which appears only in A of the extant mss, but which also features prominently in printed editions of Vergil from the first edition onwards; this epigram was therefore in circulation before the rediscovery of A in 1615, though invariably as a pair of distichs rather than a tetrastich. This also is discussed more fully in the commentary.

(E) The superscriptions of the epigrams

That the superscriptions which now feature in the mss were not (or not all) written by the author of the epigrams they head is strongly suggested by occasional incorrectness or inappropriateness: thus, for example, 167 is headed 'De Pyrrho', but its subject is Achilles, and it has been carelessly labelled from the only name in the text; 168 is entitled 'De balneis cuiusdam pauperis', but the text of the epigram gives the name of the man in question (Vita) and the author would have entitled the piece accordingly, whereas the name has been mistaken for the ordinary noun by the writer of the superscription; 118 is headed 'De Marte cinaedo', but the person in the epigram is unlikely to have been named Mars; 149 boasts a lengthy explanatory superscription, but there is reason to doubt its accuracy; and so on (see further commentary ad locc.). On the other hand, the superscriptions have a certain antiquity prior to the dates of the mss, because they appear in all the mss. ABVW for the epigrams they contain, and any differences between them are the result of textual corruption rather than different superscript traditions. Moreover, whilst most of the superscriptions merely state the obvious about the pieces they head, or give 'aliter' where more than one piece deals with the same topic,

Introduction

a limited number of them provide helpful information which is not simply derived from the texts below them. Thus 79 states 'De velo ecclesiae', and the epigram which follows is best understood as a *titulus* embroidered on a fabric hanging in a church; 120 is headed 'De Arzugitano poeta', but the adjective which appositely describes the poet's uncultured origins does not derive from the epigram which follows; and at 122 'De malis Matianis' gives the apples described a species name which the following epigrams do not provide. This all suggests that although the superscriptions are not, or not all, original (in the sense described), they probably derive from a time soon after the collection was put together.

One epigram, however, provides an intriguing piece of evidence which suggests that at least some pieces were intended to have superscriptions when they were first published: this is 172, whose conclusion, on its most likely interpretation, alludes to a name which can only have appeared in its heading (see 172.4 n.; note also 134.2 n.). This serves as a reminder that, although the mss may not now contain original headings, there is no proof that they did not exist. Indeed, the primary function of such headings is to indicate separate epigrams, which is particularly desirable when many short pieces in the same metre occur close together, as is the case with the present collection; and the need to separate one piece from another must have been as necessary when they were first published as it is now. For completeness I add that on a few occasions superscriptions appear to be missing from the mss as they now stand (e.g. 152-5; 156-7; and 161-2: see commentary); on two occasions when they are present their presence suggests that an epigram is missing (114 and 129; see also commentary on 79-80); and on one occasion a superscription may indicate separation erroneously (see 184.1 n.). On this topic generally see B.-J. Schröder, *Titel und Text*, Berlin etc. 1999, with brief treatment of the *AL* at p. 293 f.

Mention should also be made of another type of heading which features at intervals in the *AL* section of the Codex Salmasianus and of which there is a single example in the present collection. This is 'EIUSDEM', which precedes 150: similar examples show that it refers to the authorship of the pieces which it heads, though the previous heading of the type is another 'EIUSDEM' at 77, and the one prior to that is 'FLORI' at 75. Unfortunately these headings are so irregular that it is difficult to give any credence to an isolated 'EIUSDEM', and it would be rash to conclude that Florus was the author of the present collection. Nevertheless their very irregularity is enough to demonstrate that they did not originate with a scribe or annotator of the Codex Salmasianus, and enough to suggest their usefulness if they had survived in a more accurate tradition. Indeed, where authors' names are given in this way there is generally no reason to question them, if only on the grounds that the writers are mostly otherwise unknown (e.g. Lindinus at 15; Regianus at 264; Modestinus at 267; Calbulus at 373 etc.); but caution is always advisable, because on some occasions when authors are well-known and much of their work is extant, attributional headings in the Codex Salmasianus are questionable (e.g. few will believe that Martial wrote 13 or 270 (though he did write 269 (= Mart. 1.57)), or that Vergil had much to do with 250-7).

(F) **Editions which include the present collection**

Anthologia Latina, of which the present collection forms a part, is a modern designation, and derives from P. Burman the Younger's edition and especially his treatise which preceded it, the *Specimen novae editionis Anthologiae Latinae*; these works were published in Amsterdam between 1747 and 1773 and are described more fully below. *Anthologia Latina* was then the title Alexander Riese gave to his two-volume Teubner edition of 1869-70, second edition 1894-1906, which contains poems from manuscript and printed sources (the second part of the Teubner *AL* is also in two volumes and contains F. Bücheler's *Carmina Latina Epigraphica* published in 1895-7, with a supplementary volume by E. Lommatzsch published in 1926; and there is a further supplementary volume to the whole Teubner *AL*, edited by M. Ihm and published in 1895, which contains epigrams by Pope Damasus and related material). Riese's *AL* is comprised largely of short poems most of which had no home elsewhere, but by no means entirely so: it contains such extended pieces as Hosidius Geta's *Medea*, the *Pervigilium Veneris*, the *Iudicium Coci et Pistoris* and others, and a few excerpts from authors such as Vergil, Ovid and Martial which are also part of their established corpus. Some of the material which it includes had first appeared in printed editions of famous authors to whom it could be attributed, and derives largely from Leiden Voss. Lat. Q. 86 (V) or a now lost ms. once in Beauvais (known as S, on which see Riese p. xxxiii f.): thus C. Binet included a series of allegedly Petronian epigrams in his 1579 edition of Petronius (of the present collection only 101, 134, 121, 171, 145 and 137 are included); and G. Fabricius' 1561 edition of Vergil included some pieces with alleged Vergilian connections in the section headed 'Diversorum veterum poetarum in Priapum lusus' (149 and 147 only), as did J.J. Scaliger's *P.V.M. Appendix, cum supplemento multorum antehac nunquam excusorum poematum veterum poetarum*, published in 1572 (149; 144; 147; 106; 105 and 122). In 1590 P. Pithou published his *Epigrammata et poematia vetera, quorum pleraque nunc primum ex antiquis codicibus et lapidibus, alia sparsim antehac errantia, iam undecumque collecta emendatiora eduntur*, which includes much material from the Codex Thuaneus ((B); of the pieces in B from the present collection, only 116 and 118-19, which are obscene, and 131 are not included; he had also had sight of V (see W. Schetter, *Hermes* 111.1983.363 f.), from which he took 144, the only piece from this collection in his edition which is not in B). Pithou's is the first edition which bears any resemblance to what is now the *AL*, though he arranged his selection

Introduction

in four books (entitled 'Ad sacra et mores pertinent'; 'Elegia'; 'Epitaphia'; and 'Miscellanea et amissa'), and did not of course have access to the Codex Salmasianus. His anthology nicely illustrates the major dilemma which, as will be seen, forces itself upon editors of this corpus of the non-epigraphic material, namely that of arrangement: confronted with diverse types of poetry originating from different mss, written by different authors (often anonymous) at different dates, should an editor try to impose order by subject matter (as Pithou chose), by date of composition, by author, by manuscript source, or in some other way?

The next major edition was by P. Burman the Younger and was published in Amsterdam in two volumes in 1759 and 1773. It was the first to use the Codex Salmasianus and it included a commentary, with notes culled from many scholars, which is still of use; like Pithou's edition, it is arranged by subject matter (the first book deals with gods, goddesses, heroes and heroines, the second with famous humans, the third with famous places and moral, didactic and amatory subjects, the fourth with epitaphs, and the final two are miscellaneous). It is entitled, in abbreviated form, *Anthologia Veterum Latinorum Epigrammatum et Poematum sive Catalecta Poetarum Latinorum in VI Libros Digesta*. Burman had preceded this edition with comments on individual poems in his *Specimen novae editionis Anthologiae Latinae et animadversionum ad epigrammata et catalecta veterum poetarum Latinorum prodromus* (Amsterdam, 1747).

H. Meyer's *Anthologia veterum epigrammatum et poematum*, Leipzig 1835, is stated to be a revision of Burman, but a key difference lies in the ordering of the material; Meyer arranges it by chronological date of author (see his comments at pp. iii f; viii f.) and uses a single continuous sequence of numeration. But his methodology is unsatisfactory: even with a rather liberal ascription of authorship, much of the material remains anonymous and often undatable, and pieces 561 onwards (more than half) revert to Burman's order. This edition is also annotated, but Meyer's notes are less full than Burman's and often based on his. Riese (pp. iii f.) did not think highly of either Burman's or Meyer's editions because of their often uncritical approach and Burman's tendency to emend the material to accord with the canons (particularly metrical) of Augustan poetry. The criticism is fair, but both editors can still be helpful in their interpretation of what are often difficult texts.

Riese's own edition, of which details have been given above, remains the standard text, particularly for *AL* 481R and following pieces (he inadvertently included material which is medieval or later in date, but that is not a problem which affects the present collection). His arrangement of the material by the date of the manuscript in which it first appears is the most effective and logical, even if it is not aesthetically pleasing, and in particular it preserves the order of pieces in the manuscripts from which they come, which is especially significant for the present collection. At any rate, nobody subsequently has tried to impose a different methodology on the whole, or even suggested one. However, Riese's contemporary Emil Baehrens included the *AL* material in the five volumes of his *Poetae Latini Minores* (Leipzig, 1879-83; parts of some volumes were revised by F. Vollmer, Leipzig 1910-), and, like Meyer, arranged the contents by chronological date of author, the result being unsatisfactory for similar reasons (Baehrens' material is also much more extensive, as his title suggests, with the *AL* poems forming only a small part of the whole). Baehrens did however produce useful comments and conjectures on the *AL* poems he edited in these volumes, and he also still repays consultation (the present collection appears in three tranches in Volume IV, at pp. 158 f.; 281 f.; 298 f.).

Finally, D.R. Shackleton Bailey issued a new edition of part of Riese's material in his 1982 Teubner (preceded by his *Towards a Text of 'Anthologia Latina'* of 1979); it covers *AL* 1-480R, but a second volume has not appeared. This edition cannot be said to have superseded Riese's, and it omits some material included by Riese, such as the Vergilian centos, which has regrettably resulted in a different numeration for most pieces (see, for general criticism of the edition, the reviews by M.D. Reeve at *Phoenix* 39.1985.174 f. and P. Parroni at *Gnomon* 57.1985.605 f., and the article by E. Courtney at *C&M* 40.1989.197 f.). Nevertheless, it contains emendations and conjectures of which some are compelling, and its merit lies in raising such points of interpretation.

(G) Metre and prosody

The great majority of the epigrams in the collection are elegiac distichs, with 99 out of 108 pieces (92%); the only other metres used are dactylic hexameters (with five examples: 82; 105; 151; 176; 181), hendecasyllables (with three examples: 119; 138-9), and the lesser asclepiad (120). This contrasts markedly with Luxorius, who is an exponent of metrical variety: of his 90 epigrams, only 49 are elegiac distichs (54%), and he has ten in hendecasyllables, nine in dactylic hexameters, and the remaining twenty-two in a variety of ten further metrical schemes (see Rosenblum, Luxorius, 70 f.; Happ, Luxurius, 199 f.).

These statistics can be given some more context by other late epigram collections and Martial. Ausonius in his epigrams (see my commentary at p. 12) displays greater metrical variety than the author of this collection, though he similarly has a marked preference for the elegiac distich (99 out of 123 pieces, or 80%); he employs dactylic hexameters on twelve occasions, and uses seven further metrical schemes in the remaining twelve pieces (though he has no instance of hendecasyllables). Ennodius, in some 150 epigrams, uses only elegiac distichs (75%) and dactylic hexameters, apart from a single instance (256 Vogel). The Bobbio epigrams use only three metrical schemes, again predominantly elegiac distichs (56 out of 72 pieces,

Introduction

or 78%), with eight in dactylic hexameters and eight in iambic trimeters (see Speyer's Teubner edition, 101 f.). And of Martial's 1556 epigrams, 1235 are in elegiac distichs (79%), 238 in hendecasyllables (15%), 77 in choliambics (5%), with five further metrical schemes accounting for the remainder (Sullivan, *Martial*, 227 n. 22). In comparison therefore, the present collection is somewhat, but not excessively, conservative both in the variety of metres used and in the preponderance of the elegiac distich.

What is amply demonstrated by metre and prosody is the late date of the collection; the preponderant elegiacs in particular show considerable deviation from standard classical (essentially Augustan) practice. In the commentary and here I generally refer to these deviations as irregularities simply to point the difference from the Augustan benchmark; evidence suggests that, particularly as far as metre is concerned, it is reasonable to regard most of them as the practice of a later age rather than to stigmatise them as errors.

I give below a catalogue of the most obvious prosodic and metrical irregularities of the elegiac distichs and dactylic hexameters in the collection. They are based on the text printed with this commentary (most are discussed in the commentary); by way of illustration and supporting evidence I have added some information in respect of the practice of Ausonius, Luxorius and occasionally others (Vergil in particular, because he would have provided this author with an excellent appeal to precedent (see p. 12 f.)):

(a) Hiatus at the hexameter main caesura: 98.3; 102.5; 106.1; 133.1; 161.3; 166.9; 168.3; 181.3; 184.3. There are three instances in Ausonius (1.5.11; 2.3.52; 19.38); there is also Vergilian precedent at e.g. *Ecl.* 10.13; *Georg.* 1.281 and *Aen.* 3.211, and possible precedent in Augustan Latin elegiacs (for which see M. Platnauer, *Latin Elegiac Verse*, Cambridge 1951, 57 f.), though there are no certain cases in Luxorius.

(b) Hiatus at the pentameter main caesura (the first word invariably concludes with a long syllable or an 'm'): 96.6 and 8; 98.6; 102.2; 124.2; 131.2; 134.2; 143.2; 158.2; 159.2; 165.4; 188.4 and 12. There is one instance in Luxorius at 357.2, none in Ausonius or Augustan Latin elegiacs, and the instance at Mart. 3.3.4 is convincing evidence that the epigram is not genuine. Catullus provides some precedent, though in all three possible instances (66.48; 67.44; 97.2: some editors emend) the hiatus involves a final 'm' of the first word.

(c) Elision in the second hemistich of the pentameter: 96.6; 98.6; 100.2; 157.2; 174.2; 188.12. There are over twenty examples in Ausonius (see my note to *Epig.* 85.2), much the same number in Martial (see Friedlaender's commentary, p. 33), and two in Luxorius (339.2; 339.10).

(d) Multisyllabic words as pentameter endings (I give only tetrasyllables and longer): 81.2; 85.2; 96.8; 97.2; 107.2 (pentasyllabic); 109.8; 127.2; 130.2; 148.2 (pentasyllabic); 148.6; 158.4; 166.6; 167.2; 168.2; 171.10; 172.4; 178.4; 179.6; 180.6; 184.2, 6 and 8; 185.4; 186.4; 188.2. Ausonius has over thirty examples (see my note on *Epig.* 24.8), Luxorius has ten (see Rosenblum, *Luxorius*, 71 f.), and there are many in Martial (see Friedlaender, p. 30 f.)

(e) Lengthening of short syllable before the hexameter main caesura: 117.11*; 130.3; 133.1; 137.9; 145.5; note also 95.5 (lengthening at the fourth foot diaeresis). Martial has one instance at 7.44.1 (and 10.89.1 has lengthening at fourth foot diaeresis), and Luxorius has instances at 320.2*; 362.2*; 362.4* (and 361.5 has lengthening at fourth foot diaeresis). There is Vergilian precedent at e.g. *Aen.* 4.64 (see Austin's note) and often. In instances marked with an asterisk, lengthening may rather be due to the treatment of an ensuing 'h' as a consonant.

(f) Lengthening of short syllable before the pentameter main caesura: 91.6*; 102.8; 115.2; 115.6*; 124.2*. There are two examples in Martial (9.101.4; 14.77.2), four in Ausonius (see my note on *Epig.* 47.2), and three in Luxorius (323.3; 336.6 (?); 365.4). Again, in examples marked with an asterisk, lengthening may rather be due to the treatment of an ensuing 'h' as a consonant.

(g) Lengthening of short open vowel before mute and liquid of following word: 101.6; 106.11; 120.4 (lesser asclepiad); 170.1.

(h) Irregular prosody (excluding proper nouns): 80.2 rēcipit; 81.1 inpubĕs; 96.6 brĕvi; 99.8 salŭbri; 106.9 dĭcatus; 106.16 flăbella and mĕlo; 115.1 dĭcata; 117.10 cottĭdiana; 132.2 revĭsura; 137.1 lŭcubrans; 138.14 sŭbantis (?); 142.3 bŏletar; 142.4 rēnuo; 172.4 lĕgeris; 173.5 ătrămentatum (?); 174.8 salŭbrem; 181.1 hĕres; 186.2 ŏris. Luxorius affords many examples: see Rosenblum, *Luxorius*, 85 f. The note on 137.1 raises the possibility that in a few instances metrical length may have been influenced by word accent.

(i) irregular prosody of (mainly Greek) proper nouns: 91.2 Iāsonis; 106.9 Māius; 124.2 Brĭsēīda; 137.12 Fīlager (?); 140.2 Ăcim; 170.3 Īdīppum; 184.7 Palamedĕs. For Ausonius see my note on *Epig.* 12.1; for Luxorius see Rosenblum, *Luxorius*, 93 f.

Such lists of irregularity as the above tend to mask the fact that issues of metre and especially prosody may involve difficult questions of editorial principle as to where the boundaries of acceptability lie. The approach at one extreme is for editors to emend away all the irregularities they possibly can in accordance with canons of Augustan practice (which is

Introduction

Burman's tendency in his edition); at the opposite extreme the danger is an uncritical acceptance of all existing irregularities in the mss, and of introducing new ones into the text by means of conjecture and emendation. Absence of credible emendation and the metrical practice evidenced in the mss of the same author and others of similar date should act as a corrective to the former approach; the corrective to the latter is again evidence of metrical practice, allied to a reluctance to introduce irregularity into the text without something akin to corroborative proof (an example of which is Heinsius' compelling conjecture 'flābella' at 106.16). But the ground between the extremes is itself not without difficulty, to illustrate which I will give just two examples. The ms. text of the pentameter at 96.6 reads 'et brevi specie usum ad utrumque facit', thus containing the irregular scansion 'brēvi', hiatus at the main caesura, and elision in the second hemistich; an editor has to ask whether three irregularities in the same line are in combination tolerable. And at the close of the pentameter of 186.2, 'India misit oris', the prosody of 'ŏris' has to be regarded as implausible. But with obvious misgivings I have allowed both of these instances to remain in the text, with the justification that sense is ideal, that no convincing emendations are forthcoming, and that irregularities of similar type, if arguably not as extreme, occur elsewhere in the collection and other authors.

(H) The text and numeration of this edition

With some hesitation (see p. 22), the numeration of my text and commentary follows that of Shackleton Bailey's Teubner, since it will now be the most readily available text of these poems; I have included a table with cross-references to the other major editions (pp. 35 f.). References to *AL* are all to SB's edition unless otherwise specified; references to Riese's (second) edition are keyed by 'R' following the numerals.

The text which precedes the commentary is my own, though I have examined no manuscript except for the Codex Salmasianus (and that in Omont's facsimile); all textual matters are discussed in the commentary except for some minor points such as the interpretation of standard abbreviations in the mss and insignificant differences in punctuation from other editions. The mss sigla are explained above, at pp. 13-18. I mention here one specific issue: in the app. crit. both Riese and SB are liberal in their use of such terms as *vulgo, vulg., vulg. olim, edd.,* and *edd. priores*, but neither defines what, if any, differences these terms imply, with the result that they can be imprecise or misleading. I have therefore used only the term '*edd.*' in textual notes, and, unless otherwise specified either in the lemma to a note or the note itself, it signifies when a usually minor change to the ms(s) has been universally or generally accepted into the text by previous editors. The translation which heads each poem in the commentary is intended to illustrate and supplement the commentary; it has no literary pretensions.

Select Bibliography

Note: Editions of the *AL* are dealt with in the Introduction at p. 20 f. Works are generally cited by abbreviation if reference is made to them in the commentary on more than one epigram. The phrase 'op. cit.' in the commentary keys a full citation of a work in previous notes on the same epigram, unless otherwise specified. Standard commentaries on classical authors are generally not listed in the bibliography.

Works cited by abbreviation

Adams, *LSV*: J.N. Adams, *The Latin Sexual Vocabulary,* London 1982.
Adams, *Pelagonius*: J.N. Adams, *Pelagonius and Latin Veterinary Terminology in the Roman Empire*, Leiden 1995.
Adams, *Bilingualism*: J.N. Adams, *Bilingualism and the Latin Language*, Cambridge 2003.
André, *L'Alimentation*: J. André, *L'Alimentation et la cuisine à Rome,* 2nd. ed., Paris 1981.
André, *L'Anatomie*: J. André, *Le Vocabulaire latin de l'anatomie*, Paris 1991.
André, *Botanique*: J. André, *Lexique des termes de botanique en latin*, Paris 1956.
André, *Couleur*: J. André, *Étude sur les termes de couleur dans la langue latine*, Paris 1949.
André, *Oiseaux*: J. André, *Les Noms d'oiseaux en latin*, Paris 1967.
André, *Plantes*: J. André, *Les Noms de plantes dans la Rome antique*, Paris 1985.
Baumgartner, *Untersuchungen*: A.J. Baumgartner, *Untersuchungen zur Anthologie des Codex Salmasianus*, Baden 1981.
Biville, *Emprunts*: F. Biville, *Les Emprunts du latin au grec. Approche phonétique*, Tomes I-II, Louvain / Paris 1990 and 1995.
Blümner, *Privataltertümer*: H. Blümner, *Die römischen Privataltertümer*, Munich 1911.
Bonner, *Education*: S.F. Bonner, *Education in Ancient Rome*, Berkeley and Los Angeles 1977.
Brecht, *Typengeschichte*: F.J. Brecht, 'Motiv- und Typengeschichte des griechischen Spottepigramms', *Philologus Suppb.* 22.2, 1930.
Bright, *Epic*: D.F. Bright, *The Miniature Epic in Vandal Africa*, Norman / London 1987.
Busch, *Versus:* S. Busch, *Versus Balnearum. Die antike Dichtung über Bäder und Baden in römischen Reich*, Stuttgart 1999.
CAH: *Cambridge Ancient History* (vol. 14: *Late Antiquity: Empire and Successors*

Epigrams from the Anthologia Latina

A.D. 425-600, ed. Averil Cameron, B. Ward-Perkins and M. Whitby, Cambridge 2000).
Cameron, *Changing Cultures*: Averil Cameron, *Changing Cultures in Early Byzantium*, Aldershot / Brookfield 1996.
Capponi, *Ornithologia*: F. Capponi, *Ornithologia Latina*, Genoa 1979.
CCSL: Corpus Christianorum Series Latina, Turnhout 1953-.
CE: Carmina Epigraphica / Carmina Latina Epigraphica, ed. A. Riese / F. Bücheler / E. Lommatzsch, Stuttgart / Leipzig 1896-1927 (= *Anthologia Latina* vol. 2).
CIL: Corpus Inscriptionum Latinarum, Berlin 1862-.
CGL: Corpus Glossariorum Latinorum ed. G. Goetz, Leipzig 1888-1923.
Courtois, *Les Vandales*: C. Courtois, *Les Vandales et l'Afrique*, Paris 1955.
CRF, Ribbeck: O. Ribbeck, *Comicorum Romanorum Fragmenta*, 3rd. ed., Leipzig 1898.
CSEL: Corpus Scriptorum Ecclesiasticorum Latinorum, Vienna 1866-.
Cugusi, *Aspetti Letterari:* P. Cugusi, *Aspetti letterari dei Carmina Latina Epigraphica*, 2nd. ed., Bologna 1996.
D'Arcy Thompson, *Birds*: D'Arcy W. Thompson, *A Glossary of Greek Birds*, new. ed. London, 1936.
Davies, *EGF*: M. Davies, *Epicorum Graecorum Fragmenta*, Göttingen 1988.
Dölger, *Die Sonne*: F.X.J. Dölger, *Die Sonne der Gerechtigkeit und der Schwarze: Eine religionsgeschichtliche Studie zum Taufgelöb*, 2nd. ed., Münster Westf. 1970.
DS: C. Daremberg and E. Saglio, *Dictionnaire des antiquités grecques et romaines*, Paris 1877-1919.
Dunbabin, *Baiarum grata voluptas*: K.M.D. Dunbabin, 'Baiarum grata voluptas: pleasures and dangers of the baths', *PBSR* 44.1989.6 f.
Dunbabin, *Mosaics*: K.M.D. Dunbabin, *Mosaics of the Greek and Roman World*, Cambridge 1999.
Dunbabin, *North Africa*: K.M.D. Dunbabin, *The Mosaics of Roman North Africa*, Oxford 1979.
EM: A. Ernout et A. Meillet, *Dictionnaire étymologique de la langue latine*, 4th. ed., Paris 1959.
Fagan, *Bathing*: G.G. Fagan, *Bathing in Public in the Roman World*, Ann Arbor 1999.
FGH, Jacoby: *Die Fragmente der griechischen Historiker*, ed. F. Jacoby, Berlin and Leiden, 1923-58.
FHG, Müller: *Fragmenta Historicorum Graecorum*, ed. C. and T. Müller, Paris 1841-73.
FLP, Courtney: *The Fragmentary Latin Poets*, ed. E. Courtney, Oxford 1993.
Forbes, *Technology*: R.J Forbes, *Studies in Ancient Technology*, Leiden 1956-72.
Francovich Onesti, *I Vandali*: N. Francovich Onesti, *I Vandali: lingua e storia*, Rome 2002.
Friedrich, *Symposium:* A. Friedrich, *Das Symposium der XII Sapientes*, Berlin / New York 2002.
Gow-Page, *GP*: A.S.F. Gow and D.L. Page, *The Greek Anthology, The Garland of Philip*, Cambridge 1968.
Gow-Page, *HE*: A.S.F. Gow and D.L. Page, *The Greek Anthology, Hellenistic Epigrams*, Cambridge 1965.
Gramm. Lat.: *Grammatici Latini*, ed. H. Keil, Leipzig 1855-78.
Grossi Gondi, *Trattato*: F. Grossi Gondi, *Trattato di epigrafia cristiana latina e greca del mondo romano occidentale*, Rome 1968.

Select Bibliography

Hanfmann, *Season Sarcophagus*: G.M.A. Hanfmann, *The Season Sarcophagus in Dumbarton Oaks*, Cambridge Mass. 1951, vol. 1.
Happ, *Luxurius*: H. Happ, *Luxurius: Text, Untersuchung, Kommentar*, Stuttgart 1986.
Herman, *Vulgar Latin*: J. Herman, *Vulgar Latin*, trans. R. Wright, Pennsylvania 2000.
Hilgers, *Gefässnamen*: W. Hilgers, *Lateinische Gefässnamen*, Dusseldorf 1969.
HLL: *Handbuch der lateinischen Literatur*, vol. 5 (*Restauration und Erneuerung*), ed. R. Herzog and P.L. Schmidt, Munich 1989.
Hofmann, *LU*: J.B. Hofmann, *Lateinische Umgangssprache*, 3rd. ed., Heidelberg 1951.
Housman, *Class. Pap.*: *The Classical Papers of A.E. Housman*, ed. J. Diggle and F.R.D. Goodyear, Cambridge 1972.
Humphrey, *Circuses*: J.H. Humphrey, *Roman Circuses*, London 1986.
Humphrey, *Circus at Carthage*: *The Circus and a Byzantine Cemetery at Carthage*, ed. J.H. Humphrey, Ann Arbor 1988.
ICUR: *Inscriptiones Christianae Urbis Romae*, ed. J.B. de Rossi, 1st. ed., vol. II, Rome 1888.
ILCV: *Inscriptiones Latinae Christianae Veteres*, ed. E. Diehl, Berlin 1925-31.
ILS: *Inscriptiones Latinae Selectae*, ed. H. Dessau, Berlin 1892-1916.
Jones, *LRE*: A.H.M. Jones, *The Later Roman Empire 248-602*, Oxford 1964.
Kaibel: *Epigrammata Graeca ex lapidibus conlecta*, ed. G. Kaibel, Berlin 1878.
Kajanto, *Cognomina*: I. Kajanto, *The Latin Cognomina*, Helsinki 1965.
Keller, *Tierwelt*: O. Keller, *Die antike Tierwelt*, Leipzig 1909-13.
Kennell, *Ennodius*: S.A.H. Kennell, *Magnus Felix Ennodius, A Gentleman of the Church*, Ann Arbor 2000.
KS: R. Kühner, F. Holzweissig and C. Stegmann, revised A. Thierfelder, *Ausführliche Grammatik der lateinischen Sprache*: vol. 1 *Elementar- Formen- und Wortlehre*, 2nd. ed., Darmstadt 1966; vol. 2 *Satzlehre* (in two parts), 4th. ed., Darmstadt 1962-71.
Langslow, *Medical Latin*: D.R. Langslow, *Medical Latin in the Roman Empire*, Oxford 2000.
Lattimore, *Themes*: R.A. Lattimore, *Themes in Greek and Latin Epitaphs*, Urbana 1962.
Lausberg, *Einzeldistichon*: M. Lausberg, *Das Einzeldistichon,* Munich 1982.
Lewis, *Papyrus*: N. Lewis, *Papyrus in Classical Antiquity*, Oxford 1974.
LHS: M. Leumann, J.B. Hofmann and A. Szantyr, *Lateinische Grammatik*: vol. 1 *Lateinische Laut- und Formenlehre*, 5th. ed., Munich 1977; vol. 2 *Lateinische Syntax und Stilistik*, revised ed., Munich 1965.
LIMC: *Lexicon Iconographicum Mythologiae Classicae*, Zürich and Munich 1981-1999.
Lindner, *Glossar:* T. Lindner, *Lateinische Komposita: Ein Glossar, vornehmlich zum Wortschatz der Dictersprache*, Innsbruck 1996.
Lindner, *Komposita*: T. Lindner, *Lateinische Komposita: morphologische, historische und lexikalische Studien*, Innsbruck 2002.
Ling, *Painting*: R. Ling, *Roman Painting*, Cambridge 1991.
Löfstedt, *Per. Aeth.*: E. Löfstedt, *Philologischer Kommentar zur Peregrinatio Aetheriae*, Uppsala 1911.
Löfstedt, *Syntactica:* E. Löfstedt, *Syntactica: Studien und Beiträge zur historischen Syntax des Lateins*, vols I (2nd. ed.) and II, Lund 1956.
LTUR: *Lexicon Topographicum Urbis Romae*, ed. E.M. Steinby, Rome 1993-2000.
Maltby, *Lexicon*: R. Maltby, *A Lexicon of Ancient Latin Etymologies*, Leeds 1991.

Mattingly, *Fazzan: Archaeology of Fazzan: Vol. 1 Synthesis*, ed. D.J. Mattingly et al., Tripoli / London 2003.
McGinn, *Prostitution*: T.A.J. McGinn, *The Economy of Prostitution in the Roman World*, Ann Arbor 2004.
Merrills, *Vandals*: *Vandals, Romans and Berbers: New Perspectives on Late Antique North Africa*, ed. A.H. Merrills, Aldershot 2004.
MGH: AA: *Monumenta Germaniae Historica, Auctores Antiquissimi*, Berlin 1877-1919.
MGH: PLAC: *Monumenta Germaniae Historica, Poetarum Latinorum Medii Aevi: Poetae Latini Aevi Carolini*, Berlin etc. 1880-1951.
MGH:SRM:*Monumenta Germaniae Historica, Scriptorum Rerum Merovingicarum*, Hanover 1884-1920.
ML, Courtney: E. Courtney, *Musa Lapidaria*, Atlanta 1995.
MM: J. Marquardt, revd. A. Mau, *Das Privatleben der Römer*, Leipzig 1886.
Modéran, *Les Maures*: Y. Modéran, *Les Maures et l'Afrique romaine*, Bibliothèque des écoles françaises d'Athènes et de Rome 314.2003.
Müller, *De Re Metrica*: L. Müller, *De re metrica poetarum Latinorum praeter Plautum et Terentium libri septem*, 2nd. ed., Leipzig 1894.
Nielsen, *Thermae*: I. Nielsen, *Thermae et Balnea*, Aarhus 1990.
Norberg, *Introduction*: D. Norberg, *An Introduction to the Study of Medieval Latin Versification*, trans. G.C. Roti and J. de la C. Skubly, Washington DC 2004.
Neue Pauly: *Der neue Pauly: Enzyklopädie der Antike*, Stuttgart / Weimar 1996-.
NW: F. Neue and C. Wagener, *Formenlehre der lateinischen Sprache*, 3rd. ed., Leipzig 1902-05.
OCD: *Oxford Classical Dictionary*, 3rd. ed., Oxford 1996.
OLD: *Oxford Latin Dictionary*, ed. P.G.W. Glare, Oxford 1982.
Otto: A. Otto, *Die Sprichwörter und sprichwörtlichen Redensarten der Römer*, Leipzig 1890; and *Nachträge*, ed. R. Häussler, Hildesheim 1968.
Page, *FGE*: D.L. Page, *Further Greek Epigrams*, Cambridge 1981.
PG: *Patrologia Graeca*, ed. J.-P. Migne.
Pikhaus, *Répertoire*: D. Pikhaus, *Répertoire des inscriptions latines versifiées de l'Afrique romaine*, Brussels 1994.
Pischel, *Kulturgeschichte*: B. Pischel, *Kulturgeschichte und Volkskunst der Wandalen*, Frankfurt am Main etc., 1980.
PL: *Patrologia Latina*, ed. J.-P. Migne.
PLRE: *Prosopography of the Later Roman Empire*, ed. A.H.M. Jones, J.R. Martindale and J. Morris, vol. I (AD 260-395), Cambridge 1971; vols II and III ed. J.R. Martindale, Cambridge 1980-92.
RE: *Real-Encyclopädie der classischen Altertumswissenschaft*, Stuttgart 1893-.
REW: W. Meyer-Lübke, *Romanisches etymologisches Wörterbuch*, 3rd. ed., Heidelberg 1935.
RLAC: *Reallexikon für Antike und Christentum*, Stuttgart 1950-.
Roscher: W.H. Roscher, *Ausführliches Lexicon der griechischen und römischen Mythologie*, Leipzig 1884-1937.
Rosenblum, *Luxorius*, M. Rosenblum, *Luxorius, A Latin Poet Among the Vandals*, New York 1961.
Saint-Denis, *Animaux marins*: E. de Saint-Denis, *Le Vocabulaire des animaux marins en latin classique*, Paris 1947.
Salzman, *Time*: M.R. Salzman, *On Roman Time: The Codex-Calendar of 354 and the Rhythm of Urban Life in Late Antiquity*, Berkeley etc. 1990.
Shackleton Bailey, *Towards a Text*: D.R. Shackleton Bailey, *Towards a Text of*

Select Bibliography

'Anthologia Latina' (Cambridge Philological Society Supplementary Volume no. 5), Cambridge 1977.
Siedschlag, *Form*: E. Siedschlag, *Zur Form von Martials Epigrammen*, diss. Berlin 1977.
Snowden, *Before Color Prejudice*: F.M. Snowden, *Before Color Prejudice*, Cambridge Mass. 1983.
Sommer, *Lautlehre*: F. Sommer, *Handbuch der lateinischen Laut- und Formenlehre*, 4th. ed., revd. R. Pfister, Heidelberg 1977.
Souter, *GLL*: A. Souter, *A Glossary of Later Latin*, Oxford 1949.
Stern, *Calendrier*: H. Stern, *Le Calendrier de 354*, Paris 1953.
Stevens, *Image and Insight*: S.T. Stevens, *Image and Insight: Ecphrastic Epigrams in the Latin Anthology*, diss. Wisconsin / Madison 1983.
Stotz, *Handbuch*: P. Stotz, *Handbuch zur lateinischen Sprache des Mittelalters*, Munich 1996-.
Strong, *Gold and Silver Plate:* D.E. Strong, *Greek and Roman Gold and Silver Plate*, London 1966.
Stumpp, *Prostitution*: B.E. Stumpp, *Prostitution in der römischen Antike*, Berlin 2001.
Sullivan, *Martial*: J.P. Sullivan, *Martial, The Unexpected Classic*, Cambridge 1991.
Svennung, *Kleine Beiträge*: J. Svennung, 'Kleine Beiträge zur lateinischen Lautlehre', *Uppsala Universitets Årsskrift* 1936 (7).
Svennung, *Palladius*: J. Svennung, *Untersuchungen zu Palladius und zu lateinischen Fach- und Volkssprache*, Lund 1935.
Texts and Transmission: *Texts and Transmission. A Survey of the Latin Classics*, ed. L.D. Reynolds, repr. with corrections Oxford 1986.
Thébert, *Thermes romains*: Y. Thébert, *Thermes romains de l'Afrique du nord et leur contexte méditerranéen*, Bibliothèque des écoles françaises d'Athènes et de Rome, 315.2003.
TLL: *Thesaurus Linguae Latinae*, Leipzig 1900-.
Toynbee, *Animals*: J.M.C. Toynbee, *Animals in Roman Life and Art*, London 1973.
Wartburg, *Wörterbuch*: W. von Wartburg, *Französisches etymologisches Wörterbuch*, Bonn 1928-.
West, *Greek Music*: M.L. West, *Ancient Greek Music*, Oxford 1992.
Wille, *Musica*: G. Wille, *Musica Romana*, Amsterdam 1967.
Wills, *Repetition*: J. Wills, *Repetition in Latin Poetry*, Oxford 1996.
Wölfflin, *Schriften*: E. Wölfflin, *Ausgewählte Schriften*, Leipzig 1933.
Yegül, *Baths*: F. Yegül, *Baths and Bathing in Classical Antiquity*, Cambridge Mass. / London 1992.
Zarker, *Studies*: J.W. Zarker, *Studies in the Carmina Latina Epigraphica*, diss. Princeton 1958.
Ziehen, *Neue Studien*: J. Ziehen, *Neue Studien zur lateinischen Anthologie*, Frankfurt a. M. / Berlin 1909.

Concordances

Anthologiae Latinae Concordantia, ed. P.G. Christiansen et al., Hildesheim etc. 2002.
Concordantiae in Carmina Latina Epigraphica, ed. M.L. Fele et al., Hildesheim 1988.

Epigrams from the Anthologia Latina

Concordanza dei Carmina Latina Epigraphica, ed. M.R. Mastidoro, Amsterdam 1991

Miscellaneous works

Bertini, F. (ed.), *Luxoriana*, Genoa 2002.
Cameron, Averil, *Continuity and Change in Sixth Century Byzantium*, London 1981.
Castagna, L.: *Studi Draconziani (1912-96)*, Naples 1997.
Clover, F.M., *The Late Roman West and the Vandals*, Aldershot 1993.
Clover, F.M. and Humphreys, R.S. (edd.), *Tradition and Innovation in Late Antiquity*, Madison 1989.
Diesner, H.J., *Der Untergang der römischen Herrschaft in Nordafrika*, Weimar 1964.
Giardina, A. (ed.), *Società romana e impero tardoantico*, 4 vols, Rome 1986.
Happ, H., 'Zur spatrömischen Namengebung', *Beiträge zur Namenforschung* 14.1963.20 f.
L'Africa romana, Università di Sassari (conference papers), vols 1-14 Sassari / Rome 1984-.
Lepelley, C., *Les Cités de l'Afrique romaine au Bas-Empire*, 2 vols, Paris 1979-81.
Mariotti, S., *Scritti medievali e umanistici*, 2nd. ed., ed. S. Rizzo, Rome 1994.
Mariotti, S., *Scritti di filologia classica*, ed. M. de Nonno and L. Gamberale, Rome 2000.
Tandoi, V., *Scritti di filologia e di storia della cultura classica*, ed. F.E. Consolino et al., Pisa 1988.
Timpanaro, S., *Contributi di filologia e di storia della lingua latina*, Rome 1978.
Timpanaro, S., *Nuovi contributi di filologia e di storia della lingua latina*, Bologna 1994.

Two recent volumes of *Antiquité tardive* (10.2002 and 11.2003), entitled 'L'Afrique vandale et byzantine', contain various papers on the Vandal occupation of Africa.

Articles and reviews relevant to the text of AL 78-188

Courtney, E., 'Observations on the Latin Anthology', *Hermathena* 129.1980.37 f.
Courtney, E., review of *Towards a Text*, *CR* 31.1981.39 f.
Courtney, E., 'Some Poems of the Latin Anthology', *CPh* 79.1984.309 f.
Courtney, E., 'Supplementary Notes on the Latin Anthology', *C&M* 40.1989.197 f.
de Nonno, M., review of *Towards a Text*, *RFIC* 110.1982.99 f.
Keller, O., 'Einige lateinische Wortformen in der Anthologie', *RhM* 30.1875.303 f.
Lebek, W.D., review of Shackleton Bailey's Teubner edn, *CR* 35.1985.293 f.
Maehly, J., review of Riese, *ZOeG* 22.1871.550 f.
Müller, L., 'Zur lateinischen Anthologie', *RhM* 18.1863.432 f.
Müller, L., 'Zu Meyer's Anthologie', *RhM* 20.1865.633 f.
Parroni, P., review of Shackleton Bailey's Teubner edn, *Gnomon* 57.1985.605 f.
Petschenig, M., 'Beiträge zur Kritik lateinischer Schriftsteller', *ZOeG* 28.1877.481 f.
Reeve, M.D., review of Shackleton Bailey's Teubner edn, *Phoenix* 39.1985.174 f.
Schenkl, C., 'Zur lateinischen Anthologie', *WS* 1.1879.59 f.
Schneider, W.J.,'Philologisch-kunstgeschichtliche Bemerkungen zu drei Stücken der "Anthologia Latina" ', *Arctos* 32.1998.229 f.

Select Bibliography

Sedlmayer, H.S., 'Schedae Criticae', *WS* 2.1880.150 f.
Stowasser, J.M., 'Lexikalische Vermutungen zur lateinischen Anthologie I / II', *WS* 31.1909.279 f.; 32.1910.97 f.
Traube, L., 'Zur lateinischen Anthologie', *Philologus* 54.1895.124 f.
Watt, W.S., 'Notes on the Anthologia Latina', *HSCPh* 91.1987.289 f.
Watt, W.S., 'Notes on the Latin Anthology', *C&M* 47.1996.255 f.
Watt, W.S., 'Notes on the Anthologia Latina', *HSCPh* 101.2003.452 f.
Ziehen, J., 'Textkritisches zu lateinischen Dichtern', *RhM* 53.1898.270 f.
Ziehen, J., 'Archaeologisch-textkritische Bemerkungen zur Salmasianus Anthologie', *Philologus* 59.1900.305 f.
Ziehen, J., 'Geschichtlich-textkritische Studien zur Salmasianus Anthologie', *Philologus* 63.1904.362 f.
Zurli, L., 'Intorno ad alcuni carmi dell' Anthologia Latina', *GIF* 28.1997.141 f.

Concordance Between Editions

SB	Riese	Baehrens	Meyer	Burman	Pithou
78	90	4.281	298	Lux. init.	–
79	91	–	–	–	–
80	91a	4.281	–	–	–
81	92	4.281	–	–	–
82	93	4.281	–	–	–
83	94	4.282	1118	5.188	–
84	95	4.282	1119	5.189	–
85	96	4.282	854	2.268	156
86	97	4.282	653	1.123	–
87	98	4.283	1095	5.165	155
88	99	4.283	644	1.110	–
89	100	4.283	615	1.71	–
90	101	4.283	958	3.183	157
91	102	4.284	657	1.128	–
92	103	4.284	960	3.185	160
93	104	4.285	1098	5.168	–
94	105	4.285	683	1.161	–
95	106	4.285	1086	5.152	–
96	107	4.286	1103	5.173	–
97	108	4.286	952	3.175	–
98	109	4.286	953	3.176	–
99	110	4.287	894	3.31	–
100	111	4.287	954	3.178	156
101	112	4.288	956	3.179	156
102	113	4.288	955	3.181	157
103	114	4.289	957	3.182	–
104	115	4.289	959	3.184	–
105	116	4.290	1035	5.66	172
106	117	4.290	1050	5.84	176
107	118	4.291	184	1.90	59
108	119	4.298	897	3.42	–

Epigrams from the Anthologia Latina

SB	Riese	Baehrens	Meyer	Burman	Pithou
109	120	4.298	899	3.43	–
110	121	4.299	900	3.44	–
111	122	4.299	901	3.45	–
112	123	4.299	902	3.46	–
113	124	4.299	895	3.39	–
114	125	–	–	–	–
115	126	4.300	896	3.40	–
116	127	4.300	947	3.168	–
117	128	4.300	948	3.169	–
118	129	4.301	949	3.170	–
119	130	4.301	950	3.171	–
120	131	4.302	946	3.167	82
121	132	4.302	260	5.150	153
122	133	4.303	980	3.208	150
123	134	4.303	981	3.209	150
124	135	4.303	982	3.210	151
125	136	4.303	1070	5.130	159
126	137	4.304	1127	5.198	–
127	138	4.304	1128	5.199	–
128	139	4.304	562	1.7	–
129	140	–	–	–	–
130	141	4.304	565	1.9	–
131	142	4.305	567	1.11	–
132	143	4.305	568	1.12	–
133	144	4.305	569	1.13	–
134	145	4.305	243	1.140	65
135	146	4.306	667	1.144	–
136	147	4.306	668	1.145	–
137	148	4.306	961	3.186	–
138	149	4.306	962	3.187	–
139	150	4.307	918	3.80	–
140	151	4.307	626	1.85	–
141	152	4.308	627	1.86	159
142	153	4.308	630	1.87	159
143	154	4.308	631	1.88	–
144	155	4.309	712	2.21	50
145	156	4.309	951	3.172	81
146	157	4.309	1012	3.277	–
147	158	4.310	529–30	2.200–01	51–2
148	159	4.310	963	3.188	–
149	160	4.158	871-2	–	157
150	161	4.159	635	1.93	–
151	162	4.159	–	–	–
152	163	4.159	652	1.121	–

Introduction

SB	Riese	Baehrens	Meyer	Burman	Pithou
153	164	4.159	652	1.121	–
154	165	4.159	652	1.121	–
155	166	4.159	652	1.121	–
156	167	4.310	675	1.155	–
157	168	4.310	676	1.155	–
158	169	4.311	1114	5.184	–
159	170	4.311	1115	5.185	–
160	171	4.311	1116	5.186	–
161	172	4.311	681	1.159	–
162	173	4.312	665	1.138	–
163	174	4.312	654	1.125	–
164	175	4.312	905	3.49	–
165	176.1–8	4.312	1087	5.153	–
166	176.9–18	4.313	1087	5.153	–
167	177	4.313	639	1.101	–
168	178	4.313	903	3.47	–
169	179	4.314	904	3.48	–
170	180	4.314	1096	5.166	155
171	181	4.314	1093	5.162	154
172	182	4.315	943	3.163	81
173	183	4.315	942	3.162	81
174	184	4.316	185	1.99	59
175	185	4.316	1117	5.187	–
176	186	4.317	1099	5.169	–
177	187	4.317	1100	5.170	–
178	188	4.317	1101	5.171	–
179	189	4.317	641	1.107	–
180	190	4.318	1124	5.195	–
181	191	4.318	1125	5.196	–
182	192	4.318	914	3.76	160
183	193.1–6	4.318	915	3.77	–
184	193.7–14	4.319	915	3.77	–
185	194	4.319	931	3.78	–
186	195	4.320	1081	5.145	–
187	196	4.320	1080	5.144	154
188	197	4.320	891	3.15	74

Anthologia Latina

78 (90R)

Praefatio

Parvula quod lusit, sensit quod iunior aetas,
    quod sale Pierio garrula lingua sonat,
hoc opus inclusit. Tu, lector, corde perito
    omnia perpendens delige quod placeat.

79 (91R)

De velo ecclesiae

* * * * * * * * * * *

80 (91aR)

Omnia quae poscis dominum, si credis, habebis;
    quae bona vota petunt, recipit alma fides.

81 (92R)

De Christiano infante mortuo

Nobilis atque insons occasu inpubes acerbo
    decessit, lacrimas omnibus incutiens.
Sed quia regna patent semper caelestia iustis
    atque animus caelos inmaculatus adit,
damnantes fletus casum laudemus ephebi,   5
    qui sine peccato raptus ad astra viget.
Felix morte sua est, celeri quem funere constat
    non liquisse patrem, sed placuisse Deo.

Text

82 (93R)

De iudicio Salomonis

Inventa est ferro pietas prolemque negando
conservat mater, contempto pignore victrix.

83 (94R)

De cereo

Lenta paludigenam vestivit cera papyrum,
   lumini ut accenso dent alimenta simul.

84 (95R)

Aliter

Ut devota piis clarescant lumina templis,
   Niliacam texit cerea lamna budam;
congrua votiferae submittit pabula flammae,
   quae castis apibus praebuit ante domus.

85 (96R)

De magistro ludi neglegenti

Indoctus teneram suscepit cauculo pubem,
   quam cogat primas discere litterulas.
sed cum discipulos nullo terrore coercet
   et ferulis culpas tollere cessat iners,
proiectis pueri tabulis Floralia ludunt.   5
   Iam nomen ludi rite magister habet.

86 (97R)

De Bellerophonte

Bellerophon superans incendia dira Chimaerae
   victor Gorgoneo nubila tangit equo.

87 (98R)

De Chimaera

Ore leo tergoque caper postremaque serpens,
   bellua tergemino mittit ab ore faces.

Text

88 (99R)

De Lauconte

Laucontem gemini distendunt nexibus angues
 cumque suis genitis sors habet una patrem.
Quod tamen iligni violarit terga caballi,
 hinc lacerasse ferunt saeva venena virum!
Quid sperare datur superum iam numine laeso, 5
 si sic irasci ligneus audet ecus?

89 (100R)

*De templo Veneris quod ad muros
<extruendos dirutum est>*

Caeduntur rastris veteris miracula templi
 inque usum belli tecta sacrata ruunt.
Nam quae deiectis volvuntur saxa columnis,
 haec sunt murorum mox relocanda minis.
Dilati Mavors conpendia cepit amoris: 5
 per muros quaerit iam sua templa Venus.

90 (101R)

De basterna

Aurea matronas claudit basterna pudicas,
 quae radians latum gestat utrimque latus.
Hanc geminus portat duplici sub robore burdo,
 provehit et modico pendula saepta gradu.
Provisum est caute, ne per loca publica pergens 5
 fuscetur visis casta marita viris.

91 (102R)

De Medea cum filiis suis

Opprimit insontes infidi causa parentis
 Iasonis et nati crimina morte luunt.
Sed quamvis mater vivo viduata marito
 coniugis in poenam pignora cara metat,
sacra tamen pietas insanae mitigat ausus: 5
 hunc furiata premit, hunc miserata levat.

Text
92 (103R)

De homine qui per se molebat

Cum possis parvo sumptu conducere asellum,
    qui soleat teretes volvere rite molas,
cur nummi cupidus sic te contemnis, amice,
    ut cupias duro subdere colla iugo?
Linque, precor, gyros. Poteris pistore ministro   5
    candentis quadrae munus habere sedens.
Per te namque terens Cererem patiere labores
    quos quaerens natam non tulit ipsa Ceres.

93 (104R)

De formica

Verrit tetra boum gratos formica labores
    et caveis fruges turba nigella locat,
quae, licet exiguo videatur pectore, sollers
    colligit hibernae commoda grana fami.
Hanc iuste famulam nigri iam dixeris Orci,   5
    quam color et factum conposuit domino.
Namque ut Plutonis rapta est Proserpina curru,
    sic formicarum verritur ore Ceres.

94 (105R)

De Hecuba

Prole viro regnoque carens Priameia coniunx
    dura sorte venit sub iuga nunc Ithaci;
quae cupiens tantos lacrimis aequare dolores
    perpetuo planctu transit in ora canis.
Quid valeat, variis monstrat Fortuna figuris: 5
    post regnum in vico saucia latrat anus.

95 (106R)

De ansere

Aedibus in nostris volitans argenteus anser
    dulcisono strepitu colla canora levat.
Ales grata bono duplici: nam fercula mensae
    conplet et adservat nocte silente domum.
Solus Tarpeia canibus in rupe quietis   5
    eripuit Gallis Romula tecta vigil.

Text

96 (107R)

De sepia

Femineo geminum designat nomine sexum
  et candens piceum sepia claudit onus.
Utilior nullus piscis per caerula oberrat,
  cui pretium capto debuit esse duplum.
Praestat carne cibos, apicum dat felle figuras,   5
  et brevi specie usum ad utrumque facit.
Hanc potius doctos adsumere convenit escam,
  quae sapit in morsu et probat articulos.

97 (108R)

De eunucho

Quem natura marem dederat, fit femina ferro;
  nam teneri pubes viribus exuitur.
Hinc iuvenem cernis tanto sub robore mollem,
  et dubii pulcher corporis extat homo.
Coniugibus cautis placita est monstrosa voluptas;   5
  fidus enim est custos qui sine teste datur.

98 (109R)

Aliter

Incertum ex certo sexum fert pube recisa,
  quem tenerum secuit mercis avara manus.
Namque ita femineo eunuchus clune movetur
  ut dubites quid sit, vir <magis> an mulier.
Omnem grammaticam castrator sustulit artem,   5
  qui docuit neutri esse hominem generis.

99 (110R)

De balneis

Hic ubi baiarum surrexit blanda voluptas
  et rudibus splendens molibus extat opus,
rura prius, nullum domino praestantia quaestum,
  nullaque tecta tulit glebula frugis inops.
Haec nunc Bellator multo sublimis honore   5
  vestivit cameris balnea pulchra locans.
Prospera facta viri naturae munera mutant,
  cum salsum salubri litus abundat aqua.

Text

Alpheum fama est dulcem per Tethyos arva
  currere nec laedi gurgitibus pelagi.   10
Dant simile exemplum nostri miracula fontis:
  vicinum patitur nec sapit unda salum.

100 (111R)

De pantomimo

Mascula femineo declinans pectora flexu
  atque aptans lentum sexum ad utrumque latus
ingressus scenam populum saltator adorat,
  sollerti spondens prodere verba manu.
Nam cum Graia chorus diffundit cantica dulcis,   5
  quae resonat cantor, motibus ipse probat.
Pugnat, ludit, amat, bacchatur, vertitur, adstat;
  inlustrat verum, cuncta decore replet.
Tot linguae quot membra viro: mirabilis ars est
  quae facit articulos ore silente loqui.   10

101 (112R)

De funambulo

Stuppea suppositis tenduntur vincula lignis,
  quae fido ascendit docta iuventa gradu.
Quam superaërius protendit crura viator
  vixque avibus facili tramite currit homo!
Brachia distendens gressum per inane gubernat,   5
  ne lapsa gracili planta rudente cadat.
Daedalus adstruitur terras mutasse volatu
  et medium pinnis persecuisse diem.
Praesenti exemplo firmatur fabula mendax:
  ecce hominis cursus funis et aura ferunt.   10

102 (113R)

De citharoedo

Musica contingens subtili stamina pulsu
  ingreditur, vulgi auribus ut placeat.
Stat tactu cantuque potens, cui brachia linguae
  concordant sensu conciliata pari.
Namque ita <ab> aequali ambo moderamine librat   5
  atque ori socias temperat arte manus
ut dubium tibi sit gemina dulcedine capto
  vox utrumne canat an lyra sola sonet.

103 (114R)

Aliter

Doctus Apollineo disponere carmina plectro
  gaudet multifidam pectore ferre chelyn,
quam mox linguato decurrens pollice cogit
  humanum ut possit chorda canora loqui.
Amphion cithara Thebarum moenia saepsit, 5
  aurita ad muros currere saxa docens,
nec minus hac valuit reparator coniugis Orpheus,
  impia cum flexit Tartara dulcis amor.
Ars laudanda nimis, cuius moderamine sacro
  unum ex diversis vox digitique canunt! 10

104 (115R)

De pyrrhica

In spatio Veneris simulantur proelia Martis,
  cum sese adversum sexus uterque venit.
Femineam maribus nam confert pyrrhica classem
  et velut in morem militis arma movet,
quae tamen haut ullo chalybis sunt tecta rigore, 5
  sed solum reddunt buxea tela sonum.
Sic alterna petunt iaculis clipeisque teguntur,
  nec sibi congressu vir nocet an mulier.
Lusus habet pugnam, sed dant certamina pacem;
  nam remeare iubent organa blanda pares. 10

105 (116R)

Laus temporum quattuor

Carpit blanda suis ver almum dona rosetis.
Torrida collectis exultat frugibus aestas.
Indicat autumnum redimitus palmite vertex.
Frigore pallet hiems designans alite tempus.

106 (117R)

Laus omnium mensuum

Fulget honorifico indutus Ianus amictu,
  signans Romuleis tempora consulibus.
Rustica bacchigenis intentans arma novellis
  hic meruit Februi nomen habere dei.

Martius in campis ludens simulacra duelli 5
    ducit Cinyphii lactea dona gregis.
Sacra Dioneae referens sollemnia matris
    lascivis crotalis plaudit Aprilis ovans.
Maïus Atlantis natae dicatus honori
    expoliat pulchris florea senta rosis. 10
Ornat sanguineis aestiva prandia moris
    Iunius; huic nomen fausta Iuventa dedit.
Quondam Quintilis, Cereali germine gaudens,
    Iulius a magno Caesare nomen habet.
Augustum penitus torret Phaëthontius ardor, 15
    quem recreant fessum gillo, flabella, melo.
Aequales Librae September digerit horas,
    cum botruis captum rure ferens leporem.
Conterit October lascivis calcibus uvas
    et spumant pleno dulcia musta lacu. 20
Arva November arans fecundo vomere vertit,
    cum teretes sentit pinguis oliva molas.
Pigra suum cunctis commendat bruma Decembrem,
    cum sollers famulis tessera iungit eros.

107 (118R)

De Thetide

Cauta quidem genetrix, noceant ne vulnera nato,
    confirmat Stygio fonte puerperium.
Sed quia fas nulli est humanam vincere sortem
    in membris tincti dant sibi fata locum.

108 (119R)

De balneis

Aspice fulgentis tectis et gurgite baias,
    dant quibus haut parvum pictor et unda decus:
namque gerunt pulchras splendentia culmina formas,
    blandaque perspicuo fonte fluenta cadunt.
Gaudia qui gemino gestit decerpere fructu 5
    et vita novit praetereunte frui,
hic lavet. Hic corpus reparans mentemque relaxans,
    lumina picturis, membra fovebit aquis.

Text

109 (120R)

Aliter

Fausta novum domini condens Fortuna lavacruM
 Invitat fessos huc properare viaE.
Laude operis fundi capiet sua gaudia praesuL
 Ospes dulciflua dum recreatur aquA.
Condentis monstrant versus primordia nomeN   5
 Actoremque facit littera summa legI.
Lustrent pontivagi Cumani litoris antrA;
 Indigenae placeant plus mihi deliciaE.

110 (121R)

Aliter

Quisquis Cumani lustravit litoris antra
 atque hospes calidis saepe natavit aquis,
hic lavet, insani vitans discrimina ponti;
 Baiarum superant balnea nostra decus.

111 (122R)

Aliter

Flammea perspicuis coeunt hic lumina lymphis
 dantque novum mixti Phoebus et unda diem.
Denique succedit nostris lux tanta lavacris
 ut cernas nudos erubuisse sibi.

112 (123R)

Aliter

Infundit nostris Titan sua lumina bais
 inclusumque tenet splendida cella iubar.
Subiectis caleant aliorum balnea flammis:
 haec reddi poterunt, Phoebe, vapora tuis.

113 (124R)

De thermis

Delectat variis infundere corpora lymphis
 et mutare magis saepe fluenta libet;
nam, ne consuetae pariant fastidia thermae,
 hinc iuvat alterno tingere membra lacu.

Text

114 (125R)

Aliter

* * * * * * * * * * *

115 (126R)

<*De bibliotheca in tabernam mutata*>

Tecta novem Phoebi nuper dicata Camenis
   nunc retinet Bacchus et sua templa vocat.
Namque ubi tot veterum manserunt scripta virorum,
   hic potat laete dulcia vina Cypris.
Cognato semper lustrantur numine sedes: 5
   quas coluit Phoebus, has colit en Bromius!

116 (127R)

De lenone uxoris suae

Graecule, consueta lenandi callidus arte,
   coepisti adductor coniugis esse tuae,
et, quem forte procax penitus conroserat uxor,
   consueras propria praecipitare domo.
Sed praetensa catus derisit retia quidam,   5
   †quurverastatuens horemaneredomo†.
Nam semel admissus †derisit retia quidam†
   teque tuis miserum depulit e laribus.
Solus vera probas iucundi verba poetae:
   'dum iugulas hircum, factus es ipse caper.'   10

117 (128R)

Ad lenonem comitiacum

Militiae cultus et nigri tegmina panni
   cur magis exoptes, dissere, leno, mihi.
Exiguone tibi crescebat cellula quaestu,
   cum gravis adducta virgine saccus erat?
An nescis populi pastum sibi tollere paucos,   5
   unde miser fisco paupere miles eget?
Effuge vitandos, si qua potes arte, labores.
   Cur caleas tenso vivere, leno, pede?
Nam si formonsas redeas lenare puellas
   et dederit quaestus cottidiana venus,   10
non iam miles eris humilis, sed divite nummo
   fies militiae mox utriusque comes.

Text

118 (129R)

De Martio cinaedo

Quid prodest Martis nomen de nomine ductum,
    pruriat infami cum tibi clune venus?
Sors fuerat melior Cypridos si nomen haberes
    aut natura daret martia membra tibi.
Nunc utroque carens, ignoti fabula sexus,   5
    femina cum non sis, vir tamen esse nequis.

119 (130R)

De Caballina meretrice

Caballina furens, amanda nulli,
excussis modo calcibus fremebat;
quae quamvis facie micet rubenti
et vibret, Parium nitens colorem,
hirsutis tamen est petenda mulis,   5
qui possint pariles citare iunctas.

120 (131R)

De Arzugitano poeta

Praecisae silicis cautibus edite,
silvestri iuvenis durior arbuto,
trunco cum stupeas horridior, cupis
formare propriis carmina versibus
et metri variis ludere legibus.   5
Sed quis te docilem iudicet artium
quas natura dedit cordis acutior?
Solus ligna dolans fortibus asceis,
eduri resecans robora pectoris,
vatem te poterat reddere ligneum   10
qui vaccam trabibus lusit adulteris
vel qui struxit ecum fraudis Achaicae.

121 (132R)

De capone †fassanario†

Candida Phoebeo praefulgunt ora rubore,
    crista riget radiis, ignea barba micat.
Alae, colla, comae, pectus, femur, inguina, cauda
    Paestanis lucent floridiora rosis.

Text

Flammea sic rutilum distinguit pinna colorem   5
  ut vibrare putes plumea membra faces.

122 (133R)

De malis Matianis

Haec poterant celeres pretio tardare puellas,
  haec fuerant Veneri iudice danda Phryge:
nam sic ingenuo flavescunt mala colore
  ut superent auro vera metalla suo.

123 (134R)

Aliter. Laus

†His constat Veneri praelatae gratia formae†,
  haec moriente sacrum perdidit angue nemus.

124 (135R)

Aliter. Vituperatio

His contempta deum tenuit Discordia mensas,
  prodidit atque urbem his Briseida suam.

125 (136R)

De gillone

Gillo vomit gelidum vastis singultibus amnem,
  vis aliena cui frigoris addit opem.
Nam tepidum laticem curamus claudere testa,
  ut mersa imbrigenis unda nivescat aquis.

126 (137R)

De †theo†

Inguine suspensam gestas ***** <l>agunam,
  quae tibi fit turgens amphora flante noto.
Vectigal poteras figulorum reddere fisco,
  quorum tam tereti ramice vincis opus!

Text

127 (138R)

Aliter

Moles tanta tibi pendet sub ventre syringae
  ut te non dubitem dicere bicipitem.
Nam te si addictum mittat sententia campo,
  vispillo ignoret quod secet ense caput.

128 (139R)

De Iove in †pluteo†

Flexilis obliquo sinuatur circulus orbe
  inclusumque gerit machina sacra Iovem.
Vana sub aspectum duxit mendacia fictor:
  orbis rectorem quis probat orbe tegi?

129 (140R)

Aliter

* * * * * * * * * * *

130 (141R)

<De Iove et Leda>

Cygneas Genitor gestans post fulmina pinnas
  dulcia diffundit carmina virginibus,
quem retinens Leda, prenso cum gaudet olore,
  amissa agnovit virginitate Iovem.

131 (142R)

De ovo Ledae

Ledaei partus ovo monstrantur aperto,
  in cygnum verso a Iove quod genuit.
Una tribus genetrix, sed sors diversa creatis:
  sidera pars faciet, pars fera bella Phrygum.

132 (143R)

De Europa

Terga bovis credens Europa ascendit alumni
  inseditque Iovi non revisura patrem.

Text

Fraude suos Genitor celat vel conplet amores:
   nam deus in tauri corpore praedo latet.

133 (144R)

Aliter

Mentitus taurum Europam Iuppiter aufert,
   virgineos ardens pandere fraude sinus.
Humano tandem veniam donemus amori,
   si tibi, summe deum, dulcia furta placent.

134 (145R)

De Narcisso

Invenit proprios mediis in fontibus ignes
   et sua deceptum urit imago virum.

135 (146R)

Aliter

Ardet amore sui flagrans Narcissus in undis,
   cum modo perspicua se speculatur aqua.

136 (147R)

Aliter

Suspirat propriae Narcissus gaudia formae,
   quem scrutata suis vultibus unda domat.

137 (148R)

*De equa Filagri advocati. Insultatio
pro concubitu*

Causidicus pauper media sub nocte lucubrans
   cornipedis voluit terga fricare suae.
Sed cum corpus equae dextra famulante titillat,
   invasit iuvenem prodigiosa venus.
Nam qua longa solet dispendia carpere sessor,   5
   subducens durae pendula crura viae,
hanc fovet amplexu molli turdumque caballae
   adterit adsiduo pene fututor hebes.

Text

Concubitus Cressa legitur quaesisse iuvenci,
   quam gravis ira deae iussit amare pecus.   10
Par crimen flammae nostris fors intulit annis:
   Passiphaë tauro, Filager arsit equa.

138 (149R)

Aliter

Defensor probe tristium reorum,
cuius voce sacrum tonat tribunal
et palmas capiunt lares Vitenses,
cur post athla fori togaeque pompam,
gaudens monstrifero calere luxu,   5
vectricis propriae furens in usus
fessae cornipedis fricas meatum,
verso et munere dignitatis optas
admissarius esse quam patronus?
Expellas animo nimis, rogamus,   10
mores inlicite libidinantes.
Horrendum vitium est in advocato,
orando solitum movere caulas
subantis pecudis tenere gambas.

139 (150R)

De tabula picta

Hunc quem nigra gerit tabella vultum,
clarum linea quem brevis notavit,
mox pictor varios domans colores
callenti nimium peritus arte
formabit similem, probante vero   5
ludentis propriis fidem figuris,
ut, quoscumque manu repingat artus,
credas corporeos habere sensus.

140 (151R)

De Galatea

Defugiens pontum, silvas Galatea peragrat,
   custodem ut pecorum cernere possit Acim;
nam teneros gressus infigit sentibus ardens,
   nec tamen alta pedum vulnera sentit amor.
Ipsa Cupidineae cedunt elementa pharetrae,   5
   cuius et in mediis flamma suburit aquis.

Text

141 (152R)

De Galatea in vase

Fulget et in patinis ludens pulcherrima Nais,
   prandentum inflammans ora decore suo.
Congrua non tardus diffundat iura minister,
   ut lateat positis tecta libido cibis.

142 (153R)

Aliter

Ludere sueta vadis privato nympha natatu
   exornat mensas membra venusta movens.
Comptas nolo dapes; vacuum mihi pone boletar.
   Quod placet aspiciam; renuo quod saturat.

143 (154R)

Aliter

In medio generata salo nunc arte magistra
   perveni ad mensam; hic quoque nuda nato.
Si prandere cupis, differ spectare figuram,
   ne tibi ieiunus lumina tendat amor.
Quae sim, ne dubites: ludens sine nomine lympha   5
   quod Galatea vocer, lactea massa probat.

144 (155R)

De Scaevola

Lictorem pro rege necans nunc Mucius ultro
   sacrifico propriam concremat igne manum.
Miratur Porsenna virum poenamque relaxans
   mutua cum obsessis foedera victor init.
Plus flammis patriae confert quam voverat armis   5
   una domans bellum funere dextra suo.

145 (156R)

De viro quem mulier caedebat

Cum te Barbati referas de sanguine cretum,
   ut tibi cognatus sit Varitinna ferox,
cur tua femineo caeduntur tempora socco
   infamique manu barbula vulsa cadit?

Text

Desine iam tibimet auctores fingere fortes 5
    vimque tuis membris stirpis inesse ferae.
Illa Salautensi magis est de stirpe creata,
    audet quae proprium sternere calce virum.

146 (157R)

De die frigido

Sint tibi deliciae: sint ditis prandia mensae,
    munera post Bacchi sit tibi pulchra venus;
vincere nec libeat villosa veste rigorem,
    sed iungat calidum fervida virgo latus.

147 (158R)

De imagine Vergilii

Subduxit morti vivax pictura Maronem
    et, quem Parca tulit, reddit imago virum.
Lucis damna nihil tanto valuere poetae,
    quem praesentat honos carminis et plutei.

148 (159R)

De discipulo medici

Discipulum medicus quidam suscepit adultum,
    traderet ut iuveni dogma salutiferum.
Qui primo, ut iussum nosset tolerare magistri,
    publica selliferum per loca duxit ecum.
Artis prolixae breviavit tempora doctor: 5
    incepto puerum reddidit Ἱπποκράτην.

149 (160R)

De venatore qui cum aprum excepit serpentem
calcavit imprudens

Sus, iuvenis, serpens casum venere sub unum:
    hic fremit, ille gemit, sibilat hic moriens.

Text

150 (161R)

EIUSDEM

In Achillem

Inprobe distractor, pretium si poscere nosses,
   non traheres †quod pundus erat†.

151 (162R)

De Troia

Desine, Troia, tuos animo deflere labores:
   Romam capta creas; merito tua postuma regnat.

152 (163R)

De iudicio Paridis

Conubii bellique deas superavit amorum,
   cum pastor pulchram iudicat esse Cyprin.

153 (164R)

<Aliter>

Verticis et thalami pignus sublime Tonantis
   exuperat Paridis laude probata Venus.

154 (165R)

<Aliter>

Extat causa mali, malum cessisse Dionae,
   cur ruerint Graia Pergama pulsa manu.

155 (166R)

<Aliter>

Dat Veneri malum formae pro munere pastor;
   cum Iunone dolens victa Minerva redit.

156 (167R)

De Hyacintho

Discrimen vitae, ludit dum forte, Hyacinthus
   incurrit, disco tempora fissa gerens.

Text

Non potuit Phoebus fato subducere amatum,
   sed cruor extincti florea rura replet.

157 (168R)

<Aliter>

Dispersit remeans ludentis tempora discus
   et dira pulcher morte Hyacinthus obit.
Gratia magna tamen solatur fata perempti:
   semper Apollineus flore resurgit amor.

158 (169R)

De citro

Saepta micant spinis felicis munera mali;
   permulcet citri aureus ora tumor.
Hippomenes tali vicit certamina malo;
   talia poma nemus protulit Hesperidum.

159 (170R)

Aliter

Stat similis lauro citri mirabilis arbos,
   omnibus autumni anteferenda bonis.
haec ornant mensas, haec praestant poma medellam,
   cum quatit incurvos tussis anhela senes.

160 (171R)

Aliter

Omne genus mali dignum est adsurgere citro,
   vis cui multa subest corticis et medii.
Unumquemque suum referunt pomuscula sucum;
   ternus ab hoc semper carpitur ore sapor.

161 (172R)

De Daphne

Frondibus et membris servavit dextera sollers
   congruus ut sculptis posset inesse color.
Dant mirum iunctae ars et pictura decorem,
   ostendit varius cum duo signa lapis.

Text

162 (173R)

<De Marsya>

Aërio victus dependet Marsya ramo
    nativusque probat pectora tensa rubor.
Docta manus varios lapidem limavit in artus;
    arboris atque hominis fulget ab arte fides.

163 (174R)

De Philocteta

Prodentem ducibus Tirynthia tela Pelasgis
    laesa Philoctetam vulnere planta domat.
Docta manus vivos duxit de marmore vultus;
    sentit adhuc poenam, tristis et in lapide.

164 (175R)

De balneis

Una salus homini est gelidum captare lavacrum,
    ne tepidus reddat morbida membra vapor.

165 (176.1-8R)

De ansere qui intra se capit copiam prandii

Eminet impletus pullorum carnibus anser
    et varias mensae turgidus ambit opes;
inguinibus nam portat olus ventrisque soluti
    truditur e medio esitiata nitens.
Fulcit utrumque latus turdus cum turture pinguis   5
    multaque penniferum corpora condit opus.
Quis non credat ecum Graiam celasse phalangem,
    si parvus tantas anser habet latebras?

166 (176.9-18R)

<Aliter>

Plura saginato conclusit fercula capso
    aucupia et pulpas ducere docta manus.
Intus inest quodcumque placet; crescitque voluptas,
    cum scisso multas pectore prodit opes.
Cedat Cecropii lascivans bucula fabri,   5
    qua consuerat amor claudere Passiphaën;

Text

cedat et ille, dolo sollers quem struxit Epeos,
   qui gravidus bellis Pergama solvit ecus.
Maiorem in parvo haec monstrat fabrica technam;
   una capit totas anseris arca dapes.   10

167 (177R)

De Pyrrho

Placat busta patris iugulata virgine Pyrrhus
   dilectasque litat Manibus inferias.
Sors nova nymphigenae: votum post fata meretur.
   Quam pepigit thalamis, hanc habet in tumulis.

168 (178R)

De balneis cuiusdam pauperis

Vita opibus tenuis, sed parvo in caespite sollers,
   fundavit gemino munere delicias.
Nam nova congusto erexit balnea campo,
   edulibusque virens fetibus hortus olet.
Quae natura negat, confert industria parvis: 5
   vix sunt divitibus quae bona pauper habet.

169 (179R)

Aliter

Parvula succinctis ornavit iugera bais
   urbanos callens condere Vita locos.
Hic quoque pomiferum coniunxit sedulus hortum,
   qui vario auctorem gramine dives alat.
Rus gratum domino duplici iam munere constat: 5
   hinc capitur victus, sumitur inde salus.

170 (180R)

De Sphinga

Ales, virgo, lea crevit de sanguine Lai,
   Thebano nascens et peritura malo.
Haec fecit thalamos Idippum ascendere matris,
   ut prolem incestam mutua dextra necet.

Text

171 (181R)

De catto qui comedens picam mortuus est

Mordaces morsu solitus consumere mures
   invisum et domibus perdere dente genus
cattus in obscuro cepit pro sorice picam
   multiloquumque vorax sorbuit ore caput.
Poena tamen praesens praedonem plectit edacem;   5
   nam claudunt rabidam cornea labra gulam.
Faucibus obsessis vitalis semita cessit
   et satur escali vulnere raptor obit.
Non habet exemplum volucris vindicta peremptae:
   hostem pica suum mortua discruciat.   10

172 (182R)

De Aegyptio

Ex oriente die noctis processit alumnus.
   Sub radiis Phoebi solus habet tenebras.
Corvus, carbo, cinis concordant multa colori;
   quod legeris nomen convenit Aethiopi.

173 (183R)

Aliter

Faex Garamantarum nostrum processit ad axem
   et piceo gaudet corpore verna niger,
quem nisi vox hominem labris emissa sonaret,
   terreret vivos horrida larva viros.
Dira atramentatum rapiant sibi Tartara monstrum;   5
   custodem hunc Ditis debet habere domus.

174 (184R)

De Telepho

Telephus, excellens Alcidis pignus et Augae,
   externae sortis bella inopina tulit.
Nam Grai Troiam peterent dum mille carinis
   tangeret et classis litus adacta suum,
occurrens Danais forti cum pugnat Achilli,   5
   Scyria pugnanti perculit hasta femur.
Pro cuius cura consultus dixit Apollo
   hostica quod salubrem cuspis haberet opem.

Text

Mox precibus flexi Pelidae robore raso
   iniecto membris pulvere plaga fugit.   10
Monstrant fata viri vario miracula casu:
   unde datum est vulnus, contigit inde salus.

175 (185R)

De cicindelo

Igniculus tenuis pingui fulcitur olivo,
   ut frangat tenebras luminis igne sui.

176 (186R)

De capris

Lenaeos latices hircorum tergora gestant
fitque caper Bromio, fuerat qui victima, carcer.

177 (187R)

Aliter

Barbati pecoris vulgus per rura vagatur,
   pampineum gaudens laedere dente nemus.
Omnibus hinc aris Baccho caper hostia fertur
   puniturque sacro munere culpa gregis.

178 (188R)

Aliter

Sanguine Cinyphio placantur templa Lyaei,
   caprigenum cui fit victima iusta pecus.
Sed licet ulcisci nequeant animalia divos
   nec possit reddi talio numinibus,
est vindicta capris. Cassatur nomine Liber,   5
   cum hircino adversus clauditur utre deus.

179 (189R)

De Memnone

Filius Aurorae, Phoebi nascentis alumnus,
   producit gentis milia tetra suae.
Succurrens fessis fausto non omine Teucris
   pergit Pelidae protinus ense mori.

Text

Iam tunc monstratur maneat qui Pergama casus,   5
   cum nigrum Priamus suscipit auxilium.

180 (190R)

De Bumbulo

Nominis et formae pariter ludibria gestans,
   conventus nostros, Bumbule parvus, adis.
Sed ratio est si stas longis pygmaeus in armis,
   ne te deprensum grus peregrina voret.
Nec frustra ostendis proprio placuisse parenti   5
   quod turpis nomen sumpseris heniochi.
Ille habuit doctas circo prostare puellas;
   te duce lascivae nocte fricantur anus.

181 (191R)

Aliter

Cum sis patris heres teneas et, Bumbule, censum,
utile nec tibi sit pietas si inlaesa probetur,
das operam proprio auctori adversus haberi.
Discordat multum contra suscepta voluntas:
dilexit genitor prasinum, te russeus intrat.

182 (192R)

De tabula

Discolor ancipiti sub iactu cauculus astat
   decertantque simul candidus atque rubens;
qui quamvis parili scriptorum tramite currant,
   is capiet palmam quem bona fata iuvant.

183 (193.1-6R)

Aliter

In parte alveoli pyrgus velut urna resedit,
   qui vomit internis tesserulas gradibus,
sub quarum iactu discordans cauculus exit
   certantesque fovet sors variata duos.
His proprium faciunt <ars> et fortuna periclum: 5
   haec cavet adversis casibus, illa favet.

Text

184 (193.7-14R)

Conposita est tabulae nunc talis formula belli,
  cuius missa facit tessera principium.
Ludentes vario exercent proelia talo,
  russeus an nitidus praemia sorte ferat.
Pascitur a multis avide damnosa voluptas,   5
  ne foedet gliscens otia segnities.
Hoc opus inventor nimie Palamedes amavit
  et parili excellens Mucius ingenio.

185 (194R)

Aliter

Indica materies blandum certamen amicis
  offert, sed belli fert simulacra tamen.
Namque acie aequali concurrit russeus albo,
  ut gravibus damnis se domet alteruter.
Contorquet varios alternans tessera missus   5
  fataque ludentum collis et ima probant.
Pax ac pugna simul ludo iunguntur in unum,
  cum victi spoliis victor amicus ovat.

186 (195R)

De elephanto

Horrida cornuto procedit belua rostro,
  quam dives nostris India misit oris.
Sed licet immani pugnet proboscide barrus
  spondeat et saevis dentibus interitum,
fert tamen edomitus residentis iussa magistri,   5
  quoque velit monitor, cogitur ire ferus.
Vis humana potest rabiem mutare ferinam:
  ecce hominem parvum belua magna timet!

187 (196R)

Aliter

Monstrorum princeps elephans proboscide saevus
  horret mole nigra, dente micat niveo.
Sed vario fugienda malo cum belua gliscat,
  est tamen excepti mors pretiosa feri.
Nam quae conspicimus montani roboris ossa   5
  humanis veniunt usibus apta satis.

Text

Consulibus sceptrum, mensis decus, arma tablistis,
   discolor et tabulae cauculus inde datur.
Haec est humanae semper mutatio sortis:
   fit moriens ludus, qui fuit ante pavor.   10

188 (197R)

De circensibus

Circus imago poli, formam cui docta vetustas
   condidit ad numeros limitis aetherii.
Nam duodenigenas ostendunt ostia menses
   quaeque meat cursim aureus astra iubar.
Tempora cornipedes referunt, elementa colores;   5
   auriga, ut Phoebus, quattuor aptat equos.
Cardinibus propriis includunt saepta quadrigas,
   Ianus vexillum quas iubet ire levans.
Ast ubi panduntur funduntque repagula currus
   unus et ante omnes cogitur ire prius,   10
metarum tendunt circumdare cursibus orbes;
   namque axes gemini ortum obitumque docent
atque his euripus quasi magnum interiacet aequor,
   et medius centri summus obliscus adest.
Septem etiam gyris claudunt certamina palmae,   15
   quot caelum stringunt cingula sorte pari.
Lunae biga datur semper Solique quadriga,
   Castoribus simpli rite dicantur equi.
Divinis constant nostra spectacula rebus,
   gratia magna quibus crevit honore deum.   20

Commentary

78 (90R)

Preface. What I wrote playfully in boyhood, the ideas I had in my youth, and what a garrulous tongue chatters with Pierian wit, this work has included. You, reader, weigh everything carefully in your expert mind and select what pleases you.

This clearly stands as the introductory poem to a collection (the superscription labels it a *praefatio*), and the motifs in it would well suit a collection of epigrams or similar pieces. Whether that collection is the epigrams immediately following and which form the subject of this book, who the author might have been, and where the collection ends in the *AL*, are questions dealt with in the introduction (p. 1 f.).

The motifs or poetic apologies that suggest this piece introduces a collection of epigrams include: (a) 'lusit' in line 1: epigrammatic poetry is often labelled *lusus, ludus, ioci, nugae* or the product of poetic *otium*, and is characterised as light and ephemeral in tone and nature (see my note on Mart. 11.3.1); (b) 'tu, lector, corde perito / ... delige quod placeat' (lines 3-4): the reader, or patron, is sometimes modestly assumed to be more expert in epigrammatic poetry than the poet himself, and is invited to make a judgement about what he should or should not read, or even what is fit for publication in the first place (see my notes on Aus. 1.5.13; 16); (c) 'omnia perpendens delige quod placeat' (line 4): it is axiomatic that epigram collections contain good and bad pieces, though there should be something to please everyone (e.g. Plin. *Ep*. 4.14.3; Mart. 1.16; 7.81; 7.90; 9.89); and (d) 'sale Pierio' (line 2): epigrams are renowned for their mordant wit (see 2 n. below). Notably absent is any apology for obscenity, which is often part and parcel of an epigram collection containing such pieces (see my intro. to Aus. *Epig*. 1), and which would not be inappropriate in the present collection (note such pieces as 119, 137 and 138); however, that may be explained by the relative infrequency of obscene pieces, and the almost total absence of primary lexical obscenity (*fututor* at 137.8 is the only instance, though see also 137.7 n.).

One certain epigram collection in the *AL*, and which is the work of a

Commentary

single author, is that of Luxorius, who I have argued is a near-contemporary of our poet (see p. 6 f.). His series of introductory poems (*AL* 282-5) shares many motifs with this one: for example 282.1 f. 'lusus hos veteres ... / quos olim puer in foro paravi, / versus ex variis iocis deductos ... / memori tuo probandos / primum pectore'; ibid. 21 f. 'nec me paeniteat iocos secutum, / quos verbis epigrammaton facetis / diversos facili pudore lusit / frigens ingenium'; and 283.2 f. 'lector ... / nostri libelli cur retexis paginam / nugis refertam frivolisque sensibus / et quam tenello tiro lusi viscere?'

1. parvula ... iunior aetas: the sentiment modestly offers excuse both for writing in the epigrammatic genre and for not necessarily writing well. Luxorius (*AL* 282.1 f., quoted more fully in the intro. above) makes the same point: 'lusus hos veteres ... / quos olim puer in foro paravi'. 'parvula' and 'iunior aetas' are not synonymous terms here, though both refer to the early years. The former suggests an earlier stage in life than the latter (e.g. boyhood and youth): cf. Dido's 'si quis mihi parvulus aula / luderet Aeneas' at Verg. *Aen.* 4.328 f. (with Pease's note), and the progressions of age at e.g. Plin. *Pan.* 22.3 ('parvuli ... iuvenes ... senes') and Iren. *Contra Haer.* 2.22.4 ('infantes et parvulos et pueros et iuvenes et seniores').

For *aetas* + adjective describing boyhood or youth elsewhere, cf. Cat. 68.16 'aetas florida'; Cic. *Tusc.* 5.62 'improvida aetas'; *CE* 55.5 'viridis aetas'; and for the phrase *parvula aetas* cf. Jer. *Ep.* 64.15 'aetatis adhuc parvulae'. 'iunior aetas' is *iuventas* as viewed by the mature man looking back: cf. Cic. *Tim.* 46 'dis, ut ita dicam, iunioribus', with *TLL* 7.2.739.31 f.

lusit: the usual term for the writing of epigram (see intro. above).

sensit: in this literary context the verb is rather imprecise, but compare 'sensibus' at *AL* 283.3 f. Luxorius 'paginam / nugis refertam frivolisque sensibus'. The reference is to youthful ideas expressed in writing, and it develops the modest pose of the epigrammatic poetry offered in the collection being juvenilia, and to be excused as such.

2. sale Pierio: *sal* is a necessary ingredient of good epigram: cf. Mart. 8.3.19 f. 'at tu Romano lepidos sale tinge libellos: / adgnoscat mores vita legatque suos'; 7.25.3. The adjective here is pointed, and in itself a good illustration of epigrammatic wit and cleverness. Pieria was an area north of Mt Olympus sacred to the Muses, and its king, Pierus, was sometimes held to be the Muses' father (see my note on Aus. *Epig.* 35.1). In Ovid's version of the myth however (*Met.* 5.294 f.), Pierus becomes the father of nine daughters who ill-advisedly competed with the Muses in a contest, lost, and were turned into *picae* (jays, magpies or woodpeckers: for the uncertainty see Bömer's note on Ovid *Met.* 5.294-678). These birds were noted for their garrulity and imitative faculties: thus Ovid *Met.* 5.677 f. 'nunc quoque in alitibus facundia prisca remansit / raucaque garrulitas studiumque inmane loquendi', and cf. *AP* 7.423.1 Antip. Sid. (with Gow-

Page, *HE* 2.57); *AP* 9.280.5 f. (with Gow-Page, *GP* 2.158 f.); and D'Arcy Thompson, *Birds*, 146 f. The ensuing words of this epigram, 'garrula lingua sonat', show that the poet is alluding to this version of the myth, which enables him to further his modest pose by likening his youthful epigrammatic writing to bird chatter, while at the same time claiming literary credibility and pedigree with the term 'sal Pierius'.

sonat: for *sonare* of bird song cf. Verg. *Aen.* 12.474 f. 'hirundo ... nunc umida circum / stagna sonat'. The present tense of the verb contrasts with the past tense of the other verbs in the sentence ('lusit ... sensit ... inclusit') and is no doubt influenced by metrical constraint as much as anything. But it could suggest a change of focus from when the author wrote the epigrams ('parvula quod lusit ... aetas') to the contents of the book the reader now has before him ('bird chatterings').

3. hoc opus inclusit: this phrase, which occupies the first part of the hexameter line (i.e. ending at or before the main caesura) and concludes with its main verb a syntactical unit begun by subordinate clauses in the preceding couplet, is a striking type of enjambement in elegiac verse, the effect of which is to emphasise 'hoc opus' and its contents; it is evidenced twice elsewhere in the collection, though not at the beginning of poems (108.7 and 178.5). Martial offers occasional instances, and he may be the model here (the following list does not claim completeness): e.g. 7.85.1 f. 'quod non insulse scribis tetrasticha quaedam, / disticha quod belle pauca, Sabelle, facis, / laudo nec admiror', and 2.8.1 f.; 3.69.1 f.; 6.76.1 f.; 10.10.1 f. (all of which open epigrams, and in all of which the main clause is held back to line 3; there is an example not at the beginning of a poem at 4.16.5 f.). *AL* 456.1 f. Seneca is the most remarkable example, where the subordinate clauses in the opening two couplets are governed by a main verb concluding the sentence in the first foot of line 5. Examples may be added where the break occurs at the diaeresis of the fourth foot in the third line (Mart. 7.13.1 f.), or at the end of the fourth foot in the third line (*AL* 403.5 f. Seneca; 476.1 f. Petronius).

'hoc opus' must here refer to a collection of pieces. The natural inference of this introductory poem is that the pieces are the work of the person who wrote the introduction, rather than a collection of other people's work made by him. For *opus* of collected works of poetry cf. Ovid *Am.* 1. *epig.* 1 f. 'qui modo Nasonis fueramus quinque libelli, / tres sumus: hoc illi praetulit auctor opus'; Mart. 8. *pref.* 5 'hic tamen, qui operis nostri octavus inscribitur'; Quint. *Inst.* 4 *pref.* 4.

lector: an address to the reader is common in Martial (see Citroni's note on 1.1.4), but is not frequent elsewhere in epigram, though it does occur at Cat. 14b.25 and *AL* 283.2 Luxorius as well as here.

corde perito: for the heart rather than the head viewed as the seat of intelligence see my note on Aus. *Epig.* 48.2. For *peritus* of literary expertise cf. *Ep. Bob.* 47.1 ' "arma virumque" docens atque "arma virumque" peritus'

Commentary

(with *TLL* 10.1.1502.53 f.). There is also a suggestion that *cor* here refers to the memory, since the reader weighs up all the writings before making his choice ('omnia perpendens'); for its use elsewhere in this sense, cf. Plaut. *Poen.* 578; Cat. 64.231; Vulg. Prov. 3.3 'describe in tabulis cordis tui' (with *TLL* 4.937.54 f.). Finally, the reader's *cor peritum* affords a contrast to the writer's *parvula, iunior aetas*, the wisdom of experience as opposed to the impetuosity of youth.

4. omnia perpendens: the reader will have to read the whole collection to make his selection. The point must be that he can re-read or recommend favourite epigrams or groups of epigrams without having to bother with the dross. It should not be used to argue that the author did not consider the collection to be architecturally structured as a whole, or that all individual pieces stood alone and could be appreciated as such, because some pieces cannot be properly understood without knowledge of others (e.g. 122-4; 126-7; 180-81; and see p. 2 f.); it is simply a logical development of the modesty theme, in that the reader is acknowledged to be better than the author in detecting quality.

79 / 80 (91 / 91aR)

From a church hanging. Everything you ask of the Lord you will have, if you believe. What good prayers ask, meek faith receives.

Riese printed the superscription 'De velo ecclesiae' as the title to a missing epigram, and the epigram which it heads in the mss as a separate piece. In the addendum to his second edition (2.373) he referred to *ICUR* 2.240, where de Rossi comments on the epigram 'e portis ecclesiarum vela acu picta, litteris quoque insignita pendebant'. De Rossi must be correct in his interpretation: for the prevalence of inscriptional mottoes (or *tituli*) in early churches, and of tapestries and curtains, see below. Thus although there are instances in this collection where a superscription provides evidence of a missing epigram (e.g. 114; 129), this is not one of them.

Two points are raised by this first epigram after the prefatory piece. First, whether the *praefatio* before it is entirely apposite: as has been seen, that epigram is rooted in the light, even frivolous, side of the epigrammatic tradition, and the reader might expect light poetry after it, especially immediately following. It could be argued that this epigram hardly fits that description, since it is a serious motto appropriate to religious furniture in a Christian church. The answer may be that some pieces have dropped out, or that 80-4, which are all Christian in tone, have been misplaced; but, more likely, the author simply may have felt no awkwardness with his ordering of pieces. Equally at home in Christian and pagan worlds, all short poems would have been 'lusus' to him (see also the introduction, p. 4). Second, the question of authorship is raised. Did the author of the

Commentary

collection write this piece, or did he transcribe it from its setting and put it in what effectively becomes an anthology or commonplace book? This is a fundamental question with the collection which recurs, for example, in 81 and 82, but most obviously in those pieces which appear to be actual inscriptions from bathing establishments (99; 108-14; 164; 168). Various answers suggest themselves, for instance (a) that these poems were penned by a single author and were not intended for actual inscription, though they mimic its forms, but for book publication only; (b) that these poems were penned by a single author (perhaps as commissions), were intended for inscriptional use, were inscribed, and were also issued as literary pieces; or (c) that these poems were not written by a single author but were collected from their sites of inscription by him, since he found them interesting and worthy of promulgation, and were thus published in an anthology and mixed with pieces of non-inscriptional nature, whether by the collector or not. Again these issues are discussed in the introduction (see p. 4); my conclusion is that (a) or (b) is more likely the case than (c).

As for this epigram, it is accepted above that it is a motto for a 'velum ecclesiae', as its superscription states. *Vela* or *aulaea* are attested in churches from an early date; they could be used for religious purposes (i.e. veiling and unveiling objects during ceremonies), or to separate areas of the church (e.g. the nave from the aisles, or the sexes from each other in church), or they could be purely decorative, though adorned with uplifting texts or pictures. Some early churches in Rome still preserve the fittings for the rods on which ran the rings supporting the hangings (e.g. S. Giorgio in Velabro; S. Clemente; Sta Maria in Cosmedin). For some literary references see e.g. Ambros. *Hex.* 3.1.5 (*PL* 14.157); Pacian. *Ep.* 3.27 (*PL* 13.1081); Paul. Sil. *S. Soph.* 2.340 f.; with *DS* 5.671 f., esp. 674 f.

Embroidered *vela* are also well evidenced, featuring both image and text: for example Constantine gave *vela* embroidered in gold to his church in Constantinople (*Chron. Pasch.* 294 (pp. 544-5 Dindorf)) and to the Church of the Nativity in Bethlehem (Euseb. *De Vit. Const.* 3.43 (*PG* 20.1104)); cf. Paulinus of Nola's comment at *Carm.* 18.29 f. 'cedo, alii pretiosa ferant donaria meque / officii sumtu superent, qui pulchra tegendis / vela ferant foribus, seu puro splendida lino, / sive coloratis textum fucata figuris'; and *AL* 494R is an epigram celebrating a tapestry given by the Visigothic king Chintila to a Roman church in the first half of the seventh century, of which the superscription states 'in velo quod a Chintilane rege Romae dicatum est':

> Discipulis cunctis domini praelatus amore
> dignus apostolico primus honore coli,
> sancte tuis Petre meritis, haec munera supplex
> Chintila rex offert. Pande salutis opem.

Commentary

(Riese does not print the superscription but it appears in two mss, Leiden Voss. Lat. F. 82 (on which see de Rossi, *ICUR* 2.254), and Munich Clm 22227 (on which see M. Manitius, *Philologus* 62.1903.640); I have accepted Professor Reeve's suggestion of 'dicatum' for mss 'dictum'))

Similar in content to the present epigram are the *tituli* or verse inscriptions which were also a feature of early churches. They are the descendants of the mottoes that could have been found on the entrance to some pagan temples: e.g. this, from the temple of Asclepius at Epidaurus, probably written in the fifth century BC (T. Preger, *Inscriptiones Graecae Metricae*, Leipzig 1891, no. 207; Preger's selection contains other similar examples):

ἁγνὸν χρὴ νηοῖο θυώδεος ἐντὸς ἰόντα
ἔμμεναι· ἁγνείη δ' ἐστὶ φρονεῖν ὅσια.

('He must be pure who goes inside the temple which reeks of incense; purity is to think holy thoughts.') There is particularly full information about St. Paulinus' series of foundations to St. Felix at Nola (Cimitile), built around 400. Some of these buildings were decorated with both pictures and *tituli* and will be discussed further on 82 below. In *Ep.* 32 Paulinus writes to Severus with information about the *tituli* at his churches, and gives some of general application for Severus to use if he wishes. These, for example, could be inscribed above an entrance:

Pax tibi sit, quicumque dei penetralia Christi
    pectore pacifico candidus ingrederis. (*Ep.* 32.12)

Quisque domo domini perfectis ordine votis
    egrederis, remea corpore, corde mane. (ibid.)

And the physical remains of Paulinus' churches at Nola include a considerable number of biblical maxims inscribed on stones used to segregate or delineate areas of the churches: for example, 'Beatius est dare quam accipere' (from Acts 20.35); 'Dilige deum ex toto corde et proximum sicut te' (from Luke 10.27); or 'Qui parcit baculo odit filium suum' (from Prov. 13.24). Some of these have been published at *ILCV* 2472a-d, and there is a fuller collection with illustrations at A. Ferrua, 'Cancelli di Cimitile con scritte bibliche', *RQA* 68.1973.50 f.; Taf. 21 f. On *tituli* in general see E. Steinmann, *Die Tituli und die kirkliche Wandmalerei im Abendlande vom V bis zum XI Jhdt.*, Leipzig 1892, esp. 1 f.; and L. Pietri in *Mélanges d'histoire ancienne offerts à William Seston*, Paris 1974, 419 f.; with further examples at *ILCV* 1510 f.

The above discussion shows that tapestries or hangings were common in early churches, that they could be embroidered with pictures or words,

Commentary

and that those words could comprise moralising or religious maxims to improve the minds of the congregation. The present epigram fits so well into that context that it corroborates the correctness of the superscription which heads it. Lausberg (*Einzeldistichon*, 187 f.) points to literary epigrams which play on the pre-Christian precursors of this epigraphic type, and Martial opens his eighth book thus:

> Laurigeros domini, liber, intrature penates
> disce verecundo sanctius ore loqui.
> Nuda recede Venus; non est tuus iste libellus:
> tu mihi, tu, Pallas Caesariana, veni.

Similarly, though with entirely different emphasis, *Priap.* 1. Lausberg suggests that the present epigram should therefore be treated as introductory in a literary sense (i.e. entry into a collection of poems rather than a building), particularly because of its prominent position at the start of the collection. The observation is well made, but seems to me questionable because this epigram in no way characterises or advertises the nature of the verse which comes after it; it does not, for example, precede a collection which is moralising or religious in tone.

superscr: De velo (A; voto (Iuretus)) ecclesiae: Iuretus' conjecture (cf. 'vota' in line 2) is unnecessary, because a 'velum ecclesiae' is apposite for the epigram headed by this superscription: see intro. above. But 'In velo ecclesiae' might be worth consideration (cf. *AL* 494 R superscr., quoted at p. 69).

1. omnia quae poscis dominum: cf. Vulg. Mark 11.24 'propterea dico vobis, omnia quaecumque orantes petitis, credite quia accipietis, et evenient vobis'. This is close to the epigram, and may well have inspired it; but it is not close enough to use it to 'correct' the prosody of 'recipit' in line 2 (see note).

2. recipit (A); accipit (Müller; Riese); respicit (Baehrens): if the ms. reading is correct, the first syllable of 'recipit' must be metrically long. Riese considered emending to 'accipit' on the basis of the Vulgate quotation above, Baehrens to 'respicit' to correct the prosody. SB (app. crit.) rightly rejects 'respicit' on the grounds that 'alma fides' must belong to the person who prays, not the entity responding, but 'accipit' is an easy change, and the sense hardly less good than 'recipit'. The question of whether or not to accept the emendation can only be approached by examining practice elsewhere in this collection and similar poetry. There are a good number of other examples of irregular prosody in the collection, which are listed at p. 24 (as regards this particular instance, compare the lengthening of the first syllable of 'renuo' at 142.4). And there is further evidence to suggest that the author did write 'recipit' here, namely that initial syllable '*re-*'

Commentary

in verbs is not invariably metrically short, and examples where it is long could furnish incorrect analogues: thus *recido* (or *reccido*) is a present tense verb of similar form with a long first syllable (e.g. Lucr. 1.1063; 5.280; Ovid *Met.* 6.212; 10.18), perfects like *re(d)duxi*, *re(p)peri*, *re(p)puli* and *re(t)tuli*, with long first syllables, could also have been an influence, as might even nouns such as *reliquiae* and *religio* (the length of the first syllable can be short or long, depending on author and date: see Sommer, *Lautlehre*, 158 f.; *KS* 1.937 f.). It is unsurprising that prosodical irregularity with 're-' is amply evidenced in other authors of similar date: e.g. the long first syllable of 'refulsit' at Ven. Fort. *Carm.* 4.19.5 Leo; of 'remissa' at Ennod. 388.68 Vogel; and of 'regreditur' at *Aegr. Perd.* 21; the short first syllable of 'retuli' at Cor. *Joh.* 6.460; 6.596; 7.153 etc.; and there is evidence from Vegetius' practice over prose rhythm that he probably regarded the first syllable of *remedium* as long (see N. Holmes, *CQ* 52.2002.364 with n. 37). See further Müller, *De Re Metrica*, 448 f., though it should be noted that he elsewhere questioned the prosody in this instance, and suggested either 'accipit' or 'percipit', thus anticipating Riese (*RhM* 18.1863.436). But the evidence as a whole shows that 'recipit' need not be emended here.

alma fides: cf. Paul. Nol. *Carm.* 14.80 'alma fides'; 19.200 'crucis alma fides'; Ennod. 128.8 Vogel 'quos ... mens tenet alma fide'.

81 (92R)

On a deceased Christian child. A noble and innocent child died by cruel fate, instilling tears in everyone. But because the kingdom of heaven is always open to the righteous, and because a spotless soul enters heaven, let us condemn our weeping and celebrate the youth's fate; he was without sin, he has been taken off to the stars, and he thrives there. He is blessed in his death, and it is clear that by his early demise he has not deserted his father, but has pleased God.

This Christian epitaph is typical of the genre; some themes, if not most, would fit happily in and derive from pagan pieces, but the stress on the child's lack of sin ('insons', 'regna patent ... iustis', 'animus immaculatus', 'sine peccato'), and the epigram's superscription, nevertheless indicate its religious affiliations. The Vandals of North Africa were Arian Christians, though there is nothing in this epitaph or elsewhere in the collection which reflects specifically Arian thinking or doctrine.

No child's name or other clues to his identity are apparent from the piece, but that is not atypical of similar epitaphs preserved as inscriptions or as literature. Such information could be given separately in an inscription, and there is no reason why this poem could not have served an inscriptional function. I give below three examples of child epitaphs which exhibit similar topics to this one (individual themes are discussed in the notes): first, *CE* 1407 (= *ILCV* 3439):

Commentary

> Hic tenera insontis quiescunt membra sancti:
>   sanctus nomine, sanctus innocentia.
> Annorum triu fuit, mensibus quinque,
>   quem inter astra tenet alma quies.
> Ne doleas, genitor, genetrix quoque; flere desiste:
>   aeternae vitae gaudia proles habit.

Second *CE* 679 (= *ILCV* 3432):

> Hic iacet extinctus pri<mo sub limine vitae>
> angusto multum dilect<us tempore pupus>.
> Nec reor hunc lacrimis <fas esse urgere beatum>,
> corporis exutus vinclis q<ui gaudet in astris>,
> nec mala terreni sensit c<ontagia sensus>.
> Menses namque nove<m postquam super addidit anno>
> complevitque dies vitae se<x, ivit ad astra.>

And third, Luxorius' epitaph for Oageis' infant daughter Damira, of which I quote only part (*AL* 340.3 f.; 13 f.):

> Damira hic tumulo regalis clauditur infans,
> cui vita innocua est quarto dirupta sub anno ...
> Huius puram animam stellantis regia caeli
> possidet et iustis inter videt esse catervis ...

The themes of *mors immatura*, the innocence of the child, and the consolation that (s)he is better off in heaven than on earth are consistently evident.

1. nobilis: the adjective is often used of children in epitaphs: e.g. *CE* 400.2 f. 'Adtas parve puer ... taetra defungeris hora / immeritus decimo praegressus nobilis anno'; *CE* 508.1 'hic iacet Vetedinus pietatis nobilis infas'; and cf. ibid. 1313.1; 1196.7 (none of these instances are Christian). The word refers to character rather than social status.

insons: the repetition of the prefix 'in-' is notable in the opening lines of this epitaph ('insons ... inpubes ... incutiens ... inmaculatus ...'). *Insons* is another frequent adjective in these contexts: e.g. Damas. *Epig.* 44.4 Ferrua 'insontem puerum, qui poena nulla deiectus' (with ibid. 21.10; 63.5; 72.7; Ferrua suggests that in Damasus' terminology 'insons' is equivalent to 'sanctus'); *CE* 770.2 'insontem nulla peccati sorde fucatum' (and cf. *CE* 740.3; 1407.1; *ILCV* 4837.6; *CIL* 6.31934; all these examples are Christian); *CE* 430.2 'quam Parcae insontem merserunt funere acerbo'; *CE* 1165.3 f. 'animae ... piorum ... sedes insontem Magnillam ducite vestras' (and cf. *CE* 395.4; 1230.2; 1988.8; all these are pagan examples).

Commentary

inpubes: cf. *CE* 989.1 'Pistus et inpubis situs hic'; 1119.4 'Parcae nam inpubem quem rapuere mihi' (both pagan). The final syllable of 'inpubes' is irregularly short, as it is also at Drac. *Laud. Dei* 2.628 (for shortening of long final '*-es*' in late Latin see Müller, *De Re Metrica*, 423; 475).

2. lacrimas ... incutiens: for the verb cf. Lucr. 1.19 'omnibus incutiens blandum per pectora amorem'; Tert. *Apol.* 4.6. 'tantum auctori suo doloris incusserunt'; Symm. *Ep.* 1.16.2; 3.88.1; with *TLL* 7.1.1101.63 f.

3. regna ... caelestia: the phrase specifically refers to the Christian heaven: cf. *ILCV* 1312.1 f. 'in tumulo, mors saeva, iace. Caelestia regna / iste videt, cuius membra sepulta premis'; *CE* 1354.7; 1400.1; 2018.2. Damasus *Epig.* 25.5 Ferrua is similar: 'aetherias petiere domos regnaque piorum', and see further Grossi Gondi, *Trattato*, 240 f.

iustis: as Rosenblum says (*Luxorius*, 46 f.), this adjective is used in the Bible and early Christian writers to denote those who have lived 'religiose humaneque' (and they are exclusively Jews or Christians who have followed God's law); it frequently occurs in the Vulgate (e.g. Matt. 25.37; 25.46; Mark 2.17; 6.20; Luke 5.32; 14.14; John 7.24; Acts 10.22; 10.24 etc.). Luxorius pictures the pure soul of Oageis' daughter Damira with the words 'iustis inter videt esse catervis' (*AL* 340.14); and cf. *CE* 781.1 f. 'quisquis post mundum aetherias conscendere plagas / posse putat iustos, Marcellinum quo<que> credat ... / caeli sedes habitare'; Prud. *Peristeph.* 5.514.

4. animus ... inmaculatus: the adjective is almost exclusively Christian (thus *TLL* 7.1.437.17 f. has only two instances of over eighty which are non-Christian: Lucan 2.736 and Amm. Marc. 19.12.9); cf. Vulg. Job 15.14 'homo ... immaculatus ... et iustus; Lact. *Inst.* 3.12.3 'animus immaculatus'; Zeno *Tract.* 2.11.1 (*PL* 11.422) 'innocens martyr, immaculata hostia'; *CE* 787.26; 1946.3.

caelos: it is possible that the plural noun is used rather than the singular to avoid hiatus at the main caesura, though there are instances of such hiatus elsewhere in the collection (see p. 23). But it could also be explained as appropriate for the context: 'regna caelorum' is an epigraphically attested periphrasis for heaven (e.g. *CE* 1425A.4; 2193.4), and 'regna caelestia' have featured in the preceding line; cf. also *CE* 1371.8 'haec te usque ad caelos et super astra tulit'.

5. damnantes fletus: the exhortation for the living not to lament the happier dead is as frequent in pagan as Christian epitaphs (Lattimore, *Themes*, 217 f.). The particular reason given for not doing so in this instance is the prospect of immortality afforded to the child's stainless soul; the first two of the epitaphs quoted in the intro. above feature this theme, and see 3 n. above and 6 n. below.

Commentary

ephebi: the noun hardly accords with preceding 'infante' (superscr.) and 'inpubes' (line 1); the combination might conceivably be intended to suggest that the child died around the age of puberty, but it is as likely to be deliberate variation which has resulted in lexical imprecision. There is plenty of evidence elsewhere in the collection to show that the poet tends to use a variety of synonyms or near-synonyms, and to avoid repeating nouns, within the boundaries of a poem or group of poems (see notes on e.g. words meaning 'male' (97.1), 'lyre' (103.2); 'baths' (111 intro.); 'water' (125.1), 'mare' (137.2; 138.6), 'lawyer' (138.9), 'salver' (141.1), 'image' (147 intro.), 'man' (148.1), 'mouse' (171.3), 'die' (184.3), and 'elephant' (186.3)).

6. raptus ad astra viget: cf. *ILCV* 3432A.2 'quod nomen semper in astra viget'; 3433.6 'sed vivit in a<stris>'; 3434.10 'quod tales animae protinus astra petunt'; *CE* 701.5 'astra tenet nescitque mori sic luce relicta'. The concept of the soul travelling to the stars is found in both pagan and Christian epitaphs (Lattimore, *Themes*, 27 f.; 312 f.); here 'ad astra' is synonymous with 'caelestia regna' in line 3, and means heaven. 'viget' illustrates the immortality of the soul, again common in both Christian and pagan epitaph (Lattimore, *Themes*, 48 f.; 301 f.); 'raptus' hints that the deceased child has been taken by God for his own, a theme which is developed in the following couplet (and again a similar theme is found in pagan epitaphs also: e.g. Aus. *Epig.* 53.7 f.).

7. felix morte sua est: for the consolatory theme that the death of the deceased can be viewed as far as he is concerned in a positive light, see the examples in the intro. above; it amplifies the exhortation to survivors not to lament (see 5 n.).

celeri ... funere: this is typical (if obvious) phraseology of the *mors immatura* genre, that death has come early (see my note on Mart. 11.91.3). Here it is tempered by the belief that the child has been taken by God.

8. non liquisse patrem: this is a rebuttal of the traditional *mors immatura* theme of a child leaving behind grieving parents, which often takes the form that the only grief that the child has caused its parents is its death: e.g. *CE* 398.4 'liquit et orbatos miseros fidosque parentes'; 421.3 'flentes iam liqui parentes'; *CIL* 6.25022 'nullum dolorem accepi tui nisi quod fatalem diem celeriter peregisti'; with Lattimore, *Themes*, 187 f.; 198.

sed placuisse (A; properasse (Müller)) Deo: Müller's suggested emendation (*RhM* 18.1863.436) of a felicitous phrase is unnecessary. 'placuisse deo' is a fitting consolatory response to 'liquisse patrem', particularly since God is a Father himself; and much the same consolation appears elsewhere: e.g. *CE* 2016.4 'hanc placuit deo raptam adsumere sanctis'; and *AL* 661.7 f. R (on twins who predeceased their parents) 'sed dolor est nimius Christo moderante ferendus. / Orbati non sunt: dona dedere deo'.

Commentary

82 (93R)

On the Judgement of Solomon. Parental love was revealed by means of a sword, and by denying her child his mother saves him, victorious through having rejected the prize at stake.

The subject of this epigram is the famous episode from 1 Kings 3.16-28, generally known as the Judgement of Solomon. Two prostitutes had given birth but one child had died, and the women both claimed before King Solomon to be the mother of the surviving child. To settle the matter equitably he ordered that the child should be divided into two by a sword, whereupon one of the women forfeited her claim to the child so that he might be spared, but the other pressed for the order to be carried out. Solomon decreed that the true mother was revealed by the forfeit of her claim, and so gave the child to her.

The epigram is probably best understood as a type of *titulus*, a short piece of verse or prose which explained a painting or image in a church. *Tituli* have been discussed in a different and wider context on 80 above, and this piece too fits well with what is known about the decoration of early Christian churches. Thus Paulinus of Nola describes the function of *tituli* and church decoration in respect of his own foundation of Saint Felix at Nola in *Carm.* 27.580 f.:

> Propterea visum nobis opus utile, totis
> Felicis domibus pictura ludere sancta,
> si forte attonitas haec per spectacula mentes
> agrestum caperet fucata coloribus umbra,
> quae super exprimitur titulis, ut littera monstret
> quod manus explicuit ...

The decorations in Paulinus' churches encompassed scenes and images from both Old and New Testaments (*Carm.* 28.171 f.); for example, the arcade arches of the church of Saint Felix were painted with red crosses, accompanied by a *titulus* such as the following (*Ep.* 32.14):

> Ardua floriferae crux cingitur orbe coronae
>   et domini fuso tincta cruore rubet.
> Quaeque super signum resident caeleste columbae,
>   simplicibus produnt regna patere dei.

Paulinus also describes Old Testament scenes with *tituli* at this church; the *titulus* could be a monitory or improving text, such as this accompanying a picture of Joseph (*Carm.* 27.623 f.):

> Sit mihi castus amor, sit et horror amoris iniqui:
> carnis ut illecebras velut inviolatus Ioseph

Commentary

 effugiam vinclis exuto corpore, liber
 criminis, et spolium mundo carnale relinquam.
 Tempus enim longe fieri complexibus; instat
 summa dies: prope iam dominus, iam surgere somno
 tempus, et ad domini pulsum vigilare paratos.

Or it could be more descriptive, such as this on a Christianised Isaac (*Carm.* 27.616 f.):

 Hostia viva Deo, tamquam puer offerar Isac:
 et mea ligna gerens sequar almum sub cruce patrem.

Amongst Prudentius' works the *Dittochaeon* consists of a series of forty-nine quatrains which are *tituli* for Old and New Testament scenes; the twenty-first features Solomon, though as the founder of his temple rather than as the wise ruler of the present epigram. Another *titulus* from a series of five preserved in the Sylloge Lauresheimensis (Vatican City Pal. lat. 833, published at de Rossi, *ICUR* 2.150, no. 21(a)) also features Solomon and the dedication of his temple. And Rusticus Helpidius' *In Historiam Testamenti Veteris et Novi Carmina* contains a set of three-line hexameters describing and commenting on scenes from the Bible, which may have been intended for *tituli* (*PL* 62.545 f.). The present epigram accords well with this context of early church decoration.

 References to Solomon are frequent in the Church Fathers, who attributed to his authorship the Books of Proverbs, Ecclesiastes, the Song of Songs and the Wisdom of Solomon. As David's descendant, the builder of the temple, and a wise king who ruled in peace, he was sometimes held to prefigure Christ (thus e.g. Aug. *Comm. in Psalm.* 126.2 (*PL* 36.1668)). The stories associated with him furnished rich themes for Christian art, one of the earliest such artefacts extant being a late fourth-century silver reliquary at S. Nazario, Milan; an incised brown agate, thought to date from the late Empire, depicts the scene of the Judgement, with Solomon sitting on his throne holding the child by its leg, a soldier with his sword poised to slice the child in two, and the two women in front of Solomon, one kneeling (see *Dictionnaire d'archéologie chrétienne et de liturgie*, Paris 1903-53, 15.599 f. and fig. 10731); and a fourth-century bowl of North African provenance, now in the Römisch-Germanisches Zentralmuseum at Mainz, depicts Solomon at the top pointing to one woman who averts her gaze, with a second woman standing on the right and, below, a soldier with sword poised over the outstretched body of the child (on which see *Age of Spirituality, Late Antique and Early Christian Art, Third to Seventh Centuries,* ed. K. Weitzmann, New York 1979, 483 f.). Such depictions corroborate the likelihood of the present epigram being a *titulus* for an image in a church. Further on Solomon and the early church, see *The Encyclopaedia of the Early Church*, ed. A. Bernardino, trans. A. Walford,

Commentary

Cambridge 1992, 2.786; and *The Encyclopaedia of Early Christianity*, second edn, ed. E. Ferguson, New York / London 1997, 2.1076 f.

1. pietas: for *pietas* shown by parents to their children, cf. Sen. *Med.* 943 f. 'ira pietatem fugat, / iramque pietas – cede pietati dolor', with *OLD* pietas 3(b); the *pietas* relationship between parents and children is reciprocal, as is that between men and gods (see Pease's note on Verg. *Aen.* 4.382). *pietas* is here said to be 'inventa ferro', a striking phrase, because it is the imminent danger of the killing of the child in accordance with Solomon's order which elicits the display of *pietas* to him by his true mother, when she forfeits her claim to him so that he might be spared his fate. It is her *pietas* which proves her motherhood.

prolemque negando (A; necando (edd.)): 'necando' was printed by Baehrens and Riese, and this epigram did not appear in earlier editions. Riese changed his mind in his Corrigenda (2.373) and advocated 'negando'; he was right to do so, as pointed out by SB (*Towards a Text*, 18 f.), because the child was not killed and the mother's actions were designed to avert his death. SB remarks in his app. crit. that Riese's change of mind may have been prompted by J. Ziehen (*Philologus* 59.1900.305; the point had already been made by L. Müller (*RhM* 18.1863.436 f.)). Compare 144.1, where A reads 'negans' though the correct reading (as in V) is 'necans'.

2. conservat mater ... pignore (de Saumaise); conservamatrem ... pignora (A); conservat matrem ... pignore (Ziehen): in the same article in which he correctly defended 'negando' in line 1, Ziehen also defended A's 'matrem' here. He therefore punctuated the epigram '... pietas, prolemque negando / conservat matrem contempto pignore victrix', glossing the result 'sie verläugnet ihr Kind, aber sie bewahrt ihre Mutterstellung dadurch'. However, although it is the case both that *conservare* can take abstract nouns as object (e.g. 'rerum et temporum ordinem' (*Rhet. Her.* 1.15); 'valetudinem' (Plin. *Nat. Hist.* 22.14); or 'amicitias' (Cic. *Lael.* 100), with *TLL* 4.420.65 f.), and that 'mater' can stand for an abstract concept (as at e.g. Ovid. *Met.* 8.463 'pugnant materque sororque', where 'mater' means 'mens materna' (Bömer), or Claud. 36.104 'quod si non omnem pepulisti pectore matrem'), it is improbable that a reader would understand accusative 'matrem' and nominative 'victrix' in this epigram to refer to the same person, especially if it is a *titulus* for a representation of a well-known scene in which two 'mothers' feature. De Saumaise's slight emendation is therefore to be preferred.

contempto pignore victrix: *pignus* is often used in this collection in the sense 'child' (see 91.4 n.). SB (*Towards a Text*, 18 f.) takes its reference here to be 'the stake' (for which cf. Verg. *Ecl.* 3.31 'tu dic mecum quo pignore certes') rather than 'the child'. But since the child is the prize at stake for which the women argue before Solomon, both meanings are appropriate.

Commentary

83 (94R)

On a wax candle. Slow-burning wax has coated marsh-born papyrus, so that together they may give nourishment to the kindled light.

Three epigrams in the collection focus on artificial lighting, this and 84 on wax candles, and 175 on oil-fuelled lamps. Both this piece and 175 are concerned solely with the material object (for this type of epigram see Introduction, p. 2 f.), whereas 84 introduces a specifically Christian setting.

The present piece and 175 are strongly reminiscent of the epigrams of Martial's *Xenia* and *Apophoreta*, not only because of their distich form, but also their subject matter. In a series of epigrams about artificial light of various kinds (14.39-44) Martial includes one on a *cereus* (42):

> Hic tibi nocturnos praestabit cereus ignis:
> subducta est puero namque lucerna tuo.

The earliest reference to a *cereus* is Plaut. *Curc.* 9 'tute tibi puer es, lautus luces cereum', and Isidore (*Or.* 20.10.3) states the obvious: 'cereus per derivationem a cera nomen habet, ex qua formatur'. The difference between a *cereus* and a *candela* is held to be that the latter used tallow or pitch for fuel and was cheaper and no doubt less pleasant: cf. Fest. 47.27 f. Lindsay 'cereos Saturnalibus muneri dabant humiliores potentioribus, quia candelis pauperes locupletes cereis utebantur' (and see Leary's comments on Mart. 14.40 and 42 *lemmata*). There is also a poem in praise of wax for candle manufacture at *AL* 747R.

On the making of wax candles in Antiquity, which was usually accomplished by the repeated dipping of a wick in molten wax, see J. Francis, 'Lumen et Candela', in *In Altum, Seventy-Five Years of Classical Studies in Newfoundland*, ed. M. Joyal, Newfoundland 2001, 177 f.; *RE Supplb.* 13.1347 f. (Wachs), esp. 1386 f.; Forbes, *Technology*, 6.131 f. The religious and ceremonial use of candles is discussed at 84 intro.

1. lenta: the adjective connotes both the sticky, glutinous character of wax, and its slow-burning properties. For the former cf. Verg. *Georg.* 3.281 'lentum destillat ab inguine virus'; Stat. *Silv.* 3.2.67 'lentas transire paludes'; for the latter, cf. Hor. *Carm.* 1.13.7 f. 'arguens / quam lentis penitus macerer ignibus'; Ovid *Tr.* 3.11.39 f. 'saevior illo / qui falsum lento torruit igne bovem', with *TLL* 7.2.1164.11 f.

paludigenam: the adjective occurs only here and *Ep. Bob.* 48.3 'paludigenis perlucida Virgo fluentis'; J. André (*RPh* 47.1973.12) compares Greek ἑλειογενής. There is point in the adjective in that marshlands and water are not surroundings immediately associated with fire and combustion; the paradox is more explicitly made by Ennodius (14.6 Vogel): 'papyrum ad alimenta ignium limfa transmisit', and it also occurs in amatory conexts (see 135.1 n).

Commentary

vestivit: the verb alludes precisely to the method of manufacture, by the progressive clothing of the wick in layers of melted wax.

papyrum: for papyrus (processed and twisted into a rope-like material) used for candle wicks, cf. Isidore's faulty etymology (*Or.* 17.9.96) 'papyrum dictum quod igni et cereis est aptum; πῦρ enim Graeci ignem dicunt'; *AL* 84.2; schol. Juv. 3.287; Plin. *Nat. Hist.* 28.168; Paul. Nol. *Carm.* 14.100; and Lewis, *Papyrus*, 27 with n. 11.

84 (95R)

Another. In order that, as votive dedications to saints, candles may create light in churches, a sheet of wax has covered the sedge of the Nile. It provides sustenance appropriate to a votive flame, that which previously afforded homes to chaste bees.

For wax candles see intro. to the previous epigram; this epigram deals with specific Christian use of candles, and introduces some specifically Christian symbolism of bees.

Christian use of candles followed directly from pagan use, particularly, but not exclusively, as regards cults of the dead. Thus candles (or lamps) were lit in remembrance during pagan funerals and at tombs: 'assidebat aegrae fidissima ancilla, simulque et lacrimas commodabat lugenti, et quotienscumque defecerat positum in monumento lumen renovabat' (Petr. 111.4); 'candelae etiam in sepulturis ante mortuos praecedebant' (schol. Pers. 3.103); cf. Plin. *Nat. Hist.* 16.178; *Dig.* 40.4.44. There is much inscriptional evidence for the practice: e.g. *CIL* 8.9052 'ita ut statuam meam et uxoris meae tergeat et unguat et coronet et cereos II accendat'; according to Cumont the earliest reference to the custom is at *CIL* 11.1420, which deals with the cult of Gaius and Lucius Caesar at Pisa (see F. Cumont, 'Cierges et lampes sur les tombeaux', in *Miscellanea G. Mercati* 5 (= *Studi e Testi* 125.1946), 41 f.; F. Cumont, *Lux Perpetua*, Paris 1949, 48 f.). That the practice was carried over into early Christian tradition is shown by references which illustrate disquiet over it, particularly the use of artificial light in daytime: thus Canon 34 of the Council of Elvira, dating to the early fourth century: 'cereos per diem placuit in coemeteriis non incendi, inquietandi enim sanctorum spiritus non sunt' (*Concilium Eliberritanum* 34, *La Colección canónica hispana* 4, ed. G. Martínez Díez and F. Rodríguez, Madrid 1984, 253); Jerome in his reply to the attack by Vigilantius on the reverence paid to martyrs' relics defends the burning of candles at tombs while the sun is still up (*PL* 23.345 f.); and Jerome also poses the question whether lights lit before martyrs' tombs are a sign of idolatry (*Ep.* 109.1). See further *RLAC* 7.154 f. (Fackel); and D.R. Dendy, *The Use of Lights in Christian Worship*, London 1959, 92 f.; 108 f.

Votive candles are frequently attested by Gregory of Tours in the sixth

Commentary

century, though the practice predates him (cf. e.g. Lact. *Inst.* 6.2.5). He mentions, for example, a bee-keeper who offered Saint Martin his entire wax production for church candles if his bees were restored to him (*De Virt. S. Mart.* 4.15), and it seems to have been common practice for the sick to offer a candle of their own height if restored to health (ibid. 1.18; *Gloria Conf.* 21; cf. Ven. Fort. *Vita S. Radegundis* 32 (*PL* 88.509), with Dendy, op. cit. 112 f.).

The popularity of candles in the early church is further demonstrated by liturgies which grew around them. The *laus cerei* or *ad incensum lucernae* is a hymn for the lighting of candles at vespers, with examples as early as Prudentius (*Cath.* 5), Ambrose (*Hymn* 2 (*PL* 16.1409)) and Augustine (*Civ. Dei* 15.22, with M. Cutino, *Orpheus* 18.1997.396 f.), and which is also mentioned at *Per. Aeth.* 24.4 ('hora autem decima, quod appellant hic licinicon, nam nos dicimus lucernare, similiter se omnis multitudo colliget ad Anastasim, incenduntur omnes candelae at cerei, et fit lumen infinitum'). Hymns for the blessing of the paschal candle on Easter Sunday are a further development: Prudentius *Cath.* 5 was used for that purpose, and cf. Ennodius' *Benedictio Cerei* (14 Vogel). See further J. Fontaine, 'Poésie et liturgie, sur la symbolisme christique des luminaires, de Prudence à Isidore de Séville', in *Études sur la poésie latine tardive d'Ausone à Prudence*, Paris 1980, 184 f.; J. Bernal, 'La "laus cerei" de la liturgia hispánica', *Angelicum*, 41.1964.317 f.

Lastly, candles perform the entirely practical purpose of providing light in churches during the hours of darkness. Aetheria, quoted above, hints at this, as does Paulinus of Nola (*Carm.* 14.98 f.):

> Aurea nunc niveis ornantur limina velis,
> clara coronantur densis altaria lychnis,
> lumina ceratis adolentur odora papyris,
> nocte dieque micant; sic nox splendore diei
> fulget et ipsa dies caelesti inlustris honore
> plus nitet innumeris lucem geminata lucernis.

This last aspect is apparent in the present epigram ('ut ... clarescant lumina'), and Christian religious practice is also brought out in words such as 'devota' and 'votiferae'.

1. devota piis ... lumina (de Saumaise; limina (A)) templis (templo (Kay)): 'lumina' is a convincing correction, because (a) the line benefits from a noun meaning 'candles' to lead into the description of their manufacture in line 2, and (b) 'devota piis ... limina templis' is an unconvincing phrase, since *limina* are unlikely to be *devota* (whereas *lumina* are; 'limina' may have intruded into A because the phrase 'limina templi' at the end of a hexameter line was familiar to scribes: it occurs at e.g. Ven. Fort. *Carm.* 1.2.1; *Cor. Joh.* 6.98; *Laud. Just.* 2.8). 'devota' with

Commentary

'lumina' should be understood to refer to votive candles, and is picked up by 'votiferae ... flammae' in line 3. But 'piis ... templis' is not straightforward: 'devota lumina piis' is in itself a convincing, self-contained phrase, since substantival 'pii' is often synonymous with 'sancti' or 'martyres' (cf. 'turba piorum' (Damas. *Epig.* 16.1 Ferrua); 'cineres piorum' (ibid. 16.11); 'in regione piorum' (Paul. Nol. *Carm.* 18.23) etc., with Ferrua's note on Damas. *Epig.* 16.1, and W. Dürig, *Pietas Liturgica*, Regensburg 1958, 47 f.), and saints are excellent recipients of votive candles. Moreover, North Africa, and Carthage in particular, was famous even as early as Cyprian in the mid-third century for its martyr cults (*Ep.* 12.2; 39.3 Hartel), and note Augustine's comment (*Ep.* 78.3) 'numquid non et Africa sanctorum martyrum corporibus plena est'; Prud. *Peristeph.* 4.61 f.; with W.H.C. Frend, 'The North African Cult of Martyrs', *Jenseitsvorstellungen in Antike und Christentum: Gedenkschrift für Alfred Stuiber*, Münster Westf. 1982, 154 f. (= Paper XI in *Archaeology and History in the Study of Early Christianity*, London 1988); and V. Saxer, *Morts, martyrs et reliques en Afrique chrétienne aux premiers siècles*, Paris 1980, 105 f.; 239 f. This suggests that 'piis' is not an adjective which qualifies 'templis', but a noun; if this is so, 'templis' would then be locative, though, to avoid ambiguity, emendation to 'templo' (or 'templi' (Reeve)) is worth consideration.

The noun *templum* is often used in early Christian contexts to denote either the whole church building or parts of it (cf. Ven. Fort. *Carm.* 1.2.1 'quisquis ad haec sancti concurris limina templi'; Damas. *Epig.* 45.8 Ferrua 'crevit in his templis per tua damna decus'; ibid. 71.4 '(sc. Constantina) sacravit templum victricis virginis Agnes, / templorum quod vincit opus terraeque cuncta'; *ILCV* 1800.1 f., perhaps written by Ambrose himself for his foundation of what is now S. Nazario Maggiore at Milan, 'condidit Ambrosius templum dominoque sacravit / nomine apostolico, munere, reliquiis. / Forma crucis templum est, templum victoria Christi ...'). This nomenclature was perhaps facilitated by Christians being perfectly prepared on occasion to take over pagan temples suitably adapted: thus Ennodius, describing a church 'where a temple of idols had been', concentrates on its renovation rather than demolition, with the Christians allowing both the edifice and its name of *templum* to remain (98 Vogel, with Kennell, *Ennodius*, 109); and buildings such as the temple of Aphrodite at Aphrodisias and the Parthenon at Athens were converted to Christian use (see *Aphrodisias Papers I*, *JRA* supp. vol. I, ed. C. Roueché and K.T. Erim, Ann Arbor 1990, 75 f.; M. Beard, *The Parthenon*, London 2002, 49 f.).

2. Niliacam: Egypt and the Nile area are the most frequently mentioned habitats of the papyrus plant in Antiquity: thus Plin. *Nat. Hist.* 13.71 'papyrum ergo nascitur in palustribus Aegypti aut quiescentibus Nili aquis'; Mela 3.96. This area was certainly the main one (perhaps the only one) for commercial papyrus production, though papyrus was known to grow in other areas, such as the Middle East (Theophr. *Hist. Plant.* 4.8.4; Lewis, *Papyrus*, 3 f.).

texit cerea lamna: the phrase well describes the usual method of candle manufacture, by dipping the wick in hot wax to build it up layer by layer (see 83 intro.). *Lamina / lamna* usually refers to metal in sheets, but is used of other materials – e.g. Plin. *Nat. Hist.* 16.229 'eadem (sc. fagus) sectilibus lamnis ... utilis' (with *TLL* 7.2.907.14 f.).

budam: 'sedge', as stated at Don. ap. Verg. *Aen.* 2.135 'ulvam ... quam vulgo budam appellant'; papyrus, here keyed by 'Niliacam', belongs to the genus *Cyperaceae*, the sedges. The noun *buda* is rare, but also crops up in Augustine (*Ep.* 88.6; 105.3); at *Vitae Patrum* 5.10.76 (*PL* 73.925), where 'buda de papyro' is an item of bedding (I owe the reference to Dr Adams); and in glosses (*CGL* 4.211.32; 5.443.6; 5.564.33). It is probably a word of African origin (André, *Botanique*, 59 compares Berber 'tabuda'), and the name of an occupation at Cypr. *Ep.* 42 Hartel, *budinarius*, must derive from it.

3. congrua ... pabula: wax is fitting sustenance for a votive candle in a Christian context because of the symbolism attached to the bees who make it (see 4 n. below).

votiferae ... flammae: this is the flame of the 'devota lumina' of line 1. The adjective occurs also at Stat. *Silv.* 4.4.92 'votifera ... ab arbore'.

4. quae: the antecedent noun is *cera*, which has to be understood from 'cerea lamna' in line 2.

castis apibus: bees are *castae* because it was thought they reproduced asexually. The locus classicus is Verg. *Georg.* 4.197 f., a passage often cited with approval by Christian writers:

> illum adeo placuisse apibus mirabere morem,
> quod neque concubitu indulgent, nec corpora segnes
> in Venerem solvunt aut fetus nixibus edunt;
> verum ipsae e foliis natos, e suavibus herbis
> ore legunt ...

(cf. also Plin. *Nat. Hist.* 11.46 'apium enim coitus visus est nusquam'). Bees therefore readily became a symbol of purity in Christian thought (see e.g. Ambros. *De Virgin.* 1.8.40 f. (*PL* 16.200); Aug. *Civ. Dei* 15.27.4; Ennod. 14.9 Vogel; Prud. *Cath.* 3.71 f. etc.), on which see further *RLAC* 2.279 f.; E. Wimmer, *Biene und Honig in der Bildersprache der lateinischen Kirchenschriftsteller*, Vienna 1998, 82 f.

A Spanish *laus cerei*, of which the text is printed by J. Bernal (op. cit. (intro. above), 321), elaborates the same theme, describing wax in the following terms:

Commentary

quae non polluitur ex parente
cuius natura de flore
cuius ortus ex virgine
cui illa dat genetrix nativitatis originem
quae corruptionis nescit errorem ...

And P.-A. Février and C. Poinssot (*CArch* 10.1959.149 f.) discuss the symbolism of an early baptismal font from Kélibia in Tunisia, on which are carved candles and a bee. The *castae apes* are not an incidental detail in this epigram, but an important theme in it.

85 (96R)

On a negligent elementary teacher. An untrained teacher took on boys of tender age to get them to learn their elementary letters. But when he does not discipline his pupils with any terror and ineffectually ceases from eliminating their errors by the cane, the boys throw around their writing tablets and celebrate the Floralia. Now he properly has the name of 'games teacher'.

This competent if unremarkable skoptic piece satirises an elementary school teacher who is unable to keep order amongst his riotous pupils; the humour lies in the concluding pun on 'ludi magister'. Teachers at all levels were a good topic for comic writing (notably Aristophanes' *Clouds*; and cf. Juv. 7.200 f.; Mart. 9.68 (with Henriksén); 10.62; *AL* 289 Luxorius). The teacher of this epigram is at elementary level (lines 2; 6), though the terminology used is not specific about the subjects he taught (see 1 n. 'cauculo'; 2 n. 'litterulas'); for primary education in Antiquity see Bonner, *Education*, index 'teachers, primary'.

1. suscepit: for *suscipere* of teachers taking on students cf. Quint. *Inst.* 2.5.1 'susceptos a se discipulos'; it also appears in that sense at 148.1.

cauculo (AW); canculo (B); cavalo (V): for the spelling of the noun as *cauculo* rather than *calculo*, note also *cauculus* at 182.1, 183.3 and 187.8; and a gloss gives 'cauculator ψηφιστής' (*CGL* 3.310.3; 402.78). The spelling is rightly defended by O. Keller (*RhM* 30.1875.303); the change of 'dark' *l* before a consonant to back vowel *u* is also evidenced by Romance reflexes, particularly in French (e.g. *alter* and Fr. *autre*; *calx* and Fr. *chaux, chaussée*; *calidus* and Fr. *chaud*; *falsus* and Fr. *faux*; see also von Wartburg, *Wörterbuch*, 2.107, Sommer, *Lautlehre*, 132, and Adams, *Bilingualism*, 622). For the '-o' termination of the noun, cf. Fest. *Brev.* 1.1 'morem .. calculonum'; Aug. *Ord.* 2.12.35, quoted below (occasionally, as with *calculo* and *calculator*, the suffixes *-o / -onis* and *-tor / -toris* were both applied to the same stem to produce nouns of the same meaning (e.g. *aleo / -ator; lustro / -ator; pedico / -ator*)). Nouns ending in *-o / -onis*

Commentary

denote entities, usually animate, with a characteristic derived from the base of the noun (there is a treatment with full lexicon at C. Kircher-Durand, *Création lexicale: la formation des noms par dérivation suffixale*, (*Grammaire fondamentale du latin IX*), Louvain etc. 2002, 302 f.).

One might have supposed on the basis of his name that the *cauculo* would have been concerned with teaching arithmetic; he certainly is at Aug. *Ord.* 2.12.35 (*PL* 32.1012): 'quibus duobus repertis (i.e. letters and numbers) nata est illa librariorum et calculonum professio'; and cf. Isid. *Or.* 10.43 'calculator a calculis, id est lapillis minutis, quos antiqui in manu tenentes numeros componebant'; and Mart. 10.62.4. But in this instance he is specifically associated with 'litterulas' (see 2 n.), which suggests reading and writing rather than arithmetic (the *calculatores* of Isid. *Or.* 1.3.1 are also apparently teachers of elementary letters). No doubt he teaches all these subjects at elementary level; he is termed a 'ludi magister' in line 6 (and 'magister ludi' is actually glossed by 'calculo' at *CGL* 5.604.42 and 635.34), and the *ludi magister* of Mart. 10.62 likewise teaches both numbers and letters.

2. primas ... litterulas: for the adjective, which indicates elementary education, cf. Sen. *Nat. Quaest.* 6.23.4 'quisquis primas litteras didicit'; Quint. *Inst.* 2.5.1 'prima rhetorices rudimenta'; Ulp. *Dig.* 50.5.2.8. The diminutive 'litterulas' also suggests elementariness (although *litteras* would be precluded by metre): cf. Cic. *Att.* 7.2.8 'Chrysippum vero quem ego propter litterularum nescio quid libenter vidi'; Mart. 9.73.7 'at me litterulas stulti docuere parentes'.

3. nullo terrore coercet: since physical punishment is dealt with in the following line, this phrase might suggest shouting and haranguing, a trait for which primary teachers were well known (e.g. Mart. 5.84.2; 9.68.4 f.).

4. ferulis: for the use of *ferulae* in schools for physical punishment, see my note on Mart. 11.39.10.
    culpas tollere: cf. *AL* 724.10R 'in melius reparamus opus culpamque priorum / tollimus'.

5. Floralia ludunt: for a similar phrase used of schoolboys cf. Juv. 7.239 'ne turpia ludant'. The festival of the Floralia took place in spring, reaching a maximum of six days under Augustus, reducing to four by the fourth century (see in general *LIMC* 4.1.137 f.; *RE* 6.2749 f.; and *RLAC* 7.1124 f.). Whilst the festival would hardly have been celebrated as such in Christian Vandal Africa, its reputation for licence and immorality would have been well enough understood: Mart. 1. *praef.* states 'epigrammata illis scribuntur qui solent spectare Florales' (see Howell's note); Lactantius (*Inst.* 1.20.10) refers to its 'verborum licentiam, quibus obscenitas omnis effunditur'; and Augustine remarks 'tanto devotius, quanto turpius' (*Civ.*

Commentary

Dei 2.27). During the festival various items such as seeds, chickpeas and beans were thrown around (schol. Pers. 5.177 f.; Porph. ap. Hor. *Sat.* 2.3.182), just as the boys throw around their writing tablets under the tutelage of this ineffectual teacher.

6. ludi ... magister: the sobriquet of the elementary teacher, *ludi magister*, gives the epigram its concluding joke; for the appellation cf. [ps.]Ascon. on Cic. *Divin. in Caec.* 47 (= *Ciceronis orationum scholiastae*, ed. T. Stangl, 2.199.18 f.) 'omnem enim scholam ludum dixere Romani, et magistri ludi dicuntur qui primas litteras docent'. The obvious play on 'ludi' is found also at e.g. Plaut. *Bacch.* 129; *Merc.* 303; Cic. *Quint.* 3.4.6. Quintilian thought school was given the surprising name *ludus* precisely because it was not a *lusus* (*Inst.* 1.6.34); Bonner suggests it might be so called because a *ludus* was a form of military training, a mock rather than real battle, and a wider application of the term could have developed (*Education*, 56 f.); but it is actually a calque on Greek σχολή.

86 (97R)

On Bellerophon. Bellerophon, overcoming the Chimaira's dread fire, victoriously touches the clouds on the Gorgon-horse.

This is the first of a large number of epigrams in the collection on mythological themes, and it forms a linked pair with the following piece on the Chimaira (see further p. 3). It may well be ecphrastic in type, in that it could have been written to describe a work of art, presumably a painting or mosaic, or could even have been written for viewing alongside such a work, like a Christian *titulus* (see 82 intro.).

The Bellerophon myth goes back to Homer (*Il.* 6.152 f.; see also Apollod. 2.3.1 f.; Hyg. *Fab.* 57; *Astr.* 2.18; Fulg. *Myth.* 3.1; Roscher 1.763 f.). He was the son of Glaucus or Poseidon, his mother being Eurymede or Eurynome; Stheneboea (Anteia in Homer), the wife of Proetus king of Argos and Tiryns, fell in love with him and promised him her husband's throne if he reciprocated. He rejected her and she accused him of attempted seduction, so Proetus sent him to his father-in-law Iobates with a letter asking him to kill the bearer. Iobates then demanded that Bellerophon kill the Chimaira and various other monsters, expecting him to perish in the attempt, but he accomplished the task with the aid of Pegasus (cf. Hes. *Theog.* 319 f.; frag. 43a.82 f. M/W). Iobates thereupon gave Bellerophon his daughter in marriage, and he later inherited the kingship.

The scene of Bellerophon and Pegasus encountering the Chimaira was always popular in art, and remained so in late Antiquity. A fifth-century Coptic fabric, known as the Châle de Sabina, shows Bellerophon, Pegasus and the dead Chimaira in a scene similar to that suggested by this epigram (see further *LIMC* 7.1.214 f.; late representations of the

Commentary

myth are nos 13; 67; 78; 143-4; 183; 185-6; 235 (the Châle de Sabina). A recently discovered late mosaic from a house or baths at Henchir Errich in central Tunisia depicts the Chimaira and Bellerophon along with other mythological figures (F. Béjaoui, *AntTard* 10.2002.209 and fig. 34)).

It is however possible (though unprovable) that the Bellerophon story had greater resonance for the author of this epigram and his readers, because Bellerophon became an exemplar of virtuous behaviour, his image (for example) being used on Roman imperial coinage (e.g. Nero (*LIMC* 7.2.157 Pl. 136), Septimius Severus (ibid. 157 Pl. 142) and Lucius Verus (ibid. 162 Pl. 179)). It has been further suggested that Bellerophon and his fight with the Chimaira became a symbol of Christian virtue in late Antiquity, prefiguring or re-inforcing such images as the fight of Saint George and the dragon. Prime evidence for this is a fourth-century mosaic discovered in 1963 at Hinton St. Mary in Dorset, England, which features in its two main roundels both the earliest known image of Christ in Britain and the fight of Bellerophon with the Chimaira. Jocelyn Toynbee, who first published the mosaic, argued for the Christian symbolism (*JRS* 54.1964.8 f., with Pls I-VIII), and further arguments were adduced by S. Hiller, *Bellerophon, Ein griechischer Mythos in der römischen Kunst*, Munich 1970, 66 f., and M. Simon in *Mélanges d'archéologie, d'épigraphie et d'histoire offerts à Jerôme Carcopino*, Paris 1966, 889f. The alternative view, to see Bellerophon solely as a typical huntsman of virtuous nature whose story lent itself well to pictorial representation, has been promulgated by H. Brandenburg, 'Bellerophon Christianus?', *RQA* 63.1968.49 f. (and in his review of Hiller at *JbAC* 14.1971.163 f.); G.M.A. Hanfmann in *Age of Spirituality, A Symposium*, ed. K. Weitzmann, New York 1980, 85 f.; and J. Huskinson, *PBSR* 42.1974.73 f. As regards the present epigram, the only factors that might lead to a specifically Christian interpretation are its proximity to the group of evidently Christian epigrams at 79-84, and its late date; but if it was known, for example, that it served as a *titulus* for a church painting or mosaic, such an interpretation would be confirmed. However, as things stand it is unnecessary to read any religious symbolism into it, and it need have no meaning beyond that of describing an image of classical mythology, as do many other epigrams in the collection.

There is another epigram about Pegasus, Bellerophon and the Chimaira at *AL* 383, though it is incomplete because the Codex Salmasianus breaks off after the first three lines.

1. incendia dira: for the fire breathed out by the Chimaira cf. Hom. *Il.* 6.182 'δεινὸν ἀποπνείουσα πυρὸς μένος αἰθομένοιο', with Kirk's note on fire-breathing monsters at Hom. *Il.* 6.179-83; and cf. *AL* 350 Luxorius.

2. victor ... nubila tangit: the epigram depicts Bellerophon at the point of victory; he used Pegasus to take him out of reach of the opposition's weaponry by launching his attacks from on high (Euripides employed

Commentary

theatrical cranes or flying-machines to illustrate this in his *Bellerophon* and *Stheneboea*, scenes parodied by Aristophanes in his *Peace* (82 f.; 154 f.), for which see Olson's commentary at pp. xxxii-iv). Compare also Apollod. 2.3.2 and Pind. *Ol.* 13.87 f.:

σὺν δὲ κείνῳ καί ποτ' Ἀμαζονίδων
αἰθέρος ψυχρῶν ἀπὸ κόλπων ἐρήμου
τοξόταν βάλλων γυναικεῖον στρατὸν
καὶ Χίμαιραν πῦρ πνέοισαν καὶ Σολύμους ἔπεφνεν.

('And with it (i.e. Pegasus) in time he slew / With shafts from the cold vales of the desolate air / The archer-host of Amazon women, / The fire-breathing Chimaira, and the Solymoi' (trans. Bowra)).

Gorgoneo ... equo: for the epithet cf. Ovid *Pont.* 4.8.80 'Gorgonei ... equi'; *Fast.* 3.450; Stat. *Theb.* 4.61; and 'Gorgonei ... caballi' at Juv. 3.118. Pegasus was the offspring of Poseidon and Medusa: Poseidon coupled with her and Pegasus (with, in some versions of the myth, Chrysaor) leapt out when Perseus decapitated her (Hes. *Theog.* 282 f.; cf. Apollod. 2.4.2; Ovid *Met.* 4.784 f.; with *LIMC* 7.1.214 f.).

87 (98R)

On the Chimaira. A lioness as regards her face, a goat as regards her back, and a serpent at the tail, the beast shoots firebrands from her three mouths.

This epigram on a mythological theme, the Chimaira, is a companion piece to that preceding. It is similar in its description of the creature to that given by Homer (*Il.* 6.181 f.):

πρόσθε λέων, ὄπιθεν δὲ δράκων, μέσση δὲ χίμαιρα,
δεινὸν ἀποπνείουσα πυρὸς μένος αἰθομένοιο ...

('she was a lioness in front, a snake behind, a goat in the middle, breathing out a dread force of blazing fire ...'). Lucretius renders his model felicitously (5.904 f.):

qui fieri potuit, triplici cum corpore et una,
prima leo, postrema draco, media ipsa, Chimaera
ore foras acrem flaret de corpore flammam?

This epigram is less effective, with the ugly repetition in 'ore' / 'tergemino ab ore' using the noun in two different senses; with the imbalance of the tricolon in the first line, where two nouns which are ablatives of respect, 'ore' and 'tergo', are followed by the nominative adjective 'postrema' (see

Commentary

note); and with the replacement of the Greek 'chimaira' by the Latin 'caper'. There are other literary descriptions of the Chimaira at Hes. *Theog.* 319 f.; Eur. *Ion* 203 f.; Ovid *Met.* 9.647 f.; and Apollod. 2.3.1. The beast was also a popular subject in the visual arts, the usual imagery basically following the literary descriptions above, with the body and head of a lioness, the tail ending in a serpent's head, and the head of a goat (sometimes half a goat, including the front legs) rather improbably emerging from the back (see *LIMC* 3.1.249 f.).

1. ore leo tergoque caper: the ablatives are ablatives of respect; for *leo*, rather than *leaena* or *lea*, of a lioness, see 170.1 n. The poet presumably envisaged the creature with a lioness's head and body, and a goat's head emerging from its back (thus, as in other literary descriptions, its tripartite nature relates specifically to its heads, because most of it was lioness (as expressly at Eur. *El.* 474)). By using the noun 'caper' the poet forgoes use of Greek χίμαιρα (literally 'goat'), which is the feature which gives the beast its name, or perhaps was added because of its name (see West's note on Hes. *Theog.* 321, citing H. Usener at *RhM* 58.1903.171; in either case the equivalence of the part with the whole is unsatisfactory for its tripartite configuration, and Lucretius apologises for it with 'ipsa' (5.905, quoted above)).

postremaque serpens: 'postrema' is best construed in the light of passages of Lucretius and Vergil by which it is presumably influenced. Lucretius writes of the Chimaira 'prima leo, postrema draco, media ipsa, Chimaera' (5.905); and in Vergil's description of Scylla (*Aen.* 3.426 f.) he writes: 'prima hominis facies et pulchro pectore virgo / pube tenus, postrema immani corpore pistrix ...'. In both 'postrema' is a feminine nominative adjective with a noun understood, Chimaera and Scylla respectively; in this instance it appears that 'bellua' needs to be understood from the following line, though the clumsiness of the construction after the preceding ablatives has been remarked above.

2. tergemino ... ab ore: a recondite question arises as to which of the Chimaira's heads spouted fire. In Homer (quoted intro. above) it might have been the goat's or the lioness's (see Kirk's note on Hom. *Il.* 6.179-83); in Ovid (*Met.* 9.647) and Apollodorus (2.3.1) it is the goat's; in Lucretius (quoted intro. above) it might be the goat's, the lioness's, or all three; here it is certainly all three. See also 86.1 n.; and for *-geminus* adjectival compounds see my note on Aus. *Epig.* 61.1.

faces: the noun is more emphatic than 'flammas', since 'faces' are firebrands, torches used in warfare and the like, more fearsomely hostile than simple flame (e.g. Sen. *Tro.* 1073; Stat. *Theb.* 9.19); they are often associated with fierce spirits or the Furies (e.g. Verg. *Aen.* 4.472 f.; Ovid *Met.* 10.350; Val. Flacc. 4.393).

Commentary
88 (99R)

On Laocoon. The two snakes pull Laocoon apart with their coils, and one fate claims the father and his sons. Yet it's because he did violence to the back of a wooden nag, people allege that's the reason why savage poison racked the man! What hope is there when the godhead of immortals has already been offended, if a wooden horse dares to vent such anger?

Laocoon was a Trojan and priest of Apollo Thymbraeus and Poseidon; he had two sons, their mother usually named Antiope. His appearance in myth centres almost exclusively on his encounter with the Trojan horse and his family's fate. He does not feature in the Homeric epics, his first appearance being in the *Iliupersis* (*EGF* p. 62.10 f. Davies); the best-known version of his myth is in Vergil, where he vainly attempts to get Priam not to bring the wooden horse into Troy, striking it with his spear and making the Greeks' weapons inside it clang ominously (*Aen.* 2.40 f.). Although there are differences (see 4 n. 'lacerasse') there are enough similarities in the story and enough verbal echoes to suggest this poet is following Vergil: thus Vergil's snakes appear as 'gemini ... immensis orbibus angues' (2.203 f. / cf. line 1 'gemini ... nexibus angues'); they first throttle his sons to death (2.213 f. / line 2); they then both throttle and poison Laocoon himself (2.217 and 221 / lines 1 f. and 4); and the Trojan onlookers in Vergil's account assume that Laocoon has been punished for affronting the horse ('et scelus expendisse merentem / Laocoonta ferunt, sacrum qui cuspide robur / laeserit et tergo sceleratam intorserit hastam' (2.229 f.)). This last is the most effective echo in the epigram, which the author picks up with the word 'ferunt' in line 4: it is significant because the reason for the divine anger aimed at Laocoon was actually not his striking of the horse, but his coupling with his wife in front of the divine image of Apollo, whose priest he was; the Trojans misinterpreted the reason for the divine wrath behind what they witnessed, with fatal consequences (thus Serv. ap. Verg. *Aen.* 2.201, naming his source as Euphorion). The poet further demonstrates his knowledge of this in the concluding couplet (see 5-6 n.); indeed, it is no exaggeration to characterise his poem as a reflection on the workings of divine justice through the example of Laocoon, and an elucidation of what is only implicit, or even ambiguous, in Vergil's account.

Further on the Laocoon myth see Apollod. *epit.* 5.16 f. with Frazer's note; *LIMC* 6.1.196 f.; and Roscher 2.1833 f.

1. Laucontem (A): whereas Vergil uses the Greek accusative 'Laocoonta' at *Aen.* 2.230, the contracted Latinised form of the name is used here and in the superscription; the contraction goes back at least as far as Petr. 89.43 'Laoconte', and a hybrid 'Lauconta' (Baehrens' emendation of ms. 'Laoconta') occurs at Drac. *Rom.* 5.285. The name unsurprisingly often gives rise to ms. problems (e.g. at *AL* 1.2.4 the mss give variously

Commentary

'Laucoontis', 'Laocoontis', 'Laccontis' and 'Laocontis'). At *AL* 54 A gives the same superscription it gives here ('De Lauconte'), and, since the epigram following is not about Laocoon but Glaucon, Baehrens assumed that an epigram had been lost in transmission; but both Riese (in his edition) and Courtney (*C&M* 40.1989.201) must be correct in suggesting that the name has simply lost an initial 'G', as has <G>lauco in the first line of the epigram. 'De Lauconte' does however illustrate the scribe's familiarity with this form of the name.

3. quod tamen (A; namque (Meyer); sacra (Riese); tantum (Timpanaro)): ms. 'tamen' is emended by recent editors, but for no good reason: the construction 'quod tamen ... hinc ...' should be understood as exclamatory (I have punctuated the text accordingly), expressing the poet's indignant incredulity at the widespread belief that Laocoon suffered his terrible fate, which has been objectively described in the opening couplet, merely because he struck a wooden horse with his spear. 'quod ... hinc ...' is causal, and 'tamen' has an adversative sense, questioning the basis of an interpretation of events which can attribute such apparent unreasonableness to the gods' treatment of Laocoon (cf. the definition at *OLD* tamen 4: 'yet (in spite of likelihood to the contrary)'). The epigram concludes with a rhetorical question which develops this view, alluding to the implications if the gods were to treat everyone as they are alleged to have treated Laocoon. J. Ziehen (*RhM* 53.1898.271 f.) defends ms. 'tamen' on similar grounds.

iligni: deliberately echoed in 'ligneus ... ecus' at line 6, a jingle which suggests the reason for its appearance here; *ilign(e)us* refers to items made from wood of the *ilex* or holm-oak. The adjective occurs in verse also at Ter. *Ad.* 585; Verg. *Georg.* 3.330; and Claud. 24.323; this is the only occasion on which it is used of the Trojan horse.

violarit: the verb much abbreviates the story ('validis ingentem viribus hastam / in latus inque feri curvam compagibus alvum / contorsit' (Verg. *Aen.* 2.50 f.)), but implies that Laocoon has committed a crime for which punishment may be expected (cf. Liv. 6.20.16 'violatum Capitolium esse sanguine servatoris', with *OLD* violo 1(a)).

terga caballi: although *caballus* is by this date a generic term for horse without the overtones of poor quality it earlier had (see Adams, *Pelagonius*, 569 f.; *CQ* 53.2003.563 f.), it is used in a debunking sense in mythological contexts elsewhere (e.g. Juvenal's 'Gorgonei ... caballi' of Pegasus (3.118)), and such irreverence is appropriate here, in the context of the author's indignation at the apparent severity of Laocoon's punishment.

4. hinc: used here of cause not place, picking up 'quod tamen' in the previous line, and again stressing authorial indignation.

lacerasse (Oudendorp); tollerasse (A); tolerasse (Meyer; Riese);

Commentary

temerasse (Maehly) ... venena: it has been noted in the intro. above that this epigram is indebted to Vergil's account of the story, which includes the snakes both throttling and poisoning Laocoon, as they do here; but although the snakes kill the children in Vergil's account, Vergil leaves it unclear as to whether they kill Laocoon himself (they certainly injure him horribly), though his simile involving a bull injured at a botched sacrifice suggests to me that they do not finish the job (*Aen.* 2.223 f.; however, modern commentators, if they offer any comment, state that Laocoon is killed (e.g. R.G. Austin, *JRS* 49.1959.16 f., esp. 21), and it may be that our author thought likewise). Therefore 'tolerasse', which presumably lies behind A's misspelling and which would here imply Laocoon's survival, cannot be dismissed (and it is supported on these grounds by Riese in his Addenda at 1.372). On the other hand the statement in line 2 ('cumque suis genitis sors habet una patrem') strongly suggests that as far as this poet is concerned Laocoon does die with his children, and that in this detail he may not follow Vergil (there are variations over it in the other literary sources: in some (e.g. Hyg. *Fab.* 135) Laocoon and his sons are killed; in some (e.g. Apollod. *epit.* 5.18) only the sons are killed; whilst in the *Iliupersis* (loc. cit. intro.) Laocoon and one son are killed). It can further be argued that ultimately 'tolerasse' does not convince because the emphasis required in the context is on the unreasonable severity of Laocoon's punishment rather than his toleration of suffering. Oudendorp's conjecture 'lacerasse' should therefore be accepted (and is preferable to Maehly's 'temerasse' (at *ZOeG* 22.1871.565)); for *lacerare* used of the effects of poison cf. Juv. 6.624 f. 'haec potio torquet, / haec lacerat mixtos equitum cum sanguine patres'.

ferunt: see intro. above for this significant echo of Vergil's account; the meaning here is a general 'people allege that ...', with the implication being that they are in error.

5-6: quid sperare datur ... ecus?: the concluding *sententia* is better understood as a rhetorical question about man's lot in general, rather than Laocoon's fate in particular (this type of generalising conclusion is frequent in the collection as a whole (see 168.5-6 n.)). Furthermore, if the interpretation of lines 3 and 4 advanced above is correct, the tone of the question is likely to be one of indignation, illustrating the hopeless world-view of those who allege ('ferunt') that Laocoon was punished merely because he struck the wooden horse (to paraphrase: 'if men really are punished so severely for such trivia, what hope can they have for their dealings with the gods?'). However, neither ms. 'iam' in line 5, nor ms. 'cum ... audet' in line 6, is easy to understand. Taking line 6 first, the statement 'when a wooden horse ventures to show such anger' seems inappropriate to the context, because the poet ought to question its veracity, not affirm it. An objection to 'audet' has been voiced on somewhat

Commentary

different grounds by L. Zurli (*GIF* 49.1997.145 f.); his solution is to emend to 'audit (= perhibetur)', which would give good sense and attractively pick up 'ferunt' in line 4. The conjecture can however be questioned on the grounds that such a use of 'audit' with infinitive is very rare, found elsewhere only at Cat. 68.112 (see Kroll's note). But a similar result can be achieved by emending the opening 'cum' of line 6 to conditional 'si'; the tone of 'audet' is then both hyperbolic and indignant. Finally, as regards 'superum iam numine laeso' in line 5, if the above interpretation of lines 3 and 4 is correct, the phrase would contain an allusion to the Laocoon myth, and would demonstrate the poet's knowledge that Laocoon was not punished because he struck the horse, but because he had offended against a god (this gives some weight to the otherwise awkward 'iam', though it can also be said that it is used elsewhere in the collection as metrical padding (see 93.5 n.)). To paraphrase again, the poet indignantly asks 'what could anyone hope for if he has actually already offended against a god, if gods really do punish men because wooden horses get angry when struck with a spear?'. The reader can conclude that, since Laocoon was not punished by the gods because he struck the horse, there might be room for hope even when a sin of some substance has been committed; at the least, he can assure himself that Laocoon's story does not prove divine justice is entirely whimsical or disproportionate.

5. superum iam numine laeso (A); superorum numine laeso (Oudendorp): 'numine laeso' is another apposite reminiscence of Vergil (see intro. above), though of the opening of the *Aeneid* rather than the Laocoon episode: 'Musa, mihi causas memora, quo numine laeso / quidve dolens regina deum tot volvere casus / insignem pietate virum, tot adire labores / impulerit. Tantaene animis caelestibus irae?' (1.8 f.). Oudendorp's conjecture, made to get rid of 'iam', is probably not necessary (see 5-6 n. above).

6. si (Kay; cum (A)) ... audet (A; audit (Zurli)): for a discussion of the text see 5-6 n. above.

ecus (equs (A)): A has 'equs' rather than 'ecus' here (with a supralinear 'u' in a different hand), though at 166.8 it has 'ecus'; the question is one of orthography, and it is not possible to determine what spelling the author adopted, or even whether he was consistent. Some grammarians thought *equs* was correct (e.g. *Gramm. Lat.* 4.195.1 'nomina generis masculini, quae per q non per c litteram scribuntur: equs, coqus, iniqus, antiqus'; ibid. 197.30 'equs non ecus'); and both 'ecus' (e.g. *CIL* 14.3911; *CE* 1332.5, etc.) and 'equs' (*CIL* 8.4508.7) are found in inscriptions. See also Sommer, *Lautlehre*, 129.

Commentary
89 (100R)

On a temple of Venus which <was demolished to build> walls. The wonder that was an ancient temple is knocked down by crowbars, and a consecrated building tumbles down for use in war. For those stones which are rolled along after the columns have been demolished are shortly to be re-used for the merlons on the walls. Mars has abbreviated his love's postponement: now Venus seeks out her temple amongst his walls.

This epigram takes a specific event for its theme, the demolition of a temple of Venus to re-use the stone in fortification walls. It is especially interesting in being one of the few pieces in the collection offering any evidence at all for its time and place of composition which might be corroborated by external sources (see further Introduction, p. 5 f.). Unfortunately the detail is not specific enough to permit any certainty, and the best that can be done is to ask whether there is anything in the poem to support or contradict the assumption that the collection belongs in time and place to the Vandal occupation of North Africa. The conclusion will be that there is certainly no contradiction and there is even some corroborative evidence, though it is speculative.

In what follows I have made the assumption that the place in North Africa under Vandal rule that would be most likely to accommodate a temple of Venus and defensive walls is Carthage. Evidence stems largely from the walls. Most importantly we know from Procopius (*De Aedif.* 6.5.1 f.) that the invading Vandals generally destroyed existing Roman town defences to prevent the Romans getting back inside them, but that they allowed the walls of Carthage (and a few other places) to remain, though they eventually fell into disrepair and decay; and Florentinus, in his eulogy on the Vandal king Thrasamund (496-523), actually describes Carthage as 'in moenibus ampla' (*AL* 371.34). This gives a reasonable context for Carthage having city walls during the Vandal period, and for repair and rebuilding being necessary if the walls were ever needed. An obvious such occasion would have been around the time of Belisarius' invasion in 533-4, either shortly before or after it, depending on which side carried out repairs. It is thus significant that Procopius specifically draws attention to Belisarius' repair of the walls, and records Gelimer's remark on seeing them after his defeat that his neglect of them had led to his downfall (*Bell. Vand.* 1.23.19 f.); so could this epigram possibly relate to events of 533-4 (see p. 6)?

The archaeological evidence needs also to be considered. The city walls of Carthage were probably built immediately before the Vandal invasion, in around 425 (cf. *Chronica Gallica* for 425 (*MGH: AA* 9.658)). Little now remains of them, but excavations have confirmed the date of construction, the disrepair under the Vandal occupation, subsequent rebuilding under Belisarius, and the use of stone from demolished buildings for repair work (see *Excavations at Carthage: The British Mission*, ed. H.R. Hurst and S.P.

Commentary

Roskans, British Academy 1984, 1.1.13 f.; 59; *Excavations at Carthage 1976 Conducted by the University of Michigan*, ed. J.H. Humphrey, Ann Arbor 1977, 3.15 n. 36; and *New Light on Ancient Carthage*, ed. J.G. Pedley, Ann Arbor 1980, 47 f.).

A temple of Venus at Carthage is not strongly evidenced (indeed J.B. Rives, *Religion and Authority in Roman Carthage from Augustus to Constantine*, Oxford 1995, 43 can state that 'In Carthage there is almost no evidence for any cult of Venus whatsoever'). However, Cyprian refers to an area of the city 'in vico qui dicitur Saturni inter Veneream et Salutariam' (*Acta Proconsularia Cypriani* 2.5 (= *Acts of the Christian Martyrs*, Musurillo, 170.24 f.)), where 'Venerea' probably refers to a temple of Venus. *AL* 104.1 refers to a location as being 'in spatio Veneris', which may offer further evidence from this collection (though see note ad loc.). And, most interestingly, a recent re-evaluation of the sanctuary of Tanit in Carthage has tentatively identified a temple of Venus, parts of which may actually have been incorporated into the city walls (H. Hurst, *The Sanctuary of Tanit at Carthage in the Roman Period: A Re-interpretation*, Portsmouth RI 1999 (= *JRA* suppl. series 30), esp. 81 f.; 95 f.; with figs 18; 42; Hurst does not refer to this epigram). It is tempting to speculate that the initial incorporation of that structure into the walls, or (perhaps more likely given the description) the subsequent appropriation of stone from it to repair the walls, could have led to this epigram; its very proximity to the walls is significant in this context.

Although the above exposition provides no definite proof, it at least suggests that the genesis of this epigram from events which took place in early sixth-century Carthage is quite possible.

superscr.: De templo veneris quod ad muros <extruendos dirutum est> (A; *suppl.* Sched.): this superscription is unusually lengthy, the words not in A being supplied from the *Schedae Divionenses*, on which see Introduction, p. 14; the supplement is perfectly reasonable, though it adds nothing not in the epigram itself.

1. rastris: the context makes clear that these are tools for demolition work. Although a *rastrum* is usually a metal hoe (cf. Varro, *Ling. Lat.* 5.136 'rastri, quibus dentatis penitus eradunt terram, atque eruunt'; K.D. White, *Agricultural Implements of the Roman World*, Cambridge 1967, 52 f.), there is no need to question the use of the noun here. Burman reports that Oudendorp suggested 'rutris' (on which see Fantham's note on Ovid *Fast.* 4.843) because *rastra* are only agricultural implements; but Varro's language demonstrates how *rastra* could perform a demolition function in the manner of a crowbar. Vegetius (*Mil.* 1.24.5; 2.25.6) recommends *rastra* as part of military equipment for the construction of *fossae*.

veteris miracula templi: cf. 99.11 'nostri miracula fontis'; *miraculum* often refers to the seven wonders of the world (e.g. Val. Max. 4.6. *ext.* 1;

Commentary

Mela 1.85; Mart. *Spect.* 1.1; 8.36.1; Amm. Marc. 22.15.28), which suggests its tone here.

2. inque usum belli: see the intro. above for the city walls of Carthage. Evidence for the re-use of pagan temples and other buildings for fortifications can be adduced from written records: e.g. *Cod. Theod.* 15.1.36 (November 397) 'quoniam vias pontes, per quos itinera celebrantur, adque aquaeductus, muros quin etiam iuvari provisis sumptibus oportere signasti, cunctam materiam, quae oriunda (Mommsen for ms. ordinata) dicitur ex demolitione templorum, memoratis necessitatibus deputari censemus quo ad perfectionem cuncta perveniant'. For some evidence from archaeological remains other than at Carthage, see T.F.C. Blagg in *Roman Urban Defences in the West*, ed. J. Maloney and B. Hobley, London 1983, 130 f.; and S. Johnson, *Late Roman Fortifications*, London 1983, 84 f.

tecta: the noun here is a synecdoche for the building as a whole, a usage specifically remarked by Quintilian (*Inst.* 8.6.20); note also 115.1.

3. quae (Oudendorp); qua (A): A gives 'qua' here and 'haec' in line 4, and the two together cannot be correct; either 'quae ... haec (sc. saxa)' or 'qua ... hac' (Meyer's conjecture) is required. Since 'haec sunt ... relocanda minis' is the more elegant construction at line 4, Oudendorp's antecedent 'quae' should be accepted here.

columnis (Klotz); tabernis *vel* coronis; (Ziehen); catervis (A): the ms. 'catervis' is nonsense in the context, and Ziehen rightly argued that emendation needs to give an architectural feature to balance 'murorum ... minis' in the following line, and to give Venus some recognisable temple feature to look for in her perusal of the walls (*Festschrift für Otto Benndorf zu seinem 60 Geburtstage*, Vienna 1898, 49 f.). But his suggestions of 'tabernis' (which according to him can refer to a temple arcade) or 'coronis' (the top part of an entablature) are not as convincing as Klotz's more mundane 'columnis', which has the added merit that the stones would be of the right shape to roll along ('volvuntur').

4. murorum ... minis: *minae* are the projecting tops of fortified walls, namely merlons or crenellations. Thus Verg. *Aen.* 4.88 f. 'pendent opera interrupta minaeque / murorum ingentes aequataque machina caelo', on which Servius comments 'eminentiae murorum, quas pinnas dicunt'; and cf. Amm. Marc. 20.6.2; 24.2.12; 24.2.19 with *TLL* 8.994.3 f. See also D. Baatz in Maloney and Hobley op. cit. (2 n. above), 136 f.

5. dilati (A; deleti (Petschenig); dilapsi (Maehly); dilecti (Baehrens); pilati (Riese)) Mavors conpendia cepit amoris: SB rightly castigates proposed emendations in his app. crit.: '*frustra omnes; nam moras Veneris Mars praecidit*'. The 'amor' of Mars is of Venus herself, as the following

Commentary

line makes clear, and it has been 'dilatus' following the debacle when the pair were caught in flagrante by the outraged Vulcan and turned into an amusing spectacle for other immortals (Hom. *Od.* 8.266 f.). The 'amor' is rekindled by the symbolic mingling of the stones of Venus' temple with the fortifications of Mars' wall, and by the opportunity of a fresh encounter which her perusal of his walls will afford him. The ms. reading was defended on these lines by J.M. Stowasser (*WS* 32.1910.99).

90 (101R)

On a sedan. The gleaming sedan encloses modest matrons; it sparkles and it sports a long side on both sides. A pair of mules carry it under two poles, and they move the swaying cocoon forward at a modest pace. Great care has been taken to ensure that a chaste, married lady should not go through public places darkened by the sight of men.

This is the first of a series of epigrams in the collection which describe and comment on what may be termed everyday objects (see p. 2 f.). On occasion, as here, these pieces seem to go out of their way to emphasise the good qualities of an item, and have an almost promotional tone about them. In stressing how this sedan chair protects the modesty of the ladies it carries ('matronas claudit ... pudicas ... provisum est caute ...'), and suggesting the pleasure of travelling in it and the effect it has on onlookers ('aurea ... radians ... modico pendula saepta gradu'), it could stand as a reasonable piece of advertising for the manufacturer or retailer. Other epigrams which could have a similar marketing flavour are 95; 96; 122-4; 158-60; 165-6 (for produce), and 99; 108-13; 164 (for bathing establishments).

A *basterna* is a sedan chair or litter, associated with the later Empire (Serv. ap. Verg. *Aen.* 8.666; see also Blümner, *Privataltertümer*, 448); its precursors are the *sella* and *lectica* (for which see my notes on Mart. 11.98.11-12). Isidore (*Or.* 20.12.5) says of it 'basterna vehiculum itineris, quasi viae sternax, mollibus stramentis composita, a duobus animalibus comportata', which would well accord with the *basterna* of this piece; it could also be carried by porters (*CGL* 4.24.35; 5.348.5). That it was, as here, particularly associated with women is evidenced by *CGL* 5.520.24 'genus vehiculi quo nobiles Romanorum matronae vel virgines vehebantur'; but Symm. *Ep.* 6.15 shows it was also used by men. It was a vehicle in which the occupant could sleep (Jer. *in Is.* 66.20 (*PL* 24.670)), its enclosed character facilitating this. A gloss from a twelfth-century ms. (previously Sir Thomas Phillipps ms. 4626, now Brussels II 1049 (?)) was thought by R. Ellis to be close enough to this epigram to suggest it might display knowledge of it (*JPh* 8.1879.122): 'basterna: basterne etiam dicuntur quaedam matronarum in itinere vehicula quae desuper cooperta et mollioribus stramentis composita a duobus equis trahuntur'. If so, this would be one of few instances where knowledge of pieces from

Commentary

the collection can be demonstrated in external sources (see also 105.2; 106.14; 17; 19; and 171.3, with notes); regrettably it is not so, because the source is clearly Isidore (see above).

1. aurea ... basterna: the adjective is picked up in the following line by 'radians'; there is a similar *aurea carruca* at Mart. 3.62.5. The sedan was certainly not made wholly of gold, nor indeed of metal, since that would have made it too heavy to carry; 'aurea' might therefore indicate it was gilded (cf. Cic. *De Div.* 1.119, where 'sella aurea' is used of Caesar's gilded throne), or that it gleamed in the sun because of its golden or yellow colour, or that it had brass, gilt or even gold fittings. There is a curious parallel in Ennodius 332 Vogel, an epigram which is headed 'In basterna uxoris Bassi Violae':

> Quam vaga constantem retinent haec tecta decorem!
> Mittitur a domina quicquid habent pretii.
> Nam rutilat fulvum Violae de luce metallum:
> possessor radios spargit ubique suos.

The *metallum* in line 3 and the *radii* in line 4 represent the reflected moral excellence of the sedan's occupant Viola, though the conceit only has point if such sedans could be decorated with precious metal or a gleaming imitation of it.

The noun *basterna* is late, and does not appear in our sources before the fourth century (e.g. Amm. Marc. 14.6.16; Jer. *Ep.* 22.16; note that Greek βαστέρνιον and βαστερνάριος turn up at *Cat. Cod. Astr.* 1.103.25 and *IG* 3.1433.7 respectively); it is frequently glossed (see intro. above and *TLL* 2.1782.63 f.). Its origin is uncertain; Isidore's 'quasi viae sternax' (*Or.* 20.12.5) can be discounted, as can any link to the German tribe Bastarnae. The most likely possibilities are derivation from either (a) Greek βαστάζω ('carry / lift') or (b) Latin *bastum* ('stick / pole'; cf. It. bastone, Fr. bâton). In favour of (a) are the appropriateness of the βαστ- stem and its appearance elsewhere in Latin as *bastaga* and *bastagarius* ('baggage / baggage-maker'; cf. *Cod. Theod.* 8.4.11; 10.20.11 with *TLL* 2.1782.6 f.; 16 f.); as regards (b), which I prefer, *bastum* is an extremely rare noun, occurring only at *SHA Comm.* 13.3, but the derivation of *basterna* from it can be supported by the analogy of e.g. *fustis / fusterna* and *trabs / taberna*. The *-ern-* suffix is found both in temporal adjectives (*hodiernus* etc.) and in *-erna* nouns, which invariably denote objects, and of which the stem is usually related to the material out of which the object is made, a quality it possesses, or the function it serves (e.g. *caverna, cisterna, lanterna* etc.: more examples at *LHS* 1.322; *KS* 1.975 f.). It may therefore be significant that *fustis*, *trabs* and *bastum* all denote wooden items, suggesting that *basterna* may have been coined on analogy with *fusterna* and *taberna*.

claudit: throughout the collection the poet is fond of describing objects

Commentary

which contain other items within them, and the verb *claudere* and its compounds are accordingly frequent in this sense: see also 78.3; 96.2; 112.2; 125.3; 128.2; 166.1 and 6; 178.6; 188.7.

2. radians: see 1 n. above.

**latum (Vossius; palatum (AW); patulum (B); pandum (Baehrens))
... latus:** the mss reading, assuming it is 'patulum' and AW's 'palatum' is only a slip, causes concern, because 'patulum', in the sense of 'wide open', is the opposite of what is required (cf. 'claudit' in line 1, and the express prohibition of the occupants of the sedan being seen in lines 5-6). Although *patulus* can refer to broadness as well as openness (e.g. the wagons of Verg. *Georg.* 3.362; the ships of Plin. *Nat. Hist.* 36.68; and the chests of Juv. 13.74), even when so used a notion of openness still persists, as one would expect with the adjective's derivation from *pateo*. A reference which might offer support, Statius' 'patulis ... Saeptis' at *Silv.* 4.6.2, is clearly humorous ('open enclosures') and not an acceptable parallel, but in any case 'patulum' is incongruous enough here to be rejected (though it is defended by E. Wölfflin (*ALL* 1.1884.338)). However, it is not easy to find a convincing alternative, and with some hesitation I accept Vossius' 'latum' (attributed to Burman by Riese and others; but Burman explicitly says otherwise, and the conjecture is at least as old as G.J. Vossius, *Etymologicon Linguae Latinae*, Amsterdam 1662, 66). Its point is to stress the length of the vehicle's sides, pertinent in that the vehicle's occupant is able to recline (for which see intro. above); and *latus* can refer to length as well as to the more usual width (e.g. Hor. *Ars* 209, with Brink's note; *TLL* 7.2.1021.48 f.). Baehrens' 'pandum' is less convincing, because there is no reason for the sedan's sides to be curved or bowed. It can be added that 'latum ... latus' provides a punning jingle, ignoring metrical quantity, of a type which is well attested (see 158.1 n), and 'lătus ... lāti' actually occurs at Verg. *Aen.* 6.42 f. (see Austin's note).

utrimque (Scheffer); utrumque (codd.): Scheffer's small emendation is attractively idiomatic and has been accepted by editors from Burman onwards.

3. geminus: *geminus(-i)* + noun can connote two things combined into one, one thing divided into two, or, as here, two things; in this latter sense a plural construction would be more usual, but it is not invariable (cf. Verg. *Aen.* 3.535 f. 'gemino demittunt bracchia muro /... scopuli'; Sen. *Herc. Oet.* 1205 'gemina serpens'; with *TLL* 6.2-3.1740.25 f.).

duplici sub robore: the *robora* are the poles of the *basterna* by means of which it was carried by the mules: cf. Pallad. 7.2.3 'a tergo vero eiusdem vehiculi duo brevissimi temones figurantur velut amites basternarum'. The animals would have been harnessed one at the back and one at the front of the sedan (thus L. Casson, *Travel in the Ancient World*, London

Commentary

1974, 180). 'duplici' here has the same force as preceding 'geminus', i.e. there were two load-bearing poles (cf. Claud. 7.103 'duplexque ... ensis'; ibid. *carm min.* 52.81 'duplex ... anguis', with *TLL* 5.1.2267.37 f.).

burdo: the *burdo* is the male mule or sometimes the hinny (*CGL* 2.324.56 and Isid. *Or.* 12.1.60 respectively); a mule is the product of a mare and ass, the hinny of a stallion and ass. But hinnies would have been too small to be useful for carrying a chair and are not in point here. The male mule seems to have been chiefly used for carrying burdens on its back, the female for the traction of carriages, though the carrying of the chair by males here (cf. 'geminus') combines elements of both tasks (cf. Pelag. 196.2 with Adams, *Pelagonius*, 122). The noun *burdo* is also found in Luxorius (*AL* 195.6; 360.6, and as a name at 360.3); see further *TLL* 2.2248.27 f.; J.N. Adams, *RhM* 136.1993.35 f., esp. 56 f.

4. pendula saepta: 'saepta' alludes to the enclosure of the sedan in which the occupants travelled; Martial at 11.98.12 refers to a 'sella saepibus clusa', which is precisely the same idea ('saepibus' is F. Walter's excellent emendation of the mss 'saepius', and is further confirmed by this reference: see my note on Mart. loc. cit.). 'pendula' illustrates the swinging of the sedan from its poles as it is carried along.

5. per loca publica: cf. 148.4 'publica selliferum per loca duxit ecum'.

6. fuscetur (B); fugetur (A); fucetur (W): both 'fucetur' and 'fuscetur' would yield good, and to all purposes, identical meaning. Both verbs are well attested in a metaphorical sense (*TLL* 6.1.1459.84 f.; and 1652.67 f. respectively). Here 'fuscetur' makes a pleasingly explicit colour contrast with 'aurea' in line 1, and a similar contrast is found elsewhere (e.g. *CE* 1347b.19 'candida fuscatus nulla velamina culpa'); it is slightly preferable.

casta marita: synonymous with a 'matrona pudica' of line 1, a married matron of unassailable moral probity.

91 (102R)

On Medea with her sons. The trial of their faithless father destroys the innocent ones, and Jason's sons are paying for his crimes with their death. But although their mother, widowed with her husband still living, is cutting down her precious children to punish her husband, sacred parental love nevertheless alleviates the outrage of her madness: the one son she is attacking in fury, the other she is lifting up in pity.

This is another epigram on a mythological theme (on which see p. 3), examining the myth of Medea from the viewpoint of her murdered children; it has attracted recent critical attention, particularly as regards the text and import of its closing line. The vivid image of that line suggests the piece is ecphrastic in nature, and indeed the barbarian queen Medea was frequently portrayed in the arts of all periods in Antiquity. To take one example, scenes from the murder story, though avoiding the actual killing of the children, are frequent on Roman sarcophagi (see *LIMC* 6.1.386 f. (nos 50-61 for sarcophagi); and V. Zinserling-Paul, 'Zum Bild der Medea in der antiken Kunst', *Klio* 61.1979.405 f.). But the most famous ancient image of Medea, and one which gave rise to much ecphrastic poetry, was a painting by Timomachus of Byzantium (usually dated to the first century BC) which was acquired for the temple of Venus Genetrix in the Forum Julium at Rome on its dedication by Julius Caesar in 46 BC. It showed Medea preparing to kill her children: this is Antiphilus' epigram about it (*AP* 16.136):

> τὰν ὀλοὰν Μήδειαν ὅτ' ἔγραφε Τιμομάχου χείρ
> ζάλῳ καὶ τέκνοις ἀντιμεθελκομέναν,
> μυρίον ἄρατο μόχθον, ἵν' ἤθεα δισσὰ χαράξῃ,
> ὧν τὸ μὲν εἰς ὀργὰν νεῦε, τὸ δ' εἰς ἔλεον·
> ἄμφω δ' ἐπλήρωσεν. ὅρα τύπον· ἐν γὰρ ἀπειλᾷ
> δάκρυον, ἐν δ' ἐλέῳ θυμὸς ἀναστρέφεται.
> ἀρκεῖ δ' ἁ μέλλησις, ἔφα σοφός· αἷμα δὲ τέκνων
> ἔπρεπε Μηδείᾳ κοὺ χερὶ Τιμομάχου.

('When Timomachus' hand was painting Medea the murderess, dragged this way and that by jealousy and by her children, he took up the infinite task of portraying her double character, the one part inclining to rage, the other to pity. He did both in full. Look at her image: tears dwell in her menace, wrath in her compassion. Wise men have said, "Take the intention for the deed"; the children's blood was worthy of Medea, but not of the hand of Timomachus.' (Text and translation are from Gow-Page, *GP* 1.122-3.)) And this is an anonymous epigram of probably much the same date, mid-first century AD (*AP* 16.135):

> τέχνη Τιμομάχου στοργὴν καὶ ζῆλον ἔδειξε
> Μηδείης, τέκνων εἰς μόρον ἑλκομένων·
> τῇ μὲν γὰρ συνένευσεν ἐπὶ ξίφος, ᾗ δ' ἀνανεύει
> σώζειν καὶ κτείνειν βουλομένη τέκεα.

('The art of Timomachus showed the love and jealousy of Medea as she drags her children to death. She half consents as she looks at the sword, and half refuses, wishing both to save and to slay her children.' (The text is Page's (*FGE* 388), the translation based on the Loeb.)) The first of these epigrams is translated at *Ep. Bob.* 53, whilst *AP* 16.137 Philippus, on the same theme, is translated at *Ep. Bob.* 54; other probable treatments are at *AP* 16.138 and 140 anon.; 139 Julian. Aeg.; 143 Antip. Thess.; and

Commentary

AP 9.346 Leonidas Alex.; Timomachus' painting is also mentioned at Ovid *Tr.* 2.526; *Aetna* 595; and frequently in Pliny's *Nat. Hist.* (7.126; 35.136; 35.145); see further Gow-Page, *GP* 2.43 f.; Page's commentary on Euripides' *Medea* pp. lxvi-lxvii; K. Gutzwiller, 'Timomachus' Medea and Ecphrastic Epigram', *AJPh* 125.2004.339 f.; and, for possible copies of the work from Pompeii and Herculaneum, M. Beard and J. Henderson, *Classical Art: From Greece to Rome*, Oxford 2001, 29 f.

I stress two points here, because they have a bearing on the interpretation of this epigram, and particularly on the text of the final line. First, Timomachus' painting did not depict the murder of the children, but evoked Medea's conflicting emotions before the killing (some epigrams explicitly state that Timomachus refrained from showing the deaths: e.g. *AP* 16.138.6; 140.5 f.). This epigram, on the other hand, given its ecphrastic nature, describes a work of art which depicts the killing as it is taking place ('opprimit ... morte luunt ... metat ... premit ...'); a piece by Philippus, following immediately on those which describe Timomachus' painting and headed εἰς τὸ αὐτό, also describes a painting which depicts the actual murder, and it too is therefore either very freely based on Timomachus' painting, or is based on a different work, whether real or imaginary (*AP* 16.141, with Gow-Page, *GP* 2.367). That however is not crucial here; the key point is that the author of this epigram evidently does not provide an accurate description of Timomachus' painting which can be expected to accord with other literary descriptions based on it (neither does he make any mention of Timomachus). Second, the Greek epigrams usually highlight Medea's conflicting emotions of hate and pity (e.g. *AP* 16.135.3 f.; 136.1 f. (both quoted above); 138.3 f.; 139.1 f.; 140.1 f.; and 143.1 f.), making this conflict their main focus. That is also the case with the conclusion of this epigram; although I argue that it does not offer a description of Timomachus' painting, its focus on Medea's conflicting emotions nevertheless allies it as literature to the 'Timomachus' type of epigram, a Latin tradition of which is evidenced by the Bobbio epigrams mentioned above.

1. opprimit insontes infidi causa parentis: the linguistic register of the opening of the poem is distinctly legal: it is Jason's 'trial' at Medea's hands ('causa') which condemns him, he is guilty of a crime ('crimina') by reason of his adultery ('infidi'), and yet it is their children whom Medea executes ('morte luunt') to punish him ('poenam'); similarly at Sen. *Med.* 924 f. Medea says 'liberi quondam mei, / vos pro paternis sceleribus poenas date'. The verb *opprimere* also has a legal sense of consequences of judicial proceedings unfairly overwhelming defendants, witnesses or others appearing before courts (cf. Cic. *Quinct.* 7 'quo is facilius quem velit iniquo iudicio opprimere possit', with more examples at *TLL* 9.2.789.7 f.). The poet thus adeptly hints at the terrible injustice of the myth: the children are *insontes*, but are destroyed because of the actions of an

Commentary

infidus father and *insana* mother (compare his take on the Laocoon myth at 88 above).

The murderous role of Medea in this version of the myth was perhaps invented by Euripides; earlier tradition had given Medea more than two children and had not portrayed her as their intentional killer or their killer at all (e.g. schol. Eur. *Medea* 264 (= *Oechaliae halosis* frag. spur. *EGF* p. 152 f. Davies)); see Page's commentary on Eur. *Medea*, p. xxi f.; and Apollod. 1.9.28 with Frazer's note.

opprimit: the verb is picked up by 'premit' in line 6, and affords an instance of the figure of a compound verb with simplex iteration; for examples in poetry see W. Clausen, *AJPh* 76.1955.49 f. (esp. 51, for instances where, as here, the simplex is separated by some distance from the compound); 86.1965.97 f.; Wills, *Repetition*, 438 f.

2. Iasonis: the name is well-positioned and can be construed ἀπὸ κοινοῦ with 'infidi parentis' in line 1, and with both 'nati' and 'crimina' in line 2; Jason's responsibility for events is thereby emphasised. This is one of the earliest occasions in extant Latin on which 'Iason' is scanned as a disyllable with consonantal 'I'; Drac. *Rom.* 10.426 'niveam cum Iasone Glaucen' is the other ('Iason' elsewhere in Dracontius is trisyllabic). For other proper nouns with initial consonantal 'I' in Latin see Müller, *De Re Metrica*, 307; and for consonantalisation of initial iota of other Greek proper nouns transliterated into Latin, see Biville, *Emprunts*, 2.190 f.

nati: that Medea had two sons was established in the Euripidean version of the myth (*Medea* 1136 etc.; cf. Apollod. 1.9.28; Hyg. *Fab.* 25; 239; Drac. *Rom.* 10.531); Pausanias (2.3.6) gives their names as Mermerus and Pheres.

morte luunt: for similar phraseology cf. Ovid *Fast.* 4.322 'morte luam poenas'; *Ibis* 617 f.; Liv. 38.25.16; Dictys 3.10.

3. vivo viduata marito: cf. Sen. *Medea* 581 f. 'cum coniunx viduata taedis / ardet et odit'; Courtney (*Hermathena* 129.1980.43) points to a similarity with Drac. *Orest.* 431 'incolumi viduata viro'. The phrase is striking, but perhaps not as much of an oxymoron as at first appears, because *vidua* could describe a woman without a husband for any reason (i.e. being single or divorced) as well as a widow: cf. *Dig.* 50.16.242 'viduam non solum eam, quae aliquando nupta fuisset, sed eam quoque mulierem, quae virum non habuisset, appellari ait Labeo', with Mayor's note on Juv. 4.4.

4. pignora cara: children are often denoted by the noun *pignus*, since their generation guarantees the reality of a marriage and puts the seal on it (cf. Ovid. *Fast.* 2.429 f. 'maritae / reddebant uteri pignora rara suae'). The word is first used extensively in this sense by Ovid, both with explanatory nouns in apposition (e.g. *Met.* 3.134 'tot natas natosque et pignora cara nepotes'; *Her.* 6.121 f. 'prolemque gemellam, / pignora ...

Commentary

bina'), and without (e.g. *Her.* 4.120 'nec tanto mater pignore tuta fuit'); it is frequent in both constructions thereafter (*TLL* 10.1.2125.33 f.; 49 f.), as it is in this collection (also at 82.2; 153.1 and 174.1).

metat: the verb *meto* is agricultural in origin, referring to the mowing or reaping of crops; it is used in the metaphorical sense of killing at e.g. Verg. *Aen.* 10.513 'proxima quaeque metit gladio', and where it is so used it generally involves a sword if a weapon is specified (Stat. *Theb.* 9.224; Sil. It. 10.146; Val. Flacc. 3.671; with *TLL* 8.890.35 f.). Medea uses a sword to kill her children in Euripides (1277), and in Ovid (*Met.* 7.396), and it is invariably a sword with which she is depicted in the visual arts (*LIMC* 6.2 Medea nos 10; 11; 13; 14 (frescoes); 15-18 (gemstones); 19-22 (statues); 23-4 (reliefs); 29-31 (pottery) etc.); thus in Timomachus' painting she prepares herself for the deed with a sword in evidence (*AP* 16.135.3; 138.3).

5. pietas ... mitigat: cf. Verg. *Aen.* 5.783 'quam ... pietas nec mitigat ulla'; Hosidius Geta *Medea* 399 'nec te noster amor pietas nec mitigat ulla'. For the familial *pietas* of parents for children cf. 82.1 (with note).

6. hunc furiata premit, hunc miserata levat (A); hinc ..., hinc ... (Wakker); nunc ..., nunc ... (Munari); hos ..., hos ... (Lenz): the problems this line has caused are evidenced by the number of proposed emendations. The recent debate was begun by F. Munari's article 'Zu Anthologia Latina 109R' (in *Studien zur Textgeschichte und Textkritik*, ed. H. Dahlmann and R. Merkelbach, Köln / Opladen 1959, 185 f.; his arguments are largely supported by W.J. Schneider, *Arctos* 32.1998.225 f.), though Wakker's suggestion dates to 1770 and was accepted by Meyer in his 1835 edition. Meyer glosses Wakker's conjecture with the explanation 'hinc furore natos necat, hinc misericordia a noverca (i.e. Glauce) liberat'; and Munari translates his conjecture with the words 'bald beharrt sie rasend bei ihrem mörderischen Vorsatz, bald nimmt sie mitleidsvoll von ihm Abstand', apparently understanding 'ausus', supplied from line 5, as the object of 'premit' and 'levat'. These two interpretations nicely illustrate the two faults which critics find with the text as presented by the mss: (i) there can be an assumption (as by Munari) that the epigram is an ecphrastic treatment of Timomachus' painting (see intro. above), and that it therefore does not depict Medea in the act of killing her children, but in the act of contemplating their murder; and (ii) Medea murdered both her children, not one, and 'hunc ...premit, hunc ... levat' means she murdered only one. But neither of these objections is convincing. As for (i), in the intro. above I have dealt at some length with the ecphrastic epigrams on Timomachus' painting as contrasted with this one, and have concluded that this one does not depict Timomachus' scene of Medea contemplating the killings, but the murder as it is taking place (and it seems perverse to try to read it otherwise; this is also the view taken by

Commentary

F.W. Lenz (in *Miscellanea Critica, Aus Anlass des 150-Jahrigen Bestehens der Verlagsgesellschaft und des graphischen Betriebes B.G. Teubner, Leipzig*, ed. J. Irmscher et al., Leipzig 1965, 2.215 f.), though he then accepts argument (ii) in arriving at his 'hos ... hos ...' conjecture). And as for (ii), the concluding line as it appears in the mss neither states nor implies that Medea murdered only one of her sons; she is in the process of killing them both, but is at this precise moment dispatching only the first. Like the epigrams on Timomachus' painting, this one focuses on Medea's conflicting emotions, but it illustrates them in a way appropriate to the different scene. Therefore she would have been shown maternally cradling a living son in one arm whilst killing the other with her sword, thus displaying both her maternal *pietas* and her uxorial fury, though the epigram as a whole makes it clear that she is going to kill them both. And although the scenario might be thought improbable, in which Medea is murdering one son whilst simultaneously physically demonstrating her *sacra pietas* to the other, an epigram by Antipater of Thessalonica (*AP* 16.143) conjures up an even more unlikely conceit to evidence Medea's conflicting emotions, the description of which, as illustrated in the intro. above, is the focus of many of the pieces on this topic:

> Μηδείης τύπος οὗτος. ἴδ' ὡς τὸ μὲν εἰς χόλον αἴρει
> ὄμμα τὸ δ' εἰς παίδων ἔκλασε συμπαθίην.

('This is a picture of Medea. See how one eye is raised in anger, the other softened to compassion for her children.' (Text and translation both from Gow-Page, *GP* 1.30-1.))

The above interpretation is close to that of H. Heubner (*Hermes* 93.1965.355 f.), who also points out some interesting verbal parallels (italicised) with Dracontius' *Medea* (*Rom.* 10.530 f.):

> Sed postquam solos quos iusserat ignis adussit,
> tunc natos *furibunda premit*. Nam Mermerus *insons*
> et Feretus matrem blanda *pietate* vocabant.
> Ut flammas vitare queant, infantia simplex
> affectu petit ipsa necem, vel sponte pericla
> quaerit inops, passura necem mucrone parentis,
> ignari, quae mater erat, quid saeva pararet.

premit: in the light of preceding 'opprimit' (see 1 n.), 'morte luunt' (line 2), and especially 'metat' (line 4), this verb must refer to a murderous assault by the enraged mother: cf. Verg. *Aen.* 9.330 'armigerumque Remi premit' (of an attack with a sword, on which Servius comments 'opprimit, occidit'); with *OLD* premo 7(a).

levat: it is argued above that the verb refers to Medea's brief and tender cradling of a living child whilst she attacks the other; it would be a

Commentary

less convincing scene dramatically if she cradled a son already murdered, though *levare* can be used of an act of tenderness or pity in raising up a dying or dead loved one (e.g. Sil. It. 2.121 f. 'at comitis frendens casu labentia virgo /membra levat parvaque oculos iam luce natantes / irrorat lacrimis'; Stat. *Theb.* 2.630 f. 'fratris moribunda levabat / membra solo Periphas (nil indole clarius illa / nec pietate fuit) ...', with *TLL* 7.2.1233.51 f.).

For *premere* and *levare* elsewhere as paired opposites, cf. Ovid *Tr.* 1.5.75 'me deus oppressit, nullo mala nostra levante'; Drac. *Laud. Dei* 2.738 'ima levas et celsa premis', with Munari op. cit. 187 n. 9. Such contrast in the pairing gives further support to the interpretation advanced above. This line is also an isocolic pentameter concluding an epigram, for which technique see my note on Mart. 11.73.2; this again emphasises the balanced and contrasted pairing of the words in the two hemistichs.

92 (103R)

On a man who did his milling for himself. When for a small expenditure you could hire a little ass, which is used to turning the smooth millstones properly, why, my friend, are you so penny-pinching and do you so degrade yourself that you should want to put your neck under the heavy yoke? I implore you, stop your circuits. If you have a baker to work for you, you will be able to sit down and reap the rewards of your white bread. For if you grind the cereal for yourself you will suffer labours which Ceres herself did not endure in looking for her daughter.

This is a skoptic piece about a miller so mean that he refuses even to hire an animal to turn his millstone and does the job himself; he should get an ass and a baker and sit back to enjoy his fare and his profits in good capitalist fashion. Satire on misers and the greedy, particularly in epigram, is frequent, especially in Lucillius (*AP* 11.165; 171-2; 264; 294; 309; 389; 391; also *AP* 9.409; 11.168 Antiphanes; 11.325 Automedon; 11.169-70 Nicarchus; 11.173 Philippus; Hor. *Sat.* 2.3.122 f.; 142 f.; Juv. 14.124 f.; with Brecht, *Typengeschichte*, 77 f.).

The scene described in this epigram is of a grain mill which ought to be operated by an animal but is instead operated by a person. This type of mill is well known from remains at Pompeii, Herculaneum and Ostia: the animal walked round in circles, harnessed to a yoke attached to a horizontal beam projecting from a revolving upper stone (*catillus*), which fitted over and ground the grain against the conical topside of a stationary lower stone (*meta*). These rotary mills (*molae asinariae*) are known from the second century BC onwards, and evidence of them has also been found in North Africa. There is a reconstructed example at Naples, and a literary description of one in operation at Apul. *Met.* 9.11 f. See further L.A. Moritz, *Grain-Mills and Flour in Classical Antiquity*, Oxford 1958, 80 f.; 94 f.; Plate 4(b); and R.I. Curtis, *Ancient*

Commentary

Food Technology, Leiden etc. 2001, 343 f.; Plate 27 and fig. 25. Moritz (op. cit. 97 f.) discusses whether these mills would ever have been worked by human slaves rather than animals, reaching a negative conclusion on the grounds that animals would have been cheaper and more efficient, and that the archaeological remains always have a circling space large enough to accommodate an animal. There is however some evidence of humans being forced to turn the millstone like animals as a punishment: e.g. Aug. *Ep.* 185.15 '(sc. quidam patres familias) vincti ad molam et eam in gyrum ducere tamquam iumenta contemptibilia verbere adacti sunt'; and cf. Shipp's note on Ter. *Andr.* 199. Milling as a punishment, though without a task specified, is more widely attested: see Seaford's note on Eur. *Cycl.* 240. What is obvious from this is the menial and onerous task the protagonist of this epigram has taken on himself of his own volition to save some petty cash.

superscr.: per se: 'by / for himself', a clear echo of 'per te' at line 7; cf. Liv. 24.49.6 'isque ... ingenti gloria per se sine ullis Carthaginiensium opibus gessit bellum', with *OLD* per 15(b); Löfstedt's note at *Per. Aeth.* 335 f.; Adams, *Pelagonius*, 591.

1. conducere: the man need not even buy his *asellus*, but could hire it: cf. Col. 1.3.4 'conductis iumentis'; Mart. 8.61.7 'mulis ... conductis'; with *TLL* 4.159.61 f.

asellum: asses were the animal most frequently used for milling (e.g. Ovid *Fast.* 6.318; Col. 7.1.3; Juv. 8.67 with Mayor's note; Moritz, op. cit. 100); they were cheap to maintain (Plin. *Nat. Hist.* 18.44; Col. 7.1.1 etc.).

2. teretes: use would make the millstones smooth over time, though one or both would need to be striated when operated in order for the ground flour to find its way out from between them (Moritz, op. cit. 37 f.).

3. te contemnis: for reflexive *contemnere* cf. Plaut. *Mil.* 1236 'ut ipsa se contemnit', with *OLD* contemno 1(b).

5. gyros (Meyer); cuiros (A); guirios (BVW; -or (V)): there is general and frequent confusion in mss over the spelling of this noun (as also at 188.15), which can often appear as *girus* with variants such as *guirus*, *goerus* and *gurus* also attested (see *TLL* 6.2-3.2386.11 f.); for such variation in the transliteration into Latin of Greek 'γυ-' see Biville, *Emprunts*, 2.297 (gyrus); 288 (lagoena); 255 f. (upsilon generally). It is possible that the author here used the spelling 'guiros' or even 'guirios', which latter is actually the text printed by Pithou and Burman; subsequent editors have followed Meyer.

For *gyri* in milling contexts cf. Veg. *Mulom.* 2.2 'tamquam ad molam vadit in gyrum'; Aug. *Ep.* 185.15 (quoted in intro. above); Hil. *in Matth.*

Commentary

18.2 (*PL* 9.1019) 'molae opus labor est caecitatis; nam clausis iumentorum oculis aguntur in gyrum'.

pistore ministro: the *pistor* could function both as a miller (cf. the derivation of the noun from *pinsere*, 'to pound') and as a baker, and he performs both tasks here. Similarly, Martial combines the two functions when he says of Cyperus 'a pistore ... non recedis: / et panem facis et facis farinam' (8.16.4 f.), and Apul. *Met.* 9.11.1 f. gives a description of a *pistrinum* which shows the two activities taking place in the same establishment. Thus the miser is advised to acquire a 'pistor minister', do nothing himself, and sit back to enjoy his profits; 'minister' might, but need not, imply slave status.

6. candentis quadrae: as also at 96.2, the adjective refers to colour rather than heat (cf. ps.-Aug. *Vit. Christ.* praef. (*PL* 40.1033) 'nec illum satis esurire credo, qui cum panes cibarios habeat, nitidos expectat et candidos. Ita et tu, dilectissima soror, quam ego certus sum esurire nimium et sitire caelestia, cibarios interim mande panes, donec siligine candentes invenias'; and Claud. Mamert. *De Stat. Anim.* 1.21 (p. 74.4 f. Engelbrecht). *Panis candidus* was the top quality bread made from the top quality flour without impurities (see my note on Mart. 11.56.8).

For *quadra*, a segment of a round loaf of bread, cf. Verg. *Aen.* 7.115 'patulis nec parcere quadris' (with Horsfall's note), and for the process cf. *Moretum* 46 f. 'iamque subactum / levat opus palmisque suum dilatat in orbem / et notat impressis aequo discrimine quadris' (with Kenney's note). Round loaves with such segmentary markings have been found at Pompeii (see Moritz, op. cit. 217).

munus habere: the ostensible meaning is that if the miser has a *pistor* to do the work for him, he can sit down and eat his bread without having to grind the flour himself. But the context suggests there is more to it than that, because the man's operations are evidently greater than he would need for his own use (he needs an ass to operate his rotary mill). So his rewards ('munus') if he brings in a *pistor* will also be the profits of a milling and baking enterprise, which he can then reap without effort; 'munus quadrae candentis' is therefore an expression for the success of such an enterprise. In such a context, and particularly with the reference to Ceres in the following lines, 'munus' has overtones of *munera Cerealia*, Ceres' gift to humankind freely bestowed, with a suggestion of effortless abundance (cf. Ovid *Med. Fac.* 4; *Met.* 5.343; 11.121; with *TLL* 8.1664.35 f.).

sedens: the implication is of inactivity, the easy life: cf. Cic. *Att.* 9.12.3 'aediles ludos parant, viri boni usuras perscribunt, ego ipse sedeo' with *OLD* sedeo 7.

7. Cererem: the metonomy of Ceres for wheat is of the commonest (cf. Cic. *De Orat.* 3.167), though here it is used for a humorous purpose with Ceres appearing in propria persona in the next line.

Commentary

8. non tulit (codd.); pertulit (Shackleton Bailey): SB suggests 'pertulit' as 'concinnius' in his app. crit., on the grounds that 'quos' would need to mean 'quantos' if the 'non tulit' of the mss is retained (*Towards a Text*, 19). That seems hypercritical.

93 (104R)

On the ant. The dread ant sweeps up the beneficial labours of the oxen, and the little black swarm puts the harvest in its stores; although it seems to be small of girth, it skilfully collects grains which will keep it from winter famine. It is the devil's familiar, you might now justly say, since its colour and misdeeds have made it in the mould of its master. For just as Proserpina was snatched away in Pluto's chariot, so Ceres is swept up in ants' mouths.

This is the first in a series of epigrams about animals in the collection (95 is about a goose; 96 a cuttlefish; 121 a cockerel (?); 165-6 stuffed geese for eating; 171 the picaresque demise of a cat; and 176-8 goats and Bacchus); the description of everyday entities and objects is a notable feature of the collection as a whole (see p. 2 f.). Luxorius also has a series of pieces on animals, though he concentrates more on the unusual than the everyday, particularly in describing animals' interaction with man (e.g. *AL* 286 about tame fish; 287 a tame boar; 300 tame sea-birds; 325 monkeys riding on dogs' backs; 326 how bears give birth; 354 an obedient dog; 355 tame leopards; 365 a talking magpie; 370 the picaresque death of a cat).

There are a few epigrams in the Greek Anthology which feature ants (e.g. an epitaph at *AP* 7.209 Antip. Sid., with Gow-Page, *HE* 2.79; and a description of an army of ants cleverly crossing water to get some food at *AP* 9.438 Philippus); and Symphosius provides a riddle about an ant at *AL* 281.81 f.:

> Provida sum vitae, duro non pigra labore,
> ipsa ferens umeris securae praemia brumae.
> Nec gero magna simul, sed congero multa vicissim.

Vergil's ant simile at *Aen.* 4.401 f. brings in commonplace themes which are also present in this epigram (e.g. food storage (see 2 n. below); plundering to get food (1 n.; 7 n.); the blackness of the insects (2 n.); the organisation of ant columns (3 n.), and so on):

> Migrantis cernas totaque ex urbe ruentis:
> ac velut ingentem formicae farris acervum
> cum populant hiemis memores tectoque reponunt,
> it nigrum campis agmen praedamque per herbas
> convectant calle angusto; pars grandia trudunt

Commentary

obnixae frumenta umeris, pars agmina cogunt
castigantque moras, opere omnis semita fervet.

I.C. Beavis (*Insects and Other Invertebrates in Classical Antiquity*, Exeter 1988, 198 f.) comments that ancient writers pay almost exclusive attention to grain-collecting ants (species of the genus *Messor*), which forage both from the ground and from growing plants: that is clearly the case with Vergil's ants and those of this epigram. See also Keller, *Tierwelt*, 2.416 f.

This and the previous epigram both deal with aspects of the harvesting of grain, and both conclude with jokes depending on the metonymy of 'Ceres', suggesting that they might have been deliberately placed together (see Introduction, p. 3 for questions of ordering of epigrams in the collection).

1. verrit: cf. 'verritur' in line 8; there is almost a hostile tone to the verb, describing the predatory sweep of the ants as they collect together all the corn which has grown because of the labours of the oxen. Compare e.g. Lucr. 5.1226 f. 'cum vis violenti per mare venti / induperatorem classis super aequora verrit'. This hostile tone continues with the adjective 'tetra', the appellation 'famula Orci' in line 5, and the concluding simile.

For the harvesting activities of ants cf. Ovid *Ars* 1.93 f. 'ut redit itque frequens longum formica per agmen, / granifero solitum cum vehit ore cibum'; Verg. *Aen.* 4.401 f. (quoted above); Ael. *Nat. Anim.* 2.25; Beavis, op. cit. 203 f.

tetra ... formica: the adjective hints at the sinister side of the insect, which is made humorously explicit when it becomes the devil's familiar at line 5.

boum gratos ... labores: the oxen's labours are the ploughing of the fields to enable the corn to be sown and grow, labours which are 'grati' to both men and ants, because they provide them with food. The phrase has a double reference here, referring on the one hand metonymically to the 'fruges' (line 2) which are the product of these labours, but also suggesting that those labours are swept away, or rendered useless, by the ants' activities.

2. caveis: these are the storehouses of the ants' nest. They are described at Ael. *Nat. Anim.* 6.43; Plut. *Mor.* 967d-968b; Galen 3.7 Kühn, with Beavis, op. cit. 201 f.; 205 f. Cells in beehives are also sometimes termed *caveae* (e.g. Verg. *Georg.* 4.58).

fruges: Ovid refers to ants as 'frugilegae' at *Met.* 7.624. The *fruges* here are more likely to be the grown crop of corn than recently sown seed; the latter might be suggested by the immediately preceding reference to the ploughing by the oxen, but it does not suit 'Ceres' (line 8) well. Ants actually gather both sown and ripe grain (e.g. *Geopon.* 2.18.1; Beavis, op. cit. 203).

Commentary

turba nigella: for the proverbial blackness of ants cf. also Mart. 1.115.5; 3.93.3. On diminutives of colour adjectives see André, *Couleur*, 218 f.: although they often have the effect of signifying a lesser intensity of the colour concerned (e.g. Plaut. *Asin.* 400 'rufulus aliquantum'), or can be pejorative in tone (e.g. Cic. *Tusc.* 5.46 'candiduli dentes'), neither would be particularly in point here, because the whole poem stresses ants' blackness. But another use of these diminutives is to key smallness of size in the noun they qualify, as at e.g. Cic. *Att.* 16.11.1 'cerulas enim tuas miniatulas illas extimescebam'; Aus. 27.13.74 'Cadmi nigellas filias'; and Mart. Cap. 5.566 'umbilicum ... rubellulum'. Here it is not the smallness of the noun ('turba') which it qualifies that 'nigella' stresses, but the smallness of the creatures which are the constituent parts of it (see 3 n. below).

3-4. quae licet ... colligit (Maehly); quae licet ... quod legat (A); quamlibet ... quod legat (Courtney); quae licet ... quot legit (Baehrens): since the ms. reading does not offer sense, emendation is necessary. Courtney (*C&M* 40.1989.203 f.) objects to 'quae' because he does not see a reason why the statement of lines 3-4 should be put in a subordinate clause; but, for example, the relative 'quae', which is coincidentally at the same place in the following epigram, serves the same function there. Courtney's conjecture 'quamlibet' would nevertheless still be attractive if the ensuing 'sollers / quod legat' followed on convincingly, but the ellipse of a main verb seems awkward. I therefore prefer Maehly's conjecture of 'colligit' for A's 'quod legat' (*ZOeG* 22.1871.565), as do Riese and SB in their texts; confusion between 'co-' and 'quo-' in mss is common.

3. exiguo videatur pectore (A; corpore (Sched.)): the smallness of ants was proverbial, particularly in emphasising the comparative size and weight of the loads they can carry: cf. Ovid *Met.* 7.625 'grande onus exiguo formicas ore gerentes'; Verg. *Aen.* 4.402 (quoted above); Hor. *Sat.* 1.1.33 f.; Plin. *Nat. Hist.* 11.108; *Ep. Bob.* 65.1. 'exiguo ... pectore' is a descriptive ablative, and the noun carries overtones of strength and courage disproportionate to size (like Vergil's bees, which 'ingentis animos angusto in pectore versant' (*Georg.* 4.83)). The variant 'exiguo corpore' in the Schedae Divionenses is not compelling.

sollers: the adjective is frequent in the collection (see 168.1 n.). It here alludes to the ant's skill and industry in its winter provisioning, another of its proverbial qualities to go with its blackness and its smallness. This is most famously expressed at Vulg. Prov. 6.6 'vade ad formicam, o piger, et considera vias eius et disce sapientiam; quae cum non habeat ducem nec praeceptorem nec principem, parat in aestate cibum sibi et congregat in messe quod comedat'; and cf. also Arist. *Hist. Anim.* 622b20 f.; Phaedr. 4.25.13 f.; Tert. *Adv. Marc.* 1.14; Aug. *Civ. Dei* 22.24.5; with *TLL* 6.1.1091.81 f.; Beavis, op. cit. 206.

Commentary

5. famulam nigri ... Orci: cf. 173.4 f., where a black man is likened to a devil from hell. For animals as the accomplices or familiars of divinities and others cf. Ovid *Met.* 8.272 'sus erat, infestae famulus vindexque Dianae'; Juv. 14.81 'famulae Iovis' (eagles); Sil. It. 13.124 'famulamque Dianae' (a hind); Verg. *Aen.* 5.95; Val. Flacc. 3.458, etc. The name Orcus therefore refers here to the native Italian god of the underworld, equivalent to Dis and Pluto, rather than to the place over which he ruled (on the two applications of the name see H. Wagenvoort, *Studi e materiali di storia delle religioni*, 14.1938.35 f. (= *Studies in Roman Literature, Culture and Religion*, 1956, 102 f.); and G.P. Shipp, *Glotta* 39.1961.154 f.); note also 'domino' in line 6 and 'Plutonis' in line 7. Orcus is again 'niger' at Hor. *Carm.* 4.2.23; he survives in Italian *orco* and French / English *ogre*.

Ants do not appear to have a particular association with the underworld elsewhere, but they were noted as the only creatures other than man who bury their dead (e.g. Plin. *Nat. Hist.* 11.110; Beavis, op. cit. 202), which might have aided such an association.

iam dixeris: the verb is a potential perfect subjunctive; for the idiom compare e.g. Quint. 4.2.86 'quod non adroganter dixerim', and see 172.4 n. 'legeris'; with W. Kroll, *Glotta* 7.1916.132 f., and Woodcock on Tac. *Ann.* XIV, p. 28. 'iam' is metrical padding, as often in the collection, and the meaning would be quite clear without it (also at 85.6; 88.5 (? see note); 117.11; 145.5; 179.5; only at 89.6 and 169.5 does it have point). Contrast the use of *nunc*: on every occurrence it has some force (94.2; 99.5; 115.2; 118.5; 143.1; 144.1; 184.1).

6. color et factum (A; furtum (Müller)): for the association of the colour black with the underworld, devils and evil see notes on 172-3, and Dölger, *Die Sonne*, 57 f.; 64 f.; for the proverbial blackness of ants see 2 n. above. The 'factum' which suits the ant for its sinister association with Orcus is the stealing and storing of grain, set out in lines 1-4 of the poem; Müller's 'furtum' is an attractive emendation if one were needed, but there is no reason why the colourless 'factum' of the mss cannot remain. Indeed, *factum* itself can convey wrong-doing: 'supplicium pro factis dare oportet' (Cato *Orat.* frag. 134 Sblendorio Cugusi; with *OLD factum* 2(b)).

conposuit: a singular verb is used where a plural would be expected; cf. Mart. 9.70.3 'cum gener atque socer diris concurreret armis', with *LHS* 2.433.

8. verritur ... Ceres: the common metonymy of Ceres for corn permits the rather laboured comparison of the ant to Pluto by means of their pillage of mother and daughter, Ceres and Proserpina, respectively.

Commentary
94 (105R)

On Hecuba. Bereft of children, husband and kingdom, Priam's wife now by a stroke of cruel fortune comes under the yoke of the Ithacan; she wishes to match her great anguish with tears, and with her perpetual lamentation she changes into a dog's form. How powerful it is Fortune shows by varied reversals: after being a queen, a wounded old woman bays in a street.

Another epigram on a mythological theme deals with the instant of Hecuba's transformation into a bitch. For his scenario the poet generally accords with the Ovidian version of the story at *Met.* 13.565 f., which in turn was largely based on that of Euripides' *Hecuba* (esp. 1260 f.); but he focuses on Hecuba's grief rather than her anger as the factor leading to her canine metamorphosis, and although there may be some verbal reminiscences of Ovid in this epigram (see e.g. 1 n.; 6 n.), they are not particularly pronounced. One might also have expected the poet to include a detail of the myth which lends itself to a short poem (as at e.g. Aus. 12.25), namely the aetiology of the name Cynossema ('Dogsbarrow' (E.J. Kenney)), the place on the Thracian coast which was said to have been where Hecuba was buried (cf. Eur. *Hec.* 1273; Ovid *Met.* 13.569 etc.); but instead he concentrates his epigram on Hecuba as a type illustrating reversal of fortune (see 5 n.). For the Hecuba myth see esp. *LIMC* 4.1.473 f.

1. prole viro regnoque: the same trio of children, husband and homeland is found at Ovid *Met.* 13.489 f. 'quas totiens patriae dederat natisque viroque / huic quoque dat lacrimas'.

Priameia coniunx: cf. Ovid *Met.* 13.512 f. 'haec Hectoris illa est / clara parens, haec est, dicet, Priameia coniunx' (the adjective *Priameia* occurs also at Verg. *Aen.* 2.403; 3.321).

2. sub iuga nunc Ithaci: for Hecuba's enslavement to Ulysses after the fall of Troy, cf. Ovid *Met.* 13.485 f. 'quam victor Ulixes / esse suam nollet, nisi quod tamen Hectora partu / edideras (Heinsius; ediderat (codd.))'; Eur. *Tro.* 277; Apollod. *epit.* 5.23; Quint. Smyrn. 14.21 f.; Dict. Cret. 5.13. For 'Ithacus' as a substantival epithet for Ulysses cf. Verg. *Aen.* 2.104; Prop. 1.15.9; Ovid *Pont.* 1.3.33; Mart. 11.104.15; Juv. 14.287.

3. tantos lacrimis aequare dolores: for the use of *aequare* here cf. the probable reminiscence of Verg. *Aen.* 2.362 '(sc. quis) possit lacrimis aequare labores?'. Hecuba's anguish stems from her being deprived of her homeland and family, and establishes her as a good example of the reversal of fortune. She wishes to lament in a manner to reflect her grief, and to afford an external manifestation of her internal emotion, and this happens by her transformation into a howling bitch, since a baying dog

Commentary

embodies sadness and dejection (for this explanation of the metamorphosis see also Ovid *Met.* 13.571, quoted below; Dio Chrys. *Orat.* 11.154; and see 6 n. below on 'latrat').

4. perpetuo planctu transit: as remarked above, this poet concentrates on Hecuba's anguish as the basis of her metamorphosis; Ovid also mentions this (*Met.* 13.565 f., esp. 'ululavit maesta'), but focuses more on her rabid anger at the Thracian nobles who were trying to harm her after she had blinded Polymestor, the murderer of her own son Polydorus (an emotion which would manifest itself in a transformation into a barking and snarling dog rather than a baying one):

> Clade sui Thracum gens inritata tyranni
> Troada telorum lapidumque incessere iactu
> coepit; at haec missum rauco cum murmure saxum
> morsibus insequitur rictuque in verba parato
> latravit conata loqui (locus extat et ex re
> nomen habet), veterumque diu memor illa malorum
> tum quoque Sithonios ululavit maesta per agros.

Cf. also Plaut. *Men.* 714 f. and Cic. *Tusc.* 3.63 for Hecuba's anger rather than her grief being characterised in her metamorphosis.

in ora (A, corr. man. rec.); in ore (A): *in* + acc. is the usual combination for 'transire' referring to metamorphosis, and should be accepted here: cf. Ovid *Met.* 11.642 f. 'ille in humum saxumque undamque ... transit', with *OLD* transeo 6(a); for *ora* of a metamorphosed form, cf. Val. Flacc. 4.357 'tum trepida Inachiae paelex subit ora iuvencae'; ibid. 4.395; Sil. It. 17.567.

5. variis monstrat Fortuna figuris: the 'variae figurae' are clarified in the following line as Hecuba's transformation from a human to a bitch, her downfall from a kingdom to the street, and her recent wounds. She was often instanced as an example of the dire effects of a reversal of fortune (e.g. Eur. *Hec.* 58; 284 f.; 488 f.; *Tro.* 474 f.; Ovid *Met.* 13.483 f.; 13.508 f. ('modo maxima rerum, / tot generis natisque potens nuribusque viroque, / nunc trahor exsul, inops, tumulis avulsa meorum, / Penelopae munus ...'); Mela 2.26; Juv. 10.271 f.; Aus. 12.25).

6. post regnum in vico: Oudendorp (ap. Burman (1759, p. 110)) suspected 'in vico', though Burman saw it as a contrast to 'post regnum', stressing the loss of Hecuba's high status, wealth and trappings. Somewhat similarly, in Ovid's version (quoted above 4 n.) Hecuba's 'howling in sadness through the Thracian fields' is a stark contrast to her life in the royal palace at Troy. Although 'in vico' is a detail not found in earlier versions of the story, it is apt enough: Hecuba, forced out of her palace and turned into a dog, has to wander the streets as stray dogs do.

Commentary

saucia latrat anus (A); fauce latravit anus (Oudendorp); rauca latravit anus (Riese); squalida latrat anus (Shackleton Bailey); foetida latrat anus (Watt): the 'saucia' of the ms was first questioned by Oudendorp, who, objecting also to the preceding 'in vico', conjectured 'invita fauce latravit anus'; however, 'fauce' is lame, and the irregularly short first syllable this necessitates for 'latravit', which cannot be paralleled elsewhere (*TLL* 7.2.1013.23 f. (Bentley's emendation 'Lacon' for ms. 'latrans' being accepted at Phaedr. 5.10.7)), also renders his conjecture unlikely; the latter objection applies similarly to Riese's 'rauca latravit', which is further suspect on the interpretation of the epigram advanced above in that it does not suit the sound of baying. 'saucia' is also questioned by SB in his app. crit., who asks '*Num lapidibus iactis?*', and by W.S. Watt (*HSCPh* 91.1987.291), who considers it yields no satisfactory sense and suggests 'foetida' as an alternative (adducing Hor. *Ep.* 1.2.26 for the dog as an unclean animal). Yet 'saucia' can be defended, much as SB suggests. In Ovid's version of the story, quoted at 4 n. above, the Thracian nobles attacked Hecuba with weapons and stones before she retaliated and metamorphosed: 'saucia' could allude to the outcome of this scene, and would again emphasise her complete reversal of fortune, deprived of physical well-being even in canine form, as well as of home and kin. Although the Thracian nobles are not specifically mentioned in this epigram, a reader could still deduce that 'saucia', however the wounds were caused, is further evidence of a fall in fortune.

For 'latrat' and Hecuba's terrible cry of grief or rage as she metamorphoses, cf. Ovid *Met.* 13.569 (quoted 4 n. above; Ovid there uses *latrare* to reflect Hecuba's canine anger, and *ululare* (ibid. 571) to reflect her grief) and Dio Chrys. *Orat.* 33.59. Lines 3-4 of the epigram suggest that 'latrat' here is a manifestation of Hecuba's grief, and it therefore better denotes the mournful baying of a dog than its angry barking; Ovid uses *latrare* of a baying Hecuba at *Met.* 13.620 'ergo aliis latrasse Dymantida flebile visum est' and Statius also uses the verb in similar contexts of grief and loss: e.g. *Theb.* 1.550 f. 'frustraque sonantia lassant / ora canes umbramque petunt et nubila latrant', of the reaction of Ganymede's dogs to his rape; *Silv.* 2.1.12 f. 'stat pectore demens / luctus et admoto latrant praecordia tactu', of Atedius Melior's reaction to the death of his *puer delicatus* (this, as commentators say, derives from the disconcerting image of Odysseus' barking heart at Hom. *Od.* 20.13 f., but Odysseus was in a rage, whereas the relevant emotion in Statius is grief); and *Theb.* 2.338.

95 (106R)

On a goose. In our house flies a gleaming-white goose which lifts up its neck in songs of sweet-toned cackling. It is a boon of a bird on two counts: for it both furnishes courses at table and guards the house in the silence of night. Alone, watchful when the dogs were silent on the Tarpeian cliff, it rescued Romulus' buildings from the Gauls.

This rather attractive piece on a goose viewed as an edible burglar alarm is one of a series on animals in the collection (see 93 intro.); it is less fortunate than the single goose owned by Baucis and Philemon, dubbed their 'minimae custodia villae', which was spared the knife on divine intervention (Ovid *Met.* 8.684 f.). Geese as items for the table occur again at 165-6; they were also kept as household pets (cf. Caes. *Bell. Gall.* 5.12.6; Toynbee, *Animals*, 261 f.; Keller, *Tierwelt*, 2.224) and farmed for their feathers (Col. 8.13.3).

1. aedibus in nostris: it is clear from what follows, where the goose functions as a burglar alarm and as food for the table, that these are domestic rather than religious buildings.
volitans argenteus anser: the influence of Vergil is apparent (*Aen.* 8.655 f.), and this phrase is a direct borrowing:

>atque hic auratis volitans argenteus anser
>porticibus Gallos in limine adesse canebat ...

The adjective *argenteus* in this passage of Vergil has two references, both to the colouring of the bird, and to the metal of the shield given by Venus to Aeneas, on which the bird is depicted. It was subsequently used, as here, to describe (bright) colour without any suggestion of actual metal: thus Ovid uses it of the crow, a white bird before it turned black: 'nam fuit haec quondam niveis argentea pennis / ales, ... nec servaturis vigili Capitolia voce / cederet anseribus' (*Met.* 2.536 f.). The connotation is of gleaming brightness rather than a strictly silver colour, and white geese were in fact the most prized (cf. Varro, *Res Rust.* 3.10.2; Col. 8.14.3). See also André, *Couleur*, 41f.; and 143.6 'lactea massa', with note.

2. dulcisono strepitu: the adjective is rare and late (there are some instances in Terentianus Maurus (2644; 2647; 2653 etc.), Optatianus Porfirius (*Carm.* 27.4 Polara), and Martianus Capella (9.888; 9.908); see *TLL* 5.1.2198.1 f.). It is close to being an oxymoron in combination with 'strepitus', though Vergil uses *canere* (*Aen.* 8.656) as well as *strepere* (*Ecl.* 9.36) of the noise made by geese; and whilst *strepitus* does not invariably suggest a harsh or unpleasant noise (as e.g. Hor. *Carm.* 4.3.17 f. demonstrates: 'testudinis aureae / dulcem quae strepitum, Pieri, temperas'), it often does have overtones of a loud and disruptive clamour (as at e.g. Hor. *Ep.* 2.1.203 'tanto cum strepitu ludi spectantur').
colla canora: for the neck as the instrument of sound cf. Verg. *Aen.* 7.700 f. (of swans): 'et longa canoros / dant per colla modos'.

Commentary

3. ales grata bono duplici: a similar point is made about the cuttlefish in the next epigram (96.4): 'pretium ... debuit esse duplum' (i.e. the price should be double because of the double benefit given by the animal: food and ink). As punctuated in my text, in agreement with earlier editors, this phrase has an ellipse of 'est', which it would be possible to avoid by punctuating with a comma rather than a stop at the end of line 2. However, parts of *esse* are in ellipse elsewhere in the collection (e.g. 99.3; 131.3; 167.3); and it may not be coincidence that these instances all occur in the third line of elegiac poems. I therefore retain the traditional punctuation.

fercula mensae: on geese for eating see Mart. 13.73-4 (with Leary's notes) and commentary on 165-6.

4. adservat ... domum: the home security benefits of keeping geese are mentioned elsewhere, given additional resonance, as here, by the role of the birds in protecting the Capitol from sacking by the Gauls (e.g. Col. 8.13.1 f. 'eiusque generis anser praecipue rusticis gratus est, quod nec maximam curam poscit et sollertiorem custodiam quam canis praebet. Nam clangore prodit insidiantem, sicut etiam memoria tradidit in obsidione Capitolii, cum adventum Gallorum vociferatus est, canibus silentibus'). Burglars (*effractores, effractorii*) were a problem in the ancient world: 'cognoscit praefectus vigilum de incendiariis, effractoribus, furibus, raptoribus, receptatoribus ... effracturae fiunt plerumque in insulis in horreisque' (Paul. *Dig.* 1.15.3.1 f.; and cf. Sen. *Ep.* 68.4; Juv. 3.302 f., with Mayor's note).

nocte silente: the phrase is frequent (e.g. Tib. 1.5.16; Ovid *Am.* 2.19.40; *Her.* 6.96; 16.284; *Fast.* 2.692), as is the metrically useful variant *nocte silenti* (e.g. Verg. *Aen.* 4.527; Ovid *Met.* 4.84; Stat. *Theb.* 9.793). The assault on the Capitol, which will be mentioned in the following lines, also took place at night (Verg. *Aen.* 8.658; Liv. 5.47.2 f.), the prime time for burglars.

5-6. solus ... vigil: the story of the geese, M. Manlius and the saving of the Capitol in 390 BC (or possibly 387: see Walbank's note on Polyb. 1.6.1) is told by Livy (5.47). Its historicity as regards the geese, and even whether the Gauls were or were not successful in their attack, is questioned by O. Skutsch (*JRS* 43.1953.77 f.) and by N.M. Horsfall ('From History to Legend, M. Manlius and the Geese', in *Roman Myth and Mythography*, ed. J.N. Bremmer / N.M. Horsfall, *BICS* Suppl. 52.1987.63 f.). According to Cicero (*S. Rosc.* 56), both geese and dogs were maintained on the Capitol in his day for the purpose of scaring off nocturnal burglars (also Plin. *Nat. Hist.* 10.51).

5. Tarpeia ... in rupe: the Tarpeian rock is strictly that part of the Capitol from which criminals were thrown to their deaths, including Manlius

Commentary

himself (Liv. 6.20.10 f.). Here however it is a general term to describe the Capitol as a whole, which is elsewhere named 'mons Tarpeius' (Stat. *Silv.* 5.3.196), 'collis Tarpeius' (Sil. It. 6.604) and 'arx Tarpeia' (Prop. 4.4.29). The appellation is perhaps the more pointed in that the Gauls were said by Livy to have made their ascent on the Capitol via the Tarpeian rock (6.17.4; 7.10.3). For the topography of the Capitol and the route taken by the Gauls, see *LTUR* 1.226 f.; 4.237 f.; and Oakley's commentary on Livy VI-X, 1.490 f.

canibus ... quietis: the ineffectual silence of the dogs is remarked by Livy: 'sed ne canes quidem, sollicitum animal ad nocturnos strepitus, excitarent' (5.47.3; see also Col. 8.13.1 f, quoted at 4 n. above). For the prosody of 'canibus' here, with lengthening of a final closed syllable at this position in the line, cf. C. Licinius Calvus *frag.* 6.1 Courtney 'et leges sanctas docuit et cara iugavit', where the final syllable of 'docuit' is lengthened; lengthening at this place in the hexameter line is particularly frequent in Prudentius (e.g. *Ham.* 549; *Psych.* 223; 764; with L. Strzelecki, *Eos* 33.1931.490 f.); on the prosody and metre of the poems in this collection see p. 22 f..

6. eripuit: i.e. the buildings were snatched from the imminent danger of being captured by the Gauls, rather than seized from their possession (cf. Vitr. 1.1.15 'aegrum eripere de periculo').

Romula tecta: both the forms *Romulus* (e.g. 'Romula ne faciem laederet hasta Tati' (Prop. 4.4.26)) and the Greek-based *Romuleus* (as at 106.2 and e.g. Verg. *Aen.* 8.654)) are used for the adjective of the name Romulus; cf. the similar variants (useful for metrical purposes) *Augustus* and *-eus*, with *LHS* 1.286 f. The building(s) of the old Capitol to which the writer alludes might be specifically Romulan, namely the Casa Romuli (though the house on the Capitol, which is not attested before Augustan times, was probably a replica of an 'original' on the Palatine (see *LTUR* 1.241)), but are probably a generalised reference to whatever buildings happened to be on the Roman Capitol at the time of the attack (e.g. the 'aedes Iovis Feretri', alleged to have been the first Roman temple to have been consecrated, and others (Liv. 1.10.7; see further *LTUR* 1.228 f.)).

96 (107R)

On the cuttlefish. With its feminine noun it designates the two sexes, and the white cuttlefish shuts inside itself its inky load. There is no more useful sea-creature which wanders the ocean blue, and its price when caught deserved to be double. It affords food with its meat, and gives shape to letters with its bile, and though small in appearance it serves both these purposes. Experts ought to acquire it for their fuel of preference: it is tangy on the palate and puts fingers to the test.

This amusing piece fits into the category of those on animals and the

Commentary

natural world (see 93 intro.), and those which highlight the value and usefulness of the things they describe (see 90 intro.). Here the advertising aspect is especially in evidence, with the suggestion that the animal is so useful it ought to cost twice as much as it did (line 4). The epigram displays considerable subtlety in developing and illustrating its theme of the dual benefit of the cuttlefish as food and provider of writing-ink: the concluding couplet in particular operates on both literal (food) and metaphorical (literature) levels.

Cuttlefish are marine molluscs and cephalopods, distinguished by a thick internal calcified shell called the cuttlebone, by their ink sac, and by their eight arms and two larger tentacles for catching prey; they are eminently edible. All these attributes were noted in Antiquity: the black ink (e.g. [Ovid] *Hal.* 19 f.; Plin. *Nat. Hist.* 9.84; 11.8; 32.141; Ael. *Nat. Anim.* 1.34); the edibility (Apic. 9.IV Milham; Galen 6.736 Kühn); and the cuttlebone (Diosc. *Mat. Med.* 2.21 Wellmann etc.). Tertullian imaginatively employed the image of cuttlefish squirting black ink to describe blasphemers promulgating their heresies (*Adv. Marc.* 2.20.1): 'sed enim sepiae isti .. ut traductionem sui sentiunt, tenebras hinc blasphemiae intervomunt'. See further Keller, *Tierwelt*, 2.513 f.; D'Arcy Thompson, *Fishes*, 232; Saint-Denis, *Animaux Marins*, 104.

1. femineo ... sexum: cf. Varro's similar comments on animal nouns at *Res Rust.* 3.5.6 'sic aut hic aut illic turdi, qui cum sint nomine mares, re vera feminae quoque sunt. Neque id non secutum ut esset in merulis, quae nomine feminino mares quoque sunt'. Most Latin nouns for animals do encompass both genders with the same word; there are however exceptions with some nouns of the second declension, such as *agnus / agna, porcus / porca, lupus / lupa* (though on occasion the change of gender can rather signify different species, as with e.g. *picus / pica*), and with a handful of others like *leo / lea* (on which see 170.1 n.; and see generally N-W 1.915 f.). *Sepia* is no exception to the general practice; and as the poet remarks, cuttlefish come in both sexes, and apparently the extremity of the female is more rounded than that of the male, and Italian fishermen can sex them by touch (D'Arcy Thompson, 'How to Catch a Cuttlefish', *CR* 42.1928.15 f.). Aristotle also was aware of differences between the sexes in cuttlefish (*Hist. Anim.* 525a10).

2. candens piceum: for the juxtaposition of black and white cf. 172.1 n.; 187.2 n.; and Aus. 13.18.3 f. 'et caput fuligine / fucavit atra candidum'; for 'candens' see 92.6 n.

3. per caerula: for the frequent use of substantival *caerula* with reference to both the sky and the sea, see Skutsch's note on Enn. *Ann.* 54-5; the connotation of blue here adds to the colours of the animal in the previous line.

Commentary

4. capto: see D'Arcy Thompson's article cited at 1 n. above for methods of fishing for cuttlefish.

debuit esse duplum: the force of the perfect tense, when all other verbs in the piece are in the present, is not easy to determine: the thought may be that the cuttlefish ought to have been twice the price when it was landed and sold to the retailer, and it still ought to be when the retailer sells it on, with the implication that the prospective purchaser is getting a bargain. The doubling of the price is suggested by the twin functions of ink to write with and flesh to eat; compare the double benefit of the geese in the preceding poem, and Martial's comment on Trebulan cheeses: 'commendat gratia duplex' (13.33.1). *Duplus* is a proportional numeral, as is *simplus*, on which see 188.18 n.; *dupla* can stand by itself, with ellipse of *pecunia*, to mean 'twice the price' (as at e.g. *Dig.* 21.1.58.2).

5. carne: for *caro* of fish flesh, cf. Mela 2.97 'caro magnorum piscium'.

apicum ... figuras: i.e. the letters of the alphabet; for *apex* and its various meanings see my note on Aus. *Epig.* 37.4.

felle: *fel* is properly bile, though here it must refer to black ink (probably a unique instance, since no reference is made in *TLL*): the cuttlefish has an ink sac from which it squirts clouds of black ink when angry or afraid, and the metonymy of the ink with black bile thus seems reasonable. *Fel* can also carry an overtone of the bilious venom of writers (see *TLL* 6.1.423.70 f.), and it here initiates an ambiguity which culminates in the final line (see note); cf. esp. Mart. 7.25, an epigram I quote in full because it is also relevant to notes below:

> Dulcia cum tantum scribas epigrammata semper
>   et cerussata candidiora cute,
> nullaque mica salis nec amari fellis in illis
>   gutta sit, o demens, vis tamen illa legi!
> Nec cibus ipse iuvat morsu fraudatus aceti,
>   nec grata est facies cui gelasinus abest.
> Infanti melimela dato fatuasque mariscas:
>   nam mihi, quae novit pungere, Chia sapit.

Ancient ink was usually black, hence its usual name *atramentum* (cf. Cic. *Nat. Deor.* 2.127, with Pease's note; Plin. *Nat. Hist.* 9.84). But one type of ink, known as *sepia*, came from the cuttlefish; it is first mentioned at Pers. 3.13 'sed infusa vanescit sepia lympha', whereon the scholiast comments 'sepia pro atramento a colore posuit, quamvis non ex ea, ut Afri, sed ex fuligine ceteri conficiant atramentum'. Sepia ink is also mentioned by Ausonius (27.13.76; 27.14b.54), but such references are rare, and Pliny actually goes out of his way in his description of pigments and materials to say that cuttlefish ink was not used for writing (*Nat. Hist.* 35.43). He may have been factually, if fortuitously, correct in what he says, because the

Commentary

ink ejected by the cuttlefish is not itself used for writing (though it was, and still is, used in cookery (cf. Apic. 5.3.3)); the ink for writing is actually made from a processing of the ink sac. The apparent equation of the two types of ink in this epigram need not imply ignorance on the part of the author, since it is an easy assumption for reasons of poetic conciseness. On sepia ink see C. Ainsworth Mitchell, *Inks: Their Composition and Manufacture*, 4th edn, London 1937, 18 f.

6. et brevi (A); atque brevi (Meyer); eque brevi (Baehrens): the lengthening of the first syllable of such a common adjective as 'brevi', which the text of A necessitates and which is subject to easy emendation, must be questionable, but there is another instance at *AL* 354.1 Luxorius 'forma meae catulae brevis sed amabilis inde' (though it is usually emended by editors with introduction of 'est' immediately following). It is also possible that the lengthening may be due to word accent (see 137.1 n. and p. 24). I therefore retain A's text.

brevi specie: *species* refers to the outward appearance or looks of a physical entity, and the point is that the reader will be amazed that a creature as small as the cuttlefish can be so useful to man. Similarly the smallness of the ant is stressed at 93.3.

usum ad utrumque: the pentameter, as well as the irregular prosody of 'brevi', also displays both hiatus at the main caesura and elision in its second half: see further comment on the acceptability of this at p. 24 f.

facit: here synonymous with *sufficit*, as at e.g. Col. 4.13.2 'non pessime faciunt in hunc usum ... folia'; Mart. 1.51.1 'non facit ad saevos cervix, nisi prima, leones'; with Svennung, *Palladius*, 565 f.; *TLL* 6.1.122.42 f.

7. potius: this is use of a comparative where a superlative might have been expected: cf. Cass. *Var.* 1.21.1 'unicuique patria sua carior est', with Svennung, *Palladius*, 278 f.; A. Blaise, *A Handbook of Christian Latin Style, Morphology and Syntax*, trans. G.C. Roti, Washington DC 1994, 59. Syntactically it is a comparative with ellipse: *docti* should rather eat cuttlefish (sc. than anything else), because they are both nutritious and apt for aspiring authors.

doctos: a witty ambiguity, which draws the epigram together at its end, begins here. The reader has been made aware that the cuttlefish has two great benefits to bestow, food and ink, and the interconnection between the two is exemplified in this concluding couplet, where most words refer to either benefit. Thus these *docti* are not only expert writers, but also people learned in the culinary arts.

escam: this is not only a literal food for culinary *docti* to prepare, but also a metaphorical 'food' for the writer and one of the necessities of his trade, namely his ink. The specific type of the ink in question, already characterised as *fel* (see 5 n.), suggests a suitability for the more acerbic genres such as epigram. The use of food as literary metaphor is frequent

Commentary

(see e.g. J.C. Bramble, *Persius and the Programmatic Satire*, Cambridge 1974, 45 f.; 143 f. (on 'esca'); E. Gowers, *The Loaded Table*, Oxford 1993, 40 f.), though here 'esca' refers not, as it usually would, to the literary fare a writer serves his readers, but to the fare which fuels the writer, his bilious ink; there is no precise parallel for *esca* in this sense, but it is often used in a similar way of the material or tinder which fuels fire (e.g. Rufin. *Orig. in Num.* 12.2 (*PG* 12.660) 'bitumen esca et nutrimentum ignis est'; Ennod. 348.23 Vogel; Macr. *Sat.* 7.16.24).

8. sapit in morsu: the primary meaning is 'good to eat': for *sapio* in this sense cf. Mart. 13.13.1 'ut sapiant fatuae ... betae', with *OLD* sapio 1(c). This is then balanced by the following phrase, which deals primarily with writing. Both phrases however have overtones which address the other quality. Thus 'sapit in morsu' could mean in a literary context 'has real bite' of writing which is not anodyne; this is well illustrated by Mart. 7.25 (quoted at 5 n. above), where the noun 'morsu' in line 5, and the verb 'sapit' in line 8 extend beyond their basic culinary meaning to literary comment. Here, since 'sapit in morsu' refers to the writers' ink rather than their output, the inference is that ink so imbued with 'fel' will be ideal for pungent writing.

probat articulos: the primary meaning is 'tests the fingers', a balance to the previous phrase, in that writers' fingers will be put to the test when they use their sepia ink. For *probo* cf. Cic. *Caec.* 61 'non enim reperies quemquam iudicem aut recuperatorem qui, tamquam si arma militis inspicienda sint, ita probet armatum'; Sen. *Ep.* 19.11 'errat autem qui amicum in atrio quaerit, in convivio probat'; and for *articuli* of specifically writers' digits cf. Jer. *Ep.* 36.1 ego linguam et ille (sc. notarius) articulum movebamus'; Vulg. Dan. 5.5 'rex aspiciebat articulos manus scribentis'. But the phrase could equally apply to the culinary angle: the skill of gourmets' fingers will also be tested in preparing the cuttlefish for the table.

97 (108R)

On a eunuch. He whom nature made male becomes female by the knife; for the youngster's groin is shorn of its testicles. That is why you see a smooth youth with such a physique, and there is revealed a beautiful male of ambiguous body. Outrageous intercourse has given pleasure to cautious spouses; for trusty is the guard provided without a witness.

This opens a pair of six-line epigrams about eunuchs, the first of which derives its humour from a pun on the noun 'testis', the second of which exploits a play on gender.

The focus of this piece is on the eunuch as a sexual object. Slaves were often said to be castrated for sexual purposes, to serve both males

Commentary

and females. The alleged attraction in the homosexual sphere was that they retained their boyish qualities for longer: e.g. Sen. *Contr.* 10.4.17 'castratorum greges habent, exoletos suos ut ad longiorem patientiam impudicitiae idonei sint amputant'; Sen. *Ep.* 66.53 'aliquis in mulierculam ex viro versus'; Claud. 18.344 f. 'servatoque diu puerili flore coegit / arte retardatam Veneri servire iuventam'; with P. Guyot, *Eunuchen als Sklaven und Freigelassene in der griechisch-römischen Antike*, Stuttgart 1980, 59 f.; esp. 60 n. 72. And the alleged attraction in the heterosexual sphere was that they were considered to be incapable of impregnation, as at e.g. Ter. *Eun.* 665 f. 'pol ego amatores audieram mulierum esse eos maximos / sed nil potesse'; Mart. 6.67 (with Grewing's notes) 'cur tantum eunuchos habeat tua Caelia quaeris, / Pannyche? Vult futui Caelia nec parere'; Ambros. *Hexam.* 5.3.9 (*PL* 14.209) 'ut diversi generis commixtio fetus possit excludere'; with Guyot, op. cit. 63 f.; 63 nn. 94-5 (the theme is a favourite with a disapproving St. Jerome: ibid. 65 n. 112). See also Courtney's note on Juv. 6.366. The present epigram has both homo- and heterosexual comment (see notes on 'mollem' (3); 'dubii' (4); 'coniugibus cautis' (5); and 'fidus ... custos' (6)). Its precise humour is actually not easy to establish, and the concluding couplet poses problems of interpretation, but the epigram as a whole seems best read as setting up a scenario leading to an unexpected conclusion: the opening four lines would lead the reader to believe that the eunuch's attractiveness to men is the focus, but the conclusion shows him as the lover of women and wives.

1. quem natura marem dederat: for the idiom of *dare* + double accusative meaning 'to make / render someone something' cf. Verg. *Aen.* 12.436 f. 'nunc te mea dextera bello / defensum dabit'; Vulg. Ezech. 35.3 'dabo te desolatum atque desertum'; with *TLL* 5.1.1697.27 f. It is again notable how the poet likes to vary his words which denote maleness (*marem / teneri / iuvenem / homo*: the progression in age is here logical enough, because the young castrated boy grows into the attractive and youthful eunuch): see also 81.5 n.

fit femina ferro: clear alliteration (see also 104.4; 171 intro.; 172.3). For *femina* applied pejoratively to males, though not necessarily implying homosexual passivity, cf. Sil. It. 2.361 '(sc. Hannon) imbellis femina servet / singultantem animam'; *Catal.* 13.17; with *TLL* 6.1.462.16 f.

2. teneri pubes (Müller); tenerinpube (A; tenerinpubes (Sched.)); tener inpubes (Maehly): although, along with Riese and SB, I accept Müller's slight emendation (*RhM* 20.1865.636), Maehly's suggestion (*ZOeG* 22.1871.565), essentially that of the Schedae Divionenses, is worth consideration ('the young, pre-pubescent boy, is deprived of his *vires*'). On the one hand it avoids a certain duplication and lack of clarity in 'pubes viribus exuitur' (see note below), but on the other it is pleonastic itself, since 'tener' suggests 'inpubes', and it is also less graphic.

Commentary

teneri: i.e. before puberty, with the intention of keeping the eunuch boyish; for castration of children cf. Herod. 3.48.2; Mart. 9.7(8).3 f., with Guyot, op. cit. 30 n. 30.

pubes viribus exuitur: the phrase may be deliberately ambiguous, though the meaning in either sense is much the same: the testicles are removed. The most likely construction is probably (a), to understand 'pubes' to refer to the groin as a generalised location (e.g. Ovid *Ars* 2.613 'ipsa Venus pubem ... protegitur laeva semireducta manu', with *OLD* pubes 3); to understand 'viribus' as a euphemism for the testicles; and to construe 'viribus' as an ablative of separation, as is common with the verb *exuere* (cf. Hor. *Epod.* 17.15 '(sc. membra) saetosa duris exuere pellibus'; Juvenc. 3.488 'plerosque hominum vis ferrea sexu exuit'; with *TLL* 5.2.2116.42 f.; 2120.1 f.). The equivalence of 'viribus' with 'testibus' is easy enough in the context, though there seems to be no exact parallel. However, cf. *CIL* 13.1751 'L. Aemilius Carpus ... vires excepit et a Vaticano transtulit' (referring to a bull's testicles in a *taurobolium*); Plin. *Nat. Hist.* 11.60 'velut castratis viribus' (of bees which have used their sting); and compare too the verb *eviriare* and noun *eviriatio*, as equivalent to *evirare* and *eviratio*, which are found only in the *Mulomedicina Chironis*: thus at e.g. 14 (p. 8.16 f.), 'contingit ... eis eviriari. Hoc enim auctores praecipiunt, quod et nos utique intelligere debemus, iam enim partem virium cum testibus amiserunt'. The alternative construction (b) would be to understand 'pubes' to refer to the testicles (for which cf. 'pube recisa' in the first line of the following epigram, though the parallel may not be precise since *pubes* there might include the penis: see note ad loc.); and to understand 'viribus' again as an ablative of separation with 'exuitur', though referring more generally to reproductive potency (cf. Mart. 11.81.3 'viribus hic ... non est ... utilis'; in fact it would also be possible to understand 'viribus' as an ablative of manner (i.e. 'by force'; for the plural cf. Petr. 102.5 'nec posse inde custodem nisi aut caede expelli aut praecipitari viribus'), though that is less likely with 'ferro' in the preceding line).

3. hinc: causal, as at 88.4 and 177.3.

iuvenem ... mollem: this specific quality is probably intended to suggest the eunuch's appeal to males rather than females. At any rate, the adjective is immediately suggestive of passive homosexuality (see my note on Aus. *Epig.* 45.4) and can have overtones of the pre-pubescent body (see my note on Aus. *Epig.* 72.5); it is used of eunuchs also at Tac. *Hist.* 3.40.1; and Aug. *Civ. Dei* 6.7.3.

tanto sub robore: the phrase suggests the age and condition of physical prime, and as such makes a clear contrast with 'mollem': cf. Liv. 28.35.6 'aetas erat in medio virium robore'. This dichotomy of the eunuch's nature is what makes him attractive, and forms the theme of the whole epigram.

Commentary

4. dubii pulcher corporis ... homo: the phrase hints at the sexual attractiveness of the grown eunuch as well as his purely physical beauty. 'dubii' suggests the abnormal characteristics which make him desirable both to men (his *mollities*) and women (his lack of procreative power): cf. Sen. *De Prov.* 3.13 'exsectae virilitatis aut dubiae'. The abnormality is heightened by the nouns which describe him in the epigram: *mas / femina / iuvenis / homo*.

extat (Sched.); erat (A); errat (Riese): Riese justified his conjecture (which is close to A's 'erat') with the gloss 'a vera hominis figura aberrat' and by reference to Liv. 31.12.8 'foeda omnia et deformia errantisque in alienos fetus naturae visa'; but it seems improbable that *errare* would be used absolutely in this sense here, and any reader would surely understand it to mean 'wanders around'. 'extat' of the Schedae Divionenses is much more convincing, and occurs in similar contexts elsewhere in the collection (e.g. 99.2; 154.1).

5-6. coniugibus ... datur: this couplet is difficult to understand in the context of the preceding description (who are the *coniuges*, why is the eunuch a *custos*, and why is he *fidus*?); the general tenor of the opening lines has been to suggest the eunuch is sexually attractive to men, but the pun on 'sine teste' indicates that this concluding couplet should deal with his attractiveness to women. Its scenario of the closeted women whose guard provides them with the dalliance from which he is meant to protect them is so close to that of Juv. 6.O.29 f. (where their guards ignore women's affairs because they are rewarded with sexual favours for their silence) that it can reasonably be interpreted in its light:

> novi
> consilia et veteres quaecumque monetis amici,
> 'pone seram, cohibe'. Sed quis custodiet ipsos
> custodes, qui nunc lascivae furta puellae
> hac mercede silent? Crimen commune tacetur.

It is possibly significant that these lines are immediately followed by a description of the charms of eunuchs to some women, including the fact that they cannot make them pregnant. Moreover, they also illuminate the pun in the present epigram on 'custos ... sine teste' (the unguarded guard as well as the eunuch guard), by suggesting the way in which and the reason why an unguarded guard is 'fidus' ('hac mercede silent. Crimen commune tacetur.'). Might therefore lines 5-6 have been written with knowledge of and allusion to Juvenal (see also the following note)?

5. coniugibus cautis: the noun might on initial reading be ambiguous, but the next line shows the reference is primarily to wives. The adjective is certainly ambiguous: women use eunuchs because they are incapable

Commentary

of impregnation, which makes the women 'cautious' in their amours, but it transpires they are also 'cautae' in the sense that, by having guards imposed on them by their husbands, they ought to be 'secure' from extramarital activity (for this meaning of *cauta* cf. Col. 8.9.3 'cellulae cautae efficiuntur'; Mart. 2.1.11; and, intriguingly, Juv. 6.348 'cauta est et ab illis incipit uxor', from lines now often deleted from Juvenal's text, which may once have formed an abbreviation of the missing lines of the O fragment).

monstrosa voluptas: SB incorrectly says in his app. crit. that 'voluptas' here is synonymous with *deliciae*. It is a euphemism for sexual pleasure or sexual intercourse: thus Ovid *Am.* 1.10.35 'cur mihi sit damno, tibi sit lucrosa voluptas, / quam socio motu femina virque ferunt?'; Sen. *Contr.* 2.5.14 'maritus ... non vacavit in uxoris voluptates'; with *OLD* voluptas 5, and Adams, *LSV* 197 f. For *monstrosus* of abnormal sex, cf. Suet. *Tib.* 43.1 'monstrosique concubitus repertores'; *Cal.* 16.1 'spintrias monstrosarum libidinum'; with *TLL* 8.1456.18 f.

6. fidus ... custos: 'fidus' is here a παρὰ προσδοκίαν because the guard is quite the opposite of 'fidus' in his role as a guard; but he is 'fidus' as a lover to the wives whose liaisons he is supposed to prevent because he himself is unwatched and it is in his and the wives' joint interests not to spill the beans about their own dalliance (see 5-6 n. above). For amatory *custodes* see Howell's commentary on Mart. 1.73 and Gibson's on Ovid *Ars* 3.611-58; there is even a eunuch employed by a wife to keep her pathic husband from mischief at Mart. 2.54.

est: the verb is erroneously omitted from SB's text.

sine teste: for the pun see 5-6 n. above. The meaning 'testicle' derives from the meaning 'witness' (see Adams, *LSV* 67; 212), and the pun is obvious and frequent (e.g. Mart 7.62.6 'illud saepe facit quod sine teste facit'; more examples at Adams loc. cit.). On this interpretation wives can trust the guard because he is incapable of impregnation.

98 (109R)

Another. His sex, which was fixed, became indeterminate when his genitals were removed, he whom the grasping hand of profit cut when he was young. For the eunuch minces along with such a feminine behind that you would doubt what it is, man or woman. The castrator has done away with the entire art of grammar in showing that a man is of neuter gender.

This second epigram of the pair on a eunuch switches the humour to a joke on gender, namely that a eunuch is neither male nor female, but neuter. The witticism, such as it is, is not new, having featured in much the same form in Ausonius and Palladas (for which see my commentary on Aus. *Epig.* 50).

Commentary

1. incertum ex certo sexum: 'sexus' here is virtually concrete for 'virilia', as 'fert pube recisa' demonstrates (see also 100.2 n.): cf. Lact. *Inst.* 1.21.16 'amputato enim sexu nec viros se nec feminas faciunt'; Plin. *Nat. Hist.* 22.20; Juvenc. 3.488; with Adams, *LSV* 62. The fact that the 'sexus' is 'incertus' suggests that the eunuch in this instance (unlike the one in the previous epigram) may have had his penis removed as well as his testicles: thus the Galli, for example, the eunuch priests of Cybele, often or always had all their external genitals removed (Mart. 11.72.2 f., with my note).

fert: for *fero* of parts of the body in the sense *gero* ('sport' or 'have'), cf. Sil. It. 13.822 'fert frontem atque oculos terrae Lucretia fixos', with *TLL* 6.1.531.28 f.

pube recisa: for 'pubes' see 97.2 n.; for *recido* with reference to castration, cf. Ovid *Am.* 2.3.3; Petr. 23.3; with Guyot, op. cit. (97 intro.), 23 n. 25.

2. tenerum: as at 97.2 the adjective indicates that castration was carried out before puberty.

secuit: for *seco* and its compounds used of castration, see Grewing's note on Mart. 6.2.2.

mercis avara manus: for the commercial motivation for castrating slaves, cf. Mart. 9.5(6).4 'non puer avari sectus arte mangonis'; Quint. *Inst.* 5.12.19; *Dig.* 48.8.3.4; at *Cod. Just.* 6.43.3.1 and 7.7.1.5 prices for castrated slaves are shown to be two to three times those for uncastrated ones (no doubt many did not survive the operation, which would tend to increase the value of those who did). *Merx* is evidently here used more in what is the usual sense of *merces* ('payment'), though it is closer still to *lucrum*, a sense *merces* can also have (e.g. Manil. 4.401 'et quantae mercedis erunt fallacia rura!').

3. femineo ... clune (Oudendorp; crure (A)) movetur: 'clune', Oudendorp's conjecture for A's 'crure', is convincing and necessary, and confusion between the two nouns is evidenced in other mss (e.g. variant readings at Veg. *Mul.* 3.6.5). It here refers to the buttocks or posterior, as at e.g. Mart. 11.100.3 '(sc. amicam nolo) quae clune nudo radat et genu pungat'; Juv. 11.164 'tremulo descendant clune puellae'; *CGL* 5.654.7 'cinaedi, qui publice clunem agitant'. 'movetur' alludes to the manner of walking: cf. Hor. *Ars* 232 'ut festis matrona moveri diebus' (see Brink's note); Cic. *Fin.* 5.56 'inertissimos homines ... videmus tamen et corpore et animo moveri'; with *TLL* 8.1539.4 f. Whilst the phrase as a whole could have a sexual reference to movement during intercourse (note for example Juv. 2.20 f. 'de virtute locuti / clunem agitant'; schol. Pers. 1.87 'molles et obscaenos clunium motus significat'; with Adams, *LSV* 136 f.; 195; *Glotta* 59.1981.231 f.; esp. 239 f.), such a meaning seems too explicit

Commentary

for this context. It is rather a mincing gait that is described: cf. [Anon.] *De Physiogn. Lib.* 115 (*Script. Physiogn.* 2.135 Förster) '(sc. cinaedi) qui movent corpus ut mulieres'; see also Gibson's commentary on Ovid *Ars* 3.299 f.

4. vir <magis> an mulier (*suppl.* de Saumaise); vir an mulier (A); <semi>vir an mulier (*suppl.* Watt): something has dropped out from A at this point, since it is metrically deficient. Watt (*HSCPh* 91.1987.291) questioned de Saumaise's supplement, which has generally been accepted by editors, on the grounds of pleonasm (however it is not unparalleled: cf. Mart. 3.88.2 'dissimiles sunt magis an similes?'; Sid. *Carm.* 23.354 f. 'magistros / temones mage sufferant an axes'; *TLL* 8.68.48 f.). Although his 'semivir' is at first sight attractive, it does not convince because it anticipates the concluding joke on gender and does not lead into it as well as the basic 'vir ... mulier'. And for similar expressions cf. *CGL* 4.348.44 'Hermaphroditus castratus, hoc est nec vir nec mulier'; Ovid *Am.* 2.3.1 'ei mihi, quod dominam nec vir nec femina servas'.

5. castrator: the noun is extremely rare, this being the only occurrence in verse (and the only others are Tert. *Ad Nat.* 2.13; *Adv. Marc.* 1.1; and *CGL* 3.544.12 f., according to *TLL* 3.544.12 f.). The verb *castrare* is much more frequently attested.

6. neutri ... hominem generis: for the abnormal genitive of 'neuter' in the grammatical phrase 'neutri generis' see my note on Aus. *Epig.* 50.6, as also for the same joke. It is a frequent comment of grammarians that *homo* could be of either masculine or feminine gender, which makes the joke more pointed: e.g. Diom. *Gramm. Lat.* 1.301.9 f. 'sunt enim communia duum generum ex masculino et feminino, ut hic et haec homo et hic et haec sacerdos' (with *NW* 1.897 f. for more examples).

99 (110R)

On some baths. Here, where the enticing pleasure of baths has risen up and the resplendent edifice stands out from its rough-hewn foundations, there were previously fields which made no return for the owner, and the little plot of land, devoid of crops, bore no buildings. But now Bellator, an important and highly honoured man, has clothed the fields with roofs, siting his beautiful baths here. His successful project improves on nature's gifts, now that the salty shore abounds with salubrious water. There is a tale that sweet Alpheus runs through Tethys' fields and is not contaminated by the mass of sea water. The miracle of my springs affords a similar instance; the fresh water is subjected to the salty water near it, yet has no tang of it.

Commentary

This is the first of a long sequence of epigrams in the collection on bathing establishments (see also 108-14; 164; 168-9), a pleasing piece with its emphasis on poor land developed for use and profit, and its pride in the technological accomplishment of having an uncontaminated fresh-water supply at the sea's edge. Poems in praise of baths, both literary and epigraphic, form an extensive genre, for which see Busch, *Versus*, passim, and Grewing's intro. to Mart. 6.42.

Baths were one of the features of previous Roman occupation which the Vandals found much to their liking (as Procopius says at *Bell. Vand.* 2.6.5 f.) and they are often mentioned in the *AL*, both as commercial enterprises and as features of villas (cf. also 23; 194; 201-5; 265; 281.282 f.; 342; 345; 372; 873bR). The majority of baths in North Africa of which evidence remains are of the Antonine and Severan periods, and there is hardly a town which cannot boast two or three such buildings. Although the construction of the larger baths stopped after the mid-fourth century, small baths continued to be built and flourish in the late Antique period, and their very smallness can be a subject for praise (e.g. *AP* 9.609a-612; 614; 624; 784; see further Y. Thébert, *Opus* 2.1983.99 f.; esp. 112 f.). The pieces in this collection reflect such activity, and there is also evidence for the restoration of earlier buildings by private individuals. See further Yegül, *Baths*, 184 f. (for baths in North Africa); 321 f. (for the economic aspects); Thébert, *Thermes romains*, 418 f.

Various themes recur in the bath poems, often stressing their excellence and technological achievements, and these will be dealt with in the notes as they occur. These pieces often (as here) raise basic questions about poems of clearly inscriptional type in the collection: who was the author, how and why were they collected, and why do they appear in a collection? There is little doubt that most, if not all of them, must have been intended for inscription, because of the highly specific and localised detail they give: in the present piece, for example, are the name of the proprietor Bellator, the description of the way in which the baths have been built and fresh water supplied to them, and the strongly deictic localisation of the setting by the seashore ('hic ubi ...' etc.). Also, the many inscriptions which have been found in the remains of Roman baths all over the Empire demonstrate the enduring popularity of such writing (see Dunbabin, *Baiarum grata voluptas*, 16 f.). However, this need not mean that the author of the present collection toured baths and anthologised any interesting inscriptions he found; it is more plausible that he wrote them to order for inscription, and also published them in book format (see further p. 4).

E. Courtney (*Hermathena* 129.1980.37 f.) has pointed out interesting similarities between this piece and *AL* 201 by Felix on the *Thermae Alianae* (near Carthage), which he argues are not accidental: both poems are twelve lines long, and both are about baths near the sea (201.9 f.); the technology of bringing fresh water to such a location is remarked in

Commentary

both (201.9 f.); both begin with the words 'hic ubi', with the second line ending with 'opus'; both contrast previously idle land with the current useful purpose to which it is put (201.3 f.); and both end with mythological exempla. In its totality this is unlikely to be coincidence; since *AL* 201 is one of a sequence of epigrams, all twelve lines long, celebrating baths founded by the Vandal king Thrasamund, and since their length is probably dictated by the piece which contains an acrostich of 'Thrasamundus' (205), Courtney reasonably argues that it would be remarkable if Felix, author of that sequence, chanced upon this epigram of precisely the right length and subject matter to serve as model. The author of this piece is therefore likely to be the imitator, and since Thrasamund reigned from 496 to 523 the conclusion has significant consequences for the dating of the present collection (on which see p. 5 f.). More similarities between Felix's poems and the sequence at 108-14 are noted in the intro. to 108.

1. hic ubi ...: these words stand at the beginning of other epigrams and inscriptions, where they key a contrast between the present and former use or appearance of a particular site: thus e.g. Mart. *Spect.* 2.1 f. 'hic ubi sidereus propius videt astra colossus ... / invidiosa feri radiabant atria regis'; ibid. 8.65.1 f.; *AL* 115.3; 201.1 f.; *CE* 1906.1 f.; ibid. 2039.1 f.; they also occur with the same significance in other contexts (e.g. Stat. *Silv.* 2.2.54; Juv. 3.12).

baiarum: 'baiae' is here a generic noun for a bathing establishment, and it derives from the town of Baiae, the luxury resort par excellence situated on the Bay of Naples. The name was first used with wider reference than to the place to denote estates in the locality (e.g. Cic. *Cael.* 35; 38 (though see Shackleton Bailey's note on Cic. *Att.* 11.6.6); Mart. 10.14(13).3; 10.58.2), and was later used with reference to bathing establishments generally, particularly in inscriptional epigrams where the quality of the place is advertised (this perhaps explains the origin of the usage, though the term might have been used originally to denote thermo-mineral establishments of the kind for which Baiae was famous: see 109.7 n.; 111 intro.). In the present collection, it occurs with this meaning at 108.1; 112.1; 169.1; and outside it at *AL* 202.1; 372.1; *ILCV* 787.1 (=*ML* 43 Courtney); 788.1; and esp. *AE* 1968.610.1 (this is the inscription from Sullecthum quoted in the following note; its similar phraseology to this line is apparent and may well arise via a standard lexicon of North African bath epigraphy rather than from direct imitation). In this specialised sense *baiae* is mostly attested in the first line of bath poems of North African provenance. Some examples (from *TLL* 2.1684.13 f.) which might seem to be exceptions can be distinguished, because in them the noun is qualified by an adjective which indicates that the reference is to 'a second Baiae': e.g. Sid. *Carm.* 23.13 'Phocida Sestiasque Baias'; and ibid. *Ep.* 5.14.1 'calentes ... Baiae', where 'calentes' can be understood to key a place named 'Aquae Calidae'. But *CE* 1255.3 f. (= *CIL* 14.480, from Ostia), an epitaph for one Socrates

Commentary

of Tralles, is more problematic: 'omnia B(b?)aiarum lustravi moenia saepe, / propter aquas calidas deliciasque maris, / cuius honorificae vitae non inmemor heres ...'. However, it seems at least possible that 'Baiae' is there the place proper, and that Socrates was commemorated for performing some official role in connection with it, it being the only activity in the epitaph which illustrates his claim to an 'honorifica vita'. And there is at least one example from a prose text, the 'baiae calidae' of the recently edited *Galeni qui fertur ad Glauconem liber tertius* 70.16, ed. K.-D. Fischer (*AION (filol)* 7.2003.330). Although Fischer obelises the words and their context is lacunose, there is no reason to doubt them; Dr Adams informs me the text is certainly of African provenance and probably sixth-century, and I am indebted to him for the reference.

surrexit blanda voluptas: 'blanda voluptas' is a frequent phrase, especially in Lucretius (2.966; 4.1085; 4.1263; 5.178), then in Ovid (*Ars* 2.477) and Silius (15.108). For 'voluptas' characterising the delights a building has to offer, cf. a third-/fourth-century bath inscription in verse from Sullecthum (Tunisia), which begins 'en perfecta cito baiarum grata voluptas' (*AE* 1968.610; see A. Beschaouch, *RAL* 23.1968.59 f.); *AL* 299.11 Luxorius; and compare the use of *deliciae* at 109.8. The pleasure that is to be had from baths and bathing is a frequent inscriptional and literary topic, for which see Dunbabin, *Baiarum grata voluptas*, 6 f. For 'surgere' of buildings, cf. Verg. *Aen.* 1.437 'o fortunati, quorum iam moenia surgunt'.

2. rudibus splendens molibus: Busch, *Versus*, 256 f. finds the phrase difficult and relates it to Ovid *Met.* 1.7 'rudis indigestaque moles'. It is however perfectly apt: Cicero describes the spring of Arethusa at Syracuse (on which see further 9 n. below: the allusion to it is crucial to the interpretation of the whole epigram) with the words 'qui fluctu totus operiretur, nisi munitione ac mole lapidum diiunctus esset a mari' (*Verr.* 2.4.118), and the 'munitio ac moles lapidum' to which he refers are the stoneworks which prevent a fresh-water spring from being polluted by the sea. The 'molibus' here, on which the baths were built, must have served the same function, in ensuring that a natural supply of fresh water near to the sea was not polluted by sea water; they are also the foundation works, rough-hewn and gigantic ('rudibus'), on which the bathing establishment itself rose as a 'splendens opus' and 'balnea pulchra'. For *moles* of construction works at or by the sea cf. Hor. *Carm.* 3.1.33 f. 'contracta pisces aequora sentiunt / iactis in altum molibus'; Sen. *Contr.* 2.1.13 'ex hoc litoribus quoque moles iniungunt (Müller for codd. 'invehuntur')'; with *TLL* 8.1341.72 f.

The ablative 'rudibus molibus' is one of separation: for the idiom with *exstare* (effectively *exstare ex ...*) cf. Lucr. 5.1034 'cornua nata prius vitulo quam frontibus exstent'; Sil. It. 7.627 'exstabat fixo quod forte cadavere ferrum'. Thus the splendid building appears to sprout from its rough foundations.

Commentary

3. rura prius ...: 'rura' is Heinsius' certain correction of mss 'pura', and there is an ellipse of 'erant' (for other instances see 95.3 n.). It sounds a modern note that the baths are said to be a development of land which would have been no use for more productive building or for farming, because of its proximity to the sea and lack of a fresh-water supply. There is similar justification for the siting of Thrasamund's baths at *AL* 201.3 f. 'arida pulvereo squalebat cespite tellus / litoreique soli vilis arena fuit'; compare the comments about the small plots of land involved in constructing the baths of 168-9; and cf. also *Ep. Bob.* 2-3. It is a reasonable deduction from such concerns that the baths of this epigram must have been situated near a populous urban centre where land was at a premium, and Carthage would fit the bill. Luxorius reflects similar concerns: of an amphitheatre built near the sea he says 'fecundus nil perdit ager, plus germina crescunt' (*AL* 341.5 f.), and of a health spa he says it was built 'quo deserta prius solum nemus atra tenebat / tetraque inaccessam sederat umbra viam' (345.3 f.). And one Cato compliments the Vandal king Huneric on a project reclaiming land from the sea (*AL* 382). On a literary level these claims and comments may be seen as a pre-emptive riposte to charges of wanton land development and destruction of natural landscape, which had been levelled as early as e.g. Hor. *Carm.* 2.15.1 f.; 3.24.3 f.; Sen. *Contr.* 2.1.13; Mart. 3.58; Quint. *Inst.* 8.3.8 (and on which see M. Beagon, 'Nature and Landscapes in Pliny the Elder', in *Human Landscapes in Classical Antiquity*, ed. G. Shipley and J. Salmon, London / New York 1996, 284 f.; and N. Purcell, 'Town in Country and Country in Town', in *Ancient Roman Villa Gardens*, ed. E. MacDougall et al., Washington DC 1987, 190 f.). But there is no reason to doubt they also reflect genuine concerns, and that land use, particularly in or near crowded cities and towns, had to be justified; and it is a good justification that such land as this could not be put to any 'better' use than for the construction of baths.

nullum ... quaestum: this reflects the good capitalist principle that if land is useful the owner will be making a profit from it, whether from building or from farming (cf. also 92 intro.; 168 intro.).

4. glebula: used of a small plot of land as at e.g. Petr. 57.6; Juv. 14.166; with *TLL* 6.2-3.2044.82 f.; there is again the implication of moderate and laudable land use (see also 168-9).

frugis inops: despite the nearby fresh-water supply, the land would not have been able to produce crops, because until Bellator constructed his 'moles', the water was contaminated by its proximity to the sea (see 2 n.).

5. Bellator, multo sublimis honore: Bellator is presumably the landowner ('domino' line 3) and the developer of the baths, which, it is implied by line 3, are a commercial enterprise (compare the baths of Filocalus and Melania at 109; those of Vita at 168-9; with further examples

Commentary

at Nielsen, *Thermae* 1.120 with nn. 9; 11). There is recorded a 'Bellator qui et Mustelus m<a>g<ister> in pace vixit' in a sixth-/seventh-century inscription found at Ammaedara (now Haidra in Tunisia); he is described as 'urbis defensor' and is eulogised 'qui gratus populis extabas mente benigna / post hanc eternam <m>eruisti sumere bita<m>' (*AE* 1946.30; and see Pikhaus, *Répertoire*, B61 and *PLRE* 3.907). But he is probably too late in date to be the Bellator of this epigram, though the possibility cannot be ruled out. The appellation 'multo sublimis honore' is not a reference to an official title (*sublimis* seems not to be used in that way, though an extravagant range of similar official titulature is well evidenced: see R.W. Mathisen, 'Imperial Honorific and Senatorial Status' in *Law, Society and Authority in Late Antiquity*, ed. R.W. Mathisen, Oxford 2001, 179 f.), but is presumably intended to be a general indication of Bellator's civic excellence and position in society.

6. vestivit cameris: the noun derives from Greek καμάρα ('vault' or 'vaulted structure') and here refers to the domed roofs which are typical of North African baths; each room would have had its domed roof, and the effect can still be seen in, for example, the Hunting Baths at Lepcis Magna and the small baths at Bulla Regia, of which Yegül (*Baths*, 243, with figs 290-2) says 'Thanks to the exceptional state of preservation of the vaults of the Hunting Baths in Lepcis, it is possible to visualise the extraordinary effect these small baths in Bulla Regia could create with their individually expressed, vaulted and domical forms and clusters of curved and polygonal exterior surfaces'. Thus the poet here picks out the specific feature of the roof as well as the 'rudes moles' of the foundations; they would have made the establishment immediately recognisable as a set of baths.

For *camera* elsewhere used of bath roofs, cf. Vitr. 5.10.3; 8.2.4; Stat. *Silv.* 1.5.45; *AL* 372.3; *ILAlg* 1.2108. The noun survives in Romance reflexes (Fr. *chambre*; It. *camera*) and the transition of meaning from 'roof' (or 'ceiling') to 'room' can be seen in late Antiquity: e.g. [Aug.] *Serm.* 319.7 (*PL* 38.1442) 'versus in cella scripsimus ... non opus est, ut quaeratur codex; camera illa codex vester sit'; *CGL* 2.571.6 'camaria ... cubile'; with von Wartburg, *Wörterbuch*, 2.130 f.; esp. 135 f.

7. prospera facta (Riese; fata (A)): Riese's small emendation is excellent, because it picks up on the comment 'nullum domino praestantia quaestum' in line 3: the land is now put to good use, and makes a profit because of Bellator's baths.

viri: here used instead of 'eius' (see 134.2 n.).

naturae munera mutant: the phrase alludes to what has been said before about the building of the baths, and what will be said shortly about the supply of uncontaminated fresh water close to the sea. 'mutant' suggests change for the better, as at 186.7 (see note): Bellator has accomplished

Commentary

what nature did not, by de-contaminating and securing a fresh-water supply (an achievement he manages to mention explicitly twice (7-8 and 11-12), and by implication once (9-10)). For a similar argument compare 168.5 f., with note.

8. cum (A); nunc (Oudendorp); nam (Meyer); iam (Riese); cui (Shackleton Bailey): 'cum' is perfectly apposite: the seashore location now has a usable fresh-water supply, whereas it was previously contaminated, and it affords an instance of man's improvement on nature.

salsum salubri: for the jingle cf. Cic. *Orat.* 90 'quoniam quicquid est salsum aut salubre in oratione, id proprium Atticorum est'. But here 'salsum' indicates an undesirable quality, 'salubri' a desirable one: the thrust of the poem shows that 'salubri' is a reference to fresh as opposed to salt water (and for the same point cf. *AL* 201.9 f., on the Thermae Alianae, 'paruit imperiis mutato lympha sapore / et dulcis fontes proluit unda novos'). Any overtones of health are secondary; however, health is often mentioned in the bath poems in this collection and elsewhere (see 169.6 n.), and a hint of it is apt enough in stressing the excellence of the baths here.

The irregular prosody of 'salubri', with short second syllable, is repeated at 174.8; there is a tendency in late verse for naturally long penultimate syllables which include mute and liquid to be treated for metrical purposes as either long or short, by analogy with forms that can strictly be either, such as 'volucrem' (e.g. 'lavăcrum' at Ven. Fort. *Carm.* 5.5.96; 'candelăbrum' ibid. 5.5.7; with Norberg, *Introduction*, 7).

9. Alpheum fama est: the Alpheus is a river of the Peloponnese which flows through Arcadia and Elis; the story here alluded to is that of the nymph Arethusa, who was pursued by the river god Alpheus, was herself turned into a river by Artemis, and went underground until she resurfaced in Sicily, whither Alpheus followed her (Mela (2.117) claims that objects thrown in the Alpheus in the Peloponnese resurface in Sicily, but Strabo (6.2.4) will have none of such nonsense; cf. also Sen. *Nat. Quaest.* 3.26.5). That this poet is following Vergil's version of the story is suggested by the identical opening words (*Aen.* 3.694 f.):

> Alpheum fama est huc Elidis amnem
> occultas egisse vias subter mare, qui nunc
> ore, Arethusa, tuo Siculis confunditur undis.

The fresh-water Fountain of Arethusa was to be found on Ortygia, an island which lies just offshore and forms part of the city of Syracuse and part of the sweep of its great harbour, and it was an integral part of the Syracusan foundation myth (Paus. 5.7.3; cf. Pind. *Nem.* 1.1 f.). It is one of several springs which are close together on Ortygia or just off its coast; it

Commentary

was described by Cicero: 'in hac insula extrema est fons aquae dulcis cui nomen Arethusa est, incredibili magnitudine, plenissimus piscium, qui fluctu totus operiretur nisi munitione ac mole lapidum diiunctus esset a mari' (*Verr.* 2.4.118). The pertinence of the comparison of the spring to the water supply of Bellator's baths lies both in the proximity of its fresh water to the sea, and in the structures built by man to ensure its water was not polluted (see 2 n. above). The spring still exists, though it has now been enclosed by a high wall and is landscaped; an earthquake in the twelfth century destroyed the barriers described by Cicero, with the result that the water did indeed become salty. For other accounts of the myth see Verg. *Ecl.* 10.1 f. and Ovid *Met.* 5.572 f.; and for the site see M. Guido, *Sicily, An Archaeological Guide*, London 1977, 179; and E.A. Freeman, *The History of Sicily*, Oxford 1891, 1.354 f.

dulcem: in this context the adjective clearly connotes fresh water: cf. *CIL* 10.1063, the first inscription excavated from Pompeii and an advertisement for a bathing establishment, which says 'Thermae / M. Crassi Frugi / aqua marina et baln<ea> / aqua dulci Ianuarius l<ibertus>'. Busch (*Versus*, 258) aptly compares the description by Statius of the baths at Pollius Felix's Sorrentine villa: 'gratia prima loci, gemina testudine fumant / balnea, et e terris occurrit dulcis amaro / lympha mari' (*Silv.* 2.2.17 f.); he also adduces two fifth-century epigrams from Dalmatia which celebrate a fresh-water spring in similar terms, though there is an unhelpful lacuna at a key point (*CIL* 3.1894.4 'praedulcis salsam per <... Teth>yn').

Tethyos (Heinsius); tetidus (A); Thetidis (Sched.); Thetidos (de Saumaise): M. Petschenig (*ZOeG* 28.1877.483) pointed out that A has similar problems at *AL* 230.2, where Heinsius' conjecture 'Tethyos amne' should be accepted for A's 'thedidis amne'. Since Tethys, wife of Oceanus, provides a frequent metonymy for the sea (e.g. 'audiat ictus utraque Tethys' at Sen. *Herc. Oet.* 1902, with *OLD* Tethys (b)), 'Tethyos' is a likely emendation here. However the Nereid Thetis provides an equally common metonymy (e.g. 'temptare Thetim ratibus' at Verg. *Ecl.* 4.32, with *OLD* Thetis (b)), and de Saumaise's 'Thetidos' is therefore worth consideration. But prosody tells against it, since its first syllable is regularly short, whereas that of Tethys is long (similarly at Cat. 88.5 the paradosis is 'Thetis', but the correct reading, on metrical grounds, must be 'Tethys'.).

10. gurgitibus pelagi: 'pelagi' particularly suggests salt water in this context, an emphasis it carries elsewhere (e.g. Verg. *Aen.* 1.246 'mare ... pelago premit arva sonanti'; *OLD* pelagus 2); the contrast is with the fresh water of the Alpheus which is unpolluted by the great mass ('gurgitibus': cf. Lucr. 5.387 'ex alto gurgite ponti'; Lucan 7.813; with *TLL* 6.2-3.2361.63 f.) of the ocean under which it flows.

11. nostri miracula fontis: 'miracula' stresses the technological feat of building baths with a natural and uncontaminated fresh-water supply so close to the sea. For *miraculum* of buildings see also 89.1 n.; 'nostri' here refers to Bellator (note the similarly proprietorial 'nostra' etc. in the bath epigrams 110.4; 111.3 and 112.1); and 'fontis' again stresses the parallel with the Fountain of Arethusa, and suggests that the water supply of the baths is a natural spring.

100 (111R)

On a pantomimus. Declining a male physique with a feminine inflection and adapting his supple frame to both sexes, the dancer bursts onto the stage and salutes his public, promising to send forth words by his masterly gestures. For when the sweet-sounding chorus pours forth its Greek songs, he demonstrates by mime what the lead singer sings back. He fights, he clowns, he loves, he is in a frenzy, he pirouettes, he stands still; he illustrates reality, everything he does is seemly. For this man his limbs are all tongues: it is the miracle of art which enables his fingers to speak when his mouth is silent.

Although this epigram has some of the clichés one would expect about pantomimes, such as talking hands, there is plenty to give it an individual twist, particularly the cleverly contrived opening. There is evidence enough for the continuation of pantomime as an art form into the sixth century: for example there is a series of poems about it by the Agathian poet Leontius Scholasticus (*AP* 16.283 f.); Cassiodorus (*Var.* 1.20; 1.32-3) illustrates its popularity in the West under Theoderic; John Malalas witnesses the continuing interest in it in the East (*Chron.* 12.6; 15.12; 17.12 etc.; see also Proc. *Anecd.* 9.5); and Luxorius, as well as this author, has a piece on the subject (*AL* 305). There is also evidence for the restoration and continuing use of the theatres where such entertainment was staged (see *CAH* 14.940). There is therefore no reason to doubt that the author of this epigram had first-hand knowledge of the art form about which he was writing.

The popularity of pantomime is shown by the large number of epigrams and inscriptional epitaphs its artists attracted. The literary pieces are well covered in Otto Weinreich's study *Epigramm und Pantomimus* (*SHAW* 1944-48. Abh. 1), the chronological approach of which begins with the Hellenistic period (where the only sign of interest in the art is *AP* 11.195 Dioscorides), then deals with the Augustan and later periods, where the evidence is plentiful (with some twenty pieces, including the present one). The epigrams span many types, for example the honorific (e.g. *AP* 9.542 Crinagoras), the epitaphic (e.g. Mart. 11.13), the skoptic (e.g. *AP* 11.255 Palladas), and the largely epideictic (as here). Both male (e.g. *AP* 16.290 Antip. Thess.) and female (e.g. *AP* 16.283-8) performers feature in them. Weinreich's study may be supplemented by that of V. Rotolo, 'Il Pantomimo', *Atti della accademia di scienze, lettere e arti di*

Commentary

Palermo (= *Studi e testi*, 4th ser., 16.2), Palermo 1957, esp. 311 f., where he catalogues a series of forty-eight inscriptional epitaphs as well as the literary instances. And for a short history of the pantomime and its enduring popularity see M.E. Molloy, *Libanius and the Dancers*, Hildesheim etc. 1996, 52 f. I quote the following piece on the pantomime Vincentius because it is from Thamugade (Timgad) in North Africa (third century), it contains a typically North African acrostich (for which see 109 intro.), and it shares the theme of the audience's adulation of the performer with the present piece (*AE* 1956.122 = Rotolo, op. cit. 38):

> Vincentius hic est pantomimorum decus
> In ore vulgi victitans perenniter
> Non arte tantum qua solent scaenica
> Cunctis amatus set <si> quis probus bonus
> Erat per omnis innocens et continens
> Notas qui semper cum saltaret fabulas
> Tenuit theatrum usque in ortus vesperos
> Istic humatus nunc habet pro moenibus
> Vixit per annos tres et viginti virens
> Set sanctus vita gestu erat facundior

The following notes are indebted to Weinreich's treatment of the epigram at op. cit. 118 f., though I differ from him in the interpretation of the opening lines in particular.

1. mascula femineo declinans (Klotz; diribans (A); deribans (BW); derivans (edd.)) pectora flexu: Klotz's emendation of the participle 'derivans', which presumably lies behind the readings of the mss, is excellent (*Antiburmannus*, Jena 1761, 50), and was first accepted into the text by SB. With it the whole line puns on (a) the pantomime's physical movements which are required for playing both male and female roles, and (b) a grammatical play on the same words (for similar humour with gender and grammar in the collection see 96.1 n.; 98.6 n.; 118 intro.). The male pantomime can suggest femininity in his performance, and this is viewed by the poet as contrary to natural order and is reflected by the grammatical pun that the performer is 'declining male parts with female inflections' (there being additional humour in the 'male parts' being grammatically neuter). 'derivans' is unconvincing, since it is difficult to attribute to it any meaning other than a grammatical one.

Declinare is often applied to the physical movement of the eyes and head (as at e.g. Cat. 64.91; Verg. *Aen.* 4.185; Greg. Tur. *Virt. Jul.* 14), but is also used in a wider sense of general walking or a stooping posture (as at e.g. Ovid *Met.* 10.667 'declinat cursus aurumque volubile tollit'; *Vet. Lat.* Prov. 1.15 (= Lucif. Cal. *De Sancto Athanasio* 1.25, *CSEL* 14.1886.110 ed. Hartel) 'ne declinaveris pedem tuum ad semitas eorum';

Commentary

with *TLL* 5.1.192.18 f.). Here, in the context of a pantomimic dancer, it can aptly suggest the way in which a male dancer would adapt his male physique ('mascula pectora') to feminine movement in playing female parts ('femineo flexu'). But there is also a pun on the grammatical sense of *declinare*, a verb which is often used of the declension of nouns and adjectives: e.g. Varro *Ling. Lat.* 8.6 'nomina recto casu accepto in reliquos obliquos declinant'; Quint. *Inst.* 1.4.22 'nomina declinare et verba in primis pueri sciant'; with *TLL* 5.1.194.30 f. Similarly *flexus* can be used both of dancers' movements (as at e.g. Apul. *Met.* 1.4.4 'puer in ... flexibus tortuosis ... saltationem explicat'; Tert. *Spect.* 10 'de gestu et corporis flexu'; with *TLL* 6.1.909.17 f.), and of grammatical inflections (e.g. Quint. *Inst.* 1.6.15 'quae tota positionis eiusdem in diversos flexus eunt'; *Gramm. Lat.* 4.544.9 'genitivus qui primus flexum declinationis ostendit, ut puta si dicas "cuius gentis est?" '; with *TLL* 6.1.911.75 f.).

For comment on the ability of the pantomime to perform both male and female roles cf. Jer. *Ep.* 43.2 'quomodo in theatralibus scaenis unus atque idem histrio nunc Herculem robustus ostendit, nunc mollis in Venerem frangitur, nunc tremulus in Cybelem'; Liban. *Orat.* 64.70; and Cass. *Var.* 4.51.9. This ambivalence easily leads to implicit comment in the language used on the artist's sexuality, an undertone which may be present in these opening lines also: thus Lact. *Inst.* 6.20.29 'enervata corpora et in muliebrem incessum habitumque mollita impudicas feminas inhonestis gestibus mentiuntur'; Novat. *Spect.* 6.6 (*CCSL* 4.1972.175 ed. Diercks) 'homo fractus omnibus membris et vir ultra muliebrem mollitiem dissolutus, cui ars sit verba manibus expedire. Et propter unum nescioquem nec virum nec feminam commovetur civitas tota, ut desaltentur fabulosae antiquitatum libidines'; Lucian 45.2; with Weinreich, op. cit. 175 f.; Molloy, op. cit. 91 f.

2. aptans lentum sexum ad utrumque latus: again the phrase is humorously ambiguous. The word order leads the reader initially to construe 'lentum' with 'sexum' ('adjusting his pliable sex to both sides'), the image being that of the dancer adjusting his genitalia, particularly no doubt when playing female roles (for *sexus* in that sense see 98.1 n.). The other (and dominant) construction is to take 'lentum' with 'latus' and 'sexum' with 'utrumque' ('adapting his supple frame to both sexes'), suggesting as in the previous line that he was adept at both male and female roles (for *latus* used of the dancing body cf. Ovid *Ars* 3.301 'haec movet arte latus').

3. populum ... adorat: this is very Hollywood, the famed performer milking his audience by stretching out his hands and blowing kisses to them: cf. Tac. *Hist.* 1.36 'nec deerat Otho protendens manus adorare volgum, iacere oscula'; Mart. 1.3.7; Phaedr. 5.7.28; Suet. *Claud.* 12.2; Claud. 28.616; with *RE* Suppb. 5.518. Similar gestures were used in obeisance in religious contexts (*adoratio*, Greek προσκύνησις), which must have added to its significance in the theatre (cf. Jer. *In Ruf.* 1.19 'qui adorant, solent deosculari manum et capita submittere'): the audience saluted as a god.

4. sollerti spondens (Mercer); solerti spondit (A); solertis pendet (BW); sollerti et spondet (Heinsius): the sense is clear and Mercer's slight emendation plausible.

sollerti ... prodere verba manu: 'speaking hands' provide the most frequent cliché for the pantomime's art, and it appears in this epigram again at line 10. Note e.g. *AP* 16.290.6 Antip. Thess. 'ὁ παμφώνοις χερσὶ λοχευόμενος' ('the one brought into the world with hands that say everything'); *AP* 9.542 Crinagoras; Lucian 45.63; 69; Claud. 20.362 'quis voci digitos, oculos quis moribus aptet?'; Sid. *Carm.* 23.269 f. 'clausis faucibus et loquente gestu / nutu, crure, genu, manu, rotatu'; with further references at Weinreich, op. cit. 140; Molloy, op. cit. 69; and Rotolo, op. cit. 231 f. Quintilian draws a parallel between hand gestures and speech in his treatment of oratorical gesturing (*Inst.* 11.3.85 f.).

5. Graia (AW); grata (B): Schenkl (*WS* 1.1879.62) preferred AW's 'Graia (cantica)' on the grounds that pantomime troupes who toured the provinces were usually Greek-speaking, but, assuming this poem belongs to Vandal Africa, it seems unlikely that the chorus would sing in Greek because few would understand them. The adjective might more plausibly refer to the Greek mythological subjects which were typical of pantomime (cf. Lib. *Pro Salt.* 112 = *Or.* 64.112 Förster), and it is preferable to B's anodyne 'grata'. There is a similar textual point at Cat. 66.58, where ms. 'gratia' is generally emended to Baehrens' conjecture 'Graiia' (after Lachmann's 'Graia').

chorus: the pantomime chorus was said to have been introduced into performances by the famous practitioner Pylades in 22 BC, the dancers themselves having also sung the text to which they danced before that date (Macr. *Sat.* 2.7.18; with Wille, *Musica*, 178 f.; Weinreich, op. cit. 156 f.).

cantica: for *cantica* sung by pantomime choruses cf. Phaedr. 5.7.25 f. 'tunc chorus ignotum modo reducto canticum / insonuit'; Tert. *De Pud.* 8 'meminimus enim et histriones, cum allegoricos gestus adcommodant canticis, alia longe a praesenti et fabula et scaena et persona et tamen congruentissime exprimentes'; Macr. *Sat.* 2.7.14; with E. Hall, 'The singing actors of antiquity', in *Greek and Roman Actors*, ed. P. Easterling and E. Hall, Cambridge 2002, 29 f.

6. quae resonat cantor: Weinreich (op. cit. 119) suggests that 'cantor' may be a synonym for 'chorus' (though there are no instances in *TLL*); Schenkl (*WS* 1.1879.62) baldly states that it is; and Wille (*Musica*, 180 n.

Commentary

237) agrees. But 'quae resonat cantor' suggests a different activity from that in the preceding line. The pantomime chorus had its leader (cf. schol. Juv. 11.172; Lib. *Orat.* 33. 3; with Weinreich, op. cit. 157 n. 1; *RE* 18.3.856), and responsorial singing is evidenced (see West, *Music*, 388 etc.). In this performance the chorus sings a text, the chorus leader ('cantor') repeats it (so the audience can hear more clearly?), and the pantomimus dances it.

motibus ipse probat: the meaning is much the same as 'inlustrat verum' in line 8: the artist illustrates the reality of all that the chorus and their leader sing by means of the range and correctness of his gestures.

7. pugnat, ludit ...: for such asyndetic lists of nouns or verbs in epigram (*cumulatio*) see my intro. to Aus. *Epig.* 96. The point of the list here is to stress the versatility of the artist in the emotions and actions he can convey, as is also done elsewhere by reference to the multiple parts a single performer can play: e.g. Lucian 45.66; *AP* 16.289 anon.; Athen. 1.20c; Jer. *Ep.* 43.2 (quoted above at 1 n.).

bacchatur: in the context of the other verbs this probably refers to a general portrayal of frenzy and madness (as at e.g. Lucr. 5.824 'omne (sc. animal) quod in magnis bacchatur montibus'), though a specific allusion to Bacchic ecstasy would not be inappropriate since the Pentheus myth was a pantomime topic (e.g. *AP* 16.289 anon.).

8. inlustrat verum: Weinreich (op. cit. 118 f.; 144 f.) compares the opening line of the epitaph for a pantomimus at *IG* 14.2124 (= Kaibel 608) 'ἱστορίας δείξας καὶ χειρσὶν ἅπαντα λαλήσας' ('illustrating the stories and saying everything with his hands'); *AP* 11.254.1 Lucillius 'πάντα καθ' ἱστορίην ὀρχούμενος' ('dancing everything just as in the story'); and Lucian 45.63. The sense follows on from the previous line: the range of emotion and technical pantomimic skill is perfectly adapted to illuminating the story performed, and making it real.

cuncta decore replet: i.e. there is nothing crude or vulgar in the performance; Martial termed the pantomimus Paris 'Romani decus et dolor theatri' (11.13.5).

9. tot linguae quot membra viro: this is a variant of the 'speaking hands' cliché, which is itself repeated in the concluding line. It is structurally reminiscent of aphorisms like Terence's 'quot homines tot sententiae' (*Ph.* 454), which has a similar ellipse of the verb.

mirabilis ars est: compare *AP* 16.289.6 anon., on the pantomimus Xenophon: 'φεῦ θείης ἀνδρὸς ὑποκρισίης' ('oh! the divine acting of the man!').

10. facit articulos ... loqui: the construction of causative *facere* with acc. and inf., which is based on Greek ποιεῖν with acc. and inf., is found as early as Ennius (*Ann.* 439 Sk.); cf. Verg. *Aen.* 2.538 f. 'me cernere letum / fecisti'; Ovid *Met.* 7.690 f. 'hoc me ... telum / flere facit facietque diu'; Scrib.

Commentary

Larg. 180 'facit ... capitis gravitatem ... sudoresque frigidos manare'; and see P. Thielmann, 'Facere mit dem Infinitiv', *ALL* 3.1886.177 f.; esp. 180 f.; H. Petersmann, *Petrons urbane Prosa: Untersuchungen zu Sprache und Text*, Vienna 1977, 213 f.; and *LHS* 2.354.

ore silente loqui: for the oxymoron cf. *AP* 9.505.17 f. anon. (on the muse Polymnia as a pantomima):

σιγῶ, φθεγγομένη παλάμης θελξίφρονα παλμόν,
νεύματι φωνήεσσαν ἀπαγγέλλουσα σιωπήν.

(' I am silent, but speak through the entrancing motions of my hands, conveying by my gestures a speaking silence' (translation Loeb)); Nonn. *Dion.* 19.156 'αὐδήεσσα σιωπή' ('speaking silence', also of pantomime). The conceit crops up in other contexts as well (e.g. Soph. *Trach.* 814; *AP* 12.122.4 Meleager; Otto 1734; with Weinreich, op. cit. 116 n. 1).

101 (112R)

On a funambulist. The ropes of tow, which the skilled youth ascends with sure step, are made taut by the poles supporting them. How incredibly high the walker is as he stretches forth his legs and, though human, rushes along a path scarcely easy for birds! Stretching his arms to the side he controls his route through the void, lest he should miss his footing and fall from the slender rope. It is maintained that Daedalus changed country by flight, and that he clove the noonday sky on wings. That story from fiction is proved true by the present example: look, a rope and the air bear a man on his journey!

Funambulism was always a popular entertainment in the Roman world, back to the days when the audience at the first performance of Terence's *Hecyra* deserted the drama for such a display (1 f.):

Hecyra est huic nomen fabulae. Haec quom datast
nova, novom intervenit vitium et calamitas
ut neque spectari neque cognosci potuerit:
ita populu' studio stupidus in funambulo
animum occuparat.

The skill of the performer and the danger inherent in performance were the key attractions (Manil. 5.652 f.):

ac tenuis ausus sine limite gressus
certa per extentos ponet vestigia funes
et caeli meditatus iter vestigia perdet
saepe nova et pendens populum suspendet ab ipso.

Commentary

(and see also Plin. *Ep.* 9.26.3; Aug. *Ep.* 120.5; John. Chrys. *PG* 56.114). A *catadromus* (Greek κατάδρομος σχοῖνος) is often mentioned as part of the equipment, and is a rope leading up to and down from a platform at variable height (Suet. *Nero* 11.2; Juv. 14.266; Paul. *Dig.* 19.1.54); other evidence (e.g. a third-century coin from Cyzicus illustrated at *DS* 2.1362 fig. 3322, as well as the present epigram) shows a rope suspended between two high platforms. There were even animal performers, including some unlikely elephants (Suet. *Galba* 6.1; *Nero* 11.2; Sen. *Ep.* 85.41). After a boy fell to his death during a triumph celebrated by Marcus Aurelius and Lucius Verus in AD 166, mattresses or nets were used for safety reasons at some performances (*SHA* M. Ant. Phil. 12.12). For more descriptions of and references to funambulism, see Hor. *Ep.* 2.1.210; Sen. *De Ira* 2.12.5; Quint. *Inst.* 2.13.16; Juv. 14.266 f.; Lucian 41.9; *AL* 275; 281.300 f. Symphosius; with Mayor's note on Juv. 14.272; *DS* 2.1361 f.; Blümner, *Privataltertümer*, 615.

superscr.: De funambulo: the Greek equivalent is σχοινοβάτης (itself transliterated into Latin at Juv. 3.77) or νευροβάτης. Porphyrion comments on Hor. *Sat.* 1.10.28 'Pedius Publicola et Messala adeo curasse dicuntur ne Graeca Latinis immiscerent ut Messala primus "funambulum" dixerit ne "σχοινοβάτην" diceret', but that is not credible because Terence, who uses the noun *funambulus* (see intro. above), predates Pedius and Messala, and the noun itself also appears to predate σχοινοβάτης (though Lindner (*Glossar*, 79) reasonably remarks that that is probably only due to our lack of evidence). See further J. Samuelsson, *Glotta* 6.1915.264 f.

1. stuppea ... vincula: the phrase recurs at Stat. *Silv.* 3.2.26 f. *Stuppa*, Greek στύππη, is tow, the shorter, coarse fibres of flax or hemp which are separated by a process known as heckling from the fine, long-stapled fibres called 'line'. Pliny (*Nat. Hist.* 19.17) describes how the flax stalks are soaked in water, dried, then pounded on stone with a tow-hammer (*stupparius malleus*). The tow is then made into rope by *restiones* or *restiarii* (of whom there is a college at *CIL* 6.9856), though tow is not the only material used, and there were various qualities and types of rope for different purposes (Plin. *Nat. Hist.* 19.25 f.); Pliny says that hemp is preferred for rope which is not to be used at sea or in water, and that it is 'utilissimus funibus' (ibid. 29; 173), which accords well with this instance. A tow-merchant, or *stuppator*, provided the necessary material for the rope-makers, and there was a college of them at Ostia (*CIL* 14.44). See also André, *Botanique*, 306; *DS* 4.846 f. (restiarius); ibid. 1546 f. (stuppator).

suppositis tenduntur ... lignis: the 'ligna' are the high poles between which the rope was stretched and made taut when it was anchored to the ground; for the verb, cf. Hor. *Ep.* 2.1.210 'per extentum funem'; Manil. 5.653.

Commentary

2. quae (Pithou; quem (codd.)) ... ascendit: 'quem' can have no antecedent noun and needs correction. The verb 'ascendit' suggests that reference here is primarily to the rope ('stuppea vincula') by which the performer ascends to a platform at the top of the supporting poles ('supposita ligna'), from where he walks along the same or another rope to another platform: this is the *catadromus* described in the intro. above, and its ascension would have been an integral part of the act and would itself require 'fido gradu', as Manil. 5.655 f. (quoted in the intro. above) shows. Pithou's 'quae' should therefore be accepted.

docta iuventa: when it refers to people, as it must do here (cf. 'ascendit'), 'iuventa' is a collective noun (e.g. Hor. *Carm.* 3.2.14 f. 'mors ... / nec parcit imbellis iuventae / poplitibus timidove tergo'; *TLL* 7.2.742.1 f.), and is not elsewhere used of an individual. In the remainder of the epigram, however, the actions of a single performer are described ('viator ... homo ... '). Either therefore the focus shifts from the general to the specific (e.g. funambulists are skilful and young, says the poet, and he then gives a specific instance of a particularly daring performer); or 'docta iuventa' has an apparently unique reference, equivalent to 'doctus iuvenis'. The former is strained, so the latter is the more likely explanation, especially since *senecta* used in the sense *senex* affords a parallel (e.g. Sil. 8.7 'hac spirante senecta', of Q. Fabius Maximus).

3. quam (codd.); quae (edd.; *sed* iam (Baehrens); qua (Timpanaro; Shackleton Bailey)): if mss 'quam' is correct here, it is exclamatory rather than prepositional. But that makes good sense, because the action described by this line can be distinguished from that of the preceding couplet, the funambulator having made his ascent of the *catadromus* and now being pictured as walking at unbelievable height along the rope strung between the platforms. I have therefore repunctuated accordingly.

superaërius (Kay); superius (A); super aerius (BV): if 'super' is a preposition it would be best served by a preceding pronoun, but the obvious (if not only) choice of 'quae' is precluded by 'quae' in line 2 (if it is a correct emendation there). However, the difficulty can be resolved if 'superaërius' is taken as a compound adjective (and note the text of A): the height of the performer above ground is the focus of this couplet, and the more emphasis placed on it here the better for the sense of the next line. Compound adjectives with prefix *super* are rare before late Latin, but they come into their own in the Vetus Latina, Vulgate and Christian writing (note esp. *supercaelestis*, of Jesus and angels, at Tert. *De Res. Mort.* 49 etc.; there are pages of *super-* compounds in A. Blaise's *Dictionnaire latin-français des auteurs chrétiens*, Turnhout 1954). A coinage here would be possible and appropriate.

4. vixque avibus ...: although it is difficult to divorce one's thoughts from the rope ('facili tramite'), that can hardly be the author's intended

Commentary

comparison here, because birds have no need to walk on tightropes. He rather emphasises height from the ground: this performer ascends to a height which even birds with their wings would find difficult to attain.

homo: this is not the padding it might appear, because it stresses that a human can outdo a bird in the bird's own sphere.

5. brachia distendens ... gubernat: the balance of the performer may have been helped by a balancing pole, as the Cyzicus coin referred to in the intro. above illustrates. However, there is no certain indication of a pole here, and he may simply balance himself by using his outstretched arms.

6. ne lapsa (codd.; lapsu (Petschenig)) gracili (BVW; facili (A); e gracili (Binet)): M. Petschenig (*ZOeG* 28.1877.483) objected to the lengthening of the final vowel of 'lapsa' (sc. 'planta') before the opening mute and liquid of 'gracili', thus emending 'lapsa' of the mss to 'lapsu'; Binet's 'lapsa e gracili', followed by Baehrens, was conjectured for the same reason (Professor Reeve points out that 'lapsa a' would be easier). There is some force in the objection (note e.g. 'iuventa gradu' without lengthening of the final 'a' at line 2). However, S. Timpanaro, 'Alcune particularita prosodiche nell' *AL*', *Contributi di filologia e di storia della lingua latina*, 611 f. (revised from *SCO* 10.1961.166 f.), deals with three instances in the *AL* where the phenomenon occurs (also at 7.4 'cum urtica gremio prosilit' and 120.4 'formare propriis carmina versibus'), in each of which editors have emended it away. He demonstrates that in no instance is the alteration grammatically required (thus a parallel to the present instance is provided by 108.4 'blandaque perspicuo fonte fluenta cadunt'). The question is therefore solely one of metre, and that furnishes no necessity to emend: lengthening of this type is found as early as Catullus (e.g. 4.9; 4.18; 29.4), and Tibullus (1.6.34), and occurs later in Ausonius (25.10.7; 25.15.19; 26.201 (which Green accepts as special cases, though he emends at 14.3.1, on which see his note)) and especially Dracontius (e.g. *Laud. Dei* 1.145; 289; 476; with Vollmer's edition (*MGH AA* 14), index p. 442); there is actually another instance in this collection at 106.11 'aestiva prandia', where no one emends, and a further possible one at 170.1 'lea crevit', on which see note. Timpanaro also demonstrates that no differences in the practice can be established between those which occur 'in arsi' and those 'in thesi'. He also, and quite rightly, criticises editorial practice in such instances where a metrical 'licence' is rejected for metrical reasons only and in selected cases only (thus Riese, for example, emends here, at 120.4 and 170.1, but passes over 106.11 in silence).

For *gracilis* used of rope, cf. Ovid *Met.* 4.176 'graciles ex aere catenas' (with reference to Vulcan's net in which he trapped Venus and Mars), with *OLD* gracilis 1(b). The adjective stresses the rope's thinness, which is a tribute to the performer's skill (cf. Sen. *De Ira* 2.12.4). A's metrically incorrect 'facili' has no doubt intruded from line 4.

Commentary

7. adstruitur: for *adstruere* in the sense *probare* or *affirmare*, the earliest instances given by *TLL* (2.979.6 f.) are Papin. *Dig.* 46.8.3 'vulgaribus verbis ... haec quoque ... adstruentur' and Porph. ap. Hor. *Ep.* 1.17.1 (both probably third century). It is frequent thereafter.

8. medium ... diem: 'persecuisse' shows that the reference is not principally to time (as *TLL* 5.1.1054.25 suggests) but to space, though there may be an overtone of time (i.e. the middle of the sky, and the sky at noon). Compare for the former Sen. *Herc. Oet.* 1631 f. 'sedibus pulsae suis / volucres pererrant nemore succiso diem / quaeruntque lassis garrulae pinnis domus'; Claud. 36.316 'accingar lustrare diem'; with *OLD* dies 2(b). The notion of noon would also be appropriate, because disaster fell on Icarus when the wax of his wings melted at the hottest time of day.

9-10. praesenti exemplo ... ferunt: the poet concludes his epigram by humorously suggesting that Daedalus did not fly between Crete and Sicily but walked a tightrope between them in what is an intentionally ludicrous rationalisation of the myth (in fact there are more credible ones: Diodorus Siculus suggests he escaped by sea (4.77.5 f.), Pausanias that his escape involved the first journey by sail (9.11.3)).

9. firmatur fabula mendax: the phrase is a paradox, since the truth of a fiction is not confirmable (for the phraseology cf. *Aetna* 511 'si firma manet tibi fabula mendax', and for the words 'fabula mendax' concluding a hexameter cf. Lucan 10.282 and Drac. *Laud. Dei* 3.527); the point is that the myth of Daedalus flying across the Mediterranean, an evidently incredible fiction, preserves the 'truth' that he must have crossed it by tightrope, the possibility of such a feat being corroborated by the skill of the performer of the epigram. Siedschlag (*Form*, 102) gives some other epigrams in which a mythological truth is evidentially confirmed (e.g. Mart. *Spect.* 6(5); 14(12); *AP* 9.88 Philippus).

102 (113R)

On a citharode. Touching the musical strings with subtle strokes he makes his entrance, in order that he may please his audience's ears. He stands commanding in his playing and singing; his hands complement his voice, harmonised by his artistry in both. For he so balances the two of them by equal control of both, and by his artistry so regulates his hands in combination with his voice, that you become entranced by this double delight to the point where you are unsure whether the voice is singing or only the lyre is playing.

Epigrams on pantomime and tightrope-walking are followed by two on a citharode and one on a weapons dance, and it is tempting to view them

Commentary

as a group of pieces on performance arts deliberately placed together (see further p. 3). Certainly there are similarities in the way the arts are described: the pantomime's hands are said to serve two purposes (gesture and voice); the funambulist uses his limbs to perform as a bird; the citharode's instrument and voice are so attuned it seems that the two are one; and the weapon dance is paradoxically carried out in peaceful harmony. In all cases unlikely elements combine, and / or human attributes are used to superhuman effect. The emphasis on combination and harmony is particularly evident in this piece: 'concordant sensu conciliata pari' (line 4); 'aequali ... moderamine librat' (line 5); 'socias temperat ... manus' (line 6); 'gemina dulcedine' in line 7 and so on.

Riese (app. crit.) thought that two lines might have been dropped from this epigram, presumably because the companion piece (103) is ten lines long. However, there is nothing to indicate such a lacuna on the grounds of logic or sense, and there are other paired and adjacent epigrams in the collection which are of different lengths (e.g. 83-4; 142-3; 165-6; 182-3; 186-7) as well as ones of the same length (97-8; 126-7; 132-3; 141-2; 156-7; 168-9; 172-3; 184-5). The hypothesis is therefore not convincing.

Citharodes were singers of Greek or Latin lyric who accompanied themselves on the lyre (see my notes on Mart. 11.75.3 and Aus. *Epig.* 44.4). Wille (*Musica*, 330 f.) deals with their status as musical virtuosi, adducing in addition to this and the following pieces Athen. 4.183a f.; Mart. 3.4.7 f.; 5.56.8 f.; and the following inscription, which includes an acrostich (*CE* 1557):

> Musicus incanere, docte cantare solebat
> Acceptusque nimis multis magnifico ingenio,
> Receptus inter fautores prior,
> Celebri favore artem exponens suam,
> Ut quivis dederet aures suas mirifico ingenio
> Super canentis carmine doctiloquo.

Like the preceding pantomime and funambulist, the best citharodes would have had their adoring public.

1. musica ... stamina: *stamina*, referring to the vertical threads of a loom, becomes a name for lyre strings because of the visual likeness (and the weaving metaphor is continued here by preceding 'subtili', with the derivation of the adjective from *sub* + *telum*). Compare Ovid *Met.* 11.167 f. (of Apollo playing the cithara), which has a number of similarities with this epigram though not sufficient to postulate a direct influence:

> ... instrictamque fidem gemmis et dentibus Indis
> sustinet a laeva; tenuit manus altera plectrum:
> artificis status ipse fuit; tum stamina docto

Commentary

  pollice sollicitat, quorum dulcedine captus
  Pana iubet Tmolus citharae submittere cannas.

pulsu: the strings were struck by a plectrum rather than plucked (cf. Ovid *Met.* 11.168 quoted above; *Fast.* 5.667; and my note on Aus. *Epig.* 44.3).

2. ingreditur: of the performer making his entrance onto the stage, as of the pantomime at 100.3; cf. Quint. *Inst.* 10.2.22 'nec contra tragoedia socco ingreditur', with *TLL* 7.1.1569.66 f.

  vulgi auribus: for the hiatus at the main caesura of the pentameter see p. 23; there is another hiatus at the main caesura of the hexameter in line 5.

3. stat: again Ovid's picture of Apollo playing the cithara is similar (*Met.* 11.169, quoted above).

  tactu cantuque: the two nouns introduce the theme that will dominate the rest of the poem, the concord between instrument and voice; 'tactu' is immediately picked up by 'brachia', 'cantu' by 'linguae'.

  brachia: 'manus' or 'digitos' might have been expected, but compare for example Cor. *Joh.* 3.157 'infaustis admovit bracchia furtis'.

4. sensu ... pari: 'sensus' is here the artistic sensibility and awareness of the performer, as at e.g. Cic. *De Orat.* 2.184 'si est suaviter et cum sensu tractatum', with *OLD* sensus 6(b); 'pari' refers to the dual expertise in playing the instrument ('brachia') and in singing ('linguae').

5. namque ita <ab> (Baehrens); namque ita (AW); nam lira (B); nam sic (Riese): the sense is clear enough, and either 'ita' or 'sic' is required to precede 'ut' in line 7, but the wording is uncertain. The problem with 'namque ita' of AW lies in accepting hiatus both before and after the immediately ensuing 'aequali'. There are a good number of instances of hiatus in this collection (see p. 23), almost always at the main hexameter or pentameter caesura (there is one at line 2 above), but a double hiatus in such proximity would be unparalleled and probably unacceptable. Baehrens' addition of 'ab' is closer to the mss than Riese's substitution of 'sic' for '-que ita' and I therefore follow SB in adopting it.

6. ori (Riese; Shackleton Bailey); oris (codd.): Riese's suggestion 'ori' is apt in that it can be taken as a dative of advantage with 'temperat', and thereby illustrates how the citharode tempers by his art the two disparate sounds of voice and lyre until they reach the desired balance. The mss 'oris', presumably dependent on 'arte' rather than 'socias ... manus', is not impossible, but would be less apposite in implying that the performer's skill lies in his singing more than in his cithara-playing.

Commentary

8. vox utrumne (edd.; utrumque (A); utrum (W); atrum (B)) canat an ...: unsurprisingly, an 'utrum ... an' construction has been assumed in this concluding line, and editors have generally emended A's 'utrumque' and supplemented the omission of a syllable in the other mss accordingly. However, Timpanaro's interpretation of A's reading and defence of it ('*i.e. partes utrasque, vocis et lyrae*') is reported by SB in his app. crit. and adopted by him. But the logic is faulty: why would anyone who can see the performer and can hear two musical lines (voice and lyre) have doubts as to whether the lyre or voice is responsible for both of them? It would however be perfectly sensible to have doubts as to which of the two lines is the responsibility of either lyre or voice, because they are so in harmony with each other. And when only the lyre is playing (cf. 'an lyra sola sonet'), or only the voice singing, the question is the more pertinent (and the point is made again in the next epigram, where at line 4 the lyre is said 'humanum ... loqui'). The 'utrum ..an' construction, with the small emendation it involves, achieves that meaning and is surely correct.

103 (114R)

Another. Skilled in making song with his Apolline plectrum, he takes pleasure in holding his many-stringed lyre to his chest; he next traverses it with his tongued thumb and makes the singing strings sound as if human. Amphion fortified Thebes with ramparts by means of his lyre, teaching the stones to prick up their ears and scurry to the walls, and Orpheus was no less effective with his lyre as the restorer of his wife when his tender love swayed impious hell. That art is exceptionally praiseworthy by whose sacred modulation voice and fingers sing as one with their different sounds.

Another piece on an artistic performer, and another on a citharode, this epigram like its preceding companion concentrates on the excellence of the artist, which is again demonstrated by his making voice and lyre sound as one. There is considerable subtlety and wit in the supporting imagery, with thumbs growing tongues (line 3), strings singing (line 4), and stones growing ears and scurrying around to form themselves into walls (line 6).

1. Apollineo ... plectro: for the use of the plectrum in the playing of the lyre see 102.1 n., and 3 n. below. The plectrum is associated with Apollo since the lyre is traditionally his instrument, though Hermes was the inventor of both (Hom. *Hymn* 4.22 f.).

2. multifidam: this adjective usually means 'splintered', deriving its meaning from 'multi-' and 'findere'; but in this instance it derives from 'multi-' and 'fides' and is a humorous calque on Greek πολύχορδος. Lyres seem mostly to have had seven strings, but more are sometimes indicated

Commentary

by both pictorial representations and literary references (nine, ten, eleven, even seventeen strings are attested: see West, *Music*, 62 f.; Nicomachus of Gerasa's *Harmonic Handbook* (*Mus. Script. Graeci* 274.6 Janus) evidences eighteen strings). A many-stringed instrument, like this one, advertises the performer's virtuosity.

pectore ferre: the stance and method of playing of lyre players is known largely from pictorial evidence (though note e.g. Quint. *Inst.* 1.12.3; Lucian 43.14), and is described by West (*Music*, 64 f.): 'The professional citharode gave his performance standing on a podium. The player held the instrument against the left side of his body, with his left hand coming at the strings from one side through the frame and the right hand from the other .... He supported the instrument by means of a strap or sling looped round his left wrist and attached to the further side of the lyre.' To describe this as 'pectore ferre' is abbreviated, but accurate enough.

chelyn: strictly the *chelys* is, as its name suggests (Greek χέλυς, 'tortoise'), a bowl-lyre like the *barbitos* and *lyra*, while the *cithara* is a box-lyre, a bigger instrument for public performance (see West, *Music*, 48 f.); but the distinction is clearly not material in the 'lyre' nouns of this and the preceding poem ('lyra', 'chelys', 'cithara': for such variation in the poet's use of nouns see 81.5 n.).

3. linguato ... pollice: the adjective is ambiguous here, meaning both (a) 'talkative', as at e.g. Tert. *De Anim.* 3.1 'Athenis enim expertus linguatam civitatem, cum omnes illic sapientiae atque facundiae caupones degustasset'; and (b) 'tongue-shaped', as at e.g. ps.-Apul. *Herbarius* 124.18 f. 'cum foliis pinguibus ... linguatis, hoc est linguam simulantibus'. Meaning (a) suggests the ambivalence between singing and instrumental playing which is such a theme of this and the preceding epigram (and follows on with 'humanum ... loqui' in the next line), and meaning (b) suggests visually the plectrum of line 1, which, when held between thumb and finger, would make the thumb appear tongue-shaped (for which practice see M. Maas and J. Snyder, *Stringed Instruments of Ancient Greece*, New Haven and London 1989, 129 Pl. 2; 194 Pl. 10; 121 f.). For the specific reference to the thumb in playing the lyre, by both plucking and using a plectrum to strike the strings, cf. *CE* 489.3 'pulsabat pollice chordas'; Tib. 2.5.3; Stat. *Silv.* 5.5.31 etc.

4. humanum ... loqui: stringed instruments are often said to 'speak': e.g. Lucr. 4.981 'chordas loquentes'; [Tib.] 3.4.41 'sed postquam fuerant digiti cum voce locuti' (in precisely the same context as here, a citharode using a plectrum); Tib. 2.5.3 'vocales impellere pollice chordas'; with *TLL* 7.2.1668.36 f.

chorda canora: cf. Verg. *Aen.* 6.120 'fidibusque canoris' (the phrase occurs also at Hor. *Carm.* 1.12.11); Sen. *Tro.* 321 'canoram verberans plectro chelyn'.

Commentary

5. Amphion: the story of the building of the walls of Thebes with the stones moving into position under the miraculous influence of Amphion's lyre-playing makes its first extant appearance at Hes. frag. 182 M-W and was always popular (*LIMC* 1.1.718 f.). Amphion and his brother Zethus are mentioned as the founders of Thebes in Homer (*Od.* 11.260 f.), but without the miracle of the lyre.

Thebarum moenia saepsit: the meaning is 'Thebas moenibus saepsit'.

6. aurita ... saxa: cf. esp. Hor. *Carm.* 1.12.11 f. (a passage already cited at 4 n. above) 'auritas fidibus canoris ducere quercus', with reference to Orpheus' lyre-playing. It seems likely that the poet recalls Horace in this passage, though the topic of inanimate objects growing ears in the presence of an expert musician might have become a commonplace and the echo may not be a direct allusion. Nisbet-Hubbard in their note on Hor. loc. cit. also point to echoes of the Horace passage in Sidonius (*Carm.* 2.72; 16.3 f.; 23.190).

'aurita' here, like 'linguato' in line 3, is ambiguous, with the two meanings (a) 'able to hear' (as in Servius' gloss on 'auritosque' at Verg. *Georg.* 1.308: 'sensum audiendi habentes'), and (b) 'long-eared' (as at e.g. Ovid *Fast.* 6.469 'auritis ... asellis' (and see again Nisbet-Hubbard comments on Hor. loc. cit., where they postulate the same ambiguity)). The image of stones with long ears running round to form a wall is a pleasing reductio ad absurdum of the myth.

7. reparator (repetitor (Schrader); revocator (Oudendorp)) coniugis Orpheus: Orpheus is the third obvious mythical figure, along with Apollo and Amphion, associated with lyre-playing, and it is no surprise to find him here. Although 'reparator' is a rare noun, there is no cause to question it; Janus is called 'immensi reparator maximus aevi' at Stat. *Silv.* 4.1.11 because 'he ensures the continuity of time by presiding over the beginning of each year' (from Coleman's note); Oceanus is 'rutili reparator Eoi' at Avien. *Phaen.* 166; and Priam is 'gentis reparator et urbis' at Drac. *Rom.* 8.265, so there is good mythological pedigree. The verb *reparare* is used of restoring people to health or re-invigorating them (see 109.4 n.); Orpheus similarly won the right to restore Eurydice from the underworld to the earth, and from death to life, as a result of his lyre-playing.

8. impia ... Tartara: for the adjective applied to the underworld, its gods and death, cf. Drac. *Rom.* 10.436 'impie rex Erebi'; Cor. *Joh.* 4.218 'et infelicem animam mors impia clausit'; and 'mors impia' in epitaphs at e.g. *ILCV* 1217.2; 3778a.1; 4822.2; and esp. Verg. *Aen.* 6.542 f. 'at laeva malorum / exercet poenas et ad impia Tartara mittit'. Although the phrase here is Vergil's, and may derive from him, its significance is not

Commentary

the same: in Vergil it suggests that hell is the place to which the wicked properly go, whereas here and in the other instances listed it suggests hell as a kingdom which acts with *impietas* (i.e. against divine ordinance) in accepting clients who have died before their time. For the thought *TLL* (7.1.621.47 f.; 4.1226.10 f.) compares *crudelis* as applied to people who have died prematurely and left those behind distraught: e.g. *CIL* 8.21804 'Iulia ... crudelis vixit annis plus minus X'.

9. moderamine sacro ((codd.); docto *vel* certo (Shackleton Bailey); vafro (Håkanson)): in his review of *Towards a Text* (*RFIC* 110.1982.105) M. de Nonno rightly criticises SB's conjectures as hypercritical (though 'sacro' is simply athetised in the Teubner text), and defends ms. 'sacro'. And although 'sacro' might not be the expected epithet (as also at 138.2 'sacrum tribunal'), that does not render it incorrect: indeed it gives a good contrast to hell's *impietas*, and suggests that the citharode's art of balancing voice and instrument in perfect harmony is something beyond the human and is divinely ordained (this 'sacred' nature of music is also suggested, for example, by Cens. *De Die Nat.* 12.2: 'nam nisi grata esset (sc. musica) deis immortalibus, ... profecto ludi scenici placandorum deorum causa instituti non essent, nec tibicen omnibus supplicationibus in sacris aedibus adhiberetur, non cum tibicine Marti triumphus ageretur, non Apollini cithara, non Musis tibiae ceteraque id genus essent attributa ...').

10. unum ex diversis ... canunt: the conclusion is the same as at 102.10, though differently expressed. Voice and instrument are so in harmony that it is impossible to know which one is responsible for which sound.

104 (115R)

On a weapon dance. In the precinct of Venus the battles of Mars are simulated when the two sexes move against each other. For the war dance pitches the female group against the males and makes weapons move as in military fashion, though the weapons are not tipped with any hard steel, but, being made of boxwood, only give off sound. Thus do they aim their javelins turn and turn about and protect themselves with their shields, nor is man or woman hurt in their coming together. The display has fighting, but the contests bring peace, for the pleasant sounds of the organ command them back to their places on equal terms.

This final epigram of the series on performing arts (100-4) is an interesting piece on pyrrhic dancing, which was essentially a war or weapon dance whose origins lay in military training, though it had long since diversified into popular entertainment. It shares links with the previous epigrams on the citharode in that it focuses on the reconciliation of opposite or

Commentary

disparate forces, in this case males and females in the dance, in the citharode's case instrumental and vocal music.

Weapon dancing is attested on pottery decoration from the earliest classical period, as far back as the early eighth century BC, and it was widespread in the Greek city states (see S.H. Lonsdale, *Dance and Ritual Play in Greek Religion*, Baltimore and London 1993, 301 n. 9). The term by which such dancing became known, πυρρίχη (sc. ὄρχησις), is first attested at Eur. *Andr*. 1135. The origin of the name is obscure; popular aetiologies derived it from a founder named Πύρριχος (Athen. 14.631c (= Aristoxenus *FHG* 2.284 Müller); Strabo 10.3.8) or Πύρρος (i.e. Neoptolemus; ibid.; Lucian 45.9), or from the noun πυρά ('pyre'), on the grounds that the first such dance was performed round the pyre of Patroclus (Arist. frag. 519 Rose); but none convinces. The metron of two short syllables named πυρρίχιος, which is a cognate term, suggests that the dance was fast (cf. M.L. West, *Greek Metre*, Oxford 1982, 158).

Pyrrhic dances took place in various forms, sacred and secular, public and private, and with various weapons, such as swords, spears, bows and arrows, shields, or even no weapons at all (cf. Eur. *Andr*. 1130 f.; Ar. *Clouds* 989; Plato *Laws* 7.815a; Xen. *Anab*. 6.1.7 f.; with Lonsdale, op. cit. 137 f.). By the time of the Roman empire the dances were better known as entertainment than as military training (e.g. Suet. *Nero* 12.1; Fronto 9.2 vdH; SHA *Hadr*. 19.8), though there is some evidence that military aspects were not altogether lost (e.g. Amm. Marc. 16.5.10; Claud. 28.621 f.). From this epigram it is clear that one development of the pyrrhic dance was a dance illustrating the battle of the sexes. There is an earlier description of a very similar entertainment, held in a theatre in springtime, at Apul. *Met*. 10.29.4 f.: 'nam puelli puellaeque virenti florentes aetatula, forma conspicui, veste nitidi, incessu gestuosi, Graecanicam saltaturi Pyrrhicam dispositis ordinationibus decoros ambitus inerrabant, nunc in orbem rotatum flexuosi, nunc in obliquam seriem connexi et in quadratum patorem cuneati et in catervae discidium separati'. *Neue Pauly* (10.642 f.) adduces the present epigram as evidence for the late continuation of this kind of dance, surely correctly; there is no reason to suppose that the author had not seen the entertainment he describes, and indeed it is of a type which can still be seen in various folk dances. See further P. Ceccarelli, *La pirrica nell' antichità greco-romana*, Pisa and Rome 1998 (she gives a gazetteer of the surviving evidence).

1. in spatio Veneris: it is unclear whether this should be understood as an actual location, such as a space in or near what was a temple of Venus (for which see 89 intro.), or is merely a name for a dancing area for this particular type of pyrrhic dance. Whichever it is, it contrasts with the 'proelia Martis' which are performed there, and adumbrates the mock battle between the sexes of which the dance consists (for a similar contrast cf. 89.5 f.).

Commentary

simulantur: cf. 'simulacra duelli' at 106.5, with note; SHA *Maximin.* 6.2 'in<ter> se simulacra bellorum agere'.

2. sese adversum: the pronoun here is reciprocal, not reflexive; cf. 185.4 'se domet alteruter' (with note).

3. femineam ... classem: *classis* can refer to part of a land army as well as its much more frequent naval use, as at e.g. Verg. *Aen.* 3.602; 7.716 (with *TLL* 3.1281.69 f.); or to 'school' or 'class', as at e.g. Quint. *Inst.* 1.2.23; Juv. 7.151 (with *TLL* 3.1295. 39 f.); or simply to a group of people, as at e.g. Col. 1.9.8; Petr. 74.7. Here it refers to the female formation in the mock battle line-up.

confert: in the context of mock hostility this verb alludes to the commitment in battle of one group against another, as the next line elaborates. Cf. Germ. *Arat.* 655 '(sc. Diana) scorpion ingenti (sc. Orioni) maiorem contulit hostem'.

4. ... movet: the alliteration on 'm' in this line is notable, and the subject of the verb is presumably 'pyrrhica', referring to the participants rather than the dance itself ('movent' might be worth consideration, however).

5. haut ... tecta: de Saumaise's small correction of ms. 'aut' is clearly required. SB (app. crit.) glosses 'tecta' as 'munita', which must be correct: the passage from line 5 onwards stresses that no harm comes to the martial dancers because they use weapons made of boxwood; to add here that the weapons have no metal 'covering' makes good sense. It would appear from line 7 that some of the weapons used in the dance are spears or javelins ('iaculis'), so 'haut tecta' would then suggest the lack of metal tips (and cf. Liv. 26.51.4, where 'praepilati missiles' are weapons tipped with a button to prevent penetration). However, the 'buxea tela' of line 6 suggests the use of swords also, since the wood of which spear shafts were made would not be of any interest in this context; 'haut tecta' in that case suggests that the weapons have no metal cutting edges (for similar weapons compare Mart. 7.32.8 with Galán Vioque's note).

chalybis: from the Chalybes, a people of Asia Minor, probably the southern shores of the Black Sea, who were said to have discovered iron-working and to have introduced the skill to mankind (Aesch. *Prom.* 714 f.; Xen. *Anab.* 5.5.1 f.; Callim. frag. 110.48 f. (cf. Cat. 66.48 f.); Ap. Rhod. 2.1001 f. etc.). By metonymy their name is appropriated to carburised iron or steel, a use which goes back to Aesch. *Prom.* 133, and transfers to Latin (e.g. Lucan 7.518; Claud. 5.357; with *TLL* Onom.C. 369.58 f.). See further *RE* 3.2099; R. Drews, 'The Earliest Greek Settlements on the Black Sea', *JHS* 96.1976.26 f.; and, for ancient steel, J.F. Healy, *Mining and Metallurgy in the Greek and Roman World*, London 1978, 215; 230 f.; 235 f.

Commentary

6. buxea tela: boxwood was much used in manufacture, e.g. of musical pipes (Ovid *Met.* 4.30), writing tablets (Prop. 3.23.8), and combs (Mart. 14.25), though this seems to be the only mention of boxwood weapons. 'Harmless' weapons for military training are however well evidenced: Scipio in 210 BC trained his troops with wooden foils with a leather button on the tip, and javelins with similar leather points (Polyb. 10.20.3 f.); Vegetius (*Mil.* 1.11.2) says '(sc. antiqui) clavas ligneas duplicis aeque ponderis pro gladiis tironibus dabant'; and cf. Liv. 26.51.4; with R.W. Davies, *Latomus* 27.1968.75 f.

7. alterna petunt: 'alterna' indicates reciprocity, evoking the image of the dance with males and females moving against each other and sounding their wooden weapons on each other's shields. For similar instances of this neuter plural used adverbially, cf. Hor. *Sat.* 1.8.40 'alterna loquentes'; Stat. *Theb.* 7.640 f. 'sternunt alterna furentes / Hippomedon Sybarin'; ibid. 12.387.

8. nec sibi congressu (de Saumaise); ne sibi congressi (A): de Saumaise's 'nec' is required by the ensuing indicative verb, but his conjecture 'congressu' (designed to eradicate the plural participle with the singular verb 'nocet') is less certain. There are other instances of a singular verb with paired subjects which have plural qualifying attributes, as e.g. Cic. *Verr.* 2.4.92 'dixit hoc apud vos Zosippus et Ismenias, homines nobilissimi et principes Tyndaritae civitatis'; Cic. *Brut.* 108; with *LHS* 2.433. So in this case the plural 'congressi' would be logical enough with 'vir an mulier', and the singular 'nocet' would also be appropriate with that combination. But the slight change to 'congressu' avoids any confusion; a scribal error has probably crept in by homoeoteleuton.

'sibi' here might be either reflexive or reciprocal or indeed have elements of both (see 2 n. above): the dancers harm neither themselves nor their 'opponents'.

vir nocet an (A; aut (de Saumaise)) mulier: there is no need to accept de Saumaise's conjecture 'aut' for 'an': *an* is regularly used as an equivalent of *aut* or *vel*; for a similar instance cf. Aus. *Epig.* 53.3 'et iam desieras puer anne puella videri', with my note.

9. lusus ... pugnam ... certamina pacem: for similar juxtaposition cf. 185.7 f., and Claud. 28.621 f. 'belligeros ... lusus'; 'armatos ... choros' etc., with Dewar's note. It provides an effective conclusion to this epigram, which has overtones throughout of the 'militat omnis amans' theme (e.g. 'in morem militis' in line 4; 'congressu' in line 8).

10. remeare ... pares: nobody is hurt and things end as harmoniously as they began; the end of the dance suggests a happy (if utopian) outcome to its allegory of love and life.

Commentary

organa blanda: it is only at the very end of the poem that we learn that the dance, accompanied by the clashing of wooden weapons in mock battle, is also accompanied by an organ. That it sounded only to mark the end of the dance, which is its stated function here, seems an unlikely waste of resource: along with the mock weapons it would have added to the rhythm and movement of the entertainment. However that may be, it is known that ancient organs could be extremely loud: [Jer.] *Ep.* 23.1 (*PL* 30.213) describes an organ with a wind-chest made from two elephant hides, powered by twelve sets of bellows, producing a roar like thunder that could be heard a mile away (and see also Sen. *Nat. Quaest.* 2.6.5; Claud. 17.316 f.; with West, *Music*, 114 f., and J. Perrot, *L'Orgue: de ses origines hellénistiques à la fin du XIIIe siècle*, Paris 1965, for further details).

105 (116R)

In praise of the four seasons. Gentle spring picks lovely gifts from his rose-beds. Sweltering summer rejoices in the gathered crops. A head twined with a grape vine indicates autumn. Winter is pale with cold and denotes the season with his bird.

This and the following epigram depict and praise the seasons and months respectively. This piece uses stock themes without any great imagination or originality. Both pieces have close links to the visual arts and cannot be understood without reference to them; indeed they are ecphrastic in the sense that they virtually describe such images.

The popularity of the depiction of the four seasons, especially in North African mosaic, is amply attested by over eighty surviving examples, and obviously owes something to the fact that seasons are ideally suited to mosaics with four corners. They can be shown either as full-length figures or as busts, and the bust type continued later than the full-figure type. They are found primarily in private houses, largely in the social rooms such as triclinia, though some are known from public buildings, and extant examples date from the second to the fifth centuries, with a couple probably of the sixth. The iconography, namely the attributes of the various seasons, is largely constant: for example a second-century mosaic from La Chebba and now in the Bardo Museum in Tunis shows winter dancing, wearing boots and a crown of reeds, and carrying a pole from which two ducks are suspended; spring is shown crowned with roses, holding a rose in one hand and a basket of roses in the other, and is flanked by rose stems; summer is crowned with ears of corn and has a sickle in one hand, and a sheaf of ears of corn in the other; and autumn is crowned with grapes, flanked by vines, with a panther on one side and a young man loading barrels full of grapes on the other (the mosaic is illustrated at *LIMC* Horae 5.2.352). The images are virtually identical to those described in this epigram, and are typical.

Commentary

Depiction of the seasons was not limited to mosaic; for example the Season Sarcophagus now at Dumbarton Oaks, which probably originated in Rome and dates to the fourth century, shows four male seasons which, though damaged, include summer with a wreath of corn ears, autumn crowned with vine branches, spring crowned (probably) with roses, and winter (possibly) accompanied by his duck. And Philostratus (*Imag.* 2.34) describes a first century painting of the seasons with familiar attributes, spring with roses, summer with corn and autumn with grape vines.

The present epigram deals with a subject and images which would have been readily recognisable by a (North African) writer and his readership as late as the sixth century: he would have seen them all around him, and he had an equally strong literary tradition on which to draw (see below). Further on the seasons in the visual arts see D. Parrish, *Season Mosaics of Roman North Africa*, Rome 1984, esp. 11 f.; 19 f.; with catalogue nos 32; 35; 49; 57 and Plates 48b; 49; 54a; 61b-68; 78; Hanfmann, *Season Sarcophagus*, esp. 1.9 f.; 77 f.; 210 f.; P. Kranz, *Jahreszeiten-Sarkophage*, Berlin 1984, 119 f.; 154 f.; and *LIMC* Horae 5.1.510 f.

The first literary description of the four seasons which identifies them through seasonal attributes is at Athen. 5.198b (= *FGH* 627 F 2 Jacoby), quoting the (?) second-century BC Callixenus of Rhodes on the four Horae in the grand procession of Ptolemy Philadelphus. The topic is explored by Ovid in a quatrain (*Met.* 2.27 f.):

> Verque novum stabat cinctum florente corona,
> stabat nuda aestas et spicea serta gerebat,
> stabat et autumnus calcatis sordidus uvis,
> et glacialis hiems canos hirsuta capillos.

Similar brief descriptions of the seasons are frequent (e.g. Lucr. 5.737 f.; Tib. 2.1.43 f.; Hor. *Carm.* 4.7.1 f.; 9 f.; Ovid *Rem.* 187 f.; *Pont.* 3.1.11 f.; Aus. 14.11; Claud. 1.266 f.; *AL* 864R; Nonn. *Dion.* 11.484 f.), and there is a series of twelve 'tetrasticha de quattuor temporibus anni' at *AL* 567-78R (dated to the late third century by Friedrich, *Symposium*, 507 f.), of which the following is typical (571 Julianus):

> Vere gravis fundit tellus cum floribus herbas.
> Frugiferas arvis fert aestas torrida messes.
> Pomifer autumnus tenero dat palmite fructus.
> Mox humus hibernis albescit operta pruinis.

How standard the iconography is, at least for three of the four seasons, is apparent from the following brief summary of these tetrastichs: spring flowers at 567.1; 569-75.1; 577-8.1; summer crops generally or wheat specifically at 567.2; 569-75.2; 578.2; autumn vines or wine at 567.3; 569.3-78.3; it is only winter who has any significant variety (frozen rivers at 567-

Commentary

8.4; 574.4; snow at 569.4; 573.4; 576.4; 578.4; falling leaves at 572.4; 574.4; 577.4; frost at 571.4 etc.). The similarity of all this to the present epigram illustrates its literary as well as its visual pedigree (and see further on the literary aspects Friedrich, *Symposium*, 159 f.). But deictic verbs such as 'indicat' at line 3 and 'designans' at line 4, as well as the specific reference to winter's 'ales' at line 4 (on which see note), suggest here the predominance of the visual angle. It is however unclear whether the poet pictured the seasons as male or female; in mosaics they are more often female, in sculpture male, but there are variations. I have designated them as male.

1. ver ... rosetis: for the association of spring with flowers in general and roses in particular see intro. above, with Parrish, op. cit. 34 f.; Kranz, op. cit. 122 f.
  dona: gifts of nature (see 92.6 n; 106.6 n.).

2. torrida ... aestas: this is one of the few lines of the collection which is attested by citation elsewhere, namely in a poem by the ninth-century Wandalbert of Prüm (*MGH: PLAC* 2.585.264); see also 106.14 n.; M. Manitius, *Philologus* 51.1892.156 f.; and E. Courtney, *C&M* 40.1989.198. For the association of summer with crops, especially wheat, see intro. above and Parrish, op. cit. 37 f.; Kranz, op. cit. 124 f.

3. redimitus (edd.; redimito (codd.)) palmite: all editors (except for Pithou, who gives a marginal note to the same effect) plausibly prefer the more idiomatic nominative ending of the participle. For autumn's garland of vine stems see again intro. above, with Parrish, op. cit. 38 f.; Kranz, op. cit. 119 f.; for *palmes* specifically, cf. Col. 4.29.11 'autumnus deinde falcem maturis palmitibus admovet'; *AL* 571.3R, quoted above.

4. frigore pallet hiems designans alite tempus: it has been shown in the intro. above that winter is the season with a less standard iconography than the others, though cold and its manifestations are never far away (see also Parrish, op. cit. 32 f.). Winter here is also given a specific attribute, his 'ales', and it belongs much more to the world of the visual arts, particularly mosaic, than to literary antecedents. Thus Parrish (op. cit. 27) says: 'Among the different birds of seasonal content, only that representing Winter has a fixed identity in African mosaics. Winter's emblem is the duck, an object of the hunt ..., which usually appears as a pair of birds held by a personification, but is sometimes shown as a detached symbol ...'; see also the description of the La Chebba mosaic in the intro. above, with *LIMC* 5.1.510 f. nos 14; 15; 29-31; 42; Stern, *Calendrier*, 237; and Kranz, op. cit. 125 f. SB (*Towards a Text*, 20) comments 'Winter marks the end of the year – with its wing? *alite* seems to come from (p)*almite* above. The right word will be *limite* ...', and is rightly castigated by Courtney in his review of the book (*CR* 31.1981.41).

Commentary
106 (117R)

In praise of all the months. Janus is resplendent clad in his honorific garments, and he illustrates the passage of time with the consuls of Rome. Reaching out with his rustic implements at Bacchus-born vine-shoots, this man has merited the name of the god Februus. March plays battle games in the fields and brings with him milk-white bounty of the Cinyphian herd. Conducting the sacred rites of the Dionean mother, April in his celebrations claps his lascivious castanets. May, dedicated to the honour of Atlas' daughter, despoils the flowery thickets of their lovely roses. June garnishes his summer luncheon with blood-red mulberries; he takes his name from well-omened Iuventa. Previously named Quintilis, luxuriating in Ceres' crop, July derives his name from great Caesar. The sun's heat boils August to his marrow, whom, in his lassitude, a monkey jar, fans and a melon refresh. Libra's September disposes the hours to be of equal length, and carries from the countryside a trapped hare with bunches of grapes. October treads the grapes with frolicsome feet, and the sweet must foams in brimming pools. November ploughs his fields and turns them over with his fertile plough, at the time when the juicy olive feels the smooth mill-stones. Sluggish winter commends his December to all, that time when dicing skills join together masters and servants.

Short poems which catalogue the months of the year become frequent in late Latin literature, and the *AL* furnishes no fewer than six examples, excluding pieces by Ausonius which are duplicated in his collected works (these are, in addition to here, 390; 391 (the '354 Calendar' tetrastichs, on which see below); 490aR (the 'officia duodecim mensium'); 665aR (the '354 Calendar' distichs, on which see A.E. Housman, *CQ* 26.1932.129 f. (= *Class. Pap.* 3.1185 f.); and 874aR (Dracontius' 'De mensibus'). Ausonius furnishes three examples (14.2; 3; 9), and there are three early Byzantine pieces at *AP* 9.383; 384; 580 as well as John Lydus' sixth-century 'de mensibus', which discusses the Roman calendar. These pieces descend from longer poems such as Ovid's *Fasti*, which is a month by month calendar (though it now terminates with June) dealing with religious festivals, and agricultural treatises which deal with rural matters and the farming calendar on a monthly basis (e.g. Col. 11.2.1 f.; 11.3.14 f; Plin. *Nat. Hist.* 18.224 f.; Pallad. *De Agricultura* II f.). They also bear distinct similarities to the poetry on the seasons (see the preceding epigram), though the iconography of each month is much more varied and fluid than that of the four seasons. And epigraphic rustic calendars of the months, which give brief agricultural events appropriate for each month, as well as other information such as their associated zodiacal constellations and tutelary deities, are also extant (known as the *menologium rusticum Colotianum* and *Vallense*, and most easily accessible at A. Degrassi, *Inscriptiones Italiae* vol. 13.2 (1963) 284 f.).

The *AL* poems typically characterise each month in one or more of

Commentary

three ways, or with one or more related symbols or attributes: (a) official dates in the calendar, such as state and religious events and festivals; (b) astronomical activity, such as solstices, equinoxes and zodiacal signs; and (c) weather and related events, largely to do with farming, agriculture and nature in general. All of these are used in the present poem; they are dealt with more fully in the individual notes, but here is a brief preliminary catalogue: (a) state and religious events: January (consuls); April (a rite of Venus); May (the Rosalia); and December (the Saturnalia); (b) astronomical activity: September (the equinox); and (c), the weather, farming and nature, the largest category: February (vine tending); March (dancing (?) and goats); May (roses); June (soft fruits); July (wheat crop); August (summer heat); September (hunting); October (wine-making); November (ploughing and olive processing); December (winter cold). In addition this poet likes to include some etymologies for names of the months, as at May, June and July.

A notable feature of the poem is the personification of the months as male figures: there are deictic pronouns like 'hic' (line 4), and 'huic' (line 12), and cf. also 'quem' (line 16) and 'suum' (line 23); in every month there is a strong visual element with the month himself said to be performing tasks, or decorated with seasonal symbols, or whatever (thus Janus has his resplendent clothes; Februus tends his early vine-shoots; Martius attends a mock battle, and so forth); and even when the main point of the description of a month is non-visual, the poet takes care to introduce an easily recognisable visual element (thus Julius, for example, the majority of whose couplet is concerned with the origin of his name, is shown also as 'Cereali germine gaudens'). The strong visual element is not accidental of course: as with the previous poem about the seasons, most of those about the months, and this one especially, reflect parallel developments in the visual arts and describe or comment on works of art (whether real or imaginary). The background to this is well set out by D. Parrish in his article on the months at *LIMC* 6.1.479 f. (with the tables at 494-7 summarising the evidence). For the interpretation of this epigram the most significant visual representations are mosaics, particularly those from Hellin in Spain (ibid. no. 27), Ostia (no. 30) and El Djem (no. 31), and illustrations in books. The most important in this latter category is the document known as the '354 Calendar' (or '354 Chronograph') after the year for which it was produced. It was compiled by Furius Dionysius Filocalus (on whom see also 109 intro.) for one Valentinus; Filocalus' expertise lay in his calligraphy, and his written material, which is not necessarily his own, is not particularly original, but the significance of his Calendar is that the illustrations for the section dealing with the months have survived (though that oversimplifies the matter: the autograph is not extant, and the illustrations we possess date only from sixteenth-century and later copies (the best being Vatican City Barb. Lat. 2154) of a Carolingian ms., the now lost Luxemburgensis. But there also exists a

Commentary

letter of N.-C. Fabri de Peiresc who owned the Luxemburgensis and gave a detailed description of its illustrations. This can be used to corroborate those we have, as also can Leiden Voss. Lat. Q. 79, a ninth-century copy of a sixth-century ms., which has miniature illustrations set in a planisphere deriving from Filocalus' months (there is a colour facsimile in *Aratea: Kommentar zum Aratus des Germanicus. MS Voss. Lat. Q. 79*, ed. B. Bischoff et al., Lucerne 1989; the planisphere is described at p. 53 f., and features at f 93v). This all lends confidence to the supposition that the illustrations extant are essentially accurate copies of Filocalus' originals (see further on this Salzman, *Time*, 4 f.; with Appendix 1)). Verses which accompanied these illustrations in various mss have also survived, a set of tetrastichs which has a home at *AL* 391, and a set of distichs at *AL* 665aR. It is uncertain whether either of them belonged to the autograph, the scholarly consensus being that the tetrastichs are roughly contemporaneous and might have done, but the distichs are probably of earlier date (and although both show a close relationship to the illustrations, neither affords a completely accurate description of them).

The present epigram clearly stems from much the same background as the 354 Calendar in that it is an ecphrastic treatment of a work of art in which months are identified by persons carrying out tasks, or performing rites, or adorned with symbols which identify them. It might be related to a mosaic, a painting or an illustrated book, whether real or imaginary. Whatever its genesis, Filocalus' calendar affords a close parallel.

The literature on this whole topic is wide: in addition to Parrish's article already cited, see in general E. Courtney, 'The Roman Months in Art and Literature', *MH* 45.1988.33 f.; and on the 354 Calendar, see Stern, *Calendrier*; Salzman, *Time*; and H. Stern, 'Les Calendriers romains illustrés', *ANRW* II 12.2.431 f. (Table 1 at p. 468 tabulates visual images of the months, Table 2 tabulates the literary references). For the eastern or Byzantine tradition of the months and the calendar, which is similar to the western but lays greater emphasis on seasonal and agricultural symbolism, see G. Åkerström-Haugen, *The Calendar and Hunting Mosaics of the Villa of the Falconer in Argos: A Study in Early Byzantine Iconography*, Stockholm 1974. And for the continuation of the agricultural aspects of ancient characterisations of the months in the labours of medieval images of the months, see J.C. Webster, *The Labours of the Months in Antique and Mediaeval Art*, Evanston / Chicago 1938.

In the following notes, in respect of visual images I usually refer only to the numbers by which representations of the months are catalogued in *LIMC* 6.1 Menses rather than giving fuller references; those instanced are all mosaics dating to the fourth to sixth centuries (13; 15; and 16 being from Carthage), except for 33 (which is a third-century fresco from Santa Maria Maggiore in Rome), 25 (which is a seventh-century mosaic), and 26 (which is a ms. of works by Ptolemy (Vat. gr. 1291)).

Commentary

superscr.: mensuum: this fourth declension form of the genitive plural of *mensis* occurs also at Ulp. *Dig.* 48.5.30(29).5 and Apul. *Met.* 9.32.2 (the forms *mensum*, *mensorum* and *mensuorum*, as well as the standard *mensium*, are also attested: see *TLL* 8.746.23 f. On all three occasions when Vegetius (*Mil.*) uses the word, the mss offer the variants *-ium*, *-uum* and *-um* (see Reeve's morphological index ad loc.)). *KS* 1.343 compare 'alituum' at Lucr. 2.928; Verg. *Aen.* 8.27 etc.

1. fulget: January's couplet is the standard theme of the consuls opening the year, which often has reference to the consular fasti: e.g. Ovid *Fast.* 1.81 'iamque novi praeeunt fasces, nova purpura fulget'; *AL* 874a.1 f.R 'purpura iuridicis sacros largitur honores / et nova fastorum permutat nomina libris'; *AL* 391.4; *AP* 9.384.2; 9.580.1. As Ovid's 'fulget' suggests, one allusion is to the splendour of the purple colour of the consular fasti (and cf. Mart. 8.8.4; 11.4.5; 12.29(26).5; for *fulgere* elsewhere of purple cf. *Pan. Mess.* 121; Quint. *Inst.* 11.1.31). But the main allusion, as 'honorifico indutus ... amictu' shows, is to the image of a splendidly dressed official ushering in the new year. Thus in the 354 Calendar 'January is represented by a man dressed in a long tunic; a heavy toga is draped on top of the tunic, over his left arm and shoulder. The borders of the toga are ornamented with gems. On his head is a fur cap, out from which flows a long veil. He wears shoes or slippers. He is in the act of sacrifice, throwing incense on or pointing to flames that rise with much smoke ...' (Salzman, *Time*, 79). There is however some doubt as to precisely who this figure is. Stern (*Calendrier*, 266 f.) sees him as a *vicomagister* sacrificing to the Lares at the Ludi Compitales of 3-5 January, whereas Salzman (loc. cit.) takes him to be a consul who, after sacrificing at the Capitolium, made a formal announcement of vows on behalf of the State on 1 January. There is no doubt that the figure in this epigram is a consul (line 2), and, given all the literary references, he is surely the likely image of the 354 Calendar as well (for other pictorial images of consuls in calendars and other media, see *LIMC* nos 20; 25; 26). Though somewhat sporadically, the consulship continued, and continued to be used for purposes of chronology, both in the east (Constantinople) and the west (Rome), until 541 for subject consuls and until 642 for eastern emperors (see R. Bagnall et al., *Consuls of the Later Roman Empire*, Atlanta 1987, 7 f.; 47 f.).

honorifico: the sense is presumably that the splendid outfit honours the position of the consul (for luxurious consular vestments see Aus. 21.52 f.; Claud. 8.585 f.).

Ianus (Shackleton Bailey); iammsis (B); mensis (AVW): SB's objection to mss 'mensis', that January would be the only month of the twelve not mentioned by name, is forceful (the more so, in my view, since this is the first line of the poem). Courtney defends 'mensis' on the grounds that these lines would have been intended to accompany a picture (*MH* 45.1988.39 f.), but then that applies equally to the other

Commentary

eleven couplets, in which the representations are specifically named and personified; moreover, there is good reason to eliminate the word 'mensis' on the only other occasion it appears in the body of the poem (see 13 n.), and at line 4 one ms. (V) has replaced the correct reading 'nomen' with yet another 'mensis', illustrating the tendency for the word to intrude. B's 'iammsis' also gives some support to the idea that 'Ianus' could have been supplanted by 'mensis' (as a gloss perhaps). For Ianus as the month or its personified deity elsewhere, cf. Aus. 14.9.1 'principium Iani sancit tropicus Capricornus'; in the remainder of the poem the person illustrated is often given the name of the month (or its personified deity) which he represents (e.g. Februus in line 4); and compare also the Ianus of 188.8 (with note).

2. Romuleis tempora consulibus: the adjectival form *Romuleus* is used here (it means simply 'Roman'), whereas *Romulus* is used at 95.6 (see note). For *tempora* of the year and its months, cf. Lucan 5.6 'ducentem tempora Ianum'; Stat. *Silv.* 4.1.19 f.; with Housman, *Class. Pap.* 3.1188 (I understand the significance of the phrase here to be that Janus is pictured as a consul, and the succession of ordinary consuls reflects the succession of the years; as such Janus is a fitting image to introduce the annual passage of the months).

3. rustica ... intentans arma novellis: February is depicted tending the young vines. Agricultural writers show February as the key month for such tasks: e.g. Pallad. *Agric.* 3.9 f., esp. 3.20.1 'nunc locis ... calidis fodiendae sunt vites vel ... exarandae et in eisdem locis palandae aut ligandae sunt vineae'; Columella (11.2.11 f.) similarly deals with trenching vines in February, making vine props, tying up the vines and pruning the trees which support them. Different images are used for February in the 354 Calendar (cf. *AL* 391.5 f. (bird-hunting and weather) and 665a.3 f.R (weather)).

To understand the exact task the *arma* here perform would require an accompanying picture, but they could have been hoes (*LIMC* nos 15; 22), pruning-hooks (*AL* 874a.6R), spades or so forth; *arma* is used of agricultural (as opposed to military) implements at e.g. Verg. *Georg.* 1.160 (whereon Mynors compares the similar ambivalence of Greek ὅπλα); and see *TLL* 2.590.58 f. 'novellae' are vine-shoots (as 'bacchigenis' shows), as also at Cor. *Joh.* 3.327; *AL* 874a.6R.

Bacchigenis: the suffixes *-genus* (adjectival) and *-gena* (substantival) indicate parentage or origin; they are particularly frequent in Ovid, where they are often, as here, ἅπαξ λεγόμενα, and often connected with mythological genealogy (e.g. *aurigena* (*Met.* 5.250); *Faunigena* (*Met.* 14.449); *ignigena* (*Met.* 4.12); *Iunonigena* (*Met.* 4.173); *Latonigena* (*Met.* 6.160); *Martigena* (*Am.* 3.4.39); *terrigena* (*Met.* 5.325); see also Lindner, *Komposita*, 101 f.; 292 f.). The adjective (or perhaps noun in apposition)

Commentary

is appropriate here, since *novellae* are young and thereby easily 'children' with a parentage, and Bacchus, though not literally their father, was 'vitis inventor sacrae' (Enn. *Scaen.* 124 (with Jocelyn's note)).

4. hic ... Februi ...: for comment on the deictic pronoun see intro. above. Februus here is the personified god of the month. This personification is only found at a late date (e.g. Serv. ap. Verg. *Georg.* 1.43; Macr. *Sat.* 1.13.3; Isid. *Or.* 5.33.4; with Roscher 1.1470 f.).

5. Martius: the iconography of March is not certain; his natalis was on 1 March and his association with war is obvious (thus warriors feature in the images at *LIMC* nos 18; 20; 22; 26). The two pictures of this couplet, with the figure of Martius both performing some kind of mock battle, and leading a goat (and / or carrying goat products), seem most plausibly to belong to the month categories of agricultural or nature-associated events, and to describe a rustic, springtime scene (see intro. above and notes below).

in campis ludens simulacra duelli: the association of Martius and war is immediately made (cf. also *AL* 874a.5R; *AP* 9.384.5; 9.580.2), but what he is doing is not clear. The phrase 'simulacra duelli (or belli)' is encountered elsewhere: cf. esp. Lucr. 2.40 f. 'si non forte tuas legiones per loca campi / fervere cum videas belli simulacra cientis' (where 'loca campi' is also notable and may suggest a direct reminiscence here), and Verg. *Aen.* 5.585; 674; Claud. 28.573. In Lucretius however the reference is to a mock battle in military training exercises (see Fowler's note), whereas in this epigram one is more reminded of the weapon dance in 104 (e.g. 'lusus habet pugnam' (104.9) / 'ludens simulacra duelli'). That indeed would be a fitting image, since the dance of 104 is a representation of the battle between and union of the sexes, appropriate symbolism for March, springtime and the reproductive forces of nature.

The March iconography in other poems usually centres on the themes that March was previously the first month of the year (e.g. *AL* 665a.5 f.R; Aus. 14.2.3;.14.3.5 f.) or is associated with war (e.g. *AL* 874a.5 f.R), but one, connected with the 354 Calendar, offers more (*AL* 391.9 f.):

> Cinctum pelle lupae promptum est cognoscere mensem:
>   Mars olli nomen, Mars dedit exuvias.
> Tempus ver haedus petulans et garrula hirundo
>   indicat et sinus lactis et herba virens.

The illustration for the 354 Calendar is a shepherd in a goatskin (rather than the wolfskin described) with a goat and other rustic accoutrements (Salzman, *Time*, 106 f.; with figs 18; 33; 46). While it is possible that he is an allusion to a ceremony such as that of the Mamuralia of 14 March when the Salii symbolically drove Mamurius (the smith who fashioned

163

Commentary

the *ancilia* for Mars) out of Rome with clubs (on which see Ogilvie's note on Liv. 1.20.3; and H.H. Scullard, *Festivals and Ceremonies of the Roman Republic*, London 1981, 85 f.), it is equally plausible that he is nothing more than a country shepherd signifying spring, attending a springtime weapon dance with seasonal fare, as I suggest is the case in this poem.

The noun 'duellum', synonymous with *bellum*, is an old form: cf. Enn. *Ann.* 573 Sk. 'hos pestis necuit, pars occidit illa duellis'. As a disyllable it was the forerunner of *bellum* (and occurs at e.g. Plaut. *Asin.* 559); as the much more frequent trisyllable (as at Enn. loc. cit. and e.g. Hor. *Ep.* 1.2.7 as well as here) it is a metrically convenient artificiality (see Skutsch's note on Enn. loc. cit.).

6. ducit ... lactea dona: the verb suggests that an animal is present in the image, particularly since a goat is included under March at *AL* 391.11 and pictured in the 354 Calendar and at *LIMC* no. 15. But 'lactea dona' probably has wider reference: although 'lactea' might be merely a transferred epithet (i.e. 'the gift of a white goat': 'lacteus' is used of colour at e.g. Verg. *Aen.* 8.660 and Paul. Nol. *Carm.* 18.24) it could additionally suggest the presence of milk in the image (thus milk is specifically mentioned at *AL* 391.12 and *AP* 9.384.5 and often appears in visual images of March (*LIMC* nos 10; 11; 13; 15; 20)), and could also allude to the famous fleeces of these particular goats (see the note below). The 'lactea dona' would then be the fleecy animal itself and its produce, which the shepherd personifying Martius brings with him; 'dona' need not imply that these items are gifts for anyone (whether human or divine), simply that they are a benefit bestowed on man by the month in question (as similarly, for example, with such phrases as the frequent 'Cerealia dona').

Cinyphii ... gregis: the River Cinyps, which is now known as the Oued Caam and flows into the Mediterranean near Lepcis Magna, was an area famed for its goats, and in particular their fleeces: e.g. Prob. ap. Verg. *Georg.* 3.312 'Cinyps oppidum est et flumen Africae regionis Garamantum, apud quos hirci villosissimi nascuntur'; Mart. 7.95.13; *AL* 178.1; *TLL* Onom. C. 452.15 f.

7. sacra ... sollemnia: April, a male figure as are all the months in the poem, is performing a rowdy dance ('lascivis crotalis') before a statue of Venus as part of a religious ceremony. This has no exact counterpart in any known rite, though there is an interesting parallel in the 354 Calendar; this stems not so much from the written description ('contectam myrto Venerem veneratur Aprilis ...' (*AL* 391.13 f.)) but from the illustrations which accompany it. They show an elderly male dancer performing a dance with castanets before a cult statue placed in a niche, though for some unclear reason the statue too is male (see Stern, *Calendrier*, 268 f.; Pl. 9.1; Salzman, *Time*, 83 f.; fig. 34; Courtney, *MH* 45.1988.43 f.). The

Commentary

closeness of this to the description in this epigram cannot be coincidence, but it affords no solution to the precise signifance of the actions of Aprilis; the image is ludicrous to modern eyes, but there is undoubtedly no such intent behind it. There are some similarities to the ceremony of Venus Verticordia performed on 1 April and described by Ovid (*Fast.* 4.133 f.), where women ritually washed the goddess's cult statue under green myrtle, the *aition* being that lustful satyrs had seen her bathing and she had covered herself with myrtle (see Fantham's note and *RE* 8A.857 f.), but, to take only one issue, this offers no explanation for the celebrant here being a man (except, that is, that as a personification of a month a male was obligatory).

Dioneae ... matris: the epithet for Venus derives from Vergil's 'sacra Dionaeae matri ... ferebam' (*Aen.* 3.19; cf. Drac. *Rom.* 8.515). Dione is strictly Venus' mother in some versions of her myth, but the name had long been used of the goddess herself (see my note on Aus. *Epig.* 91.1). The classically correct form of the adjective is *Dionaeus* (see Housman, *Class. Pap.* 2.887 f.), but this poet is hardly classically correct, and the mss may preserve what he wrote.

8. lascivis crotalis: there is a somewhat similar portrait of a follower of Cybele at Apul. *Met.* 8.24.2 f. 'scitote qualem: cinaedum et senem cinaedum, calvum quidem sed cincinnis semicanis et pendulis capillatum, unum de triviali popularium faece, qui per plateas et oppida cymbalis et crotalis personantes deamque Syriam circumferentes mendicare compellunt'; and castanets were associated with rowdy or lewd dances (e.g. *Priap.* 27.3 'cymbala cum crotalis, pruriginis arma'; with *DS* 1.1571 f.). In the illustrations for the 354 Calendar, the celebrant's castanets are a pair of sticks with two clatters applied to the end of each, which Stern shows appear also in a fourth-century Carthaginian mosaic and elsewhere (*Calendrier*, 270; Pl. 47.2).

Aprilis: for the connection of Aphrodite / Venus with April, cf. *AL* 391.13 'Venerem veneratur Aprilis'; Aus. 14.2.4; 14.3.7 f.; with *TLL* 2.318.80 f.); Venus was the tutelary deity of the month (see e.g. the relevant entries in the *menologium rusticum Colotianum* and *Vallense*, loc. cit. intro. above). Macr. *Sat.* 1.12.8 makes an etymological connection: 'secundum mensem nominavit Aprilem, ut quidam putant cum adspiratione quasi Aphrilem, a spuma quam Graeci ἀφρὸν vocant, unde orta Venus creditur' (this etymology was old and possibly correct: cf. Varro *Ling. Lat.* 6.33; Ovid *Fast.* 4.61 f. (with Fantham's note); Maltby, *Lexicon*, 44).

ovans: the verb is used of the celebration of religious rites: e.g. Verg. *Georg.* 1.346 'omnis quam (sc. hostiam) chorus et socii comitentur ovantes / et Cererem clamore vocent in tecta'; Petr. 133.3 v.16.

9. Maïus Atlantis natae ... : the trisyllabic scansion of 'Maius' is irregular, and appears to be unique; there is another metrical irregularity

Commentary

in this line (see following note). The tetrastich of the 354 Calendar is particularly close to this couplet (*AL* 391.17 f.):

> Cunctas veris opes et picta rosaria gemmis
>   liniger in calathis, aspice, Maius habet,
> mensis Atlantigenae dictus cognomine Maiae,
>   quem merito multum diligit Uranie.

The connection of the month to Maia, daughter of Atlas and granddaughter of Oceanus (Hes. *Theog.* 938; Serv. Auct. ap. Verg. *Aen.* 8.138), is found elsewhere in the poetry about the months (also at *AL* 665a.9 f.R; Aus. 14.3.9 f.; and cf. Joh. Lyd. *De Mens.* 4.76; Macr. *Sat.* 1.12.18). An alternative ancient etymology was from 'maiores': 'hinc sua maiores tribuisse vocabula Maio / tangor et aetati consuluisse suae' (Ovid *Fast.* 5.73 f.; cf. Varro *Ling. Lat.* 6.33). But the name probably derives from the old Italian divinity Maia, daughter of Faunus and wife of Vulcan, with whom the Greek Maia became conflated in myth (see Macr. *Sat.* 1.12.18 f.; *E-M* 'Maia / Maius'; Maltby, *Lexicon*, 360).

dicatus: the irregular long quantity of the first syllable has given cause for concern (hence Pithou conjectured 'dignatus'), but it resurfaces at the same position in the line at 115.1 ('nuper dicata Camenis'), so there is no need to emend here (note however that 'dicantur' at 188.18 has the regular short first syllable). It may have arisen through similarity to *dīcere*.

10. expoliat (codd.; expolit et (Riese); exornat (Shackleton Bailey)) ... florea senta (codd.; serta (Scaliger)): the problem in this line centres on a word reported by all mss, 'senta'. If it is correct it must be an otherwise unattested neuter plural noun; but if Scaliger's slight, and prima facie tempting, conjecture 'serta' is accepted, the preceding 'expoliat' of the mss cannot be correct on grounds of sense and itself has to be emended (Riese's 'expolit et' is close to the mss, but is unconvincing; it would also require the addition of 'est' at the end of line 9). M. Petschenig (*ZoeG* 28.1877.483 f.) and E. Courtney (*MH* 45.1988.46 f.) argue for the retention of 'senta' in the sense 'senticetum' ('a thorny thicket', specifically a thicket of roses here, as 'pulchris rosis' would indicate), and this seems the best solution. The image would be almost identical to that for spring at 105.1 ('carpit blanda suis ver almum dona rosetis'), and the symbolism would be that of plucking roses while you can.

pulchris ... rosis: for the association of May with roses, cf. Pallad. *Agr.* 6.17; *LIMC* nos 11; 14; 15; 20. May was also a month in which the movable Rosalia festival was celebrated, a festival which was popular in late Antiquity and continued into the Byzantine period (see A. Hoey, *HThR* 30.1937.15 f.; Salzman, *Time*, 96 f.).

Commentary

11. ornat sanguineis ((Vinet); sanguineis ornans (codd.); sanguineis ornat (Shackleton Bailey)) aestiva prandia: the mss appear to confirm 'sanguineis ornans', but the participle has to be replaced by a verb of indicative mood because the clause would otherwise lack a main verb. SB emends 'ornans' to 'ornat', which is the simplest alteration but necessitates metrical lengthening at the main hexameter caesura; this occurs elsewhere in the collection (see p. 24), but if accepted here would entail two metrical lengthenings in the same line (the final syllable of 'aestiva' is lengthened before the initial mute + liquid of 'prandia', on which practice see 101.6 n.). On balance it seems unwise to create this by emendation and I therefore accept Vinet's correction of the participle with reversal of the word order (in his text of the whole poem, which is printed in his 1580 Bordeaux edition of Ausonius at p. 321).

sanguineis ... moris: the same phrase appears at Verg. *Ecl.* 6.22, from where it may be borrowed, and note also the 'mora cruenta' of *Copa* 21; Ovid *Met.* 4.126 f. 'madefactaque sanguine radix / purpureo tingit pendentia mora colore'; and Prop. 4.2.16. The adjective refers not only to colour but has aetiological resonance in that the black mulberry was said to have attained its colour from the blood of Pyramus (Ovid *Met.* 4.89 f.; the fruit actually changes colour from white to purple as it ripens). The tree from which the fruit comes is *Morus nigra*, native to Persia but introduced to Europe at an early date; the younger Pliny kept his garden full of them (*Ep.* 2.17.15; see also André, *L'Alimentation*, 76).

For the association of mulberries and similar fruits with June in the visual arts, a month which is arguably earlier than horticulturally accurate, see *LIMC* nos 14-16; 26; and Stern, *Calendrier*, 287f., who points out that mulberries and other soft fruits are often associated with July rather than June in both literary and pictorial depictions of the months (e.g. *AL* 391.27).

12. Iunius ... fausta Iuventa: the etymology given here (and also at Aus. 14.3.12), which derives the name of the month Junius from the goddess Iuventa, Latin equivalent of Greek Hebe, is also one of three advanced by Ovid (*Fast.* 6.65-88); his other two involve derivation from the goddess Juno (ibid. 17-64; this is the correct one), and, humorously, from the phrase 'his iunctis' (ibid. 89-96), which was used by Concordia with reference to the Romans and Sabines. Further etymologies offered derivation from 'iuniores' (Fulvius Nobilior at Macr. *Sat.* 1.12.16; it was also he who suggested the derivation of Maius from 'maiores', for which see 9 n. above), or from 'Iunius Brutus' (Macr. *Sat.* 1.12.31). See generally Maltby, *Lexicon*, 318. The epithet *faustus / -a* is rarely applied to divinities, but 'fausta Fortuna' is found at 109.1.

13. quondam Quintilis (Reeve, *ex* Quintilis quondam (Shackleton Bailey); Quintilis mensis (codd.); Quintilis, messis (Heinsius)) ... gaudens (Meyer; gaudet (codd.)): SB's 'quondam' for the 'mensis' of the mss is excellent, although it is rejected by Courtney at *MH* 45.1988.49 f. But: (a) 'quondam' could easily have dropped out of the text via consecutive words beginning with 'qu-', with the lacuna filled by the obvious 'mensis'; it may have been an even easier corruption if 'quondam' had been the first word (i.e. 'qu[ondam Qu]intilis'), as Professor Reeve suggests; (b) mss 'mensis' is a distractive irrelevance, since the poem focuses on personification of the months (see 1 n. above); and (c) mss 'Quintilis mensis ...' might imply that the month is now known as both Quintilis and Julius, whereas 'quondam Quintilis' makes it clear it has been renamed (and cf. *AL* 665a.13 f. R 'quam bene, Quintilis, mutasti nomen: honori / Caesareo, Iuli, te pia causa dedit'). Heinsius' conjecture of 'messis' for 'mensis' would deal with point (b), but is not as convincing with regard to idiom and sense. Meyer's change of 'gaudet' to 'gaudens' is desirable whether or not emendation of 'mensis' is accepted.

Cereali germine: 'germen' is here the ripened ears of corn rather than the seed: cf. Lucan 9.360 f. 'fuit aurea silva / divitiisque graves et fulvo germine rami' (where the reference is to ripe or ripening fruit), and Stat. *Theb.* 2.280 f. 'flebile germen / Hesperidum'. Sheaves of corn are also the symbol for July at e.g. *AL* 391.26; *LIMC* nos 11; 15; 18; 19; 22; with Salzman, *Time*, 99 f.; and 105.2 n.

14. Iulius a magno Caesare: cf. Aus. 14.2.7 'nomine Caesareo Quintilem Iulius auget'; *AL* 665a.13 f.R (quoted above). This line is one of three in this poem (the others being 17 and 19) which are borrowed by Wandalbert of Prüm (on whom see 105.2 n.) in his long poem on the months (*MGH: PLAC* 2.610.168; 2.613.272; 2.612.253).

The month Quintilis was renamed Julius after Caesar in 44 BC, because he had been born in that month (Dio 44.5.2; Macr. *Sat.* 1.12.34 etc.). It might also have been something of a reward for his reform of the calendar in 49 and 46 BC; prior to then the year comprised only 355 days and there had to be an intercalation of 22 or 23 days every so often; the process was so erratic that in 46 BC a year of 455 days was needed. See on this P. Brind'Amour, *Le Calendrier romain*, Ottawa 1983, 25 f.

15. Augustum: the poem concentrates on purely weather symbols for August, detailing the heat of the month and various items associated with providing some relief. There is no mention in the poem of the naming of the month after the emperor, which happened probably in 27 BC, replacing the previous name Sextilis. The *senatus consultum* by which the change was effected is preserved by Macrobius (*Sat.* 1.12.35).

The items with which the poet characterises the month, 'gillo, flabella, melo', are precisely those which accompany the illustration of August in the 354 Calendar (see Stern, *Calendrier*, 258 f.; with Pls 10.1; 16.3; 18.2); they are all also known from other representations (*gillo* at *LIMC* no. 21; *flabella* ibid. 21; 25; and *melo* ibid. 18; 20; 26).

Commentary

penitus: i.e. 'to the very marrow': cf. Curt. 7.5.5 '(sc. aestu) ora visceraque penitus uruntur'; with *TLL* 10.1.1077.66 f.

Phaëthontius: a Greek form of the adjective is also used in Latin (*Phaethonteus*), for which see Grewing's note on Mart. 6.15.1; it is particularly suggestive in describing the unpleasant and dangerous heat of the full summer sun.

16. quem (codd.); cum (Riese); quam ... ! (Baehrens): as SB says (app. crit.), the emendations are 'frustra'; August, like the other months, is described ecphrastically and personified.

gillo: this a vessel for cooling water and other liquids, and is described in greater detail at 125, on which see notes.

flabella (Heinsius); fabella (BW); fabilla (A); faula (V): although the initial short syllable of the noun is metrically irregular, and it is right to be properly circumspect in emending to a text with such irregularities, in this instance Heinsius' conjecture restores exactly the necessary sense and should be accepted (note the fan of peacock feathers in the 354 Calendar, described at 15 n. above). The same prosody is found at Drac. *Rom.* 7.30, and for metrical and prosodical aspects of this collection, see p. 24. Note that ensuing 'mĕlo' is also metrically irregular.

melo: this is the melon (*Cucumis melo*) as distinct from the watermelon (*Citrullus lanatus*); in Latin the watermelon is 'pepo' (from Greek πέπων) and the melon is 'melopepo' (Greek μηλοπέπων), which became shortened to 'melo'. Both fruits are native to Africa and would have reached the classical world via Egypt; the melon was probably introduced later, but Pliny knew of it (*Nat. Hist.* 19.67). André (*L'Alimentation*, 81) says that ancient melons were small, on the grounds that Emperor Albinus could eat ten at a sitting (*SHA* Clod. Alb. 11.3); see A.C. Andrews, 'Melons and Watermelons in the Classical Era', *Osiris* 12.1956.368 f.

17. aequales Librae September... horas: for Libra and the September equinox cf. Verg. *Georg.* 1.208 'Libra die somnique pares ubi fecerit horas'; the association was commonplace because the equinox occurs when the sun is in Libra (cf. Manil. 2.427; 3.252; Lucan 4.57; 8.467; Sen. *Herc.* 844 etc.; with *RE* 13.124). All twelve months were connected in this way with a zodiacal constellation, September's being either Virgo or Libra, which is why he is here held to belong to Libra (see e.g. Aus. 14.9, *AL* 864R, and the relevant months of the two *menologia rustica* cited in the intro. above; with *DS* 5.1054 f. and F. Boll, *Sphaera*, Leipzig 1903, 472 f.). A third-century mosaic of the months from Hellin in Spain shows a winged figure with a balance for September, clearly a personification of the equinox (*LIMC* no. 27).

In his note on Vergil loc. cit. Mynors points out that 'pares' must mean 'of equal length', not 'of equal number', because there were always twelve hours in both the Roman day and night (Cens. *De Die Nat.* 23.6); hours were

Commentary

therefore of unequal length except at the equinoxes, and that is the point poets like to make, as with 'aequales' in this line. See also E.J. Bickerman, *Chronology of the Ancient World*, London (revised edn) 1980, 15 f.

18. cum botruis: at first sight this detail of the September vignette is puzzling: why should September, who is presumably depicted as a huntsman, be carrying home bunches of grapes with his captured hare, particularly when the grape harvest and wine-making are symbols used for October in the poem? It must be intentional, however, because *AL* 391.37 f. has exactly the same image, albeit for October: 'dat prensum leporem cumque ipso palmite fetus / October'; and *AL* 665a.17 f.R similarly gives grapes for September and the vintage for October. It is also notable that the grape harvest and wine-making oscillate in both literary texts and the pictorial evidence between September and October, no doubt a reflection of reality with the ubiquity and importance of the crop (see the table at *LIMC* 6.1.493 f.; and Salzman, *Time*, 94 f.; 103 f.). But the implication of this image may simply be that September's grapes are for cooking with his hare or will constitute his dessert.

19. conterit October: cf. *AL* 391.39 f. 'iam Bromios spumare lacus et musta sonare / apparet; vino vas calet ecce novo!'; *LIMC* nos 18; 20; 26; and see 18 n. above for grapes and the vintage associated with September and October.

lascivis calcibus: note also 'lascivis crotalis' at line 8; the adjective here has no pejorative overtones, suggesting the jolly frolicking of peasants engaged in grape-crushing.

20. dulcia musta: cf. Verg. *Georg.* 1.295 'aut dulcis musti Volcano decoquit umorem', with Mynors' note. Here the 'dulcia musta' is the trodden grape juice and pulp of the pressing, whereas Vergil refers to the later process of turning some of it into a syrup.

21. November: as regards November's iconography, cf. *LIMC* no. 20 for ploughing, and 33 for ploughing and olive gathering; the making of olive-oil occurs in November at Pallad. *Agric.* 12.17 and *AL* 874a.21R. Other poems on the months use religious rites for their November symbolism (e.g. *AL* 391.41 f.), or astronomical signs and the weather (*AL* 665a.21 f.R; Aus. 14.2.11; 14.3.21 f.).

vomere vertit (Sannazarius); nomine bestie (codd., *sed* **vestit (A)); numine Vestae (Scaliger):** editors generally accept Sannazaro's conjecture 'vomere vertit' for the corrupt 'nomine bestiae' (?) of the mss, though the fact that 'vomere vertit' essentially repeats the preceding 'arans' may give rise to some unease. If Scaliger's 'numine Vestae' yielded reasonable sense for the context it would be well worth consideration, particularly since A also has 'arat' rather than 'arans' in the line. But

Commentary

it is not convincing: the festival of the Vestalia took place in June, not November (Ovid *Fast.* 6.249 f.); Vesta's sphere was hearth, home and domestic animals rather than agriculture; and even when deities are shown presiding over months, that associated with Vesta is December (see C. Long, 'Gods of the Months in Art', *AJA* 93.1989.590 f.).

22. teretes ... molas: the same words are used of the stones of a rotary mill for the grinding of wheat at 92.2; here they belong to an olive mill (*mola olearia*), which was constructed to a different design and was used to crush the olives before they were pressed (see A.G. Drachmann, *Ancient Oil Mills and Presses*, Copenhagen 1932, 41 f.; with 143 fig. 9 and 144 fig. 10).

23. pigra ... bruma Decembrem: 'bruma' is the cold weather of winter, though it is welcome in this concluding couplet because it enforces inactivity and rest from the toil of the other months, and because it heralds the festival of the Saturnalia. For the same symbolism for December cf. Aus. 14.2.12; 14.3.23 f.; *AL* 391.47 f. 'pigra' has an active sense here (cf. *Rhet. ad Herr.* 4.43 'frigus pigrum (sc. dicimus) quia pigros efficit').

24. ... famulis tessera iungit ...: the themes of gaming or gambling and of servants being elevated to their masters' level are typical of the Saturnalia and symbolise it. The December illustration in the 354 Calendar shows dice and a dice-shaker ready for play (Stern, *Calendrier*, 283 f., with Pls 13.1-2); cf. *AL* 391.48 'nunc tibi cum domino ludere, verna, licet', and Salzman, *Time*, 74 f. On the Saturnalia generally see Leary's commentary on Mart. XIV, 1 f.; and for the connection with dice and gambling see my note on Mart. 11.6.2.

107 (118R)

On Thetis. She is indeed a mother with foresight who, in order that wounds cannot harm her son, tempers her offspring in the waters of Styx. But because it is ordained that nobody can overcome the human lot, the Fates leave room for themselves in the limbs of the one immersed.

This short epigram on a mythological topic stands in isolation between the pieces on the calendar and a series of bath poems. It is possibly ecphrastic, the work of art it describes being an image of Thetis dipping Achilles in the Styx, though it might be simply epideictic, more 'rhetorical' in nature, its point lying in the neat expression of lines 3-4. SB announces '*finem deesse puto*' in his app. crit., and indicates a corresponding lacuna in his text; but there is no need for such a supposition (133, for example, is also a mythological quatrain with the first two lines setting up the scene of Jupiter and Europa, and the second two providing authorial comment).

Commentary

The myth of Achilles being dipped by his mother Thetis in the Styx to render him impervious to wounds and /or to give him immortality receives surprisingly late attestation in the literary record: it does not appear until Statius (*Ach.* 1.134; 269 f.). Yet there is evidence in the visual arts which goes back to the Hellenistic period, and which probably confirms a Hellenistic origin for this part of the story (see *LIMC* 1.1.41 f., nos 5-18). The scholiast in his comment on Stat. *Ach.* 1.134 gives the basic account: 'Thetis cum cognovisset fata Achillis, timens de morte eius in Stygem paludem intinxit, et toto corpore invulnerabilis fuit excepta parte qua tentus est'. Earlier versions of this element of the myth are more colourful, and reflect less well on the mother: Hesiod (frag. 300 M-W) says in his *Aigimios* that Thetis, in order to test whether her children were immortal or not, since they had an immortal mother but mortal father, immersed them in boiling water, thereby proving their mortality; but Peleus stopped her when she came to Achilles. A similar but fuller tradition has Thetis using fire for her test, or, in some versions, as a means to give her children immortality (Ap. Rhod. 4.865 f.; Apollod. 3.13.6); Peleus rescued Achilles when only his ankle had been incinerated, and replaced it by exhuming the relevant joint of the fleet-footed giant Damysus (Ptol. *Heph.* 4 (*Mythographoi*, ed. Westermann, p. 195.15 f.)). In all versions, sketchy though some now are, it was Achilles' heel that was left as his vulnerable part, and it is through a wound there that he meets his end (see Frazer's notes on Apollod. 3.13.6 and *epit.* 5.3; Bömer's note on Ovid *Met.* 12.580 f.; and *LIMC* 1.1.41).

Another epigram of the *AL* (192) deals with this myth and has a similar point:

> Pande manum genetrix; totus tingatur Achilles.
> Tu faci<e>s natum mortis habere locum.

1. cauta quidem: 'quidem' is answered by 'sed' in line 3; Thetis can be as caring and protective towards her son as she likes, but she cannot get round the ordained limits of fate. For the structure of 'quidem' as the second or third word of an epigram with 'sed' following, cf. Mart. 2.1.1; 4.69.1; 10.63.1; 13.52.1; 14.158.1; Aus. *Epig.* 37.1 (and note Ovid *Pont.* 4.8.1; *Tr.* 3.4.1). It is effective in the conversational and anecdotal tone it gives ('well, yes, of course x is the case, but ...').

2. confirmat: the verb is used quite literally of 'hardening up' people, making them robust and healthy: e.g. Col. 5.12.2 'pueri abundantia lactis confirmabuntur'; Mart. 6.43.3 'me Nomentani confirmant otia ruris' (with *TLL* 4.219.54 f.). It can also take a legal sense of 'acknowledgment': e.g. *Dig.* 29.7.2.4 'confirmare hereditatem'; ibid. 1.7.38 'confirmare adoptionem' (with *TLL* 4.221.56 f.). Thus Thetis' action is designed both to secure invulnerability and robustness for Achilles, and to confirm her

Commentary

maternity of him by making him immortal or at least invulnerable. The two meanings of 'puerperium' help this, both abstract 'birth' and concrete 'offspring' (for the latter cf. Stat. *Theb.* 4.279 f. 'quercus laurique ferebant / cruda puerperia' with *OLD* puerperium (b)).

3-4. sed quia ... locum: a similar point is made by the scholiast on Stat. *Ach.* 1.269-70 'Thetis cum sciret [eo] quod a Peleo Achilles mortalis esset, in Stygem paludem eum intinxit et toto corpore impenetrabilem fecit excepta corporis parte qua eum tenuerat. Pro nefas! Novum genus calamitatis! Ibi mortis locum reliquit, ubi eum est mater implexa'. And cf. also *AL* 192, quoted in the intro. above.

108 (119R)

On some baths. Look at the baths gleaming with their roofs and gushing torrents, to which an artist and the water lend no little beauty: for the splendid ceilings sport lovely shapes, and pleasant streams flow from the clear spring. He who aims to take this enjoyment with a double benefit, and who knows how to enjoy life as it passes by, let him bathe here. Here, refreshing his body and relaxing his mind, he will soothe his eyes with the pictures and his limbs with the waters.

This piece begins a lengthy sequence of epigrams about baths and bathing (108-14), a favourite theme of the *AL* in general and this collection in particular, and a literary vogue which reflects the popularity of bathing in Vandal North Africa (on which see 99 intro., where the interrelationship between that epigram and the sequence by Felix on the Thermae Alianae at *AL* 201-05 was also remarked: there are further, though less significant, similarities between Felix's poems and those of this sequence, for which see the notes at 109 intro. (at end); 109.1; 109.2; 109.4; 111.2; and 113.3).

There is a question over the extent to which the present group of epigrams constitutes a cycle. Busch (*Versus*, 331 f.; esp. 340) argues that they relate to a single bathing complex, with 108-10 being about the whole complex, 111-12 about the caldarium, and 113-14 (the latter of which is missing) about the frigidarium. On the one hand the poems are placed together in the ms., and they are all clearly inscriptional in nature: cf. 108.1 'aspice'; 108.7 'hic ... hic ...'; the acrostich 'Filocali' and telestich 'Melaniae' in 109; 110.3 'hic'; 111.1 'hic'; 112.4 'haec'; 113.4 'hinc'. And they share similarities of phrasing: e.g. 109.7 'lustrent ... Cumani litoris antra' / 110.1 'Cumani lustravit litoris antra'; and 110.3 'hic lavet' / 108.9 'hic lavet'. On the other hand (as Busch loc. cit. states) there is no particular linkage between the addressees (e.g. 108 is addressed to people of Epicurean disposition; 109 to the reader; 110 to one tired of Baiae; 111 to the reader; and 112 to the sun); and the superscription of

113, 'De Thermis', is discarded to fit his theory, with it and the missing 114 (if it belongs to this cycle: see 115 intro.) being made to refer to a frigidarium, which is not necessarily their subject (Busch, *Versus*, 338 f.). Nevertheless the links and similarities between most of the pieces are undeniable and have point, particularly if, as I suggest, the comparisons with Cumae and Baiae in the earlier epigrams (109.7 f.; 110.1 f.; 110.4) provide help in understanding the energy sources for heating the baths detailed in the later epigrams. I therefore accept the main thrust of Busch's argument, that these pieces do constitute a cycle about one bathing establishment. It follows that it is an establishment with which Filocalus and Melania are in some way connected (see 109 intro.), and that it is probably centred on the use of hot springs, and is in essence a spa (see 111 intro.). For such establishments see Thébert, *Thermes romains*, 369 f.; Yegül, *Baths*, 92 f.; and R. Jackson, 'Waters and Spas in the Classical World', in *The Medical History of Waters and Spas*, ed. R. Porter, London 1990, 1 f.: they ranged from the basic, offering little more than use of the spring, to the magnificent, where huge complexes were furnished with suites of both naturally and artificially heated water and rooms (Filocalus' baths would presumably have been relatively modest).

The cleverly exploited theme of this opening epigram is the dual attractiveness of the baths' water supply and their decoration. Lines 1-2 describe both ('tectis et gurgite' / 'pictor et unda'); lines 3-4 give a brief description of decoration and water supply in turn; and lines 5-8 pick up on the dual pleasure this gives the bather, with water to soothe his body and pictures to relax his mind.

Pictorial decoration of baths is known from literary, epigraphical and archaeological evidence; it seems to have taken the form of painting as often as mosaic, which on the one hand is surprising because of problems to be expected with ambient humidity, but on the other would have been cheaper (for a general treatment of decoration of baths, particularly with statuary and mosaic, see Dunbabin, *Baiarum grata voluptas*, 12 f.). Sidonius (*Ep.* 2.2.5 f.) gives an interesting description of the lack of decoration at his own baths, which suggests what it was like elsewhere: 'interior parietum facies solo levigati caementi candore contenta est. Non hic per nudam pictorum corporum pulchritudinem turpis prostat historia, quae sicut ornat artem, sic devenustat artificem ... Quid plura? Nihil illis paginis impressum reperietur quod non vidisse sit sanctius. Pauci tamen versiculi lectorem adventicium remorabuntur minime improbo temperamento, quin eos nec relegisse desiderio est nec perlegisse fastidio' (Sidonius' use of written texts for decoration in baths also shows how the epigrams of this series might have served for actual inscription.) For further literary or inscriptional evidence of paintings at baths, cf. *POxy* 896 col.1 (of AD 316); *POxy* 2145 (AD 186); *ILS* 5713; *ILS* 5732; with Busch, *Versus*, 235 n. 30. Archaeological remains offer, for example, paintings in the baths of the House of Menander at Pompeii; the dome of the Forum Baths at Herculaneum, which was painted with an assortment of fishy creatures to give bathers the sensation of swimming in an aquarium; and the Hunting Baths at Lepcis Magna, the upper zone of the entire south wall of the frigidarium of which boasts a monumental painting of a leopard hunt (see Ling, *Painting*, 92; 96; 136; and Yegül, *Baths*, fig. 198). The brief description this epigram gives of the decorations, 'pulchras ... formas', suggests figurative images, but whether of animals, fishes, nudes or something else is guesswork. For mosaic decoration in baths, see Dunbabin, *Baiarum grata voluptas*, 21 f.

1. aspice: Martial also uses the imperative of a verb of seeing to arrest the reader's attention in this kind of deictic context: e.g. 4.3.1 'aspice quam densum tacitarum vellus aquarum / defluat in vultus Caesaris ...'; 5.31.1; 13.58.1, with further examples, Latin and Greek, at Siedschlag, *Form*, 9.

fulgentis ... baias: the use of 'baiae' as a generic noun for baths has been discussed at 99.1 n. The participle here emphasises both the physical splendour of the building's gleaming stone work and flowing water (cf. Sen. *De Tranq. Anim.* 1.8 'tecta ipsa fulgentia'), and their excellence in an abstract sense: cf. *AL* 194.1 f. Luxorius, on Hilderic's baths: 'Hildirici regis fulget mirabile factum / arte, opere, ingenio, divitiis, pretio'.

tectis: the roofs of the buildings, a particular feature of North African baths, are highlighted, as they are also at 99.6 'vestivit cameris balnea pulchra locans' (see note) and *CE* 1910.1 'splendent tecta Bassiani fundi'. Although the reader will call to mind the baths as viewed from outside, it will become clear as the epigram progresses that his attention is drawn rather to their inside decoration.

gurgite: most Latin nouns denoting bodies of water are imprecise: *gurges*, even apart from its reference to whirlpools and vortices, can denote springs, fountains, lakes, rivers, seas and oceans or the water in them (see e.g. *TLL* 6.2-3.2361.55 f.). In this piece the water is not only labelled *gurges*, but variously *unda, fons, fluenta* and *aquae*. Such vocabulary could be applicable to more than one source of water supply, though the emphasis laid on it in this epigram by the varied vocabulary suggests that it is something of which the establishment is particularly proud and on which it trades (plenty of it, flowing not stagnant, of high quality etc.). If this is so, it would accord with the theory that it was supplied by natural hot springs (see 111 intro.); and compare the similar stress laid on the water supply of Bellator's baths (99.2 n.; 7 n.; 9 n.).

2. pictor: for decoration of baths see intro. above; *pictor* can refer to artists working either with paint or mosaic (for the latter usage see M. Donderer, *Die Mosaizisten der Antike und ihre wirtschaftliche und soziale Stellung: eine Quellenstudie*, Erlangen 1989, 27 f.).

Commentary

3. splendentia culmina: cf. *AL* 345.1 f. Luxorius, on a bathing establishment: 'ardua montanos inter splendentia lucos / culmina'; *AL* 201. 5 and 205.6 Felix. The phrase picks up 'tectis' in line 1.

4. ... fonte fluenta: both nouns are again imprecise (see 1 n.), though they would well suit the baths' water supply being a natural spring. The noun *fluenta* (the singular is infrequently used: *TLL* 6.1.949.32 f. for examples) can be used either without qualification, as here and at 113.2, or with a descriptive genitive or other attribute (e.g. 'Gorgonei ... fontis ... fluenta' (Fulg. *Myth.* 1.*pref*.22); 'gurgitis aestivi ... pura fluenta' (Prud. *Symm.* 2.790)). A fourth-century inscription from Calama (Algeria) commemorates the restoration of a *piscina* 'quae antea tenuis aquae pigra fluenta capiebat, nunc ve<ro ... und>arum intonantium motibus redundantem ... restituit' (*CIL* 8.5335).

5. gaudia ... gemino ... fructu: the line is striking, bringing together the descriptions of the decoration of the baths and the water supply of the opening quatrain. 'fructu' shows that the 'gaudia' are not only pleasurable, but of benefit to the bather in the two ways which the closing couplet will elucidate. As often in the collection, the poet is fond of items that have more than one use, and of expressions to illustrate them: cf. 95.3; 96.4; 102.7; 103.10; 159.3; 169.5.

6. vita ... praetereunte frui: this is the frequent 'carpe diem' theme, an enticement to potential bathers (for it see Nisbet-Hubbard's note on Hor. *Carm.* 1.11.8).

7. hic lavet: for the striking enjambement see 78.3 n.
 corpus reparans: for the idea that bathing is physically reinvigorating see 109.4 n., and for the idea that it is of direct benefit to health see 169.6 n.
 mentemque relaxans: for the idea that bathing is an aid to mental relaxation and reducing stress (though here it is specifically looking at the pictures in the baths that is claimed to produce the benefit), cf. Aug. *Conf.* 9.32 'visum etiam mihi est ut irem lavatum, quod audieram inde balneis nomen inditum, quia Graeci βαλανεῖον dixerint, quod anxietatem pellat ex animo'; Claud. *Appx.* 12.11 f. Hall ('*De Lavacro*') 'huc ades, o Florens, et festa luce relaxa / mentis onus, nebulasque fuga ...'.

8. fovebit (de Saumaise); fobit (A): this is an example of A's carelessness necessarily corrected (the same type of error, involving the omission of letters from words, also occurs in A at 82.2; 99.7; 104.5; 104.8; 108.2; 109.5; 124.1; 135.1; 140.2; 162.1; 167.4; 175.1; 183.6; 185.2; 186.5; and 188.4. I have not commented on all instances in the notes). For *fovere* of the pleasant effect of bathing in usually warm water, see Mart. 1.62.4 with Citroni's note.

Commentary

109 (120R)

Another. The good fortune of the proprietor founded these new baths, and invites the road-weary to hurry here. The overseer of the establishment will gain her satisfaction from praise of the operation while her guest is refreshed by the sweet-flowing waters. The first letters of the verses spell out the founder's name, and the outermost ones enable the manager's name to be read. Let ocean-goers visit the grottoes of the Cumaean coast; let these local delights give me greater pleasure.

This second epigram of the series of seven on baths raises fundamental points for the collection as a whole, particularly concerning date and authorship (for which see pp. 4 and 5 f.). Many questions centre around the acrostich FILOCALI and telestich MELANIAE, the identities of those named, and their inter-relationship with the various descriptive nouns of the persons referred to in the epigram ('domini' (line 1); 'fundi praesul' (line 3); 'condentis' (line 5); 'a(u)ctorem' (line 6); and 'mihi' (line 8)). My conclusions, explained further in the remainder of this introduction and in the notes below, are that Filocalus and Melania are not known from elsewhere, that neither of them is the author of this epigram, that both were involved in the building and running of the baths to which the epigram relates, that their date and that of the epigram is consonant with a sixth-century origin, and that the epigram relates to baths in North Africa, perhaps Carthage.

I begin with the acrostich FILOCALI and telestich MELANIAE. The acrostich was first recognised by L. Müller (*RhM* 20.1865.633 f.), who correctly emended the ms. spelling 'hospes' in line 4 to 'ospes', a reading which had previously obscured it. The emendation is confirmed beyond any doubt by line 5 ('monstrant versus primordia nomen'), and by a particular fondness for acrostichs in North African verse inscriptions (see below). Although this acrostich is now universally acknowledged, the telestich MELANIAE is not: e.g. Riese (app. crit.) says '*Nihili est telestichon quod Hugenus et Thielmannus ... putarunt se agnoscere MELANIAE: nam u. 5 sq. de illo loquuntur, de hac vel hoc tacent*'; this has apparently convinced SB, who marks the acrostich in his text and comments on it in his app. crit., but neither marks nor comments on the telestich. However, Thielmann (*ALL* 4.1887.600) must have been correct to identify the telestich, as must also M. Manitius (*RhM* 51.1896.162): it is impossible that an eight-letter telestich should appear coincidentally in an epigram which already sports an eight-letter acrostich, and that it should be, like the acrostich, the genitive singular of a personal name. It is in fact highly unlikely that it would appear coincidentally anywhere else, in support of which statement may be adduced one of the odder pieces of scholarly research, an article by I. Hilberg (*WS* 21.1899.305 f.) in which he lists all accidental acrostichs in Latin poetry from Ennius to Corippus: he finds only three of eight letters or more in length ('laniabor' at Val. Flacc. 4.177 f.; 'Dictaeis'

Commentary

at Claud. 20.434 f.; and 'petiique' at Ven. Fort. *Vit. S. Mart.* 2.139 f.), thereby confirming the deliberate sixteen-line acrostich 'Italicus scripsit' at *Ilias Latina* 1 f. and 1063 f. (on which see Scaffai's commentary (second ed.) at p. 11 f.; that there is an acrostich is certain, though some relatively minor emendation is necessary, and Scaffai suggests, as have others, that the author may have been Baebius Italicus, *cos. suff.* AD 90). This proves that a coincidental telestich in this epigram is an impossibility (even discounting the unlikelihood of the double instruction for finding an acrostich at lines 5 and 6 if the telestich is not recognised), and the piece must be interpreted accordingly.

The next question to pose relates to the identity and functions of the various persons mentioned in the epigram. These fall into three categories:

(A), and presenting no problem, the people using the bath, who are described as 'fessos viae' (line 2) and 'ospes' (line 4), and who will appreciate the facilities with which they are provided.

(B), and most problematic, the persons who are said to have some capacity in the ownership, construction or running of the establishment: thus line 1 refers to a 'dominus' whose *Fortuna* is portrayed as 'condens lavacrum'; line 3 mentions the 'fundi praesul' who will take pleasure in the guests' or customers' praise; line 5 states that the acrostich refers to the 'condens'; and line 6, as it stands in the ms., states that the acrostich refers to the 'auctor'. Despite the difficulties of interpretation, some of this seems reasonably clear: the 'condens' of line 5 ought to be the 'condens lavacrum' of the first line, and, if that is so, he is also the 'dominus' of the first line and the Filocalus of the acrostich (since he is male, and Melania is surely female, the appellation 'dominus' gives confidence). But then who is the 'auctor' of line 6 (I refer to 'auctor' in this introduction although I argue in the note ad loc. for emendation of the text)? The terms themselves offer little help because of their imprecision: in architectural and euergetical vocabulary 'auctor' and 'condens' can mean much the same, i.e. the builder or founder of a building, and both nouns can also be used metaphorically of authors of literary works (see notes ad locc.). Therefore I would revert to an argument of probabilities: given that the epigram sports both an acrostich and a telestich, given that two separate lines (5 and 6) of the epigram give instruction on how to solve such puzzles, and given that Filocalus can be identified as the 'condens lavacrum', it is reasonable to conclude that line 6 as a whole, and 'auctor' in particular, should refer to the telestich and Melania. Since the 'praesul fundi' of line 3 can also be plausibly distinguished from the 'condens lavacrum' of line 1 (see 3 n.), it too is likely to refer to Melania. Although the precise details may remain obscure, I suggest that the epigram refers to, or honours, two people, Filocalus and Melania, who both had some capacity or function in constructing or running a bathing establishment. This conclusion agrees in many aspects with that of E. Courtney (*Hermathena* 129.1980.41), though I differ from him over the significance of 'auctor' (see line 6 n.).

Commentary

And (C), there is 'mihi' in the concluding line. The epigram is inscriptional in nature, especially in the sense that it is difficult to divorce understanding of it from its particular place and time (cf. 'huc' in line 2; the invitation to the weary traveller; the circumstantial detail of Filocalus and Melania and their roles; and the instructions in lines 5-6 on deciphering acrostich and telestich), and that involves reading it as if it were inscribed on the walls of the baths to which it relates. In such a context the concluding first person wish 'lustrent ... placeant ... mihi' would relate to the protagonist of the epigram and founder / owner of the baths, Filocalus, who effectively recommends his reader / clients to enjoy the local facilities and shun fancy foreign establishments, as he does himself (compare the proprietorial 'nostra' at 110.4; 111.3; and 112.1). Such advertising technique is still common: 'I like this, you trust me, so you should do as I do, or buy what I buy'.

I now consider whether it is possible to identify more specifically the Filocalus and Melania of the acrostich and telestich. J. Evans-Grubbs and E. Courtney (*CPh* 82.1987.237 f.) suggested that 'Filocalus can be identified with a subdeacon known from the correspondence of Augustine as *Hipponensium primarius* and *vir honorabilis* [*Ep.* 222-3 = *PL* 33.999 f.] and Melania with the younger of two aristocratic Roman ladies of this name. She and her husband decided to live a life of Christian asceticism, sold off their estates in Western Europe and North Africa, and settled at Thagaste *c.* 410-17. As a noted philanthropist she might well have suggested the erection of baths, and indeed put up some or all of the money for their construction' (this is Courtney's summary at *ML* 266). A. Cameron (*CPh* 87.1992.140 f.) identifies the builder of the baths as the elder Melania, grandmother of the younger, born *c.* 340, widowed *c.* 372, who spent twenty-seven years in the east, returning briefly to Rome in *c.* 400 (the precise chronology is uncertain); and he identifies Filocalus as the 'auctor' (line 6) of the epigram and the calligrapher and friend of Pope Damasus, whose floruit was *c.* 350-80 (and whose role in the composition of the 354 Calendar has been noted at 106 intro.; see further on him Ferrua's edition of Damasus' epigrams, 21 f.). Cameron also adduces a reference in the *Life of Melania* (in ch. 21 of both the Greek and Latin versions, ed. Rampolla del Tindaro, 1905), where Melania is said to have donated a property at Thagaste, which specifically had a 'balneum', to the Church. Finally, J. Dingel (*WS* 19.1985.173 f.) suggests that the telestich MELANIAE, particularly if it is not referred to by line 6, may simply indicate that Melania was Filocalus' mother or wife. On the two Melaniae see further *PLRE* I, Melania 1 and 2; D. Gorce's edition of the Greek *Life of Melania* (Paris 1962), 20 f.; 41 f.; and E.A. Clark, *The Life of Melania the Younger*, Lewiston etc. 1984.

But in my view (agreeing with Busch, *Versus*, 230 f.) these theories should be treated with caution. Courtney (loc. cit.) rightly says of Cameron's identification of the calligrapher Filocalus and the elder Melania that (1) they had no known connection with Africa (though it should be pointed out it is known that Melania had estates there), and (2) Filocalus' fame was as a calligrapher / engraver, not as an author, and even if he were described as the composer / engraver of the piece, this would entail that 'condens' in line 1 requires a different sense from 'condentis' in line 5, which must be implausible. It can be added that this Melania and Filocalus are not connected with each other elsewhere, and that the link to the baths is at best tenuous. As regards Courtney's identification of the younger Melania and subdeacon Filocalus, it can be objected (1) that they have no other known connection with each other, even though they are both connected with Africa and Augustine; (2) that although Melania was known for her philanthropy, this lay in Christian good works and the foundation of religious houses rather than baths; and (3) her Life specifically states that she did her best to go nowhere near a bath (ch. 2, both Latin and Greek versions), which makes her an unlikely provider of a secular bathing establishment. And Dingel's hypothesis also seems improbable: a reader of this epigram, faced with the two instructions on decipherment in lines 5 and 6 together with an acrostich and telestich in the poem, would surely not assume that both instructions relate to the acrostich, and that the telestich therefore contains the name of a relative; he would assume, rightly in my view, that something is wrong with the instructions (see 6 n. below). My conclusion is therefore that the Filocalus and Melania of the epigram are not known from elsewhere, and there is no reason why their date cannot be consonant with a sixth-century provenance for it.

Whatever their identity, Filocalus and Melania are shown as beneficent proprietors of the baths who have built them and provide a necessary and excellent service to their clients and guests; this euergetic tone is frequent in pieces of this type. In the *AL* it is particularly associated with the Vandal kings (cf. 201.7 f.; 202.4; 204.2 and 7; 205.7; with M. Chalan et al., 'Memorabile Factum', *AntAfr*, 21.1985.207 f.), and gifts to a local community of whole baths, or free access, or of their upkeep or the provision of heating or oil, are all well evidenced inscriptionally (see esp. Fagan, *Bathing*, 104f.; 128 f.; 233 f. (where he catalogues over two hundred and fifty euergetic bathing inscriptions)). Bellator in *AL* 99 and Vita in 168-9 are comparable: the inscriptions at these baths not only advertise the wares, but also record the useful social function they fulfil, and in that way they honour the proprietors.

Finally in this introduction I deal with acrostichs and telestichs on a more general level. This will largely focus on inscriptional evidence, but the practice in Latin literary texts can be found as early as Ennius ('Q. Ennius fecit' from Cic. *De Div.* 2.111 (= *Incerta* 53 Vahlen), discussed by Courtney, *FLP* 30); and see further Müller, *De Re Metrica* 578 f.; E. Courtney, *Philologus* 134.1990.3 f. (correcting and supplementing examples collected by G. Barbieri, *MGR* 23.1975.328 f.; 364 f.; 401); G.

Commentary

Damschen, *Philologus* 148. 2004.88 f.; and, for Greek literary examples, E. Vogt, *A&A* 13.1967.80 f. The evidence for Latin inscriptional acrostichs, telestichs and the like is collected by J. Zarker, *Orpheus* 13.1966.125 f., and supplemented by G. Sanders, *Lapides Memores*, ed. A. Donati et al., Faenza 1991, 183 f. (= *Roczniki Humanistyczne* (*Lublin*) 27(3).1979.57 f.). They catalogue a total of eighty-six relevant inscriptions from the second century AD onwards, forty of pagan origin and the remainder Christian, the predominant areas of production being Italy with thirty-seven examples and (significantly for this piece) North Africa with thirty-one. The majority of the inscriptions are funerary, the next largest category being those about buildings or other objects. A recently published third-century acrostich poem commemorating building works carried out by the centurion M. Porcius Iasucthan at the military outpost of Bu Njem in North Africa is discussed by J.N. Adams (*JRS* 89.1999.109 f.).

Acrostich and telestich together feature in inscriptions at *CE* 1615; 1616; 1916; 1977 (all from North Africa) and 726 and 727 (from Rome); an acrostich / telestich is also found at *AL* 6aR, but the most intricate example of all is *AL* 205, an inscription of twelve lines written by Felix for the Thermae Alianae near Carthage, which has not only acrostich, telestich and mesostich, but positions the mesostich of each line at the nineteenth letter, and the telestich at the thirty-seventh.

1. fausta ... Fortuna: 'fortuna' may be general good fortune, but Fortune as a goddess is often associated with bathing establishments (e.g. *CIL* 2.2701; 3.789; 7.273; with Nielsen, *Thermae*, 1.146 n. 7), so the author may have intended a greater resonance. Before the acrostich of the epigram was recognised, it was suggested that 'fausta fortuna' was the key to the identity of the builder or owner of the baths, and comparison was made with 'Fausti balnea' at Mart. 2.14.11 (thus e.g. Burman, 1759, 486). Such plays on names, especially in the first word of the epigram, are found elsewhere, and there is another probable example in another bath poem in this collection at 168.1 (see note): e.g. *CE* 1829, an epitaph for Liberalis, which begins 'Liber et exuctus cura, germane, subisti'; or *CE* 1187 on Prima, beginning 'Prima aetate tua rapta es, karissima coniunx'; or *CE* 439, on Vera, an acrostich epitaph beginning 'Ver tibi contribuat sua munera florea grata'; with J.W. Zarker, *Orpheus*, 13.1966.148. Such a play is not necessary here, given the acrostich, but the name Filocalus Faustus for the proprietor is an intriguing possibility.

lavacrum: *lavacrum / -a* can refer to the whole bathing complex as well as a single pool in it: e.g. *AL* 205.4 Felix 'praecelsa lavacra'; Eutr. 8.20.1 'opus ... lavacri, quae Antoniae appellantur', with *TLL* 7.2.1032.61 f.

2. properare: the invitation to prospective bathers to hurry to visit baths is also found at *AL* 203.11 Felix 'hic Thrasamundiacis properet se tinguere thermis'.

Commentary

viae (Heinsius); vitae (A); viros (de Saumaise): 'fessos vitae' is unmetrical, and 'fessos viros' is lame; Heinsius' small emendation to 'viae' is excellent. For *fessus* + gen., cf. Stat. *Theb.* 3.395 'Tydea ... fessum bellique viaeque'; Symm. *Ep.* 1.13.2 'tabellarius vigiliarum fessus astabat'. It is also possible 'viae' here might depend on 'huc' (cf. Pers. 3.15 'hucine rerum venimus?'), but the link to 'fessos' is more pointed. Riese (in his addenda at 2.373), picking up on a suggestion by J. Ziehen (*Philologus* 63.1904.366 f.), suggested that 'Vitae' might be a place name (i.e. 'here to Vita') on the strength of 'Vitenses' at 138.3 (see note), but he does not convince (all tired people obviously will not want to go to Vita for a bath).

3. fundi ... praesul: this refers to Melania on the interpretation advanced in the intro. above. For *praesul* of someone put in charge of something, cf. Pallad. *Agric.* 1.6.18 'agri praesulem non ex delectis ... servulis ponas'; *SHA* Did. Jul. 9.4 'reprehensum in eo praecipue, quod eos, quos regere auctoritate sua debuerat, regendae rei publicae sibi praesules ipse fecisset'; it can often have the sense of acting on behalf of others, as these examples show, as also does its application to intercessory saints (e.g. Ambr. *De Obit. Theod.* 16 (*PL* 16.1391); Paul. Nol. *Carm.* 13.26).

For *fundus* referring to a bathing establishment cf. the acrostich poem *CE* 1910.1 (from Sidi Abdallah) 'splendent tecta Bassiani fundi cognomine baiae'.

4. ospes (Müller); hospis (A): Müller's orthographic emendation is certain (see intro.; it occurs in other inscriptions (*TLL* 6.2-3.3020.6 f.)); the customer of baths is also termed *hospes* at 110.2, *AL* 203.7 Felix, and e.g. Stat. *Silv.* 1.5.60 'si Baianis veniat novus hospes ab oris'.

dulciflua: the adjective is found elsewhere only in Dracontius (*Laud. Dei* 1.166) and three times in later authors (according to *TLL* 5.1.2187.27 f.). It alludes here to the fresh- rather than sea-water supply of the baths (see 99.8 n.).

recreatur: the theme of physical re-invigoration is common in the poems about bathing: cf. 108.7 f.; 169.6; 202.5 f.; 372.12.

5. condentis: picking up 'condens ... lavacrum' in line 1; it is argued in the intro. above that the phrase refers to Filocalus as the builder and founder of the baths and the owner of the land on which they stood. For *condere* and derivatives referring to the instigation of building and other works cf. Verg. *Aen.* 1.447 (of a temple); Liv. 34.35.11 (of a *castellum*); Col. 1.5.7 (of a villa); Amm. Marc. 31.1.2 (of a *lavacrum*); *CIL* 6.31916 (of *balneae*); with *TLL* 4.152.43 f. *condere* can also be used of literary creation, as Curt. 8.5.8 'conditor carminum'; Juv. 11.180 'conditor Iliados' etc., though I argue in the intro. above and notes below that that is not the reference here.

Commentary

monstrant versus primordia nomen: A's singular verb 'monstrat' is corrected in the ms. itself to the plural which 'primordia' requires. J.M. Stowasser (*WS* 31.1909.281) suggested that 'versus' is incorrect because it ought to be plural, though his remedy, the conjecture of an adverbial 'verso' to key the telestich, can be discounted. The solution lies elsewhere: an ellipse such as 'primordia (omnis) versus' has to be understood. In order to guide a reader's eye the initial letter of each line would almost certainly have been highlighted in some way in the actual inscription: such letters are sometimes coloured, carved in a different style, set apart from the rest of the line, or whatever, to draw attention to their special significance (for examples see Zarker, *Studies*, 40 f.). For 'primordia' cf. *CE* 511.10 'inspicies, lector, primordia versiculorum', and 273.9 f. (= *ML* 39.9 f.) 'ut tamen et lector nomen <cognosce>re possis, / singulae declarant exordia <litter>ae primae', both keying acrostichs.

An explicit instruction of the type which keys the acrostich here is often encountered in acrostich poems: thus e.g. *CE* 108.10 f. 'attonitus capita nunc versorum inspice, / titulum merentis oro perlegas libens: / agnosces nomen coniugis gratae meae'; also *CE* 109; 273.10 f.; 1814.8; *AE* 1925.41; *AL* 484a.8R, with many instances at Zarker, *Orpheus* 13.1966.144 f. But such explicit help is not always proffered: the complex combination of acrostich, mesostich and telestich at *AL* 205 is one such example.

6. actoremque (Kay); auctoremque (A): on the face of things the ms. 'auctoremque' is convincing because it is the kind of word one expects in the context, since it is virtually synonymous with *conditor / condere* (see 5 n. above) in both building (e.g. later in this collection at 169.4, of a bath-owner also termed 'dominus'; Front. *Aqu.* 7.3 'cui (sc. aquae) ab auctore Marciae nomen est'; *CE* 273.7 'tam laudati operis dominus ve<teranus> et auctor'; *AL* 205.7; *CE* 577.1; *AE* 1937.31; with *TLL* 2.1205.5 f.) and literary senses. But before considering this further, the wider import of line 6 needs examination. As it stands in the ms. it keys the acrostich ('facit littera prima legi'), as does the preceding line. But why two instructions to exactly the same end? Add the fact that the epigram also sports a telestich and that the person to whom it refers is different from that in the acrostich, and it is surely inconceivable that the instructions of both lines refer only to the acrostich. One of them must key the telestich, and it is more convincing to emend line 6 both on textual grounds, and because the identification of the 'condens' of line 5 with that of line 1 can then be maintained (see the next note). In what follows I therefore understand this line to refer to the telestich and to Melania.

Reverting to 'auctoremque', is it probable that it here refers either (1) to the builder / founder of the baths, or (2) to the author of the inscription? As regards (2), although it is not usual for the author of an inscriptional epigram to refer to himself in the body of the poem, the practice does occur and is sometimes coupled with an acrostich. Caution over the evidence is

Commentary

necessary, because it can be unclear whether the claim made relates to the authorship of the piece, the commissioning of it, physically inscribing it on stone, dedicating a building, or some other function: thus, for example *CE* 477.1 f., an epitaph from Tusculum on M. Publicius Unio, says 'te rogo, praeteriens fac mora et perlege versus / quos ego dictavi et iussi scribere quendam', and is a likely claim of authorship; whereas *CE* 512, an epitaph involving an acrostich on the centurion L. Praecilius Fortunatus, says 'hic ego qui taceo, versibus mea vita demonstro ... / titulos quos legis, vivus meae morti paravi' and need not imply that Fortunatus wrote the piece (and for other similar examples, where the nature of the claim cannot always be determined, see e.g. *CE* 271; 321; 521; 727; 735; *AE* 1947.31; and line 33 of Iasucthan's piece (see intro. above, with Adams, op. cit. 113); and see further Cugusi, *Aspetti letterari*, 23 f.; Adams, *Bilingualism*, 84 f. For stonemasons and calligraphers similarly claiming authorship for their work, note particularly Pope Damasus' friend Filocalus (see intro. above) with Damas. *Epig.* 18 and Ferrua's note). However, suffice it to say that a claim to literary authorship being made in this poem is possible. What makes it doubtful is the context: given the similarity between its meanings and that of 'condens', how is the reader of the piece expected to divine from this single word that the subject of the preceding five lines, the baths themselves, has suddenly been dropped, and that the poet has decided to comment on literary matters? I also note that where in other inscriptions a claim to literary authorship (or other such accolades) is made, it is made at some length and with greater clarity than a single ambiguous noun. Although, therefore, the reference of 'auctoremque' to Melania as author cannot be ruled out, it is improbable.

As for (1) above, a real problem again lies in the similarity of the term to that of 'condens'; thus Courtney (*Hermathena* 129.1980.41) suggests it signifies 'the person who suggested to Filocalus that the baths be built'. But that is surely too fine a distinction for any reader to be expected to draw, and seems to me no more likely a hypothesis than (2).

Overall 'auctoremque' gives rise to such problems that emendation is worth consideration, and the palaeographically easy 'actoremque' suggests itself (the ms. corruption would have been the easier since 'auctor' is so readily suggested by the whole context, and it is common in any case (see Stotz, *Handbuch* 2.172)). It would indicate that Melania was the person who managed the establishment which Filocalus had built. *Actor* is frequent in this sense of 'agent': cf. Plin. *Ep.* 3.19.2 'utraque (sc. praedia) ... sub eodem procuratore ac paene isdem actoribus habere'; *CIL* 12.2250 'actoris huius loci'; 13.2243 'actoris praediorum horum'; 13.2533 'Valentinus actor fundi Ammatiaci'; with *OLD* actor 6(a) and *TLL* 1.447.15 f. As regards baths, there is an *exactor thermarum Traianarum* (of uncertain function) at *CIL* 6.8677 (early second-century, from Rome), and *curatores* and *vilici* of baths are also epigraphically evidenced (see Fagan, *Bathing*, 321 f. nos 265-73). Here, 'actor' would also be synonymous with 'praesul fundi'

Commentary

(see 3 n.), and give good sense in distinguishing the functions of Filocalus and Melania. If the emendation is correct, the implication is that the epigram was written contemporaneously with Melania's running of the establishment, because the nature of her job is of transitory interest only. I would argue that this places it in the first half of the sixth century (see p. 5 f.).

summa (Courtney); prima (A): the principal reasons for accepting Courtney's conjecture (loc. cit. and *ML* 266; he does not however print it in his own text) are given in the note above, and 'summa' would key a telestich (for its reference to the last item of a sequence, cf. Quint. *Inst.* 6.4.22 'in argumentis ratio est, ut potentissima prima et summa ponantur; illa enim ad credendum praeparant iudicem, haec ad pronuntiandum'). Again, it is possible to see how the corruption occurred once 'auctoremque' had arisen and the existence of the telestich was not apparent: a scribe saw no difference between an 'auctor' and a 'condens' and therefore made this line say the same as the preceding one.

7. pontivagi: a ἅπαξ λεγόμενον.

Cumani litoris antra: the phrase is repeated in the first line of the next poem. *Antra* may not immediately suggest the bathing establishments to which one expects reference to be made, but note Mart. 4.57.1 f. 'dum nos blanda tenent lascivi stagna Lucrini / et quae pumiceis fontibus antra calent', where the 'antra' are evidently places connected with bathing. There were indeed many thermo-mineral baths fed by hot springs in the myrtle groves on the hills between Cumae and Baiae, which used the naturally occurring sources of hot water created by the volcanic activity of the area (Vitr. 2.6.2; Cels. 2.17.1; J.H. D'Arms, *Romans on the Bay of Naples*, Cambridge Mass. 1970, 139 f.), and the 'antra' which housed them may have been natural features or man-made structures (see, for the hot springs of the area around Cumae and Baiae, Plin. *Nat. Hist.* 3.60 and Sen. *Nat. Quaest.* 3.24.3, with H. Lavagne, *Operosa Antra*, Rome 1988, 625 f.). The poet here cites the luxurious bathing places of Southern Italy as examples of exotic and unnecessary distraction to those who use Filocalus' baths, probably with the added implication that his baths also were based around naturally occurring hot water (see intro. to 111); note that when he mentions the Fountain of Arethusa in connection with Bellator's baths, his comparison is no mere poetic flight of fancy, but gives important clues for the understanding of the whole epigram (see 99.2 n.; 9 n.).

8. indigenae ... deliciae: for *deliciae* used of places rather than the more usual persons, and with particular reference to North African baths, cf. 168.2 and *ILCV* 787.6 (= *ML* 43.6); the usage is reminiscent of the similarly localised 'baiae' in connection with these establishments (see 99.1 n.), though it also occurs elsewhere (e.g. Plin. *Nat. Hist.* 19.50 'hortorum

Commentary

nomine in ipsa urbe delicias agros villasque possident'). 'indigenae' is a substantive used attributively to qualify another noun: cf. Val. Flacc. 6.294 'indigenis sacratus aquis ... sacerdos', with *TLL* 7.1.1170.65 f. For the sentiment of this concluding couplet, that bathing pleasure can be found close to home rather than in distant resorts, compare Mart. 6.43.

110 (121R)

Another. Whoever has frequented the grottoes of the Cumaean coast and has swum often as a guest in the warm waters, let him bathe here, avoiding the perils of the wild ocean; our baths eclipse the attractions of Baiae.

This third epigram in the series on bathing establishments has close connections with the preceding two: e.g. 'Cumani ... litoris antra' is repeated from 109.7; '(h)ospes' is also found at 109.4 in the sense of 'guest' or 'customer'; 'hic lavet' is repeated from 108.7; and the unnecessary ocean voyage of line 3 is a theme found also at 109.7 f. Further on these linkages see intro. to 108.

1. Cumani ... litoris antra: see 109.7 n.

2. calidis ... aquis: for the naturally hot water at Cumae see 109.7 n. The focus here and in the epigram as a whole is on hot water, a topic shared by the following two pieces (see 111 intro.).

3. insani: a stock epithet for the wild and unpredictable sea (e.g. Verg. *Ecl.* 9.43; Prop. 3.7.6; Ovid *Her.* 7.53), and almost a transferred epithet here in that people who contemplate such travel must be mad, given the local facilities available.

   discrimina: the metaphorical sense of 'danger' is prevalent, but the literal one of 'separation' (cf. *discernere*) is also relevant, since the sea separates North Africa from the south of Italy. For 'discrimen' in the latter sense, cf. Cic. *De Lege Agr.* 2.87 '(sc. duo maria) cum pertenui discrimine separentur'; Plin. *Nat. Hist.* 3.100 'ad discrimen maris'.

4. Baiarum: on this occasion the noun is not the idiomatic, generic 'baths' (on which see 99.1 n.), but refers to the actual Baiae, the Roman spa town par excellence, with its plethora of thermal baths (see Yegül, *Baths*, 94 f.). Baiae is often used as a standard of excellence in the bathing sphere: 'nullae sic tibi blandientur undae, / ... non Phoebi vada principesque Baiae' (Mart. 6.42.3 f.; also Stat. *Silv.* 1.5.60 f.; Aus. 16.345 f.; *Ep. Bob.* 48.1; Sid. *Carm.* 18.12; *AL* 23.1 f.).

Commentary

111 (122R)

Another. Blazing light here mingles with clear water, and sun and water are mixed to give a new daylight. In fact so much light gets down into our pools that you can see naked people blush for themselves.

This and the following epigram deal with the power sources for the heating and lighting of the baths. Busch (*Versus*, 333 f.) draws attention to the links between 110-12: 111 and 112 deal with the sun and its heat and light, and have 'lumina' in their first lines; all epigrams feature deictic pronouns (110.3 'hic'; 111.1 'hic'; 112.4 'haec'), being inscriptional in type; and they use different words for 'baths' ('balnea' in 110; 'lavacra' in 111; 'baiae' in 112), which are all qualified by 'nostra / nostrae' (see further 108 intro.). He (ibid. 336f.) also considers there to be such a close correspondence between 111-12 and a section of a letter of Sidonius written in 465 (*Ep.* 2.2.4), in which he describes a caldarium in his villa, that he uses the letter as a *terminus post quem* for dating the epigrams ('... einige Formulieren, die so eng mit den Epigrammen ubereinstimmen, das sie geradezu als eine weitere mögliche Vorlage zu betrachten sind'). This would be significant if it were demonstrable, and would tally well with a sixth-century date, but to my mind the evidence is too thin to convince.

It is notable that in 110-12 no artificial heating system is mentioned in connection with these baths, and at 112.3 f. (see notes) it is specifically stated that fire was not the source used for heating rooms, and that solar power was. There is evidence which corroborates such technology: the positioning of rooms in baths to face south-west and benefit maximally from natural light and heat is attested by e.g. Vitruvius (5.10.1; 6.4.1), Pliny (*Ep.* 1.3.1; 5.6.26) and Statius (*Silv.* 1.5.45 f.), and by archaeological remains. The use of window glass (e.g. Sen. *Ep.* 86.6; Plin. *Nat. Hist.* 36.189) and the heat-retentive properties of marble (cf. Mart. 6.42) could also have assisted in maximising solar power. And it might even have been possible for the sun to be used to heat water directly in suitable metal tanks before it went to the pools, but there is little evidence for such practice in the ancient world (though Suet. *Aug.* 82.2 refers to Augustus' being showered with water 'egelida ... vel sole multo tepefacta', and Vitr. 5.10.1 refers to bronze tanks), and it is little attested before the nineteenth century (according to K. Butti and J. Perlin, *A Golden Thread: 2500 Years of Solar Architecture and Technology*, Palo Alto 1980, 113 f.). So a question remains in the present instance: if the establishment had no artificial means of heating at all, then water, let alone rooms, could not have been effectively heated on days without sun; on the other hand, if the water was artificially heated, there would seem to be no reason why the rooms to and near which it went could not also be heated artificially, and there would be little point to the author's boast about the absence of 'subiectae flammae' (112.3). A credible explanation is that these baths were built

Commentary

around hot springs, the combination of which with maximal use of the sun would provide both the necessary hot water, and warm or steamy rooms when required. In particular, this would give added significance to the previous comparisons of the establishment with Baiae and Cumae, which are the obvious comparators for baths using natural hot springs (see 109.7 n.; 113.3 n.), and to the stress the epigrams put on the water supply (see 108 intro.). This is not to claim that all comparisons of baths to Baiae or Cumae imply the use of hot springs, but when other evidence, such as explicit reference to the absence of fire, points in the same direction, such an implication is strengthened. Furthermore, there are many examples from late Antiquity of epigrams explicitly celebrating baths built around hot springs (e.g. *Ep. Bob.* 1; 38; 58; *AP* 9.626-7; 630; 632; *AL* 264-5; with L. Robert, *Hellenica IV*, Paris 1948, 76 f., and Busch, *Versus*, 345 f.), including more instances from Vandal Africa (e.g. *AL* 345 Luxorius and *ML* 43 Courtney). Thébert, *Thermes romains*, 369 f. deals with the archaeological evidence for such spas in North Africa, of which there were many, though he comments that they have received inadequate scholarly attention; indeed, the main feature which indicates their presence is precisely the absence of a means of supplying artificial heat.

1. flammea ... lumina: the phrase refers to Allecto's eyes at Verg. *Aen.* 7.448 f.; here it is sunlight, which is stressed in this piece as a key feature, whereas in the following epigram the focus is on solar heat. For light as a prized and desirable quality of baths, cf. Mart. 6.42.8 f. 'nusquam tam nitidum vacat serenum: / lux ipsa est ibi longior, diesque / nullo tardius a loco recedit'; Stat. *Silv.* 1.5.45 f.; Plin. *Ep.* 1.3.1; Sen. *Ep.* 86.8; Sid. *Ep.* 2.2.4; with Dunbabin, *Baiarum grata voluptas*, 8 f.; Busch, *Versus*, 41 and n. 18; and Howell's note on Mart. 1.59.3. Yegül (*Baths*, 382) comments: 'The opening of large windows facing south and west was another attempt to maximise access to the sun's energy. Naturally, no small part of the incentive was the appreciation of well-lighted bathing halls and enjoyment of the view while bathing.'

perspicuis ... lymphis: for the importance of the clarity of bathing water, no doubt also a good indication of its cleanliness or otherwise, cf. Mart. 6.42.19 f. (quoted at 4 n. below), with Grewing's note.

2. novum ... diem: the same point is made by Luxorius (*AL* 194.3 f.): 'hinc radios sol ipse capit, quos huc dare possit; / altera marmoribus creditur esse dies'; and *AL* 202.2; 204.12; 205.2 (all Felix). The image here is of the light reflected from the pools (see 4n. below).

3. denique: the adverb might be temporal (i.e. 'the sun has *eventually* reached such a position and its light is so intense that ...'), or used to emphasise the conclusion to which the poet is leading from his premise of

Commentary

the efficient concatenation of light and water (i.e. '*in fact*, what happens is that ...').

succedit: the 'sub-' prefix is significant, because the reflected light appears to come up from under the water in the pools. This effect may have been achieved or enhanced by the use of mosaics of glass tesserae in the pools, which are a common feature of North African baths (see F. Sear, *Roman Wall and Vault Mosaics*, Heidelberg 1977 (= *MDAI(R)* Suppl. 23), 145 f.).

4. nudos erubuisse sibi: the reflexive pronoun 'sibi' is a pleonastic dative of disadvantage; cf. Aug. *Gen. c. Manich.* 1.1.2 (*PL* 34.174) 'de imperitia sua erubescant sibi' (with J.N. Adams, *JRS* 89.1999.125). Much the same observation on the embarrassing side effects of particularly good light in a bathing complex is made at Sid. *Ep.* 2.2.4 'intra conclave succensum solidus dies et haec abundantia lucis inclusae ut verecundos quosque compellat aliquid se plus putare quam nudos'; and a similar point is differently expressed at Mart. 6.42.19 f. 'quae tam candida, tam serena lucet / ut nullas ibi suspiceris undas / et credas vacuam nitere lygdon' (and also at Mart. 4.22). The poet's reference here to the blushes of the naked bathers is nothing to do with prudery, but simply emphasises that the light is so good and the water so clear that all bodily imperfections are unavoidably illuminated, even for their owners. Nude bathing, at least for men, was always the norm (see Nielsen, *Thermae*, 140 f.; Busch, *Versus*, 463 f.).

112 (123R)

Another. Titan pours his light into our baths, and the splendid room keeps the sunlight shut inside. Let the baths of others grow hot with flames underneath; these baths will be able to be made steamy by your flames, Phoebus.

This epigram forms a pair with that preceding, and its connections with that piece and others are discussed in the intro. to 111, as also are the questions it raises about the ways in which the water and rooms of the baths were heated.

1. Titan: a variant for 'Phoebus' (line 4). For Titan as the sun cf. Verg. *Aen.* 4.119; Ovid *Met.* 10.79; and Sen. *Herc. Oet.* 722: he is so called because he is the son of the Titan Hyperion (Hes. *Theog.* 371 f.; Apollod. 1.2.2; with West's note on Hes. *Theog.* 134).

bais: generic for 'baths' (see 99.1 n.).

2. cella: the noun is often used of individual rooms in a bathing complex: e.g. a frigidarium (Plin. *Ep.* 2.17.11), a *cella unctuaria* (*CIL* 8.4645), and a *cella solearis* (*SHA* Carac. 9.4).

Commentary

3. subiectis ... flammis: an allusion to the furnace and hypocaust system of heating which these baths specifically do not have (see 111 intro.).

4. haec reddi poterunt (A (*sed* -uerunt); haec radiis poterunt (Oudendorp); haec radio poterunt (Petschenig); accendi poterunt (Baehrens); incendi poterunt (Burman)), | Phoebe, vapora tuis (Mariotti; foebi, vapore suo (A); Phoebe, vapore tuo (Heinsius; Burman; Baehrens); Phoebe, tepere (*vel* calere) tuis (Oudendorp); sole tepere tuo (Petschenig); sole vapora suo (Riese); calda vapore tuo (Sedlmeyer)): this is a *locus conclamatus* but not *desperatus*, at least as far as its general import is concerned. It is clear enough from what has preceded that it must mean that since the relevant rooms of the baths are not artificially heated but are hot, the heat is produced by the sun's power alone. How it says what it means is another matter.

S. Mariotti's discussion (at *BPEC* 7.1959.56 f. (= *Scritti di filologia classica*, Rome 2001, 274 f.)) of previous conjectures and his own is excellent, and his solution, accepted by SB, is unlikely to be bettered. In brief, he accepts necessary metrical emendations to A's text ('poterunt' for 'potuerunt'; and 'Phoebe' for 'Phoebi', a vocative which in turn necessitates emendation of 'suo'). What is then amiss is that 'haec' lacks an attribute after 'reddi'; Petschenig (*ZOeG* 28.1877.484) thought that 'calda' might be supplied from the preceding 'caleant' in line 3, but that is harsh and improbable. The idea of 'vapor' which A contains is right for the context, so conjectures such as Oudendorp's and Petschenig's, which involve its complete removal, can be discounted; and Burman, Baehrens and Sedlmeyer (*WS* 2.1880.150 f.) similarly stray a long way from the received text. But Riese's suggestion of adjectival 'vapora' for substantival 'vapore' in A gives 'haec reddi' exactly the required attribute (though his further alteration of 'Phoebi ... suo' to 'sole ... suo' is again not close to the paradosis and would involve a corruption difficult to explain palaeographically). Mariotti therefore suggests retention of 'Phoebe' (for the metrically impossible 'Phoebi'), acceptance of Riese's 'vapora' (for 'vapore'), and emendation of 'suo' to 'tuis (sc. flammis)'; it is only the third of these conjectures which represents a radical departure from the paradosis, and 'suo' would have been a natural scribal change after 'vapore' had replaced 'vapora'.

For the adjectival form *vaporus* (rather than *vaporosus* or *vaporifer*) cf. e.g. Nemes. *Ecl.* 4.63 'ter ture vaporo'; and Prud. *Peristeph.* 6.115 'hos cum defugeret vaporus ardor' (and cf. the analogies of *odorifer / odorus; soporifer / soporus*). 'vapora' here would suggest steam (cf. 'tepidus ... vapor' at 164.2, another bathing context; and 'cohaeret hypocauston et, si dies nubilus, immisso vapore solis vicem supplet' at Plin. *Ep.* 5.6.25); steam could be produced in a solar-powered environment by the evaporation of water on marble or stone in the enclosed, windowed space indicated by line 2, and it would be a good sign of the efficiency of solar power. If the baths

Commentary

were built around hot springs (as suggested in 111 intro.), those springs could have added to the effect; indeed, some hot springs gave off vapours which were specifically harnessed for use by bathers (see e.g. Cels. 2.17.1 on Baiae), though there is no direct claim of that in this case.

113 / 114 (124 / 125R)

On the hot rooms. It is a delight to immerse the body in different waters, and a pleasure to change pools with greater frequency; for instance, in order that the hot rooms should not breed contempt through familiarity, from here it will do you good to dip your limbs in another pool.

This final extant epigram of the cycle on baths and bathing is followed in the ms. by the superscription 'aliter' above an epigram (115) which has nothing to do with baths. It is usually assumed that this means an epigram about baths has been lost at some stage in the transmission, but it is equally plausible that the missing piece dealt with the same subject as that of 115 (see further 115 and 129-30 intros).

The focus of this epigram is on the pleasures and benefits of moving around from one kind of water to another: 'delectat' (line 1); 'libet' (line 2); 'ne ... fastidia' (line 3); and 'iuvat' (line 4). Its superscription 'De Thermis' is doubted by Busch (*Versus*, 339 f.), who would alter it to 'De Frigidario', in support of his thesis that since 108-14 form a cycle about a specific set of baths, this piece should be about a frigidarium after the heated rooms of 111-12. In my view, however, he goes too far in emending 'hinc' in line 4 to 'hic' (see note) and in alleging that the superscription has intruded from 'thermae' in line 3. However it is understood the epigram is just as much about 'thermae' as a frigidarium, and it explicitly refers to the former and not to the latter.

The theme of the bather moving around the baths from hot to cold water is, as Busch points out, known elsewhere, particularly in the following piece by Sidonius on a *piscina* (*Carm.* 19):

> Intrate algentes post balnea torrida fluctus
>   ut solidet calidam frigore lympha cutem;
> et licet hoc solo mergatis membra liquore,
>   per stagnum nostrum lumina vestra natant.

The attractions of changes in the temperature of the various waters at baths are also remarked at Plin. *Ep.* 5.6.25 f., and see notes on 164. It is likely that such is the subject of this epigram. In fact it reads well as a humorous attempt to persuade the frequenters of hot facilities to remove themselves and give others a chance; they have to be enticed by repeated assurances of pleasure and benefit.

Commentary

2. et (Meyer); ut (A) .... magis (A); maris (Meyer); vagis (Shackleton Bailey): Meyer's conjecture of 'et' for 'ut' should probably be accepted on grounds of sense, but his removal of 'magis' and substitution of 'maris' does not convince, because sea water is not in point. SB's 'vagis' is even less convincing: it is intended to denote wandering bathers (*Towards a Text*, 21), but (a) the omission of a noun is awkward to say the least, and (b), with 'mutare ... fluenta' in the same clause, a reader would naturally suppose that 'vaga' are replacing 'fluenta' (for the construction cf. Verg. *Georg.* 1.8 'Chaoniam pingui glandem mutavit arista'). M. Petschenig (*ZOeG* 28.1877.484) defended A's 'magis', construing it with 'libet', and comparing 117.2 'cur magis exoptes?'. But the word order makes it more likely that it should be taken with 'saepe': for *magis* used to form comparative adverbs cf. Plaut. *Most.* 197 'insperata accidunt magi' saepe quam quae speres'; Cic. *De Orat.* 1.52 'magis assidue'; Vict. Vit. 2.11 'magis violenter iussus est pergere' (with Wölfflin, *Schriften*, 152 f.). The sense would be elliptical ('more often than you do now'), and the tone beseeching ('wouldn't you like a change?'), an interpretation supported by the next line.

3. nam: 'nam' is one of the most frequent words in the collection (21x), and occasionally its logical connection with the context is not transparent. However, one of its uses is to introduce a specific example illustrating the truth of a more general preceding statement (note the definition 'for instance' at *OLD* nam 3(c); *KS* 2.2.116); thus here, it introduces a humorous application of the general principle that bathers like a change of water temperature, by suggesting that they should vacate the hot rooms they invariably favour and try something different. See also 140.3 n.

consuetae pariant fastidia thermae: *thermae*, like *balnea*, usually refers to a bathing complex, but must here refer only to the hot rooms of the baths (if it were understood to refer to the complex, the suggestion of the epigram would be for bathers to move from the establishment they are frequenting to another one, on the grounds that familiarity breeds contempt, which is most improbable). Similarly, in his pieces on the Thermae Alianae, Felix uses the noun to evoke the hot rooms: 'expavit subitas Vulcanus surgere thermas / et trepida flammas subdidit ipse manu' (201.11 f.; cf. 202.1). So readers and bathers are in these lines advised to move round from the hot rooms to ones with different water temperatures, which makes good sense for the context (see intro. above). Indeed, hot bathing was sometimes considered bad for the health (see 164.1 n.), so customers could reasonably be advised to temper themselves with cold water. Pliny makes a similar point: 'si natare latius aut tepidius velis, in area piscina est, in proximo puteus, ex quo possis rursus adstringi, si paeniteat teporis' (*Ep.* 5.6.25). There is also here an implication that the hot rooms were the most popular, natural enough if hot springs are

Commentary

the attraction, and that bathers needed encouragement to let others have a turn.

4. hinc (A); hic (Shackleton Bailey): 'hinc' gives perfectly good sense. The epigram has centred on the pleasures for bathers in changing from one kind of water (hot) to another and, if imagined as inscribed in the most frequented hot room, the exhortation to move elsewhere is comprehensible and amusing (for the inscriptional nature of the present cycle see 108 intro.). Furthermore, if 'hic' is read it would mean that the reader / bather has already moved to the different room, and the recommendation to do so would then be much less pertinent.

lacu: for *lacus* of a pool at baths cf. Aus. 16.342; *AL* 203.6; with Busch, *Versus*, 338 n. 145.

115 (126R)

<*On a library converted into a tavern.*> This building which was recently dedicated to the nine Muses of Apollo is now occupied by Bacchus, and he calls it his temple. For here, where all those writings of the men of old were housed, Cypris beatifically quaffs sweet wines. Premises are always frequented by related divinities; Apollo lived here, but, look, Bromius lives here now!

A superscription has fallen out either from the missing previous epigram or here: editors assume that the superscription 'Aliter' of the ms., which heads 115, belongs to a previous piece in the cycle on baths, but it is just as possible that it is correctly placed and a previous epigram on this subject has been lost (see also 129-30 intro.).

There is no reason for not taking this unusual and interesting epigram at face value. It is inscriptional or ecphrastic in nature ('hic' line 4) and, in a humorous manner, details the change in function of a building from a library to something else. What that something else was is a matter for conjecture, but Riese's supplement of the superscription in his text, 'De bibliotheca in triclinium mutata', which is adopted by SB, is implausible. From what it says, the epigram is best interpreted as describing a former public (rather than private) library dedicated to learning, which has since been turned into a tavern or tavern with brothel attached, and I have altered the supplement accordingly: this is considered further in the notes below.

A series of epigrams by Palladas (*AP* 9.180-83) about a temple of Tyche which was converted into a tavern is curiously close in subject matter. Here is *AP* 9.183:

Καὶ σὺ Τύχη λοιπὸν μεταβαλλομένη καταπαίζου
μηδὲ τύχης τῆς σῆς ὕστατα φεισαμένη·

Commentary

ἢ πρὶν νηὸν ἔχουσα, καπηλεύεις μετὰ γῆρας,
θερμοδότις μερόπων νῦν ἀναφαινομένη.
νῦν ὁσίως στένε καὶ σὺ τεὸν πάθος, ἄστατε δαῖμον,
τὴν σήν, ὡς μερόπων, νῦν μετάγουσα τύχην.

('And of thee too, Fortune, they make mockery now thou art changed, and at the end thou hast not even spared thy own fortune. Thou who hadst once a temple, keepest a tavern in thy old age, and we see thee now serving hot drinks to mortals. Justly bewail thine own mischance, fickle goddess, now that thou reversest thine own fortune like that of mortals' (text and translation from Loeb)). The similarity may extend beyond the subject matter, because the epigrams by Palladas work best if the name of the person behind the bar at the tavern is named Tyche, like the goddess who was the previous occupant. In our epigram too there is humour with names: SB observes (app. crit.) that Cypris in line 4 is *pro feminae nomine habendum*', because the goddess herself would not be drinking sweet wine in a tavern; and a good case can also be made for Bacchus and Bromius in lines 2 and 6 being sobriquets of the tavern-keeper (see notes ad locc.). It makes an amusing scenario that two all-too-human 'divinities' have opened a tavern in what was once a library dedicated to Apollo and the Muses.

The setting of the epigram, a converted library, would accord perfectly well with a late antique North African origin. In the pre-Vandalic period Apuleius mentions a library at Carthage (*Flor.* 18.8, with Hunink's note), and he refers to 'bibliothecae publicae' in which books on magic could be consulted (*Apol.* 91). In Timgad one Marcus Julius Quintianus Flavius Rogatianus gave his home town 400,000 HS to fund a library, in which he was buried; and others are known (see R. Cagnat, 'Les Bibliothèques municipales dans l'empire romain', *Mémoires de l'institut national de France, Académie des inscriptions et belles-lettres* 38.1909.1 f., the article which also contains the first publication of the Timgad inscription; L. Casson, *Libraries in the Ancient World*, New Haven and London 2001, esp. 109 f. (which also deals with the library at Timgad, one of very few which have been excavated and of which the plan is known); and H. Blanck, *Das Buch in der Antike*, Munich 1992, 168 f.).

1. Phoebi ... Camenis: these are the real Apollo and his Muses (cf. his title Apollo Musagetes), appropriately suggesting the scholarly and decorous world of libraries, and a humorous foil to the 'deities' who have replaced them. The cultured Apollo has obvious connections with libraries; thus Augustus built a library adjoining the Temple of Apollo on the Palatine (Suet. *Aug.* 29.3).

nuper dicata (A); nuperque dicata (Heinsius); nuper devota (Sedlmeyer); nuper dictata (Baehrens); nuper dignata (Courtney): the text has been emended by editors here for prosodical reasons (for Sedlmeyer see *WS* 2.1880.151, for Courtney see *CR* 31.1981.40 (who,

Commentary

however, is not convinced emendation is necessary)): the long quantity of the first syllable of 'dicata' is irregular. Heinsius' conjecture, which is in full 'Phoebo tecta novem nuperque dicata Camenis' ('Phoebo' being a correction by a later hand in A), is largely accepted by SB ('tecta novem Phoebo nuper<que> dicata Camenis'), who comments (*Towards a Text*, 21): 'The standard of versification in the group to which this epigram belongs warrants replacement of *dicata*'. But it does not, because exactly the same irregular quantity appears at 106.9 (see note ad loc.), where SB accepts it; and there are plenty of other metrical and prosodical irregularities in the collection (see p. 23 f.).

2. Bacchus: whilst the name could simply denote the god in order to indicate the change of function of the building, it is much more pointed if it refers to the tavern-keeper or owner, either as his given name, or more likely as a working *nom de guerre* (and see also Bromius at 6 n. below). This suggestion is supported by the facts that one of the few named persons probably connected with the catering trade is the 'Capella Bacchis' inscribed on the wall of an inn at Pompeii (*CIL* 4.8238, with T. Kleberg, *Hôtels, restaurants et cabarets dans l'antiquité romaine*, Uppsala etc., 1957, 88 f.), and that the divinely entitled Cypris of line 4 is undoubtedly a person (see note; for some other late evidence for similar nicknames cf. R.W. Mathisen, 'Phoebus, Orpheus and Dionysus, Nicknames and the Literary Circle of Sidonius', in *Studies in the History, Literature and Society of Late Antiquity*, Amsterdam 1991, 29 f.). Moreover Bacchus is itself an attested personal name: there are three examples from the mid-sixth century at *PLRE* 3.162 f.; there is a Bromius who had a son named Bacchus at *CIL* 8.19540; there is a fourth-century saint who bears the name and who is usually paired with St. Sergius; and there are other instances at *TLL* 2.1666.38 f.

templa (Shackleton Bailey); tecta (A): SB's conjecture seems excellent (though Courtney considers it 'ruinous' at *CR* 31.1981.40). It enhances the humour of the tavern-keeper named Bacchus when he refers to his emporium as a 'temple'; 'templa' can refer hyperbolically to buildings which are not temples (cf. esp. Lucr. 2.28 'nec citharae reboant laqueata aurataque templa', where 'tecta' is actually a variant in a citation by Macrobius (*Sat.* 6.4.21): see Fowler's note); 'tecta ... templa ...' reinforces the change in function of the building (and the two nouns are a frequent alliterative pairing: see Wölfflin, *Schriften*, 276); and the neutral 'sedes' of line 5, which could refer to either a religious or another building, picks up 'tecta / templa' well. It would also have been easy for a duplicated 'tecta' to have replaced 'templa' in the ms.

3-4. ubi ... hic: see 99.1 n.; this formula keys the change in use of the building.

Commentary

4. laete (Riese); laeta (A): although the final short vowel of A's 'laeta' immediately preceding the main caesura would not of itself be reason for emendation (particularly since the other two pentameters of this epigram display the phenomenon, and for such lengthening generally in the collection see p. 24), it is immediately and awkwardly followed by the similar terminations of 'dulcia vina'. On the other hand, 'laeta' is often used to describe a goddess, especially Venus, on a visit to mankind (see Grewing on Mart. 6.21.2), and so would be very apposite for the 'divine' Cypris here. But 'laete' can make the same point, and surely the poet would have used the adverb to avoid any ambiguity; Riese's conjecture should therefore be accepted. At the beginning of this line SB prints 'his' rather than A's 'hic' in his text, which appears to be a simple error.

Cypris: SB rightly says (app. crit.) that this must here be a woman's name, not a reference to the goddess (and it is frequently so attested: see *TLL* Onom. C. 800.79 f.); the short quantity of the first syllable is less frequent than long, and reappears in this collection at 118.3 and 152.2. So who is Cypris? She might be a barmaid, but then one would expect her to be serving wine rather than drinking it as she does. The obvious explanation is that she provides what her name suggests, sex (as Bacchus / Bromius provides what his name suggests, drink (see 2 n. above)); see also Cypris at 118.3, with note, and, for the common association of Bacchus and Venus (or drink and sex), see Nisbet-Rudd on Hor. *Carm*. 3.18.6-7; 3.21.21. For evidence of inns and hotels also offering sexual services cf. Ulp. *Dig*. 23.2.43.9 'si qua cauponam exercens in ea corpora quaestuaria habeat (ut multae adsolent sub praetextu instrumenti cauponii prostitutas mulieres habere)', with further references at Kleberg, op. cit. 2 n. above, 89 f.; Stumpp, *Prostitution*, 194 f.; McGinn, *Prostitution*, 15 f.

5. cognato ... lustrantur numine: the implication of this statement, as elaborated in the following line, would appear to be that temples are inhabited by related gods, and that if a temple is rededicated the rededication is to a relative. Thus Apollo and Bacchus have the same father, Jupiter, and are thereby 'cognata numina'. But the point is humorous: since Apollo (the god) used to inhabit these premises, and they are now run by Bacchus (the tavern-keeper), it proves that this is a family seat. For similarly flippant reasoning cf. Ovid *Fast*. 3.425 f. 'ortus ab Aenea tangit cognata sacerdos / numina: cognatum, Vesta, tuere caput!' (where Vesta is urged to protect Augustus, a *cognatum numen* in that he was descended from Venus through Aeneas, Venus being Saturn's granddaughter, whilst Saturn was also Vesta's brother).

lustrantur: the meaning of the verb here is simply 'move round or about / frequent', with Bacchus now moving round the building as Apollo used to (*OLD* lustro 2), though its religious origins in purification rites have an apposite tone in the context of this 'temple'. There might however be a further overtone in that 'lustra' can denote inns and brothels (cf. Non.

Commentary

p. 333.9 M. 'lustra etiam lupanaria dicuntur'; Porph. ap. Hor. *Sat.* 1.6.68 'lustra non ferarum cubilia tantum, sed et popinae dicuntur'), 'lustrantur' thereby hinting at the current use of the place.

6. Bromius: this is the same person as the Bacchus of line 2, the tavern-keeper, who now appropriates another of the god's names; and like Bacchus, Bromius is known as a personal name for humans (e.g. Juv. 6.378; *CIL* 8.19540 (cited at 2 n. above); with *TLL* 2.2204.30 f.).

116 (127R)

On a man who pimps for his own wife. You wretched Greek, skilled in your customary art of pandering you began to act as your wife's pimp, and had been accustomed to fling out of his home anyone into whom your wife had happened to get her claws by her allures. But one clever fellow scorned the nets you had stretched out for him, †and himself determined to stay in your house†. For once let in †he won over your wife† and drove you wretched from your home. You are all that is needed to prove true the jocund poet's words: "While you were cutting the goat's throat you were yourself made a gelding." '

This skoptic piece is on the well-worn subject of the man who prostitutes his own wife, the *leno maritus* (on whom see H. Herter, *JbAC* 3.1960.75 n. 96; McKeown's note on Ovid *Am.* 2.19.57-8; Mayor's note on Juv. 1.55 with addendum; and Stumpp, *Prostitution*, 197 f.). There are serious textual problems, particularly around lines 6-7, which make proper comprehension difficult, but the mise-en-scène would appear to be that the husband and wife entrap clients for financial gain, resulting in their total ruin; the twist in the tail is that the biter is bit, because a canny client turns the tables on the husband and throws him out of his home (presumably usurping his bed and trade). Precisely how he achieves this is not clear because the reason is hidden by the defective text, but reasonable hypotheses can be suggested (see 6 and 7 nn.).

Luxorius also writes about a *leno maritus* at *AL* 317, and about *lenones* at 297 and 303.

1. Graecule (W); gregule (A); grecula (B): there is no reason to doubt that 'Graecule' is correct. SB (app. crit.) understands it as a cognomen, but it is not so attested elsewhere although the feminine 'Graecula' is (Kajanto, *Cognomina*, 204). However, it is in any case simply the contemptuous diminutive of *Graecus*, found at e.g. Juv. 3.78 and frequently (see esp. B. Isaac, *The Invention of Racism in Classical Antiquity*, Princeton etc. 2004, 390 f.). A xenophobic slant is appropriate for the context (whether or not its allegation true) and also gives bite to the following phrase 'consueta arte' ('just like the Greeks').

Commentary

lenandi: the verb *lenare*, a derivative of the noun *leno*, is rare, and is attested only in the *AL* (also at 117.9 and 297.9) and schol. Juv. 6.233.

2. adductor: the noun occurs only here in the sense of *leno* (*TLL* 1.603.35 f. compares Greek προαγωγός) and only once elsewhere, Iren. *Contra Haer.* 1.13.6 'te viae duce at adductore utentes' (where *TLL* loc. cit. compares Greek προαγωγεύς). But cf. Ter. *Ad.* 965 'scortum adducere'; *Haut.* 1041 f. 'adducere ante oculos – pudet / dicere hac praesente verbum turpe (i.e. 'scortum')'; Plaut. *Merc.* 924; 'adducta virgine' at 117.4; and 'te duce' at 180.8 (see note). *Adducere* is also used of e.g. putting a mare to the stallion (Varro *Res Rust.* 2.7.9).

3. procax: indicating sexual allure and provocation, as at e.g. Aus. 13.107.1 'procaces Naides'; *SHA* Maximin. 27.1 'ipse autem pulchritudinis fuit tantae ut passim amatus sit a procacioribus feminis, nonnullae etiam optaverint de eo concipere'; cf. Fest. 290.24 f. Lindsay 'est ... procare poscere ... unde etiam meretrices procaces'.

penitus conroserat: the verb is used literally of amatory biting at *AL* 428.5 'felix si qua tuum conrodit femina collum', and of the corrosive effects of rust at Eug. Tol. *Hex.* 380 'rubigo latens quae viscera ferri conrodat'. The sense here is metaphorical, and is echoed in the hunting imagery of line 5: the wife sinks her teeth into the pair's victims like a vampire, and they are so ensnared by her that there is no escape until they are bled dry. For the intensifying effect of 'penitus' see 106.15 n.

4. consueras: this picks up 'consueta' in line 1; the alliteration on 'con-' in the first four lines is marked, and suggests the mechanically run racket by which a procession of clients has been bled dry: 'consueta ... coniugis ... conroserat ... consueras'.

propria praecipitare domo: this gives rise to an ambiguity, in that 'propria' might key either the client's (= *sua*) or the *leno*'s (= *tua*) house. In both cases the reader would have to supply some of the scenario for himself, though the context of an entrapment racket (see intro. and 5 n.) necessitates the implication being the ruin of the client. This is well achieved if the *leno* boots the client out of the client's own home, since it is easy to deduce that he has been made homeless because he has had to give all his property, even his home, to the *leno* and his wife; it also provides an effective balance to line 8, when a client turns the tables and ejects the *leno* from the *leno*'s home (note its emphatic opening 'teque tuis'). It is not as convincingly achieved if the *leno* ejects the client from the *leno*'s house, because the implication of that would only be that the *leno* had got rid of a client, for which there could be many explanations other than the client's ruin. I stress this point because it also has relevance to the text of line 6 (see note). For *praecipitare* with bare ablative, cf. Ovid *Fast.* 5.634 'pontibus infirmos praecipitasse senes'.

Commentary

5. praetensa ... retia: the hunting metaphor implies that the objective of the *leno* and his wife is relieving clients of money and property (for 'praetensa retia' cf. Col. 8.9.3 'praetentis retibus, quibus prohibeantur volare (sc. aves)'; Plin. *Nat. Hist.* 9.29 etc.). The method of the pair presumably involves entrapment: adulterers caught in flagrante would be punishable by law, so threat of exposure would afford opportunity for blackmail and for leaving the wife's lovers destitute. Apuleius provides a similar instance in his *Apologia* (75), where, inter alia, he accuses his prosecutor Herennius Rufus of prostituting his wife and blackmailing her clients: 'hic iam illa inter virum et uxorem nota collusio: qui amplam stipem mulieri detulerunt, nemo eos observat, suo arbitratu discendunt; qui inaniores venere, signo dato pro adulteris deprehenduntur, et quasi ad discendum venerint, non prius abeunt quam aliquid scripserint'. See further T.A.J. McGinn, *Prostitution, Sexuality and the Law in the Roman World*, Oxford 1998, 177 f.; 182 f.

6. †quurverastatuens horemaneredomo† (A); curvarastuens hac remanere domo (B); cur verastuens hac remanere domo (W); conversa statuens sorte manere domo (Burman): there is clearly severe corruption in the mss here, which is made worse in the following line, where the second hemistich is a duplication of that of line 5. Burman (1759, 611), followed by Meyer, omits lines 6 and 7 from his text altogether, but gives suggestions for their restoration in his notes. Deletion is a remedy worth consideration, on the grounds, for example, that the lines might have intruded from marginal glosses, but an explanation of how the tables were turned on the *leno* is desirable, and 'nam' in line 7 offers hope that there was one.

E. Courtney (*C&M* 40.1989.204) agrees with SB's comment (app. crit.) that Burman's emendation of line 6 is incorrect, '*neglecta vel perversa sententia*', and suggests by way of illustration 'in vestra statuens ipse manere domo'. Burman's conjecture should not however be dismissed out of hand, because it is as close as possible to the mss texts, and because it would make tolerable sense if 'propria' in line 4 is to be understood in the sense 'tua'. Since, however, 'propria' there should be understood in the sense 'sua' (see note), I have athetised the whole line as being beyond repair, and have translated Courtney's supplement by way of example.

7. †derisit retia quidam† (codd.): the repetition of the end of line 5 is untenable. Preceding 'nam semel admissus' ought to be the prelude to an explanation of how the client turned the tables, so the missing words should carry the implication of 'he won over your wife' or 'he found a way to blackmail you' (preferable to Riese's illustration 'tenuit mox omnia felix' and Burman's 'tenuit bona, credita servans', in that those supplements essentially repeat what will be said in line 8).

Commentary

9. iucundi ... poetae: this is Martial, and the epithet is appropriate for the most famous Latin epigrammatist because his field is *ioci, lusus* and the like (see 78.1 n.). Although *iucundus* is not etymologically connected with *iocus* (it derives from *iuvare*: Cic. *Fin.* 2.14), popular etymology made this obvious connection, as is evidenced by the frequent spelling *iocundus* (cf. Isid. *Or.* 10.125; *TLL* 7.2.592.4 f.).

10. 'dum iugulas hircum, factus es ipse caper': this is a verbatim quotation of Mart. 3.24.14, the concluding line of an epigram which tells the story of a priest sacrificing a goat and enlisting the help of a local rustic to assist in castrating it before death; unfortunately while performing the sacrifice the priest revealed his large hirnea which the local hacked off, according to what he believed to be ritually appropriate; the thereby castrated priest was changed from a 'Tuscus' to a 'Gallus' and became a 'caper' himself. The quotation here is apposite in that the *leno*'s relationship to his victims has been similar to that between the priest and the animals he sacrifices, and in that *caper* in both cases is applied to the castrated protagonist, literally in Martial, metaphorically here (i.e. the *leno* has been deprived of wife, trade and home by his client). It is an interesting point whether the *AL* poet and his readers were aware of or concerned about the context of the quotation, or whether it had become proverbial for 'the biter bit'. For the practice of concluding an epigram with a quotation from another author see my note on Aus. *Epig.* 102.6, where Ausonius quotes verbatim the latter part of Mart. 6.11.10, which is also a concluding line.

The meaning of 'caper' in the quoted line of Martial and here must be 'gelding', though the noun does not usually connote castration of the animal. There is however an interesting passage in Gellius (9.9.9 f.), where he compliments Vergil's translation (at *Ecl.* 9.23 f.) of Theoc. *Id.* 3.3 f., though he excludes one thing from the compliment: 'nisi quod "caprum" dixit, quem Theocritus ἐνόρχαν appellavit – auctore enim M. Varrone is demum Latine "caper" dicitur qui excastratus est'. The explanation may be that 'gelding' was an ancient meaning of the Latin noun which survived in the language of sacrifice.

117 (128R)

On a pimp of high military rank. Why you should sooner opt for a soldier's life and the garb of a black cloak, tell me pimp. Was your strong-room only growing with small profits when your purse was heavy after you had pimped girls? Do you not know that a few people filch the provisions of the rank and file for themselves, which is why the wretched soldier, the fiscus impoverished, goes lacking? Steer clear of avoidable toil by any ruse you can. Why should you be so enthusiastic, pimp, to live by busting a gut? For if you revert to pimping beautiful girls and cheap sex makes you your profit, no longer will you be a rank and file soldier, but, with enormous piles of cash, you will shortly be Count of the Two Militias.

The epigram about the *leno maritus* is followed by one about a different type of *leno*. He is contemplating giving up his trade to join the army (or, more likely, he has already made the move: cf 'redeas' in line 9) and the epigram explores whether his career change is financially profitable, the conclusion being that it is a mistake. The climax of the piece is a joke about a military title of the highest rank which is set up by plenty of circumstantial detail of army life and its disadvantages; to become rich and powerful it is better to be a pimp than a soldier, and better still to be a pimp for the army (see 12 n; superscr. n.).

See also 116 intro., and for a discussion of prostitution and the military see Stumpp, *Prostitution*, 186 f.

superscr.: Ad lenonem comitiacum (A (*ex* comitianum)): both forms *comitiacus* and *comitianus* are attested designations of officials, and both are late and relate to the Western empire. 'comitiacus' is the more likely to be correct here, because it is an essentially military title. It is first attested at *CIL* 5.7530 (AD 432) 'Disiderius comitiacos', and is frequent in Cassiodorus' *Variae*, which relate to the first part of the sixth century (e.g. 6.13 superscr. 'formula magistri scrinii quae danda est comitiaco, quando permilitat'; 7.31.2 'si quos etiam comitiacorum ad comitatum iudicaveris esse dirigendos'). As a title it probably derives from the *comes et magister militum*, under whom the *comitiacus* would have served (though the rank is in itself high); the duties included financial ones (Cass. *Var.* 5.6; 8.27), which is relevant here. See further *TLL* 3.1797.80 f.; *RE* 4.715 f.; T. Mommsen, *Neues Archiv der Gesellschaft für ältere deutsche Geschichtskunde*, 14.1888.469 f.

SB (app. crit.) remarks that this superscription is '*ex ultimo versu expressum ceteris parum intellectis*'; it clearly does link with 'militiae utriusque comes' in line 12, which is a humorous appellation (see note). But there is no reason why the title 'leno comitiacus' in this superscription is not similarly humorous, not an official appellation of course, but indicative of the kind of career to which this man should aspire in order to achieve wealth and power.

1. nigri tegmina panni: given the context of the *leno*'s choice of a military career being criticised by the poet and the suggestion that he is a mere 'miles humilis' (line 11), the generally pejorative overtones of 'pannus' ('rag, scrap of cloth, poor clothes') ring true. But a precise reference is not easy to establish, since both 'pannus' and 'tegmen' are imprecise: 'tegmina panni' could, for example, be the covering of a canvas tent, the covering of a ragged cloak or tunic, or even the covering of a bandage (for *pannus* in this latter sense, cf. Cels. 3.21.14; 8.10.1E; Scrib. Larg.

131; Pelag. *Mul.* 213), and it is also possible that the phrase is military parlance of a specific place and time. Since however it is paired with the generalised 'militiae cultus', it seems likely that the *pannus* is something generically applicable to soldiers. A cloak or tunic would be applicable to all soldiers all the time and is therefore preferable to a tent, which would only be applicable to soldiers not housed in barracks but on campaign or manoeuvres (see for such tents R.W. Davies, *Latomus* 27.1968.75 f.). The significance of 'nigri' is also questionable: it might be that the soldiers of whom the protagonist is one had an emblematic black part of their uniform (N. Fuentes in *Roman Military Equipment, The Accoutrements of War*, ed. M. Dawson, Oxford 1987, 41 f.; esp. 51 f., from admittedly scanty evidence, cites Strabo (3.3.7) in evidencing auxiliaries from some Northern Spanish tribes who wore black, though white (surprisingly) is the commonest colour for military apparel where any evidence is available), or it might be that the adjective simply describes grime and filth (cf. 'pulvere Troico / nigrum Merionen' at Hor. *Carm.* 1.6.14 f.). Because the view of military life here propounded is negative, the latter sense seems the more likely (Corippus (*Joh.* 2.134 f.) describes the cloaks of soldiers in unflattering terms which evoke a similar image: 'horrida substrictis dependens stragula membris / ex umeris demissa iacet').

3. cellula: this is a repository for money (as *TLL* 3.761.41), probably envisaged as a strong-room rather than a chest: cf. Varro *Ling. Lat.* 5.182 '(sc. asses) non in arca ponebant, sed in aliqua cella stipabant'; Paul. *Dig.* 1.15.3.2 'cum vel cella effringitur vel armarium vel arca', in both of which quotations 'cella' is distinguished from 'arca', both being used for the safekeeping of money.

4. cum (A); nec (Baehrens); non (Riese): A's reading here makes good sense, since the clause suggests that wealth should accumulate when the pimp's 'saccus' is heavy from each act of pimping. 'cum' is preferable to both Baehrens' and Riese's conjectures, which do not so clearly imply that the trade of *leno* was a profitable one, though obviously not as profitable as its practitioner had hoped, since his 'cellula' has not filled up quickly enough. It is also a good argument for the poet to entice the *leno* back to his old trade by emphasising to him that he actually did make a good living out of it.

adducta virgine: for *adducere* used of the act of pimping, cf. 'adductor' at 116.2. The singular 'virgine' does not mean that the pimp had only one girl; either the clause as a whole implies that each act of pimping provided an addition to his wealth, or 'virgine' could be a collective singular (for which see Löfstedt, *Syntactica*, 1.12 f.). Neither does it mean the pimp's girls were virgins (though he might have advertised them as such); *virgo* can in any case be used oxymoronically of e.g. a *nupta* (Hor. *Carm.* 2.8.23) or an *adultera* (Ovid *Her.* 6.133).

Commentary

5. populi pastum sibi tollere paucos: the *leno* is unaware that army provisions are siphoned off by the few, and it is implied in the following line that this thieving extended to army pay as well. 'populi pastum' must here refer to the provisions of the ordinary soldiery: *pastus* in this sense is known also from highly specific references to *pastus primipili*, the process by which a *primipilus* of one province had to convey provisions to an army in another province (e.g. *Cod. Th.* 8.4.8; *AE* 1927.45; with Jones, *LRE* 459); and for *populus* used in a military context, cf. Amm. 20.7.5 'Persarum populus omnis' (den Boeft-den Hengst-Teitler in their note gloss the noun as *militaris multitudo* and illustrate the frequency of the usage in Ammianus).

tollere: for *tollere* in the sense 'steal', cf. Cat. 12.3 'tollis lintea neglegentiorum' with *OLD* tollo 11; 'sibi' is a dative of advantage.

6. unde … fisco paupere: 'unde' is causal: the soldier is needy because the *fiscus* has felt the consequential effects of the purloining of the 'pauci'. The *fiscus* is presumably the treasury of the military quarters (e.g. *CIL* 8.12609 'adiutor tabulariorum fisci castrensis'), and 'fisco paupere' should be construed as an ablative absolute rather than as dependent on 'eget'. The point is to provide a stark contrast with the *leno*'s previous life: then he was concerned with purses and strong-boxes, now he will be lucky even to get basic essentials.

7. labores: i.e. the typical soldier's life, which it is suggested the *leno* can avoid if he combines his old and new occupations.

8. cur (Shackleton Bailey); ut (A): it is difficult to see how 'ut' can be correct because, on the most likely interpretation, the command of line 7 ('avoid hard work') would not result in the outcome of this line.

caleas: for *calere* in the sense 'vehemently desire' cf. Claud. 10.287 'calet obvius ire' with *TLL* 3.148.71 f.

tenso vivere … pede: this is imaginative idiom if the text is sound, though there must be some doubt over the appositeness of a naval metaphor in an army context. But SB's explanation (*Towards a Text*, 21) that it is the equivalent of the Greek πάντα κάλων ἐκτείνων gives it a convincing meaning (the Greek phrase is a metaphor from sailing and means literally 'letting out to the full every sheet (or brailing-rope)' and metaphorically 'to make every effort' (see Eur. *Med.* 278 with Page's note); the nautical Latin phrase 'plenis velis' has the same metaphorical meaning (cf. Cic. *De Domo* 24; Petr. 45.10; with Otto velum 2)). For *pes* in the requisite nautical sense cf. esp. Lucan 8.185 f. 'sed quo vela dari, quo nunc pede carbasa tendi / nostra iubes?' (note also 'tendi'); Sen. *Med.* 321 f. 'prolato / pede transversos captare notos'; with *OLD* pes 12(b). 'tenso pede' thus literally means 'with the sheets / brailing-ropes stretched tight (through the impact of wind on the sails)', and connotes a life of hard and unrewarding toil.

Commentary

9. redeas lenare: 'redeas' strongly hints that the *leno* has already changed trade and is in the army; he is now advised to revert to pimping. For the rare verb *lenare* see 116.1 n.; for the infinitive after 'redeas' compare the similar infinitive of purpose after *ire* and other verbs of motion (e.g. Mart. 11.1.3 'numquid (sc. tendis) Parthenium videre?', with *LHS* 2.344 f.; *KS* 2.1.680 f.).

10. cottidiana venus: the implication of the adjective is both of frequency (cf. Cic. *ad Brut.* 1.16.1 'non solum enim usitatum, sed etiam cotidianum est aliquid audire de te'; Mart. 4.37.9) and of cheapness (cf. Mart. 11.1.2 'cultus Sidone non cotidiana'), the clients being impoverished but plentiful soldiers; 'venus' is a euphemism for sexual intercourse (see 118.2 n. and 146.2 n.) and Martial's 'plebeia venus' (2.53.7) is a similar expression. 'cottidiana' has an irregularly short quantity in its second syllable (it has an irregularly short first syllable at Mart. 10.65.8 and 11.1.2); this is unparalleled elsewhere, though for what it is worth 'cottidie' is so scanned at *CE* 629.9 (barely literate in any case).

11. divite nummo: an ablative absolute like 'fisco paupere' at line 6 above; 'nummus' is here simply 'money' (as at e.g. Mart. 13.3.6 'si tibi tam rarus quam mihi nummus erit'), while 'dives' indicates a large quantity of it (as at e.g. Liv. 21.43.9 'tempus est iam opulenta vos et ditia stipendia facere'). This particular phrase occurs also at Drac. *Laud. Dei* 3.44 f. 'semper avarus inops, pauper sub divite nummo / aestuat'.

12. militiae ... utriusque comes: this title is a real one, though it is humorously adapted to the context. Gildo, son of King Nubel of Mauretania and protagonist of Claudian's *De Bello Gildonico*, is entitled 'comes et magister utriusque militiae per Africam' at *Cod. Th.* 9.7.9. He had served in the Roman army but led a revolt in 397 and was killed in battle the following year. His title indicates the bringing together of the two posts of *magister equitum* and *magister peditum* and denotes a person at the very summit of the military. Although the title was extraordinary it was not unique (cf. *Cod. Th.* 1.21.1), but the fact that Gildo was both African and exceptionally wealthy suggests he specifically might be in the poet's mind here. His fame would have survived his death, and an allusion to him would not prevent a sixth-century date for this poem. See further on Gildo and his title *PLRE* I. 395 f.; Jones, *LRE*, 175; 183; A. Cameron, *Claudian, Poetry and Propaganda at the Court of Honorius*, Oxford 1970, 93 f.; A.E.R. Boak, *HSCPh* 26.1915.73 f.

On one level therefore, this concluding couplet indicates that when he reverts to his former trade the *leno* will become as rich and powerful as a Gildo; but 'utriusque militiae' no doubt has a double meaning, one type of 'militia' being the literal soldiering of an army career, the other type being the metaphorical soldiering of 'militia amoris', and a career in pimping.

Commentary

The implication is that the man is advised to combine his trades, and become a wealthy pimp for the military.

118 (129R)

On Martius, a pathic. Of what help is your name derived from Mars' name when desire itches in your infamous anus? It would have been a better outcome if you were named Cypris, or if you were endowed by nature with limbs like Mars. But as it is you lack both, you freak of gender unknown, and, though you are not a woman, you are nevertheless unable to be a man.

This skoptic epigram on a passive homosexual focuses on the inappropriateness of his name (for similar humour with names in epigram see my intro. to Aus. *Epig.* 21). Although the text poses problems, the general outline is clear: Martius is a *cinaedus* who either should have been named Cypris, looking and behaving as he does, or should have had physical attributes better suited to his given name. As it is, he occupies the no-man's-land between male and female. Both the theme, a variation on the play of gender between masculine, feminine and neuter (for which see also 98 intro.), and the structure of the epigram, with its humorous concluding paradox (for which cf. e.g. Mart. 4.71.6; 7.75.2; 8.20.2; 11.61.14; and 11.99.8), are common. Epigrams on *cinaedi* also feature in Luxorius (*AL* 290; 331).

superscr.: De Martio (Riese; Marte (codd.)) cinaedo: I accept Riese's conjecture (Burman had suggested 'In Martium cinaedum') because the first line of the epigram, on which the title is evidently based ('Martis nomen de nomine ductum'), implies that the required name is derived from Mars rather than actually is Mars; SB (app. crit.) reasonably remarks that it would be no surprise if the superscript writer had actually written 'De Marte cinaedo', which poses a dilemma for an editor (I have given the writer the benefit of the doubt). Martius, a common enough nomen, is obviously not the only possibility for the context, but it is nicely echoed by 'Martia membra' in line 4.

1. nomen de nomine (AW; de me (B); de numine (Schenkl; Baehrens)): SB (app. crit.) dismisses Schenkl (*WS* 1.1879.62) and Baehrens as 'nihil agentes', and rightly so; for similar repetition cf. Ovid *Ars* 3.93 'quis vetet adposito lumen de lumine sumi', with Gibson's note; Mart. *Spect.* 9(7).6 'inque omni nusquam corpore corpus erat'; 7.61.2.

ductum (Burman; dictum (codd.)): (*nomen*) *ducere* is a common expression for etymological derivation, the meaning pertinent here: cf. Hor. *Sat.* 2.2.56 'Canis ex vero ductum cognomen'; Don. ap. Ter. *Eun.* 51 'naviter a navi ductum'; Quint. *Inst.* 1.5.8; 1.6.13; 1.6.28, and frequently.

Commentary

2. pruriat ... venus: of the locus of sexual desire. For *venus* in this sense cf. Verg. *Georg.* 4.516 'nulla venus, non ulli animum flexere hymenaei'; Liv. 39.43.5 'vino et venere amens'; Ovid *Am.* 2.4.39 f. 'capiet me flava puella; / est etiam in fusco grata colore venus'. *Venus* is often a euphemism for sexual intercourse (for which see Adams, *LSV* 188 f.), which is of relevance here, but it is the desire rather than the act which bests suits 'pruriat'. *Prurire* in this sense usually has a personal subject (e.g. Cat. 88.1 f. 'cum matre atque sorore / prurit'), but is found in a transferred sense also at Mart. 11.81.4 'sine effectu prurit utrique labor'.

The collocation of Venus and Mars, which here gives an effective juxtaposition, is one to which the collection as a whole is partial: it occurs also at 89; 104 and 106.

infami ... clune: the adjective is appropriate to a context of passive homosexuality: cf. Gell. 1.5 tit.; and at schol. Juv. 2.107 passive homosexuals are termed 'infames' without further qualification (which raises the possibility that 'infami' here might be construed with 'tibi' rather than with 'clune', or ἀπὸ κοινοῦ with both). *Clunis* is used with the meaning 'anus' also at Mart. 9.47.6 'in molli rigidam clune libenter habes' (and see Adams, *LSV* 115).

3. Cypridos: see intro. and superscr. n. above, with 115.4 n. (the latter also for the prosody); Cypris here is promulgated as a name suitable for a *cinaedus*, which can only be a *nom de guerre*. This appears to be the only instance in Latin where the Greek genitive formation is used; 'Cypridis' is elsewhere the norm.

si (Burman); ut (codd.); cum (Baehrens): 'sors fuerat melior ut ...' is a more awkward construction than 'sors fuerat melior si ...', though Burman's conjecture was probably intended to avoid the lengthening of the preceding syllable that 'ut' involves. The two points together tip the balance in favour of accepting the conjecture.

4. aut (Oudendorp); et (codd.); nec (Shackleton Bailey): the following line ('nunc utroque carens') shows that neither of the hypothetical situations posited in lines 3 and 4 currently applies: therefore, as things stand, the man is neither called Cypris nor is endowed with 'Martia membra' (because as a *cinaedus* he is effete). SB's 'nec' can accordingly be ruled out; mss 'et' is not tenable either, because calling someone with 'Martia membra' by the name Cypris is not an example of 'sors melior'. Therefore Oudendorp's 'aut' should be accepted, because then either an effete *cinaedus* would have been named Cypris (and not Martius), or someone with 'Martia membra' (and by implication not an effete *cinaedus*) would have been named Martius, and both would be examples of 'sors melior'.

5. ignoti fabula sexus: for *fabula* used personally of an object of gossip

Commentary

cf. Tib. 1.4.83 'parce, puer, quaeso, ne turpis fabula fiam'; Hor. *Epod.* 11.8 'heu me, per Urbem ... / fabula quanta fui', with Mankin's note.

6. femina ... vir: for the play on gender see intro. above; cf. Ovid *Am.* 2.3.1 'ei mihi, quod dominam nec vir nec femina servas', with McKeown's note.

119 (130R)

On Caballina, a prostitute. Caballina was on fire, lovable to no one, and recently she was shouting out whilst lashing around with her heels; although she rushes along, her face ruddy, and trembles all over, radiant with Parian whiteness, she nevertheless needs to be taken in hand by some hairy mules who can get females yoked to them going at the same pace.

This epigram is obscure and difficult, though its superscription baldly states that it is about a prostitute named Caballina. That it is about a human female with an equine name, and not a horse, is largely corroborated by the phrase 'amanda nulli' (line 1), the description of beauty in lines 3-4, and particularly the name itself (see 1 n.). Courtney's exposition (at *CR* 31.1981.41) is helpful: the poem targets the unfortunate habit of a woman kicking during sex, and its conclusion indicates that she should be coupled with mules able to urge on their yoke-partners whilst keeping them in step, whereas in her excitement she ignores Ovid's precept 'ad metam properate simul' (*Ars* 2.727). Although the epigram is ponderous and not completely successful, it manages to maintain an intriguing ambivalence between a spirited mare which has to be tamed, and a dangerously oversexed woman who also needs corrective treatment.

The general topic in erotic poetry of the likening of human females to mares, and particularly young girls to fillies, is of course a theme which can be traced back to the earliest Greek lyric (e.g. Alcman frag. 1.46 f.; Semonides frag. 5 West; Anacreon frag. 417 *PMG*; and for its endurance see Hor. *Carm.* 2.5 with Nisbet-Hubbard's intro.). This poem adapts the theme to an invective purpose (see 1 n. below).

The hendecasyllables in which this epigram is written afford the first variation from dactylic hexameters or elegiacs in the collection (see further p. 22 f.); they are appropriate for light verse, and are often associated with ribaldry and obscenity (cf. Quint. *Inst.* 1.8.6; Plin. *Ep.* 4.14.2 f.). They are used again at 138, which is another obscene piece involving an equine theme.

1. Caballina: to be understood as a personal name, probably a nickname (cf. Bacchus, 115.2 n.), derived from *caballus* (although it is not attested as a personal name elsewhere, other names from the same stem are

Commentary

(e.g. Caballius at *CIL* 6.32664 and Caballus at *CIL* 3.4890 and Mart. 1.41.17)). It is key to the epigram, because on it depends the humour of the ambivalence between human and horse which runs through the poem, especially in the horse-like kicking which characterises the protagonist; and it must be relevant that mares were considered to be the most highly-sexed mammals, with Aristotle specifically saying that excessively over-sexed women were known as mares (*Hist. Anim.* 572a10 f., with Watson's intro. to Hor. *Epod.* 12 (p. 385)).

The form of the name is itself significant, particularly the suffix '-ina' (I am grateful to Dr Adams for suggestions). It suits on one level as a typical female name, famous from examples such as Agrippina and Messalina, though there are many female cognomina even closer in type: thus Kajanto provides a list of names derived from mammals amongst which are evidenced, inter alia, the females Capellina, Cervina, Leonina, Tigrina and Soricina (*Cognomina*, 325 f.). The '-inus / -ina' suffix is frequent in Latin nomenclature generally, and one function is to signify various degrees of consanguinity (see M. Leumann, *Kleine Schriften*, Zürich / Stuttgart 1959, 63 f. (= 'Sache, Ort und Wort: Jakob Jud zum sechzigsten Geburtstag', *Romanica Helvetica* 20.1943.150 f.)); so here the name Caballina with the meaning (for example) 'the daughter of Caballus' would stress the woman's equine descent and nature.

But there may be additional overtones, some of which suggest the suitability of the name for a prostitute: (1) the adjective 'caballina' is used as a substantive, with ellipse of *caro*, to mean 'horse-meat': it is found in that sense at *CGL* 3.565.42 'ippia ... cavallina', and many other animal names take the '-ina' suffix to denote their meats (e.g. Plaut. *Capt.* 849 (*porcina*; *agnina*); Nep. *Ages.* 8.4 (*vitulina*); SHA *Prob.* 4.6 (*caprina*); esp. the list at *CGL* 3.316.36-66; with *LHS* 1.327 f.). Indeed, a (male) cognomen which probably reflects such a derivation is famous, namely Catilina, denoting a person who likes eating dog-meat (see M. Niedermann, *Mnemosyne* 3.1936.276 f.; Leumann, op. cit. 75). Here the resonance of the name or nickname would be rather different, suggesting a woman who actually can be termed 'horse-meat', because, as a prostitute, she can be bought, sold and used as meat (for other expressions using *caro* as a sexual term, cf. Mart. 11.102.1 f. 'non est mentitus qui te mihi dixit habere / formonsam carnem, Lydia, non faciem'; and Martial's description of himself as 'carnarius' in amatory matters at 11.100.6). Compare the Pompeiian prostitute name 'Asellina' (*CIL* 4.7863 (where the plural 'Asellinas' is used, which might suggest it is a nickname) and 7873; there is a catalogue of prostitute names at McGinn, *Prostitution*, 297 f.). Or (2), a less vituperative though given the context less likely allusion would be for '-ina' to have diminutive force, its import then being an affectionate 'my little mare'. Words of such formation and with such meaning are not common, but note e.g. the race-horse names Aquilinus and Passarinus (*CIL* 6.10053 and 10056), and the diminutive nouns *columbinus* (*Ed. Diocl.* 4.29; Cael. Aur. *Acut.* 1.94), *micina* (Sor. *Gyn.* 1.130) and *titina* (ibid. 1.131), with other examples in M. Niedermann, '-inus als Diminutivsuffix im späteren Volkslatein', in *Sprachgeschichte und Wortbedeutung: Festschrift Albert Debrunner*, Bern 1954, 329 f.

For the prosody of the name, with a short syllable beginning the line, see 138.14 n. 'subantis'.

furens: the context indicates that the reference is to sexual arousal: cf. Hor. *Carm.* 1.13.11 f. 'sive puer furens / impressit memorem dente labris notam'; Mart. 11.49(50).1 f. 'nulla est hora tibi qua non me, Phylli, furentem / despolies'. It would also suit a rampaging horse, as at e.g. Verg. *Aen.* 11.609 f. 'furentisque / exhortantur equos'; Petr. 134.12 v.12.

2. excussis ... calcibus: *excussus*, of parts of the body, signifies their use at full stretch and with full force, as at Ovid *Her.* 4.43 'excusso iaculum vibrare lacerto'; Petr. 95.4 'simulque os hominis palma excussissima pulsat'; Drac. *Satisf.* 138 '(sc. leo) unguibus excussis', with *TLL* 5.2.1312.25 f. Applied to the *calces* of a horse it would indicate the animal lashing out with its hooves, and applied to the *calces* of a human it indicates lashing out with the heels. In this context, particularly in consideration of the conclusion of the epigram, it suggests Caballina reaches a speedy and violent climax, and one unpleasurable for her clients ('amanda nulli'); it may also be of relevance that use of the *calces* can imply aggression towards the other party (see 145.8 n.).

fremebat: the verb continues the theme of uncontrollable and extreme excitement, on this occasion vocally displayed. Again, the verb suits both humans (cf. Verg. *Aen.* 9.636 f. 'Teucri clamore sequuntur / laetitiaque fremunt animosque ad sidera tollunt'; Plin. *Ep.* 4.11.5 'fremebat enim Domitianus'), and horses (cf. Verg. *Aen.* 12.82 'poscit equos gaudetque tuens ante ora frementis'; Hor. *Epod.* 9.17 'frementis verterunt bis mille equos').

3. quamvis facie micet rubenti: again the phrase could refer to human or mare. For *facies* of equine 'faces' cf. Varro *Ling. Lat.* 9.92 'equos eadem facie'; Pelag. *Mul.* 47; with *TLL* 6.1.48.84f.; and for 'red' coloration of equines cf. Varro *Res Rust.* 2.8.6 'hinnus qui appellatur, est ex equo et asina, ... plerumque rubicundior'; Plin. *Nat. Hist.* 10.180; Stat. *Theb.* 6.301. Indeed earlier Latin had specific nouns for horses of chestnut or bay colour, such as *spadix* (Verg. *Georg.* 3.82; Gell. 2.26.9) and *badius* (Varro *Sat.* 361 Cèbe), while later Latin used adjectives such as *russeus* (Pallad. 4.13.3) or *rubeus* (Ambr. *De Trin.* 27 (*PL* 17.539)): see further H. Blümner, *ALL* 6.1889.406; *TLL* 5.2.735.59 f. A mare with a 'rubens facies' would therefore be one with a chestnut or bay head, though the next line shows the overall colour of this one is skewbald since it has a white body. A woman with a 'facies rubens', in conjunction with the marble white of the following line, would be considered beautiful, red and

Commentary

white in combination being what might now be termed a 'peaches and cream' complexion (see 121.1 n.); 'quamvis' indicates that the comment is favourable and affords a reason to find her attractive.

Interpretation of the verb 'micet' is more complex. Applied to the woman it would again have a positive tone, suggesting a pleasing effect on the eye of the beholder and the glow of a radiant complexion: cf. Stat. *Silv.* 2.6.44 f. 'primoque micantes / flore genae'; Sen. *Ep.* 115.14 'dulce si quid Veneris in vultu micat'. But applied to a mare it suggests rapid physical movement (thus *OLD* mico 1(a): 'to make a sudden rapid movement or a series of movements'): cf. Verg. *Georg.* 3.84 'stare loco nescit, micat auribus et tremit artus'; Calp. Sic. 6.53 'illi ... micat acre caput'; on both occasions when Pelagonius uses the verb it suggests movements of a horse which are irregularly rapid ('auriculis micat' (404) as a symptom of madness; 'oculis ... semper micantibus' (291) as a symptom of illness). This overtone is further suggested by 'vibret' in the following line (see note). It is therefore plausible, in the context of the prostitute with equine characteristics, that 'facie micet rubenti' could suggest not only her complexion, but also her enthusiastic mobility in love-making, evidenced by her face reddening through effort. The 'quamvis' of the clause would indicate this to be a good technique in principle, but the epigram as a whole demonstrates that it is taken to excess by her habit of kicking.

4. vibret, Parium nitens colorem: cf. 121.6 'ut vibrare putes plumea membra faces', which is a description of the highly coloured wings of a bird compared to the visual effect produced when torches are waved about (the same epigram also has the verb *micare* at line 2, used of the effects of light). But while that image is striking, the one in this line is more problematic: (1) it is difficult to construe 'colorem' as the object of 'vibret'; (2) 'nitens' is virtually redundant if 'vibret' governs 'colorem' and refers to the effects of light and colour; and (3) what would be the relevance of intermittent or flashing light in any case? It is therefore attractive to understand 'vibret' as intransitive, and 'Parium colorem' as an internal accusative dependent on 'nitens', and I have repunctuated the line accordingly. As applied to a mare the image of lines 3-4 would be of the characteristic shaking of head and body which accompanies its whinnying ('fremebat' in line 2); the white colour would refer to its body rather than its head (i.e. it is a skewbald). As applied to the woman the phrase would suggest, as does 'micet', movement during sex (for *vibrare* used intransitively in a sexual context, cf. Apul. *Met.* 2.7.3, 'lumbis sensim vibrantibus'), and her white colour would complement the red of the preceding line as a sign of her beauty (see note thereon).

Parium ... colorem: for Parian marble as a yardstick of whiteness cf. Hor. *Carm.* 1.19.6 with Nisbet-Hubbard's note, and for whiteness and human beauty see 121.1 n. White was also the colour of the most prized

Commentary

horses, those ridden by kings, generals and triumphators (e.g. Plin. *Nat. Hist.* 7.110).

5. hirsutis ... mulis: the mare or woman, beautiful though she is, is to be courted by 'hirsuti muli', the reason being made explicit in the following line. But the ambivalence between mare and woman is difficult here. With *caballina* viewed as the spirited mare, the cure is for her to be linked in a yoke with hirsute mules who will get her to travel at the right pace in a team (whether this would actually have an effect I know not, but for a spirited mare to be yoked with mules could easily be seen as a degrading punishment). When Caballina is viewed as the prostitute the reader has to determine the nature of the 'hirsuti muli' who will provide a cure for her sexual problem; it seems best to understand them to be hairy, insensitive and stupid clients whose unappealing nature will oblige her to keep to a suitable pace. Hirsuteness was not considered a desirable quality in a lover (cf. Verg. *Ecl.* 8.34; Suet. *Tib.* 45).

6. pariles citare iunctas: 'iunctas' are animals yoked to the plough, carriage or whatever, the gender showing they are here female, which is necessary for the climax of the epigram and the association of them with Caballina; 'pariles' should be taken closely with 'citare', indicating that the yoked animals travel in unison at the same speed. Whilst 'citare' is used of animals in the sense of getting them to move (e.g. Sil. It. 16.423 f.'citatos / verbere quadrupedes'), it must here have an ambiguous sexual sense to maintain the ambivalence between horse and woman, with 'pariles citare iunctas' indicating a road to simultaneous orgasm (Courtney aptly compares Ovid's 'ad metam properare simul' (see intro. above); further examples are collected by Adams at *LSV* 144 f.).

120 (131R)

On the poet of the Arzyges. Scion of a slab of quarried flint, young man denser than woodland arbutus, although you are more uncouth and dim than a tree trunk, you wish to form poems with your own verses and to play with various rules of metre. But who would judge you capable of learning such skills as a more acute kind of intellect gave? Only someone chopping logs with hefty axes, hewing the solid heart of your dense sensibilities, was able to turn you into the wooden poet who fashioned the cow with its adulterous planks and who constructed the horse of Greek trickery.

The epigram attractively lampoons a bad poet, a favourite target of epigrammatic and comic writing generally (see my intro. to Mart. 11.93), and one also found in Luxorius (*AL* 311). An opening comparison of the aspiring poet to insensate wood and stone is developed into an allegation that he must actually have been hewn out of wood, and is wrapped up in

Commentary

a conclusion which divulges that even his subjects are literally wooden, Pasiphae's cow and the Trojan horse: a wooden poet writes about wooden subjects in wooden verse.

This is the only piece in the collection which is not written in dactylic hexameters, elegiacs or hendecasyllables, and it features the lesser asclepiad. There is intent in this, because it allows a direct echo of Horace, whose first ode of his first book is in this metre (see 1 n. below), and it provides the wooden poet who would like to write in different metres (line 5) with a mocking illustration of how to do it. Luxorius uses this metre in six poems (*AL* 284; 309; 311 (also about a bad poet); 318; 351; 356).

superscr.: De Arzugitano (BW; Arzucitano (A)) poeta (Burman; evete (A); fuet(a)e (BW); vate (Meyer)): there must be some doubt over both conjectures 'poeta' (which is preferred by SB) and 'vate' (preferred by Riese), though either gives good sense; but if the mss can cope with the obscure adjective 'Arzugitano', it is strange they have difficulty with such an obvious noun. It should also be noted that there is nothing in the epigram itself which explains why 'Arzugitano' appears in the superscription (though it again makes good sense), and that it is one of a few instances where a superscription in the collection gives such additional information (see further p. 18 f.).

Arzugitanus derives from the name 'Arzyges', a tribal group of people the precise location of whose territory (the Arzugis) is disputed, but probably lay around the southern margins of Byzacena (modern southern Tunisia); they would thus have lived on the fringes of the area of Roman, and later Vandal, rule and influence, but essentially within it (see A. Rushworth in Merrills, *Vandals*, 95 f.; Modéran, *Les Maures*, 364 f.). The adjective *Arzugitanus* is found only at Aurel. *Ep.* (*PL* 20.1011) and Dion. Exig. *Can. Eccl.* 52 (*PL* 67.197) apart from here, though the preface of Pelagonius' work on veterinary medicine is addressed to one Arzygius (see Adams, *Pelagonius*, 115 f.), whose name must be connected to the tribe. The point of the designation here is to show that the would-be poet is a native African, and therefore to be regarded as unromanised (unvandalised too for that matter) and hence incompetent; such localised xenophobia resurfaces later in the collection (see 172-3), so it fits in well. SB (app. crit.) compares Martial's use of 'Abderitanus' to indicate stupidity at 10.25.4 (and cf. Juv. 10.49-50 with Courtney's note), and Catullus describes the would-be poet Suffenus in terms which lampoon a similar unurbanised rusticity (22.9 f.).

1. praecisae: this suggests quarrying activity (cf. Aug. *Serm.* 336.1 (*PL* 38.1471) 'de silvis et montibus ligna et lapides praeciduntur'), and is pointed in that it will later be alleged that human hands have literally fashioned the wooden poet into what he is (lines 8 f.).

Commentary

silicis: stone affords a common simile for stupidity: cf. Plaut. *Poen*. 291 'tu es lapide silice stultior', with Otto 911; Hofmann, *LU* 88.

cautibus: *cautes* are usually cliffs or rock faces, but are here perhaps a slab of stone (since they are formed of 'praecisae silicis') as at e.g. Col. 10.66 f. 'nos abruptae tum montibus altis / Deucalioneae cautes peperere'; *cautes* also can allude to insensitivity and stupidity (cf. Verg. *Ecl.* 8.43).

edite: a clear echo of the first line of the first book of Horace's Odes 'Maecenas atavis edite regibus', a poem in the same uncommon metre. Some other similarities of vocabulary might be coincidental (e.g. 'arbuto' (line 2 / Hor. *Carm*. 1.1.21); 'docilem / indocilis' (line 6 / Hor. *Carm*. 1.1.18)), but this is not.

2. silvestri ... arbuto: the comparison is to *Arbutus unedo* (Greek κόμαρυς) the strawberry tree. For the adjective cf. Col. 7.9.6 'pomiferisque silvestribus, ut sunt ... arbutus'; Prob. ap. Verg. *Georg*. 1.148 'arbuta sunt arbusculae, quae in silvis frequenter nascuntur, quos plerique unedones vocant' (popular etymology of 'unedo' suggested the trees were so called because once you have eaten one of their tempting strawberry-like fruits you will not want another (cf. Plin. *Nat. Hist.* 15.99)). This seems to be a unique instance of this tree being used as a measure of stupidity and insensitivity, but it suits well. Its wood was known to be dense: cf. Theophr. *Hist. Plant.* 5.9.1 'ἄνθρακες μὲν οὖν ἄριστοι γίνονται τῶν πυκνοτάτων, οἷον ἀρίας, δρυὸς, κομάρου' ('the best charcoal comes from the densest woods, such as oak, holm-oak, arbutus'). It is a native of North Africa as well as of Southern Europe and 'the wood is white, hard and heavy, but brittle and with little elasticity' (J.C. Loudon, *Arboretum et Fruticetum Britannicum*, London 1838, 2.1117). Current uses of the wood are for the carving of spindles, stools and small articles of furniture, though the tree is largely grown for the decorative purposes of its strikingly reddish bark (I am grateful to Dr M. Nesbitt of the Royal Botanic Gardens, Kew and Mr N. Humphrey of the Victoria and Albert Museum for information).

durior: *durus* can suggest general stupidity (e.g. Mart. 5.56.10 'si duri puer ingeni videtur') but also literary insensitivity and ineptitude (e.g. Cic. *Att.* 14.20.3 'Atilius, poeta durissimus'; Hor. *Sat.* 1.4.8 'durus componere versus').

3. trunco: for *truncus* of an insensate lump cf. Cic. *Pis.* 19 'tamquam truncus atque stipes'; *De Nat. Deor.* 1.84 'qui potest esse in eiusmodi trunco sapientia'; Ovid *Am.* 3.7(6).15 'truncus iners iacui'; with Otto 1695. Compare also Catullus' alder (17.18 f.).

horridior: *horridus* can suggest general uncouthness (as at e.g. Juv. 6.10 'horridior glandem ructante marito'; Apul. *Socr.* 22 'horridi, indocti incultique') but, like *durus*, can also be a term of literary criticism (e.g. Liv. 2.32.8 'prisco illo dicendi et horrido modo'; Tac. *Dial.* 18. 1 'sunt enim horridi et impoliti et rudes et informes').

Commentary

4. formare ... carmina: there is more than a hint of the prosaic here, suggesting a carpenter working with wood rather than the inspiration of the poet; poetic inspiration is dealt with at lines 6 f., and see the notes below on 'lusit' (11) and 'struxit' (12).

propriis (codd.); e propriis (Heinsius): Heinsius' supplementary 'e', which is introduced to obviate lengthening of the final syllable of 'formare' before the initial mute and liquid of 'propriis', is not necessary (see 101.6 n.). 'propriis' is here used in the sense 'tuis', as elsewhere in this collection (116.4; 138.6; 180.5; 181.3; *proprius* is also used in the sense 'suus', as at 134.1; 136.1; 139.6; 144.2; 145.8; 183.5; 188.7).

5. metri variis ludere legibus: 'ludere' has no dominant implication here of the light verse of epigram (for which see 78 intro.), because the poet aspires to epic themes (lines 10-11). It rather suggests that the poet plays around with all different kinds of metre without sensitivity or competence, a carpenter rather than a poet. For *lex* of the rules of metre, cf. Ovid *Pont.* 4.12.5 'lex pedis'; Plin. *Ep.* 4.14.8 'metri lege'; Aus. 11.3.3 'lege metrorum'.

7. natura ... cordis acutior (AW; cordas ('i' *supra* 'a' *scriptum*) auctior (B); ... cordibus auctior (Oudendorp); ... cordis amantior (Klotz)): there is no need to doubt the text of AW, which is entirely apposite. The contrast is with the poet of wooden sensibility at lines 1-5, and the difference between his lack of inspiration and that of the true poet is here made explicit. *Cor* is commonly used of the seat of the intelligence and intellect (cf. Mart. 14.191.1 'ut perhibent doctorum corda virorum', and my note on Aus. *Epig.* 48.2), though here it may also embrace notions of poetic inspiration. For *acutus* as a term of literary criticism, cf. Cic. *De Orat.* 1.191 'hominem acutissimo omnium ingenio'; *Brut.* 225; Plin. *Ep.* 5.5.1, with *TLL* 1.464.78 f.

dedit: *dare* is often used of the gifts of nature to man (e.g. Cic. *Quinct.* 11 with *TLL* 5.1.1684.82 f.), but the perfect indicative reads rather awkwardly. Perhaps 'docet' or 'decet' (Reeve) is worth consideration.

8. solus ligna dolans ...: the point is that this poet is so wooden that only a (rustic) carpenter could have created him: thus 'ligna dolans' results in the 'vatem ligneum' of line 10. This and the following line are close in their imagery and wording to Cic. *Luc.* 101 'non enim est e saxo sculptus aut e robore dolatus, habet corpus habet animum, movetur mente movetur sensibus'. Martial's use of the phrase 'inutile lignum' (7.19.1), with an ambiguous reference to bad poetry, is also similar.

asceis: *asceae* / *asciae* are basic tools of forestry and carpentry, with various uses such as cutting, hollowing or planing (Isid. *Or.* 19.19.12 with *DS* 1.464 f.; *TLL* 2.762.51 f.). Here the noun 'ligna' and adjective 'fortibus' imply heavy work, which will not lead to the fashioning of a sensitive poet.

Commentary

9. eduri (Reeve); et duris (codd.); et duri (Heinsius); tam duri *aut* praeduri (Shackleton Bailey); haec duri (Håkanson): a genitive adjective seems certain, since the mss ablative 'duris' could only qualify 'fortibus asceis', which would be inapposite or otiose; but further reference to the poet's insensibility is attractive. Although mss 'et' could be retained and make sense (as Heinsius suggested; also Courtney at *CR* 31.1981.42), Reeve's suggestion 'eduri' leads better into the humorous conclusion to the line and is palaeographically convincing. Whilst *edurus* is a rarely attested adjective (only once in Tertullian and once in Ausonius apart from Vergil and Servius: *TLL* 5.2.125.47 f.), it is used by Vergil with specific reference to trees (*Georg.* 4.145 'eduramque pirum'; probably also ibid. 2.65). Its use here would be particularly effective in that it would emphasise the unexpectedness in the context of the noun which it qualifies ('pectoris': see below); and an allusion to Vergil would be typical of the poet of this collection, who knew his Vergil well (see p. 12 f.).

eduri ... robora pectoris: there is a suitably epic tone to this phrase, given the poet's subject matter which will shortly be revealed, and it would usually be understood in a metaphorical sense to illustrate obdurate courage. But here, humorously, it is to be understood partly at a more literal level, of the block of wood that is the poet, and partly at a metaphorical level, suggesting stupidity and insensitivity (cf. Hor. *Carm.* 1.3.9 'robur et aes triplex' with Nisbet-Hubbard's note; Ovid *Am.* 1.11.9 with McKeown's note; Ovid *Am.* 3.6.59); 'pectoris' is a παρὰ προσδοκίαν for 'arboris' or some type of tree.

10. vatem ... ligneum: for *ligneus* of stupid or insensitive people, cf. Sid. *Ep.* 5.7.4 'ad intellegendum saxei, ad iudicandum lignei'; Aus. *appx* A4.9.1 f. Green (of a pantomimus) 'saltavit simius idem / ligneus ut Daphne, saxeus ut Niobe'; Mart. 10.100.6.

11. qui ... lusit: SB (*Towards a Text*, 22) says '... we are to understand that it would take a more than usually expert carpenter to make such a block of wood into a poet', and Courtney (*CR* 31.1981.42) similarly considers that 'qui lusit' describes 'solus' of line 8. However, an alternative interpretation is possible and in my view preferable, namely that 'qui lusit' picks up 'vatem ligneum' from line 10 (even though the third person 'lusit' is perhaps awkward after the second person 'vatem te ... reddere ligneum'). This arguably suits the word order better; it allows 'lusit' to echo 'ludere' from line 5, since both words would refer to the same person; it introduces the additional jibe that the wooden poet has written about literally wooden subjects; and it gives better invective (to claim that some anonymous rustic and his heavy tools fashioned this poet is more vituperative than to claim that 'a more than usually expert carpenter' fashioned him, because renowned craftsmen like Daedalus or Epeos could be expected to fashion good wooden poets, as wooden poets go). On this

Commentary

interpretation 'lusit' is ambiguous: it refers both to writing (for *ludere* + acc. in this sense cf. Stat. *Silv.* 2.7.55 'ludes Hectora Thessalosque currus'; Mart. 12.94.8 'ludo levis elegos'), and to fashioning materials (cf. Stat. *Silv.* 4.6.48 f. 'nec qui polit arma deorum / Lemnius exigua potuisset ludere massa', with *TLL* 7.2.1781.48 f.); its subject is the poet with the lumberjack approach to the hacking out of wooden poetry from wooden topics.

vaccam trabibus ... adulteris: this is the wooden contraption in the form of a cow, built for Pasiphae by Daedalus, by means of which she was able to couple with the bull of which she was enamoured, and thus produced the Minotaur (see my intro. to Aus. *Epig.* 65). For the bold use of the adjective 'adulteris' transferred to the planks of wood forming the contraption which enabled adultery to be committed, cf. Horace's reference to Paris' 'adulteros cultus (or crines)' at *Carm.* 1.15.19 f.; there is also present here the idea of 'counterfeit', in that the wooden cow was no cow, but a device built to deceive (compare the similar ambiguity with 'adultera clavis' at Ovid *Ars* 3.643).

12. vel: *vel* is here used in the sense *et*, as on the only other occasion it occurs in the collection (see 132.3 n.). *LHS* (2.502) and Stotz (*Handbuch* 4.413) illustrate the frequency of this usage in late Latin; it is also found in earlier writers, as at e.g. Verg. *Aen.* 6.769 f., 'pariter pietate vel armis / egregius', where the meaning is not that Silvius Aeneas will be renowned for either his moral or military prowess, but for both; and at Claud. 26.131, 'donis invicta vel armis', where Fabricius is unconquered by bribes and arms, not by only one of them (see also Fordyce's note on Cat. 45.6 f.). Thus here the argument is that the poet has written about both Pasiphae and the Trojan horse, and his woodenness is evident from either work.

qui struxit: 'struxit' is ambiguous in the same way as 'lusit'; for *struere* applied to poetic composition, cf. Ovid *Pont.* 2.5.19 'structos inter fera proelia versus'; Hor. *Ep.* 1.3.6; with *OLD* struo 3(a). The traditional designer and builder of the wooden horse was Epeos, on whom see 166.7 n.

121 (132R)

On a red (?)cockerel. His white face glows with sunlike ruddiness, his crest is stiff with spikes, his fiery beard glisters. Wings, neck, head-feathers, breast, leg, loin, tail – they are more brightly coloured than roses of Paestum. The flaming plumage is of such a distinctively fiery colour that you might imagine the feathered limbs are waving torches.

This epigram about a red-coloured bird derives much of its effect from an anthropomorphic treatment: standard amatory themes of red blending with white and the cataloguing of admired parts of the body (especially in

Commentary

lines 1, 3 and 4) place the bird on a level with an elegiac poet's love-object. The concluding couplet is also particularly successful in describing the rippling effect of light playing on the bird's feathers.

The superscription aims to give a definition of what the object described in the epigram actually is, as is often the case; but editors necessarily emend the text of the mss, and I deal with the detail of this in the relevant note. Here it needs to be said that the first two words of the superscription in all the mss are the same ('de capone'), but the third is corrupt ('fassanatio' (A); fassanario (BVW)); emendations usually produce the same outcome, namely that the bird described is a pheasant, *Phasianus colchicus*, so called after the River Phasis on the Black Sea, which is where pheasants were thought to have originated (see Coleman's note on Stat. *Silv.* 4.6.8). This result is not certainly incorrect, and the emphasis in the poem on red coloration would in some ways accord well with a pheasant. But some points raise serious doubt: for example, pheasants do not have combs on their heads and this bird does ('crista riget radiis' line 2), and the bird of the emended superscription (basically a *capo Phasianus*) is linguistically improbable (a *capo* is a cockerel, either castrated or not, and *Phasianus* refers to a pheasant, but though these birds are both gallinaceous they belong to separate species).

This however is Columella's description of the cockerel (8.2.9): 'atque in his quoque sicut in feminis idem color (cf. 8.2.8 robii coloris) ..., sublimes, sanguineaeque nec obliquae cristae, ravidi vel nigrantes oculi: brevia et adunca rostra: maximae candidissimae aures: paleae ex rutilo albicantes, quae velut incanae barbae dependent: iubae deinde variae, vel ex auro flavae, per colla cervicesque in humeros diffusae: tum lata et musculosa pectora, lacertosaeque similes bracchiis alae ...'. His description of the comb and wattles, but particularly the emphasis on red and white coloration, are similar to this poem and to my mind, in combination with the other points already made, suggest it describes a cockerel rather than a pheasant (there is a similar description at *Geopon.* 14.16); this is assumed in the following notes. Further information can be found at e.g. S. Madge and P. McGowan, *Pheasants, Partridges and Grouse*, London 2002, 292 f. (cockerel); 322 (pheasant); Keller, *Tierwelt*, 2.131 f. (cockerel); 145 f. (pheasant); V. Hehn, *Kulturpflanzen und Haustiere*, ninth edn repr. Hildesheim 1963, 326 f.; Capponi, *Ornithologia*, 260 f. (cockerel); 408 f. (pheasant).

superscr.: De capone †fassanario† (BVW; fassanatio (A)); De gallo gallinaceo (Binet); De capone Phasiano (Burman); De capone Phasianacio (Riese): see intro. above for the basic questions which arise concerning the correctness of this superscription. *Phasianus* is used as a substantive for both male and female pheasants (see Leary on Mart. 13.72 lemma), but is also rarely an adjective (*SHA* Tac. 11.5 'fasianam avem') which it would need to be here if Burman's conjecture is correct.

Commentary

Other cognate attested forms are *fasianarius*, a ἅπαξ λεγόμενον at Paul. *Sent.* 3.6.76 (of someone who tends pheasants), and *fasianinus* at e.g. Anthim. *De Obs. Cib.* 38; Riese's 'Phasianacio' is an editorial confection to get as close as possible to the jumble exhibited in the mss. *Capo* is also an uncommon word, usually denoting a castrated cockerel or capon, as at Mart. 3.58.38, 13.63 and Pelag. *Mul.* 123, but also used of an uncastrated cockerel at Iren. *Contra Haer.* 2.12.4 ('uti ... generent sine alterius complexu quemadmodum gallinae sine caponibus') and, probably, Petr. 59.2; on no occasion, however, is it used either adjectivally or substantivally with reference to a bird of another species (*TLL* 3.354.8 f.). I conclude from this that the mss do not mask 'Phasiano' or a similar adjective, and that the bird described is not a pheasant; I have therefore obelised the adjective. Given the emphasis on the colour red throughout the piece, perhaps a colour adjective is required (e.g. by way of example only 'phoeniciato' (cf. Isid. *Or.* 12.1.49) or 'phoenicino' (cf. Dioscor. Lat. 3.163 (= *Romanische Forschungen* 10.1899.443.18) 'florem fenicinu habens'). There is however no reason to doubt 'capone', since the noun can refer to a cockerel. In my view Binet found the correct subject, if not wording, with his radical emendation 'De gallo gallinaceo', which was printed in their texts by all editors before Meyer.

1. candida ... rubore: this highly Ovidian (cf. *Her.* 21.217 'candida nec mixto sublucent ora rubore'; *Am.* 3.3.5 f. 'candida, candorem roseo suffusa rubore, / ante fuit; niveo lucet in ore rubor'; *Her.* 20.120 with Kenney's note) and anthropomorphic description is humorously applied to a bird. White suffused with red is a commonplace ascription of beauty (in addition to the Ovid passages cited, cf. Musaeus 58-9 with Kost's note; Bömer's note on Ovid *Met.* 3.423; Prop. 2.3.11 f.). Columella's description of a cockerel, quoted in the intro. above, details the bird's red crest, white ears, and wattles 'ex rutilo albicantes', which this line would admirably suit.

praefulgunt: third (rather than second) conjugation *praefulgere* is very rarely attested (*TLL* 10.2.656.3 f.), though third conjugation *fulgere* is common, and is actually attested earlier than the prevalent second conjugation form (the third at e.g. Pacuv. *Trag.* fr. 229 Ribbeck; Lucr. 5.1095; Verg. *Aen.* 6.826; the earliest instances of the second are Cic. *Arat.* 96; Cat. 66.61; see *TLL* 6.1.1507.48 f.); this variability was noted by ancient grammarians (Priscian at *Gramm. Lat.* 2.445.3, and Servius on *Aen.* 4.409). Third conjugation *effulgere* also is found at e.g. Verg. *Aen.* 8.677, and some other verbs with both second and third conjugation forms are *fervere*, *stridere* and *tergere* (see Stotz, *Handbuch*, 4.177 f.). See also 166.5 n. 'lascivans'.

2. crista riget radiis: its comb is virtually the cockerel's symbol (cf. Varro *Res Rust.* 3.9.5; Col. 8.2.2; Mart. 9.68.3, with *OLD* cristatus 1), and it is pronounced and spiky. This spikiness is presumably the quality conveyed

Commentary

by 'riget radiis', the structure being viewed as a membrane with radial supports. The text therefore seems sound though there might be some residual concern, both in that this is the only phrase in the poem which has no reference to colour, and in that 'radii' have a specific reference in ornithological terminology to spurs (particularly those of the cockerel: e.g. Plin. *Nat. Hist.* 30.96).

ignea barba micat: 'barba' refers to the bird's wattles: cf. Col. 8.2.9 'paleae ex rutilo albicantes, quae velut incanae barbae dependent'; Plin. *Nat. Hist.* 30.96. *Igneus* as a colour adjective can describe various shades of red, but here is almost scarlet (as at Lucan 10.125, and cf. André, *Couleur*, 114 f.; note also Gellius' discussion of 'red' adjectives at 2.26.2 f.).

3. alae ... cauda: the catalogue of body parts is again a standard topic in descriptions of beauty, lending further anthropomorphic tone to the poem: see e.g. *AP* 5.132.1 f. Philodemus (with Sider's note), and Ovid *Am.* 1.5.19 f. (with McKeown's note; he comments that the rhetorical rules for such an ἔκφρασις προσώπου prescribe description from the top of the body downwards (Aphthon. *Progymn.* p. 37.9 f. Rabe), though there is no attempt to adapt that to the bird here).

comae: this is the only item in the catalogue which is not readily identifiable, but since the other parts in it are feathered, the reference is clearly to the bird's head-feathers.

4. Paestanis ... rosis: roses are here used as a yardstick of redness (cf. also *roseus* with the comments of André, *Couleur*, 111). For Paestan roses cf. Mart. 4.42.10 'Paestanis rubeant aemula labra rosis'; they are also regularly mentioned for their outstanding qualities of scent (e.g. Ovid *Pont.* 2.4.28; Prop. 4.5.61; Mart. 5.37.9) and frequent flowering (Verg. *Georg.* 4.119; Mart. 12.31.3). See Grewing's note on Mart. 6.80.6 and H. Blümner, *Die Farbenbezeichnungen bei den römischen Dichtern*, Berlin 1892, 166.

5. flammea ... pinna: for the red feathers of the cockerel cf. Varro *Res Rust.* 3.9.4 f.; Col. 8.2.7; Plin. *Nat. Hist.* 10.117 (both Varro and Columella refer also to black feathers on the wings), with H. Blümner, *ALL* 6.1889.407 f.

rutilum ... colorem: *rutilus* describes a 'rouge vif' (André, *Couleur*, 85 f.) and is often used of fire (e.g. Verg. *Aen.* 8.430; Ovid *Met.* 12.294; Val. Flacc. 5.450).

distinguit (codd.; distinquit (A)); distendit ((*vel* diffundit *vel* dispergit) Shackleton Bailey): SB comments (*Towards a Text*, 22) '*flammea* and *rutilum* seem to mean the same colour; cf. Avien. *Arat.* 81 'rutilo flagrat coma flammea crine'. How can red plumage *distinguish* red colour?'. Although *distinguere* can be used in colour contexts, especially by Pliny (e.g. *Nat. Hist.* 8.69 'albis maculis rutilum colorem distinguentibus, unde appellata camelopardalis'; ibid. 10.3 'caeruleam roseis caudam pinnis

Commentary

distinguentibus'), SB does highlight a difficulty, and in the quotations from Pliny the significance of *distinguere* (one of colour contrast) is much clearer than here. All the colour emphasis of this epigram has been on red, often flame, and it will climax in the concluding line with the image of the bird's feathers as a flaming torch. If 'distinguit' is correct here, it has to mean something like 'its fiery feathers make its flaming coloration so distinctive that you would think ...'; but in the context that seems possible (compare e.g. Sen. *Contr.* exc. 5.8 'vult aliquo imperio, aliqua potestate distingui'; Sil. It. 1.78 'ut fari primamque datum distinguere lingua / Hannibali vocem' (of Hannibal's learning to utter coherent sound), and esp. Apul. *Flor.* 10 '(sc. Amor) ubique distinxit amnium fluores, pratorum virores'), and I have retained the ms. reading.

6. vibrare: cf. 'vibret' 119.4 n.; the verb is here strikingly used to suggest that the movement of the bird's red feathers creates an effect of colour like the flickering of flames when lit torches are waved around.

122 (133R)

On Matian apples. It is these which were able to slow down speedy girls by their value, it is these which had to be given to Venus when the Phrygian was judge: for these apples so glister with natural colour that they outdo the actual metal with their gold.

This is the first of a trio of epigrams on *mala Matiana*, or dessert apples, and one which shows the poet in laudatory vein (virtually advertising, as has been previously remarked: see 90 intro.). All three pieces look at the apples through comparisons with famous examples in myth, of which there are many; A.R. Littlewood's useful article, 'The Symbolism of the Apple in Greek and Roman Literature' (*HSCPh* 72.1967.147 f.) gives an overview of the topic and will be referred to in the following notes. The point of the comparisons is to stress the excellent quality and appearance of *mala Matiana*.

The precursor of this type of epigram, a description of everyday comestibles with a literary overlay, can be found in Martial's *Xenia* and *Apophoreta*, and there is a particularly close parallel to the present trio of epigrams at 13.37 (*mala citrea*), where the fruit, which is there citrons rather than apples, is deemed to have come from one of the great gardens of myth:

> Aut Corcyraei sunt haec de frondibus horti
> aut haec Massyli poma draconis erant.

Similar praise of apples can be found at Priap. 16 and *AL* 281.267 f. Symphosius.

Commentary

superscr.: De malis Matianis: it is apparent from the epigram which ensues that its subject is apples, but the title, as is occasionally the case (see p. 18 f.), gives additional information with the epithet 'Matianis'. Although Isidore thought the name derived from a place (*Or.* 17.7.3), it is certain that these apples were named after a person: 'reliqua cur pigeat nominatim indicare, cum conditoribus suis aeternam propagaverint memoriam, tamquam ob egregium aliquod in vita factum? Nisi fallor, apparebit ex eo ingenium inserendi nihilque tam parvum esse quod non gloriam parere possit. Ergo habent originem a Matio, Cestioque et Mallio, item Scaudio ...' (Plin. *Nat. Hist.* 15.49, in a section dealing with apples). Cnaeus Matius was an *eques* and friend of Augustus who wrote on agricultural matters and is most likely to be identified with the person after whom the specific apple variety was named (Plin. *Nat. Hist.* 12.13; Tac. *Ann.* 12.60; Col. 12.4.2; 12.46.1; with *RE* 14.2210). His apples are also mentioned at e.g. Col. 5.10.19; 12.47.5; Ed. Diocl. 6.65 (where they are listed as the best grade of apple, and cost twice as much as the next best variety), and he had a ragoût named after him too, *minutal Matianum* (Apic. 4.3.4). It is interesting that the (probably sixth-century) Latin Dioscorides uses *malum Matianum* to translate μῆλον (3.99 (= *Romanische Forschungen* 10.1899.420.25); 3.149 (= ibid. 437.6)), suggesting that it eventually became a generic term for the dessert apple, no doubt to distinguish it from other species of *mala* (see 158.1 n.); that is not the case here, however, because the whole point of the epigram is that the apples are of the highest quality. Matius would be pleased to know that his apples and his name have passed in various ways into Romance languages (*REW* 5427): e.g. Old Sp. *mazana*, Sp. *manzana* ('apple'); Sp. *manzanilla* ('camomile', whence also the sherry variety); and Fr. *mancenille* (whence Eng. *manchineel*), the poison guava tree of the Caribbean and Mexico, whose attractive apple-like fruits 'have poisoned Spanish conquistadores, shipwrecked sailors and present-day tourists' (*Encyclopaedia Britannica*).

1. haec poterant: all three epigrams are couched in strongly deictic terms (the first words are 'haec', 'his' and 'his'), which adds to the advertising tone. 'poterant' here expresses a fact rather than a contingency: 'these apples were able to ... (and did)' rather than 'these apples were able to ...(but did not; i.e. these apples could have ...'). This is shown by the indicative mood of the verbs in the mythological exampla of the two following epigrams ('perdidit', 'tenuit', 'prodidit'). Thus the poet hyperbolically suggests that the *mala Matiana* he has to hand and advertises are of such excellence that they actually are the famous apples of the myths he cites, which were of course all renowned for excellence and quality: this is also Martial's technique in 13.37 quoted above.

celeres pretio ((p̄cio (V); tio (BW); *om.* A)) tardare puellas (codd.); celeris plantas (gressus (Baehrens)) tardare puellae

Commentary

(Shackleton Bailey); celerem pretio (stadio (Sannazarius)) tardare puellam (Heinsius): this is an obvious allusion to the myth of the swift Atalanta and her being vanquished in a foot race by her suitor Melanion or Hippomenes, who, as a diversionary tactic, threw into her path three golden apples which Venus had given him for the purpose. However, the text has caused problems for two reasons: (1) 'celeres puellas' is plural, and Atalanta was singular; and (2) 'pretio' (if that is what lies behind the mss) is according to SB 'certe haud ferendum'. W.S. Watt (*HSCPh* 91.1987.291 f.) agrees with both criticisms, adopting Heinsius' 'celerem puellam' in respect of (1), and seeking an instrumental ablative, such as 'specie', for (2).

But of the objections to the received text (1) seems slight: 'celeres puellas' is a generic plural of a type often used by Martial, for example, though usually with personal names (e.g. 1.24.3 'qui loquitur Curios adsertoresque Camillos?'; 8.56.5 with Schöffel's note; *LHS* 2.19; and, more generally, Löfstedt, *Syntactica*, 1.38 f.). Since the mythological reference is clear, a rather dismissive 'all those quick girls like Atalanta' is apposite enough (she is identified as simply 'pernix puella' in the admittedly fragmentary Cat. 2b.11 f.). As for (2), 'pretio' can supply the instrumental ablative sought by Watt (and L. Zurli (*GIF* 28.1997.146 f.) points out that Lucan uses the noun of the apples of the Hesperides at 9.365: 'abstulit arboribus pretium nemorique laborem / Alcides'). *Pretium* is often used to refer to a bribe (e.g. esp. Hor. *Carm*. 3.16.8 'converso in pretium deo', alluding to Jupiter's conversion into a shower of gold in order to seduce Danae, where *pretium* is both concrete 'gold' and abstract 'bribe'; Verg. *Aen*. 6.621 f. 'vendidit hic auro patriam ... fixit leges pretio atque refixit'; Cic. *Verr*. 2.5.27); and it can have the more abstract meaning of 'value' (e.g. Plin. *Nat. Hist*. 33.5 'quibus (sc. crystallinis) pretium faceret ipsa fragilitas'; *AL* 194.2 Luxorius; 385.25). The latter sense is perhaps most appropriate here, because it equates the excellence, and therefore cost, of the *mala Matiana* with the value of the gold of the apples by which Atalanta was diverted (and for their value being her motive cf. First Vatican Mythographer 1.39.2 'tunc Atalante, cupiditate colligendorum malorum retenta, superata est'); *pretium* is again used in this sense at 150.1. So on the assumption that 'celeres pretio tardare puellas' originally stood in the text, there is no reason to emend it.

2. haec: strictly this is plural for singular and seems clumsy, because only one apple was awarded to Venus as her prize; but use of the singular was not available to the poet because of the preceding 'haec' and the plural subject of the epigram (note the similar 'his' at 124.1). The point is that any or all of the *mala Matiana* could be believed to be the one which was Venus' prize.

fuerant ... danda: pluperfect for imperfect (cf. 'poterant' in line 1), a frequent idiom (see *LHS* 2.321).

iudice ... Phryge: the Judgement of Paris is another myth featuring a

Commentary

prominent role for a golden apple; but though the story of the judgement itself is early (Hom. *Il.* 24.28 f.; there is a full telling at Ovid *Her.* 16.53 f.), the prize of the apple is not attested until much later (first at Apul. *Met.* 10.32.4; Hyg. *Fab.* 92 and Lucian 78.7(5).1 f.), when it became appropriately identified with the Apple of Discord which Eris had thrown amongst the goddesses Aphrodite, Hera and Athene to foment dissent over their relative beauty, after she had herself been excluded from the celebration of the marriage of Peleus and Thetis (for which see 124.1 n.). This episode led directly to the contest which Paris judged (see further Littlewood, op. cit. intro., 150 f.; *LIMC* 7.1.176 f.; T.C.W. Stinton, 'Euripides and the Judgement of Paris', *JHS* Suppl 11.1965 (= *Collected Papers on Greek Tragedy*, Oxford 1990, 17 f., esp. 22 n. 24); and M. Davies, 'The Judgements of Paris and Solomon', *CQ* 53.2003.32 f.).

The bald 'Phryx' is not used elsewhere to denote Paris, though he is called 'Phrygius pastor' at Verg. *Aen.* 7.363 and 'Phrygius hospes' at Sen. *Tro.* 70 f. The tone is contemptuous: this may reflect the late allegorical interpretation of the myth of the Judgement as a precursor to that of Heracles at the cross-roads, with Athena representing the contemplative life, Hera the active, and Aphrodite the hedonistic (cf. Fulg. *Myth.* 2.1; 3.7), though since it led to the Trojan War Paris' decision could be criticised in any case.

3. flavescunt: the verb *flavescere* and adjective *flavus* often allude to the glister of gold (e.g. Verg. *Aen.* 1.592; Ovid *Met.* 8.701; Mart. 14.12.1).

4. auro ... suo: for *aureus* used of the colour of apples cf.Verg. *Ecl.* 3.71; 8.52; Aus. 27.16.1; *AL* 209.1 Petronius.

123 (134R)

Another. A eulogy. †In these apples is embodied Venus' radiant beauty which won the contest†, these are the apples the sacred garden lost when its serpent died.

The second of the trio of epigrams on the *mala Matiana* is headed 'laus', while the final one is a 'vituperatio'; the praise or blame lies in interpretation of mythological tales in which apples have featured, though in the 'laus' the praise seems to relate to the excellence and beauty of the apples (the text of the first line does not however yield convincing sense: see note), while in the 'vituperatio' the blame lies in the evil uses to which apples have been put.

1. †his constat Veneri praelatae gratia formae†: the problems raised by this line are significant enough to suggest significant textual corruption: the line apparently instances the prize apple from the Judgement of Paris

Commentary

as a mythological example of a high-quality apple. But: (1) is it likely that the apple of the Judgement is employed a second time (cf. 122.2), when the other five mythological examples in 122-4 are all different? (2) why is the verb 'constat' in the present tense, when the other five examples all have verbs in past tenses, which key them as affording mythological exempla? (3) what governs the dative 'Veneri': is it 'constat', or 'praelatae', and what sense could either make? (4) what, and whose, is the 'gratia formae'? and (5) how is 'his' to be construed? I cannot offer plausible answers, so I have athetised the whole line (the translation above gives the best sense I can make of it, though I have had to emend 'Veneri' to 'Veneris'; I also note that two key words, 'constant' and 'gratia', recur in close proximity at 188.19-20, though without aiding understanding here).

gratia formae: the phrase also occurs at e.g. Ovid *Met.* 7.44; Stat. *Silv.* 3.4.66; and Claud. *Carm. Min.* 30.224.

2. haec ... nemus: this is a reference to the golden apples of the Hesperides, which were protected by a fierce snake and stolen by Heracles as the last of his labours after he had killed the guardian. Hyginus identifies the snake as the offspring of Typhon and Echidna and says that it was catasterised as the constellation Serpens after death (*Fab.* 30.12; *Astr.* 2.3); it was a popular subject with fifth-century BC red-figure vase painters, who depicted a large snake coiled round the apple tree it protects, its head poking out of the branches (and an analogue of the snake of the Garden of Eden: see *LIMC* 5.2.287 f.; 5.1.394 f.). The myth of the apples of the Hesperides was a favourite in Antiquity, and Littlewood (*HSCPh* 72.1967.163 f.) has collected over a hundred examples in an incomplete catalogue. Golden apples in other myths, such as the Judgement of Paris and Atalanta's race, are sometimes said to be derived from this source (e.g. Colluth. 59 f.; First Vatican Mythographer 1.39.2). The apples are used elsewhere as the yardstick of apple excellence: for example, Juvenal's Virro serves his honoured guests apples 'credere quae possis subrepta sororibus Afris' (5.152), whilst the less deserving get rotten fruit discarded by a performing monkey.

124 (135R)

Another. An attack. It is with these apples that despised Discord held the immortals' attention as they dined, and these are the apples with which Briseida betrayed her city.

The praise of apples of the previous epigram now shifts to condemnation, with the Apple of Discord providing an obvious example of a mythological bad apple; but the second example gives rise to difficulties of interpretation.

Commentary

1. his: for the plural, here and in the next line, rather than the more logical singular pronoun, see 122.2 n.

contempta ... Discordia: Discordia (or Eris) is termed 'contempta' because she was the only immortal not to be invited to the marriage of Peleus and Thetis, and she took her revenge by means of the golden Apple of Discord, which became the prize in the beauty competition between Aphrodite, Hera and Athene, of which Zeus appointed Paris to be judge. The goddesses tried to bribe him, Hera offering power and wealth, Athena bravery and cleverness, and Aphrodite the hand of Helen: by accepting the latter he started the Trojan War, and therefore the apple thrown by Discordia is an excellent exemplar in this *vituperatio*. Although Discordia's role in fomenting trouble amongst the goddesses at the marriage of Peleus and Thetis is known from early mythography (it appears in the *Cypria*: see Davies, *EGF* 31.5 f. Proclus), her exclusion from the celebration and her use of the Apple of Discord are only attested in later literary sources (Hyg. *Fab.* 92 is a full account; cf. Lucian 78.7(5).1 f.; Third Vatican Mythographer 11.20 (G.H. Bode p. 240)). In some versions the apple was inscribed (e.g. Lucian loc. cit. says 'ἐπεγέγραπτο δὲ "Ἡ καλὴ λαβέτω" ' ('it was inscribed "Let the beautiful one win me"')), which may be of relevance to the second line of this epigram (see note). See also 122.2 n.; Apollod. *epit.* 3.2 with Frazer's note; *LIMC* 7.1.176 f.

deum tenuit (A; genuit (BW)) ... mensas (Baehrens; mensam (Kay); mensa (codd.)): 'deum' is genitive plural, though the whole clause is rather forced. If it is correctly transmitted and Baehrens' necessary conjecture, or something similar, is accepted, 'tenuit' is used in the sense 'held the attention of' and 'mensas deum' means 'the gods as they dined' ('tenuit' is unlikely to mean 'physically held on to', both because the detail would not be particularly relevant, and, since Discordia had been excluded from the celebrations, she had to roll her apple from the doorway of the dining-hall (e.g. Hyg. *Fab.* 92.1)). For *mensa* metonymically of diners at table, cf. Sil. It. 11.439 'atque haec (sc. carmina) e multis carpsit mollissima mensae', with *OLD* mensa 6; *mensam* might here be preferable to *mensas*, suggesting that the gods dined at one special table.

2. prodidit (edd.; providit (BW); prodedit (A); perdidit (Hagen)) atque urbem his Briseida suam: this line is problematic; Riese says 'non intelligitur' and SB obelises the entirety. But a reasonably strong case can be made for the text printed by earlier editors, which involves only a slight correction of the mss in the first word. The questions are (1) what does it mean, and (2) does what it means make sense in the context? A subsidiary question is whether the line is metrically acceptable.

Regarding (1): the line can only have a meaning if 'Briseida' is a nominative, but that is possible. 'Briseida' is of course the Greek accusative form of the name Briseis, and is attested as such in Latin transliteration (e.g. Prop. 2.8.35); however, there are indications that it could well have become a nominative in late Latin. There is evidence from other accusative Greek nouns which similarly give rise to Latin nominatives in '-a', and which include proper nouns: e.g. Latin nominative 'lampada' from the Greek accusative λαμπάδα (Fulg. *De Aet.* 140.19 Helm); 'hebdomada' from ἑβδομάδα (Gell. 3.10.14); 'absida' from ἀψῖδα (Paul. Nol. *Ep.* 32.17); 'sphinga' from σφίγγα (Hyg. *Fab.* 67.3); Ancona from ἀγκῶνα, and especially Luxorius' nominatives 'Lacedaemona' and 'Laida' (*AL* 346.3 and 369.1 respectively); in the present collection there are also the possible nominatives 'syringa' from accusative σύριγγα at 127.1 (see note), and 'Garamanta' from Γαράμαντα at 173.1 (see note); see further on the phenomenon Stotz, *Handbuch*, 4.25; E. Courtney, *C&M* 40.1989.201 f.; *KS* 1.498 f. The nominative *Briseida* is not elsewhere attested, though the incorrectly formed Latinate accusative *Briseidam* suggests how easily it might have been supplied (*Briseidam* is found at e.g. Hyg. *Fab.* 106.1; 106.3; schol. ap. Cic. *Orat.* Gronovianus D, 2.311 Stangl; and Dares 13; 'Chryseidam' occurs at Hyg. *Fab.* 121.1).

This evidence is strengthened by the survival in medieval tales of aspects of this myth, especially the story of Troilus and Cressida. When that story first appears, the heroine is named Briseida (in the twelfth-century Benoît de Sainte-Maure's *Roman de Troie*, e.g. lines 5275-6 'Briseida fu avenant: / Ne fut petite ne trop giant'); but in Boccaccio's retelling (in *Il Filostrato* of 1338) she had become Criseida, the name which then found its way into Chaucer (Criseyde) and Shakespeare (Cressida). The reasons for the confusion over the name may not be clear and are not relevant to the matter in question (see e.g. E. Talbot Donaldson, 'Briseis, Briseida, Criseyde, Cresseid, Cressid: Progress of a Heroine', in *Chaucerian Problems and Perspectives*, ed. E. Vasta and Z.P. Thundy, Notre Dame / London 1979, 3 f.), but the eventual shift in the nominative forms of both Briseis and Chryseis is apparent. 'Briseida' can therefore be accepted as a nominative here, and the line means 'and with these apples Briseida betrayed her city'.

This leads into question (2) above: does this make sense in the epigram as a whole? Initial reaction is favourable, because the clause suggests myths of the type where a city is betrayed by a girl in love with its enemy attacker (typically Scylla and Nisus at Ovid *Met.* 8.6 f., and see Hollis' commentary on lines 1-151 for more instances). If an apple featured in such a story which involved Briseis, it would be an excellent example of another bad apple for the *vituperatio*. Although the evidence is thin, there is some: Littlewood (op. cit. at 122 intro., 151 f.) points to a scholium on Hom. *Il.* 6.35 (= Hes. frag. 214 M-W) in which it is said that Achilles, when besieging towns around Troy during the Trojan War, came to one previously called Monenia but now called Pedasos; the siege was difficult and the Greeks were about to give up when 'a maiden' in the city, enamoured of Achilles, took an apple, inscribed it, and threw it to the Greeks. It said:

Commentary

μὴ σπεῦδ' 'Αχιλλεῦ πρὶν Μονηνίαν ἕλης·
ὕδωρ γὰρ οὐκ ἔνεστι· διψῶσιν κακῶς.

('Do not hurry away, Achilles, before you take Monenia; for there is no water in it; they are terribly thirsty.') Achilles took the advice and the town. We also know from Homer that Achilles won Briseis during the sack of a city (*Il.* 16.57), which he identifies as Lurnessos (*Il.* 2.690); however, in the *Cypria* (*EGF* frag. 21 Davies) the city was Pedasos (see also on this myth Lightfoot, *Parthenius*, 496 f.; and M. Cuypers, 'The Sack of Methymna in the *Lesbou Ktisis*', *Hermathena* 173-4.2002-03.117 f., esp. 124 f.). In total this remains inconclusive but significant: it is a reasonable possibility that the poet of this epigram knew a version of a myth in which Briseis / Briseida betrayed her city by means of an inscribed apple, and that this furnished him with a good example for his *vituperatio*.

Metre and prosody also need consideration in this line. The hiatus at the main caesura of the pentameter is evidenced elsewhere in the collection and is not a significant issue (see p. 23). The prosody of Brīsēĭda is unparalleled and the precise reverse of the orthodox Brĭsēīda, but there is plenty of evidence of major irregularity in the prosody of Greek proper names in late poetry: compare for example Luxorius' 'Clĕōbŭlus' at *AL* 346.13 (with Rosenblum, *Luxorius*, 93 f.), Dracontius' 'Īphīgĕnĭa' at *Orest.* 52, or 'Ăcis' (see 140.2 n.) and 'Īdīppus' (i.e. Oedipus; see 170.3 n.) in the present collection. See generally Norberg, *Introduction*, 12 f.

My overall conclusion is that, although there is obviously room for doubt, the line should stand as it is in the mss, with only slight emendation of the first word (Lausberg, *Einzeldistichon*, 351 f. comes to much the same conclusion).

125 (136R)

On a monkey jar. The monkey jar vomits out an icy river in huge gulps; an external force adds the boon of coldness to it. For we take pains to enclose warm water in the jug so that it can be immersed in rainwater and chilled.

The *gillo* (from which noun ultimately derives Eng. liquid measure 'gill') has already been encountered in the poem on the months (106.16), where it is one of three items listed under August which do something to alleviate the heat; the longer description of it here illustrates the same qualities, and makes it clear that it is a vessel used to cool water. Such vessels, as well as ones for cooling wine, occur occasionally in classical literature, but perhaps not as often as would be expected given the premium that must have been placed on cool drinks in summertime: an anonymous epigram (*AP* 11.244, probably first-century AD) describes a brass boiler which is so inefficient that it ought to be used as a water cooler in summer; Martial describes a *lagona nivaria* for cooling liquids, though he explicitly says that snow was used to achieve refrigeration (14.116-18 with Leary's notes); and *gillo* is glossed by Greek βαύκαλις at Cass. *Inst.* 4.16.1 and *CGL* 4.346.15; 596.10, while vessels of the same type called βαυκάλιον / καυκάλιον are also evidenced (in the references of Olympiodorus and Alexander Aphrodisias cited below).

This epigram suggests that the *gillo* was made of terracotta ('testa' line 3, and cf. Cass. *Inst.* 4.16.1 'gillonem fictilem'); Vandal Africa, as previously Roman Africa, was a prolific manufacturer and exporter of pottery to the Mediterranean area and beyond, so *gillones* may well have been a local product (see P. Reynolds, *Trade in the Western Mediterranean AD 400-700: The Ceramic Evidence*, BAR International Series 604, Oxford 1995, 28 f.; 53 f. etc.; Merrills in Merrills, *Vandals*, 8 f., with n. 22; N. Duval et al., *AntTard* 10.2002.177 f.). Terracotta vessels of similar type were used for cooling water in the Bahamas until recently (they are known as water monkeys or monkey jars). They are effective: the porous pottery refrigerates or cools by means of evaporation, and can lead to drops in the temperature of the liquid contained of up to 25° C (see Forbes, *Technology*, 6.106 f.; P. James and N. Thorpe, *Ancient Inventions*, London 1995, 320 f.; and compare the cooling container encased in wickerwork at Mart. 2.85.1 f.). When this type of vessel is mentioned in the ancient sources it can be remarked, as here, that it makes a gurgling sound when its contents are poured, or that if tilted too quickly it does not release them (as e.g. Olympiodorus on Arist. *Meteor.* 348a14 (p. 93.6 f. Stüve); Alex. Aphrod. *Probl.* 1.94 (in *Physici et Medici Graeci Minores*, ed. Ideler): this suggests it had a narrow spout which would contribute to the cooling process (and cf. 'claudere' line 3). It is also said at line 4 of the poem that the water to be cooled is cooled by 'imbrigenae aquae', which suggests the *gillo* would be kept in as cold an environment as possible, perhaps a running stream or a shaded tub. The three factors together (evaporation via terracotta, the narrow spout and the immediate external environment) should have given rise to a considerable cooling effect.

1. gillo: *gello* and *gellunculus* are also found, though all the nouns are rare (*AL* 106.16; Cass. *Inst.* 4.16.1; Cass. Felix 42, with *TLL* 6.2-3.1730.2f.). A *gillonarius* makes an intriguing appearance at *Lex Visigoth.* 2.4.4 'ut non immerito palatinis officiis liberaliter honorentur, id est stabulariorum, gillonariorum, argentariorum, coquorum quoque praepositi'; and see Hilgers, *Gefässnamen* no. 177.

vomit ... vastis singultibus: for the intermittent gurgling or vomiting effect caused by the vessel's narrow spout, see intro. above. The image, which is aural as well as visual, is graphically hyperbolic and the vocabulary might equally suggest a volcanic eruption (cf. 'vomat' at Lucr. 1.724) or a person vomiting. The same effect is remarked by Pliny (*Ep.* 4.30.6) in his musings on an intermittently flowing spring:

Commentary

'quod in ampullis ceterisque generis eiusdem videmus accidere, quibus non hians nec statim patens exitus. Nam illa quoque, quamquam prona atque vergentia, per quasdam obluctantis animae moras crebris quasi singultibus sistunt quod effundunt'.

amnem: the poet varies the nouns he uses for 'water': also 'laticem' (line 3), 'unda' and 'aquis' (line 4).

2. vis aliena: this imprecise term is elaborated in lines 3-4; the point is that warm water has gone into the vessel and cold has come out, so some external process must have operated to achieve the cooling.

3. curamus claudere: this phrase might be intentionally more allusive than (for example) simple 'inserimus': the vessel's narrow opening (see intro.) would entail as much effort in inserting the water as it would in extracting it, so careful hands would be required ('curamus'); and the same narrowness of the entrance leads to the enclosure ('claudere') of the water which plays a part in its cooling (see intro.).

4. mersa ... unda: the participle suggests that once the warm water has been shut in the vessel, the vessel and its contents are immersed in 'imbrigenae aquae'.

imbrigenis (A); indigenis (BVW): the majority reading 'indigenis', presumably a noun in apposition, can hardly be correct. A's 'imbrigenis' is a ἅπαξ λεγόμενον, but more convincing, and means 'imbri genitis' on the lines of *fluctigenus, nubigenus* and such compounds (see Lindner, *Komposita*, 105 and *TLL* 7.1.427.1 f.). Its significance here would be to specify fresh water as a coolant; given that the terracotta of which the vessel was made was porous, immersion in sea water would taint the contents.

nivescat: the verb is again rare, attested elsewhere only at Tert. *Pall.* 3, where it refers to colour; *Lewis and Short* are incorrect in alleging a colour reference here ('turn snow white'), because the context shows it must refer to temperature.

126 (137R)

On †theus†. You sport a flask hanging down from your groin *****, which turns into a swollen amphora when the wind blows. You could have paid potters' tax to the tax office, since you excel their product with such a smooth swelling!

This and the following epigram are imaginative (if difficult) pieces about a man with an inguinal hernia or similar affliction, though this one lacks crucial words in its superscription and first line. Greeks and Romans were neither squeamish nor politically correct in poking fun at the physical and mental ailments and peculiarities of others, and here

Commentary

we have no exception. Similar humour about hernias, usually but not always associated with old men, can be found at e.g. *AP* 6.166 (Lucillius); 11.404 (Lucian); Lucil. 331-2 Marx (332-3 Krenkel); Mart. 3.24; 12.83; Juv. 6.326; 10.205; *CE* 49 (= *ML* 82 Courtney).

The effectiveness of the present epigram works in more than one way, stemming both from the visual image of the affected scrotum as a large terracotta pot of varying sizes and such perfection that potters' tax could be paid on it, and from the verbal plays on words alluding to the scrotum and the unexpected and imaginative language in which the piece is couched. W.J. Schneider (*Arctos* 32.1998.229 f.) has suggested an illuminating parallel with the visual arts: *grylloi* (on which see Plin. *Nat. Hist.* 35.114 with *Neue Pauly* 5.6 f.) are grotesque statuettes which caricature deformed people, often with enormously swollen heads and genitals, and Schneider provides an illustration of a statuette from Smyrna now in the Louvre which shows a male torso with a normal-sized penis but hugely enlarged scrotum. The visual humour of this type of image is close to the verbal humour of the epigram (and see also 127.2 n. for a painting of a man with a huge hernia). Schneider uses this parallel to supplement the first line of the epigram ('inguine suspensam gestas, o grylle, lagunam'), which might be considered a step too far. However, another intriguing piece of evidence is supplied by Luxorius in a (textually problematic) epigram about a useless charioteer who habitually falls out of his chariot and gets his horses' legs broken (*AL* 322). The charioteer is described with the words 'ast ego non aliud quam turgida (Burman; turbida (A)) membra notavi (Schubert; notabo (A)) / inflatumque caput papulis (Doehner; populis (A)) et amica ruinis / brachia'; and the epigram concludes 'non iste humano dicatur semine natus; / hunc potius Grillum (Shackleton Bailey; grillum (Schubert); grifum (A)) proprium vocat Africa circo'. If the emendation 'G(g)rillum' is correct in the final line, it is clear evidence that the word could be applied pejoratively to persons with deformities involving swelling like the *grylloi* caricature statuettes. In sum, 'o G(g)rille /-ylle' merits serious consideration as a supplement in the first line of the present epigram, though see further 1 n. below.

superscr.: De †theo† (A): A's text makes no sense; as SB says (app. crit.), '*Theus vel theum quid sit vel hic quid sibi velit mihi quidem in tenebris est ...*', and he suggests that it might belong to a missing epigram (for similar omissions see 113/14 intro.; 129/30 intro.), though even then it would almost certainly require emendation. Schneider (loc. cit. intro.) suggests 'De Lecythio', from Greek ληκύθιον, a pottery vessel which might have a possible alternative reference to a hernia (he adduces Dover's note on Ar. *Frogs* 1200 and G. Anderson *JHS* 101.1981.130, as well as the use of 'laguna' in line 1 of this piece (see note)), but that is too speculative for serious consideration (and 'De G(g)ryllo' would seem to me more plausible, if Schneider's supplement in line 1 is accepted).

Commentary

1. suspensam ... <l>agunam: a *laguna* (from Greek λάγυνος; Latin offers the various spellings *lagoena*, *lagona* and *lagena* as well as the change of termination; see 92.5 n. for similar issues with *gyrus* and the transliteration into Latin of Greek upsilon) is a vessel characterised as narrow-necked, two-handled and of bellying-out shape, and it was generally used for containing wine or water (see Hilgers, *Gefässnamen*, no. 205; Leary's notes on Mart. 14.116). The image it conveys will only become apparent at the conclusion of the epigram ('tereti ramice'), where it is revealed as a scrotum swollen by an ailment; the image may suggest a scrotum of normal size which becomes swollen by the ailment detailed in line 2, but more probably it suggests an abnormal scrotum of which the abnormality increases in line 2 (see 4 n.). It is the body of the vessel, the part which bellies out, which pictures the scrotum, while the narrow neck would suggest the (normal) penis.

It is not surprising that the use of *laguna* with these overtones is unique, but other vessels of suitable shape could be used to picture male genitalia: Greek ληκύθιον has been noted above (though the overtones (if any) in Aristophanes are disputed); ἀλάβαστος occurs at e.g. Ar. *Lys.* 947; and *vas* and its derivatives are so used in Latin (e.g. Petr. 24.7; *Priap.* 68.24; with Adams, *LSV* 41 f.).

For the lacuna displayed by the ms. text of this line, see intro. above; Schneider's supplement 'o grylle' (perhaps 'o Grille') is ingenious, but the interjection 'o' with vocative does not appear elsewhere in the collection, and is rare in what Eleanor Dickey terms low register poetry (*Latin Forms of Address from Plautus to Apuleius*, Oxford 2002, 227). Somewhat reluctantly, I therefore retain the lacuna.

2. turgens amphora: the image continues with the *laguna* swelling into an *amphora*, a jar of the same basic shape but much larger size (Hilgers, *Gefässnamen*, 35 f.; no. 15); 'turgens' makes a link between the scrotum, which can increase and decrease in size because of the hernia, and the images of the pottery vessels, which are fixed and solid. The reader might not yet understand the allusions of the images, because the 'turgens' vessel could at this stage suggest erection of the penis rather than scrotal affliction (and see the next note).

flante noto: this phrase, somewhat strange for the context, must explain how the swelling of the *laguna* into an *amphora* occurs. Taking the scrotal image, the assumption that the swelling is due to internal air is neither unreasonable nor unlikely (although *notus* is not paralleled in this sense, *ventus* is (e.g. Col. 6.30.8, with *OLD ventus* 4(b)), and the fact that the south wind is warm and moist (cf. Ovid *Met.* 1.264; Hor. *Epod.* 10.19) is helpful. For similar phraseology in the specific description of a hernia cf. Cels. 7.18.17 f.: 'at si is (sc. tumor) vehementer increvit, renititur sicut uter repletus et arte adstrictus. Venae quoque in scroto inflantur, et, si digito pressimus, cedit umor circumfluensque id, quod

Commentary

non premitur, attollit et tamquam in vitro cornuque per scrotum apparet ...'. Significantly, Paulus Aigineta (6.64.3 Heiberg) describes a condition termed πνευματοκήλη, which is 'a hirnea containing air or gas' (the definition is from the *Oxford English Dictionary*, s.v. pneumatocele). More generally, erection is often said in medical (and sub-medical) texts to occur because of inflation (e.g. Galen 4.214 ; 8.442; and 13.318 Kühn; ps.Arist. *Probl.* 4.26; 13.6; 30.1 etc.), and the ambivalence of the *laguna / amphora* imagery has been remarked in the preceding note. Compare also expressions such as Horace's 'simul ac venas inflavit taetra libido' (*Sat.* 1.2.33) and Vergil's 'inflatum ... venas' (*Ecl.* 6.15).

3. vectigal ... figulorum: for pottery manufacture as a continuing major industry of Vandal Carthage, see 125 intro. The identification of the *laguna* and *amphora* as earthenware vessels gives them the correct colour for the scrotal comparison.

Taxes on traders are evidenced in the ancient world from various times and places: for example, Constantine instituted a general tax on trading (Zosimus 2.38); Libanius (*Or.* 46.22) speaks of a cobbler whose only asset was his knife, but who still had to pay a trade tax at Antioch; potters were specifically exempted from tax at *Cod. Th.* 13.1.10, which suggests they were subject to it at other times and places; and Suetonius suggests Caligula taxed everyone for everything (*Gaius* 40-1). So although there is no definite evidence of a tax on potters in North Africa under the Vandals, there is no reason to doubt the existence of one (and there are inevitable and no doubt true allegations of rapacity in taxation matters against Vandal kings and their officials: e.g. Victor Vit. 2.2; *AL* 336-7 Luxorius). See also the comments of R. Duncan-Jones, *Structure and Scale in the Roman Economy*, Cambridge 1990, 175 f. (on local revenue raising); A.H.M. Jones in *The Roman Economy*, ed. P.A. Brunt, Oxford 1974, 35 f. (= *Recueils de la Société Jean Bodin* 7.1955.161 f.); and Jones, *LRE* 110; 431 f.

poteras ... reddere: see 122.1 n. for the meaning of 'poteras'.

fisco: there is perhaps another play on words: *fiscus* is of course a treasury, probably a local one here, which derives its name from the basic meaning of the word ('bag' or 'moneybag'). However, there is some evidence that along with other words of similar meaning (such as *follis*; *folliculum*; *scrotum*; compare Fr. *bourse*; Germ. *Hodensack*) it might also denote the scrotum: explicitly, though it would seem uniquely, Isid. *Or.* 11.1.105 'fiscus est pellis in qua testiculi sunt' (quoted at *CGL* 5.201.5). It would resonate as an appropriately humorous place to which this particular sufferer can pay tax.

4. tam tereti ramice: it is revealed that the reason why the subject of the epigram should pay potters' tax is that his scrotal swelling, which looks like various earthenware vessels, is so smooth and rounded that

Commentary

it would appear to be a better piece of workmanship than any pot. It is only with this phrase (subject, however, to the first line lacuna) that the meaning of the images of the epigram becomes clear.

Ramex and *rames* (pl. *ramices, ramites*) have various references. The original meaning (1) seems to have been the bronchial tubes, and then by extension the lungs themselves (as at Plaut. *Merc*. 138; *Poen*. 540; Varro *Sat*. 192; 561 Cèbe, often in the phrase *ramices rumpere*, 'to burst the lungs'). The image of a network of tubes probably led to the noun being applied to (2) the transverse bars, perhaps withies, of a rustic fence (as at Col. 9.1.3). But the meaning most often attested, as here, is (3), an ailment affecting the scrotum, an inguinal hernia, varicocele, enterocele or hydrocele (the image of a network of knotted tubes or veins would have helped the shift in meaning, and the phrase 'ramices rumpere' might have helped in also suggesting the cause, real or imaginary, of such maladies). Thus for example Non. Marc. 166.4 (p. 244 Lindsay) 'ramites dicuntur pulmones vel hirnea'; Marc. *De Med*. 33.60 (p. 257.19 f. Niedermann) 'testiculorum tumentia et ydrocelae puerorum sive ramites'; Plin. *Nat. Hist*. 20.251 'testium vitia et ramices'; Paul. Aeg. 6.62; *CGL* 3.604.53; Cael. Aur. *Tard. Pass*. 5.128; and see André, *L'Anatomie*, 124 (who also suggests that meaning (1) above strictly belongs to *rames*, and meaning (3) to *ramex*, though there is confusion in the sources between the two).

127 (138R)

Another. Such a large syringe hangs under your belly that I would have no hesitation in saying you were two-headed. For if you should be sentenced to the field of execution for punishment, the executioner would not know which head to cut off with his sword.

This is the second of the pair of epigrams about the man suffering from a scrotal ailment. The humour now switches to alleging he has two heads, and that if he had to be executed the executioner would not know which to cut off. The parallel with the *grylloi* statuettes is again helpful (see 126 intro.). This is an occasion where it would be difficult to understand the piece without its companion; there the concluding 'tereti ramite' shows the point behind the word play, but there is no such clue here (see further p. 3).

1. moles tanta: for *moles* of massiveness of parts of the body, cf. Sil. It. 13.195 'membrorum mole Taburnus'; ibid. 14.529 f. 'corporis alti / terribilis moles' (of Polyphemus); ibid. 16.46; and Heinsius' brilliant emendation of Ovid *Met*. 15.230 'solidorum mole tororum' (for mss 'solido(a)rum mor(t)e fero(a)rum', although one ms. (Paris lat. 8000) has 'mole').

Commentary

syringae (Petschenig); siringi (A); syringis (Burman); Siringi (Lessing): a genitive dependent on 'moles tanta' is required. SB (following Riese) is incorrect in his app. crit. with the comment 'siringae (*sic*) *Petschenig*', because Petschenig conjectured 'syringae' (*ZOeG* 28.1877.484). If Petschenig is correct the noun has taken its formation here from the Greek accusative singular σύριγγα, a phenomenon already noted with the name Briseida at 124.2 n. (there are more examples from the medical lexicon at Langslow, *Medical Latin*, 79). The Greek-derived genitive 'syringis', suggested by Burman, would however also be possible, since both forms *syrinx* and *syringa* are attested in medical terminology (cf. Theod. Prisc. *Eup.* 81 'syringes'; 85 'syringa', in both cases referring to fistulas; Veg. *Mul.* 1.28.7 'syringis medicaminibusque diversis', where *syringae* refer to injections or syringes; and cf. ibid. 2.27.2 'syringotomium', which is a knife for excising a fistula). As will be apparent from what follows, I prefer 'syringa' because of the sense of 'syringe' it has in Vegetius and because of the support of similar nominative formations. It is also worth noting that the instability in transliteration of Greek upsilon is again apparent here (for which see 92.5 n. gyros).

There is nevertheless an issue as to the meaning of 'syringae' or 'syringis' in this context (Langslow (*Medical Latin*, 11 f.) comments on the imprecision of Latin medical terminology, when one noun may not only have different meanings, but can even be used in the same passage with different meanings: he illustrates this with the word *fistula*, and *syringa*, essentially its synonym, would serve equally well). Its pathological sense of 'fistula' is inappropriate, because a fistula is not a scrotal swelling: it is a tubular structure, an artificial passage between two body surfaces, which can either be deliberately created by a surgeon or be the result of an ulcerous wound. Moreover, a term for an ailment is not necessarily what is required, since in the previous epigram the nature of the ailment was conveyed by the metaphors of *laguna* and *amphora*, and similar allusiveness might be expected here. Another meaning of 'syringa' is however convincingly apposite: a type of medical syringe known in the Roman world was the bladder syringe or catheter, essentially a bellows-like contraption with a bag of animal skin attached to a nozzle, and used to inject liquids into, or suck them out of, parts of the body (cf. Paul. Aeg. 6.59.25 f. Heiberg '... τῷ καθετῆρι προσαρμόσαντες τὸ δέρμα ἢ κύστιν βοείαν διὰ τῆς τοῦ καθετῆρος ἐνέσεως ἐγκλύσομεν' ('having fixed the skin or leather bellows to the catheter we will carry out the injection through the insertion of the catheter'), with G. Majno, *The Healing Hand*, Cambridge Mass. 1975, 160 fig. 4.16). This furnishes an ideal image: not only the large bag and nozzle which resemble the male genitalia with the swollen scrotum caricatured as a second head, but additionally the inflation and deflation of the bag / scrotum which was also described as part of the ailment in the previous epigram (line 2 'flante noto', with note).

Commentary

2. bicipitem: the two heads are of course the one on top of the neck and the swollen scrotum, which is of the same shape, size and colour. There is an extraordinary painting from the Suburban Baths at Pompeii which shows a naked writer encumbered by a huge hernia reaching almost to his knees, the visual impact of which well complements this verbal 'two-headed' humour (it is illustrated in M.D. Grmek and D. Gourévich, *Les Maladies dans l'art antique*, Paris 1998, 331, fig. 265; see also p. 330 f., with figs 264, 266-7).

3. addictum ... campo: for *addictus* of punishment of the condemned cf. Hor. *Epod.* 17.11 'addictum feris alitibus atque canibus'; Apul. *Met.* 2.29.5 'addictus noxio poculo'; Aug. *Civ. Dei* 12.21 'morti addictus bestialiter viveret'. The datives in these illustrations suggest that 'campo' here is the punishment to which the man would be condemned, though it also functions as a local dative with 'te mittat'. SB (app. crit.), on the basis of *SHA* Aurel. 23.5 ('solum denique ex omnibus, qui oppugnabantur, campus accepit'), comments '*i.e. sub terram*'; but 'campus' is rather a designation of a place of execution, as also at *SHA* Tyr. Trig. 26.4 'fratrem Theodoti qui Aemilianum ceperat, ad campum deductus victus est et occisus', and cf. Cic. *Rab. Perd.* 10. It is perhaps strange that this meaning is so infrequently attested, but its sense here is certain enough from the context.

4. vispillo: the noun (which can also be spelled 'vespillo') is rare and occurs first in Martial, where it denotes an undertaker (1.30.1 with Citroni's note; 1.47.1); Martial, in adjacent lines, links a *vispillo* with an executioner (2.61.3 f.): 'postquam triste caput fastidia vispillonum / et miseri meruit taedia carnificis' (I.-X. Adiego (*AFB* 16.1993.9 f.) unconvincingly suggests that the evident meaning of the noun in the present epigram was due to a misunderstanding by the poet of this passage). Paul. *Fest.* 506.16 f. Lindsay specifically states that *vespillones* were undertakers for the poor: 'vespae et vespillones dicuntur, qui funerandis corporibus officium gerunt, non a minutis illis volucribus, sed quia vespertino tempore eos efferunt, qui funebri pompa duci propter inopiam nequeunt'. And the noun *vespellio*, which must be related, is associated in the jurists with disreputable traders and thieves, and is generally held to denote a robber of corpses (*Dig.* 46.3.72.5; 21.2.31). Unsurprisingly, there is confusion between the nouns *vi(e)spillo* and *vespellio* (if indeed they are correctly identified as separate words with differentiated meanings): thus Fulg. *Serm. Ant.* 2 'vispillones dicti sunt baiaules, quamvis Antidamas Eracleopolites vispillones dixerit nudatores cadaverum, sicut in historia Alexandri Macedonis scripsit dicens: "Plus quam trecentos cadaverum vispillones repperiens crucibus fixit." Tamen Mnaseas scribit in Europae libro Apollinem, posteaquam a Iove victus atque interfectus est, a vispillonibus ad sepulturam

Commentary

delatus est.' It is however apparent from what he does in line 4 that the reference here must be to an executioner; although the noun is not so used elsewhere, its association with death and low social status make such an extension of meaning plausible.

128 (139R)

On Jupiter †in an enclosure†. A revolving circlet is encircled by a ring at an angle to it, and the sacred contraption sports Jupiter inside. Its maker has fashioned empty lies to look at: who thinks it true that the ruler of the universe is enclosed in a globe?

This puzzling epigram is ecphrastic in nature, describing an artefact or object in the first couplet, then commenting on it in the second. The superscription reads 'De Iove in pluteo', but although *pluteus* boasts a variety of meanings none seems applicable here, and the correctness of this title may be doubted (on the titles see further p. 18 f.; on *plutei* see also 147.4 n.).

The key to the epigram obviously lies in determining what it describes, and I therefore begin by listing some features from the body of the piece which need to be explained by any solution: (1) the object is an 'orbis' (line 4); (2) the object is three-dimensional, since Jupiter can be enclosed or covered by it ('tegi' line 4); this conclusion is also suggested by the extraordinary agglomeration of words connoting curving, circles and globularity in the opening line; (3) the object is a 'machina sacra' (line 2), which suggests it has a function of some kind and is not purely decorative; 'machina' again suggests three-dimensionality; and (4), whatever the object is, it has to be capable of illustrating the epigram's concluding paradox, that the ruler of the 'orbis' is himself contained in or covered by this particular 'orbis'.

Most interpretations of the epigram start from its superscription 'De Iove in pluteo'; and *pluteus* has its attractions, not least in being a noun of such a wide range of meanings that it can accommodate most theories, and so it needs to be fully examined (bearing in mind, of course, the description in the body of the epigram). A *pluteus* in military terminology is an assembly of osier work, animal skins and other materials which was designed to protect besiegers; Vegetius (*Mil.* 4.15.5) describes *plutei* as 'qui ad similitudinem absidis contexuntur e vimine', and this well illustrates the curved shape which is so stressed in this epigram. Even in military terminology *pluteus* can have wider reference to objects made largely of wood used for general screening and protection (as at e.g. Vitr. 4.4.1; 5.1.5; Caes. *Bell. Gall.* 7.41.4 etc). This notion of fencing and enclosure extends outside the military sphere to fencing in general (Paul. *Fest.* 259.10 f. Lindsay) and, significantly, to the enclosure of sacred areas (Liv. 10.38.5 f., where the area is also circular; and *plutei* are dedicated

Commentary

to deities in some inscriptions (e.g. *CIL* 10.472; 3778-9)). Building on this Lambertz in his *RE* article (21.977 f.) interprets *pluteus* in this epigram as 'das elliptisch gebaute Häuschen' which encloses Jupiter inside it as a machine of war encloses besiegers and equipment. But whilst this would provide reasonable references for the sinuosity and sacredness described in the epigram, it does not convince in respect of 'machina' or the thrice mentioned 'orbis'; furthermore, the *pluteus* of Lambertz' evidence is not a 'Häuschen' but an enclosure.

Ziehen (*Neue Studien*, 11) picked up on another reference of *pluteus*, that of a feature in a library: 'et iubet archetypos pluteum servare Cleanthas' (Juv. 2.7; cf. Sid. *Ep.* 2.9). It is not however certain what the *pluteus* in libraries was: *OLD* pluteus 2(b) suggests a small barrier of some kind; Courtney (Juv. loc. cit. n.) suggests a wall-bracket; Braund (Juv. loc. cit. n.) suggests a shelf; Ziehen suggests a niche in the wall, and compares *imagines clipeatae*, which are bas-reliefs generally depicting sculpted heads or busts protruding from a circular, shield-like sculpted background (for which see Plin. *Nat. Hist.* 35.13 with E. Espérandieu, *Recueil général des bas-reliefs de la Gaule romaine*, Paris 1908, 2.30 f., no. 892). But whilst this interpretation again might convince with regard to sinuosity, it fails because it probably does not give sufficient weight to 'orbis' and 'tegi' (Ziehen actually conjectures 'regi' to obviate the latter concern), and it certainly does not give enough weight to 'machina'. Stevens (*Image and Insight*, 135 f.) takes this interpretation in a slightly different direction, adducing the types of grand silver platters or dishes which have portrait busts soldered onto them, with pagan gods and goddesses being popular fifth-century subjects (for which see Strong, *Gold and Silver Plate*, 151 f.; 197 f.; Pls 36a; b). But this interpretation is open to much the same objections as Ziehen's.

My conclusion is that 'in pluteo' of the superscription cannot be cajoled into producing an object which matches the description of it given by the epigram it heads. In tentatively advancing another interpretation I therefore ignore the superscription and use only the epigram itself to determine what the object might be. The emphasis on 'orbis' and similar words, the frequent references to circles and curves in the first line, and the term 'machina sacra', would together well describe a mechanical representation of the universe in the form (for example) of a skeleton celestial globe, which was used to demonstrate the orbits of the planets and other celestial bodies around a central earth (the modern nomenclature of these globes can be imprecise, and they are sometimes referred to as orreries, armillary spheres or even astrolabes). The best known of these instruments in the ancient world was made by Archimedes and brought to Rome in 212 BC, where it was later seen by Cicero (*De Repub.* 1.22): 'hoc autem sphaerae genus, in quo solis et lunae motus inessent et earum quinque stellarum, quae errantes et quasi vagae nominarentur, in illa sphaera solida non potuisse finiri, atque in eo admirandum esse inventum

Commentary

Archimedi, quod excogitasset, quem ad modum in dissimillimis motibus inaequabiles et varios cursus servaret una conversio' (the reference to 'illa sphaera solida' suggests that Archimedes' second globe was hollow and of the skeleton type); cf. also Cic. *Tusc.* 1.62 f.; *De Nat. Deor.* 2.88 (with Pease's note)). It was still famous in Lactantius' time: 'an Archimedes Siculus concavo aere similitudinem mundi ac figuram potuit machinari, in quo ita solem lunamque composuit ut inaequales motus et caelestibus similes conversionibus singulis quasi diebus efficerent ...' (*Inst.* 2.5.18). Claudian (*Carm. Min.* 51.5 f.) and Firmicus Maternus (1 proem. 5) also refer to it.

The manufacture of a celestial globe can be deduced from the instructions at Ptol. *Alm.* 5.1 for the making of a similarly constructed armillary sphere, designed to illustrate the fundamental circles of the heavens around the earth (on which see G.J. Toomer, *Ptolemy's Almagest*, London 1984, 217 f. with Fig. F): in essence an outer metal ring contains a series of pivoted rings inside it which can be turned and moved independently of each other in three dimensions. The effect of these rings within rings would be well conveyed by the sinuosities of the first line of the epigram, and the globe itself, as a model of the universe, would be well termed a 'machina sacra'; it is also hollow, and it is possible to imagine a decorative statuette of Jupiter, ruler of the universe, imprisoned inside (as a part of the base on which it would need to stand, for example). The object described in the epigram need be no Archimedean masterpiece, but a celestial globe would fit the description the poet gives more satisfactorily than anything which could be termed a 'pluteus'.

Further on celestial globes and armillary spheres, see A. Schlachter and F. Gisinger, *Der Globus, seine Entstehung und Verwendung in der Antike*, Berlin 1927 (= *Stoicheia* 8), passim, esp. 46 f.; G. Thiele, *Antike Himmelsbilder*, Berlin 1898, 27 f.

superscr.: De Iove in †pluteo†: for the reasons given above I obelise 'pluteo'; perhaps 'globo'?

1. flexilis obliquo sinuatur circulus orbe: the line instantly evokes astronomy and planetary motions: cf. esp. Manil. 3.225 'sed iacet obliquo signorum circulus orbe' (of the zodiac); and for these words in general astronomical use cf. e.g. Suet. frag. p. 215.10 Reifferscheid 'in ambitu septem caelestium orbium primum inferiore sphaerae circulo luna est constituta'; Manil. 5.695 '(sc. Arctos) numquam tincta vadis sed semper flexilis orbe'; with *TLL* 9.2.100.22 f. (obliquus); *OLD* orbis 7 and 15; *OLD* circulus 3.

If it describes a celestial globe, 'flexilis circulus' is here a ring mapping an orbit and which can be revolved accordingly, 'obliquus orbis' is the same at an angle to it, and 'sinuatur' describes the bellying-out of the one ring in relation to the other (see Fig. F in Toomer, op. cit. for a drawing which

Commentary

illustrates this). For 'orbes' of constituent parts of globes and spheres, cf. Lact. *Inst.* 3.24.6 'aereos orbes fabricati sunt quasi ad figuram mundi', and for their movement cf. ibid. 2.5.18 (quoted in the intro. above).

2. machina sacra: 'machina' exactly characterises a celestial globe, in that it is a man-made object which performs a function. It can also describe aspects of the celestial clockwork which it is the function of the instrument to elucidate: cf. Lucan 1.79 f. 'totaque discors / machina divolsi turbabit foedera mundi'; Lucr. 5.96; Manil. 2.807; Stat. *Silv.* 2.1.211. 'sacra' stands in antithesis to 'machina', a man-made instrument, in that the fabric of the universe is not man-made but divine, and it also honours Jupiter, the imprisoned inhabitant of the globe.

3. sub aspectum: 'to the sight', as at e.g. Cic. *Tim.* 52 'si neque sidera neque sol neque caelum sub oculorum aspectum cadere potuissent'; Amm. Marc. 22.8.9; *TLL* 2.802.63 f.

duxit mendacia: *ducere* is appropriate both to fashioning works of art (see 166.2 n.) and to fabricating lies (e.g. Cic. *Q. Rosc.* 48 'unde hoc totum ductum ... mendacium est?').

fictor (Meyer); pictor (A): Meyer's conjecture is certain: 'fictor' is much the more apposite noun in the context of a celestial globe, it suits 'duxit' much better than would 'pictor', and it is preferable for any interpretation of the epigram discussed in the intro. above (because the object described is a 'machina').

4. orbis rectorem ... orbe tegi: there is a play on two senses of 'orbis' which mirrors that on 'machina' in line 2: it is both the celestial globe itself and the universe which it describes. A statuette of Jupiter imprisoned inside the globe would suggest to a viewer the falsehood that the god is subservient to the universe, rather than the truth that he is its ruler. Jupiter is given the title 'rector universi' at Sen. *Nat. Quaest.* 2.45.1.

129 / 130 (140 / 141R)

<*On Jupiter and Leda.*> The Father sports swan feathers after he has put down his thunderbolts, and scatters his pleasant songs to the girls; Leda holds him back and, as she exults in the swan she has clasped, with her virginity gone she recognises Jupiter.

Epigram 130 lacks a proper superscription in the ms. and is headed 'Aliter'. This suggests the loss of an epigram between 128 and this one; editors assume that 'Aliter' belongs to the missing epigram, and that therefore its subject was the same as that of 128. But it seems more probable (or at least just as probable) that this epigram has its proper title, and that the missing piece was therefore on the same subject: a copyist is more

Commentary

likely to miss out a complete piece than read the superscription of one and attach the body of another (see also 113/14 intro.). On the superscriptions in the collection, see further p. 18 f..

This is the first of a sequence of seven grouped pieces on mythological themes. There is some evidence of deliberate ordering, in that the following epigram deals with the outcome of the union between Leda and Jupiter which this one describes, and it is followed by a pair on another of Jupiter's liaisons in animal disguise (Europa), which are in turn followed by three distichs on Narcissus; and Jupiter has also been featured as the protagonist in the different context of the descriptive 128. On ordering in the collection, see further p. 3.

The present piece is strongly ecphrastic, describing the scene of Jupiter as the swan courting and coupling with Leda. The episode was a popular one in Roman and late Antique art (*LIMC* 6.1.236 f.; 245 f.; 6.2.114 f., nos 39 f.), especially in North African mosaics (see Dunbabin, *North Africa*, index Leda); note also the hexameter found on a fragment of decorated earthenware (*CE* 345) 'Iuppiter in cycno cum Leda iunxsit amorem' and *AP* 5.307 Antiphilus, an ecphrastic epigram about a painting of Zeus and Leda.

1. cygneas ... pinnas: cf. Ovid *Tr.* 4.8.1 'iam mea cycneas imitantur tempora plumas'; for *cycnus* and *olor* see 3 n.

Genitor: a solemn word, as Skutsch says on Enn. *Ann.* 108 Sk., where it is applied to Romulus. Consequently it is found more frequently in epic than elsewhere when it is used as the title of a deity: cf. Verg. *Aen.* 8.427; 9.630; 12.200; 12.843; Claud. 36.18 (in all cases referring to Jupiter); it recurs at 132.3.

post fulmina: in the phrase 'gestans post', 'post' might be either spatial or temporal. Since this is an ecphrastic epigram, the image of Jupiter's swan wings setting off his thunderbolts in front of them might seem apposite; and thunderbolts are indeed portrayed in the visual arts (cf. Liv. 22.1.17; Amm. Marc. 23.4.12; Aug. *Civ. Dei* 5.26.1 etc.). However, *LIMC* has no example which would match this image, and, more fundamentally, if Jupiter had displayed his thunderbolts so openly, one would have thought that even the gaggle of impressionable girls would have seen through his singing swan disguise (and they do not: lines 3 f.). The temporal meaning (essentially 'depositis fulminibus') is therefore preferable.

2. dulcia ... virginibus: this detail of Jupiter singing before her companions as well as Leda herself appears unique to this epigram in extant literature, though there is some evidence from the visual arts: a fourth-/ fifth-century Coptic relief shows Leda with two naked female companions and Jupiter as the swan (*LIMC* 6.1.237; 6.2. Leda no. 52), and a late mosaic from Nea Paphos in Cyprus shows Leda with the swan and three ladies in attendance (ibid no. 50). Note also the First Vatican

Commentary

Mythographer's telling of the Europa myth, quoted at 132 intro., where again Jupiter's prey is accompanied by 'virgines' as he seduces her.

diffundit: for the uncompounded verb *fundere* used of song, cf. Cic. *Tusc.* 1.64; Lucan 1.449; Stat. *Silv.* 5.5.34; Claud. *Carm. Min.* 40.4; with *TLL* 3.469.78 f. *Diffundere* is used of song also at 100.5 (a chorus), and is used in a different sense of sound at e.g. Lucr. 4.569 '(sc. pars vocum) praeterlata perit frustra diffusa per auras'. The prefix 'dis-' (of which this poet is fond: cf. 88.1; 100.5; 101.5; 103.1; 106.17; 117.2; 121.5; 141.3; 157.1; 171.10; 181.4) here suggests the swan is wholeheartedly serenading all the *virgines*, liberally scattering about his songs (cf. F. Stolz, *ALL* 13.1904.110; *OLD* 'dis-').

carmina: swans were noted not only for their swan-song (as at e.g. Cic. *Tusc.* 1.73; Ovid *Met.* 14.430; Mart. 13.77) but also for song generally (cf. Lucr. 4.181; Verg. *Ecl.* 9.29 with Coleman's note).

3. retinens: the swan's song is so effective that it is Leda who makes the initial advance to him, possibly to anticipate the other girls.

olore: the swan has also been termed *cycnus* in line 1, and the nouns are interchangeable (e.g. Porph. ap. Hor. *Carm.* 3.28.15 'oloribus id est cycnis'; Serv. ap. Verg. *Aen.* 11.580 'olorem Latine ita dicimus; nam cycni graece dicuntur'); and Jupiter as a swan can be *olor* (e.g. Manil. 1.339; Stat. *Theb.* 10.504) or *cycnus* (e.g. Ovid *Her.* 17.55; Mart. 9.103.2). Although there are two species of swan which would have been known in the ancient world, the whooper (*Cygnus cygnus*), which is the more vocal, and the mute (*Cygnus olor*), which is however not entirely mute, there appears to have been no distinction made between them (see W.G. Arnott, *G&R* 24.1977.149 f.).

4. agnovit: the poet uses the perfect tense of this verb, after the preceding present tenses of 'diffundit' and 'gaudet', when he could easily have written 'agnoscit'; but he generally has no problem with mixing perfect and historic present tenses within epigrams (see e.g. 85; 137; 152; 171).

131 (142R)

On Leda's egg. Leda's offspring are shown in the egg which has hatched, the egg she laid impregnated by Jupiter when he had metamorphosed into a swan. She is one mother for three children, but different fates attend their births: part will make stars, part will make the ferocious Trojan War.

This epigram deals with the aftermath of the preceding one, when Leda lays an egg from which hatch the Dioscuri and Helen. The myth of the births is one which displays many variations over precise parentage, with Nemesis also featuring on the female side and Tyndareus on the male,

Commentary

and over precise offspring, with Clytemnestra sometimes as a second daughter. The piece is again ecphrastic, perhaps describing a mosaic which depicted the hatching of the egg. Aus. *Epig.* 61 is similar, though he uses a version of the myth which features Nemesis and Tyndareus as well as Jupiter and Leda: see my intro. to that epigram for a discussion of the myth and representations of it in the visual arts.

1. ovo ... aperto: there is a fourth-century mosaic from Trier which shows precisely this scene, illustrated at Dunbabin, *Mosaics*, 85, fig. 85.

2. in cygnum verso a (codd.; e (Kay)) Iove quod (Baehrens; quos (codd.)) genuit (Oudendorp; tenuit (codd.)): both language and metre remain questionable, even after what appears to be the minimum necessary emendation. Oudendorp's conjecture of 'genuit' is likely, since *gignere* is the *vox propria* for the laying of an egg (cf. Cic. *De Nat. Deor.* 2.129 'pisces ... ova cum genuerunt relinquunt'; Plin. *Nat. Hist.* 10.212 'de iis quae ova gignunt incertum est'; Aus. *Epig.* 61.3) and the preceding clause requires a verb on which it can logically depend; if that is correct 'quos' of the mss, whilst perhaps possible, is much inferior to Baehrens' 'quod', which switches the pronoun from qualifying 'partus' to qualifying 'ovo'. 'tenuit' might have arisen in the mss because it goes better with the preceding preposition 'a'; where *gignere* is used of the mother, and the father is also mentioned, he usually appears as a dative (e.g. Verg. *Aen.* 1.617 f. 'Aeneas quem Dardanio Anchisae / alma Venus ... genuit'), as a bare ablative (e.g. Verg. *Georg.* 4.322 f. 'quid me praeclara stirpe deorum / ... invisum fatis genuisti?), or as an ablative with 'ex' (e.g. Tac. *Ann.* 12.3 'quem ex Cn. Ahenobarbo genuerat'). The preposition 'a' in this line seems barely tolerable, and, coupled with the hiatus it causes at the caesura (though for hiatus elsewhere in the collection see p. 23) and the almost perverse word order (the logical order would be 'quod genuit a Iove verso in cygnum'), it is even more suspicious. However further convincing emendation is not obvious (though 'e' for 'a' is worth considering), and I therefore accept the text favoured by modern editors; 'Leda' has to be supplied from preceding 'Ledaei' as the subject of 'genuit'.

3. una tribus genetrix: the three children are the Dioscuri and Helen; as often in this version of the myth, the fourth child, Clytemnestra, is omitted (see my intro. to Aus. *Epig.* 61).

4. sidera pars faciet: one might have expected a construction along the lines of 'sidera pars fiet', but the meaning is clear and the ensuing 'pars fera bella Phrygum' has to be accommodated to the same verb. This 'pars' is the Dioscuri, who in one version of their myth were catasterised as the constellation Gemini (Eur. *Helen* 138 f.; ps.-Eratosth. *Catast.* 10; Ovid *Fast.* 5.693 f.), though the better-known version is of their alternating

Commentary

time spent in the underworld and with the gods, an outcome of their mixed immortal (Jupiter) and mortal (Tyndareus) paternity (see Frazer's note on Apollod. 3.11.2).

132 (143R)

On Europa. Europa mounted the bull's back, believing it reared in the herd, and took her seat on Jupiter; she would never see her father again. The Father disguises and fulfils his amours by trickery: for the god conceals himself, a ravisher in a bull's body.

This is the first of two pieces on the subject of Europa and the bull; they follow on well from the preceding pair on Leda and the swan in that both pairs deal with a liaison of Jupiter in animal form with a human female. Like the epigrams on Leda, this pair are ecphrastic and probably describe works of art; the subject was a favourite, particularly in the mosaics of which North Africa furnishes its share of examples (see *LIMC* 4.1.84 f. nos 144 f., where no. 164 is a particularly fine example from Djemila (Cuicul), dated to around AD 400; Dunbabin, *North Africa*, index 'Europa').

The Europa myth goes back to Homer (*Il.* 14.321 f.), where Zeus speaks of the daughter of Phoinix who bore him Minos and Rhadamanthus, though he does not name her; Europa's father is thereafter usually said to be the Phoenician king Agenor. The actual role played by the bull is a significant variable in the story, since he can be viewed as Jupiter metamorphosed, Jupiter disguised, Jupiter's agent, or rationalised away completely (see 4 n.). This is the First Vatican Mythographer's version (2.46.2 f.): '... Iuppiter in formam speciosi tauri conversus eam vitiavit hoc modo. Cum Mercurius iussu patris in Phoenicem transgressus esset, ut armenta illius regionis ad litus compelleret, Iuppiter in taurum conversus est. Cum se iumentis Agenoris regis immiscuisset et in amorem sui spatiantes in arena virgines coegisset, [ac] paulatim singulis alludens, novissime Agenoris filiam – cuius in amorem compulsus averterat figuram – insidentem sibi tergo in insulam Cretam detulit ibique concubiti<bu>s eius fruitus est' (on the three Vatican Mythographers and their sources see the useful treatment of J. Chance, *Medieval Mythography from Roman North Africa to the School of Chartres AD 433-1177*, Gainesville etc. 1994, esp. 158 f.; 300 f.; all three are medieval in date, the first two belonging to s. viii / ix, the third to s. xii, but all preserve earlier material); see further *LIMC* 4.1.76 f.; Roscher 1.1410 f.

1. credens ... alumni: Europa trusts the bull because she thinks him one of her family's herd (it is usually said to belong to her father Agenor (see Ovid *Met.* 2.836 f.)); *alumnus* in reference to animals is to ones suckled or reared by another animal or a person, as specified in the context: e.g. Hor. *Carm.* 3.18.1 f. 'Faune ... / per meos finis et aprica rura / lenis incedas

Commentary

abeasque parvis / aequus alumnis'; Mart. 13.41.1 'lacte mero pastum pigrae mihi matris alumnum / ponat ...'; Juv. 14.246 f. 'magistrum / ... leo tollet alumnus'. For Jupiter's trickery in disguising himself amongst the herd cf. the First Vatican Mythographer quoted in the intro. above; Ovid *Met*. 2.850 f. 'mixtusque iuvencis / mugit'; and at Hor. *Carm*. 3.27.44 f. it is clear that the bull has wormed himself into Europa's affections before seducing her.

2. non revisura patrem (A); non reditura patri (Burman): SB accepts Burman's conjecture, made to avoid the irregular prosody 'revĭsura', saying '*quod scribit Riese multis horum carminum locis prosodiam neglegi, non est ita*'. But the collection displays plenty of examples of irregular prosody, not all of which SB removes (see 115.1 n. and p. 24). Moreover, Müller (*De Re Metrica*, 455) discusses instances in late authors where the vowels *a*, *e* and *i* can occasionally be shortened if (a) they have a long vowel following, and (b) they are not in the penultimate syllable of a word (e.g. 'creătura' at Sid. *Carm*. 15.92; 'verĕcundo' at *AL* 340.8 Luxorius; 'ferĭtura' at Maxim. *Eleg*. 5.97 and 'ferĭturus' at Drac. *Laud. Dei* 3.106). This may be accepted as a similar instance (it is the phenomenon of the shortening of an unstressed syllable; see 137.1 n).

3. Genitor: see 130.1 n.; the noun contrasts with preceding 'patrem'.

  celat vel complet: *vel* is best understood in the conjunctive sense *et*, as also at 120.12 (see note).

4. in tauri corpore praedo latet: the words perhaps suggest that Jupiter has not in this instance fully metamorphosed into the bull; he has hidden himself inside a bull, which would be a reason why Europa cannot distinguish him from the herd (see 1 n.). There are different degrees of rationalisation which can be apparent in this element of the story: (1) Jupiter can metamorphose fully into a bull (this is the commonest version, as at e.g. Hes. frag. 140 MW; Ovid. *Met*. 2.846 f.; First Vatican Mythographer 2.46.2 f., quoted in the intro. above; Apollod. 3.1.1); (2) Jupiter can use a bull as his agent (as at e.g. Aesch. frag. 99 Radt; Apollod. 2.5.7 (= Akousilaos *FGH* 2.F29 Jacoby)); (3) Jupiter can dress up as a bull or put himself inside one (e.g. Clem. *Hom*. 5.13 (*PG* 2.184) and here); or finally (4), a literal bull is dispensed with and becomes, for example, the shape or sign of a ship on which Europa is carried away (as at e.g. Lycoph. 1298 f.; Fulg. *Myth*. 1.20; Isid. *Or*. 8.11.35).

133 (144R)

Another. Impersonating a bull Jupiter carries off Europa, burning to spread her virginal thighs by his trickery. We really should excuse humans' affairs if, greatest of gods, you enjoy pleasurable adulteries.

Commentary

This second of the two epigrams about Jupiter and Europa is similar to the first in telling the myth briefly in the opening couplet and making a comment on it in the second. It perhaps alludes to a different version of the myth with Jupiter actually metamorphosing into a bull (see 1 n.), and its moralistic conclusion, that if gods can behave disgracefully humans should be able to, is particularly interesting (see 3 n.).

1. mentitus taurum Europam ...: 'taurum Europam' produces the metrical irregularities of hiatus and lengthening at the caesura; both can be paralleled individually in the collection, but this would be the only instance of the two together. Burman, following Oudendorp, changed the order of words to 'Europam, taurum mentitus ...', and this merits serious consideration; but given the many instances of irregularity of metre in the collection (see p. 23), the balance of probability seems to me to favour acceptance of the metre here rather than textual emendation. For *mentior* + accusative in the sense 'impersonate', cf. Val. Flacc. 7.211 f. '(sc. Venus) mentitaque pictis / vestibus ... Circen'; Rut. Nam. 1.259 '(sc. Iuppiter) faciem mentitus et ora iuvenci'; with *TLL* 8.780.31 f. The language perhaps suggests a full metamorphosis in contrast to that of the previous epigram (see 132.4 n.).

2. virgineos ... pandere ... sinus: epic phraseology is given a risqué twist (for epic cf. e.g. Verg. *Aen.* 8.711 f. 'maerentem corpore Nilum / pandentemque sinus'; Stat. *Ach.* 1.101 f. 'conubialia pandunt / antra sinus'): 'sinus' is here almost a euphemism for *cunnus* (Adams, *LSV* 90 f. details two different uses of this euphemism, the one poetic as at e.g. Ovid *Fast.* 5.256 'et tacto concipit illa sinu', the other medical as at e.g. Soran. Lat. (Mustio) p. 9.3 'quid ipse sinus muliebris? ... quem vulgo connum appellant'; the former derives from *sinus* in its application to any hole or cavity, the latter is a calque on medical Greek 'γυναικεῖος κόλπος'). For epic phraseology being put to obscene use see 137.7 n.

3-4. humano ... placent: for similar thinking, that the gods' promiscuous and disgraceful behaviour might serve as a justification for humans, cf. Ter. *Eun.* 586 f.; Sen. *De Vita Beata* 26.6 'sic vestras halucinationes fero quemadmodum Iuppiter optimus maximus ineptias poetarum, quorum alius illi alas imposuit, alius cornua, alius adulterum illum induxit ... quibus nihil aliud actum est quam ut pudor hominibus peccandi demeretur, si tales deos credidissent'; *AL* 247.143 f. Reposianus 'criminis exemplum si iam de numine habemus, / quid speret mortalis amor? quo vota ferenda?'; with W. Bühler, *Europa, ein Überblick über die Zeugnisse des Mythos in der antiken Literatur und Kunst*, Munich 1968, 37.

4. summe deum: cf. Verg. *Aen.* 11.785 'summe deum' (of Apollo); Ovid *Met.* 4.756 'summe deorum' (of Jupiter); Sil. It. 15.362 'summe deum' (of Jupiter).

Commentary

dulcia furta: for this phrase, and for the *furta* of gods in their love affairs, cf. Cat. 68.140 'omnivoli plurima furta Iovis'; Prop. 2.30.28 'dulcia furta Iovis'; Verg. *Georg.* 4.346 'Martisque dolos et dulcia furta', on which Servius comments 'id est adulterium'; with Galán Vioque's note on Mart. 7.74.3.

134 (145R)

On Narcissus. He has found his flame in the middle of the spring, and it is his own reflection that burns the deluded man.

This piece heads three epigrams about Narcissus which display close similarities: all concern Narcissus alone (there is no Echo); all are single distichs; all feature the moment from the myth when he gazes on his reflection in the water; all refer explicitly to his narcissism; and all are ecphrastic in that they describe a scene from another medium, such as a mosaic or painting, whether real or imaginary. There are plenty of paired or triplicate epigrams in the collection (see p. 3), but these show the least variation among themselves; the poet is attempting variation through the imagery and language he uses to describe a single, though pivotal, scene in the Narcissus myth.

Ovid's is the main telling of this myth (*Met.* 3.339 f.); whilst it is possible to detect similarities of language with our epigrams, particularly in the metaphor of burning love and its juxtaposition with the water which is the setting of the story (e.g. 'accendit et ardet' (*Met.* 3.426); 'uritur' (ibid. 430) and 'ignes ... urit' (134.1-2); 'ardet ... flagrans' (135.1)), it would be difficult for such coincidence to be avoided, and no especially pointed reminiscence of Ovid is detectable. Narcissus, particularly after Ovid, was a popular subject in the visual arts: for depictions of him at the spring gazing at his own reflection see *LIMC* 6.1.704 nos 1-24 (no. 12 is a mosaic of this type from the baths at Henchir-Thina, now at Sfax, which dates to the late third century). Note also Aus. *Epigs* 108-10 for another late trio of epigrams about Narcissus, though they are more varied than this in subject matter and metre, on which see my intro. to 108.

1. proprios ... ignes: for the use of *proprius* as equivalent to *suus / tuus* in this collection, see 120.4 n. For *ignis* as the object of erotic desire, cf. Ter. *Eun.* 85 'accede ad ignem hunc, iam calesces plus satis'; Verg. *Ecl.* 3.66 'meus ignis Amyntas'; Ovid *Am.* 2.16.11; *Her.* 16.104; with *TLL* 7.1.295.74 f. And for the conceit of water not extinguishing the flames of love, see 135.1 n.

2. virum: this noun is incongruously applied to Narcissus, an archetypal adolescent who would never feature amongst examples of *virilitas*; it is however an inappropriate instance of a usage categorised by *OLD* vir 6

Commentary

(see also *KS* 2.1.618 Anm. 1) as a reference to a person previously named or referred to, with or without emphasis, to avoid inflected cases of *is* in dactylic verse (there are other examples at 88.4; 99.7; 144.3; 147.2 and 174.11; I note the only occurrence of any part of 'is' in the whole collection is at 182.4). Narcissus has however not been previously mentioned except in the superscript (and he is named in the two following pieces); this may therefore be evidence that the poet assumed his book would be published with superscripts (on which see further p. 18 f.), though the myth is so well-known that its referent would not be in doubt.

135 (146R)

Another. He burns with love of himself, Narcissus aflame at the bank of the spring, as soon as he views himself in the clear water.

1. ardet ... flagrans: as with *ignis* (134.1 n.), both these fire words are often metaphorically used of love and passion: for *ardere* cf. Verg. *Aen.* 4.101; Ovid *Her.* 16.104; and for *flagrare* cf. Cat. 67.25; Mart. 7.26.8.

flagrans Narcissus (de Saumaise; fraglansnarcis (A)) in undis: the phrase 'in undis' undoubtedly constitutes a paradox with 'ardet ... flagrans', playing on the conceit that water cannot extinguish the flames of love (cf. 134.1; 140.6; *ILCV* 787.3 f. (= *ML* 43.3 f.); Ovid *Her.* 16.124 'quanta per has nescis flamma petatur aquas', with Kenney's note for further references; although it is a conceit, the image nevertheless derives from the natural world, because the ancients were well aware of underwater volcanic activity: see e.g. Sen. *Nat. Quaest.* 2.26.3 f.). But what is the precise meaning of 'in undis'? At first sight 'Narcissus in undis' would be taken to refer to Narcissus' reflection, but since he is the subject of 'perspicua se speculatur aqua' in the following line that is nonsensical. SB (*Propertiana*, Cambridge 1956, 80 n. 2) takes 'in undis' to mean 'on the fountain bank', adducing Prop. 1.3.6 'qualis in herboso concidit Apidano' (where 'in herboso Apidano' must refer to the banks of the River Apidanus, though 'herboso' helps). That seems to be the only solution for the text as it stands, but to understand 'in undis' in this context as having anything but its natural meaning gives cause for suspicion. The text of this line has however had to be slightly emended and supplemented because of A's defective 'fraglansnarcis in undis'; might 'fraglans' be hiding something other than 'flagrans'? And 'fraglans' itself is noteworthy; it is such a common variant of *fragrans* in mss (occasionally of *flagrans*: in the Salmasianus also at 16.39R and 18.65R) that it is possible it was a word in use in colloquial speech. Mss confusion between *fragrans*, *flagrans*, *fraglans* and even *flaglans* (cf. Hyg. *Fab.* 152.2) is rife (see *TLL* 6.1.1237.65 f. (*fragrans* / *fraglans*); 846.26 f. (*flagrans* / *fraglans*)).

Commentary

136 (147R)

Another. Narcissus swoons at the loveliness of his own form, Narcissus enslaved by the looks of the water which he scrutinises.

1. suspirat ... gaudia: for *suspirare* + acc. of the person or thing swooned over, cf. Tib. 1.6.35 'absentes alios suspirat amores', the first attested occurrence of the idiom, with Murgatroyd's note. 'gaudia' is the personified object of desire (as 'ignes' in line 1): cf. Ovid *Her.* 19.41 f. 'iamne putas exisse domo mea gaudia, nutrix, / an vigilant omnes et timet ille suos?'

2. scrutata ... unda: the participle might be understood to have an active force from deponent *scrutari* (i.e. 'whom the water scrutinises and enslaves with its features (Narcissus' reflection)'), or perhaps a passive force, from either *scrutari* or *scrutare* (i.e. 'whom the water which he scrutinises enslaves with his features (his reflection)'). For the form *scrutare* cf. Vet. Lat. John 5.39 'scrutate scripturas'; Prisc. *Gramm. Lat.* 2.396.15, with P. Flobert, *Les Verbes déponents latins des origines à Charlemagne*, Paris 1975, 314; and for the past participle of *scrutari* being used with passive force, cf. Sen. *Ep.* 110.13 'ista sollicite scrutata varieque condita'; Amm. Marc. 28.1.10, with Flobert, op. cit. 367. Since the meaning is much the same with either construction, and since the reciprocity of the relationship between Narcissus and his reflection suits such epigrammatic wordplay, the poet might have intended both.

137 (148R)

On the mare of the lawyer Filager. A lampoon on his intercourse with it. A poor lawyer who was burning the midnight oil wanted to rub down the back of his horse. But as he was massaging the mare's body with ministrations of his right hand, thoughts of monstrous intercourse overcame the young man. And so with soft embrace he fondles her where, drawing up his feet from the hard road to swing freely, he usually sits to undertake his long journeys, and he rubs against the mare's thing with his ever-ready penis, a fucker with dulled sensation. The Cretan girl, it is said, sought intercourse with a bullock when the goddess's harsh anger made her fall in love with the animal. Fate has brought the crime of a similar passion to our age: Pasiphae burned for her bull, Filager for his mare.

This is the first of a pair of epigrams concerning the topic of bestiality: a lawyer couples with his mare. It is unusual that the protagonists are a male human and a female animal; such episodes elsewhere usually feature a human female and a male animal (though the extract from Gellius quoted at 2 n. below provides another exception): e.g. Hor. *Epod.* 12.1 (with Watson's note); Lucian 39.51; Apul. *Met.* 10.19 f.; Juv. 6.334; Plin. *Nat. Hist.* 8.155; *AL* 216.6 f. Coronatus; 360.6 Luxorius (though

Commentary

this is merely a play on names); Ennod. 132.1 f. Vogel. There are also some examples from magical papyri cited by J. Gwyn Griffiths in his commentary on Apul. *Met.* XI, 25 f.; and there are of course instances in myth, some of which have appeared previously in this collection (130-3; see also J.E. Robson, 'Bestiality and Bestial Rape in Greek Myth', in *Rape in Antiquity*, ed. S. Deacy and K.F. Pierce, London 1997, 65 f.).

There are also epigrams which attack the sexual proclivities of lawyers, such as Mart. 11.30; Aus. *Epig.* 99; and *AL* 290; 335 Luxorius. In this epigram (and its pair) however, the lawyer is not the shiftless and incompetent creature who usually graces the pages of legal satire; quite the reverse, he is hard-working and travels a lot (137.1; 137.5; 138.3), and he impresses the courts and wins cases (138.2 f.). This tends to highlight the contrast with his sexual behaviour, though his implicit lack of free time might also explain it.

For a similar type of epigram compare Aus. *Epig.* 72, where Ausonius narrates the remarkable episode of a boy who turned into a girl, and then contrasts and compares it with mythological cases of sex reversal. Similarly here, the reader will be astonished at happenings in real life which he might have considered belong only to the tales of myth.

superscr.: Filagri (A); Philagri (edd. *praeter* Riese): it surprises SB that Riese follows the ms. spelling here and in line 12 (see his app. crit.; and indeed Philager is a name attested elsewhere: e.g. *CIL* 6.4893; 8012; 24074). But the similar spelling 'Filocali' at 109 is certain because of the acrostich which contains it. Also, if 'Philager' here were intended to be Greek-based, it would have an irregularly long first syllable at line 12. 'Filager' could be a name of non-Greek provenance, and even if it is Greek of a sort, the Filocalus of 109 is sufficient support to retain the ms. spelling here.

1. causidicus: this noun occurs in verse as early as Lucr. 4.966, and is frequent in Martial and Juvenal (see Citroni's note on Mart. 1.97.2). This seems to be its first appearance in verse subsequently; possibly, given the obscene content of the epigram, it is a deliberate reminiscence of Martial.

pauper ... lucubrans: the epithets are connected: since the lawyer is poor he has to work at night. *Lucubrare* often has the overtone of burning the midnight oil to work or study (e.g. Liv. 1.57.9; Sen. *Contr.* 1. pref. 17; Plin. *Ep.* 3.5.8); apart from Varro *Sat.* 219 Cèbe and Phaedr. *appx.* 15.14 this is the only instance in verse, and the first syllable is irregularly short (see further p. 24). It can be remarked that in about half the examples of irregular prosody in the collection (excluding names) there might be an effect due to shortening of unstressed long vowels or lengthening of short vowels stressed under the accent (as well as here cf. 'récipit' (80.2); 'inpúbĕs' (81.1); 'brĕvi' (96.6); 'flăbélla' (106.16); 'cottīdiána' (117.10);

'revīsúra' (132.2); 'bŏlétar' (142.3); 'rĕnuo' (142.4); 'ătrămentátum' (173.5)). J.N. Adams (*JRS* 89.1999.114 f.) gives some interesting evidence which specifically links the phenomenon of such accentual, rather than classically quantitative, prosody with North Africa (such as comment by grammarians and others on the disregard of quantitative distinction in words by North African Latin speakers (e.g. Consentius, *Gramm. Lat.* 5.392.1 f.); the accentual hexameters of the third-century (or later) Christian poet Commodianus; and the prosody of the third-century verse inscriptions from Bu Njem with which his article deals). Nevertheless, it is evident both that this collection is written in what is basically sound quantitative verse, and that not all departures from it would fit an accentual explanation in any case (see p. 24). If there is any influence of accentual prosody, it would therefore need to be regarded as a variation from the norm, whether deliberate or not.

2. cornipedis: the poet varies terminology for the mare (also 'equa' at line 3, and 'caballa' at line 7); *cornipes* of horses appears first as an adjective in Vergil (*Aen.* 7.779), then as a substantive at Sen. *Phaedra* 809 and Lucan 4.762; 8.3, gaining vast popularity as a kenning in epic (e.g. Statius 15x; Silius 33x; Corippus 13x). It occurs again in this collection at 188.5. Apart from here, the only instances of its being of certain female gender are Ennod. 263.22 Vogel 'ieiunae cornipedis sessor visceribus cibos extrahat' and Cypr. Gall. *Num.* 601 (*TLL* 4.960.35 f.). See also K. Rittweger, *ALL* 7.1892.328 f.

voluit terga fricare suae: on first reading this phrase can appear entirely innocent, referring to the rubbing down or currying of the mare. This action is more often described by the compound *defricare* (e.g. Col. 6.30.1 'nec minus cotidie corpora pecudum quam hominum defricanda sunt, et saepe plus prodest pressa manu subegisse terga, quam si largissime cibos praebeas ...'; Sen. *Ep.* 87.10; Pelag. 402; *Mul. Chir.* 216), but the simple *fricare* is also so used (e.g. *Opus imperf. in Matth.* hom. 42 (*PG* 56.867) 'mollibus manibus nodosam eius (sc. tauri) fricat cervicem'; with *TLL* 6.1.1320.14 f.). For the application of the practice generally in Antiquity see P. Vigneron, *Le Cheval dans l'antiquité gréco-romaine*, Nancy 1968, 1.25 f. However, an obscene double entendre is cleverly introduced, because the scene painted in the epigram is of the *causidicus* going to his mare with the intention of giving her a rub-down, and that act then suggesting another to him; and this phrase is equally appropriate for both acts. For *fricare* used in an erotic sense of manual stimulation cf. 180.8 and note; *CIL* 10.4483 'cunnu tibi fricabo' (these instances have female objects); Mart. 11.29.8; Petr. 92.11 (these instances have male objects); with *TLL* 6.1.1320.21 f. and Adams, *LSV* 184. For *tergum* in an erotic context (though location is imprecise in this double entendre) cf. Aus. *Epig.* 100.6 'tergo femina, pube vir es'.

There is an almost identical instance of the pun on *fricare* preserved

Commentary

in a squib lampooning the low-born consul Ventidius Bassus (Gell. 15.4.3 (= Courtney *FLP, versus populares* no. 3)): '... qui Ventidium Bassum meminerat curandis mulis victitasse, ut vulgo per vias urbis versiculi proscriberentur:

> Concurrite omnes augures, haruspices;
> portentum inusitatum conflatum est recens,
> nam mulos qui fricabat consul factus est.'

3. dextra famulante titillat: on the one interpretation this action can innocently describe the act of currying the mare; on the other it has an erotic significance (*titillare* is not usually a sexual word, but cf. Aus. *Epig.* 115.16 'titillata ... voluptas'; and for use of the right hand in genital stimulation cf. Mart. 11.29.1 f. 'languida cum vetula tractare virilia dextra / coepisti'). The action involved in currying, and the vocabulary descriptive of it, again suggests to the *causidicus* the act of bestiality.

The idiom of noun + *famulare* in an ablative absolute construction is late: cf. Claud. 26.512 f. '(sc. Stilicho) iniquos / fortuna famulante premit'; Paul. Nol. *Carm.* 21.824 f. 'auxit / natura famulante tuum manus (sc. Dei) alta decorem'; Drac. *Rom.* 8.560 'famulantibus undis' (of a scene with Jupiter carrying off Europa). The verb is all but pleonastic; in this instance it could easily be omitted without detracting from the sense.

4. invasit iuvenem: for *invadere* of an idea or emotion suddenly overcoming a person, cf. Sall. *Cat.* 5.6 'hunc ... lubido maxuma invaserat rei publicae capiundae'; the meaning here, it transpires, is 'invasit animum iuvenis' (cf. Apul. *Met.* 5.15.1 'sororis invadunt animum').

prodigiosa venus: the adjective connotes a parting from the norms of nature or acceptable behaviour: cf. Ovid *Met.* 9.727 f. 'cognita quam nulli, quam prodigiosa novaeque / cura tenet veneris' (of lesbianism); and Mart. 1.90.8 'mentiturque virum prodigiosa venus' (again of lesbianism, but nevertheless possibly the source of the phrase here). *Venus* is often used euphemistically of sexual intercourse (see Adams, *LSV* 188 f.), though here it is clear from what ensues that it refers to a desire to perform a sexual act rather than the act itself (see also 118.2 n.; 146.2 n.).

As in the first three lines, it is probable that the reader is intentionally misled by another double entendre in this line: until he reads on, he might suspect that the denouement of the epigram is going to be a sexual assault on the *causidicus* himself. Thus *invadere* + accusative can allude to assault or sexual penetration (cf. e.g. Mart. 11.28.1 f. 'invasit medici Nasica phreneticus Eucti / et percidit Hylan'), and 'prodigiosa venus' could be interpreted to suit such a meaning (e.g. for *venus* used with the sense *mentula* see Adams, *LSV* 57).

Commentary

5. nam qua ... : SB glosses '*Sc. equa*' in his app. crit., but 'qua' is a relative adverb and its reference is '*sc. parte equae*': the lawyer's focus is not on mares, but on particular parts of a particular one (see also 7 n.). The sexual schema suggested by the poet is presumably of the lawyer having to stand on something in order to effect penetration of the mare between its hind legs, while at the same time leaning over on to the animal's back, caressing those areas of it on which he would normally be seated. The schema in the following epigram is different (see 138.14 n.).

longa ... dispendia (Shackleton Bailey; quadrupia (A); quadruvia (Riese)): Riese (app. crit.) says he does not doubt that this poet can use the noun *quadruvium* with the meaning 'road' or 'route' ('notio ... viae'); but such a meaning is not found elsewhere, and it is surely difficult for 'quadru-' to lose all significance of crossroads, a noun which 'longa' does not happily qualify. SB's objection to 'quadruvia' is therefore convincing, and his conjecture 'dispendia' provides excellent sense: cf. *Gramm. Lat.* 7.544.37 'compendia, via cita; dispendia, via per circuitiones difficilis'; Mart. 9.99.5 'tu qui longa potes dispendia ferre viarum' (with Henriksén's note); and cf. the definition at *OLD* dispendium 3: 'extra expenditure in terms of distance (caused by a detour or out of the way journey), extra or excessive distance'. Although the corruption in A is not easy to explain palaeographically, the sense given by 'dispendia' is so apposite that SB's conjecture should be accepted.

carpere: for *carpere* of travel, cf. Hor. *Sat.* 1.5.94 f. 'utpote longum / carpentes iter et factum corruptius imbri'; Ovid *Fast.* 5.496 'carpebant socias ... vias'; Sil. It. 5.28.

sessor: for *sessor* of riders on the backs of animals cf. Sen. *De Const. Sap.* 12.3; Suet. *Jul.* 61; Veg. *Mul.* 1.56.35; 1.62.1. For *sedere* similarly used see J.N. Adams, *JRS* 85.1995.125.

6. subducens ... pendula crura viae: *subducere* + accusative and dative means to withdraw a part of the body from something: e.g. Ovid *Pont.* 1.5.24 'subducunt oneri colla perusta boves'; Juv.1.15 'et nos ergo manum ferulae subduximus'; and 'pendula' is here proleptic (i.e. the rider's feet swing freely and do not come into contact with the ground: cf. Ovid *Am.* 3.2.63, also of a rider: 'sed pendent tibi crura').

7. hanc fovet amplexu molli: construe 'hanc (sc. equam) fovet, qua ...' (see 5 n. 'qua'). For the phraseology cf. Verg. *Aen.* 8.387 f. 'dixerat et niveis hinc atque hinc diva lacertis / cunctantem amplexu molli fovet', describing Venus' embrace of Vulcan, and probably echoed here (for Vergilian lines elsewhere being re-used in obscene contexts see Aus. *Epig.* 75.8 with my note). For *fovere* in erotic contexts, cf. Tib. 1.8.30 'ut foveat molli frigida membra sinu'; Ovid *Her.* 19.62; with *TLL* 6.1.1219.32 f.

molli turdumque (Ziehen *ex* Baehrens); mollitur dumque (A); molli cunnumque (Riese): the slight re-ordering of the ms. text to

Commentary

'molli turdumque' (which was printed in his text by Baehrens, though with the second word obelised) has been independently defended by J. Ziehen (*Philologus* 63.1904.372) and F. Skutsch (*Glotta* 3.1912.104) on the strength of some other bird names used to refer to human genitalia, which are listed by F. Bücheler at *ALL* 2.1885.118 f. Adams (*LSV* 31 f.) gives various appellations of this type for the penis, such as *strutheum*, *titus* and *turtur*, but points out that they are less frequently attested for female genitalia (*LSV* 82), though 'barbata chelidon' at Juv.6.O.6 (cf. Ar. *Lys.* 770) is one instance, and Greek ἀηδονίς at Archil. 263 West is another. *Turdus* in the sense *cunnus* would however be unique; accordingly Riese, followed by SB, dispenses with it and emends to the explicit 'cunnumque'. The choice is finely balanced, but Riese's conjecture would have more force if A had bowdlerising tendencies (which is clearly not the case: 'fututor' appears in the very next line and A has no problem recording it, and A also has no problem with *cunnus* at *AL* 297.12; 312.3 and 5 Luxorius). It is therefore not easy to see why 'turdumque' should have replaced 'cunnumque', and the balance lies in favour of retaining the ms. text and its metaphorical ἅπαξ λεγόμενον (the reference of which is perfectly clear from the context). Note also 138.7, where 'meatus' is used in a unique sense to refer to the mare's sexual organs.

caballae: this, surprisingly, seems to be the only surviving instance of the female noun, though *caballus* is common (*TLL* 3.4.39 f.); *cavalla* survives in Italian. E. Wölfflin (*ALL* 7.1892.318) suggests it was coined here for metrical reasons, but it must also have had a colloquial circulation (see G. Rohlfs, *Die lexikalische Differenzierung der romanischen Sprachen*, Munich 1954, 76 f.).

8. adterit: for *terere* in a sexual sense, cf. Petr. 87.8 'utcumque igitur inter anhelitus sudoresque tritus, quod voluerat accepit', with Adams, *LSV* 183 f. on such uses of the verb and also its compounded forms.

adsiduo pene: the unexpected adjective might suggest either prolonged maintenance of erection (compare the similar use at e.g. Cic. *Clu.* 16 'assiduo fletu'; Cat. 64.71 'assiduis ... luctibus'), or frequent acts of intercourse (cf. Prop. 3.11.56 'assiduo lingua sepulta mero'; 3.16.26 'qua facit assiduo tramite vulgus iter').

fututor hebes: there seem to be no literary occurrences of the noun between its frequent use in Martial and the *Priapea* and its reappearance here (see Citroni's note on Mart. 1.73.4, and cf. note on 'causidicus' in line 1 above). The qualifying 'hebes' sits somewhat oddly with the preceding 'adsiduo pene': its usual meanings of dim-wittedness or laziness are unlikely, because the lawyer's sexual activity is both voluntary and enthusiastic. It can however also refer to a dulling of sensual experience, as at Ovid *Ars* 3.799 f. 'infelix, cui torpet hebes locus ille, puella, / quo pariter debent femina virque frui'; Liv. 5.18.4 'sensus oculorum atque aurium hebetes'. So it may here suggest, in combination with 'adsiduo

Commentary

pene', that the lawyer's congress with the mare has been so prolonged that he has lost all pleasurable sensation in it.

9. concubitus: the noun is a common euphemism for sexual intercourse, particularly in verse, going back to Plaut. *Amph.* 1136 (and cf. Tib. 2.5.53; Ovid *Ars* 1.377; *TLL* 4.99.79 f.).

Cressa: for the lengthening of the final syllable before the hexameter caesura see p. 24. This Cretan girl is Pasiphae, who is identified by her myth rather than this adjective, which is also used by itself with reference to Ariadne (Ovid *Her.* 2.76), Aerope (Ovid *Ars* 1.327), Telethusa (Ovid *Met.* 9.703), and Phaedra (Juv. 10.327). For Pasiphae as a mythical exemplar of bestiality see also Apul. *Met.* 10.19.3; 10.22.4.

iuvenci: also at Verg. *Ecl.* 6.46 with reference to the bull of which Pasiphae was enamoured.

10. quam gravis ira deae: this does not follow the usual version of the myth, which is that Minos had enraged Poseidon over a sacrificial bull, whereupon Poseidon took his revenge by making Minos' wife Pasiphae fall in love with a bull (see Apollod. 3.1.3 with Frazer's note). The variant the poet here adopts is either that Pasiphae herself had outraged Venus by failing to observe her rites and was punished by falling in love with the bull, or alternatively that the Sun had outraged the goddess by disclosing her affair with Mars to her husband Vulcan, and that she then took her revenge on Pasiphae, daughter of the Sun, in this way (see Hyg. *Fab.* 40.1; First Vatican Mythographer 1.43.1 f. respectively).

pecus: the noun not infrequently, as here, refers to a single animal rather than a herd: e.g. Sen. *Thy.* 225 f. 'est Pelopis altis nobile in stabulis pecus, / arcanus aries, ductor opulenti gregis'; Ovid *Ars* 3.249; Mart. 5.31.8; with *TLL* 10.1.952.8 f. *Pecus / pecudis* is much more frequently used of single animals, as it is at 138.14.

11. flammae: perhaps here not simply of the flames of passion, but of the object of that passion (cf. Hor. *Carm.* 1.27.20 'digne puer meliore flamma', on which see Nisbet-Hubbard's note); compare 'proprios ignes' at 134.1 (with note).

138 (149R)

Another. Upright defender of the wretched accused, at whose voice the esteemed tribunal thunders and your home town of Vita carries off victories, why, after the labours of the forum and the ceremonial of the toga, do you enjoy basking in monstrous depravity and, burning to have your way with your mount, rub the opening of the tired horse, and, the responsibility of your position traduced, opt to be a stallion rather than a patron? You should expel from your mind, we beg, these illegally libidinous

Commentary

traits. It is a terrible vice in an advocate, that one accustomed to sway the courts by his pleading should hold the hind legs of a mare in heat.

This second of the pair of epigrams about the lawyer who practises bestiality with his mare is also one of the few in the collection not written in dactylic hexameters or elegiacs. Its hendecasyllables suit the obscene subject (see 119 intro.).

1. tristium reorum: cf. Martial's 'maestorum ... anhelitus reorum' (4.4.8), also a hendecasyllabic line.

2. sacrum ... tribunal: the significance of 'sacrum' is not immediately apparent, but it is a favourite adjective in the collection (also at 91.5; 103.9; 106.7; 123.2; 128.2; 177.4; cf. 'sacrata' at 89.2), and it does not always feature in contexts with any particularly divine significance (e.g. 103.9). The tribunal here is not in any sense ecclesiastical, but secular (see line 4); the significance of the adjective may therefore be nothing more than 'highly revered', indicating an institution to be regarded with the utmost respect.

3. lares Vitenses: this seems to be the equivalent of 'your home town of Vita', though there is no close parallel (perhaps the point is that the lawyer often acted in cases on behalf of his town, and won). A proper name 'Vita', though with a long first syllable, also occurs at 168.1 and 169.2, where it belongs to a person. There was however a town called Vita of which we have knowledge and which would make an appropriate reference here: it was in Byzacena (modern Tunisia), was probably the home town of Victor Vitensis, the historian of the Vandal invasion of North Africa, and had its own bishop in the fifth century (*Notitia provinciarum civitatum Africae*, *MGH AA* 3 p. 67).

4. athla fori: *athla* in Latin often refers to the labours of Hercules, and, with the exception of Hyg. *Fab.* 91.4 ('in athlo funebri'), only occurs as a plural noun; it is also used in an astrological sense by Manilius (3.162 etc., with *OLD* athlum 2). Hercules' labours would here provide a suitable allusion for the hard-working lawyer; similarly a freedman at Trimalchio's dinner describes his ascendancy in his former master's house with the words 'haec sunt vera athla' (Petr. *Sat.* 57.11).

togaeque pompam: *toga* stands by metonymy for the law and legal process (cf. Liv. 22.26.2 'togaque et forum placuere'), while *pompa* is its ceremony. The whole line, indeed the whole of the opening quatrain, is grandiloquent and redolent of the solemnity and might of the law: a stark contrast to the lawyer's sexual activities.

5. monstrifero ... luxu: this is the equivalent of 'prodigiosa venus' at

Commentary

137.4. For *monstrifer* (*monstrum* is a noun frequently compounded: e.g. *monstriger, monstrificabilis, monstrificus, monstrigena, monstriparus, monstrivorus*), cf. Stat. *Theb.* 10.796 'monstrifero coitu', of Jocasta's incestuous union with Oedipus. For *luxus* of sexual excess or depravity, cf. *Epit. de Caes.* 41.8 '(sc. Licinius fuit) avaritiae cupidine omnium pessimus neque alienus a luxu venerio'; Aus. *Epig.* 75.5 'capitalis luxus'; *AL* 318.7 f. Luxorius 'ego te non puto virginem / in luxum capere'; *AL* 338.6 Luxorius.

calere: used of mental passion and arousal at e.g. Hor. *Sat.* 2.3.79 f. 'quisquis luxuria tristive superstitione / aut alio mentis morbo calet'; the verb also frequently applies to the fires of love (cf. Mart. 7.32.12 with Galán Vioque's note).

6. vectricis propriae: as in the previous epigram (137.2 n.), the poet varies the nouns by which he refers to the mare (also 'cornipes' at line 7 and 'pecus' at line 14). 'vectrix' does not appear to be used as a substantive in this sense elsewhere, though it is used of a ship at Paul. Nol. *Ep.* 49.8.

7. fessae cornipedis: on 'cornipes' see 137.2 n.; the mare is tired either because of her long journeys, or because of the amount of sexual activity she affords the lawyer.

fricas meatum: for 'fricare' see 137.2 n. Here 'meatum' uniquely refers to the opening of the mare's sexual organs (as Svennung, *Palladius*, 584 and J. Ziehen, *Philologus* 63.1904.372 state). It can be applied to various other bodily apertures, such as nostrils (Plin. *Nat. Hist.* 28.197), mouth (Prud. *Peristeph.* 10.938), rectum or colon (Pelag. 210.3) etc.

9. admissarius: the noun (the word is also used adjectivally) refers to male animals kept for stud purposes, particularly stallions but not exclusively so (see E. Wölfflin, *ALL* 7.1892.315). Thus Varro *Res Rust.* 2.7.1 'mares, quos admissarios habeo ... singulos in feminas denas'; Col. 6.27.10 'si admissarius iners in venerem est'. As with English 'stallion', the term can be transferred to humans, as it is here and also at e.g. Plaut. *Mil.* 1112 'ad equas fuisti scitus admissarius'; Cic. *Pis.* 69; Sen. *Nat. Quaest.* 1.16.2.

patronus: synonymous with 'defensor' in line 1, though more elevated in tone; the lawyer of these two epigrams is also termed 'advocatus' (138.12) and 'causidicus' (137.1), a titular variety to match that of his mare (137.2 n.).

10. rogamus: the conversational phraseology of *rogare* + subjunctive is typical of Martial: cf. 1.35.13 'parcas lusibus et iocis rogamus'; 1.96.2 'nostro rogamus pauca verba Materno / dicas'; 6.35.5; 8.2.8; and 'rogo' similarly at 6.5.2 and 7.95.18. The idiom is also frequently found in subliterary Latin (e.g. *Tab. Vindol.* III.831 'rogo iubeas dari', with J.N. Adams, *CQ* 53.2003.546 and 85 n.).

Commentary

11. inlicite: this is the only instance of this adverb in verse.

libidinantes: the verb is applied not only to humans (as at e.g. Mart. 7.67.13), but also to animals, as at Vet. Lat. Jer. 5.8 (= Greg. Iliberr. *in Cant. Cant.* 2.26 (*CCSL* 69.1967.187 ed. Bulhart)) 'equi libidinantes ad uxores proximi sui hinniebant'; and esp. Porph. ap. Hor. *Epod.* 12.11-12 'subare proprie sues dicuntur, cum libidinantur' (see also 14 n. 'subantis' below). An overtone of animal lust would be appropriate here.

13. solitum (edd.); sonitum (A); solito (Shackleton Bailey): although SB's conjecture 'solito' (*Towards a Text*, 22) makes the construction slightly easier (he also removes the comma placed by most editors at the end of line 12 so that 'solito' picks up 'advocato'), the previous editors' preference 'solitum' is possible, is closer to the ms. 'sonitum' (which itself is not supportable), and avoids the awkwardness in the jingle 'advocato / orando solito'.

caulas: *caulae* are lawyers' enclosures in front of judges at tribunals, and here metonymically stand for the judiciary. The noun refers to apertures or openings in Lucretius (e.g. 3.255 'diffugiant partes per caulas corporis omnis'); to animal pens in Vergil and elsewhere (e.g. *Aen.* 9.59 f. 'ac veluti pleno lupus insidiatus ovili / cum fremit ad caulas'); and then to enclosures for people in religious and legal environs (cf. Serv. ap. Verg. *Aen.* 9.59 'in sacris aedibus et in tribunalibus saepta, quae turbas prohibent, caulas (de Saumaise; clausas (codd.)) vocamus'; *CGL* 4.27.18; 216.3).

14. subantis: for *subare*, which denotes an animal in heat, cf. Lucr. 4.1199 f. 'ipsa quod illarum (sc. animalium) subat ardet abundans / natura et Venerem salientum laeta retractat'; and Porphyrion quoted above at 11 n.; the verb is applied to a human female at Hor. *Epod.* 12.11 (see Watson's note), and even to human and divine males, Jupiter at Tert. *Apol.* 14.3, and Epicurus at Jer. *Ad Jovin.* 2.379 (*PL* 23.334). The scansion of the first syllable may here be long and therefore prosodically irregular, though there is one other instance of a short syllable opening a hendecasyllabic line in the collection ('Caballina' 119.1), and the total sample is relatively small (at 29 lines); Luxorius also affords an example ('mori' at *AL* 302.7).

tenere (A; timere (Shackleton Bailey)) gambas: *gamba* (*camba* is also attested) derives from Greek καμπή ('bending' or 'joint'); for similar changes from Greek 'κ' to Latin 'g' cf. κυβερνᾶν / gubernare; κωβιός / gobius (more examples at LHS 1.151 f.). It belongs in Latin largely to veterinary writers apart from this instance (e.g. Pelag. 219; 329; Veg. *Mul.* 2.49.1; *Mul. Chir.* 26; 692 etc.; but for its use in non-veterinary contexts to denote a human leg, rather than as might be expected only a part of it, see J.N. Adams, *IF* 87.1982.98 f.); it properly refers to the hock of a horse, the joint in the back legs which corresponds to the knee (*genu / geniculum*) in the front legs (see Adams, *Pelagonius*, 399; 401; 408). The context

257

Commentary

here however is that the lawyer's 'horrendum vitium' is evidenced by his holding the mare's 'gambae'; since he has just been labelled a would-be stallion (line 9), and since his mare is sexually receptive ('subantis'), this action of his, which is the denouement of the epigram, must allude to his having intercourse with the mare, as he does in the previous epigram. But that would be physically impossible if he holds the animal's hocks, and therefore *TLL* (6.2-3.1688.15 f.) is surely correct in interpreting 'gambae' here to be used with a less specific reference (e.g. to the mare's hind legs; for other evidence for such an extension of meaning of the noun cf. *CGL* 5.495.59 'crura: gambae; tibiae', and Adams loc. cit. above). SB's conjecture of 'timere' for 'tenere' (*Towards a Text*, 22) is unnecessary, and would provide a weak conclusion to the piece.

139 (150R)

On a panel painting. This face which the black panel sports, which a thin outline has clearly delineated, the painter, taming his varied palette, extremely experienced in his skilful art, will next render like its original, with reality proving the truth to nature of the artist in his forms, to the extent that you believe that whatever parts of the body are painted by his hand have bodily sensations.

This intriguing but convoluted and muddled epigram apparently describes the outline drawing of a panel painting which awaits coloration by the painter; unfortunately it has such problems of text and interpretation that certainty over the basic subject matter, let alone points of detail, is difficult to achieve. The praise of the poem is however directed specifically at the painter, who may or may not also be the person who has drawn the outline.

M. Borda (*La pittura romana*, Milan 1958, 392) says of the process involved in making pictures like the one this epigram describes: 'I ritratti sono dipinti su sottilissime tavolette di legno (tiglio, cedro, cipresso, platano, quercia, sicomoro); se dipinti a tempera hanno un' imprimatura bianca di creta e colla, o colla e gesso; se ad encausto, la preparazione avveniva con una spennellatura bianca o nera a tempera; il disegno della figura veniva tracciato a tinta chiara a grandi tratti, con rapidi tocchi. Seguirà la pittura ad encausto, eseguita col pennello e con la spatola (come dimostra la macrofotografia ...)'; see also Ling, *Painting*, 157 f. Unsurprisingly there is little surviving evidence for the presumably secular panel paintings of the type described in the epigram, but the mummy portrait busts from Fayum in Egypt, which date from the first to fourth centuries, give a good idea of technique (see S. Walker and M. Bierbrier, *Mummy Portraits from Roman Egypt*, London 1997), a first-century AD portrait painting from Hawara, which is still in its frame, survives (see R. Cormack, *Painting the Soul: Icons, Death Masks and*

Commentary

Shrouds, London 1997, fig. 19), and a framed portrait of a woman on a black background can be seen in Room XXV of the Museo Arqueológico at Seville. Also of note are the two remaining panels of a third-century portable triptych now in the John Paul Getty Museum, which feature busts of Isis and Sarapis painted in tempera on wood, and which are particularly interesting in that they are precursors of the Christian icon painting which would have been in or near its infancy when this epigram was written (the earliest surviving icons are dated to the later sixth century: see esp. K. Weitzmann, *The Icon: Holy Images*, London 1978, Fig. V; Pl. 1; and passim; *Late Antiquity, A Guide to the Postclassical World*, ed. G.W. Bowersock, P. Brown and O. Grabar, Cambridge Mass. / London 1999, 627 f.; Cormack, op. cit. 64 f.).

The painting of this poem may arguably be on a larger scale than a portrait bust (see 7-8 n.), but the purpose for which it was painted, its location, and its subject matter are not apparent. It would probably have been an honorific or commemorative piece, but other purposes for ancient portraiture are known: there are, for example, literary references to paintings which shipwrecked persons carried around with them, depicting the disaster that had befallen them, in order to facilitate begging (Juv. 14.301-2, with Courtney's note), and to votive paintings which were offered in thanks for the aversion of calamity (Hor. *Carm.* 1.5.13, with Nisbet-Hubbard's note).

The metre of this poem is the hendecasyllable, for which see p. 22.

1. nigra ... tabella: this can only indicate that the panel on which the painting is to be made is black, and that black is therefore the background colour on which the painting will be made; it need not imply that it would remain black in the finished product. There is some evidence for such a technique in surviving wall paintings (see P. and L. Mora and P. Philippot, *Conservation of Wall Paintings*, London etc. 1984, 89 f., with Pls 60-1), and see Borda's remarks above about preparation for encaustic painting.

gerit (Riese; gerens (A)) ... vultum (Petschenig; vultu (A)): the two parallel introductory clauses which result when Riese's emendation 'gerit' is accepted are by no means certain, but they yield reasonable sense and stay reasonably close to A's text, which cannot stand as it is. The 'vultus' here is elaborated by the following line, and is an outline drawing; there is no reason why it cannot refer just to the face, even though it seems from later in the epigram ('artus' line 6) that the painting might be a fuller portrait.

2. linea quem brevis (Riese; qua morevis (A); quem more vos (Sched.)): A and the Schedae Divionenses offer nonsense; Riese's emendation is convincing because it gives good sense and is palaeographically plausible (the 'b' of 'brevis' having been misread as 'o' with further corruption following). For *linea* as the line of a drawing cf. Plin. *Nat. Hist.* 35.81 f., where he describes a drawing and painting

Commentary

competition between Apelles and Protogenes, in which *linea* frequently occurs (e.g. 'adrepto ... penicillo lineam ex colore duxit summae tenuitatis per tabulam'); Quint. *Inst.* 10.2.7 'non esset pictura nisi quae lineas modo extremas umbrae quam corpora in sole fecissent circumscriberet'; with *TLL* 7.2.1436.40 f. The adjective 'brevis' suggests that although the outline drawing is still an incomplete product achieved with minimum line, the identity of the 'vultus' is nonetheless apparent ('clarum'): compare Pliny's 'summae tenuitatis' at *Nat. Hist.* 35.81, quoted above.

Underdrawing of paintings would be an expected technique of preparation, though the lack of surviving evidence for it is hardly surprising; but some support can be adduced from similar technique in fifth-century manuscript illumination, notably the Vatican Vergil (Vat. lat. 3225) and the *Itala* Quedlinburg fragment of the Bible (on which see *CAH* 14.888 f., with further references).

3. varios domans colores: 'domans' implies that the painter, who is the focus of the epigram, judiciously selects colours from his palette to achieve his lifelike effects; the colours are wild and untamed until he applies them and creates order. Horace similarly describes the grape turned into wine as 'prelo domitam Caleno' (*Carm.* 1.20.9) and Pliny (*Nat. Hist.* 16.171) describes tibia-playing with the words 'multa domandae exercitatione et canere tibiae ipsae edocendae'.

4. callenti ... arte: *callens* usually applies to the person, but cf. also Jer. *Ep.* 82.6 'tam argutum ... et callens ingenium'. It is here almost pleonastic with 'nimium peritus', emphasising the painter's skill and knowledge of his craft.

5. formabit (Petschenig); formavit (A): the preceding 'mox' by no means guarantees a future tense since it only indicates that one event takes place after another and is often used with past tenses, but the sense of the epigram strongly supports Petschenig's conjecture (*ZOeG* 28.1877.484 f.), and mss confusion between '-vit' and '-bit' is common (see 161.1 n.). The opening describes a 'nigra tabella' with an outline drawing, but the poet would hardly use the adjective 'nigra' if the object were the finished product. It makes better sense for the object the poet describes to be understood as a sketch that the painter is about to complete by application of colour, rather than as a sketch which has been fully completed by the painter, since under the latter circumstances the sketch would not be visible to the reader-viewer and would not be of interest to him. Martial too describes a partially completed portrait of himself at 7.84.1 f.

similem: 'like the original': cf. Stat. *Silv.* 5.1.1 'manus ... similis docilis mihi fingere ceras', with *OLD* similis 8. Verisimilitude is the usual yardstick of ancient art criticism (see my intro. to Mart. 11.9), and the

Commentary

remainder of the poem elaborates and exemplifies the concept introduced by this adjective.

5-6. probante vero (Burman; viro (A)) ludentis (Shackleton Bailey; ludentam (A); ludentem (edd., *sed* indens iam (Baehrens)) propriis fidem figuris: the vocabulary suggests that this clause develops the idea of verisimilitude, which will continue into the closing lines; but the construction is so compacted and obscure that deeper textual corruption than is implied in the discussion which follows cannot be ruled out. The text of A is 'probante viro / ludentam probriis fidem figuris'; 'probriis' is only orthographic variation on 'propriis', but 'viro' and 'ludentam' evidently require emendation and are problematic, whilst the sense of 'fidem' is also not beyond doubt. I will deal with the issues in turn:

(1) In this art-critical context the slight emendation of 'viro' to 'vero' is plausible, and is accepted into the text by Burman and most subsequent critics and editors (e.g. Ziehen (*BPhW* 1919.1051 f.), Petschenig (*ZOeG* 28.1877.484 f.), Riese, Baehrens and SB), who understand it as the ablative of abstract *verum* used in the sense 'veritas naturae' (it adds weight that it also has this sense at 100.8). E. Courtney's suggestion (*CPh* 79.1984.311) that 'verum' here means 'the original' (adducing Claud. 35.42 f. 'nulli sic consona telae / fila nec in tantum veri duxere figuras') is a more specific application of this interpretation.

(2) To what does 'fidem' refer? Riese glossed it in his app. crit. as '*sc. spectantium*' (printing the text 'ludentem propriis fidem figuris'); SB criticises this in his app. crit. (though the criticism is more based on 'ludentem' than 'fidem': '*sed vultus ita fidem ludens ut artus corporeos habere sensus credas mihi quidem non probatur*'), and convincingly offers instead the gloss '*I.e. fidelem repraesentionem*', interpreting 'fidem' in the light of 162.4 'arboris atque hominis fulget ab arte fides', where it refers without doubt to the verisimilitude of a statue of the flayed Marsyas ('fides' is an emendation, though certain: see note ad loc.).

(3) Finally A's 'ludentam', which is nonsense. Some editors and critics from Burman onwards (e.g. Courtney, loc. cit.) have emended to the palaeographically close 'ludentem', which however seems impossible to interpret with any conviction (see SB's comment referred to in (2) above); some have suggested 'iam' or 'tam' lies behind the final syllable and have added a preceding participle (thus 'indens iam' (Baehrens); 'ludens tam' (Hagen)), but this would involve a break in sense at the end of line 5 and a new clause beginning line 6, which again does not convince. SB's conjecture 'ludentis' (which he glosses '*i.e. pingentis*' in his app. crit.) consequently seems the best option, though it cannot be beyond question in such a generally problematic context. For *ludere* used elsewhere of painting or sculpting, cf. Sen. *Contr.* 10.5.8 'ne Parrhasii manus temere ludat coloribus'; Stat. *Silv.* 1.3.50 f. 'quicquid et argento primum vel in aere minori / lusit et enormis manus expertura colossos' (the implication

Commentary

behind this use of the verb is of the apparently effortless ease with which a great artist creates masterpieces).

My conclusion from this is that lines 5-6 may be best construed and translated as follows: 'probante vero' (ablative absolute, meaning 'with reality demonstrating', sc. either from a comparison of the sitter for this particular portrait with the product when it is finished, or from reader-viewers' everyday perceptions of human faces and what constitute convincing representations of them), 'fidem ludentis' (object of 'probante', meaning 'the verisimilitude achieved by the painter'), 'propriis figuris' (dative dependent on 'fidem', meaning 'in the images or forms he is about to paint', sc. in this particular portrait, which as yet is only an outline sketch).

7-8. ut, quoscumque ... habere sensus: the hypothesis already advanced about the verisimilitude that will be demonstrable on the painter's completion of the portrait is developed to advertise the more general conclusion that whatever 'artus' he paints are so close to nature that the reader-viewer may think they are the living thing. These 'artus' might belong to the particular portrait of the epigram (and suggest that it is larger than a portrait bust), but it is perhaps more likely that they have a wider, general reference to the painter's work and skill.

7. repingat: the prefix implies that the painter uses the colours of his palette to complete the outline previously sketched.

140 (151R)

On Galatea. Fleeing the sea, Galatea scours the woods to catch sight of the guardian of the flocks, Acis; for in her passion she skewers her tender soles on thorns, yet her love does not feel the deep wounds of her feet. The very elements yield to Cupid's quiver; his flame smoulders even in the midst of water.

This is the first of a series of four epigrams about the nymph Galatea; the following three are variants on a single idea, that of an image of Galatea which decorates a platter or salver, but this one stands on its own as a telling of part of her myth. It is ecphrastic in that the poet paints a specific scene, that of Galatea desperately pursuing her beloved Acis, and then comments on that scene. As often with this type of epigram, the poet might have in mind a specific painting or mosaic which featured Acis with Galatea looking for him (lines 1-2). A Pompeiian wall painting and two third-century mosaics from Africa feature the two characters, though the scene is different (*LIMC* 5.1.1000 f, with nos 25; 26; 47).

In myth Galatea was the daughter of Nereus and the sea nymph Doris, and is closely connected with Sicily. The giant Polyphemus fell in love with

Commentary

her, and in the usual version of the story she was unimpressed, though in some versions she succumbed to his wooing and bore him children; the contrasts this myth offered between Polyphemus' uncouthness and his love for the nymph made it popular with Hellenistic writers. Ovid gives the first literary account which completes the triangle with the shepherd Acis, with whom Galatea was in love (though the myth in all probability predates him); on discovering this liaison Polyphemus tried to flatten Acis by throwing half a mountain at him, but Galatea transformed him into the river which bears his name (*Met.* 13.750 f., with Bömer's note, and cf. Sil. It. 14.221 f.; the river is identified with the modern Jaci (see E. Manni, *Geografia fisica e politica della Sicilia antica*, Rome 1981, 94 f.)). In the four poems on the theme in this collection there is no mention of Polyphemus, and the poet concentrates on the nymph alone at 141-3 with Acis added only in this epigram. The particular scene is not taken directly from Ovid (and it is unlikely that it originated with this poet), though it accords well enough with the outline of his story: the concluding couplet shows it is intended to illustrate the passion of love, and it would provide a relationship which offers a pointed contrast to Polyphemus' infatuation with Galatea. For the myth and its variants see *LIMC* and Bömer locc. cit.; Gow's preface to Theoc. *Id.* 6; and Hopkinson's commentary on Ovid *Met.* XIII, p. 35 f.

1. defugiens (Müller); diffugiens (A): although this poet is fond of the 'dis-' prefix (see 130.2 n.), it is questionable here: its force with *fugere* is usually to indicate diverse persons fleeing in diverse directions, rather than a single person fleeing something, as is required here (cf. Isid. *Diff.* 1.231 'fugiunt pariter, diffugiunt divisi' with *TLL* 5.1.1106.73 f.). Whilst this is not conclusive, it tips the balance in favour of Müller's slight emendation, which undoubtedly has the right shade of meaning (cf. Cic. *De Repub.* 2.34 'defugit patriam vir liber ac fortis'; Sen. *Herc. Oet.* 675 'quisquis medium defugit iter').

pontum, silvas: the juxtaposition emphasises how Galatea has moved out of her proper element as a sea nymph, and how her love for Acis has driven her onto the alien and dangerous land. This is significant for the impact of the concluding couplet (see 5 n.).

peragrat (A); peragrans (Shackleton Bailey): SB's emendation is unnecessary, particularly if ms. 'nam' is retained in the following couplet, as I argue it should be. For *peragrare* of thorough searching, cf. Verg. *Georg.* 4.53 'saltus silvasque peragrant', with Mynors' note.

2. Acim: the short first syllable of the name, whether referring to the shepherd or the river, is found only here (except possibly at Claud. 36.332 'flumen Acin', which editors often emend to 'flavum Acin' because of the prosody (see Hall's note)); for other prosodical irregularity with proper names in the collection, see p. 24. The Latinate accusative is also only found

Commentary

here; Latin elsewhere uses the Greek accusative *Acin* (as at Ovid. *Met.* 13.861; 874; 884; Claud. loc. cit.), though *Acidem* appears at Sol. 5.17.

3. nam (A); tam (Baehrens); iam (Oudendorp): A's 'nam' is by no means secure but the obvious emendations of 'iam' and 'tam' are not improvements. See note on 'nam' at 113/14.3; here it is best understood as simply introducing evidence that Galatea has left the sea for the land in her passion for Acis (her feet are badly hurt, which would not usually happen).

teneros gressus: these are Galatea's feet (or more accurately her soles) rather than the steps she makes with them; cf. Lucr. 6.1116; Petr. *Sat.* 30.7 'ceterum ut pariter movimus dextros gressus', with *TLL* 6.2-3.2327.1 f. Their tenderness is evidence not only of her delicate femininity, but also of her inexperience of running on land.

4. alta ... vulnera: this (or 'altum vulnus') is a frequent epic phrase (e.g. Verg. *Aen.* 10.857; 11.817; Lucan 1.32; Sil. It. 9.155), stressing Galatea's physical wounds, to which her passion makes her insensible. For such dulling of the lover's senses see Gow's note on Theoc. *Id.* 10.20.

5. Cupidineae ... pharetrae: for similar phrases cf. Stat. *Theb.* 6.9 'Apollineae ... pharetrae' and Sen. *Agam.* 614 'Herculea ... pharetra'. It is Cupid's arrows rather than his quiver that are in point here (and the poet could easily have written 'Cupidineis ... sagittis'), but the quiver exemplifies his full armoury.

cedunt elementa: this is almost certainly A's text, though with typical carelessness it gives 'cedunt telementae'; and it is sound, as SB says (*Towards a Text*, 23), objecting to Riese's 'laedunt tormenta' ('tormenta' being a conjecture by Baehrens). The thought expressed is that all the universe is subservient to the powers of love: 'omnia vincit amor, et nos cedamus amori' (Verg. *Ecl.* 10.69). This is made explicit in the next line by the conceit of love's flame burning even in water (fire and water themselves being *elementa*), and it encapsulates the preceding lines of the poem, where Galatea's passion is such that she is willing to change her sea home for dry land, and where she does not feel the pain of the thorns which lacerate her feet.

For *elementa* symbolising all creation, cf. Apul. *Met.* 11.25.3 'tibi (sc. Isidi) respondent sidera, redeunt tempora, gaudent numina, serviunt elementa'; *Pan. Lat.* 5(8).10.4 'vicisti ... ipsa elementa, quibus animamus et vivimus'; ibid. 8(5).4.2; Lact. *Inst.* 2.13.12 'admirantes elementa mundi, caelum, solem, terram, mare'.

6. cuius: i.e. 'Cupidinis', supplied from the adjective in the preceding line.

in mediis flamma ... aquis: for the topic that love's flames cannot be extinguished by water, see 135.1 n.

Commentary

suburit: of the smouldering fire of love, which is ready to flare up at any time: cf. Theoc. *Id.* 3.17 'ὅς με κατασμύχων καὶ ἐς ὀστίον ἄχρις ἰάπτει' ('his slow fires torture me to the very bones' (Gow)), with Gow's note; also Headlam's note on Herodas 1.38; and Gow-Page, *HE* 2.163.

141 (152R)

On Galatea on a salver. The loveliest of Naiads sports playfully and she shines out even on the salver, making the diners' faces blush by her beauty. May the waiter not be slow in splashing around the sauce accompaniment in order that the arousing image may lie hidden, covered by the food on it!

The subject of Galatea continues from the previous epigram, but this and the next two concentrate on a piece of tableware, a dish which shows the nymph disporting herself naked in the sea (for her nakedness see 143.2 n.). The point is the same in all three, though expressed with considerable wit and invention: the naked girl is so beautiful that she will prevent the diners who gaze on her from eating, if they are not careful.

Representations of Galatea alone are rare in the visual arts, for a reason which is clear from 143.5 f.: unless she is named or identified from other characters in her myth there is no way of distinguishing her from many another beautiful nymph (thus Homer catalogues thirty-three Nereids at *Il.* 18.39 f., including Galatea (45); Hesiod lists forty-nine at *Theog.* 240 f., including Galatea (250); Apollodorus has forty-five at 1.2.7, again including Galatea; and so on). *LIMC* (5.1.1000 f.) therefore can produce only two certain images of Galatea alone, and they are certain only because she is named.

Ecphrastic epigrams which describe decorated tableware or other vessels, such as this and its two companion pieces, are common enough: thus *AP* 9.406 Antigonus, about a frog decoration on a crater (with Gow-Page, *GP* 2.17); 9.541 Antip. Thess., describing the constellations carved on a pair of bowls (with Gow-Page, *GP* 2.55); 9.585 anon. on a dish with decorations of Venus and Cupids; 9.749 Oenomaus on an Eros carved on a bowl; 9.771 Julian. Aeg. on a phiale with fish decorations; and 9.822 anon. on a dish with decorations of the zodiac. And the type becomes a particular favourite of Ennodius, who describes a set of seven dishes with animal decorations (129 Vogel), a *caucum* with Pasiphae and the bull (133; 136; 136a; 136b Vogel, with Kennell, *Ennodius*, 115), and *scutellae* depicting more of Jupiter's amours (232; 232a; 233 Vogel). Particularly similar to the present pieces is *Anacreontea* 57 (probably of late date), which describes in modestly erotic detail a naked Aphrodite cavorting in the sea, an image engraved on a platter; the poet says of the artist and his subject (9-19):

Commentary

ὁ δέ νιν ἔδειξε γυμνάν,
ὅσα μὴ θέμις δ' ὁρᾶσθαι
μόνα κύμασιν καλύπτει.
ἀλαλημένη δ' ἐπ' αὐτὰ
βρύον ὥς, ὕπερθε λευκᾶς
ἁπαλόχροον γαλήνας
δέμας εἰς πλόον φέρουσα,
ῥόθιον παρ' οἶμον ἕλκει.
ῥοδέων δ' ὕπερθε μαζῶν
ἁπαλῆς ἔνερθε δειρῆς
μέγα κῦμα χρῶτα τέμνει.

('He showed her naked, covering with the waves only what ought not to be seen. Roaming over the waves like sea-lettuce, moving her soft-skinned body in her voyage over the white calm sea, she pulls the breakers along her path. Above her rosy breasts and below her soft neck a great wave divides her skin' (Loeb))

The type of table decoration which is described in the present pieces is silver plate which has either been engraved, or more probably decorated in relief (see 141.1 n. patinis; 143.6 n. lactea massa). It was popular in late Antiquity and a number of excellent examples survive, usually because they were part of treasure troves (see Strong, *Gold and Silver Plate*, 196 f.; and esp. J.M.C. Toynbee and K.S. Painter, 'Silver Picture Plates of Late Antiquity AD 300 to 700', *Archaeologia* 108.1986.15 f., with e.g. Pl. 16c, a fourth-century plate from Baku decorated with a naked nymph astride a hippocamp; and Pl. 17c, a sixth-century plate allegedly from Carthage with a half-clothed Nereid astride a sea-lion).

Epigrams 141-3 have received some recent critical attention, largely because of criticism of SB's Teubner text and his previous comments at *Towards a Text*, 23: esp. W.J. Schneider, 'Zu Tisch mit der schönen Galatee', *C&M* 50.1999.189 f.; and P. Paolucci, 'Il "Ciclo di Galatea" ', *BStudLat* 32.2002.111 f. It will be apparent from the following notes that I largely concur with their comments.

1. fulget et: the verb alludes both to the metal of which the salver described is made (see 143.6 n.), and to the beauty of the nymph who is the subject of the decoration (cf. Ovid *Med.* 68 'fulgebit speculo levior illa suo'; Sen. *Phaedra* 651); 'et' emphasises the fact that the nymph's beauty is as apparent from the decoration of the salver as it would be in the flesh.

in patinis: plural for singular; the object is also termed *vas* (141 superscr.) and *boletar* (142.3 n.), and described as 'lactea massa' (143.6 n.). None of these terms is well defined, but they would all suit a large salver or serving dish (cf. Varro *Ling. Lat.* 5.120 'patenas a patulo dixerunt'). Silver vessels described as *patinae* occur at e.g. Paul. *Sent.* 3.6.86 and *SHA* Claud. 17.5; with Hilgers, *Gefässnamen*, 72 f. and no. 283. It must be doubtful whether salvers like the one described would ever have been used for serving food rather than as a table display. There is the practical difficulty of getting food off the relief decoration, and the whole raison d'être of such ware is to reflect the owner's taste and wealth; so when the servant is here instructed to cover the decoration with food and sauces, the command is humorous.

ludens: of the nymph disporting herself; the verb is repeated at 142.1 and 143.5. There is also a strong hint of erotic titillation and the interest Galatea will awake in the diners who gaze on her (for such overtones of the verb see my note on Mart. 11.104.5).

2. inflammans ora (codd.; corda (Baehrens)): SB follows Baehrens' conjecture, merely labelling the mss 'ora' as 'grotesque' (*Towards a Text*, 23). It is the case that *inflammare*, when applied to persons, is almost invariably used metaphorically in respect of their emotions, especially love and lust (e.g. Cic. *Tusc.* 5.16 'libidinibus inflammatum et furentem'; Mart. 10.86.1 'nemo nova caluit sic inflammatus amica'; with *OLD* inflammo 2). However there is also evidence that *inflammare* can be used with the meaning 'to make blush' (Cass. *in Psalm.* 43.16 (*PL* 70.315) 'nube sanguinea facies eius inflammata rutilavit'). The mss reading is therefore likely to be sound, with 'inflammans ora' illustrating the diners' embarrassment at being caught ogling the nymph.

3. congrua (codd.; pinguia (Shackleton Bailey)) ... iura: SB comments (app. crit.) of his emendation 'sc. quo figuram melius celent', adducing e.g. Scrib. Larg. 189 'ius pingue agninum' at *Towards a Text*, 23, where he also remarks of ms. 'congrua' 'appropriate to what?'. Schneider (loc. cit. intro.) responds that it might be appropriate to the image of Galatea, so that she is obscured from view and does not distract the diners (line 4). It might also, or better, be appropriate to the 'positis cibis' of line 4, since *ius* is a liquid, no doubt here a sauce of some kind, which could be served as an accompaniment to other food (cf. Hor. *Sat.* 2.4.38 'ignarum quibus est ius aptius'). The addition of such a sauce would cover up any parts of Galatea that the food had not obscured.

diffundat (codd.; difundat (A)); defundat (Shackleton Bailey): although Paolucci (op. cit. intro., 116 with n. 25) supports SB's conjecture on the grounds that *defundere* is the usual culinary term (cf. Cels. 6.6.1K), *diffundere* is much better suited to the context. The waiter is asked to splash the sauce about in all directions so that the offending image can be covered as quickly as possible. The poet is very partial to the prefix 'dis-' (see 130.2 n.).

4. tecta libido: 'libido' refers to the erotic image of the nymph; somewhat similar are the instances of *libido* in art at Plin. *Nat. Hist.* 33.4 'in poculis libidines caelare iuvit ac per obscenitates bibere'; and 35.72

Commentary

'(sc. Parrhasius) pinxit ... tabellis libidines, eo genere petulantis ioci se reficiens'. But here it is not so much the image which is itself an instance of *libido* (i.e. sexual activity depicted in art), it is rather the image of the naked nymph which arouses *libido* in the viewer (i.e. pornography).

142 (153R)

Another. The nymph, accustomed to disport herself in private swimming at the beach, decorates the table, moving her lovely limbs. I do not want fancy food; put down the salver empty, as far as I'm concerned. Let me look at what gives me pleasure; I reject what fills me up.

1. ludere: see 141.1 n.

privato ... natatu: the nymph's secluded, nude (cf. 143.2 n.) swimming is spied upon by the voyeuristic diner, an invasion of her privacy which titillates him.

2. exornat mensas: cf. 159.3 'haec ornant mensas'.

3. comptas nolo dapes: this is a reference to haute cuisine; cf. Isid. *Diff.* 1.112 'inter comptum et compositum: comptum cura, compositum natura'; Tac. *Germ.* 14.3 'nam epulae et quamquam incompti, largi tamen apparatus pro stipendio cedunt'.

vacuum ... boletar: the point of 'vacuum' is clarified by the following line; this diner, unlike the ones in the previous epigram, does not want any food to be put on the salver because he wishes to ogle the naked nymph. *Boletar* is a rare noun, and this is its only appearance in verse (where it is given an irregular short first syllable); it derives from *boletus* ('mushroom'), though its function is not specifically connected with mushrooms in extant references (for which see Leary's comments on Mart. 14.102) – perhaps the name derives from the shape? A weighty silver *boletar* puts in an appearance at *SHA* Claud. 17.5 ('boletar halieuticum argenteum librarum viginti'), where also it must be some kind of decorative dish (see Hilgers, *Gefässnamen*, no. 56).

4. renuo: for the (irregular) long quantity of the first syllable, compare 'rēcipit' at 80.2 with note thereon.

saturat (codd.); stimulat (Shackleton Bailey): SB has missed the point, as Schneider says (op. cit. 141 intro., 190 f.). The speaker is not rejecting the erotic delights of the salver with the Galatea decoration, but asking to see it unobscured by any food (the precise opposite of the request in the previous epigram). The arrangement of the concluding couplet is subtle and effective: the speaker does not want fancy food on the salver (first clause) and accordingly rejects it (fourth clause); he wants the salver to be empty (second clause) in order to ogle Galatea (third clause).

Commentary

143 (154R)

Another. Born in mid-sea, now, by the art of a master, I have come to the dining table; here too I swim naked. If you want to eat, put off gazing at my lovely figure so that your hungry passion does not divert your eyes. Do not doubt who I am: I am a nameless nymph disporting herself – that I am called Galatea the salver's milky mass indicates.

1. in medio generata salo: a birth at sea befits a Nereid, and the phrase also alludes to the derivation of Galatea's name (see 6 n.).

arte magistra: cf. Verg. *Aen.* 8.442 'nunc manibus rapidis, omni nunc arte magistra', with *TLL* 8.88.45 f. for more references.

2. mensam (A); mensas (Heinsius): Heinsius' conjecture was made to eliminate the hiatus at the main caesura, but this is common enough in the collection (see p. 23). However, the fact that the plural appears at 142.2 lends the conjecture some support.

nuda nato: this is the first occasion in the trio of epigrams on the decorated salver when Galatea's nakedness has been made explicit, though in the other poems her diversion of the diners' gaze implies it.

3. differ spectare figuram: 'differ' is pointed: it implies that diners may look at Galatea after they have eaten, so she does not spoil their appetite. Thus the poet offers a third approach for diners confronted by the Galatea salver: do not look (141); do look (142); only look once you have eaten (143). For *figura* of a beautiful figure, cf. Prop. 1.2.7 'non ulla tuae est medicina figurae'; Ovid *Am.* 1.10.14 'nunc mentis vitio laesa figura tua est'.

4. ieiunus (A; ieiuno (Maehly)) ... amor: 'ieiunus' is unexpected but can stand. The reader would expect the epithet to be applied to the diner because the order to him not to eat would entail his hunger; but the epithet is instead applied to the passion he will feel if he looks on her before he eats, implying that it will never be satiated however much he gazes.

lumina tendat (A); inguina tentet (Maehly); lumina tentet (Burman): there is nothing amiss with the ms. text: the poet's insatiable love for Galatea's beauty would occupy his gaze and keep him from eating. For *tendere* used with reference to the eyes, the gaze, etc. as object, cf. Verg. *Aen.* 2.405 'ad caelum tendens ardentia lumina frustra'; ibid. 5.508 'pariterque oculos telumque tetendit'; and for *tendere* applied to emotions as object cf. Ovid *Am.* 3.11b(11).33 f. 'luctantur pectusque leve in contraria tendunt / hac amor, hac odium'. Maehly's conjecture 'inguina', which SB follows, is entirely unconvincing.

5. lipha (*i.e.* lympha (A)); nympha (Burman): A's 'lympha' is not demonstrably incorrect, though it may be only an example of his carelessness: note 'nympha' at 142.1 above, though that of itself proves

Commentary

nothing. *Lympha*, however, occurs elsewhere as a synonym of the Greek-derived *nympha*: thus Hor. *Sat.* 1.5.97 f. 'dein Gnatia lymphis / iratis exstructa dedit risusque iocosque'; *CIL* 5.3106 'Nymphis Lymphisque Augustis ob reditum aquarum ...'; Aug. *Civ. Dei* 4.34 'Nymphas Lymphasque coluerunt'; with J. Wackernagel, *ALL* 15.1908.218 f. (= *Kleine Schriften*, Gottingen 1969, 2.1224 f.). The poet might here be using a somewhat recherché noun for variation (see 81.5 n.), and I have therefore retained it in the text.

6. quod ... vocer: for the subjunctive, where classical Latin would normally use the indicative, cf. Vulg. Gen. 42.33 'ait nobis "sic probabo, quod pacifici sitis ..."'; the idiom is found as early as Cicero (*Att.* 9.10.10; *ad Brut.* 1.15.9), and compare *dicere quod* + subj. at 174.8 n.

lactea massa probat: Galatea's name was connected with the milky froth of the sea (γαλακτόχρως ἀφρός) by Eustathius (ap. Hom. *Od.* 18.42, p. 1131.5), and whether or not the connection with γάλα ('milk') has any etymological truth, the nymph's whiteness is often remarked (e.g. Duris *FGH* 76 F58 Jacoby; Theoc. *Id.* 11.19 f.; Verg. *Ecl.* 7.37 f.; Lucian 14.3 etc.), and her name invites this sort of popular etymology. The poet is however subtle in his introduction of the milk topic: 'lactea massa' (compare λευκοτέρα πακτᾶς ποτιδεῖν at Theoc. 11.20) would at first sight suggest cheese or something made from milk (cf. Ovid *Met.* 8.666 'lactis massa coacti'; Mart. 8.64.9 'massam ... lactis alligati'), but that is not the reference here. It refers to the silver of the salver on which Galatea provides the decoration. Silver is often used as a yardstick of whiteness (as at e.g. Mart. 1.115.2 f 'loto candidior puella cycno, / argento, nive ...', with Citroni's note), and although *massa* usually denotes an unfashioned lump when it refers to metal, it can have wider application to chunky manufactured items (e.g. especially Mart. 3.31.4 'sustentatque tuas aurea massa dapes'; 14.192.1 'multiplici quae structa est massa tabella'). Thus Galatea's milky name and her identity are revealed by the milky silver of the vessel she graces.

Poems in the collection often conclude by offering an explanation or proof of something that has preceded: various verbs can key this, such as *probare* (also at 116.9; 128.4), *monstrare* (e.g. 94.5; 166.9; 174.11 and 179.5) and *ostendere* (e.g. 161.4).

144 (155R)

On Scaevola. Mucius assassinates the attendant instead of the king and now voluntarily burns his own hand to ashes in the sacrificial flame. Porsenna admires him, remits his punishment and, though the victor, enters into an equal truce with the besieged. It benefits its country more in the flames than by the help it had vowed with weapons, the single right hand which allays a war with its funeral.

Commentary

This epigram is ecphrastic in nature (note 'nunc' with present tense verbs), and describes a scene from one of the most famous episodes of early Roman history, when C. Mucius Scaevola voluntarily burned his right hand before the Etruscan king of Clusium, Lars Porsenna, who was besieging Rome in an attempt to restore the deposed king Tarquinius Superbus. This episode was often featured as an *exemplum virtutis*, particularly of the patriotic endurance of physical pain (see Mart. 1.21 with Howell and Citroni). The canonical version is that of Livy (2.12.1-13.5), who describes the key moments which also feature in this epigram: Mucius, intending to enter the Etruscan camp and kill Porsenna, came upon the king sittting with his scribe and mistakenly slew the latter; apprehended and about to be tortured he 'dextram ... accenso ad sacrificium foculo inicit' (2.12.13); whereon Porsenna was so impressed by his patriotism, particularly when he learned that there were hundreds more to follow in Mucius' footsteps, that he made peace with Rome (2.12.15-13.4). In a different version of part of this story, known only in abbreviated form, Porsenna's siege of Rome was successful and he took the city and imposed a humiliating treaty on it (cf. Tac. *Hist.* 3.72; Plin. *Nat. Hist.* 34.139); so when in this epigram Porsenna is labelled 'victor' (line 4), it is probably an allusion to this alternative tradition, in which case the poet has conflated the two accounts. It can be argued that Mucius' heroism appears the greater for it, because as victor Porsenna would have had little motive beyond admiration of his heroic act to make a treaty with Rome.

On the story (a 'romantic tale' according to *OCD* 1227), see Ogilvie's commentary on Livy I-V, 262 f.; and R. Heikkinen, 'A Moral Example in Seneca: C. Mucius Scaevola', in *Utriusque linguae peritus, Studia in honorem Toivo Viljamaa*, ed. J. Vaahtera and R. Vainio, Turku 1997, 63 f.

1. lictorem: the unlucky attendant with whom Porsenna is sitting when Mucius comes upon them is variously described: he is a *lictor* here; a *scriba* at Liv. 2.12.7 and a γραμματεύς at Dion. Hal. 5.28.2; and a *satelles* at Mart. 1.21.1.

pro rege: it is a common element of the story that it was because of his failure to identify the king that Mucius punished himself by immolating his hand (e.g. Sen. *De Prov.* 3.5; *Ep.* 24.5; Val. Max. 3.3.1; Sil. It. 8.383 f.).

necans (V); negans (A): compare 82.1, where A correctly has 'negando', though editors have sometimes mistakenly emended to 'necando'; but 'necans' must be correct here.

2. sacrifico ... igne: cf. Liv. 2.12.13, quoted in the intro. above; Mart. 1.21.2 'ingessit sacris se peritura (sc. dextra) focis'; Sil. It. 8.385; the detail of the flame being sacrificial is significant because Mucius' hand is effectively sacrificed by him to redeem his failure.

concremat: *TLL* 4.92.76 f. states that this verb is only found twice in verse (at Sen. *Phaedra* 1216; *Phoen.* 346), but this is a third instance.

Commentary

3. Porsenna: the name is variously spelt and prosodically treated: Porsenna at e.g. Verg. *Aen.* 8.646 and here; and Porsena (with short second syllable) at Mart. 1.21.6 and 14.98.2.

4. mutua (Shackleton Bailey; maxima (A)) ... foedera: A's 'maxima' is meaningless in this context (cf. SB, *Towards a Text*, 23; E. Courtney, *C&M* 40.1989.202). Although Courtney finds SB's conjecture 'mutua' to be 'no more likely than e.g. *mitia* or *mox rata*' (and 'mitia' is separately proposed by W.S. Watt, *HSCPh* 101.2003.452), it does have considerable merit. SB adduces by way of support Claud. 10.66 f. 'nutant ad mutua palmae / foedera, populeo suspirat populus ictu, / et platani platanis alnoque adsibilat alnus'; and the attraction of 'mutua foedera' here is that it tells the reader something that he did not know and that it is pertinent to know, namely that the treaty Porsenna entered with Rome was on equal terms, and since he was 'victor' he need not have entered such a treaty.

victor: see intro. above.

5. plus flammis ...: Howell (Mart. 1.21.8 n.) aptly compares the similar sententiae at Mart. 1.21.7 f. 'maior deceptae fama est et gloria dextrae: / si non errasset, fecerat illa minus'; Sid. *Carm.* 5.76 f. 'steterat nam corde gelato / Scaevola et apposito dextram damnaverat igni / plus felix peccante manu'; Sen. *Ep.* 66.53; and Drac. *Laud. Dei* 3.397 f.

quam voverat armis (A, armis *ex* maris); quam forvesaturis (V): the text of A has usually been found wanting by editors and has therefore been emended: thus Riese, followed by SB, conjectured 'quam iuverat armis'; Baehrens conjectured 'quam proderat armis'; Petschenig conjectured 'quam voverat aris' (*ZOeG* 28.1877.485); and early editors printed 'quam fortibus armis'. But Ziehen (*Philologus* 59.1900.311) and Courtney (loc. cit. at 4 n.) are correct in their defence of it: in Courtney's words 'the text is simple enough and means "quam voverat <se conlaturum esse> armis"'. Mucius had told the senate he was going to commit a great feat of arms, and he had told Porsenna he had failed by not killing him (cf. Liv. 2.12.5; 2.12.9 'hostis hostem occidere volui'). Further, the contrast between the military failure of the hand and its sacrificial success is pointed elsewhere: e.g. Sen. *De Prov.* 3.5 'regem quem armata manu non potuit exusta fugat'; *Ep.* 24.5.

The subject of the verbs 'confert' and 'voverat' is 'una dextra' of line 6, which stands *pars pro toto* for Mucius: this is unusual but (1) his right hand is the part of him around which the action of the story is focused; (2) it is further personified by having its own funeral (line 6); and (3) the conclusion of Mart. 1.21, quoted above, similarly personifies it.

6. domans bellum: i.e. by persuading Porsenna into offering the treaty; for the phrase, cf. Stat. *Silv.* 1.1.79 f. 'tu bella Iovis ... longo Marte domas'; Cor. *Joh.* 1.127; 4.273; 7.271.

Commentary

145 (156R)

On a man who used to be hit by his wife. Given that you claim descent from the line of Barbatus in order that ferocious Varitinna may be related to you, why are your temples beaten by a lady's slipper, and why has your little goatee fallen out, plucked by her demeaning hand? Stop at once pretending that you have heroic ancestors and that the strength of a fierce line courses in your limbs. She is rather the descendant of Salautensian line, who has the courage to lay low her husband with her heel.

Although the details of this epigram are obscure, because the humour depends on proper names which were exemplary to the writer but whose significance is now lost, its general thrust is unmistakable. An unnamed husband is lampooned for giving himself a falsely heroic family tree while letting his wife beat him black and blue with her slippers; it is she who is more of warrior descent. These general topics appear elsewhere: for the claiming of a false ancestry see my intro. to Aus. *Epig.* 26, and for husband-beating wives see 3 n. below.

1. cum ... cretum: for similar absurdly boastful claims about the family tree cf. *AL* 310.1 f. Luxorius 'fingis superbum quod tibi patrum genus ...'; Mart. 5.17.1 f.; Juv. 8.40 f.; and Aus. *Epig.* 26.3 f.

Barbati (ABW); Barbatae (V): this fierce-sounding name is echoed, and mocked in connection with the lampooned husband, when his own 'barbula' is tweaked out by his wife (line 4). Since he claims descent from this Barbatus in order to get himself related to Varitinna (line 2), it is a likely supposition that Barbatus lived closer to the present than Varitinna, and it is a possibility that Barbatus was mortal and Varitinna mythical or divine, in much the same way that descent from the Julio-Claudians, for example, would automatically appropriate their remoter mythical and divine ancestors (see also 2 n. below).

Although Barbatus here is unknown, the name is the only one in the epigram which appears in other contexts. It is an old Roman cognomen, belonging to e.g. the consul of 449 BC, M. Horatius Barbatus, to the consul of 298 BC, P. Cornelius Scipio Barbatus, and to others. Barbati are also known from a time and place roughly contemporary with this epigram: there is a Christian from Carthage who probably bears the name (*CIL* 8.14170 'Bar<b>atus'), and a cavalry commander under Belisarius who was in Africa with him from 533 to 536 (Proc. *Bell. Vand.* 1.11.7; 2.3.4 etc., with *PLRE* III Barbatus (1)).

2. Varitinna ferox: this particular name is not known elsewhere, but pertinent names with a 'Var-' stem are attested. There is for example a sixth-century native North African leader named Varinnus who features in Corippus (*Joh.* 7.417 f.), where he is labelled 'belliger ille terribilis quondam'. Even more relevant, there appear to be native North African gods similarly named (though the interpretation of the names can be disputed): e.g. 'PLUT<ONI> Variccalae' at *CIL* 8.17330; 'Varsissima' at *AE* 1948.114; and 'Varsutina Maurorum' at Tert. *Ad Nat.* 2.8.4 (see further K. Jongeling, *North African Names from Latin Sources*, Leiden 1994, 146 f.; and F. Vattioni, 'Per una ricerca sull' antroponimia fenicio-punica', *Studi Magrebini* 11.1979.119; 12.1980.1 f.) It is possible that the 'Var-' stem derives from 'Bar-', which in turn derives from 'Baal' (see *LIMC* 8.1.183 Varsissima; 6.1.382 Mauri Dei); a divine ancestry with such associations would be ideal for this context. Other names with an '-inna' suffix are actually attested in native North African nomenclature (e.g. Nafaminna and Mininna (both females); Susrinna (male): see Jongeling's catalogue for details); since the suffix occurs in some Roman names of Etruscan origin, such as T. Vestricius Spurinna (see J. Hadas-Lebel, *Le Bilinguisme étrusco-latin*, Louvain etc. 2004, 333 f.), it may have been appropriated in latinising native African names.

3. femineo ... socco: this is of course a humorously effete item with which a man with warrior aspirations should be beaten by his wife (for specifically ladies' slippers elsewhere, cf. Suet. *Gaius* 52, where they are an item of Caligula's idiosyncratic wardrobe; *Ed. Diocl.* 9.20-1, where 'socci viriles'and 'socci muliebres' are distinguished; and Plin. *Nat. Hist.* 37.17). Pallades (*AP* 10.55.5) characterises a man less dominated by his wife than most as one who can claim not to be beaten by her footwear; and for other such beatings, cf. Ter. *Eun.* 1027 f. 'qui minus quam Hercules servivit Omphalae? ... / Utinam tibi conmitigari videam sandalio caput!'; Pers. 5.169 'solea, puer, obiurgabere rubra'; and Lucian 79.15(13).2. According to Hesychius, a Greek verb had been coined for the act of whacking with slippers: βλαυτόω from βλαύτη ('slipper').

caeduntur tempora (A; tergora (Müller); pectora (BVW)): A's 'tempora' is surely correct here (though 'tergora' is preferred by Riese and SB). A full-frontal assault around the ears, accompanied by a vicious beard-tweaking, is more humorously humiliating than a beating on the back; and in the lines of Terence quoted in the note above, it is similarly the head which is belaboured. 'pectora' was preferred by early editors such as Burman because of 'calce' in line 8 (they thought the woman's foot needed to be in the slipper when it struck, and that she would therefore not be able to reach the man's head; Müller possibly suggested 'tergora' for the same reason (*RhM* 20.1865.635); but the objection is pedantic). Meyer, it should be noted, retained 'tempora'.

4. infamique manu: the adjective here has an active force, as Riese says ('*i.e. cuius plaga tibi infamiae est*'); this is rare, but cf. Ovid *Rem.* 254 'non anus infami carmine rumpet humum'; Nep. *praef.* 5; Quint. *Inst.* 3.7.21 'et est conditoribus urbium infame contraxisse aliquam perniciosam ceteris gentem'; with *TLL* 7.1.1342.3 f.

Commentary

barbula vulsa cadit: the husband's beard is not like that of the fierce warrior stock from which he claims descent and which is personified by Barbatus; it is effete and manicured (cf. Heges. 4.25.2 'vellicare barbulam'). For exactly the same contrast, cf. Cic. *Cael.* 33 'aliquis mihi ab inferis excitandus est ex barbatis illis, non hac barbula qua ista delectatur sed illa horrida quam in statuis antiquis atque imaginibus videmus'. The diminutive noun is unsurprisingly rare in verse, but also occurs at Lucil. 321 M. (= 324 K.); *CE* 1399.4.

7. illa Salautensi (W; -is (ABV)) magis est de stirpe creata; illa sed audaci mage fit de ... (Binet): given the build-up to this conclusion, this phrase must mean that the wife can claim the ancestry to which her husband aspires, because she is more virile than he. It is therefore a reasonable asumption that Barbatus and Varitinna are also 'de stirpe Salautensi'; that the adjective derives from a proper noun is more than probable (Stowasser's (*WS* 31.1909.279) removal of it on the grounds it is unattested elsewhere can be discounted, particularly when he replaces it with Latin which is equally unattested ('sat aut(h)enti'); Binet's emendation would be better if one were needed). According to Keune (*RE* 1A.1850), the name behind *Salautensis* might relate to either a person or place, but given the context the former seems preferable.

8. sternere: this is emphatically humorous language; the verb is, for example, a favourite euphemism in epic of warriors 'laying low' and killing their opponents (e.g. Verg. *Aen.* 11.483 f. 'Tritonia virgo / ... ipsum / pronum sterne solo'; 10.119 with Harrison's note).

calce: for the heel used in fighting, cf. Plaut. *Poen.* 819 'incursat pugnis, calcibus'; Sen. *Ep.* 80.3 'et pugnos pariter et calces non unius hominis ferat'; with *TLL* 3.195.73 f. The lady kicks her husband as well as hitting him with her slippers and pulling out his beard.

146 (157R)

On a cold day. May you have a splendid time: may you lunch on expensive food, and after the gifts of Bacchus may you have satisfying love-making; and may it give you no pleasure to overcome your stiffness with fleecy clothes, but may a fiery girl join her warm flanks to yours.

This hedonistic wish for a day of wine, women and song with which to dispel the cold belongs in its essentials to Greek sympotic epigram, the roots of which go back to themes in Homer, Theognis, the Greek lyric poets (especially Anacreon) and others, and which in its turn influences similar pieces in the output of Latin poets such as Catullus, Horace and Martial (the secondary literature is extensive, but see e.g. G. Giangrande, 'Sympotic Literature and Epigram', *Entretiens Hardt* 14.1968.93 f.; esp.

Commentary

127 f.; M.L. West in *Sympotica: A Symposium on the Symposion*, ed. O. Murray, Oxford 1990, 272 f.; K. Gutzwiller, *Poetic Garlands*, Berkeley etc., 1998, 115 f.; and O. Murray, 'Symposium and Genre in the Poetry of Horace', *JRS* 75.1985.39 f.). The general theme is well-trodden and hackneyed, though the poet has here tried to inject some life into it by his contrast of the warmth offered by a *fervida virgo* to the chill of the day on which he sets his piece, and by an adept double entendre (line 3 n.).

superscr.: De die frigido: 'Immo nocte, opinor' comments SB (app. crit.), prosaically; day time is just as suitable, with a riotous lunch party being more out of the ordinary and therefore enjoyable than one in the evening (see Fordyce on Cat. 47.6).

1. deliciae: as defined at *OLD* delicia 1(a), 'an activity or sim. which affords enjoyment, a pleasure, delight': cf. Cic. *Mur.* 13 'tempestivi convivi, amoeni loci, multarum deliciarum comes est extrema saltatio'; Sen. *Contr.* 5.5 *exc.* 'deliciis tuis, dives, ardebimus'. The 'deliciae' are here defined by the subsequent references to eating, drinking and love-making, and I have punctuated accordingly.

ditis prandia mensae: the phrase makes good sense, and there is no need to accept a conjecture such as Baehrens' 'ditis gaudia mensae'. The *prandium* is typically the mid-day meal (Blümner, *Privataltertümer*, 381 f.), so suits the epigram's superscription. 'ditis mensae' refers to the quality of the food (for *mensa* metonymically of food, cf. Hor. *Sat.* 2.4.87 'quae nisi divitibus nequeant contingere mensis'; Mart. 5.44.7 'captus es unctiore mensa' etc.; for *dives* of food, signifying the food of the rich man's table rather than 'rich' food, cf. Stat. *Theb.* 5.187 'ditibus indulgent epulis'; *AL* 469.12 f. 'i nunc et vitae fugientis tempora vende / divitibus cenis'). The presence of food evokes the setting of the Roman *convivium* rather than the Greek symposium.

2. pulchra venus: since 'venus' is defined as the services of the *fervida virgo*, the noun here stands metonymically for sexual intercourse (as elsewhere in this collection: cf. 117.10; 118.2; 137.4, which have varied shades of meaning for the metonymy). For the offer of sexual activity along with drink and food at the *convivium* see 115.4 n.

3. villosa veste: this is the equivalent of winter woollens and the like (cf. *Moretum* 22 'cinctus villosae tergore caprae'), worn to warm the body in cold weather, though the *fervida virgo* will perform the function on this occasion. The same humour is employed in a different way by Martial (14.147): 'stragula purpureis lucent villosa tapetis. / Quid prodest si te congelat uxor anus?'

rigorem: 'rigorem' is both unexpected (note the assonance with *frigorem*) and humorous: its primary reference is indeed to stiffness

Commentary

caused by the cold weather (as at e.g. Lucr. 5.746 f. 'bruma nives adfert pigrumque rigorem / reddit hiemps'; Sen. *Nat. Quaest.* 2.31.1 'stat fracto dolio vinum nec ultra triduum ille rigor durat'), and on this level the wish is that the guest will not need to keep on his clothes, despite the chill, because the *fervida virgo* will warm him up. But the notion of sex and the *fervida virgo* gives it an obvious sexual reference as well (e.g. Apul. *Met.* 2.16.6 'arcum meum ... vigorate tetendi et oppido formido ne nervus rigoris nimietate rumpatur'; and both the adjective *rigidus* (cf. Mart. 9.47.6 'in molli rigidam clune libenter habes'), and verb *rigere* (e.g. Mart. 6.73.8 'rigeat mentula') are frequent in this sense). Adams (*LSV* 46 n. 1) points to the medieval use of *rigor* in the sense *mentula* at e.g. William of Blois, *Alda* 509 'tunc sedet ille tumor, pendet rigor ante superbus'. Here the meaning of 'stiffness' or 'sexual arousal' evidenced in Apul. loc. cit. is pertinent, with 'vincere' referring to the mastering or controlling of an emotion or impulse (e.g. 'dolor' is mastered at [Sen.] *Oct.* 221, and 'ira' at Justin 9.18.14).

4. iungat ... latus: another euphemism for sexual intercourse; for similar expressions cf. Lucr. 4.1193 '(sc. mulier) complexa viri corpus cum corpore iungit'; Ovid *Am.* 1.4.43 f. 'nec femori committe femur nec crure cohaere / nec tenerum duro cum pede iunge pedem', with Adams, *LSV* 180.

fervida: again ambiguous: the girl will literally warm the man in place of his winter woollens, but she will also be erotically stimulating (cf. Apul. *Flor.* 16 'amator fervidus').

147 (158R)

On an image of Vergil. An enduring portrait has rescued Maro from death and his image restores a man whom his Fate has taken away. Loss of the light has been powerless as far as such a great poet is concerned; the distinction of his poetry and this portrait illumination make him present.

In this ecphrastic epigram an image of Vergil is described which, along with his poetry, secures his victory over death and ensures his immortality. The image is designated variously *pictura*, *imago* and *pluteus*. Of these *imago* is the most wide-ranging noun and might embrace any type of physical representation of the poet, whether a statue, an *imago clipeata*, a painting, a mosaic, or a manuscript illumination; *pictura* narrows the field effectively to the final three of these; and *pluteus* is a problematic term with various meanings, though the basic concept which it seems to maintain in all its incarnations is that of a curved enclosure of some kind (see 128 intro., which also deals with *imagines clipeatae*). In view of the duality of the concluding phrase of the epigram ('honos carminis et plutei') the interpretation favoured here is that the poet describes an

Commentary

illumination of Vergil in a book which contains his works, though the possibility that it may be a painting or mosaic cannot entirely be ruled out (and there is, for example, a famous mosaic of Vergil from Sousse, illustrated at Dunbabin, *North Africa*, Pl. LI.130; see also *RE* 8A.1493 f. Vergilporträts).

If this epigram does indeed describe a portrait illumination, it would belong to a type of classical art for which there is some evidence. Varro's *Hebdomades*, for instance, contained seven hundred images of famous people (Plin. *Nat. Hist.* 35.11); Martial refers to the frontispiece of a book of Vergil's works which had a portrait of the author (14.186 'quam brevis immensum cepit membrana Maronem! / Ipsius vultus prima tabella gerit'), and perhaps to similar portraits of Sallust (14.191) and himself (1.1; 7.84); and the Priapea seem to have been adorned with a representation of the god (*Priap.* 1). And extant mss from late Antiquity and subsequently afford some evidence for the portraiture to which the literary sources allude: the Vatican Vergil (Vat. lat. 3225), dated to *c.* 400, has an offset from a lost page following the end of *Aen.* VI, of which the shape and traces of colour suggest that *Aen.* VII was headed by Vergil's portrait in an illuminated medallion format (like an *imago clipeata*); a Vatican Terence (Vat. lat. 3868) of Carolingian date has an illumination of a medallion portrait of the author, which is placed in the centre of an easel panel and held by two actors; and a late Byzantine medical ms. in the Ambrosian library at Milan (E 37 sup.) has over sixty portraits of famous physicians in medallion portraits (see K. Weitzmann, *Ancient Book Illumination*, Cambridge Mass. 1959, 116 f.). The ways in which this type of illuminated portrait was framed on the page would well suit the description 'pluteus' in the epigram (see further K. Weitzmann, *Studies in Classical and Byzantine Manuscript Illumination*, Chicago / London 1971, 105 f.).

The interesting textual transmission of this epigram may also shed a light on these questions (M.D. Reeve, *Phoenix* 39.1985.175 f. terms it 'a most unusual if not unique distribution'). The only extant ms. containing the piece is A, which was not rediscovered until 1615 (see p. 13 f.); however this epigram, separated into two adjacent distichs, appears in works printed well before that date. It features, for example, in editions of Vergil from the editio princeps (Rome 1469) to the Aldine of 1517 under the general heading 'Diversorum veterum poetarum in Priapum lusus', in Fabricius' 1561 edition of Vergil and Scaliger's of 1572, and in Pithou's selection from what is now the *AL*. In these it is usually attributed to Hilasius, who is otherwise known only as a probably fictitious author amongst the twelve to whom the *Carmina duodecim sapientum* are attributed (Hilasius is the author of *AL* 506, 517, 528, 539, 550, 561, 572, 583, 594, 605, 616 and 627R; for the genesis of the cycle and the attribution of the work to a single author see Friedrich, *Symposium*, 8 f., and for Hilasius, ibid. 421 f.). The attribution occurs because in the printed editions this piece was added to

Commentary

the group of epigrams in the *Symposium* which are epitaphs for Vergil (555-66R), and it usually follows that by Hilasius; it is accompanied by the similarly extraneous 'Mantua me genuit ...' (Courtney *FLP*, P.Vergilius Maro 2). One can only speculate about the details, but transmission may not have been through any now lost ms. of the *AL*; the lines might have been discovered, for example, as the accompaniment to an illumination of Vergil in a now lost ms. of his works, performing precisely the function for which it is suggested above they were written. The 'Hilasius' transmission also exhibits a variant reading in line 3 (see note).

1. subduxit morti vivax pictura: cf. 156.3 'fato subducere amatum'; the rescue from death is a variation on the hackneyed topic that a work of art breathes life into its subject (which is usually betrayed by key words such as ἔμψυχος, ἐμψυχόω, ἔμπνους, ζωή, *vivo*, *spiro* and *anima*; note 'vivax' here): see my intros to Mart. 11.9 and Aus. *Epig.* 63, and F. Bömer, *Hermes* 80.1952.121 f. The topic of rescue from death is repeated in line 3, where it is linked both to the portrait image of Vergil, and to his poetry. 'vivax' suggests not only that the image will have a long life, but also that it gives life to the deceased poet (cf. Ovid. *Met.* 1.419 f. 'semina ... / vivaci nutrita solo').

2. Parca: the Fates are usually plural; when there is only one, as here, the implication is of a Fate which governs an individual's life and death (e.g. Hor. *Carm.* 2.16.39; Ovid *Tr.* 5.3.14; Pers. 5.48).

3. lucis damna: *lux* is a metonymy for *vita*, as at e.g. Cic. *Verr.* 2.5.75 'ipsis piratis lucis usuram tam diuturnam dedisti'; Lucr. 3.80; [Tib.] 3.3.9; with *TLL* 7.2.1910.6 f.

  valuere (A); nocuere (edd.): 'nocuere' appears in the 'Hilasius' transmission of the epigram as well as being preferred by editors of the *AL* up to and including Meyer, so it might have (lost) ms. authority rather than being editorial conjecture (see intro. above). Although 'nocuere' makes good sense, A's 'valuere' is the *lectio difficilior* and suits the sense of the poem better (to say that death has had no power over the immortal poet is more vivid than to say that it has done no harm to him); 'tanto ... poetae' is a dative of disadvantage.

4. praesentat: following on from the theme of rescue from death, the poem concludes with Vergil's poetry and portrait making his presence a reality. Thus similarly Pliny on the images contained in Varro's *Hebdomades* (*Nat. Hist.* 35.11): ' ... immortalitatem non solum dedit, verum etiam in omnes terras misit, ut praesentes esse ubique ceu di possent ...'; and Alc. Avit. 84 (*MGH AA* 6.2 p. 95.5) 'ut affectui vestro litterarum praesentarer officio, qui cuperem et occursu'.

  carminis et plutei: see intro. above.

Commentary

148 (159R)

On the student of a doctor. A certain doctor took on an adult student so he could pass on his health-giving doctrine to the young man. In order to get to know how to tolerate his master's commands, he first led a saddled horse through public places. The teacher shortened the time for acquiring a skill it takes long to learn: right at the beginning he turned the boy into a Hippocrates!

Epigrams and other satire and comedy about doctors and the medical profession are frequent in both the Greek and Latin traditions (see e.g. Howell and Citroni on Mart. 1.30; Grewing on Mart. 6.31; Sullivan, *Martial*, 87 f.; 167 f.); the focus is usually on the practitioner's incompetence, though in this instance that theme is avoided and the tale of the doctor and his student serves largely to deliver the concluding pun on the name Hippocrates (though the joke itself is lame, allusions to Hippocrates and medical terminology are more subtly employed than might at first appear). Luxorius also has two epigrams which deal with the medical profession (*AL* 297; 304).

The training of doctors in the ancient world ran the range from the passing of knowledge from father to son to a completely academic and bookish approach. On-the-job learning and first-hand experience was the usual route, as appears to be the case in this epigram, and there are some vignettes of doctors doing their rounds accompanied by their students (cf. Mart. 5.9; Philostr. *Vit. Ap.* 8.7.14); but we also hear, at one extreme, of characters like Thessalus of Tralles, who turned cooks, dyers and cobblers into doctors on his six-month course (Galen 10.5; 19 Kühn), and, at the other, of the famous medical school at Alexandria, which flourished in the fourth to sixth centuries (e.g. Amm. Marc. 22.16.18). See further J. Scarborough, *Roman Medicine*, London 1969, 122 f.; and I.E. Drabkin, 'On Medical Education in Greece and Rome', *BullHistMed* 15.1944.333 f.

It is significant for the context of this particular epigram that there were writers in Latin on medical matters who date to the late fourth and fifth centuries, and whose origins, and presumably places of work, were in North Africa (so the author of this piece was writing for an audience who may well have had everyday experience of contemporary medicine and its practitioners). The most famous of them is Caelius Aurelianus (c. 400), but works by Theodorus Priscianus (slightly later), and Cassius Felix are also extant. The last-named is particularly interesting, because his *De Medicina* is dated precisely to 447, which places him as writing under Vandal rule. These writers all seem to have been fluent in Greek, the language traditionally associated with medicine, and there is evidence that Theodorus' first language was Greek: so the translation of Hippocrates' most famous aphorism and the Greek-based punch-line of this epigram are redolent allusions to the medical profession (see 6 n. below). See further Langslow, *Medical Latin*, 53 f.; 125 f. (Theodorus);

Commentary

56 f.; 121 f. (Cassius); and A. Fraisse's introduction to the Budé edition (2002) of Cassius Felix.

1. discipulum ... adultum: the student is termed variously 'adultus', 'iuvenis' (line 2) and 'puer' (line 6), and although Latin is not always precise about such denominations of age, there may here be intended a retrogression which illustrates the training the student receives: an adult becomes a boy (or servant) through being taught to do only what his teacher instructs. However, see also 81.5 n. for the poet's tendency to use a variety of sometimes imperfectly synonymous nouns.

2. dogma salutiferum: this is a grand term, which suggests the doctor / teacher has developed medical doctrine which he can pass on. The noun *dogma* actually has a pertinent medical usage: e.g. Cass. Fel. *praef.* 'placuit mihi ut ex Graecis logicae sectae auctoribus omnium causarum dogmata in breviloquio latino sermone conscriberem'; and, appropriately for this epigram, Cassius entitles Hippocrates 'dogmatum princeps' (ibid. 1.3; later writers categorised followers of Hippocrates as either Dogmatics or Empiricists).

3. ut iussum ... magistri: it is not immediately apparent how the action the student has to perform, that of leading a horse through public areas, will teach him the required subservience, but the answer is revealed by the joke on the name Hippocrates at the end of the epigram. It is probable that further humour, a debunking *annominatio* on 'dogma salutiferum' and 'selliferum ecum', is intended, particularly since the detail 'selliferum' is not relevant to the main joke on Hippocrates.

4. selliferum: the *sella equestris* is the riding saddle, a use of the noun found only from the fourth century (*Cod. Th.* 8.5.47, of the mid-fourth century, details price restrictions for it): cf. Veg. *Mul.* 3.6.2 'nam ut viliora ministeria taceamus, equus tribus usibus vel maxime necessarius constat: proeliis circo sellis', and see Adams, *Pelagonius*, 110 f.

5. artis prolixae breviavit tempora: *prolixa* is the opposite of *brevis*: cf. Paul. Nol. *Ep.* 37.1 'per epistolam brevem quidem verbis, sed caritate prolixam'; ps.-Soran. *Quaest. Med.* 17 (*Anecdota Graeca et Graecolatina*, ed. V. Rose, Berlin 1870, 2.250) 'esse illa (sc. vitia) aut prolixa aut brevia'; and esp. the Latin Hippocrates quoted below. The verb *breviare* is found first in Manilius (3.434), four times in Quintilian, and frequently from the third century onwards (*TLL* 2.2170.70 f.).

The phrase as a whole appositely sets up the concluding joke, in that it is a humorous play on one of the most famous of Hippocrates' *Aphorisms* (1.1 (4.458 Littré)), and discloses that this teacher has found a way to abbreviate the time necessary for learning and acquiring a complex skill:

Commentary

'ὁ βίος βραχὺς, ἡ δὲ τέχνη μακρὴ', usually Latinised as 'ars longa, vita brevis' (cf. Sen. *De Brev. Vit.* 1.1). A late Latin translation of the *Aphorisms* actually renders these words 'vita brevis, ars autem prolixa' (the text has been edited by I. Müller-Rohlfsen, 'Die lateinische ravennatische Übersetzung der hippokratischen Aphorismen aus dem 5/6 Jahrhundert n. Chr.', *Geistes- und sozialwissenschaftliche Dissertationen* 55, Hamburg 1979). The meaning behind what the poet has written is only apparent with knowledge of the aphorism.

doctor: despite the medical context, 'doctor' is simply a synonym of 'magister'; its specific application in English to medical doctors is of medieval derivation, though it is remarkable that in ten columns of references in *TLL* (5.1.1773.6 f.) to *doctores* of many and varied spheres, that of medicine is absent.

6. incepto: as SB remarks (app. crit.) this must be an adverbial equivalent of *principio* (if the text is correct), a use not elsewhere attested. The sense of 'beginning' for substantival *inceptum* is however attested: e.g. Hor. *Ars* 126 f. 'servetur ad imum / qualis ab incepto processerit'; *CE* 457.3 'nonus ab incepto currebat mihi tem<po>ris annus'. *TLL* (7.1.923.41 f.) considers that 'incepto' here is substantival ('i.q. facinus, res gesta'), but that is unlikely; preceding 'primo' and 'artis prolixae breviavit tempora' argue strongly for a temporal adverb.

reddidit Ἱπποκράτην **(Riese; ipograten (A); Hippocratem (Burman); Hippocraten (Shackleton Bailey)):** the phrase recalls Cat. 74.4 'et patruom reddidit Harpocratem'. To understand the joke the name of the great doctor must be literally translated and interpreted, so that the pupil is turned into a 'Hippocrates' not because of the medical skill he has acquired, but because he 'masters horses' (by having to lead one through public places). An epigram by the Hellenistic poet Rhianus preserved by Athenaeus (11.499d = Gow-Page, *HE* 1.3246 f.) similarly reserves its humour for a two-edged reference to Hippocrates in the final word (though the humour does not depend on a literal translation of the name, and in fact is obscure: see G. Giangrande, *Entretiens Hardt* 14.1968.142 f.; G. Luck, ibid., 395 f.).

The joke is interesting here, because it is one of the very few instances in the collection where a knowledge of Greek is either evident in the author or presupposed on the part of the reader (see further p. 12). This raises the question of whether the name should be printed in Greek or Latin script. I follow Riese in thinking that the balance lies in favour of Greek for three reasons: (1) it points the reader unavoidably in the direction of the humour and how the puzzle of the epigram is to be solved (similar issues arise with Ausonius' epigrams, though he was well versed in Greek (see my note on 86.2)); (2) A's reading 'ipograten', with its missing 'H' and its Greek termination, might suggest textual descent from an original Greek script; and (3) the use of Greek would of itself key the medical

Commentary

profession and suggest aspiration to, though not necessarily possession of, medical knowledge (note particularly the highly Greek-based lexicons of late North African writers on medicine such as Theodorus Priscianus and Cassius Felix: see intro. above).

For other instances of epigrammatic humour with the etymology of names, see F. Grewing in *Toto Notus in Orbe*, ed. F. Grewing, *Palingenesia* 65.1998.340 f.; W.J. Schneider, *Mnemosyne* 54.2001.712 f.; Siedschlag, *Form*, 91 n. 13; Sullivan, *Martial*, 246; and Aus. *Epig.* 21 with my intro.

149 (160R)

On a hunter who, when he had killed a boar, imprudently trod on a snake. Boar, youth and snake met at one fatal event; this one roars, that one sighs, this one hisses as he dies.

This distich is one of the small genre of Greek and Latin epigrams which are highly condensed versions of *historiolae* or monitory fables (the term *historiola* has a slightly different application in magical texts, where it is used of abbreviated narratives incorporated into a spell: see D. Frankfurter in *Ancient Magic and Ritual Power*, ed. M. Meyer and P. Mirecki, Leiden etc. 1995, 457 f.; R. Kotansky in *Magika Hiera*, ed. C.A. Faraone and D. Obbink, Oxford 1991, 112). Further on the genre see O. Weinreich's article 'Zu antiken Epigrammen und einer Fabel des Syntipas', *AIPhO* 11.1951.417 f.; Lausberg, *Einzeldistichon*, 365 f.; and my intro. to Aus. *Epig.* 23. The condensation of the fable in this distich is remarkable, and, as Weinreich says, it would scarcely be intelligible at all without a superscription to explain it; for other instances of similarly constructed epigrammatic *historiolae* in *AL*, cf. 387 and 905R.

The popularity of the particular *historiola* of this epigram with anthologists and the like is demonstrated by another version which appears in various mss (Leipzig Rep. I. 4°. 74 (s. ix); St. Gall 899 (s. ix) and St. Petersburg F14.1 (s. viii-ix)):

> Anguis, aper, iuvenis pereunt vi vulnere morsu:
> sus iaculo extinctus, serpens pede, ille veneno.

All three mss puzzlingly add a third line ('quae pede comprimitur, subtrahit ipsa pedem'), which apparently derives from *AL* 18.2. Two of them give the superscription 'De iuvene qui aprum occidit et ipse a serpente percussus est', whilst the St. Petersburg has 'Hos versus Homerus de Evandro fratre Alexandri regis errante in silva et pugnante contra aprum et draconem et inventi sunt postea tres mortui'. The picture is further complicated by a group of mss which more or less conflate the above distich with that of our epigram (e.g. Paris lat. 8093 (s. ix); Paris lat. 8069 (s. x-xi); and Vat. lat. 3257 (s. xii)):

Commentary

> Sus, iuvenis, serpens casum venere sub unum,
> sus iaculo extinctus, serpens pede, ille veneno.
> Anguis, aper, iuvenis pereunt vi, vulnere, morsu:
> hic fremit, ille gemit, sibilat hic moriens.

The superscription in this group of mss is lengthy and begins 'Versus VIRGILII', and this ascription to Vergil, which persisted into printed editions of his works such as those by Fabricius and Scaliger (though they rejected the ascription, and also printed a third version of the couplet), helps in explaining the popularity of the poems. A line of another epigram which is also clearly based on the same story is found at Berne 611 (f. 207, s. x): 'anguis pressa perit, fera telo, virque veneno' (see also D. Schaller and E. Könsgen, *Initia Carminum Latinorum Saeculo Undecimo Antiquiorum*, Göttingen 1977, nos 798-9; 15908-09; and H. Walther, *Initia Carminum ac Versuum Medii Aevi Posterioris Latinorum*, Göttingen 1959, no. 18931). And finally, in a short poem based on the same scenario by Hildebert of Lavardin (1055 – c. 1133, Archbishop of Tours 1125), a peasant in a wood comes across a boar, which he shoots with an arrow, the boar falls dead on a snake and crushes it to death, and the snake ejects venom which kills the peasant; the poem concludes (*PL* 171.1446; cf. J.B. Hauréau, *Les Mélanges poétiques d' Hildebert de Lavardin*, Paris 1882, 139):

> saucia, contrita, sparsus, telo, pede, viru,
> bestia, vipera, vir, sternitur, aret, obit.

The above demonstrates the enduring popularity of this kind of highly compressed poetastery, which also affords an enticement to superscript writers to offer explanations longer than the poems and to festoon them with some inventive literary pedigrees. The present example is not especially adept, because without the superscription (or some prior knowledge of the tale) it is difficult to work out why each of the three protagonists meets his fate. There is however another issue, which concerns the explanation of the tale offered in the superscription; in stating that the hunter both shoots the boar and then inadvertently treads on the snake, it renders misleading the claim in the first line of the epigram that the protagonists 'casum venere sub unum', because two 'casus' trigger events, and one of them, the hunter's inadvertent treading on the snake, is only a lame coincidence in the episode and is causally unconnected with his shooting of the boar. So perhaps the scenario the poet intended is as it was later more fully set out by Hildebert: the hunter shot the boar, the boar as it fell dead squashed the snake, and as a result the snake spat out its poison to kill the hunter. Although that will inevitably stretch the reader's credulity, it makes the story more interesting and better explains 'casum venere sub unum'. Similarly as regards the alternative distich quoted above, the proper interpretation may be that the 'pede' belongs not to the hunter but

Commentary

to the boar in its death throes (for *pes* of an animal's hoof, cf. Hor. *Sat.* 2.3.314 (in a similar context) with *TLL* 10.1.1907.21 f.), as might also 'vi', the method of the snake's demise, which in any case hardly suits the action of a hunter stepping on a snake by chance.

1. sus: 'sus' is here synonymous with 'aper', as is shown by the superscript and its interchangeability with 'aper' in the poems quoted in the intro. above; as a monosyllable it is a useful variant. Earlier examples of its reference to a boar, rather than to a domestic pig, are infrequent, and mainly in a debunking context (e.g. Mart. 11.11.18 'sus Calydonius'), though not invariably (e.g. Ovid *Met.* 8.272, also of the Calydonian boar); see Bömer's note loc. cit., Mynors' note on Verg. *Georg.* 3.255, and *OLD* sus 1(c).

2. hic fremit: the verb is rarely used of boars, *TLL* (6.1.1282.43 f.) citing only Apul. *Met.* 8.4.4, but it is a good parallel: an enraged, hunted animal is described as 'impetu saevo frementis oris totus fulmineus'.
moriens: to be taken ἀπὸ κοινοῦ with all three nouns in the line.

150 (161R)

Against Achilles. Wicked dismemberer, if you knew how to demand its proper value, you would not drag around †that which was worth its weight in gold for you.†

A group of epigrams on mythological themes begins with this mutilated distich about Achilles; it is followed by five further distichs on aspects of the Trojan War, and two quatrains on Hyacinthus (156-7).

Since this epigram lacks the conclusion of the second line, it is not possible to be certain that it was complete in a distich, but given the five epigrams of that length which follow, and given that it is possible to supplement it to provide a good structure and sense, the hypothesis need not seriously be challenged. The lacunose second line reads 'non traheres quod pundus erat' in the ms.; this is the beginning of a dactylic hexameter, and since the next epigram is a dactylic hexameter distich it may be that we should supplement accordingly here. Editors and critics diverge over whether to assume a hexameter line (as does e.g. Riese) or a pentameter (as does e.g. SB).

The setting of the piece is a humorously mercenary view of Achilles' treatment of the slain Hector's body; in the Homeric version, Priam ransoms Hector's body, which has been protected by Apollo from laceration and dismemberment during Achilles' repeated dragging of it round the walls of Troy. For this purpose Priam fills chests with rich clothing and other fabrics, precious metals and ten talents of gold (*Il.* 24.228 f.); Homer's one-line reference to gold in this passage (which however may be interpolated: see McLeod's and Richardson's notes on 24.232) picks up on a previous comment by Achilles to the dying Hector that he would not ransom his body even if Priam should offer Hector's weight in gold for it (22.351 f.): 'οὐδ' εἴ κέν σ' αὐτὸν χρυσῷ ἐρύσασθαι ἀνώγοι / Δαρδανίδης Πρίαμος' ('not even if Priam, descendant of Dardanus, should instruct me to weigh your body against gold'). This threat seems to have led to an alternative version of this part of the myth that the ransom for Hector's body was agreed between Achilles and Priam to be Hector's weight in gold, but it was so heavy that not enough gold could be found in Troy; so Polyxena added her jewellery to the scales to tip the balance, and Achilles was so smitten by her that he offered to take her instead of the gold (cf. Serv. ap. Verg. *Aen.* 3.321 (quoted in full at 167 intro.); Dares 27; Dict. Cret. 3.27; this version might have been used by Aeschylus in his lost play *The Phrygians* or *The Ransom of Hector*, and see also Ennius' *Hectoris Lytra* frags 67-82 Jocelyn). It is the detail of the ransom with gold to the weight of Hector's body which suggests this variant of the myth lies behind the present distich, as evidenced by its witty pun on 'distractor' and with further clues in 'pretium' and 'pondus' (see notes).

Achilles' treatment of Hector's body is also the subject of *AL* 44, and see further *LIMC* 4.1.483.

superscr.: EIUSDEM: on the implications of this scribal heading see p. 19 f.

1. inprobe distractor: Achilles is 'inprobus' because he goes beyond the bounds of acceptable behaviour in trying to defile Hector's corpse by dragging it round the walls of Troy. He is literally a 'distractor' in that he tries to dismember the corpse, though Apollo averts that result. But 'distractor' has another sense which is relevant here, that of a vendor who splits up the item he sells into smaller lots (asset-splitting in financial terminology). This sense of the verb *distrahere*, which later also develops the meaning 'sell' without any implication of fragmentation (see J.H. Schmalz, *BPhW* 13.1893.1090 f.), occurs in Tacitus (*Ann.* 6.17) and Suetonius (*Vesp.* 16.1), and there is a virtually identical play on words to that here at Gell. 20.1.19: 'quid enim videri potest efferatius, quid ab hominis ingenio diversius, quam quod membra et artus inopis debitoris saevissimo laniatu distrahebantur, sicuti nunc bona venum distrahuntur?' (note also Cic. *Sulla* 59). The point of the ambiguity in this epigram is that Achilles, intending to be a literal 'distractor' of Hector's corpse, would also become a financial 'distractor' to his disadvantage, because if Hector's body disintegrated it would weigh less and be less profitable to ransom.

pretium si poscere nosses: the phrase continues the humour with the financial ambiguity: if Achilles knew how to negotiate over the ransom for his asset, he would not try to fragment it behind his chariot. L. Zurli

Commentary

(*GIF* 28.1997.148 f.) proposes 'si noscere posses', but there is no need for emendation.

2. non traheres quod pundus (A; funus (Burman)) erat: this is not the only occasion in the *AL* on which A (and other mss) present lacunose lines: cf. also 212.2-3; 272.2. Since the line is incomplete, and since 'pondus' (which it is reasonable to assume lies behind A's 'pundus') can have an easy reference in the context of the story of the epigram, it is not necessary to entertain Burman's conjecture (though SB does (app. crit.), and suggests by way of illustration 'non traheres <lucro> quod <tibi> funus erat'). W.S. Watt (*HSCPh* 91.1987.292; 101.2003.453) suggests the supplements 'non traheres <auri> quod <tibi> pondus erat', and similar sense would need to emerge if a hexameter reconstruction of the line is preferred. 'traheres' picks up 'distractor' in line 1.

151 (162R)

On Troy. Cease, Troy, from lamenting in your mind over your travails: captured, you give birth to Rome; deservedly does your posthumous daughter rule.

This dactylic hexameter distich addressed to Troy plays on the metaphor of Troy as the mother of Rome; Troy suffers the pains of labour (see 1 n. labores) and gives birth to Rome, and her 'posthumous' child (see 2 n.) is all-powerful. As was noted by Riese, there is a similarity of wording between the epigram and some fragments of Ennius preserved by Cicero (at *De Fin.* 2.106 and *De Orat.* 3.167), which Skutsch tentatively attributes to a speech of Scipio Africanus in the *Annals* (see Skutsch's *operis incerti fragmenta annalibus fortasse tribuenda*, no. vi, with p. 754 f.). Points which suggest an allusion here to Ennius are: (1) Skutsch's truncated line vi.6 reads 'desine Roma tuos hostis', and probably continued with the infinitive 'to fear'; the beginning of this epigram, addressed to a personified Troy ('desine Troia tuos ...'), would seem to be an echo. (2) The 'labores' of Skutsch's line vi.7 'nam tibi moenimenta mei peperere labores' are echoed in the 'labores' of the epigram. And (3), more specifically, the context in which Cicero (*De Fin.* 2.105) introduces the Ennian lines when he quotes them is 'suavis laborum est praeteritorum memoria'. In the epigram, on one meaning of 'labores', Troy is bidden to forget her past toils, which are painful (the Trojan War), and to console herself with the birth of Rome: thus whilst Ennius' Scipio took pleasure in recalling his labours, probably as a reason for Rome not to fear her enemies, the Troy of the epigram takes no pleasure in her labours as regards the war, but can console herself with her labour over Rome's birth. Although this is necessarily speculative in view of the scrappiness of the Ennian fragments, an allusion to them in this epigram seems probable.

Commentary

There is a series of epigrams which personify Troy at *AP* 9.152-5 Agathias, the last of which focuses on Troy's resurrection as Rome.

1. animo (A); nimium (Maehly); tandem (Shackleton Bailey); iam iam (Watt): there is no convincing reason to doubt the ms. text: Troy is addressed as a person, she can weep and give birth to Rome, so why should she not have an *animus*? The ablative 'animo' is limitative: cf. Enn. *Ann*. 201 Sk. 'sed ego hic animo lamentor' with Skutsch's note, adducing this line. L. Müller (*RhM* 18.1863.437), also supporting 'animo' here, adduced Prop. 2.1.23 'regnave prima Remi aut animos Carthaginis altae' (where, although *animi* belong to a city, they have a different reference from 'animo' here). A contrary view is taken by SB (*Towards a Text*, 24) and W.S. Watt (*HSCPh* 91.1987.292).

labores: on first reading the reader will understand the *labores* over which Troy is bidden not to weep to be her failed struggle in the Trojan War. But the second line of the epigram will lead to a different interpretation, that Troy is personified as a mother who has laboured and given birth, and that though she has died in that childbirth, her child, Rome, survived and thrives. For *labor* in the latter sense, cf. Plaut. *Amph*. 488; Aus. 14.25.31 f. 'quod legitimos Lucina labores / praevenit'.

2. tua postuma: i.e. your posthumous daughter, since Troy died in giving birth; for *postumus / -a* used substantivally of children born at or after the death of a parent (usually the father), cf. Gaius *Inst*. 2.131 '(sc. testamentum) postea agnatione postumi sive postumae rumpitur'; Amm. Marc. 21.15.6 'uxorem autem praegnantem reliquit, unde edita postuma'; with *TLL* 10.2.220.8 f.; 24 f.

152 (163R)

On the Judgement of Paris. The goddess of the loves triumphed over the goddesses of marriage and war when the shepherd judged Cypris to be beautiful.

The sequence of mythological epigrams continues with a clutch of four rather drab distichs on the Judgement of Paris, a myth which is popular in this collection (see also 122.2 n.; 124.1 n.). The separation into four separate pieces was made by L. Müller (*RhM* 20.1865.635), with the latter three being given supplemental superscriptions by Riese. Since there is no connection in language or logic between the distichs, the separation is almost certainly correct (see p. 19, and for similar issues in Ausonius see my intro. to *Epig*. 39).

1. conubii: 'dea conubii' describes Hera / Juno as goddess of marriage

Commentary

(see Roscher 2.588 f.); elsewhere she is regularly entitled 'pronuba' (e.g. Verg. *Aen.* 4.166; Ovid *Her.* 6.43; *Met.* 6.428 etc.).

This noun raises a frequently debated point of prosody, as to whether and when the second syllable of *conubium* should be treated as metrically short or long (it can be long by virtue of the following 'i' being treated consonantally), a debate which was noted as early as Servius (on *Aen.* 1.73). Either scansion would be possible here, as it would in most other instances. The issues are discussed at e.g. Müller, *De Re Metrica*, 303; P. Maas, *ALL* 13.1904.433; J. Wackernagel, *Festschrift P. Kretschmer*, Vienna 1926, 289 f. (= *Kleine Schriften*, Göttingen 1969, 2.1280 f.); Munro's note on Lucr. 3.776; and Austin's note on Verg. *Aen.* 4.126 (a good summary).

bellique: Athena / Minerva is often a goddess of war (see *RE* 15.1790 f.), and is given such titles as *belligera* (Mart. 7.1.1), *bellica* (Ovid *Met.* 2.752), *bellatrix* (ibid. 8.264), *pugnax* (Ovid *Tr.* 3.9.7) and *virago* (Stat. *Theb.* 11.414).

amorum: a striking ellipse of 'dea' is made easier by the preceding 'deas' (and is further evidence of the technique of compression in epigram which has been remarked at 149 intro.). The use of plural *amores* to characterise Aphrodite / Venus is perhaps intentional: the plurality suggests weightier responsibility than the singular 'conubium' and 'bellum' of the other goddesses, and it also produces a balance in the line with two goddesses who preside over a single responsibility each, and one goddess who has plural responsibilities. A plurality of *amores*, *cupidines* or even *Veneres* is however a common topos from Hellenistic poetry onwards (cf. Horace's 'mater saeva Cupidinum' at *Carm.* 1.19.1, with Nisbet-Hubbard's note).

153 (164R)

<*Another.*> The exalted child of the Thunderer's head and the exalted wife of the Thunderer's marriage-bed are both defeated by Venus, who is approved by Paris' commendation.

1. verticis et thalami pignus: 'pignus sublime Tonantis' has to be understood ἀπὸ κοινοῦ with 'verticis' and 'thalami' in this learnedly peculiar phrase. As applied to 'verticis' *pignus* has a meaning ('child', as the guarantee of the reality of a marriage: see 91.4 n.) which is frequent in this collection, and it alludes to the birth of Minerva from the head of her father Jupiter (cf. *Priap.* 1.4 'de patrio vertice nata dea'; Hes. *Theog.* 924, with West's note on 886-900). But 'pignus' can allude to relationships other than that of parents and children, including that of husbands and wives (e.g. Liv. 2.1.5 'priusquam pignera coniugum ac liberorum ... animos eorum consociasset'), and can even mean concretely 'wife' (e.g. Petr. 108.14 line 3 'vehit decepti pignus Atridae'). So as applied to 'thalami', Jupiter's other 'pignus' is his wife Hera.

Commentary

sublime: the figurative sense of the adjective predominates, but the literal meaning would also suit a punning reference to the birth of Minerva from Jupiter's head.

154 (165R)

<*Another.*> The cause of the calamity is clear: to have ceded the apple to Dione is why Troy fell, razed by Greek hands.

1. mali, malum: for similar plays on the different meanings and metrical quantities of *malum*, cf. Plaut. *Amph.* 723 f. 'enim vero praegnati oportet et malum et malum dari / ut quod obrodat sit, animo si male esse occeperit'; Aus. 27.16.3 f. 'unum nomen utrisque, sed est discrimen utrisque: / poma ut mala voces, carmina vero mala'; and note also Cic. *Fam.* 9.20.1 (with Shackleton Bailey's note). Burman (1759, p. 94) quotes a monkish jingle on the apple eaten by Eve: 'mala mali malo mala contulit omnia mundo'. There are similarities with phrases like the Homeric 'Ἄρες Ἄρες' (*Il.* 5.31), much imitated subsequently, where metrically different forms of the same word appear in close proximity (see Nisbet-Hubbard's note on Hor. *Carm.* 1.32.11 'nigroque' for more examples); here, however, the different prosody keys different words.

For this particular *malum*, the Apple of Discord, see 122.2 and 124.1, with notes.

cessisse: to be understood in a transitive sense with Paris as the unnamed subject; Venus was alleged to have bribed Paris for his judgement in her favour by offering him the hand of Helen, and thus the Trojan War was triggered.

Dionae: Dione is here a synonym of Venus (as often elsewhere), though she was also Venus' mother in some versions of her myth (see 106.7 n.).

2. cur ruerint (Oudendorp); cum ruerit (A); corruerunt (Ziehen); quo ruerent (Riese): A's text, with its singular verb, has to be emended, and Oudendorp's conjecture is the best, both palaeographically close and restoring good sense.

Graia Pergama pulsa manu: the meaning of the participle is 'impulsa', an instance of simple for compound verb (for which see generally *LHS* 2.298 f.; E. Löfstedt, *Vermischte Studien zur lateinischen Sprachkunde und Syntax*, Lund 1936, 117 f.); given also 'manu' and the reference to the fall of Troy, there may be an illusion to Seneca's 'cuius (i.e. Agamemnon's) impulsum manu / cecidit … concussum Ilium' (*Agam.* 920 f.) and 'cuius (Achilles) unius manu / impulsa Troia' (*Tro.* 204 f.). There is similar phrasing at Prop. 3.1.25 'nam quis equo pulsas abiegno nosceret arces', which again refers to the fall of Troy, but where the apparent equation of the wooden horse with a battering-ram makes the use of the uncompounded verb more straightforward.

Commentary

155 (166R)

<*Another.*> The herdsman gives the apple to Venus as the prize for her beauty; tearful and defeated, Minerva goes back home with Juno.

1. formae pro munere: cf. Verg. *Aen.* 1.27 'iudicium Paridis spretaeque iniuria formae' (of Juno).

pastor: a frequent sobriquet for Paris (see Nisbet-Hubbard's note on Hor. *Carm.* 1.15.1), particularly favoured by Dracontius (fourteen instances). It alludes to his occupation on Mt. Ida immediately before he was chosen to judge the contest between the three goddesses. Compare his sobriquet 'Phryx' at 122.2.

2. cum Iunone ... redit: this bathetic line, which closes the sequence of four dull distichs on the Judgement of Paris, is also the most attractive, in the picture it paints of the two dejected losing goddesses trudging off home after the contest which has been judged by a herdsman.

156 (167R)

On Hyacinth. While exercising Hyacinthus runs into the crisis of his life, having his temples split open by a discus. Phoebus was unable to bring his loved one back from his fate, but the blood of the dead boy fills the fields with flowers.

The current sequence of epigrams on mythological themes ends with two about Hyacinthus, a boy from Amyclae near Sparta with whom Apollo fell in love; he was killed by a discus thrown by Apollo, the result either of an accident (as at e.g. Hes. frag. 171 M-W; Eur. *Helen* 1471 f.; Ovid *Met.* 10.178 f.; Apollod. 1.3.3; 3.10.3), or of deliberate interference by Zephyrus, the west wind, who had also fallen for the boy, but was rejected by him in favour of Apollo and took his revenge by blowing the discus off course so that it hit and killed Hyacinthus (as at e.g. Philostr. *Imag.* 1.24; Lucian 79.16(14).2). Apollo turned the boy's blood into the flower which bears his name (see 4 n.), and it is the origin of the flower which most interests the poet in these two epigrams; he does not specifically deal with responsibility for the boy's death, merely stating he was hit by the discus (though see the note on 'remeans' at 157.1).

There is nothing in these epigrams which proves them to be ecphrastic, in that they describe a work of art, but equally there is nothing to prevent it, and the scene of the martyred boy with his blood producing flowers would lend itself to visual treatment. Such pictures are described by Martial (14.173 with Leary's intro.) and Philostratus junior (*Imag.* 14), which for no good reason are labelled 'sans doute imaginaires' by *LIMC* (5.1.550), and Pliny (*Nat. Hist.* 35.131) mentions a Hyacinthus painted by Nicias.

Commentary

1. discrimen vitae: cf. Cic. *Verr.* 2.2.76 'minus ad vitae nostrae discrimen'; ibid. 2.5.157 'hoc capitis vitaeque discrimen'; with *TLL* 5.1.1362.7 f. for other examples of the use of this frequent phrase.

ludit dum forte Hyacinthus (Sched.); ludit · desorteiaquintus (A): the reconstruction in the Schedae Divionenses of the text presented by A is accepted by editors. It should not pass unremarked because 'ludit dum forte' is weak, but 'incurrit' in the following line governs 'discrimen vitae', which means that 'ludit' must belong to a subordinate clause and requires a conjunction. 'ludit' is apposite in the context: cf. Ovid *Met.* 10.182 'actusque cupidine lusus'; ibid. 200 f. 'nisi si lusisse vocari / culpa potest'.

3. non potuit Phoebus ...: Apollo attempts to prevent Hyacinthus' dying of his wound at Ovid *Met.* 10.185 f., but 'nil prosunt artes; erat immedicabile vulnus'.

fato subducere: cf. 147.1 'subduxit morti'.

4. cruor extincti: Apollo transforms the boy's blood into the flowers that bear his name; cf. Ovid *Met.* 10.210 f.:

> ecce cruor, qui fusus humo signaverat herbas,
> desinit esse cruor, Tyrioque nitentior ostro
> flos oritur formamque capit, quam lilia, si non
> purpureus color his, argenteus esset in illis.
> Non satis hoc Phoebo est (is enim fuit auctor honoris):
> ipse suos gemitus foliis inscribit et AI AI
> flos habet inscriptum, funestaque littera ducta est.

The precise flower envisaged by the poets as the 'hyacinth' is much debated (Ovid's is probably imaginary in any case, since it is not botanically identifiable), but it is evident from the descriptions that no one species was universally so named, with the flower now known as the hyacinth (*Hyacinthus orientalis*) being only one amongst many; star hyacinths, larkspur, iris and lily also seem to be described by various authors (see *Neue Pauly* 5.767 f.; S. Amigues, 'Hyakinthos, Fleur mythique et plantes réelles', *REG* 105.1992.19 f.; M.J. Mellink, *Hyakinthos*, Utrecht 1943, 111 f.).

157 (168R)

<*Another.*> The rebounding discus splattered his temples as he exercised, and beautiful Hyacinthus died a cruel death. A great kindness nevertheless compensates for the fate of the exterminated boy: Apollo's love always springs up anew with a flower.

This epigram is not separated from 156 in A; the suggestion that it should be separated was made by P. Burman senior (uncle of Burman junior),

Commentary

and was adopted by Burman junior (1759, 108) and subsequent editors. It is undoubtedly correct, because the opening couplet presents the same scene as that of the opening couplet of the preceding epigram, both closing couplets deal with Apollo's transformation of the boy's blood into flowers, and both epigrams contain the name Hyacinthus. See p. 18 f. for other questions over the separation of epigrams in this collection.

1. dispersit (A); discerpsit (Petschenig); dispertit (Stowasser): the verb *dispergere* is ideal for the context and needs no emendation: cf. Ter. *Ad.* 782 'an tibi iam mavis cerebrum dispergam hic?'; Sen. *Herc. Fur.* 1007 'cerebro tecta disperso madent'.

remeans: this participle might suggest that Hyacinthus threw the discus and it boomeranged back at him; but that is neither the flight of a discus, nor is it the happening of the myth, in which either Apollo threw the discus and Zephyrus redirected it to kill the boy, or Apollo threw it and it accidentally hit Hyacinthus (see 156 intro.). Since the west wind does not feature explicitly in either epigram, the latter version is probably intended here; Ovid (*Met.* 10.182 f.; the text is the *OCT*) describes the calamity with the words 'protinus imprudens actusque cupidine lusus / tollere Taenarides orbem properabat, at illum / dura repercusso subiecit pondere tellus / in vultus, Hyacinthe, tuos', and similarly 'remeans' here appears to mean that the discus bounced back up from the ground and hit the boy as he ran to collect it.

ludentis tempora discus: cf. 156.1 f. 'ludit ... disco tempora'.

2. dira pulcher morte: the sandwiching of 'pulcher' is pertinent, alluding not only to the boy's beauty when alive, but also to his continuing beauty after death in the flowers that bear his name.

morte Hyacinthus: for elision in the second half of the pentameter in this collection see p. 23.

3. fata perempti (Shackleton Bailey); mortepemti (A); morte percmtum (Burman sen.); sorte peremti (Baehrens); amore perenni (Petschenig): Burman senior's conjecture for the evidently corrupt ms. text involves the least change to it to restore some sense, but 'morte' is virtually pleonastic with 'peremtum', and it is certainly pleonastic with 'morte' and 'obit' in line 2 (indeed it may well have intruded from line 2). Both Baehrens' and Petschenig's conjectures leave 'solatur' without an object, which might be acceptable if they added revelation in another direction, but they do not; SB's 'fata perempti' gives excellent sense and should be accepted. The concept 'solatur fata perempti' also accords well with Ovid's version of the story, where Apollo's acceptance of responsibility for the boy's accidental death and his inability to restore him to life lead him to offer Hyacinthus eternal memorials in music, song and the flower that bears his name (*Met.* 10.196 f.).

Commentary

4. semper ... flore resurgit: i.e. the flowering each spring of the hyacinth reflects Apollo's love, and is the boy's eternal memorial and consolation in death.

158 (169R)

On the citron. Protected by thorns the gifts of the fertile fruit tree glister; the golden globe of the citron soothes the mouth. Hippomenes won his race with such a fruit; such fruits the grove of the Hesperides provided.

This is the first of a group of three epigrams on citrons, somewhat similar to those on the *mala Matiana* (122-4), particularly in stressing the qualities of the fruit and adducing supporting examples from myth; as often in this collection, the tone is almost that of advertising (see 90 intro.).

SB remarks in his app. crit. to the superscription of this piece ('De citriu') 'sed tituli auctor hic quoque erravit; nam versus de malo scripti sunt'; but the fact that the tree on which the fruit grows has thorns is enough to prove him incorrect. Courtney (*C&M* 40.1989.200) points this out, but his suggestion that the fruit described is the lemon is also incorrect, not only because of some echoes of and allusions to the citron in Vergil (see 1 n. and 2 n. below; 159.1 n. and 4 n.), but also because lemons (and oranges) were not known to Greeks and Romans, or at any rate were not grown by them and not imported. They seem to have been introduced to the Mediterranean area only in the tenth century from the Yemen by Arab traders (see André, *L'Alimentation*, 78 f; 78 n. 67; *Neue Pauly* 2.1223 f.; G. Piccaluga in *Aevum Inter Utrumque, Mélanges offerts à Gabriel Sanders*, ed. M. van Uytfanghe and R. Demeulenaere, The Hague 1991, 313 f.).

The citron tree (*Citrus medica*: 'medica' refers to its supposed place of origin) admirably fits the description in the epigram of a thorny tree or shrub which produces *mala* (on which term see 1 n. below). It is small, growing to a height of around 3.5 m., has irregular, spreading, spiny branches, and produces bright yellow, furrowed, oval or oblong fruits about 12-15 cm in length. As regards the fruit, the inner portion of the rind is thick, white and fleshy, while the outer is thin and fragrant; the pulp is firm and can be either acidic or sweet. The variety known to the ancient world may have been acidic, since the only uses for it were in medicine or in perfumery (Theophr. *Hist. Plant.* 4.4.2 f.; Plin. *Nat. Hist.* 23.105; Isid. *Or.* 17.7.8), or, to a limited extent, in culinary flavouring (Apic. 4.3.5; Apicius also has a process for preserving citrons at 1.21). It is nowadays used for by-products such as candied peel, but the fruit as such is not eaten. The citron should not be confused with another tree which was also known in Latin as *citrus* and which provided sought-after wood for tables and other items; that is *Callitris quadrivalvis*, a native of North Africa, and a large evergreen conifer of the cypress family.

Commentary

superscr.: De citro (edd. *post* Meyer); De citriu (A); De citrio (Sched.; Burman): either small correction of A could be correct here; this and the following two epigrams are strictly about the citron fruit, rather than the tree, and though *citrium*, *citreum* and *malum citreum* are the more usual terms for the fruit, this author uses *citrum* in that sense (see 2 n. below and 160.1 n.); the superscript-writer could reasonably have written here either 'citro' or 'citrio'.

1. saepta ... spinis: cf. Theophr. *Hist. Plant.* 4.4.2, describing the attributes of the citron tree: 'ἀκάνθας ... λείας δὲ καὶ ὀξείας σφόδρα καὶ ἰσχυράς' ('smooth and very sharp and strong thorns').

micant: the verb alludes to what is made explicit in the following line and in the mythological exempla of lines 3 and 4: these fruits glister in the light like gold (thus the Sun's palace is 'clara micante auro' (Ovid *Met.* 2.2), and the golden fleece 'micet arbore sacra' (Val. Flacc. 5.203)); they are depicted as a treasure protected by the thorns of the tree.

felicis munera mali: 'mali' (from *malus*) is here the fruit tree; at line 3 'malo' (from *malum*) is the fruit. Both nouns can refer to trees or fruit other than apples (and see also 'poma' at line 4, with note): thus, for example, *malum Persicum* is the peach, *malum Punicum* the pomegranate, and *malum cotoneum* the quince, and *malus Persica* etc. the trees on which they grow (see André, *Plantes*, 152 f.). The identification of the tree here is apparent from the superscription, from the fact the tree is thorny, and from the evident allusion to a passage of Vergil (*Georg.* 2.126 f.), where he describes the citron tree: 'Media fert tristis sucos tardumque saporem / felicis mali ...'. Vergil's phrase 'felicis mali', which is borrowed in this epigram, shows *felix* used in its original sense of 'fruitful' or 'making fruitful, and so beneficent' (see Mynors' note); it also contains a humorous pun, in that 'felicis mali' understood in another sense is an oxymoronic 'lucky bad luck' (see 154.1 n., and for metrical quantity being ignored in such puns see J.N. Adams, *SIFC* 53.1981.200 n. 3).

2. permulcet citri (Riese); quetulitutcirci (A); cui legit, ut citri (Maehly); pellicit, ut citri (Shackleton Bailey); quas tulit ut circi (Traube): assuming A reads 'quae tulit ut circi', the ms. text has led to various flights of editorial fancy. Efforts to preserve 'circi' are futile: J.M. Stowasser (*WS* 32.1910.97 f.) retained all of A's supposed text here, emended the ensuing 'aureus' to 'laureus' (cf. Verg. *Georg.* 2.131 and 159.1 n. below), and glossed the result 'illa malus ora fert (i.e. similis est) ut circi laureus tumor' (!). Emendation to 'ut citri' is also no help, since the reference is to a citron (or conceivably a citron tree), not a fruit (or tree) which looks like one. But Riese's 'permulcet citri', though it is not easy to see how the corruption in A would have arisen, gives ideal sense, because one of the few uses to which the citron was put was precisely to soothe sore throats and sweeten the breath (cf. 159.3 with note; Verg. *Georg.*

295

Commentary

2.134 f. 'animas et olentia Medi / ora fovent illo et senibus medicantur anhelis'; Theophr. loc. cit.).

As implied above, it seems likely, because of ensuing 'aureus tumor', that 'citri' should here be derived from 'citrum' (the fruit) rather than 'citrus' (the tree), as 'citro' certainly does at 160.1 (see note); although grammatically a plural might have been expected after 'munera', use of the singular leads well into ensuing 'malo'.

citri aureus: for the hiatus at the main caesura of the pentameter, see p. 23.

tumor: of the swelling of ripe fruit; cf. Ovid *Met.* 15.77 'tumidaeque in vitibus uvae'; Verg. *Georg.* 2.102.

3. Hippomenes ...: for the mythological comparators in this couplet cf. *Priap.* 16.1 f. 'qualibus Hippomenes rapuit Schoenida pomis, / qualibus Hesperidum nobilis hortus erat'; Mart. 13.37 (headed 'mala citrea') 'aut Corcyraei sunt haec de frondibus horti / aut haec Massyli poma draconis erant'. For the myth of Atalanta and Hippomenes (in some versions Melanion), see 122.1 n.

tali ... malo: the same mythological exempla which are used regarding apples at 122-4 are here employed with reference to citrons. This is not unique: for citrons rather than apples featuring in these myths, cf. Athen. 3.84a; Juba ap. Athen. 3.83b (= *FGH* 275 F6 Jacoby); Mart. 13.37, quoted above; with West's note on Hes. *Theog.* 215; Piccaluga, op. cit. intro., 317 n. 15.

4. talia poma: *pomum*, like *malum*, refers not only to apples but also to virtually any fruit which grows on trees. Isidore (*Or.* 17.7.8), in describing the fruit of citron trees, uses the nouns as synonymous: '... quod eius pomum ac folia cedri odorem referant. Malum eius inimicum venenis ... Haec arbor omni pene tempore plena est pomis'; and cf. André, *Botanique*, 257.

nemus ... Hesperidum: for the myth of the Apples of the Hesperides and the snake which guarded them in the Garden see 123.2 n. Juba (loc. cit. 3 n. above) refers to the citron as 'μῆλον Ἑσπερικόν' (cf. also Antiphanes frag. 59 K-A), and glosses give similar terms (*CGL* 3.26.22; 358.75). This is further evidence that the citron rather than the apple was sometimes regarded as the fruit of the Garden (see 3 n. above).

159 (170R)

Another. The wonderful citron tree stands like the laurel, and it is to be preferred to all autumn's bounty. These fruits of it garnish dinner tables, these fruits provide medicines when a gasping cough racks doubled-up old men.

Commentary

This second of the trio of epigrams on the citron tree and its fruit has clear echoes of Vergil (1 n.; 4 n.), as does the previous piece.

1. similis lauro (Stowasser); similis auro (A): Stowasser's conjecture (*WS* 31.1909.290) has much more force than does his similar 'laureus' at 158.2 (see note). Whilst the lengthening of the final syllable of 'similis', which is required if A's text is accepted, could conceivably be justified (see p. 24, and the examples elsewhere in the *AL* collected by Courtney at *C&M* 40.1989.201 f.), the author of this trio of epigrams evidently knows and uses the Vergilian description of the citron tree, and Vergil describes it as 'ipsa ingens arbos faciemque simillima lauro' (*Georg.* 2.131). Furthermore, the tree does not 'look like gold', though its fruit does (cf. 158.2; the connection would explain the easy corruption here). This tells strongly in favour of the Vergilian allusion in this phrase, and for the correctness of Stowasser's conjecture.

The citron tree actually bears little resemblance to the laurel or bay tree, but Vergil has taken his description from that of Theophrastus (*Hist. Plant.* 4.4.2) in which the noun δάφνης ('laurel' or 'bay') is to be found, though it has probably intruded into the text from a gloss (see Mynors' note on Verg. loc. cit.). The misdescription has been perpetuated here.

arbos: *arbos* is an old form of *arbor* (cf. Paul. *Fest.* p. 14.9 Lindsay 'arbosem pro arbore antiqui dicebant'; Prob. *Gramm. Lat.* 4.20.9; Isid. *Or.* 1.27.23; 17.6.3 (where Isidore unconvincingly attempts to distinguish different meanings for *arbos* and *arbor*)); compare e.g. *labos* and *honos*, with *LHS* 1.179. It adds further proof for this line being an allusion to Vergil that 'arbos' is the noun he uses in his description of the citron tree (quoted above).

2. autumni anteferenda: autumn is traditionally the time of the harvest and of fruit-gathering, especially apples (cf. Sall. *Hist.* frag. 3.98D Reynolds; Verg. *Georg.* 4.134; Ovid *Rem.* 187 etc.), though the citron bears fruit at all seasons (Theophr. loc. cit.); that could be one reason for its preferability.

For the hiatus at the main caesura of the pentameter see p. 23.

3. poma: for *pomum* used of fruits other than apples see 158.4 n.

medellam: here probably concrete 'medicine' rather than the more abstract 'cure', as also at Gell. 17.16.3 'ipsum autem regem adsiduo talium medelarum usu a clandestinis epularum insidiis cavisse'; Aus. 21.76; 77; Pelag. 283. Such a medicine would be a syrup, which is also said to soothe the throat at 158.2: cf. Plin. *Nat. Hist.* 23.105 'faciunt oris suavitatem decocto eorum colluti aut suco expresso'.

4. incurvos: of the effects of old age, as at e.g. Ter. *Eun.* 336; Ovid *Met.* 14.659; Amm. 24.1.10.

Commentary

tussis anhela senes: yet another reminiscence of Vergil's description of the citron (*Georg.* 2.134 f.): 'animas et olentia Medi / ora fovent illo et senibus medicantur anhelis'; note also *Georg.* 3.496 f. 'et quatit aegros / tussis anhela sues'; *AL* 202.5 'senibus ... anhelis'.

160 (171R)

Another. Every kind of fruit ought to rise to the citron, which has much goodness in its rind and pulp. Each and every little fruit gives a juice of its own; from this one three flavours at once invariably tickle the tastebuds.

1. omne genus mali: the noun must here be *malum* rather than *malus*, because the comparison which follows is with a fruit, not a tree; and its reference is to all kinds of fruit growing on trees, not only apples (for which see 158.1 n.).

adsurgere: a metaphorical use, 'to rise to' in the sense of 'to give precedence to', which is humorous in its anthropomorphism of the fruits. For the idiom, cf. Verg. *Georg.* 2.98; Aus. 24.2 'Constantinopoli assurgit Carthago priori'; *AL* 189.87; with *TLL* 2.938.28 f.

citro: like 'mali' preceding this must be the fruit, not the tree (*TLL* 3.1208.51 f. is in error); for *citrum* of the fruit, cf. Cass. Fel. 81.4, 'tria grana de medio citri tolles et teres', with *TLL* loc.cit. 18 f.

2. corticis et medii: these are the rind and flesh of the fruit respectively. For *cortex* cf. Vulg. Cant. 6.6 'sicut cortex mali Punici genae tuae'; the rind of fruits is often to be found in medicinal recipes (e.g. Cels. 6.7.2; Scrib. Larg. 248). For *medium* used substantivally elsewhere, cf. Cels. 4.15.3 'ex malo cotoneo medium'; Plin. *Nat. Hist.* 10.148 'medium ovi'; Cass. Fel. quoted at 1 n. above.

3. unumquemque suum (A); unum quaeque suum (Hagen; Baehrens): the precise phrasing of the opening of this line is open to doubt, but the contrast between this line and the next is that though all *pomuscula* can provide juice, the citron is a special *pomusculum* in that it provides threefold flavour (i.e. from juice as well as from the rind and pulp already mentioned). The conjecture offered by Hagen and Baehrens for A's 'unumquemque suum' is generally adopted by modern editors (e.g. Riese and SB; see also Baehrens at *RhM* 31.1876.613), but 'unum ... suum ... sucum' seems at best inelegant and wrongly emphasised (obviously every fruit gives only one kind of juice; it is the fact that the citron has more than one *sapor* that is of interest). However Löfstedt (*Per. Aeth.* p. 337 n. 1) defended the ms. 'unumquemque suum' by analogy with a construction which is frequent with 'suus quisque', where by enallage *quisque* is attracted into agreement with the noun which *suus* qualifies (e.g. Verg. *Ecl.* 7.54 'strata iacent passim sua quaeque sub arbore poma'

Commentary

('its fruits lie scattered about under each tree'); Caes. *Bell. Civ.* 1.83.2 'aliae totidem (sc. cohortes) suae cuiusque legionis subsequebantur' ('and the same number of cohorts followed, each from its legion'); with more examples at *KS* 2.1.645 Anm. 6; *OLD* quisque 2(d)). Thus here 'unumquemque' ought to agree with *pomuscula* (if that were possible) but is attracted into agreement with 'suum sucum'. Retention of the received text therefore seems preferable to emendation.

4. ternus ab hoc ... sapor: the threefold flavour which, it is implied, distinguishes the citron from other fruits, is attributable to the *cortex* and *medium* of line 2 and the *sucus* which is introduced in line 3; the antecedent to 'ab hoc' is supplied from 'pomuscula' in line 3.

161 (172R)

On Daphne. A skilled hand took care that the sculpted boughs and limbs could have an appropriate colour. Art and coloration together produce a wonderfully apposite effect, when variegated marble depicts two entities.

This is the first of three interconnected ecphrastic epigrams with mythological themes. They all concern statues, they all celebrate the skill of the (anonymous) sculptors, and the first two focus as much on the technological as the aesthetic triumph of the sculpture. This epigram describes a statue of the metamorphosing Daphne which is made from variegated marble, carved so that the tree elements of the finished piece are suitably brown or green in their natural colour, whilst the flesh sections are suitably pink or white. The next epigram describes a statue of the flayed Marsyas and the tree from which he hangs suspended, and there are surviving examples of that type (see 162 intro.), though none survive of the Daphne type here described. These statues were carved from single blocks (as line 4 suggests), and in both the present cases more than one object is depicted in the finished artefact (Daphne and the bush into which she metamorphoses, Marsyas and the tree from which he hangs). This is in itself a technological accomplishment to be celebrated by the poet (on which see my note on Aus. *Epig.* 34.2), but that accomplishment is all the greater in the present instances, because suitable sections of the variegated marble blocks have to be accommodated to the relevant entities depicted to give the correct coloration. Some examples of the type of marble which might have been used for the Daphne sculpture here described can be found in *Marble in Antiquity: Collected Papers of J.B. Ward-Perkins*, ed. H. Dodge and B. Ward-Perkins, London 1992, Appx. 1, which catalogues the main quarries of the decorative stone used in the Roman world (possible candidates are, for example, cipollino from Carystus in Euboea, or verde antico from Thessaly, illustrated at Pl. II c

Commentary

and f); and see also *Radiance in Stone: Sculptures in Colored Marble from the Museo Nazionale Romano*, ed. M.L. Anderson and L. Nista, Rome 1989, 14 f.; 21 f.

The classic telling of the myth of Daphne's metamorphosis is that of Ovid (*Met.* 1.452 f.), and representations of her in the visual arts centre almost exclusively on her pursuit by Apollo and transformation; she is well enough represented in North Africa, with mosaics from El Djem and Tebessa, and through influence on Coptic art (see *LIMC* 3.1.344 f.; with nos 4-7; 16; 18; 29; 40a). See further Y.F.-A. Giraud, *La Fable de Daphné, Essai sur un type de métamorphose végétale dans la littérature et dans les arts jusqu' à la fin du XVII siècle*, Geneva 1968; and my intro. to Aus. *Epig.* 114.

1. frondibus et membris: the paired nouns introduce the theme of the epigram, with the boughs belonging to one part of the statue, the limbs to the other.

servavit (Sched.); servabit (A); servivit (Shackleton Bailey): although SB's conjecture is prima facie attractive, because 'servivit' could directly govern the datives of 'frondibus et membris', the smaller correction made to A's text by the Schedae Divionenses is perfectly supportable (and A often exhibits confusion between 'v' and 'b': see Riese, xlii f.; M. Spallone, *IMU* 25.1982.61 f.). *Servare* can be used in the sense *observare*, and can take *ut / ne* clauses: e.g. Col. 8.5.13 'servat autem qui subicit, ne singula ova in cubili manu componat ...' (well translated in the Loeb 'the man ... is careful not to ...'); Liv. 39.14.10 'servarent ne qui nocturni coetus fierent'; Plin. *Nat. Hist.* 17.124; with *TLL* 9.2.213.43 f. Therefore 'servavit' here should be construed as governing the 'ut' clause of line 2, 'frondibus et membris' should be construed with 'sculptis' in line 2, and there should be no punctuation at the end of the first line.

dextera sollers: a unifying theme in these three epigrams: cf. 'docta manus' at 162.3 and 163.3.

3. iunctae ars et pictura: Riese (app. crit.) rightly interprets 'ars' as the art of the sculptor, though it is rather 'pictura' that merits explanation: it describes the naturally variegated colouring of the marble. Similarly, *pictura* is often used by Pliny to denote natural coloration and shades of colour: thus trees 'tunc se novas aliasque quam sunt ostendunt, tunc variis colorum picturis in certamen usque luxuriant' (*Nat. Hist.* 16.95), and he also uses the noun with reference to patterned gems (2.207), animals (7.7), snake markings (8.85) and peacock colours (24.162). It should not here be understood to refer to painting (i.e. the stone being partly painted to achieve the desired effects): 'varius lapis' in the next line suggests otherwise; the technological achievement of ensuring the correct coloration of the separate entities of the group, which is the basis of the opening couplet, would hardly merit such praise if the feat had

Commentary

been achieved by a coat of paint; and the phrase 'ars et pictura' would be unnecessarily unbalanced (on the interpretation advanced the nouns make a witty pairing, with 'pictura' mischievously suggesting art, but actually referring to nature, the phrase being a play on 'ars et natura').

4. varius ... lapis: cf. Sen. *Tro.* 836 'ferax varii lapidis Carystos' (for the significance of Carystus marble see intro. above); Sen. *Ep.* 8.5.

duo signa: these are the two entities which make up the finished sculpture, Daphne and the bush into which she is metamorphosing.

162 (173R)

<*On Marsyas.*> From a lofty branch the defeated Marsyas hangs down, and the natural red coloration shows how his chest is tensed. A skilled hand has polished the marble into differently coloured limbs; the lifelikeness of tree and man shines forth from such artistry.

This second piece about a statue depicting a scene from myth shares many themes with that preceding (see intro. thereon), to the extent that in A it has become conflated with it (a misinterpretation of 'duo signa' at 161.4 might also have been a cause). Heinsius, before conjecturing 'aerio' for A's nonsensical 'erio' as the opening word, had suggested 'ex illo' in order to maintain this connection, but Marsyas and his tree and the metamorphosing Daphne are clearly differentiated subjects (for questions of separation in the collection see p. 19).

The myth of Marsyas and his ill-advised musical contest with Apollo, which culminated in his being flayed alive, is first evidenced by Herodotus (7.26), though it was obviously well established by that date. Plato first attributed hubris to him (*Symp.* 215b), whilst Latin authors tended to emphasise his arrogance and stupidity (Ovid *Fast.* 6.706 f.; Apul. *Flor.* 3 etc.) and the cruelty of his punishment (Ovid *Met.* 6.385 f.). An epigram by the Hellenistic Alcaeus of Messene (*AP* 16.8) describes a depiction of the binding of Marsyas, whilst another by Archias of Mytilene describes his dead body being buffeted by wind as it hangs from the tree (*AP* 7.696). Herodotus (loc. cit.) says Marsyas' skin could be seen at Calaenae near Apamea in Phrygia, and Pliny (*Nat. Hist.* 16.240) says that the tree from which he was hung and flayed could still be viewed in his day by travellers to the same area.

Marsyas was a popular subject in the visual arts, with over four hundred known representations depicting scenes from all parts of his myth: his challenge to Apollo, the contest, the judgement, and his binding and flaying. Statues of the hanging Marsyas, bound and hung from a tree immediately before his flaying alive, which is the subject of this epigram, number well over fifty extant examples. They fall into two basic groups, which are known as the red and white types. The red is the more animated, depicting

Commentary

Marsyas' chest thrust out and his muscles tensed, whilst the figure in the white type merely hangs down from the tree: 'the muscles of the "red" replicas are expanded to their greatest extent, and their veins project like thick rope-like cords. The hair is disordered ... and the face is distorted by the asymmetrical line of the mouth and the furrows of the forehead and brows. The individual muscles of the "white" replicas are, in contrast, barely indicated, and the play of veins across the surface is not as marked. The features of the face are symmetrical; the mouth is straight and barely open; the hair is swept back from the face above the forehead and at the sides' (A. Weis, 'The Hanging Marsyas and its Copies, Roman Innovations in a Hellenistic Sculptural Tradition', *Archaeologica* 103.1992.19). The red type is the earlier, beginning in the first century BC and continuing through to at least the late fourth century AD, whilst the white type begins in the first century AD and continues to much the same date. Although the red type is so termed because of the predominantly red marbles of which it is made, and the white similarly, the adjectives describe types rather than colour, because the colours of the marble used vary.

Weis (op. cit. 27, with Pls 1; 4; 9; 13) illustrates the present epigram by reference to a Marsyas of the red type now in Karlsruhe, carved from red-violet pavonazzetto marble; it has been heavily restored after suffering bomb damage in 1944, it came from Tusculum, and it probably dates to the second century AD. This is Weis' description of it: 'the satyr is attached to the tree across the shoulders and by means of smaller supports disguised as branches or a tail at the small of the back, beneath the feet and behind each leg. The curve of the satyr's back and two conveniently placed "tree-limbs" cover the major point of attachment; the branch which supports the feet is set at a diagonal that stops just short of the toes so it is not visible from the front and not observable from the side. The monument is thus composed of two closely connected columns of marble, but the artist, through a brilliant manipulation of the connecting struts, has given the impression that the satyr and the tree are two separate objects, one suspended from the other'.

See also P.B. Rawson, *The Myth of Marsyas in the Roman Visual Arts*, Oxford 1987, 3 f. (for the myth); 53 f.; 140 f.; Frazer's note on Apollod. 1.4.2; and *LIMC* 6.1.366 f.

1. aerio (Heinsius); erio (A); pierio (Sched.): Heinsius' conjecture is excellent; *aerius* is an adjective often applied to trees (e.g. 'aeria ... ab ulmo' (Verg. *Ecl.* 1.58); 'aeriam ... ornum' (Val. Flacc. 8.113); 'aerios pityonas' (Mart. 12.50.1)), alluding to lofty height. Pliny (*Nat. Hist.* 16.240) says of the tree alleged to be the one from which Marsyas was suspended 'quae iam tam magnitudine electa est', though here the implication of the adjective is to illustrate how the sculptor has overcome the technical challenge of keeping Marsyas' feet well clear of the ground.

Commentary

dependet: for the suspension of Marsyas from the tree as a prelude to his flaying cf. *AP* 7.696.2 Archias; Ovid *Fast.* 6.707 f.; Hyg. *Fab.* 165.5.

Marsya: for this metrically convenient and frequent Latin termination of the nominative of Greek names of '-as' form, cf. *Marsya* also at Hor. *Sat.* 1.6.120 and Mart. 2.64.8; with other examples at *N-W* 1.60.

2. nativusque ... rubor: the reference is to the colour of the marble from which the sculpture is fashioned (cf. 161.3 'pictura', with note). This is likely to have been pavonazzetto or Phrygian marble, a rare and expensive stone which came from Docimion in Phrygia, modern west central Turkey (which appositely also happens to be the area in which the Marsyas myth is set: see intro. above). The red coloration of this marble would be ideal not only in suggesting the constriction of Marsyas' muscles as he hangs bound from the tree, but also in luridly suggesting the punishment of being flayed alive which awaits him (gruesomely described by Ovid at *Met.* 6.385 f.). See A. Weis, 'Material Limitations and Exotic Materials in the Copying of a Hellenistic Statuary Type', in *Classical Marble: Geochemistry, Technology, Trade*, ed. N. Herz and M. Waelkens, Dordrecht etc., 1988, 219 f.; and J.B. Ward-Perkins, op. cit. at 161 intro., 29 n. 35; 158.

pectora tensa: the phrase describes the tensed muscles of his constricted chest as Marsyas hangs from the tree (for which see intro. above).

3. docta manus: repeated at 163.3, at precisely the same position in the line (see note).

varios ... in artus: these 'artus' are not only those which belong to Marsyas, but also the boughs of the tree from which he hangs (compare 161.1 'frondibus et membris' of the sculpture of the metamorphosing Daphne). For *artus* used metaphorically of parts of trees (as English 'limbs'), cf. *Culex* 137 f. 'hic magnum Argoae navi decus addita pinus / proceros decorat silvas hirsuta per artus / ac petit aeriis contingere motibus astra'; Pallad. *De Insit.* 47 'nexilibus gemmis fecundos implicat artus vitis'; and for other analogy between trees and men, see R.G.M. Nisbet, 'The Oak and the Axe: Symbolism in Seneca *Hercules Oetaeus* 1618 f.', in *Collected Papers on Latin Literature*, ed. S.J. Harrison, Oxford 1995, 202 f.

limavit: the verb signifies the final stage of the fashioning of a statue, that of smoothing and polishing the surface (cf. the synonymous *polire*, with my note on Aus. *Epig.* 62.3).

4. fides (Cannegieter); figis (A): 'fides' must be correct: it denotes verisimilitude, as at 139.6 (see note).

Commentary

163 (174R)

On Philoctetes. His foot injured by a wound subdues Philoctetes into handing over his Tirynthian weapons to the Pelasgian leaders. A skilled hand has chiselled his living features from the marble: he still feels his agony, wretched even in stone.

The final epigram of the trio on statues with a mythological subject concerns the wounded Philoctetes giving up his bow and arrows to the Greek leaders. His myth has many variations of detail, but the well-known outline is that his weapons had been given to him (or to his father Poeas) by Hercules as a reward for lighting his funeral pyre on Mt Oeta, and that he had sailed with them to Troy as the leader of a contingent of archers, but was left behind on Lemnos because of the fetid stench of a wound to his foot caused by a snake bite. Helenus had however prophesied that Troy would not fall without Philoctetes and / or his bow, so a contingent of Greeks (Ulysses alone or with others) was sent to prise him off Lemnos and get the weapons. By various stratagems, and the assistance of Hercules as a deus ex machina, they succeeded (Hom. *Il.* 2.718 f.; *Cypria* (Proclus) frags *EGF* p. 32.64 f. Davies; Soph. *Phil.* passim; Apollod. *epit.* 3.27; with *LIMC* 7.1.376 f.).

The wounded Philoctetes was a popular figure in the visual arts. Three epigrams at *AP* 16.111-13 describe pictures or statues of him, stressing the expression of his pain as does this epigram (lines 3-4); Polygnotus painted a Philoctetes surrendering his arms (Paus. 1.22.6); and three late Etruscan alabaster funerary urns also depict the scene of the handing over of the weapons (illustrated at *LIMC* 6.2.643; 7.2.325); for surviving portrayals of his sufferings on Lemnos see also *LIMC* 7.1.379 f., nos 21-69. Stevens (*Image and Insight*, 66 f.) suggests that this epigram describes a relief rather than a statue, but this is only on the grounds that it depicts more than one figure (Philoctetes and 'duces Pelasgi'). Whilst this might be correct, the epigram follows two about statues which depict more than a single entity (Daphne and the bush, Marsyas and the tree), and other statue groups are known (e.g. Niobe and her children (Aus. *Epig.* 57, with my intro.), Laocoon and his). It is therefore possible, if not probable, that the description is of a statue group.

1. prodentem (A); probentem (Stowasser); arcentem (Courtney): SB, retaining the ms. text, comments (app. crit.) '*Cf. Serv. in Aen. 3.402*', where Servius details a version of the myth in which Philoctetes receives his wound to the foot because he had betrayed Hercules' confidence in disclosing the site of his pyre. Courtney (*C&M* 40.1989.200) asks why this is relevant to Philoctetes agreeing to 'betray' Hercules' weapons to the Greek leaders; he therefore rejects the ms. 'prodentem' in favour of 'probentem' (a contracted form of 'prohibentem', found also at e.g. Lucr. 1.977; 3.864: see J.M. Stowasser, *WS* 31.1909.290), or his own conjecture

304

Commentary

'arcentem'. But *prodere* need not descend as far down the moral scale as betrayal, since it can also connote surrender of or handing things over to an enemy (e.g. Liv. 22.60.16 'Hannibalem post paulo audistis castra prodi et arma tradi iubentem'; Ter. *Heaut.* 479), or mean simply 'give' (e.g. Plin. *Ep.* 4.14.1). The force of the participle here could thus be proleptic, in that the pain of Philoctetes' wounded foot subdues him into handing over his weapons to people he has good reason to regard as his enemy, because that is the only way he will escape from Lemnos and get his wound healed (although such motivation plays only a subsidiary part in extant tragedy (e.g. Soph. *Phil.* 1424; 1437 f.), it is dominant in e.g. Quintus of Smyrna's account (9.410 f.)). For the prolepsis of the participle compare e.g. Verg. *Aen.* 7.350 'fallitque furentem', describing the effect on Amata of the bite of Allecto's poisonous snake (see Horsfall's note).

ducibus ... Pelasgis: Ulysses and Neoptolemus make up the Greek delegation in Sophocles' play, whilst Euripides uses Ulysses and Diomedes, Aeschylus uses Ulysses alone, and there are other variants (see Frazer's note on Apollod. *epit.* 5.8).

Tirynthia tela: Hercules was Tirynthian, and the adjective points to the pedigree of Philoctetes' weapons and the part of Hercules in the story (see intro. above, Soph. *Phil.* 801 f.; Diod. Sic. 4.38.4; Ovid *Met.* 9.229 with Bömer's note; Hyg. *Fab.* 102).

3. docta manus: a frequent metonymy for artistic or other skill: e.g. Tib. 1.8.11 f. 'quid ungues / artificis docta subsecuisse manu?'; *CE* 1414.3 'docta manus', of a doctor; *AL* 329.1 Luxorius; with *TLL* 5.1.1758.81 f. Note also 161.1 'dextera sollers'; 162.3 'docta manus'; 166.2 'docta manus'.

vivos ... vultus (Burman; sensus (A)): A's 'sensus' has probably replaced 'vultus' because of the ensuing 'sentit' in line 4; but it is not beyond all probability, because it is precisely Philoctetes' pain and emotion that is emphasised when good representations of him in the visual arts are described: e.g. *AP* 16.112.4 anon. 'ἀλλὰ καὶ ἐν χαλκῷ τὸν πόνον εἰργάσατο' (Loeb 'but he wrought in the brass even the pain'); ibid. 111.3 f. Glaucus; ibid. 113.1 f. Jul. Aeg. However, his face is also a focus of these descriptions, and epigrams specify the depiction of tears in his eyes as a sign of his pain (e.g. *AP* 16.111.3; 113.7). Burman's conjecture allows this epigram to make both points, the pained face in this line, and the portrayal of emotion in line 4; and it also provides a convincing reminiscence of Verg. *Aen.* 6.848 'vivos ducent de marmore vultus' (for Vergilian echoes in the collection see p. 12 f.).

4. sentit adhuc poenam, tristis et in lapide (A, *ex* sentitadhucsensuspena tristis et in lapidem); ... tristis et inde lapis (Burman): Burman's conjecture, made because ecphrastic epigrams often attribute feeling to stone or the like (e.g. Aus. *Epig.* 58.7 f.; *AL* 268.4

f.), is worth consideration, but his 'inde' is mere padding and the trope about sentient stone is present anyway.

Philoctetes' suffering is described in terms of his *tristitia*, which stems from his wounded foot and ten-year isolation on Lemnos, and in terms of *poena*. It would be natural to consider *poena* in terms of crime and punishment, and such an implication could be accommodated here: although Philoctetes' injury was not usually stated in his myth to have been a punishment for some misdemeanour, a variant preserved by Servius (ap. Verg. *Aen.* 3.402) held that it was caused by one of Hercules' poisoned arrows, which had attacked its new owner because he had broken his promise to Hercules not to divulge the site of his pyre; and another variant at Hyg. *Fab.* 102.1 said that Juno had punished Philoctetes because she had been angered by his building of Hercules' pyre. However, *poena* can have shades of meaning which do not imply the cause and effect of crime and punishment, but focus more on the outcome of punishment as felt by the person punished, that is physical or mental pain or deprivation. Thus Seneca (*Ep.* 5.4 f.): 'hoc contra naturam est, torquere corpus suum et faciles odisse munditias et squalorem adpetere et cibis non tantum vilibus uti sed taetris et horridis ... Frugalitatem exigit philosophia, non poenam'; Juv. 3.278 f. 'ebrius ac petulans, qui nullum forte cecidit, / dat poenas, noctem patitur lugentis amicum / Pelidae'; Plin. *Nat. Hist.* 2.27; *AL* 247.180. This foreshadows the dominant meaning of some reflexes of *poena* in Romance languages, such as Fr. 'peine' (*REW* 6628); and such a meaning is more appropriate in this context, where the focus is on the accuracy of the depiction in statuary of Philoctetes' pain and suffering.

164 (175R)

On some baths. Man's one salvation is to go and get a cold bath, so that sultry steam does not render the limbs debilitated.

For the frequent topic of baths and bathing in the collection see 99 intro. This distich stands in curious isolation, separated by three pieces from the next pair on the theme (168-9); 99 is similarly isolated, but it is a much more substantial twelve-line piece (for the ordering of epigrams in the collection see p. 3). Busch (*Versus*, 340 f.) in his treatment of this piece points out its similarity to 113 both in its content of the contrasting of different water temperatures and in its structure.

1. una salus ...: the line is a witty parody of Verg. *Aen.* 2.354 'una salus victis nullam sperare salutem', a line which is also quoted verbatim at Sen. *Nat. Quaest.* 6.2.2, and interpolated by one ms. family at the end of Veg. *Mil.* 3.21.6.

gelidum (Shackleton Bailey; calidum (A)) ... lavacrum: SB adduces *AL* 281.242 Symphosius, where A similarly has 'calidis' (which is

Commentary

incorrect) and Baehrens' conjecture 'gelidis' may be correct. Since 'tepidus vapor' in the following line of this epigram renders limbs 'morbida', which is a bad effect, it must be likely that the reader is here bidden to have a cold bath, not a hot one. It would not seem logical for the reader to be advised to have a hot bath rather than subject himself to 'tepidus vapor' (see 2 n.), and SB's conjecture should therefore be accepted (see also note on 'captare' below).

Although evidence can be adduced for ancient belief in the health-giving effects of both hot and cold waters (for hot water cf. Suet. *Aug.* 82.2; Plin. *Nat. Hist.* 29.10; with Fagan, *Bathing*, 87 n. 13; for cold water cf. Hor. *Ep.* 1.15.4; Cels. 1.1.2; Plin. *Nat. Hist.* 29.26; my note on Mart. 11.47.6), attacks on the enervating and effeminising effects of hot water began early (e.g. Ar. *Clouds* 1044 f.) and continued into Latin literature (e.g. Liv. 23.18.12; Plin. *Nat. Hist.* 29.10; *SHA* Alex. Sev. 53.2, with Fagan, *Bathing*, 88 n. 15); and it is in any event more likely that bathers would need encouragement to take cold baths rather than hot (cf. 113.3 n.).

captare: this is the equivalent of the English idiom 'go and get': cf. Verg. *Ecl.* 2.8 'nunc etiam pecudes umbras et frigora captant' (and ibid. 1.52); Stat. *Silv.* 4.4.17 'frigora captant'; Sen. *De Vita Beata* 7.3 'voluptatem ... tenebras captantem': it is notable that what is gone and got in all these instances is cool and shade, which lends some further support to SB's conjecture 'gelidum'.

2. tepidus ... vapor: cf. 112.4 'haec reddi poterunt, Phoebe, vapora tuis' (with note); *vapor* in a bathing context suggests steam, and so the reference here might be to a *laconicum* or sauna, as Busch suggests (loc. cit. intro.). He adduces Sid. *Ep.* 2.9.9 for a similar scenario and the contrast between hot and cold bathing: 'coctilibus aquis ingerebamur quarumque fotu ... resoluti aut fontano deinceps frigore putealique aut fluviali aqua solidabamur'. Nevertheless 'tepidus' does here give pause for thought, because in combination with 'vapor' it is almost an oxymoron and its overtones are pejorative (cf. Prop. 1.13.26 'nam tibi non tepidas subdidit illa faces'; with *OLD* tepidus 3(a)); it might suggest the steam is not as hot as it should be, or, more likely, that there is something 'wrong' in the heat it provides, because it renders limbs 'morbida'.

165 (176.1-8R)

On a goose which contains a whole banquet inside it. Filled with chicken meat the goose towers up and, swollen, encloses various treats for the table; for in its groin it holds vegetables, and a gleaming sausage is extruded from amidst its relaxed bowels. Juicy thrush and turtle-dove shore up both of its sides, and the winged creation hides many carcasses. Who would not believe that a horse hid a phalanx of Greeks, if a little goose has such hidden capacity?

Commentary

This and the following epigram, rather attractive pieces about stuffed geese, are not separated in A, and Riese, despite being aware of G. Loewe's arguments for separation, keeps them as one. But Loewe is surely correct (*Acta Soc. Phil. Lipsiensis* 6.1876.356 f.): 166 is essentially a repetition of this piece (165.2 'varias ... ambit opes' / 166.4 'multas ... prodit opes'; 165.3 'ventrisque soluti ...' / 166.4 'scisso ... pectore'; 165.8 'si parvus ... anser' / 166.9 'maiorem in parvo'; and esp. the openings, where the stuffing of the goose with other goodies is described, and the endings, where the finished product is compared to the Trojan horse and its contents). It can further be argued that the separated pieces are convincing entities, with the initial description of the whole bird and its various stuffings and appurtenances concluded by comparison with similar mythological 'stuffings'. Given also that separation is necessary elsewhere in the collection (see p. 19), the argument for it here is sound, and Loewe's supplement of 'Aliter' as the superscription for 166 should be accepted, as it is in SB's text.

The stuffed goose which the epigrams describe is clearly a luxurious and extravagant item, a centrepiece for a dinner party. Roman cuisine was fond of stuffed meat and fowl generally: Apicius gives recipes for stuffed sucking-pig (8.7.1; 14), stuffed hare (8.8.3; 9), stuffed dormice (8.9) and stuffed chicken (6.8.14), amongst others; a sequence of epigrams in the *AL* describes various kinds of stuffing (217-22); and Cato gives instructions in his *De Agricultura* (89 f.). But these epigrams take the practice to an extreme, with the stuffed animal concealing a regression of other cooked animals and stuffings inside it, like a set of Chinese boxes. Where such creations are mentioned elsewhere, it is often in a context of disapproval, such as sumptuary laws (cf. esp. the *porcus Troianus* 'quasi aliis inclusis animalibus gravidum, ut ille Troianus equus gravidus armatis fuit' (Macr. *Sat.* 3.13.13)) or satire (cf. Petr. *Sat.* 36.1 f.; 40.4 f.; 69.6). There is however no such disapproval detectable in the present instances, where the geese are described only as objects of interest. See further on culinary stuffing, E. Gowers, *The Loaded Table*, Oxford 1993, 70 f.; 112 f.

superscr.: copiam (Riese); cupia (A); cupedia (Reinesius): Riese's rather prosaic 'copiam' is the more likely emendation of A's 'cupia', though Reinesius' 'cupedia' is well worth consideration: the noun is rare but makes appearances from Plautus onwards, and it is sometimes neuter, as in the conjecture here, sometimes feminine, and usually is spelled with double 'p'. *Cup(p)edia* are comestible delicacies: cf. Paul. *Fest.* p. 42.9 Lindsay 'cuppes et cupedia antiqui lautiores cibos nominabant, inde et macellum forum cupedinis appellabant. Cupedia autem a cupiditate sunt dicta ...'; Non. Marc. p. 120.10 Lindsay. At Plaut. *Stich.* 714 'nil moror cuppedia' they are a kind of hors d'oeuvre or tapas; at Gell. 6.16.6 they are luxury overseas foods of various kinds; at ibid. 7.13.2 they are tit-bits taken to a dinner; and at Amm. Marc. 25.2.2 they are the kind of food

Commentary

an emperor might eat. They seem however to be properly regarded as exquisite culinary delicacies rather than as large dishes or parts of them, and for that reason 'copiam' better defines what will be described in the epigram.

prandii: see 146.1 n.; it seems unlikely that the *prandium* envisaged here is the mid-day meal, because that was usually a light meal. This is rather dinner; for *prandium* with this wider reference see *TLL* 10.2.1125.44 f.

1. anser: goose does not seem to have been a particularly prized eating bird, except for its liver (Stat. *Silv.* 4.6.9; Mart. 3.82.19; 13.58 etc.). However Columella gives a guide to the rearing of geese on the farm (8.14), as does Cato (*Agr.* 89), and see also André, *L'Alimentation*, 120.

2. turgidus (Müller); torridus (A): there is nothing to be said in favour of 'torridus', and Müller's conjecture 'turgidus' (*JKPh* 93.1866.556), which emphasises the bulging carcass of the bird, must be correct (cf. *AL* 218.1 (of a stuffed animal) 'turgida membris / ex aliis crescit').

ambit: for *ambire* used with reference to one item which contains another, cf. Plin. *Nat. Hist.* 33.54 'et quota pars ea fuit aureae domus ambientis urbem'; Amm. Marc. 14.6.4 'ex omni plaga, quam orbis ambit immensus'.

3. olus: (*h*)*olus*, Greek λάχανον, includes root and green vegetables, which would either have been roasted inside the bird or chopped up into a vegetable stuffing (see André, *L'Alimentation*, 34).

ventrisque soluti: the image evoked by this phrase is scatological, though the language is euphemistic; *ventrem solvere* is medical terminology for defecation (see Mart. 11.88.4 with my note). The bird is described as though it were excreting the 'esitiata nitens' which no doubt suggestively bursts out of its engorged rump. The verb 'truditur' (line 4) would also suit the euphemistically-phrased imagery (for similar euphemisms see Adams, *LSV* 243 f.; *Mul. Chir.* 229 uses as a substantive the adjectival form 'farciminalis' (from *farcimen*, 'sausage') to refer to horse dung).

4. esitiata (A); isiciata (Gronovius): both *esit(c)iatus* and *isiciatus* are attested adjectival forms, deriving from the noun *esicium* or *isicium* (*TLL* 7.2.492.15 f.; 27 f.). Varro (*Ling. Lat.* 5.110) comments on 'insicia' 'ab eo quod insecta caro, ut in carmine saliorum <prosicium> est' (and cf. Macr. *Sat.* 7.8.1); whether or not there is any etymological truth in this, the definition of chopped meat (or fish) is borne out by the evidence. *E(i)sicium* was sausage-meat or forcemeat which could be used to stuff animals or birds, or could be turned into sausages, rissoles and the like (cf. Don. ap. Ter. *Eun.* 257.4). Apicius (2.2.6) lists the basic ingredients, which in his descending order of preference are based on meat of peacock, pheasant, rabbit, chicken and pork, and his entire second book deals with the mincing of meat; *Ed. Diocl.* 4.14 adds beef, and *SHA* Heliog. 19.6 adds fish. The piglet of the *Testamentum Porcelli* apportions his body with the words 'et de meis visceribus dabo donabo sutoribus saetas, bubulariis intestina, esiciariis femora'.

'Esitiata' is however strictly an adjectival form, and might here need to be considered as an ellipse (and *TLL* loc. cit. comments '*sc. gallina, ut vid.*'): thus in Apicius there are 'vulvulae isiciatae' (2.3.1), 'circellos isiciatos' (2.5.4) etc., and 'De esiciata' in the superscription to *AL* 217 must be an ellipse (the opening of the epigram reads 'amisit proprias vacuato corpore carnes / accepitque novas', where 'novas (carnes)' illustrates the effects of being *esiciata*, but 'amisit' has no noun to show what is *esiciata*). However, it is possible 'esitiata' may here be a substantive ('sausage'), because (a) it has a qualifying adjective in 'nitens', and (b) the image of a sausage would well suit the humour with 'ventris soluti' (note also substantival 'farciminalis' at 3 n. above).

5. fulcit utrumque latus: this and the next line apparently deal with the external presentation of the bird: it has been stuffed to such fullness that it needs external supports, and these are provided by a thrush and dove, or thrushes and doves, on both sides.

turdus cum turture: for thrushes and turtle-doves as high quality foods see Mart. 13.51 and 53, with Leary's notes.

6. multaque (A; pulpaque (Baehrens); vulvaque (Riese)) penniferum (Burman; perniferum (A)) corpora condit (Shackleton Bailey; pandit (A)) opus: if it is correct that this couplet describes the external presentation of the bird (see 5 n. above), SB's text, which I follow, is convincing (*Towards a Text*, 24), though I understand 'condit' to refer to items outside rather than inside the bird. A's 'perniferum', which would be a ἅπαξ λεγόμενον, is unconvincing, because we have been told what the 'opus' of the goose contains, and it is not a ham; and A's 'pandit', considering the conclusion of the epigram in the next couplet is a reference to everything the goose hides, is the opposite of what is required (it can be added that Baehrens' and Riese's introductions of 'pulpa' and 'vulva' respectively add to the confusion rather than dispel it). But SB's restoration of the text gives good sense: the 'wing-bearing creation' of the goose 'hides' (sc. with its outstretched wings, still with their feathers to add to the visual impact and camouflage) 'many carcasses' (sc. comprising or in addition to the supports of thrushes and doves already mentioned) in its presentation at table. The compound adjective 'pennifer' also occurs at Sid. *Carm.* 2.309 'flectis penniferos ... armos'; for 'opus' compare 'haec ... fabrica' at 166.9.

7. ecum: for another stuffed animal compared to the Trojan horse, cf. the *porcus Troianus* at Macr. *Sat.* 3.13.13, quoted in the intro. above.

Commentary

8. parvus: the bird is small only in comparison to the Trojan horse.

latebras: cf. Vergil's description of Trojan suspicion of the wooden horse (*Aen.* 2.38) 'aut terebrare cavas uteri et temptare latebras'; the noun often refers to the hidden recesses of body or soul (e.g. Plaut. *Cist.* 63 'in latebras apscondas pectore peritissimo'; Verg. *Aen.* 10.601 'tum latebras animae pectus mucrone recludit'; Stat. *Theb.* 8.585; with *TLL* 7.2.992.83 f.). The 'latebrae' of the goose would include not only its insides, but the cover provided by its outstretched wings.

166 (176.9-18R)

<*Another.*> A hand skilled at moulding poultry and meat has enclosed many dishes in the fattened container. Inside it is whatever delights; and one's pleasure grows when the breast is cut and it gives birth to many delicacies. Let the Cecropian workman's rampant heifer, in which passion used to enclose Pasiphae, give precedence! Let that also give precedence which Epeos, expert in trickery, built, the horse which, pregnant with war, destroyed Troy! This fabrication shows greater skill on a small canvas; one goose container holds a complete banquet.

For the arguments for separation of this from the preceding piece see 165 intro.; in this epigram the focus shifts slightly to the skill of the chef in the preparation of the stuffed goose, a skill which is compared in its execution to two great fabricated containers of myth, Pasiphae's heifer and the Trojan horse. Trickery and exhibitionism in the kitchen always impressed ancient writers: compare for example Martial's Caecilius, who served up gourds made to look like other food for every course of a banquet (11.31 with my intro.), and Petronius' Trimalchio, with his liking for deceptive foods (see E. Courtney, *A Companion to Petronius*, Oxford 2001, 83 f.).

1. saginato ... capso: the phrase is picked up by 'anseris arca' in the concluding line, and it is not until then that the 'container' is revealed to be the goose carcass. The 'capsus' here, in a unique usage, is a metaphor for the hollowed-out container of the goose's body (though there are similar instances at Vell. 1.16.2 'clausa capso (*campo*, Watt) aliove saepto diversi generis animalia', and at Isid. *Or.* 20.12.3, of that part of a carriage which contains passengers). The participle 'saginato' is ambiguous, indicating both that the bird itself has been 'fattened' for the table (cf. Prop. 4.1.23 'saginati ... porci'), and that the resultant carcass has been 'stuffed full' with other foods (cf. Apul. *Met.* 4.27.7 'mellitis dulciolis ventrem saginare').

2. aucupia et (Tollius; hocupiat (A)) pulpas: Tollius' emendation looks certain: the nouns refer respectively to the meat of fowl and other animals, which has probably been used to make stuffings, sausages and forcemeat (cf. 'ducere'); compare 'pullorum carnibus' at 165.1. *Aucupium* can denote either the act of fowling, or, as here, its product, the birds caught (cf. Cat. 114.3 'aucupium omne genus'; Sen. *De Prov.* 3.6).

ducere docta manus: the words suggest artistic creation as well as technological accomplishment (see 163.3 n. for the frequently used 'docta manus'); for *ducere* in the sense of making or moulding works of art, cf. 128.3; 163.3; Mart. 3.40(41).1 f. 'Mentoris manu ducta / lacerta'; Pan. Lat. 2(12).44.5 'haec ... gesta sollertes manus ducant'; with *OLD* duco 23(a).

4. prodit: the image is almost that of giving birth (cf. Apul. *Met.* 9.33.6 '(sc. gallina) praematurum ... prodidit partum'), and the subject of the verb is 'saginatus capsus' rather than 'docta manus'. Compare the image of defecation in the previous epigram (lines 3-4) and the pregnant Trojan horse at line 8.

opes (edd.); apes (A); aves (Burman): A displays his carelessness again; the correction printed by editors from Burman onwards is more convincing than his alternative conjecture.

5. Cecropii ... fabri: this is Daedalus, and a unique appellation, though Juvenal (1.54) calls him 'faber volans' in a debunking reference.

lascivans bucula: the verb, usually *lascivire* of the fourth conjugation, is here uniquely given a first conjugation termination, no doubt influenced by metrical considerations, though there is no reason why it cannot also reflect popular usage (it is an appropriately promiscuous verb: at Charisius p. 469.12 Barwick it has a second conjugation termination). A handful of other verbs behave similarly, for example *dementire / -are* (*TLL* 5.1.478.73 f.; 66 f.), *praesagire / -are* (*TLL* 10.2.810.18 f.; 813.11 f.); *insignire / -are* (*TLL* 7.1.1909.65 f.; 58 f.); *singultire / -are*, though subtle distinctions of meaning between the conjugations can be alleged (see Stotz, *Handbuch*, 4.191 f.). See also 121.1 n. 'praefulgunt'.

Whilst *lascivia* can denote the typical gambolling behaviour of heifers at play in the fields, such is not the typical behaviour of heifers with Pasiphae inside them, and 'lascivans' here clearly has sexual overtones to hint at her myth.

7. Epeos: Epe(i)os, son of Panopeus of Phocis, was, with Athena's help, the traditional designer and builder of the Trojan horse (Hom. *Od.* 8.493; 11.523); he is later designated a sculptor (e.g. Plat. *Ion* 533a; Paus. 2.19.6) or an architect (Apollod. *epit.* 5.14); see further *LIMC* 3.1.798 f.

8. gravidus bellis: for the image of the pregnant Trojan horse cf. Enn. *Scaen.* 26 Jocelyn 'nam maximo saltu superavit gravidus armatis equus / qui suo partu ardua perdat Pergama' (note, as here, the male pregnancy); Verg. *Aen.* 2.237 f. 'scandit fatalis machina muros / feta armis'; Ovid *Ars*

Commentary

1.364 'militibus gravidum laeta recepit equum'. Compare also Verg. *Aen.* 10.87 'quid gravidam bellis urbem et corda aspera temptas?'.

9. haec ... fabrica: *fabrica* can allude both to the act of craftmanship (e.g. Lucr. 4.513; Sen. *Ep.* 95.56 'non est necesse fabro de fabrica quaerere quod eius initium, quis usus sit'), or, concretely, to the artefact made (e.g. Pallad. 1.7.4 'si vicinus est fluvius, ubi statuimus fabricae sedem parare'; *AL* 202.1 'nobilis exsultat baiarum fabrica thermis'). It here has the latter meaning, because ensuing 'technam' would otherwise be pleonastic.

technam: Greek τέχνη is the exact equivalent of Latin *fabrica*, and here creates a witty juxtaposition of nouns. Although Latin *tech(i)na* is frequent in the comedians (e.g. Plaut. *Bacch.* 392; *Capt.* 642; Ter. *Heaut.* 471 etc.), it appears to fall out of use thereafter, and this seems to be the first subsequent occurrence.

167 (177R)

On Pyrrhus. Pyrrhus placates his father's tomb by cutting the girl's throat and he makes the offering they crave to his father's Manes. It is a novel destiny for the one born of a nymph: he gets what he desired after his death. The girl he engaged for his marriage bed he possesses in the grave.

This epigram on a mythological subject, which stands in isolation (for the ordering of epigrams in the collection see p. 3), describes the sacrifice of Polyxena by Pyrrhus at his father's tomb. Pyrrhus is usually the son of Achilles and Deiodamia, though in some versions of the myth his mother is given as Iphigenia; he is known as Neoptolemus in the Homeric epics (*Il.* 19.327; *Od.* 11.506), but is Pyrrhus in the *Cypria* (*EGF* frag. 16 Davies). He fought at Troy, where he killed Priam and a clutch of his sons (Verg. *Aen.* 2.526 f.). In this piece he is shown slaying Polyxena, Priam's daughter by Hecuba; it might be ecphrastic since it describes a single scene, though there are no specific words to key such an interpretation (there are however some paintings of the scene described at Paus. 1.22.6 and 10.25.10). In the earliest tellings of the myth Polyxena was killed by Ulysses and Diomedes (*EGF Cypria* frag. 27 Davies; *EGF Iliupersis* p. 62.35 f. Davies), but the usual version, as here, attributes her death to Pyrrhus (e.g. Eur. *Hec.* 521 f.; Ovid *Met.* 13.449 f.; Sen. *Tro.* 938 f.; Quint. Smyrn. 14.304 f.). The opening of the epigram suggests, and the conclusion confirms, that in the killing Pyrrhus was carrying out his father's wishes: Euripides (*Hec.* 37 f.; 107 f.) and Seneca (*Tro.* 181 f.) similarly describe Achilles' ghost rising from his tomb to demand Polyxena as his blood-due, whilst in Quintus Smyrnaeus (loc. cit.) Achilles appears to Pyrrhus in a dream and threatens to prevent the Greek fleet sailing if Polyxena is not sacrificed to him.

Commentary

Achilles' falling in love with Polyxena as an outcome of his ransoming to Priam of Hector's body has been briefly discussed at 150 intro. Servius gives two versions of the myth which are both similar to the scenario of this epigram: 'Achilles, dum circa muros Troiae bellum gereret, Polyxenam visam adamavit et conditione pacis in matrimonium postulavit. Quam cum Troiani fraude promisissent, Paris post Thymbraei Apollinis simulacrum latuit et venientem Achillem ad foedus missa vulneravit sagitta. Tum Achilles moriens petiit ut evicta Troia ad eius sepulcrum Polyxena immolaretur, quod Pyrrhus implevit' (ap. Verg. *Aen.* 3.321). And 'et alius ordo fabulae huius: cum Graeci victores in patriam vellent reverti, e tumulo Achillis vox dicitur audita querentis quod sibi soli de praeda nihil impertivissent. De qua re consultus Calchas cecinit Polyxenam Priami filiam, quam vivus Achilles dilexerat, eius debere manibus immolari. Quae cum admota tumulo Achillis occidenda esset, manu Pyrrhi aequanimiter mortem dicitur suscepisse; invenitur enim apud quosdam quod etiam ipsa Achillem amaverit, et ea nesciente Achilles fraude et insidiis sit peremptus' (ibid.). Cf. also Dict. Cret. 3.2 f.; 4.10 f. In Servius' version Achilles died before he could marry Polyxena; there are indications elsewhere that she was slain to be his bride in the afterworld, which is what the conclusion to this epigram suggests (see 4 n. below). For the myth see further *LIMC* 6.1.773 f.; 7.1.431 f.

superscr.: De Pyrrho: this furnishes evidence that the superscriptions were not the work of the poet (on which see p. 18 f.): the epigram is about Achilles, but only Pyrrhus' name appears in it, so the title is given to him.

1. busta patris: for the apposite location of Polyxena's slaying at Achilles' tomb cf. *EGF Iliupersis* frags 35-6 Davies; Eur. *Tro.* 264; *Hec.* 37 f.; Ovid *Met.* 13.452; and Servius, quoted above.

2. litat: for *litare* + the object of the gift offered in prayer or supplication ('dilectasque inferias'), cf. Prop. 4.1.24 'pastor ... exta litabat ovis'; Stat. *Silv.* 1.4.128.

3. nymphigenae: a ἅπαξ λεγόμενον to denote Achilles, alluding to his mother, the Nereid Thetis cf. Lindner, *Komposita*, 101 f.

votum post fata meretur: this is explained by the following line, in that Achilles consummated his wish to marry Polyxena after his death.

4. quam pepigit thalamis: for the phrase cf. Val. Flacc. 3.495 'thalamis et virgine pacta'. Achilles had hoped to celebrate marriage to Polyxena in the bridal bed, but actually possesses her in the grave. *Pactio* is a stage before the formal marriage ceremony in the process of engagement of bride and groom: thus Servius comments on 'pactae coniugis' (Verg. *Aen.*

Commentary

10.722) 'hic ordo est, conciliata primo, dein conventa, dein pacta, dein sponsa'. Although its precise nature is not established, it seems to refer to a formal betrothal rather than a marriage settlement. The woman is the object of the *pactio* made between the intended groom and her parents (cf. Cat. 62.28), and a woman who is *pacta* is roughly equivalent to one who is *sponsa* (thus Treggiari, *Marriage*, 138 f.). Here the word used is pointed, because although Achilles was effectively engaged to Polyxena, he was slain before he could formally marry her; the marriage was consummated post mortem, after her sacrifice at his tomb. For the idea cf. *AP* 9.117.1 f. Statyllius Flaccus; Sen. *Tro.* 942 f. 'Polyxene miseranda, quam tradi sibi / cineremque Achilles ante mactari suum, / campo maritus ut sit Elysio, iubet'; and Philostratus actually recasts the myth with Polyxena killing herself so that she may marry Achilles in the afterworld (*Vit. Apoll.* 4.16.4; *Heroicus* 51.5 f.); see further C. Fontinoy, 'Le sacrifice nuptial de Polyxène', *AntClass* 19.1950.383 f.

tumulis: there is an intended balance and *annominatio* with 'thalamis' at the end of the first hemistich of the line, but the plural noun is elsewhere used of the grave of a single individual (e.g. Prop. 4.7.54; Mart. 9.30.5).

168 (178R)

On the baths of a poor man. Vita, a man of limited means but resourceful with his small plot of land, has created a delightful place which has two benefits. For he has built some new baths on a narrow piece of land, and its thriving garden is fragrant with edible produce. What nature denies, industry confers on men of slender means; the blessings this poor man has are scarcely available to the rich.

An attractive pair of epigrams on baths, the last on this popular subject in the collection, concentrate on themes which have been encountered before: 99 in particular emphasises the importance attached by the poet to land use and land development; and land that can be used for farming should be used for farming, and not for the projects of the rich or the comforts of the idle (see 99 intro. and 3 n. for these themes). Thus in the present epigrams not only is the site on which the baths are built small (168.1; 3; 169.1), but the plot is used for growing nutritious food as well as the baths (168.4; 169.3 f.). The owner, who is poor (168.1; 168.5 f.), can be congratulated on his industry (168.5 f.) and on the double benefit he gets from his plot, health from both bathing and good food (168.2; 169.5 f.).

The establishment described may be part of a villa complex (despite the claims of poverty), or might be a small commercial enterprise, though in these two epigrams there is no suggestion that the baths are open to the public (see further 99 and 108 intros).

Superscr.: cuiusdam pauperis: this is evidence that the superscriptions

Commentary

were not written by the author, but are scribal additions. The *pauper* is named Vita in the epigrams, and it is because he has misunderstood it as the common noun that the scribe has contented himself with an imprecise 'cuiusdam' (on the superscriptions see p. 18 f.).

1. Vita: as Riese comments (app. crit.), this must be a name and it belongs to the owner / proprietor of the baths and garden; although it is almost certainly intended that the noun is ambiguous, in that the epigram does praise a 'vita opibus tenuis' which is evidenced by the establishment, the subsequent verbs 'fundavit' and 'erexit' require a subject, and when 'Vita' recurs at 169.2 it can only make sense as a name (for similar ambiguity with proper names in the first word of epigrams see 109.1 n.). Vita is however a very rare personal name, this being the only apparent instance except the Julia Vita of *CIL* 6.20729 (though Vitalis is of course common); it may conceivably be a homophonic assimilation or translation into Latin of a local African name (for the phenomenon see Adams, *Bilingualism*, 172; 219 f.; 238).

opibus tenuis: 'opibus' is an ablative of respect, as at Apul. *Met.* 11.25.5 'tenui patrimonio'.

sollers: signifying a person who is clever and resourceful, and able to get the most out of his assets, like Ulysses (Stat. *Ach.* 1.784) or Nature (Cic. *Nat. Deor.* 2.128); it is a favourite adjective in this collection (also 93.3; 100.4; 106.24; 161.1).

2. gemino munere: compare the similar theme at 108.5 f. 'gemino ... fructu', where the twin benefits of bathing in nourishing both body and mind are expounded. The twin benefits here, as will become clear in the following couplet, are the 'balnea' and 'hortus', putting the small plot of land to maximal use.

delicias: cf. 109.8 'indigenae placeant plus mihi deliciae' (with note); 'deliciae' here includes baths, garden and the location generally.

3. congusto (A); in angusto (Sched.); congesto (Müller): there is nothing to choose on grounds of meaning between A's 'congusto' (a contraction of *co-angusto*) and 'in angusto' of the Schedae Divionenses, because both denote the small, narrow strip of land which the establishment occupies (cf. 'parvo in caespite' in line 1). Although *congustus* is a rare adjective, it does occur elsewhere, for instance: (1) in an anonymous *Descriptio orbis terrae* (see T. Sinko, *ALL* 13.1904.544 *lines* 51 f.), which contains the sentence 'iacientes retias in congusta loca fluvii suscipiunt ventura'; (2) at Ven. Fort. 1.11.21 f. 'congusta prius subtraxit fana sacerdos / haec nisi perficeret quae modo culta placent' (where some mss give the metrically suspect opening words 'nec angusta', which are nevertheless accepted by most editors); and (3) in the Latin Soranus (*Gyn.* p. 9.1 f. Rose), which describes the 'sinus muliebris' with the words 'intus autem

Commentary

est spatiotissimus, foris vero congustus' (and the noun *congustia* occurs at e.g. Jord. *Get.* 33 (167)). *TLL* comments (3.1384.12; 81) that with both adjective and noun the best mss usually give the contracted form (*con-*). The evidence thus suggests that A's text is supportable, so I retain it (as also W. Heraeus (*ALL* 15.1908.575 f.)).

4. edulibusque ... fetibus: although the neuter plural *edulia* as a substantive is much commoner, *edulis* is found as an adjective at e.g. Hor. *Sat.* 2.4.43 'vinea summittit capreas non semper edulis'; *fetus* is generally used of fruiting plants rather than vegetables (see *OLD fetus* (2) 4(a)), but is here indeterminate since the garden provides both fruit and herbs (169.3-4).

5-6. quae natura negat ... pauper habet: other epigrams in the collection conclude with a sententia of this type, where a specific example is broadened into a general principle, often one with moralising overtones (cf. 80; 81; 88; 97; 107; 133; 186; 187; 188), and this one is apposite enough here, extolling the poor man whose industry has given him a richness greater than money. In one ms. (C) which contains other pieces from the *AL*, this concluding couplet surfaces as a complete epigram; it is not uncommon for memorable sententiae or other passages to be thus excerpted and take on a more solitary existence (e.g. *AL* 256 and 263 (Ovid); 258 (Propertius)). Such recycling might have been made easier in this instance because the first line is clearly an echo of Juvenal's epigrammatic 'si natura negat, facit indignatio versum' (1.79), which is also echoed in Corippus' 'quos doctrina negat, confert victoria versus' (*Joh.* praef. 33, where 'confert' suggests possible allusion to this couplet as well).

5. natura ... industria: the point made is the same as that made with respect to Bellator's baths at 99 (see 3 n.; 7 n.): the land in an undeveloped state was not and could not be put to significant productive use like agriculture or farming, so when it is used for baths, and in this case an allotment too, the justification for what might otherwise be reprehensible development is that the plot was no good for anything else; and specifically, Nature is seen as a force who does not necessarily act in her own or man's best interests, and can therefore be 'improved' by man. For *industria* being the human enterprise that can tame nature, cf. Cicero's description of Demosthenes' overcoming his stammer (*De Orat.* 1.260): 'in quo tantum studium fuisse tantusque labor dicitur, ut primum impedimenta naturae diligentia industriaque superaret'.

parvis (Müller); paucis (AC); Vitae (Kay): mss 'paucis' is hardly acceptable in this context because the contrast in this concluding couplet must lie between the industrious poor and the rich, based on the example of Vita's productive baths: to allege that there are few industrious poor

Commentary

would be at best irrelevant to the argument, at worst deleterious (in his app. crit. SB considers construing 'paucis' with the following 'divitibus', which would require strong punctuation after 'industria': the sense would be reasonable, but he is no doubt right to reject the idea because the strong break in sense after the fifth foot would be alien to this collection (and difficult for a reader to pick up without the aid of punctuation)). If 'paucis' cannot stand, Müller's conjecture 'parvis' is the best option, understanding *parvus* as in the English idiom 'the little man', indicating low status, here primarily in economic terms: cf. Hor. *Ep.* 1.7.44 'parvum parva decent'; Mart. 3.31.5 'fastidire tamen noli, Rufine, minores'; with *TLL* 10.1.566.41 f. Alternatively, 'Vitae' might be considered (it could easily have been replaced by a scribe who did not recognise it as a proper name, or who wanted to turn a specific comment into a general sententia).

169 (179R)

Another. Vita, resourceful in founding an urban venue, crowned his small plot with compact baths. Here he also industriously added a fruitful garden, which feeds its creator richly with various herbs. The estate is now a boon to its owner with its double benefit: one gives him food, the other affords him health.

1. parvula succinctis: the idea of compactness of building and the optimal use of a small plot of land is carried over from the preceding epigram into these opening words. Although 'succinctis' here has a dominant sense of compactness (as it does as early as e.g. Mart. 2.1.3 'at nunc succincti quae sint bona disce libelli'), it might still retain a suggestion of its *cingere* root, with the idea of the 'iugera parvula' acting as a constraining belt round the baths to restrict their size.
bais: see 99.1 n.

2. urbanos ... condere (Watt; fundere (A)) ... locos: A's text has rightly aroused suspicion; SB athetises 'locos', and conjectures for 'fundere' have been made by Courtney ('urbanos callens reddere Vita locos' at *CR* 31.1981.41) and Watt ('urbanos callens condere (*vel* vincere) Vita locos' at *HSCPh* 91.1987.292; 101.2003.453). However, epigraphic evidence suggests there is nothing amiss with 'urbanos ... locos': it is a regular boast in bath inscriptions that establishments offer their services 'more urbico', presumably suggesting cleanliness and sophistication: e.g. *CIL* 11.721 'in praedis / C. Legianni Veri / <b>alineum, more urbico / lavat<ur> / <et> omnia commoda praestantur'; *AE* 1933.49 'omnis humanitas urbico more praebetur'; *CIL* 14.4015; with Fagan, *Bathing*, 316 f., nos 254 f. The 'loci urbani' are therefore equivalent to the 'deliciae' of 168.2, evoking a sophisticated establishment bathers would expect to encounter only in urban centres. *Fundere* however is not equivalent to *fundare* (168.2),

Commentary

for which a synonym is required; Watt's 'condere' is excellent (cf. 109.1 'condens ... lavacrum').

callens: a much rarer adjective than *callidus*, which is here precluded by metre; it occurs in verse only at Iuvenc. 1.258 and Prud. *Hamart.* 224 and here. It is the equivalent of 'sollers' at 168.1.

3. hic (A); his (Riese): 'hic' is the adverb rather than pronoun (though Riese's conjecture 'his' is not without merit, because it avoids any confusion with 'qui' in line 4).

pomiferum ... hortum: clearly the 'edulibusque virens fetibus hortus' of 168.4; the adjective emphasises the usefully productive rather than merely decorative function.

sedulus: compare Vita's 'industria' at 168.5.

4. vario ... gramine: these are probably herbs or similarly useful plants (cf. Ser. [med.] 18 'gramina mentae'; 205 'chelidonio ... gramine'; 747 'gramen hyoscyami'; 1002 'gramina rutae'); they could be grown under the trees of the 'pomifer hortus'. *Varius* is a frequent adjective in the collection: e.g. 94.5; 113.1; 120.5; 139.3; 161.4; 162.3; 165.2; 174.11; 184.3; 185.5 and 187.3.

auctorem: here the founder of the establishment, Vita (see 109.6 n.).

5. duplici ... munere: the twin benefits of garden and baths; cf. 'gemino munere' at 168.2.

6. salus: the benefit to health of bathing is often advertised in the bath epigrams of this collection (e.g. 99.8; 108.7; 109.4; 164.1 f.), elsewhere in the *AL* (e.g. 202.5 f.; 202.11 f.; 203.8; 372.12), and in other epigraphic evidence (e.g. *AE* 1929.7b.8 (= *ML* 40.8 Courtney); *CE* 1754.1 (= ibid. 43.1); *ILCV* 1901.1 f.). Medical and other sources quite rightly uphold the truth of the assertion with frequency, and statues of deities of health such as Asclepius and Hygieia were often found in baths (Fagan, *Bathing*, 85 f. assembles much evidence).

170 (180R)

On the Sphinx. A winged creature, a human female, and a lioness, she was born of Laius' line, to be in birth and death a curse on Thebes. She it was who made Oedipus mount his mother's bed, so that their incestuous offspring might be slaughtered by each other's hand.

This is another lone-standing epigram with a mythological theme (see 167; 174; and p. 3); it concerns the Sphinx, and may be ecphrastic in the sense it could have accompanied a representation of the Sphinx in the visual arts, whether statue, painting, or book illustration. Certainly the

Commentary

Sphinx was always a popular subject, and her physical composition in this epigram, a combination of human female with wings and a partially leonine body, is the commonest type (Eur. *Phoen.* 806; 1019; 1042; Apollod. 3.5.8; Aus. 15.40; she can also be partially canine, as at e.g. Aesch. *Sphinx* frag. 236 Radt): see *LIMC* 8.1.1149 f.

The earliest reference to the myth of the Sphinx is at Hes. *Theog.* 326. There are many variations of her parentage: Hesiod says she is the daughter of Orthus and Chimaira (loc. cit. with West's note), Apollodorus gives her father as Typhon and her mother as Echidna (3.5.8), and others held her father to be Laius, as is the case here (Lysimachus of Alexandria, *FGH* 382 F4 Jacoby; Paus. 9.26.2). There is a satisfying compactness to the allusive version of the myth the poet presents, with the Sphinx at its centre: as daughter of Laius her birth is a disaster for his kingdom of Thebes because she terrorises it (this was sometimes said to be due to divine punishment for Laius' abduction of the boy Chrysippus: Peisandros *FGH* 16 F10 Jacoby); it is Laius' son Oedipus who kills her and as a reward wins Laius' widow Jocasta for his wife; and the sons of that incestuous marriage, Polyneices and Eteocles, kill each other in the war of the Seven Against Thebes. Although the Sphinx can hardly be held directly responsible for all this calamity, it could not have happened without her presence at key moments, so she is appositely described as 'Thebano nascens et peritura malo'.

On the myth see further L. Edmunds, 'The Sphinx in the Oedipus Legend', *Beitr. zur klass. Philol.* 127.1981.12 f.; and idem, *Oedipus, The Ancient Legend and its Later Analogues*, Baltimore / London 1985.

superscr.: De Sphinga (AB); De Sphinge (W): the combination of AB are likely to show the correct termination for the noun: for such Latin formations from the Greek accusative, and their declension accordingly, cf. 'Briseida' at 124.2 (and note). First declension *sphinga* is also found at Hyginus *Fab.* 67.5 ('Sphingae'), though he also uses nom. 'Sphinx' (e.g. *Fab.* praef. 39; 67.4; 151.1) and abl. 'Sphinge' (ibid. 67.5).

1. ales, virgo, lea (AW; leo (B)): the three asyndetic nouns take a singular verb ('crevit') because they form the constituent parts of a single being; the epigram on the Chimaira (87) is similar in its effect. For the form 'lea' cf. Serv. ap. Verg. *Georg.* 3.245 'leaena autem graecum est ... nam nos "hic" et "haec leo" dicimus. "Lea" namque usurpatum est, quia in "o" exeuntia <masculina> feminina ex se non faciunt, ut ... "leo" '; nevertheless, *lea* is common enough in verse, particularly Ovid, not least for the differences from *leo* it affords in declension and metre (e.g. Lucr. 5.1318; Ovid *Met.* 4.102 (and frequently); Stat. *Theb.* 10.414 etc.). Here however the form 'leo' (as in B) might be preferred, because AW's 'lea' necessitates lengthening of the final 'a' before the initial mute and liquid of 'crevit'. Against this it can be argued that 'lea' is found in two of the

Commentary

three mss; that it is fitting for the poet to denote a lioness unambiguously as a constituent part of the female Sphinx (though cf. Aus. 15.40 'leo' of the Sphinx, and 'leo' at 87.1, referring to a constituent part of the Chimaira; for *leo* elsewhere of lionesses see *TLL* 7.2.1166.61 f.; 82 f.); and that similar metrical lengthening is found elsewhere in the collection (cf. 101.6 'ne lapsa gracili' with note and the article by Timpanaro there cited). The balance is slightly in favour of 'lea'.

crevit de sanguine Lai: the phrase should be understood metaphorically, not literally (which has however been suggested: e.g. she is born from the blood of the slain Laius according to Edmunds, op. cit. (1981) 12 f.). Laius is elsewhere recorded as the Sphinx's father (see intro. above), and for the wording cf. 145.1 'cum te Barbati referas de sanguine cretum'; Verg. *Aen.* 2.74 'hortamur fari quo sanguine cretus'; Lucr. 4.1214.

3. haec fecit thalamos ... ascendere: the Sphinx caused Oedipus' marriage and downfall, though only in the sense the events would not have happened without her. Edmunds (op. cit. (1981) 15 f.) points out that the function of the Sphinx in the myth is to enable Oedipus to win his bride and marry his mother, because the killing of Laius would not by itself have effected that. For the idiom of causative *facere* + inf., see 100.10 n.

I(Y)dippum ascendere (Svennung); idippum conscendere (AB, *sed* concedere (B)); oedippum concedere (W); Idipum conscendere (de Saumaise): the prosody of the name is a problem here, and is irregular whatever solution is adopted. If 'conscendere' (assuming that it lies behind what the mss report) is correct, de Saumaise's correction of mss 'Idippum' (or 'Oedippum') to an anapaestic 'Idipum' is necessary. But the available evidence, though slender, tells against that: (1) as for the orthography, at *AL* 62 *superscr.* A has 'De Iocasta et Idippo', while at *AL* 190.84 both A and B have 'ungellam (h)ydippi' (which editors usually emend, though the metre it produces is correct). And (2) the shift of the diphthong *oe* (for Greek οι) to long *i* or *y* is well attested in late Latin (many examples, especially from Marcellus' *De medicamentis*, are collected at Svennung, *Kleine Beiträge*, 30 f.; and see also S.W. Omeltchenko, *A Quantitative and Comparative Study of the Vocalism of the Latin Inscriptions of North Africa, Britain, Dalmatia and the Balkans*, Chapel Hill 1977, 400 f.). This suggests that 'Idippum' should be retained here, and to restore metre elsewhere Svennung's conjecture 'ascendere' is required in place of mss 'conscendere' (op. cit. 39). For contrary views, in support of de Saumaise's conjecture, see O. Keller, *RhM* 30.1875.303 f.; and E. Courtney, *C&M* 40.1989.202.

4. mutua dextra: 'mutua' refers to the hands of the 'incesta proles', Eteocles and Polyneices, who killed each other.

Commentary

171 (181R)

On a cat which died from eating a magpie. Accustomed to consume gnawing mice with its bite, and to kill that species hateful to households with its teeth, a cat seized a magpie in mistake for a mouse in the dark, and voraciously swallowed its talkative head in its mouth. However, instant agony punished the greedy plunderer, for the horny beak blocked its ravening maw. Its throat obstructed, its vital airway stopped, the thief, stuffed full, perished from its consuming wound. There is no precedent for this vengeance of a murdered bird: a dead magpie slaughters its enemy.

This unusual epigram, about a cat which dies of choking whilst trying to eat a large bird which it improbably mistakes for a mouse, belongs to a sub-genre of epigram which details picaresque deaths of animals; it flourished around the time of the Philippan Anthology and is well represented in the ninth book of the Greek Anthology (e.g. 1 Polyaenus of Sardis; 10; 417 Antip. Thess.; 14; 86; 310 Antiph. Byz.; 94 Isidorus of Aegae; 227 Bianor; 17; 18 Germanicus Caesar; 410 Sabinus; 339 Archias of Mytilene). Straight epitaphs on animals are related (for which see G. Herrlinger, 'Totenklage um Tiere', *Tbn. Btr. Alt.* 8.1930), as are epigrams which describe picaresque human deaths (see my intro. to Mart. 11.41). Although this epigram might also seem close to the territory of fable, there is nothing strikingly similar in the ancient fabular corpus and its origins lie rather in the epigrammatic tradition. Compare also Luxorius' similar piece entitled 'De catto qui, cum soricem maiorem devorasset, apoplexiam passus occubuit' (*AL* 370); and from the House of the Faun at Pompeii there is a famous mosaic of a cat with its paw on a large bird, which may well be intended to be a night scene because of the dark blue background (illustrated at Keller, *Tierwelt*, 1.72 fig. 21).

This piece is notable for the emphasis it puts on the greed of the cat ('morsu ... consumere / sorbuit / praedonem ... edacem / rabidam ... gulam / satur / escali vulnere / raptor') and its fondness for alliterative effects ('m' in lines 1-2; 'c' in lines 3-4; 'p' in line 5; and 's' in lines 7-8).

3. cattus: the noun is rare and late, with an instance in Palladius (4.9.4), one in Luxorius (*AL* 370.1), and a handful of other cases; it also features in some glosses (e.g. *CGL* 5.176.16 'cattus Latinum est'; 5.605.11 'murilegus catus'; 5.607.34), and Isidore (*Or.* 12.2.38) derives it from an otherwise unattested verb 'cattat (= videt)'; *FEW* 2.520 suggests it is of African origin. Female *catta* occurs at *CGL* 5.422.39 'cattas muriceps (= muricipes?)' and Vet. Lat. ep. Jerem. 21 (at *Geremia*, ed. A. Penna, Turin 1954, 437; cf. Vulg. Baruch 6.21); in a much earlier occurrence at Mart. 13.69.1 it almost certainly refers to a kind of bird rather than a mammal (see Leary's note). Greek κάττα and κάττος occur in scholia as synonyms of αἴλουρος (e.g. schol. Callim. *Hymn. Cer.* 110a), and the cat was domesticated in Egypt and must have been well known in Roman North

Commentary

Africa (Toynbee, *Animals*, 87 f., points out that the cat never achieved the popularity of the dog as a pet in the ancient world).

in obscuro: i.e. at night; cf. Fulg. *Myth.* 3.4 'nocte, id est in obscuro'; Liv. 41.2.6; Sen. *Ep.* 122.4.

pro sorice: the *sorex* (also spelt *saurex, surex, sorix, surix, sores*) is strictly the shrew, though in later Latin the difference between it and *mus* was not maintained (cf. *Epit. de Caes.* 41.10; *AL* 370.1 Luxorius); and 'mures' in line 1 (with 'invisum domibus genus' in line 2) strongly suggests that this author regarded *sorices* as a synonym. It has been noted (81.5 n.) that the poet likes to vary his substantives, and he does not always employ precise equivalents.

'Sorice' here has its classically regular long first syllable, whereas Luxorius (*AL* 370.1 (cf. also 196.1); see Happ's note) shortens it. This line, used as a prosodic illustration, gave rise to an intriguing reference in the ninth-century Mico of Saint-Riquier's *Libelli Prosodiaci*, where it is stated 'sorice. cattus in obscuro cepit pro sorice picam. Sofocles. orat.' (*MGH: PLAC* 3.292.356). A gloss in a s. xii ms. which was once in the Phillipps collection (details are given at 90 intro.) derives from this and recasts it: 'sorex mus unde Sofocles catus in obscuris cepit pro sorice picam', and the statement is repeated in the s. xiii-xiv Paris lat. 7598 (see further Riese's app. crit. and addendum; R. Ellis, *J. Philol.* 8.1879.123; M. Manitius, *RhM* 50.1895.316; M. Ihm *RhM* 52.1897.212; M. Spallone, *Stud. Med.* 29.1988.621 f.). From this a fictitious Latin Vandal poet named Sofocles was born, allegedly the author of this epigram. L. Traube (*RhM* 44.1889.478 f.) astutely explained his genesis: Mico's treatise is in alphabetical order, and it contained immediately before the entry on 'sorice' a comment on the prosody of the name *Sofocles*, with the intention of adducing an illustration from Horace (*Ep.* 2.1.163 'quid Sophocles et Thespis et Aeschylus utile ferrent'). But this previous entry somehow became truncated to the ghostly 'Sofocles. (H)orat.', while also being conflated with the comment on 'sorice' and the illustration taken from this line. In trying to make sense of the resultant jumble subsequent writers discovered a new Sofocles.

picam: either a jay or a magpie (see 78.2 n.).

4. multiloquumque: jays and magpies were famed for their garrulity: cf. Mart. 7.87.6 'pica salutatrix'; 14.76.1 'pica loquax'; and at Petr. 28.9 a 'pica varia' is kept in a gold cage to greet Trimalchio's guests (the bird in this epigram is almost certainly envisaged as a domestic pet, making its loss the greater and the cat's demise all the more deserved).

sorbuit: the verb, intensified by 'vorax', well suits the action of the fatally greedy cat: cf. Stat. *Silv.* 4.3.29 'sorbebatque rotas maligna tellus', where Coleman comments that the verb 'is used of whirlpools, marshes, quagmires and the like into which persons or objects disappear'; and note also Verg. *Aen.* 3.422 (of Charybdis); Sen. *Phaedra* 1049.

Commentary

5. poena tamen praesens: the reference is perhaps more to physical pain than punishment, since the latter notion is present in the ensuing verb 'plectit'; see 163.4 n. The phrase is also found in Juvenal, where the context of satirised greed is so similar as to suggest a deliberate echo here (cf. also 'gulam' at line 6 below): 'quanta est gula quae sibi totos ponit apros ... / Poena tamen praesens, cum tu deponis amictus / turgidus et crudum pavonem in balnea portas' (1.140 f.).

praedonem ... edacem: for *praedo* used of animals cf. Mart. 2.75.9 (lion); 14.217 (hawk); Drac. *Rom.* 8.360 (lion); and for *edax* of animal greed cf. Ovid *Am.* 2.6.33 (vulture); Hor. *Epod.* 2.34 (thrushes); and Sen. *Ep.* 60.3 (unspecified).

plectit: in classical Latin the verb is found only in its passive forms, when it means 'to be beaten' and thus 'to be punished' (see Nisbet-Hubbard's note on Hor. *Carm.* 1.28.27); the active form is found only later, as also at e.g. Aus. 19. *praef.* 5.

6. cornea labra: although *TLL* (7.2.811.36) specifically states that *labrum* is not used of birds' beaks, it is here; for *corneus* describing beaks, cf. Ovid. *Met.* 8.546; *Priap.* 83('Quid hoc novi est?').13.

gulam (*ex* guilam; AV): the noun can have a literal sense of 'throat', as at e.g. Phaedr. 1.8.7 f. 'gruis / gulaeque (sc. lupi) credens colli longitudinem', and a metaphorical sense of 'greed', as at e.g. Mart. 1.20.3 'quid dignum tanto tibi ventre gulaque precabor'. Both are relevant here, though the former predominates.

7. faucibus obsessis: cf. Verg. *Georg.* 3.508 'obsessas fauces premit aspera lingua'.

vitalis semita: cf. Hor. *Ep.* 1.18.103 'semita vitae' (echoed at Juv. 10.363), where the phrase has a metaphorical sense entirely different from its literal use here.

8. et satur: Riese comments '*corruptum*', but for no good reason, as SB says; the cat is demonstrably 'satur' with half a magpie sticking out of its mouth.

escali: apart from here, the adjective is only found at *Dig.* 33.10.8 'argentum escale et potorium', where it has a different sense.

raptor (A); captor (BVWP): A is preferable, since the cat's greed is the focus of the epigram (see intro.).

9. peremptae (W); pemit (A); parente (B); phente (V); praereptae (P): for W's uniquely correct readings see p. 15.

10. pica ... mortua discruciat: the point made is reminiscent of that at 167, where the dead Achilles has a similarly dramatic effect from beyond the grave. The verb *discruciare* here has its original sense of physical

324

Commentary

torture (cf. Cic. *Phil.* 13.37 'ut ille Trebonium et, si posset, etiam Brutum, Cassium discruciatos necaret') rather than the commoner sense of mental torture; *TLL* (5.1.1363.80 f.) evidences a meaning of 'kill' (Marcell. *Med.* 4.22 'stercus scrofinum ... lindines peduculosque discruciat'), which would also be apposite: the cat dies an agonising death from suffocation with the bird lodged in its throat.

172 (182R)

On Aegyptius. From out of the rising day issued forth night's progeny. Under the sun's rays he alone has blackness. Crow, charcoal, soot match his colour exactly; the name which you can read befits an Ethiopian.

This and the following epigram deal with a black man, and though this one limits itself to comments about colour, its companion is altogether more vituperative, labelling him 'faex Garamantarum' and likening him to a demon from hell. The general term for a black person in the classical world was *Aethiops* (from Greek αἴθω and ὄψ ('burnt face')), as in the last line of this piece; blacks were thought to originate from south of Egypt and the southern fringes of North West Africa, but there was migration northwards (both voluntary and through slave-trading) and well-documented interaction with the Greco-Roman world. Although 'Ethiopians' were always a yardstick of blackness, differences between racial types in the darkness of skin pigmentation were well appreciated (e.g. Philostr. *Vit. Apoll.* 6.2), and the protagonist of the present epigrams must be a black African. The subject is large: see further F.M. Snowden, *Blacks in Antiquity*, Cambridge Mass. 1970, 2 f.; Snowden, *Before Color Prejudice*, 5 f.; *LIMC* 1.1.413 f.

There are intriguing similarities between this epigram and a piece by Luxorius (*AL* 288), which needs to be quoted in full:

De auriga Aegyptio qui semper vincebat

Quamvis ab Aurora fuerit genetrice creatus
   Memnon, Pelidae conruit ille manu.
At te Nocte satum, ni fallor, matre paravit
   Aeolus et Zephyri es natus in antra puer.
Nec quisquam qui te superet nascetur Achilles:
   dum Memnon facie es, non tamen es genio.

S.T. Stevens ('The Circus Poems in the Latin Anthology' in Humphrey, *Circus at Carthage*, 1.153 f.) has suggested that these two pieces (172 and 288), together with 173 and 179, show such similarities that they were written by contemporaries about one particular black man, who is identified as a charioteer only in the superscription to *AL* 288. Leaving aside 179, which is evidently about the Memnon of myth only, there are attractions in linking 172-3 with Luxorius' epigram quoted above: these lie not so much in their common themes (e.g. the protagonist being the progeny of night), which could arise independently, but in the similarity of their superscriptions. This epigram sports a bare 'De Aegyptio' but that of Luxorius describes 'Aegyptius' as a charioteer who was always victorious. SB comments in his app. crit. to the superscription of this epigram '*Titulum* De Nigro *esse oportuit; cf. 173.2*' and a personal name needs to be found because the denouement of line 4 requires it (see note). If however 'Aegyptius' is understood to be a personal name both here and in Luxorius' superscription, the interpretation of the whole piece is clearer. In support of this it can be argued that the superscription writer of the present piece would have written 'De Aethiopi (or -e)' if he had had no further information to impart (note the further comments at 4 n. below); that Aegyptius is an attested African name (*CIL* 8.7924 and *Tablettes Albertini* XI. 20; XIII.37; XVI.5; even if it were not so attested it would be possible for it to be the sobriquet of a black charioteer – cf. 115 intro. for such names); and that the Garamantes, to which tribe this man belongs, probably included black people (see 173.1 n.), and were also famous for their chariot skills (see Mattingly, *Fazzan*, 87 f.). Ultimately the identification of the man of this and the following epigram with the charioteer of *AL* 288 can only be speculative, not least because there is nothing in them to suggest the protagonist was a charioteer and they are hostile towards him whereas Luxorius is complimentary, but the more important point to establish is that 'Aegyptius' in the superscription may not only indicate race or nationality, but could be a personal name.

1. ex oriente die: although it might mislead (cf. temporal 'exoriente die') this phrase here refers to place ('processit'); 'die' is pleonastic in that 'ex oriente' would suffice, but it is pointfully added as a contrast to the 'noctis alumnus' who comes from there. For the same contrast cf. Apul. *Flor.* 6 'non ... miror ... quod isdem Indis ibidem sitis ad nascentem diem tamen in corpore color noctis est'; and for the adjacent pairing of antonyms for black and white, see 96.2 n.

The Ethiopians feature as a (mythical) tribe as early as Homer, where the gods banquet with them (*Il.* 1.423 f.; *Od.* 1.22 f. etc.), and they were usually held to dwell in the east, their king being Memnon son of Eos (Mimn. 12.9 West; Aesch. *Prom.* 809; with West's note on Hes. *Theog.* 985). Thus this Ethiopian is said to come from the direction of the rising sun.

noctis ... alumnus: cf. *AL* 288.3 quoted above; 296.3 '(sc. virgo) quam Nox atque Erebus tulit Chaosque'; Mart. 1.115.4 'sed quandam volo nocte nigriorem'.

processit: the main sense is literal, as at 173.1 'nostrum processit ad axem'; but the metaphorical sense of 'take one's origin from' is also

Commentary

present (cf. 'alumnus'), to stress the paradox of the black man who comes from the halls of dawn (for *procedere* in this sense cf. Lucr. 2.270; Sen. *Suas.* 6.27). A similar paradox is presented in the next line.

2. solus habet tenebras: cf. Manil. 4.723 f. 'Aethiopes maculant orbem tenebrisque figurant / perfusas hominum gentes', where 'tenebrae' denote dark skin pigmentation. The paradox here is that even in broad daylight the man remains black. There may also be the suggestion that the sun's rays are the agency through which (cf. 'sub') the skin becomes and remains black (as at Manil. loc. cit.; Plin. *Nat. Hist.* 2.189).

3. corvus carbo cinis: the alliteration on 'c' in this line is notable (see also 97.1 n.). For *carbo* as a yardstick of blackness cf. Ter. *Ad.* 849; for *corvus* cf. Petr. 43.7; Apul. *Met.* 2.9.2 'corvina nigredine caeruleos columbarum collis flosculos aemulatus'; *Conv. et Pass. S. Afrae* 6 (*MGH: SRM* 3.58.7 f.) 'Aegyptius quidam nigrior corvo'; *cinis* does not seem to be so used elsewhere, though cf. 'cinis ater' at Verg. *Aen.* 4.633.

multa (codd.); cuncta (Baehrens): in view of the alliteration on 'c', Baehrens' conjecture is tempting. However, replacement of 'cuncta' by 'multa' in the mss would be less likely than the reverse, and the inference must be that they preserve the truth. There may be intentional humour in the unexpected.

4. quod legeris nomen ... (codd.); quod legitur nomen ... (Oudendorp); quodque gerit nomen ... (Shackleton Bailey); quod dederis nomen ... (Klotz); quod legeris nomen, convenit: Aethiopis (Riese): whatever the text, a name which is apposite to the concluding word of the epigram, 'Aethiopi', has to be found; the question is from where. Although mss 'quod legeris nomen' exhibits prosody of the perfect of *legere* (a short first syllable) which cannot be paralleled, irregularities almost as extreme are evidenced elsewhere in the collection (see p. 24), so perhaps that fact of itself should not rule out the paradosis. What is convincing is that the phrase has a pertinent, and almost precisely paralleled, meaning. Compare the following instances from epitaphs: 'tu quicunque titulum nostrum legeris, / rogo ne velis tribus sepulcris molestari' (*CE* 1884); 'quisque praeteriens titulum scribtum legeris, / tactus pietate hoc praecor ut dicas: Ianuaria, sit tibi terra levis' (*CE* 133); 'bene sit tibi qui me legeris' (*CIL* 6.8534b); and 'opto valeas qui legeris' (*CIL* 6.25512). In these inscriptions *tituli* giving at least the name of the deceased are either extant or have to be assumed; and the examples quoted all demonstrate an epigraphic use of the potential perfect subjunctive of *legere* (or less likely, the future perfect: compare 'dixeris' at 93.5, with note) to key to the reader that there is pertinent information to be read elsewhere in the inscription, though outside the immediate text. Applied to the epigram under consideration, this suggests that a reader may find

Commentary

the relevant name, if he has not already done so, and, since it is not in the body of the epigram, it can only be in its superscription or *titulus*. In the intro. above I have suggested that the extant 'De Aegyptio' might provide a name which has already been read and which would suit this black person ('quod ... nomen convenit Aethiopi'). But it is clear that all the extant superscriptions in the mss are not the work of the poet behind the collection (see p. 18 f.), so the original superscription to this epigram might have contained a more obvious or effective name. However that may be, this is a rare piece of good evidence that an author intended that some or all of his epigrams would have superscriptions when they were published (again, see p. 18 f.).

As regards the suitability of the name for 'an Ethiopian' at a lexical level, although *Aegyptius* often refers to people of native North African as distinct from black African characteristics, it is also found as a synonym of 'Aethiops' (thus St. Perpetua of Carthage, on the eve of her martyrdom, was engaged in a struggle with the Devil in the form of an 'Aegyptius foedus specie' (*Pass. Perpet.* 10 (= *Acts of the Christian Martyrs*, 118 Musurillo); cf. Paul. *Fest.* p. 26.10 Lindsay 'Aegyptinos Aethiopas'); and there are further instances of the interchangeability of these words in the passages cited at 173.4 n.

173 (183R)

Another. The dregs of the Garamantes have come to our part of the world and the uncouth black man glories in his pitchy body; if the voice which issued from his lips did not sound human he would terrify the living as a horrible demon. Dreadful Hell should get hold of the blacked-up monster for itself; the House of Dis ought to have him as its doorkeeper.

This second epigram on the black man is more hostile in tone than the first, mixing straightforward insult with adverse comment on colour, but concentrating on the image of the black as a portent of ill fortune and a demon in human form. For a general treatment of the black as ill-omened see Snowden, *Before Color Prejudice*, 83 f.: he cites such instances as the Ethiopian who was said to have met the troops of Brutus and Cassius before they went into battle and lost (Florus 2.17.7 f. etc.); a theatrical performance featuring Egyptians and Ethiopians which was held to be a portent of Caligula's assassination (Suet. *Gaius* 57.4); and the Ethiopian encountered by Septimius Severus as a premonition of his death (*SHA Sev.* 22.4 f.).

See also 172 intro. for the tentative identification of this Ethiopian with the 'Aegyptius' of *AL* 288 Luxorius.

1. faex: for *faex* as a pejorative term cf. Cic. *Fam.* 7.32.2 'sed quoniam tanta faex est in urbe'; Juv. 3.61; Apul. *Met.* 8.24.2; with *TLL* 6.1.171.10 f.;

Commentary

it means simply 'dregs', and the plural 'faeces' did not become an English euphemism for excrement until the seventeenth century.

Garamantarum (codd. *ex* garamentarum (A); caramentarum (B)); Garamantum iam (Shackleton Bailey): SB objects to the heteroclite formation 'Garamantae', though his conjecture 'Garamantum iam' is not convincing and is metrically suspect. Courtney (*C&M* 40.1989.204) reasonably suggests the form 'Garamantae' could be based on the Greek accusative (for similar instances cf. 124.2 n.); the mss reading should be retained.

'Garamantes' is the usual name of these people. They were termed Ethiopians by some authors (e.g. Solinus 30.2; Ptol. *Geog.* 1.8.5; Isid. *Or.* 9.2.128), but were distinguished from them by others (e.g. Strabo 2.5.33; 17.3.19); the main point is that they may well have comprised both black and North African people (thus at *AL* 324 Luxorius writes about Myrro, who likes 'foedae puellae'; a 'foeda puella' is characterised as 'Garamas' without further description, whereas a 'pulchra puella' is simply 'Poenica'). They were known to Herodotus (4.183.1) and are called 'perusti' by Lucan (4.679) and 'furvi' by Arnobius (*Adv. Nat.* 6.5); they fall from historical sight after the seventh century. They lived in what is now southern Libya (Fazzan) on the edge of the Sahara, their main town being Garama (Plin. *Nat. Hist.* 5.36; Ptol. *Geog.* loc. cit.), which lies due south of Lepcis Magna and is the modern Djerma, also spelt Germa or Jarma. See esp. Mattingly, *Fazzan*, and *AntAfr* 37.2001.45 f.; Modéran, *Les Maures*, 267 f.; and E.M. Ruprechtsberger, *Die Garamanten, Geschichte und Kultur eines libyschen Volkes in der Sahara*, Mainz am Rhein 1997.

nostrum processit ad axem: *axis* is often used of land, deriving that sense as part of the development in meaning of the noun *axis* from the heavens, to part of the heavens, to the land covered by part of the heavens; thus e.g. Paul. Nol. *Carm.* 11.59 'quo me locarit axe communis pater'; Claud. 26.203 'nostro procul axe remotam'.

2. piceo ... corpore: for pitch as a yardstick of blackness, cf. Ovid *Her.* 18.7 'pice nigrius'; Mart. 1.115.5; with Otto 1433 and *Nachträge*, 284.

verna: the noun is intended as an insult, an overtone it has as early as Plaut. *Amph.* 1033. Its implication here is probably not of (home-born) servile status (note that the man 'nostrum processit ad axem', which might suggest he migrated of his own volition), but rather of the uncouthness and lack of civilisation that was alleged of *vernae*: thus for example Mart. 1.41.1 f. 'urbanus tibi, Caecili, videris. / Non es, crede mihi. Quid ergo? Verna ...', where 'verna' is pond life with no veneer of *urbanitas* (see Howell's and Citroni's notes). Cf. the derivatives *vernilis*, *vernilitas*, *verniliter*, all of which carry much the same connotations.

niger: SB understands this as a personal name, though I have taken a different interpretation of the epigram (see 172 intro.).

quem: gramatically 'cuius' would be expected. If 'quem' is retained

Commentary

in the text, it has been attracted into agreement with 'hominem'; but emendation might be considered (Courtney (op. cit. 1 n.) suggests 'qui'; better perhaps to sacrifice ensuing 'sonaret' for 'probaret').

3. vox hominem ... sonaret: cf. Verg. *Aen.* 1.327 f., where Aeneas comments to Venus, 'namque haud tibi vultus / mortalis, nec vox hominem sonat', of which this line may be a deliberate reminiscence.

labris emissa: the reader's attention is drawn to the distinctive lips of the black man.

4. vivos (Baehrens); visos (codd.); visu (Riese): E. Löfstedt (*Eranos* 8.1908.96 f.) defended mss 'visos', adducing [Aus.] *Epig.* 144 (= *Ep. Bob.* 31), where the text reads 'Stella prius visis fulgebas Lucifer, at nunc / extinctus cassis lumine Vesper eris'. He argues that editors emend 'visis' there and 'visos' here 'aus mangelnder Kenntnis des oben erörterten eigentümlichen Sprachgebrauchs', and considers the past participle has an active sense in both cases. But *Ep. Bob.* 31.1 is a translation of *AP* 7.670.1 Plato 'ἀστὴρ πρὶν μὲν ἔλαμπες ἐνὶ ζωοῖσιν Ἑῷος' ('Of old among the living thou didst shine the Star of morn' (Loeb)), and the Bobbio epigrammatist was nothing if not literal in his translations; Schenkl's emendation of 'vivis' for 'visis' is therefore likely to be correct. Baehrens' 'vivos' here is less certain, and mss 'visos' could even have its passive sense (i.e. 'people on whom he has gazed': cf. 90.6 'visis ... viris'), but coupled with his excellent conjecture 'larva' (see following note), 'vivos' makes an equally convincing distinction between live humans and demons from Hell, and should be accepted.

larva (Baehrens); labra (codd.): note that the mss also give 'terrerent' in agreement with 'labra'. J. Ziehen (*Philologus* 63.1904.370) tried to defend 'labra' on the grounds that a comment on the black man's lips is apposite, but (a) there already is one in the preceding line, (b) there is no reason why the lips should be less terrifying if the man can speak, and (c) Baehrens' emendation makes excellent sense and leads perfectly into the conclusion of the epigram; 'labra' has simply intruded from 'labris' in line 3.

A *larva* is variously glossed as *diabulus, simulacrum, daemon vel umbra errans* (*CGL* 2.585.6; 7; with 4.359.24), and the noun is used of the living as an insult (e.g. Plaut. *Cas.* 592; Petr. 44.5); *larvae* can be the restless spirits of the dead (e.g. Apul. *Socr.* 15 'qui ob adversa vitae merita nullis sedibus incerta vagatione ceu quodam exilio punitur, inane terriculamentum bonis hominibus, ceterum malis noxium, id genus plerique larvas perhibent') and go abroad at night and fly through the air (Petr. 62.10; Apul. *Apol.* 64; Amm. Marc. 14.11.17 etc.), but this Ethiopian is seen as a fit doorman for Hell, and as such is part of the essentially Christian iconography which pictured devils and demons as black. Thus the devil who appeared to St. Perpetua on the eve of her martyrdom was

Commentary

'Aegyptius foedus specie' (see 172.4 n.); a female demon appears in the *Acts of Peter and Simon* (ch. 22) described as 'mulierem quendam turpissimam in aspectu, Ethiopissimam neque Aegyptiam, sed totam nigram' (*Acta Apostolorum Apocrypha*, ed. R.A. Lipsius, repr. Hildesheim 1959, 1.70); in the *Vita Beati Antonii Abbatis* ch. 4 the devil is 'puer horridus atque niger' (*PL* 73.130); in an encounter with Melania the Younger the devil disguised himself as a young black man (ch. 54 Gorce); and there are more Ethiopian devils or demons in the apocryphal *Acta Joannis* (p. 124.2 f. Zahn), and Gregory of Tours' *Liber de miraculis Andreae* ch. 22 (= *MGH: SRM* 1.838.38 f.); see further Dölger, *Die Sonne*, 52 f.; 54 f. Black devils and demons also put in appearances in contemporary visual arts: see O.A. Erich, 'Die Darstellung des Teufels in der christlichen Kunst', *Kunstwissenschaftliche Studien* 8.1931.90 f.; J.M. Courtès in J. Devisse, *The Image of the Black in Western Art*, series ed. L. Bugner, Cambridge Mass. / London 1979, 2.1.19 f.; 59 f.; and generally, Snowden, *Before Color Prejudice*, 100 f.

This context makes Baehrens' conjectures 'larva' and 'vivos' all but certain; the black demon from Hell would terrorise the living, but that fear is assuaged once they find out he talks as, and is, a human.

5. dira atramentatum (W; *om.* dira (Kay)); dira atrementatu (A); dira adramenta tu (B); dira (H)adrume(n)ta tuum (edd.; *sed* dira Hadrumentarum (Baehrens); dira, Adramente, tuum (Shackleton Bailey)); dura adamante suum (Courtney): the conjectures '(H)adrume(n)ta', 'Adramente' and 'Hadrumentarum' all refer to Hadrumetum, a town which is the modern Sousse and lies about 100 km south of Carthage. One might ask why it is allegedly introduced into the epigram at this point. E. Courtney (*C&M* 40.1989.204 f.), correctly in my view, dispensed with any reference to a place, and conjectured 'dura adamante suum rapiant sibi Tartara monstrum'. However W's 'atramentatum' (with A and B closely adjacent) would provide an ideal sense; the verb would derive from *atramentum* ('blacking', 'black ink'), and an 'atramentatum monstrum' would be an appositely pilloried 'blacked-up devil' who is now humorously debunked, since the fear he evoked has dissipated once he has been exposed as human. For what it is worth, the verb *atramentare* can be found at Virg. gram. *Epit.* 1 (p. 5.18 Huemer) '(sc. Latinitatis) genera sunt xii, quorum unum usitatum fitur, quo scripturas Latini omnes atramentantur', and ibid. 15 (p. 89.2 Huemer).

However, there is a problem in the prosody of 'atramentatum' here, since the first two syllables are both irregularly shortened. But it might be possible that this is an instance of the shortening of unstressed long vowels before the accent (on which see 137.1 n.; compare also 'sacramenta', with irregularly short second syllable at Damas. *Epig.* 14.6); an alternative remedy, which would restore quantitative metre, would be deletion of the line's initial word 'dira'. The unusual participle is such a good fit for

Commentary

sense, and provides such effective alliteration with 'Tartara monstrum', that editors should be reluctant to dispense with it.

Tartara monstrum: cf. *AL* 195.1 f. 'Servandus spurcus medicus monstrumque medentum / qui se Tartareo missum de carcere finxit'.

6. custodem hunc Ditis: cf. the similar description of the ant at 93.5 f. 'hanc iuste famulam nigri iam dixeris Orci / quam color et factum composuit domino'.

174 (184R)

On Telephus. Telephus, excellent child of Alcides and Auge, waged an unexpected war for which foreign powers were responsible. For while the Greeks were bound for Troy with their thousand ships and their fleet had been driven towards and was anchored at his coast, he opposed the Danaans, and when he was fighting heroic Achilles the Scyrian spear struck through his leg as he fought. Regarding a cure for this Apollo was consulted, and he said that the enemy's spear would bring health and relief. Next, scrapings were taken from the spear of Peleus' son, who had been moved by his entreaties, and when the powder was injected into his limbs the wound vanished. What happened to him illustrates the miraculous with its change of fortune: by that which dealt the wound was his health restored.

This penultimate mythological epigram of the collection is also at twelve lines the longest of that type; it deals with Telephus' fight with Achilles, his wound, and the paradox of his cure by the spear which had wounded him.

Auge's father had been warned by an oracle that his brothers-in-law would die by his grandson's hand, so to prevent her becoming pregnant he made her a priestess, but she succumbed to Hercules' attentions at the temple of Athena in Tegea, and Telephus was the result (Apollod. 2.7.4, with Frazer's note). He became king of Mysia, to where the Greek fleet sailed in error on its first attempt to reach Troy, and he attacked the Greeks as they disembarked, being wounded in the thigh by Achilles. Apollo told Telephus that the wound could only be healed by its cause, so he visited Agamemnon at Mycenae and on Clytemnestra's advice kidnapped the baby Orestes and threatened to kill him if he was not helped. Agamemnon co-operated because he had had an Apolline oracle that he could only take Troy with Telephus' assistance; so Telephus agreed to show the way to the Greek fleet, in return for which Achilles used his spear to cure his wound (see Apollod. *epit.* 3.20; *LIMC* 7.1.856 f.; and C. Preiser's edition of Euripides' *Telephus*, 172 f.).

1. Alcidis: in classical Latin verse the genitive of '-ides' patronymics is

Commentary

'-idae', this '-idis' form being 'barbarous' (Housman, *Class. Pap.* 2.826 n. 3), and a clear sign of its late date of composition. Heinsius indeed emended to 'Alcidae' here, though unnecessarily (but note 'Pelidae' at line 9): 'Alcidis' is also found in Dracontius (*Rom.* 2.65), along with 'Atridis' (8.449) and 'Tydidis' (8.647).

pignus: 'child', as often in the collection (see 91.4 n.).

2. externae sortis (codd., *sed* sorsis (A)); externi Martis (Heinsius); extremae sortis (Struchtmeyer): the phrase in the mss is not an easy one and has been regarded with suspicion (J.J. Struchtmeyer's conjecture is from *Animadversionum Criticarum Libri Duo*, Hardervici 1755, 41). But it need not be doubted. There is in fact convincingly similar phraseology at Liv. 9.42.1, 'Fabius, alienae sortis victor belli', where the reference is to a war which Fabius had won, although it had been someone else's responsibility to fight it. Thus here 'externae sortis bella' are wars for which foreign powers were responsible, and in which Telephus had no interest; they were also 'inopina' to him, because he became tangentially embroiled only when Greek warriors who had lost their way landed on his doorstep. This is borne out by the fact that, despite being Priam's son-in-law, he did not take any part in the subsequent war at Troy, though his son Eurypylus did (Apollod. *epit.* 5.12; Hyg. *Fab.* 101.5).

bella ... tulit: cf. Hor. *Ep.* 1.18.55 'Cantabrica bella tulisti'; Sil. It. 10.67 f. 'qui nunc contraria bella / ipsi ferre Iovi valeat'; with *TLL* 2.1836.41 f.

3. nam ... peterent dum (Kay; cum (codd.)) mille carinis: although there is no problem with postponement of the subordinating conjunction 'cum' to follow its verb (e.g. there are more instances in this collection (118.2; 161.4) and well over twenty in Martial, from a cursory look at Siedschlag's concordance), it is inelegant here when it can be mistaken for a preposition because of the immediately following ablative. An easy remedy is to emend to 'dum', which in turn prompts the reverse change of 'dum' to 'cum' in line 5 (again, in e.g. Martial 'dum' is sometimes postponed to follow its verb (e.g. 7.54.4; 9.64.3; 11.41.1)); one could also argue that the alteration marginally improves the sense.

mille carinis: the round number of a thousand ships goes back at least to Aesch. *Agam.* 45; Thucydides said there were twelve hundred (1.10.4); and apparently 1,186 can be counted in the Homeric catalogue (see Mayor's note on Juv. 12.122).

4. litus adacta suum: cf. Sil. It. 12.447 'ad litus adacta'; 'suum' refers of course to Telephus.

5. cum (Kay); dum (codd.): see 3 n.

6. Scyria (W; Syria (AB)) ... hasta: Achilles' famous spear, which only

333

Commentary

he could wield, had been given to his father Peleus by the centaur Cheiron (Hom. *Il.* 16.141 f.; see Janko's note on ibid. 130-54). Scyros is the island in the Sporades to which the young Achilles was sent by his mother in an attempt to avoid his fate in the Trojan war, and where he was installed at the court of Lycomedes disguised in girl's clothing (Apollod. 3.13.8). But the connection of the spear with Scyros is somewhat oblique, and the epithet here employed is unexpected. However, Ulysses was sent by the Greeks to prise Achilles away from Scyros, and he established the boy's identity by bringing the girls at the court a spear and shield concealed amongst more feminine gifts; Achilles chose them (Ovid *Met.* 13.162 f.; Stat. *Ach.* 1.841 f.; Hyg. *Fab.* 96). Only in Ovid's version is there a suggestion that the spear brought by Ulysses was identical with Cheiron's gift (13.180), though the supposition is not unreasonable and presumably gives the connection with Scyros that provides the epithet here. There is nothing to be said in favour of 'Syria', the variant in A and B.

pugnanti: for this type of repetition (cf. 'dum pugnat' in line 5), where a participle in a subsequent clause picks up a preceding verb, see Wills, *Repetition*, 311 f. ('participial resumption'). It is particularly frequent, and more adeptly employed than in this rather awkward instance, in Ovid (ibid., 316 f.); for example, 'demere temptabat laevi quoque robora postis / Cinyphius Pelates: temptanti dextera fixa est / cuspide …' (*Met.* 5.123 f.); and 'atque ubi sit quaerit; quaerenti iterumque vocanti / …prosiluit' (*Met.* 6.656 f.). It is a technique used also by prose writers (see Landgraf's commentary on Cic. *S. Rosc.* 32 (p. 80 f.)).

7. pro cuius cura consultus …: 'pro' is an unexpected preposition here (*de* and *super* are much more frequent: *TLL* 4.583.14 f.; 35 f.), but there is another example at Jul. Val. 2.29 'proque supplicum civium consulit voluntate'. For this part of the myth cf. Hyg. *Fab.* 101: 'Telephus … in pugna Chironis hasta percussus dicitur, ex quo vulnere cum in dies taetro cruciatu angeretur, petit sortem ab Apolline, quod esset remedium. Responsum est ei neminem mederi posse nisi eandem hastam qua vulneratus erat'.

8. hostica … opem: this motif of the wound being healed only by the weapon which caused it is the focal point of the epigram (see lines 11 f.) and was well rehearsed in earlier literature, especially Ovid (*Am.* 2.9.7 f.; *Rem.* 43 f.; *Met.* 12.111 f.; *Pont.* 2.2.25 f.), but also elsewhere (e.g. Prop. 2.1.63 f.; *AL* 226.28 f.). Pliny adduced the cure as evidence of the remedial efficacy of rust (*Nat. Hist.* 25.42; 34.152), but it is clearly an instance of sympathetic magic (Apollod. *epit.* 3.20, with Frazer's note).

quod (BW; quo (A)) … haberet: the idiom of a verb of saying or knowing with *quod* + subjunctive is found as early as e.g. Plaut. *Asin.* 52 'scio filius quod amet meus' and *Bell. Hisp.* 36.1 'legati … renuntiaverunt quod Pompeium in potestate haberent', and it becomes frequent in late

Commentary

Latin (see P. Cuzzolin, *Sull' origine della costruzione 'dicere quod': aspetti sintattici e semantici*, Florence 1994, esp. 106 f.; 189 f.; *LHS* 2.576 f.).

salubrem: for the irregular prosody of the short second syllable cf. 99.8, where the same word is similarly scanned at the same place of the line.

9. robore ... raso (A; sato (BW); sacro (Pithou)): *robur* is strictly the wooden spear shaft, as at e.g Verg. *Aen.* 10.479 'ferro praefixum robur acuto', and then by synecdoche the spear as a whole, as it is here. It was not the wood of the spear that was used to heal Telephus' wound, but rust shaved from the metal head which had made the wound: thus in Eur. *Telephus* frag. 35 Preiser (= frag. 724 Nauck) 'πριστοῖσι λόγχης θέλγεται ῥινήμασιν' ('is magicked away by the filings sawn off the spear'); and cf. Plin. *Nat. Hist.* 25.42; 34.152; Apollod. *Epit.* 3.20. A's text is clearly correct.

10. pulvere: the rust was administered in powdered form: cf. Cels. 4.27(20).1D 'adiecto ... contritae rosae pulvere'.

175 (185R)

On a lamp. The slender little flame is supported by rich olive-oil so that it may shatter the dark with the fire of its light.

This distich on a *cicindelum*, which here is clearly an oil-fuelled lamp, is similar in content and structure to 83 on a wax candle: the first line details the technology behind the light source, whilst the second lauds its efficacy.

For a discussion of ancient lamps and lanterns see Forbes, *Technology*, 6.164 f. The body of lanterns could be made of bronze, iron, pottery or wood, and they had windows which were often made of horn shaved down to the desired thinness to emit light, since glass was not widely available until the seventh century. The fuel for them was usually olive oil, as here, to which salt was added to dye the oil, alleviate spluttering, impart a yellow colour to the flame, and perhaps also prevent overheating. A substitute fuel was castor oil, which was said to give off a strong smell and was found at the poorer end of the market, and mainly in Egypt and other countries where the castor bean was readily available (cf. Herod. 2.62; Greg. Tur. *In Glor. Mart.* 5 (for olive oil), and Herod. 2.94.2; Plin. *Nat. Hist.* 15.25 (for castor oil)).

superscr.: De cicindelo: the noun is found with many different spellings and in all three genders: e.g. *cicendula* (Serv. ap. Verg. *Aen.* 1.727); *cicindela* (*CGL* 2.338.24); *cicindile* (ps.-Aug. *Serm.* 265.2 (*PL* 39.2238)); *cicindelum* (Greg. Tur. *Hist. Franc.* 4.31 and here) and others. It refers to an insect, the glow-worm or firefly (cf. Plin. *Nat. Hist.* 18.250 'lucentes vespere per arva cicindelae - ita appellant rustici stellantes volatus, Graeci vero lampyridas'; Paul. *Fest.* p. 37.17 f. Lindsay; I.C. Beavis, *Insects and Other Invertebrates in Classical Antiquity*, Exeter 1988, 175 f.), as well as to a source of light (both the candle, as at Mart. 14.40; and the lamp, as at Isid. *Or.* 20.10.2 and here).

1. pingui ... olivo: for *pingue* of the viscosity of olive oil cf. Verg. *Ecl.* 5.68; Stat. *Theb.* 6.576 etc.

fulcitur (A); nutritur (Petschenig): Petschenig's conjecture (*ZOeG* 28.1877.485) is based on the nutritional phraseology at 83.2 'dent alimenta' and 84.3 'submittit pabula', which describe the role of the fuel in providing a flame and light. But there is nothing wrong with ms. 'fulcitur', as he recognises ('stütze sich auf das Oel').

2. luminis igne sui: SB obelises 'luminis igne' and comments (app. crit.) '*Poetam non insulsum haec scripsisse vix credo. Vide ne scripserit* igne lucerna suo'. But it might equally be argued that the poet reverses the expected 'lumine ignis' to stress the ambivalence of fire and light in the context; the phrase seems no more 'insulsum' than many another in the collection and elsewhere.

176 (186R)

On goats. Goatskins hold Lenaean liquid and the goat, who had been his victim, becomes Bromius' prison.

This epigram begins a set of three on the relationship between Bacchus and goats; it may be deliberate organisation that each grows longer by a distich (see further p. 3). They centre on the goat's notoriety as a nibbler and destroyer of young vines, said to be the reason why it was a popular sacrifice to the god: 'non aliam ob culpam Baccho caper omnibus aris / caeditur' (Verg. *Georg.* 2.380 f., with Mynors' note (the line is echoed at 177.3); and cf. Serv. ap. loc. cit. 'per contrarietatem immolantur ... ut caper, qui obest vitibus, Libero'; Varro *Res Rust.* 1.2.18 f.; Ovid *Fast.* 1.357; Mart. 3.24.1 f.; *AL* 177). In this epigram and 178 this piece of rustic lore sets up the joke that the goat used to be Bacchus' sacrificial victim, but the relationship is now reversed, because Bacchus (a common metonymy for wine) is imprisoned in goatskins. An epigram on the same general topic by the Philippan poet Evenus describes the revenge of the gnawed vine on the goat by providing the grapes for the wine at its sacrifice (*AP* 9.75); it is quoted at Suet. *Dom.* 14.2, where it is said its circulation was responsible for Domitian changing his mind about an edict to cut down vines. F. Rodríguez Adrados (*History of the Greco-Latin Fable III*, Leiden and Boston 2003, 562 f.) highlights the fabular aspects of the story.

Commentary

This and the next two epigrams also appear in a ms. (Berlin Diez. B. Sant. 66) which contains a miscellany of material and may have been written in Charlemagne's scriptorium around AD 800: see *Codices Selecti Phototypice Impressi*, vol. 42, Graz 1973 (intro. B. Bischoff, esp. 23 f.); M. Spallone, 'Ricerche sulla tradizione manoscritta dell' *AL* (*AL* 181, 186-188, 379 Riese): itinerari testuali nell' età carolingia', *Stud. Med.*, 29.1988.607 f. (arguing that the epigrams in Diez. B. Sant. 66 were not copied from A, but from a separate, indirect tradition); and C. Villa, 'La tradizione di Orazio e "la biblioteca di Carlo Magno" ', in *Formative Stages of Classical Traditions: Latin Texts from Antiquity to the Renaissance*, ed. O. Pecere and M.D. Reeve, Spoleto 1995, 299 f. (arguing that Diez. B. Sant. 66 is Veronese in origin).

1. Lenaeos latices: cf. Verg. *Georg.* 3.509 f. 'profuit inserto latices infundere cornu / Lenaeos'; it is likely that this poet borrowed his erudite phrase from there (see p. 12 f. for the extensive Vergilian influence on the collection). The Lenaia was a festival dedicated to Dionysus which was celebrated in January (on which see H.W. Parke, *Festivals of the Athenians*, London 1977, 104 f.); for *latex* of wine, cf. Lucr. 2.657; 5.15; Verg. *Aen.* 1.686 'laticemque Lyaeum'; Val. Flacc. 4.533 'Bacchi latices'.

hircorum tergora: these are goatskins (though the coupling with the verb 'gestant' is not felicitous, because the meaning that initially comes to mind is of goats carrying items on their backs). For *tergus* and *tergum* used of a container made out of animal hide, cf. Ovid *Met.* 14.225 'bovis inclusos tergo'; ibid. 15.305; and for a similar metonymy cf. Mart. 7.2.2 'Martis Getico tergore' (of a shield). Goatskins are evidenced as wine containers at all periods: e.g. Hom. *Il.* 3.247; Plin. *Nat. Hist.* 28.240; *Ed. Diocl.* 10.13a; Jer. *Vita Malchi* 8 (*PL* 23.57); with *DS* 5.613 f.; *MM* 458 n. 4.

gestant: i.e. 'continent'.

2. caper ... carcer: for this type of punning (*annominatio*) at the conclusion of an epigram, cf. Mart. 11.18.26 f. 'nam quo tempore praedium dedisti / mallem tu mihi prandium dedisses', with my note.

victima: i.e. a sacrificial victim (see intro. above).

177 (187R)

Another. The drove of the bearded herd wanders through the countryside, delighting in damaging vine groves with their teeth. This is the reason why the goat is brought as a sacrifice to Bacchus at all his altars, and the herd's sin is punished by its becoming a sacred offering.

For the connections between, and epigrams about, Bacchus and goats see 176 intro.

Commentary

1. barbati pecoris: for *barbatus* characterising goats cf. *Priap.* 86.16 Bücheler 'barbatus ... hirculus'; Phaedr. 4.9.10; Mart. 11.84.18.

2. laedere dente nemus: see 176 intro., and cf. 171.2 'perdere dente genus'.

3. omnibus hinc aris Baccho ...: the similarity to Verg. *Georg.* 2.380 is so marked that the borrowing must be intentional: 'non aliam ob culpam Baccho caper omnibus aris / caeditur'.

4. sacro munere: i.e. by becoming a sacrificial offering to the god, a frequent sense of *munus* (e.g. Verg. *Ecl.* 3.63; *Aen.* 6.637; Ovid *Am.* 2.13.24).

178 (188R)

Another. Lyaeus' temples are placated with Cinyphian blood, and caprine animals are his just sacrifice. But although animals cannot take revenge on gods, and neither can the law of talion be visited on deities, the goats get vengeance. 'Liber' is deprived of his title when the hostile god is enclosed in a goatskin.

The last epigram of the trio about the goat as a sacrificial victim of Bacchus centres on the novel idea that sacrifices cannot usually get their own back on the gods to whom they are dedicated, but the goat is the exception because after death he imprisons Bacchus when he is turned into a wineskin. The god is not then 'Liber'.

1. sanguine Cinyphio: for the epithet see 106.6 n.
   Lyaei: for the title ('the one who sets free', from Greek λύω) see Jocelyn's note on Enn. *Scaen.* 52. It is appropriate here in emphasising Bacchus' connection with wine and intoxication; Vergil refers to wine as 'laticem Lyaeum' (*Aen.* 1.686).

2. victima iusta: the goat is rightly sacrificed to Bacchus because it destroys young vines (see 176 intro.); this is the common theme which runs through this trio of epigrams.

3. sed licet ulcisci nequeant: for a similar theme cf. Tib. 1.6.30 'contra quis ferat arma deos?', with Murgatroyd's note. But this takes the argument a stage further: not merely how it is possible to resist the gods, but how it is possible be avenged on them.

4. reddi talio: the *lex talionis* of 'an eye for an eye' was included in the Twelve Tables ('si membrum rupsit, ni cum eo pacit, talio esto' (8.2)),

Commentary

though it did not outlive the Republic and may have been abolished by the Lex Aebutia (cf. Gell. 16.10.8). The principle was however occasionally applied at a later date (e.g. castration for castrators at Just. *Nov.* 142.1); it should not be confused with the similar principle of mirror punishment, whereby for example the feet of a runaway slave were the object of his punishment (see my note on Aus. *Epig.* 17.1). See further *RE* 4A.2069 f. The principle of talion when applied to the present situation would be that animals should sacrifice gods as recompense for being sacrificed to them; though that cannot happen, the goats get some sort of vengeance ('est vindicta capris').

5. est vindicta capris: there is a double significance to the phrase: on the one hand the goats get some 'vengeance'; but *vindicta* is also a type of legal manumission for slaves and an assertion of liberty (see Ogilvie's note on Liv. 2.3-5; and A. Bürge, *Römisches Privatsrecht*, Darmstadt 1999, 47 f.), and goats are therefore also alleged to be more at liberty than the god, because, despite being Liber, he is deprived of his freedom in the wineskin. For the enjambement of this line see 78.3 n.

cassatur nomine Liber: *cassare*, formed from the adjective *cassus*, is a late confection, appearing in literary sources only from the fourth century onwards (e.g. *AL* 810.5R 'cassato solito vigore pennae'), when it also becomes reasonably frequent in legal texts (see *TLL* 3.519.84 f.). The verb means 'cassum vel irritum reddere' and the construction here is based on adjectival *cassus* + ablative, meaning 'devoid of' (e.g. Lucr. 3.562 'cassum anima corpus'; Verg. *Aen.* 11.104 'nullum cum victis certamen et aethere cassis'). Thus the god Liber ('The Free One') is deprived of his title when he is bottled up in a wineskin. This play on words is found elsewhere: cf. Petr. 41.6 f. (for the elaborate puns in the passage see Housman, *Class. Pap.* 3.962 f.); *AL* 212.2 f. 'Bacchum servire coegi, / quamvis Liber erat' (for some medieval versions of this epigram see A. Riese, *ZOeG* 18.1867.433 f.; K. Smolak, *WS* 15.1981.233 f.); and *AL* 252.

6. hircino ... utre: for goatskins as wine containers see 176.1 n.
adversus ... deus: i.e. hostile to goats.

179 (189R)

On Memnon. The son of Aurora, nurseling of the rising sun, leads forth fearsome thousands of his people. He goes to help the weary Trojans, but with an unpropitious omen, and by so doing presses on to certain death by Pelides' sword. Now already the disaster that awaits Troy is made manifest, when Priam accepts this black help.

This is the last epigram on a mythological theme in the collection and it

Commentary

features Memnon; the portrayal of him as a black man of ill omen has links to other epigrams in the immediate vicinity which comment adversely on blacks and pygmies (172-3; 180-1); see 172 intro.

Memnon was traditionally the son of Eos and Tithonus (and thus nephew of Priam) and was king of the Ethiopians, his myth being told in the lost *Aithiopis* (*EGF* p. 45 f. Davies); he is mentioned in Homer (*Od.* 11.522) and Hesiod (*Theog.* 984 f.). He fought at Troy and killed many Greeks, most notably Nestor's son Antilochus (*Od.* 4.187 f.), until he was killed by Achilles (Apollod. *epit.* 5.3). The lament of Eos for her son is a favourite scene in the visual arts (*LIMC* 6.1.448 f.) and in Hellenistic and later literature (e.g. Ovid *Met.* 13.586 f.; Quint. Smyrn. 2.549 f.). Various monuments were connected with Memnon, most notably the colossal sighing statue at Luxor (Plin. *Nat. Hist.* 36.58; Juv. 15.5; Paus. 1.42.2).

Separate traditions of his myth associated Memnon with both Susa (e.g. Herod. 5.54.2; Strabo 15.3.2; Paus. 10.31.7) and Ethiopia (e.g. Hes. *Theog.* 985; Curt. 4.8.3; Dio Chrys. *Or.* 11.114) or both together (Paus. 1.42.2; Dict. Cret. 4.4). In archaic art his attendants are usually depicted as black, but never Memnon himself; it is Latin poets who first describe him as black (e.g. Verg. *Aen.* 1.489; Ovid *Am.* 1.8.3 f.; Manil. 1.767; Sen. *Agam.* 212 etc.), and he is used as an exemplar of blackness by Luxorius at *AL* 288.1 f. See also Roscher 2.2653 f., esp. 2661 f. (colossi), 2669 (blackness).

1. filius Aurorae, Phoebi nascentis alumnus: cf. 172.1 'ex oriente die noctis processit alumnus'. Here 'Phoebi nascentis alumnus' is primarily a reference to place, to locate Memnon's kingdom of Ethiopia in the east (see 172.1 n.); but since 'Phoebus nascens' is the dawn, or Aurora, the phrase on another interpretation would be almost synonymous with the preceding 'filius Aurorae'. An allusion may also be intended to the fact that it was at dawn that the colossal statue at Luxor which became so closely associated with Memnon was said to sigh (Philostr. *Her.* 26.16; Paus. 1.42.2; and passim in the many inscriptions and epigrams which were carved on the monument itself (collected by A. and É. Bernand, *Les Inscriptions grecques et latines du Colosse du Memnon*, Paris 1960)).

2. milia tetra: for *milia* of large military forces cf. Verg. *Aen.* 1.491; 10.761; Stat. *Theb.* 8.481; Val. Flacc. 6.60; the forces are 'tetra' because they are black (note 'nigrum auxilium' line 6, and compare the 'tetra ... formica' of 93.1). Philostratus (*Imag.* 2.7.2) says Memnon struck terror into the Greeks because before his time black people were only a myth.

3. fausto non omine: the phrase is clumsy (presumably a metrical necessity for 'non fausto / infausto omine'), and postponed 'non' seems to be rare, but note 'degener haud Gracchis consul' at Sil. It. 4.515, with some more examples of postponed 'haud', though usually qualifying an adverb,

Commentary

at *TLL* 6.2-3.2558.61 f. In fact emendation would not be difficult (e.g. 'non fausto (or infausto) fessis succurrens omine Teucris'), but accounting for the word order in the ms. would be.

There is in extant literature no particular oracle, augury or omen connected with Memnon's assistance of Priam which would be pertinent here; however, in the absence of the complete *Aithiopis* that should occasion no surprise, and the existence in the tradition of an augury which either predicted Memnon's death if he went to Troy (line 4, with note), or (less probably in my view) warned Priam against accepting Memnon's help (lines 5-6), or both, need not be doubted. In the same vein, for example, Proclus' summary of the *Aithiopis* states that Thetis foretold Achilles that if he fought Memnon he would kill him but would himself be killed shortly afterwards (*EGF* p. 47.15 f. Davies; and see M.L. West, 'Iliad and Aithiopis', *CQ* 53.2003.1 f.).

4. pergit ... mori: cf. Plin. *Ep.* 3.16.10 'cum Thrasea gener eius deprecaretur ne mori pergeret', where the concluding words mean 'that he should not persevere in his intention to die'; similarly here, it seems that Telephus has been warned that if he perseveres in going to Troy to assist the Trojans, he will die. By going, he effectively signs his own death warrant.

protinus: the import of the adverb here is not the usual temporal 'immediately' (because Memnon actually accomplished much at Troy before his death), but emphasises the inevitability of 'pergit ... mori'. Thus *OLD* protinus 4 'at the same time, by the same action', adducing Quint. 8.3.10 'fugientia in altum cacumina oleae ferro coercebo: in orbem se formosius fundet et protinus fructum ramis pluribus feret'. Once Memnon chooses to go to Troy, he is a dead man.

5-6. iam tunc ... auxilium: it is difficult to read this couplet with modern eyes and not assume that racist comment lies behind it, and such an implication may well be present given invective elsewhere in the collection about black Africans (esp. 173; cf. also 180; 181; and Luxorius' comment at 288.6 'dum Memnon facie es, non tamen es genio'). But it may not be intended: the Africans' colour might, for example, be taken as a presentiment of the eventual burning of Troy, or it might be in point simply because black was the colour of ill omen, an association which could be extended to black people (see 173 intro.).

180 (190R)

On Bumbulus. Sporting a name as ludicrous as your figure you join our troupe, little Bumbulus. But there's a reason for that, if, being like a pygmy, you stand amidst long spears so that a migrating crane does not grab and swallow you. And you broadcast to the world how you have delighted your father in having assumed the name of a depraved charioteer. He kept girls skilled in prostitution at the circus; with you as the pimp randy old women are screwed at night.

This interesting piece is also one of the most puzzling in the collection: it is difficult to understand the subject, and even more difficult to understand the logic and reasoning behind the statements it contains. It is however clear that the protagonist is of very small build, that he has joined 'conventus nostros', that he has a father (who appears again in the following epigram), and that he is morally base. But connections between these facts are obscure: what are 'conventus nostros', why has Bumbulus joined them, why should his assumption of the name Bumbulus please his father, who is the 'ille' of line 7, and what precisely are 'ille' and Bumbulus engaged in doing? It is unusual for an irrisory epigram to impart so much information with such little clarity; and it is unfortunate that on an occasion when a superscription could be of help, it stays silent (only 'De Bumbulo').

In the following commentary I have raised these questions of interpretation and suggested answers, though no doubt others equally or more plausible could be advanced. This is a brief summary: Bumbulus, a dwarf, has joined a troupe of spear-carrying entertainers to give himself some protection from being carried off and eaten by cranes, which is what happens to the very small; he has adopted his odd name from that of a notorious charioteer; it is sarcastically suggested that this has pleased his father, because Bumbulus has outdone his namesake in depravity; and the charioteer pimped some genteel call-girls at the circus, whilst Bumbulus is a pimp for some randy old women. I also understand Bumbulus to be a dwarf who is compared to a pygmy (line 3) rather than to be himself a pygmy, though if he were it would not seriously affect the interpretation of the epigram as a whole; but it seems improbable that a pygmy would gain entry to 'conventus nostros', and that the poet would not make more of the fact if his target were a pygmy. Whether Bumbulus was a real person or not is an open question; since the allegations about him are specific and unusual, the likelihood is that he was real.

A skoptic tradition in Greek and Latin epigram against thin, light and small people is well developed (see my intro. to Mart. 11.101); to modern sensibilities it is strange that humour directed at fat people is almost non-existent. Luxorius too wrote on dwarfs (the obscure *AL* 200) and pygmies (291). On dwarfs in the Greco-Roman world see R.S.J. Garland, *The Eye of the Beholder: Deformity and Disability in the Greco-Roman World*, London 1995, index 'Dwarfism'.

1. nominis et formae ... ludibria: Bumbulus' 'forma' is a source of humour because he is exceptionally short; the name is not elsewhere attested (there is a Bombylas at *CIL* 6.35239) although he has taken

Commentary

it from a charioteer (line 6). The humour of it presumably lies in its sound, its rarity and its closeness to, perhaps derivation from, the Greek βομβύλιος, the bumblebee (cf. Ar. *Wasps* 107; Athen. 11.784d etc.), which was so called because of its droning (Greek βόμβος). There seems to be no particular insect lore which might explain more fully the humour of the name here, but no doubt a dwarf pimp who has adopted the name Mr Bumblebee would amuse some.

2. conventus nostros ... adis: cf. 173.1 'nostrum processit ad axem'. *Conventus* is a vague term, its meaning extending as widely as 'region' or 'locality' (e.g. Isid. *Or.* 14.5.21 'regiones partes sunt provinciarum, quas vulgus conventus vocat'; Juv. 8.129, with Courtney's note), though here it probably refers to a gathering of people for a purpose. The clue to that purpose lies in the following line ('sed ratio est': see note), where the characterisation of the gathering is that it is equipped with 'longa arma'; given the remainder of the epigram with its circuses and prostitution, it is unlikely to have a military context, so perhaps a troupe of performers or entertainers of some kind would be most likely (Courtney, *CR* 31.1981.41 f., suggests a similar interpretation).

Bumbule parvus: for other instances of mixed forms of address (vocative + nominative) cf. Aus. 11.3.9 f. 'bonus frater ... nate pius'; Sid. Ap. *Carm.* 9.290 'tu ... o dignissime Quintianus alter'; *AL* 71.144 'Aeneas ingrate meus'; with J. Svennung, *Anredeformen*, Lund 1958, 246 f.; 272 f.; 274 f.; Löfstedt, *Syntactica*, 1.96 f. Many instances can however be construed in other ways: here, for example, the line might be punctuated 'conventus nostros, Bumbule, parvus adis'.

3. sed ratio est si stas (Shackleton Bailey); sed ratio est mixtus (A); sed ratio est: extas (Riese); sed ratio est: metuis (Watt): it needs to be determined what the 'ratio' is, and what it explains. The conjunction 'sed' suggests that the fact to be explained is what has preceded, namely that a small person named Bumbulus has joined 'conventus nostros'. With SB's conjecture (*Towards a Text*, 25), the reason why Bumbulus has made such a strange choice is that, since he will stand like a pygmy amongst 'longa arma', the cranes will not eat him. This makes good sense: it was the signature myth about pygmies, to whom Bumbulus is likened because of his stature, that they were annually attacked and carried off as food by cranes (see 4 n. below). A's 'sed ratio est: mixtus' is untenable here because a main verb is needed in the second clause; Riese's conjecture 'extas' gives the opposite of the sense required; and Watt's conjecture 'sed ratio est: metuis' (*C&M* 47.1996.256) is unconvincing, because 'longis ... in armis' surely explains Bumbulus' means of protecting himself, and does not describe a situation from which he needs to escape.

longis pygmaeus in armis: 'longis ... in armis' is glossed by SB as '*i.e pene, puto*' (app. crit.). This is entirely inappropriate: there is no conceivable

Commentary

connection between the length of Bumbulus' penis and either his joining the 'conventus' or his not being carried off by cranes. The 'longa arma' should be understood to be actual spears (cf. Enn. *frag. var.* 14 Vahlen 'longis hastis'; Verg. *Aen.* 9.229 'stant longis adnixi hastis'), because if Bumbulus stands amongst people of average size holding long spears the cranes will find it impossible to attack him, long though their necks are. For the phrase 'in armis' cf. Verg. *Aen.* 9.376 'quive estis in armis?'; and esp. Juv. 13.168, quoted below; and for the significance of 'longis' here (that 'length' is a defence against attack by long-necked cranes), cf. *AL* 281.95 Symphosius (describing a crane) 'nec vereor pugnas, dum non sit longior hostis', and Lucil. 168 Marx (173 Krenkel) 'longior hic quam grus, grue tota, cum volat olim'.

4. ne ... grus peregrina voret: Courtney (*CR* 31.1981.42) well points to the influence of Juv. 13.167 f. on this and the preceding line ('longis in armis', in particular, would seem a riposte to Juvenal's 'parvis ... in armis'):

> Ad subitas Thracum volucres nubemque sonoram
> pygmaeus parvis currit bellator in armis,
> mox inpar hosti raptusque per aera curvis
> unguibus a saeva fertur grue. Si videas hoc
> gentibus in nostris, risu quatiare ...

Pygmies (the term derives from Greek πυγμή ('fist'), an allusion to their size) were known to Homer (*Il.* 3.3 f.), though, as with the Ethiopians (see 172-3), a basis in fact became elaborated with flights of fancy about exotic tribes and peoples. Thus by far the best-known and most regularly retailed 'fact' about them was their annual fight with migrating cranes, which allegedly attacked them, carried them off, and ate them (cf. also Hecataeus *FGH* 1 F382a-b Jacoby; Basilis *FGH* 718 F1; *AP* 11.265 Lucillius; Ovid *Fast.* 6.176; Mela 3.81; Plin. *Nat. Hist.* 7.26; Juv. 6.504 f.; *Priap.* 46.3; the story was so entrenched that the very presence of cranes was taken to indicate pygmies living nearby, whether in Thrace (Plin. *Nat. Hist.* 4.44), Caria (ibid. 5.109), or India (ibid. 6.70)). See further *LIMC* 7.1.594 f.; V. Dasen, *Dwarfs in Ancient Egypt and Greece*, Oxford 1993, esp. 175 f.; P. Janni, *Etnografia e mito, la storia dei pigmei*, Rome 1978, 19 f.

peregrina: the migratory habit of cranes was well-known and well-rehearsed (e.g. Hom. *Il.* 3.3 f.; Herod. 2.22.4; Eur. *Helen* 1478 f.; Arist. *Hist. Anim.* 597a; Plin. *Nat. Hist.* 10.58 f.). The common crane breeds in northern Europe and winters in North Africa amongst other places; migrating cranes would have been a familiar sight to Carthaginian residents (see E.K. Urban et al., *The Birds of Africa*, London etc. 1986, 2.132 f.; Capponi, *Ornithologia Latina*, 280 f.).

Commentary

5. nec frustra ostendis: the connection with what has preceded seems tenuous: the author has apparently moved away from Bumbulus' size and 'conventus nostros' to deal with his strange name and the pleasure his having assumed it allegedly gives his father. 'nec frustra ostendis' I take to be litotes ('nor are you ineffectual in showing ...' meaning 'and you broadcast to the whole world ...'), and I understand the statement the phrase introduces to be heavily ironic: his father cannot be at all pleased either that Bumbulus has adopted a notorious charioteer's name, or that he has outdone him in sleaziness by pimping old women, gaining a wide notoriety in the process. The relationship with his father is also central to the following piece, when the father has died and Bumbulus has thrown all filial obligation to the winds.

proprio: i.e. 'tuo', as elsewhere (see 120.4 n.).

6. quod ... sumpseris: dependent on 'placuisse'.

turpis nomen ... heniochi: this is the only occasion in extant Latin literature where Greek ἡνίοχος is found in transliteration, other than as the name of a constellation or a people. The reason for the choice of the Greek term here is not apparent, though it might for instance signal that Bumbulus, the name with which the epigram is concerned, is of Greek derivation and to be interpreted in that knowledge (see 1 n. above and 116.1 n. for a specific connection of pimping with Greeks), or it might conceivably have some specific local significance (e.g. that some chariot-racers in North Africa were so termed, or that chariot-racers who were also pimps were so termed). The reason for the charioteer's turpitude is given in the concluding couplet.

7. ille: the logical connection is again not altogether clear, and the pronoun might belong to either Bumbulus' father or to the charioteer from whom he has taken his name. But the latter is much the more likely (despite SB, *Towards a Text*, 25), because the concluding lampoon involves activity at the circus, which fits the charioteer, and it is activity of a disreputable kind, which fits his turpitude (which would otherwise be unexplained); moreover there would be little point in introducing the charioteer to the epigram if 'ille' does not refer to him.

doctas circo (Baehrens; circi (A)) prostare (edd.; prostrare (A)) puellas: Baehrens' emendation 'circo' should be accepted: the place of work of a *heniochus* is the circus, and it would be a suitable location for his acting as a pimp (cf. Juv. 3.65 'ad circum iussas prostare puellas'; there are further references for the availability of prostitutes at the circus at McGinn, *Prostitution*, 22 f.). Ms. 'circi', which would depend on 'doctas', makes little sense, because the girls' knowledge of the circus is immaterial in the context. And there is also nothing to be said for A's 'prostrare', a verb which does not exist, though Riese put it in his text.

Commentary

8. te duce: 'dux' here presumably has the sense 'pimp', though there seems to be no exact parallel; compare however 'adductor' at 116.2 and 'adducta virgine' at 117.4 (see notes).

nocte: again the significance of the detail is not clear; perhaps the *heniochus* pimped at the circus by day when races were held (when there could have been a wealthy, discerning clientèle), whilst Bumbulus had to do his work at night (presumably both less glamorous and with rougher trade).

fricantur: in an obscene context *fricare* usually refers to masturbation: e.g. Mart. 11.29.8 'nil opus est digitis; sic mihi, Phylli, frica'; schol. Juv. 6.238 'manu sua penem fricat sibi'; Petr. 92.11; and see also 137.2 n. Here the sense is probably 'futuuntur'; Adams, *LSV* 184, with reference to this instance, evidences a change in meaning of reflexes of the verbs *fricare* and *sollicitare* in Romance languages from masturbation to *fututio*.

181 (191R)

Another. Since you are your father's heir, Bumbulus, and have possession of his property, and since there is no advantage to you in demonstrating that your filial piety is intact, you are ensuring that you are considered antagonistic towards your begetter. Your inclinations go completely against your undertakings: your father fancied a Green, a Red gets into you.

This second piece on Bumbulus the dwarf, which again gives his father a prominent role, is as obscure as the first. If the text and some key emendations are sound, it seems to mean that now Bumbulus has inherited his father's estate he no longer needs to display any *pietas* towards him, so he has broken free and supports a different circus faction from his father; that preference is, however, expressed in sexual terms. Again we have to assume that this type of epigram is skoptic in type, but its location in a specific place and time makes its interpretation tendentious without local knowledge.

1. cum (Traube; Shackleton Bailey; dum (A)) sis: SB's proposal was anticipated by L. Traube (*Philologus* 54.1895.127). It seems a necessary and logical correction, though consideration of it requires an overview of the piece as a whole: from the third line onwards it is evident that Bumbulus is acting in a manner which his father would not have wished, and his being his father's heir and getting his hands on his money (lines 1-2) is the reason for his conduct; a causal 'cum' rather than A's conditional 'dum' is therefore required.

heres: the short quantity of the first syllable is found only here and Cypr. Gall. *Exod.* 542, but there is plenty of evidence of irregular prosody in the collection (see p. 24).

Commentary

censum: this is the father's property and thus Bumbulus' inheritance, so it would appear that the father has died (see line 2).

2. inlaesa (Shackleton Bailey); laesa (A): it is difficult to imagine circumstances in which it would be advantageous ('utile') for a son to be able to demonstrate a lack of *pietas* towards his father, particularly when inheritance is under consideration. SB's conjecture should therefore be accepted: since Bumbulus has inherited and no longer needs to be able to demonstrate *pietas* towards his father, he can now do as he pleases.

3. proprio auctori: for *proprius* in the sense *tuus* see 120.4 n. For *auctor* in the sense *pater* cf. Drac. *Rom.* 7.16 f. 'auctor Achillis ... Aeacides'; it is a rare use, though much commoner in signifying the founder of a race or dynasty (e.g. Verg. *Aen.* 4.365; 7.49; Hor. *Carm.* 1.2.36; with *TLL* 2.1204.30 f.), which suggests it has an inappropriately elevated tone here.

The metre of this line is notable: there is hiatus at the main caesura followed by elision in the fourth foot (see p. 23 f.).

4. discordat ... contra suscepta: this seems to be the only occasion on which *contra* is used with *discordare* (*a / ab* being usual, *cum* rare), though the idiom is clear enough (cf. such expressions as 'it goes against the grain'). 'suscepta' here must be undertakings or promises about support of circus factions (see following note) which Bumbulus had made to his father (for *suscipere* in this sense, cf. Liv. 10.39.17 'hinc iuris iurandi adversus foedera suscepti exsecrationes horrens', with *OLD* suscipio 8(b)): i.e. Bumbulus, now he has inherited, wants to act in a way of which he knows his father would have strongly disapproved.

5. dilexit ... : in the context of circus factions the verb need only mean 'liked' or 'supported', but the ensuing 'russeus intrat' suggests it may have a more sexual tone as well ('loved').

russeus: the Blues and Greens were always the larger and better supported faction colours, but Reds and Whites, though nowhere near as popular, never disappeared, even being attested into the fifth and sixth centuries; the emperor Anastasius, for example, was remarkable for supporting the Reds (see A. Cameron, *Circus Factions*, Oxford 1976, 45 f.; 71 f.). However, one can see how Bumbulus' support of a clearly minor faction and abandonment of family loyalties might have alienated his father, had he been alive.

intrat: an obscene sense for the verb here (i.e. 'pedicat') is easy enough to understand and is surely intended as a παρὰ προσδοκίαν conclusion to the piece, though (surprisingly) the only reasonably close parallels seem to be Mart. 11.99.6 'nimias intrant Cyaneasque natis' (of clothes) and Juv. 10.317 'moechos et mugilis intrat' (see *TLL* 7.2.63.22 f.); contrast

Commentary

and compare 'inire', which is often instanced with a sexual reference, for which see my note to Aus. *Epig.* 112.2 'inesse'.

182-185 (192-194R)

General introduction

This group of four epigrams deals with the game of *tabula*, a board game of a popular and enduring type which has many similarities with modern backgammon and kindred games. The basics of the ancient game are ascertainable from what these epigrams tell us, sometimes supplemented by other sources and, with caution, by analogy from later forms of the game; however, their focus is on generalities and moralising aspects rather than the details of the game, and some points remain obscure. Since none of the pieces can be understood without some knowledge of the game, both the equipment for playing it and the way it was played, I will preface them with an outline discussion.

The relationship between the four epigrams 182-5 needs first to be considered: they deal with the same subject matter, but are they a sequence in any broader sense? Might they, for instance, describe a game of *tabula* in chronological order, from the setting-up of the board to the end of play? At the extreme, might the epigrams have become separated in the ms. tradition but originally have formed a single piece (although long by the standards of the collection at twenty-six lines, this would almost be matched by 106 at twenty-four lines)? As regards the evidence of the mss, 183-4 are joined together in A, which is how they are printed in Riese's text; A gives 182 and 185 as separate pieces, and the only other mss witnesses, B and W, offer only 182. This of itself argues for separation, at least into three pieces, and there is in any event more evidence to adduce for separate pieces erroneously becoming joined in ms. traditions than for single pieces becoming dismembered (see my note on Aus. *Epig.* 39.1 with references). But there are also strong supporting arguments: the separate pieces all end with moralistic sententiae or similar, a type of closure which is relatively common in this collection (see 168.5-6 n.); the opening of 185, 'Indica materies blandum certamen amicis / offert', would be abrupt and unexpected if introduced three-quarters of the way through a longer poem, since the composition of board, pieces and accessories has been described earlier; and, although 182 might in its first line be a convincing description of a game about to start (cf. 'astat'), it becomes evident that it is better read as a description of a game in progress (if the poet had wanted to suggest otherwise, he would not have used the present tenses 'decertant' and 'currant'). I therefore conclude that the link between the complete group of four epigrams is their subject, and that they should not be interpreted as a chronological or other sequence; a much stronger case can however be made for not separating 183 from 184 (for which see 184.1 n.).

Commentary

I have said above that the description of the game which these epigrams provide should be interpreted, inter alia, by (judicious) analogy from its modern descendants like backgammon. However, this should evidently be a last resort, and I therefore begin a consideration of the game by extracting from the epigrams the basic details about it which they provide, and then introduce evidence from other ancient descriptions of the same and similar games before finally considering modern analogues.

The game is known as *tabula* (182 superscr.); it is played on a board (183.1) by two players who use differently coloured (red and white) pieces (182.1 f.; 183.3 f.; 185.3 f.); the players have alternate throws of the dice which control the moves of the pieces (182.1; 183; 184.2); a *pyrgus* is used for rolling the dice (183.1 f.); both luck and skill are involved in the game (182.4; 185.3 f.; 185.6); the game is a 'war' game (184.1; 184.3; 185.2); the objectives of the moves in the game are (a) for pieces to travel along a route of *scripta*, by implication with the aim of moving them through and off the board (182.3; 185.3 f.) and (b) to obstruct the opponent's progress by inflicting losses on him, that is by removing his pieces from play (185.4); the game is played for a prize and /or involves gambling (184.5 f.; 185.8); and the game should be played in the proper spirit (185.1; 185.7 f.). Necessary information missing from this seemingly long list is: (1) a description of the layout of the board on which the pieces moved; (2) a description of how the opponent's pieces can be attacked; (3) the number of pieces each player has; (4) the number of dice used for each throw; and (5) the disposition of the pieces at the start of the game. Other evidence from ancient sources now needs to be introduced.

A board game called *tabula* is described by Isidore at *Or.* 18.60 f. ('tabula luditur pyrgo, calculis, tesserisque' (18.60)); he says of the dice and board (18.64) 'nam tribus tesseris ludere perhibent propter tria saeculi tempora: praesentia, praeterita, et futura; quia non stant, sed decurrunt. Sed et ipsas vias senariis locis distinctas propter aetates hominum ternariis lineis propter tempora argumentantur. Inde et tabulam ternis discriptam dicunt lineis'. So three dice were used, and the route along which the pieces moved on the board was made up of *loci* in sixes and *lineae* in threes; there is plentiful archaeological and other literary evidence which shows boards with this basic layout: for present purposes a good example is a stone board found at Ostia (*CIL* 14.5317) which is marked thus:

CCCCCC	*	BBBBBB
AAAAAA	*	AAAAAA
DDDDDD	*	EEEEEE

This pattern of three lines (*lineae*) of symbols with two sets of six spaces or squares (*loci*) per line is reflected in boards where words are used rather than simple letters (the words often form maxims or sentences; numerals are not found, which is unsurprising in the absence of Arabic numerals); e.g. *CIL* 13.3865 (from Trier):

> VIRTUS   IMPERI
> HOSTES   VINCTI
> LUDANT   ROMANI

A sequence of such pieces can be found at *AL* 495-506R, and many examples are known from archaeological remains (more than fifty are collected by M. Ihm in 'Römische Spieltafeln', *Bonner Studien Reinhard Kekulé*, Berlin 1890, 230 f.; and there is an illustration of a board which has thirty-six inlaid squares and was found in a tomb at Qustul, Nubia in W.B. Emery, *Nubian Treasure*, London 1948, 46 with Pl. 32). The game with which such board layouts is associated is often called *ludus duodecim scriptorum* (it must be so called because each line (*linea*) of the board has twelve spaces or squares, *scripta* thus being synonymous with Isidore's *loci*; the number of lines might have varied), but other evidence as well as Isidore's description of the *tabula* board (quoted above) proves the close similarities of the two games (it is summarised by Baumgartner, *Untersuchungen*, 129 f.). Indeed it may well be, since *ludus duodecim scriptorum* and *tabula* are the only Roman board games known which were played with both dice and pieces, that they were identical in all significant respects, or that *tabula* was a standardised variety of *ludus*; *tabula* was the name that survived into Romance languages (see below).

As regards the movement of pieces on the *tabula* board, particularly the way in which opposing pieces interacted, Isidore again provides useful information (*Or.* 18.67): 'calculi partim ordine moventur, partim vage: ideo alios ordinarios, alios vagos appellant; at vero qui moveri omnino non possunt, incitos dicunt. Unde et egentes homines inciti vocantur, quibus spes ultra procedendi nulla restat'. This information can be supplemented with a complicated epigram by Agathias (*AP* 9.482), where he sets out in great detail the position that had been reached in a game of *tabula* played by the emperor Zeno immediately before he made a legendarily disastrous throw of the three dice; although the language Agathias uses, particularly to describe specific squares on the board, is highly obscure, the rules by which the players had reached the position in the game which he describes were brilliantly analysed by L. Becq de Fouquières (*Les Jeux des anciens*, Paris 1869, 371 f.; see also R.G. Austin, *JHS* 54.1934.202 f.), who was able to draw the following conclusions: each player had fifteen pieces (as is also the case at *AL* 8.55); pieces had to be moved in accordance with the throw of the dice if they could be moved; a player's two pieces or more on a square of the board defended that square from the opponent's pieces; a single piece on a square of the board could be removed by an opponent's piece moving to that square and would then

Commentary

have to re-enter the board at the start; and none of a player's pieces could be moved off the board until they had all passed beyond a certain point on it. This fleshes out Isidore's description: thus 'calculi partim ordine moventur' refers to two or more pieces on a square; 'partim vage' refers to single pieces on a square; and 'inciti' refers to pieces which cannot be moved at all on a particular throw.

The above description also demonstrates the closeness of *tabula* to modern backgammon and similar games, evidence from which can now be introduced. To begin with the similarities: backgammon is a board game played by two players with fifteen pieces each; each player has to travel a set course through the points of the board (points being the equivalent of *loci* or *scripta*), with the aim of getting all his pieces to the other end and off the board; players have alternate throws of the dice; and pieces can be removed by the opposing pieces if they are unprotected on a point (such pieces are known as 'blots'), though two or more pieces on a point protect it. Two obvious differences are that *tabula* was played with three dice, whereas backgammon is played with two, and that *tabula* used a thirty-six square board whereas backgammon uses a twenty-four point board (and lays out the board differently). The latter difference may however be more apparent than real: if we look again at the board from Ostia illustrated above (*CIL* 14.5317), a striking feature of it (which as far as I am aware has aroused no comment) is the line with the letter 'A', since it contains two sets of six 'A's whereas the other letters only have one set of six each. This can be explained by considering the beginning of the game: in modern backgammon the pieces are placed on predetermined points of the board, but there is no suggestion that that was the case in *tabula*. Pieces presumably had to be entered on to the board (as is suggested by 183.1 f., where at the roll of the dice 'discordans cauculus exit'); if this was done on to squares which both players had to travel at the game's start, the game would not only be very slow to begin at all (since many pieces would necessarily sit on unprotected squares and be immediately removed by the opponent's throw), but the effects of luck at the beginning would be much greater than any use of skill. So the double set of 'A' squares suggests that each player had his own set of six at the start of the course through which to enter his pieces on to the course proper, which begins with the 'B' squares, both players from that point moving their pieces along the same course. Backgammon overcomes these problems of the start by putting the pieces on predetermined points, but in effect both games use boards with twenty-four squares (and indeed in the game of *tabula* described by Agathias which is discussed above, the number of 'effective' squares on the board and to which reference is made is twenty-four, but there is no reason why it could not have had the additional twelve 'starter' squares). Backgammon also involves the pieces moving around the board in opposite directions, which further removes the element of luck from the start of the modern game (there

Commentary

is no suggestion that *tabula* pieces moved in this way: indeed 182.3 'qui quamvis parili scriptorum tramite currant' suggests they did not).

For the sake of completeness I give other references to the game of *tabula* which have not been discussed above, though they add nothing of significance: Aus. 11.1.25 f.; *AL* 70; 328; and possibly *AL* 8R (De alea); there are also some references which detail various attempts to ban the game (for which see 184.6 n.); and Baumgartner, *Untersuchungen*, 129 f. gives a catalogue which additionally includes all references to *ludus duodecim scriptorum*. Both the name and game of *tabula* survived into Romance languages, with e.g. It. *tavole*, Sp. *tablas*, Port. *taboas*, Fr. *tables* all being games of the backgammon type (and cf. also English *tavel* and *tables*). Backgammon, the modern British form of the game, arose in the early seventeenth century, but its continuity with earlier forms has been shown above; indeed, in its terminology of 'home and away tables' for sections of the board it demonstrates that continuity admirably.

Literature concerning *tabula, ludus duodecim scriptorum* and their descendants is large: see Baumgartner, *Untersuchungen*, passim, esp. 93 f.; 129 f.; Friedrich, *Symposium*, 81 f.; R.G. Austin, 'Roman Board Games I and II', *G&R* 4.1935.24 f. and 76 f.; T.J. Leary, 'Some Roman Board Games', *Akroterion* 35.1990.123 f.; *RE* 13.1979 f. 'Ludus duodecim scriptorum' (Lamer); G. Carbone, *Il centone 'De alea'*, Naples 2002 (a commentary on *AL* 8R); H.J.R. Murray, *A History of Board Games Other Than Chess*, Oxford 1952, 29 f.; R.C. Bell, *Board and Table Games From Many Civilizations*, revised edn, New York 1979, 1.30 f.; 34 f.; and (for sociological aspects) N. Purcell, 'Literate games: Roman urban society and the game of *alea*', in *Studies in Ancient Greek and Roman Society*, ed. R. Osborne, Cambridge 2004, 177 f.

182 (192R)

On tabula. The differently coloured pieces await the capricious throw, and white and red fight it out with each other. Although they travel along the same path of squares, he will win the victory palm whom good fortune favours.

superscr.: De tabula: the name of the game is derived from the board ('tabula') on which it was played; it is an indication of its popularity and ubiquity that the designation 'the board' was enough to identify it. The noun *tabula* could take qualifying adjectives if necessary: for instance *tabula latruncularia*, used for playing the game of *latrunculi* (Sen. *Ep.* 117.30); *tabula lusoria*, a board for playing both *latrunculi* and *ludus duodecim scriptorum* (Mart. 14.17, with Leary's commentary); or simply *tabula aleatoria* (Paul. *Fest.* p. 7.17 Lindsay). In this sequence of epigrams the board is actually termed 'alveolus' on the one occasion it is mentioned (183.1 n.), perhaps to avoid confusion (see also 184.1 n.). At *AL* 328.7

Commentary

and 9 Luxorius refers to the board as *tabula* and to a single game played on it as 'una tabula', and the superscription to the epigram terms the over-enthusiastic player it describes as 'tablista furiosus'; note also 187.7 'tablistis'; 187.8 'tabulae'.

1. discolor ... cauculus: singular for plural (cf. 187.8): two sets of fifteen pieces, differently coloured, were used in the game (see 182-5 intro. above); one set was usually white, the other red or black (white and red in the present epigrams; white and black at e.g. Petr. 33.2; *Laus Pis.* 194; and *AP* 9.482). *discolor* can mean either 'variegated in colour' with reference to a single item (as at e.g. Ovid *Am.* 3.2.78; Sen. *Nat. Quaest.* 1.3.1 'formam arcus discoloris'), or, as here, indicate that one item differs in colour from another, particularly pieces in board games (e.g. Ovid *Tr.* 2.477; Mart. 14.17.2; *AL* 187.8): on this see B. Zucchelli in *Mnemosynum, Studi in onore di Alfredo Ghiselli*, Bologna 1989, 557 f. For *cauculi*, the pieces or counters in the game, cf. *Laus Pis.* 192 f.; Mart. 2.48.2; 14.17-18; Juv. 11.132; Plin. *Ep.* 7.24.5 etc; for the form 'cauculus' rather than 'calculus' see note on 85.1 'cauculo'.

astat: it seems clear from the following lines that the verb does not refer to the beginning of a game, with the pieces 'standing ready' in their starting pools, but to the course of a game, where pieces 'await' the throw of the dice so that they can be moved (see 182-5 intro. above).

2. simul: the adverb implies reciprocity as also at 185.7, and e.g. Ven. Fort. *Carm.* 1.6.22 'certantesque simul'; Greg. Tur. *Hist. Franc.* 2.35 'simul locuti'; see P. Thielmann, *ALL* 7.1892.385.

3. parili scriptorum tramite: the *scripta*, as in the *ludus duodecim scriptorum*, are the squares on the board, which could be designated by letters or more abstract designs (see 182-5 intro. above): cf. Ovid *Ars* 3.363 f. 'est genus in totidem tenui ratione redactum / scriptula (*de Saumaise*; spicula (*codd.*)), quot menses lubricus annus habet'. The 'parilis trames' is the route set out on the board and along which the pieces travel, the phrase suggesting that they travelled in the same direction, unlike in modern backgammon.

4. is (W; his (AB)) capiet palmam: although 'his' could refer back to 'qui', W's 'is' is preferable because of the succeeding 'quem'; it thus refers to the winning player. It is, however, the only occasion on which any part of 'is' appears in the collection; the poet clearly avoids the pronoun (see 134.2 n.)

quem bona fata iuvant: it is true that a player needs luck to win, especially with the throws of the dice, but the author also rightly stresses the skill which is equally necessary for victory (183.5 f.); this is by no means only a game of chance.

Commentary
183 (193.1-6R)

Another. In a part of the board the urn-like dice-tower has been fixed, and it spews out the dice from the steps inside it; on their throw the differently coloured pieces exit, and the vagaries of fortune favour the two contestants. Skill and luck make for both of them their test: the one gives protection when things go badly, the other provides good fortune.

1. in parte alveoli: cf. Val. Max. 8.8.2, on Mucius Scaevola, a well known player of *ludus duodecim scriptorum* (see 184.8 n.), who 'alveo quoque et calculis interdum vacasse dicitur'. *Alveus / alveolus* are terms for the gaming board, whether used for *ludus / tabula* or other games (see *OLD* alveus 5; alveolus 2). The name may have arisen because some boards had raised sides to prevent the pieces or dice from rolling off (thus Lamer at *RE* 13.1981). The *pyrgus* (see following note) must have been on a part of the board where the dice could roll out freely without affecting play.

pyrgus: from Greek πύργος ('tower'), also known by the Latin name *turricula*, this is a tower-shaped container which had an arrangement resembling steps inside; the dice were put in at the top, and rolled down the steps and out onto the board. The implication here is that the *pyrgus* was affixed to the board ('resedit'), and the whole device was designed to prevent any cheating in the rolling of the dice; note also Mart. 14.16; Isid. *Or.* 18.61; and *AP* 9.482.24 Agathias. A *pyrgus* is shown in an illustration for December in the 354 Calendar (Stern, *Calendrier*, Pl. 13.1-2), and one has been reconstructed from pieces found with a *tabula* board in a tomb at Qustul in Nubia (see 182-5 intro. above). The *fritillus* served a similar function but was a dice-shaker rather than a fixture of the gaming board (see my note on Mart. 11.6.2).

velut urna: the comparison is not of shape, but of function: as lots were cast from an urn without favour or cheating, so the *pyrgus* assured fair play in the rolling of the dice.

2. internis ... gradibus: for these internal steps see the note above on *pyrgus*, and cf. Sid. *Ep.* 8.12.5 'hic tessera frequens eboratis resultatura pyrgorum gradibus expectat'; *AP* 9.482.24 Agathias 'πύργου δουρατέου κλίμακι κευθομένῃ' ('from the wooden *pyrgus* with its hidden ladder').

tesserulas: *tesserae / tesserulae* are six-sided dice, whereas *tali* are generally a four-sided variety; cf. Mart. 14.15; Isid. *Or.* 18.61; 64; Gell. 18.13.2; see however 184.2 n.

3. sub quarum iactu: cf. 182.1 'ancipiti sub iactu'.

discordans cauculus exit: for the 'discordans cauculus' see 182.1 n.; the verb 'exit' strongly implies, if it does not prove, that pieces were introduced onto the board by throws of the dice (exiting from a starting pool), whereas in modern backgammon they are placed on the board on

Commentary

fixed starting points: see 182-5 intro. above. Thus the pieces are here being moved on throws of the dice from their starting pool onto the lines of the board from which they will start the game proper (the 'A' line in the layout of the board from Ostia described in the 182-5 intro. above). As the poet goes on to say, even these preliminaries involve luck and skill.

5. his (Baehrens; hic (A)) proprium (A; ambiguum (Scriverius)) ... periclum: Baehrens' small emendation to A's text is necessary, because 'ars et fortuna' making 'periclum' for themselves is pointless; 'his' is needed to refer to the two contestants of line 4, and 'proprium periclum' belongs to them. 'periclum' needs to be understood in its neutral sense of 'trial' or 'test' rather than its adverse sense of 'danger', because the following line shows that 'ars et fortuna' can act beneficially for the players; for *peric(u)lum facere* see *TLL* 10.1.1458.58 f.

<ars> (*suppl.* **de Saumaise**): a syllable has dropped out of the text, and de Saumaise's supplement looks certain: it provides the necessary monosyllabic feminine substantive to accompany 'fortuna' in line 5 and balance 'haec' and 'illa' in line 6; for the thought cf. Ter. *Ad.* 739 f. 'ita vitast hominum quasi quom ludas tesseris: / si illud quod maxume opus est iactu non cadit, / illud quod cecidit forte, id arte ut corrigas'. For the omission of words by A elsewhere, cf. 98.4 and 102.5.

6. haec ... illa ...: since *fortuna* rather than *ars* provides good luck ('favet'), it is *ars* that protects against bad luck; 'haec' is therefore *ars*, and 'illa' is *fortuna*.

cavet ... favet: for similar rhymes, cf. Plaut. *Pseud.* 64 'amores ... mores'; Ter. *Eun.* 236 'pannis ... annis'; Fronto 34.10 vdH 'palantes ... balantes'; Apul. *Met.* 9.14.4 'saevus ... scaevus'; Sen. *Ep.* 63.11 'unica ... tunica'; with *LHS* 2.704 f.

184 (193.7-14R)

Such are the positions for war which have now been drawn for a game of *tabula*, and the roll of the dice signals the start. The players fight out battles with their different throws of the dice, to see whether red or white has the luck and carries off the prize. Many people avidly nurture a ruinous passion, so that mounting indolence does not besmirch their leisure time. Its inventor Palamedes was extremely fond of this creation, as was Mucius, who excelled at it with an equal talent.

1. conposita est tabulae nunc talis formula belli (edd.); ... nunc malis formula bellis (A) ... non tristis formula belli (Shackleton Bailey); ... simulati formula belli (Courtney); ... nunc magni formula belli (Watt): this is a problematic line. A's 'malis' has to be emended, because it is unmetrical and affords no sense: 'talis formula

355

Commentary

belli', printed by all editors except SB (who in his text athetises 'nunc malis'), involves minimal change and gives reasonable sense ('talis' being construed as a nominative adjective, not an ablative noun). 'nunc' is of particular note, because if it is correct it suggests a close connection between this and the preceding epigram, which raises questions over the separation of the epigrams (see 182-5 intro. above). If, as I have argued above, 183 describes the procedure for the moving of the pieces in the opening of the game, before the game proper gets under way, 'nunc' would have a significant force: the pieces have *now* been entered onto the board in their starting positions, and battle-lines are drawn accordingly ('talis formula belli'). 'tabulae' then means 'for this particular game of *tabula*' (cf. *AL* 328.9 f. Luxorius 'hic si forte unam tabulam non arte sed errans / vicerit'). The conjectures detailed above (SB's from his app. crit.; Courtney's at *C&M* 40.1989.205; Watt's at *C&M* 47.1996.257) seem to me less convincing than such an explanation, and therefore, like Riese, I would not follow Scriverius in separating this epigram from that preceding (though I have retained the separation in the text to adhere to SB's numeration).

2. missa ... tessera principium: if the above interpretation is correct, 'principium' refers to the start of the game proper, after the pieces move from their starting squares (see also 183.3 n.).

3. proelia: for the metaphor of war to describe the game in these epigrams, cf. 'belli' (184.1); 'belli ... simulacra' (185.2); 'pugna' (185.7); and 'victi ... victor' (185.8). *Tabula* is a war game in that pieces can be removed from the board by the opponent's pieces under certain circumstances; it is also a race game, in that the objective is to be the first to move all your pieces through the course of the board and past the finish (see 182-5 intro. above).

talo (A; fato (de Saumaise)): *talus* must here be used as equivalent to *tessera*, the six-sided die used in the game of *tabula* (see 183.2 n.), so de Saumaise's conjecture is unnecessary. The choice of word is influenced by 'tessera' in the preceding line and the poet's practice of avoiding repetition of substantives, which sometimes leads him to use imperfect synonyms (see 81.5 n.).

4. nitidus: referring to the whiteness of the natural ivory from which the white pieces are made (see 185.1 n.); the adjective is used of ivory also at Ovid *Met.* 2.3.

praemia: the game is played for a prize (the following lines suggest it may have been money), as often elsewhere (e.g. *AL* 70.10 f.; 318 superscr.; 328.8; 495R; 497R; 499R; 500R).

5. pascitur a multis: who are 'multi'? It seems the poet has moved

Commentary

away from his mention of the prize for a specific game to a generalised *sententia* about the many who play board games for money. If so, his observation is commonplace: e.g. Ovid *Ars* 3.373; Mart. 14.19.1; Juv. 14.4; ps.-Cypr. *Lib. de aleatoribus* passim, esp. *PL* 4.831; and cf. Friedrich, *Symposium*, 88 f.

6. ne foedet: the argument of this line is worth comment (and unexpected after the preceding remark about 'damnosa voluptas'), since it implies that games have to be played for money in order to keep people interested, and people who are not interested in them necessarily vegetate. To some extent this reads like a pre-emptive strike against those who wanted to ban the playing of games for money and gambling generally, such as Justinian (*Cod. Just.* 3.43), the bishops at the council of Elvira in the early fourth century (canon 79, *Concilium Eliberritanum*, ed. G. Martínez Díez and F. Rodríguez, *La Colección canónica hispana 4*, Madrid 1984, 268), and others (cf. Isid. *Or.* 18.68). Palamedes was similarly said to have invented dice and associated games to alleviate soldiers' boredom and avert mutiny: 'nam et tabulam ipse invenit ad comprimendas otiosi seditiones exercitus, ut Varro testatur' (Serv. ap. Verg. *Aen.* 2.81); this comment therefore makes a good prelude to the mention of Palamedes in the next line.

7. inventor ... Palamedes: Palamedes, a hero of legendary cleverness, was said to have invented, inter alia, κύβοι (Soph. frag. 479 Radt), *tesserae* (Plin. *Nat. Hist.* 7.202; Paus. 2.20.3), *tali* (Sid. Ap. *Carm.* 23.491 f.) and *tabula* (Serv. loc. cit. 6 n.; schol. ap. Stat. *Ach.* 1.93); see *RE* 18.1.2506. The final syllable of this Greek name is here irregularly short; for similar instances in late poetry see Müller, *De Re Metrica*, 423, and for prosodical irregularity with proper nouns in this collection, see p. 24.

nimie: the adverb is late and rare: e.g. Pallad. 4.10.27; Aug. *Conf.* 2.9; Macr. *Sat.* 6.6.6; with *NW* 2.595.

8. Mucius: Q. Mucius Scaevola was a famous player of *ludus duodecim scriptorum* (Cic. *De Orat.* 1.217; Val. Max. 8.8.2; Quint. *Inst.* 11.2.38; with *RE* 13.1980); this again suggests the essential equivalence of *ludus* and *tabula* (see 182-5 intro. above).

185 (194R)

Another. The produce of India affords a pleasant contest for friends, but nevertheless involves mock battles. For red clashes with white in equal formation, so that they may conquer each other with heavy losses. Alternate shakes of the dice roll out varied numbers, and the 'peaks' and 'troughs' put the players' fortunes to the test. War and peace are joined with each other into one by this game, when the victor triumphs in the spoils of the vanquished as a friend.

Commentary

1. Indica materies: the equipment used for this game is of high quality, and the reference to ivory foreshadows the following two epigrams about the elephant, especially 187.5 f., where the specific use of ivory in the manufacture of *tabula* items is highlighted. See further R.G. Austin, *G&R* 4.1935.80 f.

blandum certamen amicis: a key theme is introduced, that although *tabula* is a competitive war game it is in essence only a pleasant diversion for friends, and should be played in the appropriate manner (and not like the demented *tablista* of *AL* 328 Luxorius, or the losing player in the *Cento de alea* who trudges home penniless and in tears (*AL* 8.105f.R)). Dice games elsewhere are labelled *blandum* (e.g. Ovid *Pont.* 1.5.46; Mart. 4.14.7; 5.84.3) and *certamen* (Quint. *Inst.* 11.2.38; Aus. 11.1.25).

2. belli ... simulacra: see 106.5 n. for the phrase; 184.3 n. for *tabula* as a war game.

3. acie aequali: this is not synonymous with 'parili tramite' (182.3), but a reference to the fact that the forces in the game are equally balanced, each player having fifteen pieces (see 182-5 intro.).

4. gravibus damnis: these losses during the play of the game are the 'elimination' or 'killing' of single, unaccompanied pieces by an opponent's piece which lands on the same square; such pieces have to leave the board and be re-entered from the start, to their player's obvious disadvantage (see 182-5 intro. above).

se domet alteruter: 'se' is here used in a reciprocal sense (as at 104.2): compare Verg. *Aen.* 7.472 'certatim sese Rutuli exhortantur in arma'; Hor. *Ars* 119 'sibi convenientia'; Apul. *Met.* 4.5.6 'secum eos animadverteram conloquentes'; Min. Fel. *Oct.* 9.2 'occultis se notis ... noscunt'; in descriptions of battles 'adversum se' becomes common in this sense (e.g. Iren. *Contra Haer.* 4.9.2; Dict. Cret. 2.4 etc.); and see further *OLD* se 8; P. Thielmann, *ALL* 7.1892.380 f.; *LHS* 2.177. For *alteruter* in contexts of reciprocity, where it even becomes used adjectivally (e.g. Aug. *Ep.* 211.10 'alterutro delectantur ardore'), see Löfstedt, *Per. Aeth.* p. 337.

5. missus: of throws of the dice also at *AL* 8.43R, and cf. 184.2 'missa ... tessera'.

6. collis et ima probant (A); colus et urna probant (de Saumaise); talus et urna probant (Shackleton Bailey): 'collis et ima' provides the most obscure technical phrase in the whole group of epigrams; '*non intelligitur*' says SB (app. crit.), basing his conjecture 'talus et urna' on de Saumaise's 'colus et urna'. But a strong suggestion that the text is sound is given by *AL* 8.49f.R, where a board for playing *tabula* is described:

Commentary

Vos, O Calliope, precor adspirate canenti,
quae loca, quive habeant homines, ubi sistere detur.
In summo collem, qui plurimus; alter ab illo
est locus, quem iuxta sequitur, qui deinde sub ipso
hic locus est partis semper sublimis: at illum
quinque tenent ebuli bacis minioque rubentem.
Terna tibi haec primum fundo volvuntur in imo.
Sunt alii, quos ipse via sibi repperit usus.

Although this is hopelessly obscure (Carbone's commentary is some help), 'collis' at line 50 recalls 'collis et ima' in this epigram, and appears to refer to a specific part of the board. The main clue from the present epigram is that the interplay between *collis* and *ima* is a crucial test of the players' skill ('probant'), and it is therefore a not unreasonable assumption that it is better for pieces to be on the 'collis' than in the 'ima'. Thus, for example, 'collis' might represent the squares closest to the end of the board, and 'ima' might represent the squares at the start (in backgammon this would be the 'home' and 'away' tables respectively), or 'collis' might represent all the playing squares of the board, and 'ima' the place from which taken pieces have to restart. Other explanations might be equally plausible, but there is no convincing reason to doubt that 'collis et ima' is sound textually, though not enough is known about the terminology of the game (which might also display some local variants) to be sure of the precise meaning. Equally obscure terminology can be found in the names Agathias gives to some squares on the board at *AP* 9.482.9 f.

For similar use of the neuter plural *ima* as a substantive, cf. Verg. *Georg.* 1.401 'at nebulae magis ima petunt'; Ovid *Met.* 7.278; with *TLL* 7.1.1400.13 f.

7. simul: suggesting reciprocity, as at 182.2 (see note).

186 (195R)

On the elephant. The beast, awesome with its tusked trunk, goes on its way; rich India has sent it to our shores. But though the elephant fights with its colossal trunk and guarantees death with its fierce tusks, nevertheless it has been tamed completely and carries out the orders of the master who sits on it, and where the mahout wants, the wild animal is forced to go. Human power can ameliorate feral savageness. Look, the great beast is afraid of a puny man!

The final group of epigrams in the collection consists of two on the elephant, the first concentrating on the power and fierceness of the beast, which can nevertheless be tamed by humans, the second focusing more on the uses to which the dead animal can be put, particularly as regards

Commentary

its ivory. It at first sight seems odd that the animals are imported from India (line 2) if this collection of poems was written in and describes Africa. But written sources are clear that the (North) African elephant had disappeared over time from its habitat in what is now Morocco, Algeria and Tunisia, exploited for use in war by the Carthaginians, and for amphitheatres and ivory by Romans (Pliny comments on this at *Nat. Hist.* 8.7). They were around in the early third century (Solinus 25.2), and a mosaic at Piazza Armerina shows some being shipped to Italy in the later fourth century. But Themistius (*Orat.* 10.140a), also in the fourth century, says they had died out, and Isidore in the seventh century says that only India now produces them, though Africa used to (*Or.* 12.2.16). The explanation for this must be that the large African bush elephants (known now as African elephants) have their habitat south of the Sahara, whilst a smaller species or sub-species (*Loxodonta cyclotis*) is a forest elephant now found only in western equatorial Africa. It is the latter animal which had been eliminated from North Africa, evidenced by the fact that ancient writers describe the African elephant as smaller than the Indian (e.g. Polyb. 5.84.6; Plin. *Nat. Hist.* 8.27), whilst the reverse would now be the case. Importation of Indian elephants to North Africa in the fifth and sixth centuries is therefore plausible. See further H.H. Scullard, *The Elephant in the Greek and Roman World*, London 1974, 30 f.; Toynbee, *Animals*, 32 f.

1. cornuto ... rostro: the expression is strange, because *cornua* naturally refers to the elephant's tusks, but *rostrum* to its trunk: thus Varro, *Ling. Lat.* 7.39 'cum ... in Lucanis Pyrrhi bello primum vidissent apud hostis elephantos, ... quadripedes cornutas (sc. appellaverunt); nam quos dentes multi dicunt, sunt cornua'; Isid. *Or.* 12.2.14 'rostrum autem proboscida dicitur, quoniam illo pabulum ori admovet; et est angui similis, vallo munitus eburno'; Plin. *Nat. Hist.* 8.7 (where Pliny specifically states that the proper word for 'tusks' is 'dentes'); ibid. 18.2. Presumably the author intentionally refers to both tusks and trunk in a composite expression, because he goes on to describe them separately in lines 3-4; 'cornuto ... ore' at Mart. *Spect.* 22(19).3 is a similar if more elegant expression, though the text is problematic (see Housman, *Class. Pap.* 3.1101 n. 1).

procedit: perhaps in a show or procession of some kind?

2. oris (A); †orist† (Shackleton Bailey); agris (Burman); haris (Watt): the prosody of 'oris' with a short first syllable is unprecedented and possibly unacceptable in a disyllabic word which begins with a long syllable and was in common use. But there are irregularities, if not as extreme, elsewhere in the collection (see p. 24); at any rate, proposed emendations are not convincing (because a balance to 'dives India' is required), and ms. 'nostris ... oris' gives the right sense. I therefore accept

Commentary

it; if the prosody is considered unacceptable the best option is to obelise, as SB does.

3. pugnet: for the elephant using its trunk as a weapon in battle cf. Arist. *Part. Anim.* 2.17 (661a.25 f.); 4.6 (682b.35 f.).

proboscide: the long first syllable is another instance of irregular prosody (the irregularity recurs at 187.1); it is probably influenced by the preposition 'pro', as *TLL* suggests (10.2.1478.27 f.).

barrus: the noun is rare, occurring first in extant literature at Hor. *Epod.* 12.1 (see Watson's note) and sporadically thereafter, and it is perhaps of Indian provenance (Isid. *Or.* 12.2.14 with *TLL* 2.1757.34 f.). The cognate verb and noun *barrire* and *barritus* are used of elephants' trumpeting: cf. Veg. *Mil.* 3.24.5 'elephanti in proeliis magnitudine corporum, barritus horrore, formae ipsius novitate homines equosque conturbant'; *SHA* Geta 5.5 'elephanti barriunt'. As often (see 81.5 n.), the poet likes variety for the nouns to denote the animal in this pair of poems; also *elephans, belua, monstrum* and *ferus*.

4. spondeat ... interitum: the verb is here used as an effective intensification of 'minari': the elephant's tusks do not merely threaten death, they guarantee it.

dentibus: the usual word for 'tusks': see 1 n. above.

5. edomitus (edd.; et domitus (A)): the function of 'et' in A's text is peculiar: it draws especial emphasis to the participle ('nevertheless it carries out (and what is more, tamely!) the orders of ...'), but in an idiom which merely emphasises the obvious. The slight emendation made by earlier editors (Burman and Meyer) gives the participle a more convincing emphasis, and I therefore follow them.

iussa (A); iura (Shackleton Bailey): Courtney (*C&M* 40.1989.197) points out that although SB prints 'iura' in his text without further comment, A reads 'iussa'. If 'iura' is merely an error, it is an interesting one (cf. Ovid *Met.* 2.47 f. (of Phaethon and Sol) 'rogat ... alipedum ius et moderamen equorum'); there is however nothing wrong with 'iussa', and it should remain.

magistri: the *magister* here is the mahout who controls the animal (as at Ovid *Tr.* 4.6.7; Pliny uses the term *rector* (*Nat. Hist.* 8.3)); if the poet envisages a battle context, as seems likely from lines 3-4 and 'ferus' in line 6, the Indian elephant could also carry armed soldiers in a howdah, whereas the African was not large enough.

6. monitor: in this context the *monitor* is most plausibly the same person as the *magister*, unless he is an additional attendant who walks in front of the beast and assists in guiding it (thus, for example, a *monitor* can also be a *paedagogus* (cf. Sen. *Ep.* 94.8)).

Commentary

7. mutare: here meaning *domare*, because the implication is of change for the better, as at 99.7 (see note); compare Tac. *Hist.* 1.52.1 'sordes et avaritiam Fontei Capitonis ... mutaverat'; Pallad. 3.25.2; with *TLL* 8.1724.60 f.

187 (196R)

Another. Prince of great animals, the elephant, savage with its trunk, terrifies with its black bulk and flashes with its white tusks. But though the beast which so bristles with danger of various kinds should be fled from, the death of a trapped animal is nevertheless worth a great deal. For those bones of mountainous strength on which we gaze come in useful for man's purposes. From them comes the sceptre for consuls, ornament for tables, their paraphernalia for *tabula* players, and the differently coloured pieces for *tabula*. This is the eternal changeability of the human condition: in death he becomes a plaything, who was before a terror.

1. monstrorum princeps: for *monstrum* of elephants cf. Sil. It. 9.570 f. 'appellitur atra / mole fera, et monstris componitur Itala pubes'; 10.101 (and frequently); Drac. *Laud. Dei* 1.307 'eburnea monstra'. For *princeps* of animals cf. Varro *Ling. Lat.* 6.12 'princeps gregis' (a ram); Manil. 2.227 (a bull); Mart. 13.85 (a fish); Hyg. *Astr.* 2.24.1 (a lion).

proboscide: for the irregular prosody see 186.3 n.

2. mole nigra: all mss (ABV) reverse the order of these words, with A and B showing further errors. For *moles* of elephants cf. Sil. It. loc. cit. 1 n. (and see also 127.1 n.); and for *niger* of elephants cf. Hor. *Epod.* 12.1 (with Watson's note); Sil. It. 9.240; Mart. 6.77.8 (with Grewing's note); there is a suggestion of black as the colour of foreboding and evil (see 173.4 n.).

micat: suggestive of rapid movement as well as of flashing light; see 119.3 n. The white tusks contrast with the black body (cf. the description of the cuttlefish at 96.2, with note).

3. vario ... malo ... gliscat: *gliscere* is rarely used of animate subjects, though here it perfectly suits the elemental power of the beast and the fear it engenders (cf. Sil. It. 5.512 f. 'arenti robore gliscens ... Volcanus'); 'vario ... malo' qualifies 'gliscat', not 'fugienda', despite the word order.

4. excepti (Shackleton Bailey); ex certis (codd.); expertis (Burman sen.); excelsi (Watt): the mss text is meaningless. SB rightly criticises Burman senior's conjecture 'expertis', which has won general favour with editors: Burman junior in his commentary interpreted 'pretiosa' in the following phrase in the sense 'costly to the hunter' (since hunting elephants involves expense and danger), with 'expertis' referring to those

362

Commentary

who have killed elephants (which is awkward Latin in any case). But it is clear from what follows that the animal's death is valuable rather than costly (because of the ivory it provides); what is here needed, therefore, is a link between the awesome power of the animal (lines 1-3) and the value it creates in death (lines 5 f.). SB's 'excepti' provides that in introducing the concept of hunting and killing more emphatically than Burman's 'expertis'; *excipere* in a hunting context means 'to lie in wait for an animal', 'to attack an animal when it comes along', or 'to catch and kill an animal in a trap' (cf. Verg. *Ecl.* 3.18; Hor. *Carm.* 3.12.12; with SB, *Towards a Text*, 26; and Leary's note on Mart. 14.30.1). Watt's 'excelsi' (*C&M* 47.1996.257) omits the hunting reference and is less convincing.

mors pretiosa: there is a curious and elephantine parallel at Petr. 119.14 f. 'et ultimus Hammon / Afrorum excutitur, ne desit belua dente / ad mortes pretiosa'. The phrase 'ad mortes pretiosa' is difficult to understand, but the meaning '... whose tusks make an elephant precious enough to kill elephants' is feasible, given the general context of other beasts sought by Rome which are not killed (i.e. elephants are difficult to capture alive, because they are valuable dead and therefore often killed).

5. montani roboris ossa: 'montani roboris' is a striking phrase, with the adjective used in a metaphorical sense it does not appear to have elsewhere. *Mons* is however well enough attested as a comparator of size (cf. Sen. *Thy.* 1083 f.; Drac. *Laud. Dei* 1.286), and Isidore (*Or.* 12.2.14) even managed to derive the noun *elephantus* from Greek λόφος ('mountain'). *Ossa* is rarely used of elephant tusks, *TLL* (9.2.1098.71 f.) giving only one example in Prudentius (*Peristeph.* 10.150) and two in Arnobius (*Nat.* 1.39; 6.13), all of which are characterised as 'per contemptum dictum'. But there is no contempt in this instance, rather a pathetic contrast between the mountainous animal and the tusks it provides for human use by its death.

6. humanis veniunt usibus apta: this line is so similar to Drac. *Laud. Dei* 1.579 f. that imitation is likely: 'quod generant terrae, quod flammae, pontus et aer / usibus humanis data sunt haec cuncta venire' (see further p. 7). For *venire* in the sense of *esse* or *fieri*, see J. van Wageningen, *Mnemosyne* 47.1919.343 f. (the earliest example he cites is Verg. *Aen.* 5.344 'gratior et pulchro veniens in corpore virtus', where 'veniens' supplies a missing present participle of *esse*; cf. also Prop. 1.18.14; 2.34.81; the usage is frequent in Manilius (e.g. 4.375; 382; 457 etc.)). The idiom of *devenire* = *fieri* should be particularly noted (at e.g. Soranus p. 54.15 Rose; with *TLL* 5.1.850.51 f.; 77 f.), since it leads to Fr. *devenir*; and *ire* also is found in the sense *esse* (see my note on Aus. *Epig.* 53.7).

7. consulibus sceptrum: for consular sceptres, a late emblem of that office, cf. Amm. Marc. 29.2.15; *SHA* Aurel. 13.4; Claud. 1.205; Prud.

Peristeph. 10.148 f.; Cass. *Var.* 6.1.6 (AD 511) 'consulatus te decoramus (i.e. Theoderic) insignibus, pinge ... validam manum victoriali scipione nobilita'. Although ivory is only specified by Prudentius amongst these references, sceptres made of it are known from other contexts (such as those awarded to triumphators (e.g. Juv. 10.43)), and in the considerable number of extant ivory diptychs from late Antiquity which depict consuls, the consul usually holds a sceptre in his left hand; see W.F. Volbach, *Elfenarbeiten der Spätantike und des frühen Mittelalters*, 3rd. edn, Mainz am Rhein 1976, nos 1-65a with Pls 1-37; C.L. Connor, *The Color of Ivory*, Princeton 1998, 60 f.; fig 2.

mensis decus: for ivory used in the manufacture of tables, usually table legs, see Mart. 14.91 with Leary's note.

arma tablistis: cf. 185.1 'Indica materies' (with note), which shows the use of ivory in the manufacture of the equipment for board games; since the *tabula* pieces are the subject of the following line, the reference here should be to the dice and perhaps the board. The syncopated form *tablista* occurs also at *AL* 328 *superscr.* Luxorius, and reflects Greek ταβλιστής (found at *CGL* 2.450.62); the Greek equivalent of Latin *tabula* was invariably τάβλα / τάβλη. For similar cases of syncope, which can survive in Romance reflexes, cf. *saeculum / saeclum*; *fabula / fabla*; *stabula / stabla*; there is a long list at *App. Probi, Gramm. Lat.* 4.197.20 f. (see also G. Grösser, *ALL* 6.1889.117 f.; Müller, *De Re Metrica*, 456 f.); and for *tabla* specifically cf. Fr. 'table'; Sp. 'tabla' etc. (*REW* 8514).

8. discolor ... cauculus: cf. 182.1 'discolor ... cauculus', with note; one set of the pieces would have been naturally-coloured ivory, the other painted red or black.

9. haec est humanae ... sortis: for this type of concluding sententia in the collection see 168.5-6 n. This one is not very apposite, because elephants do not provide an example of 'humana sors', neither does their fate in being turned into artefacts particularly reflect 'humana sors'. The intention seems to be a generalised 'the powerful dead can no longer terrify', but the expression of the sentiment is more impressive than its connection to the context; indeed, one might wonder whether it properly belongs to this epigram, though the sententia which concludes the previous epigram argues for a similar conclusion being required here.

188 (197R)

On circus races. A circus is a mirror of the heavens, and the learned men of old fashioned its form in accordance with numbers of the celestial region. For the openings of the starting stalls represent both the months, which are born in groups of twelve, and the signs of the zodiac, which the golden sun passes as it rushes by. The horses reflect the seasons, the colours the elements; the charioteer attaches four horses to his chariot, as does Phoebus. The starting stalls shut in the chariots with hinged doors for each; Janus, raising his flag, gives them the order to start. But when the bars are drawn back and let loose the chariots, and one has got to go in front of the others, they strive to complete orbits with circuits of the turning posts; for the two axes of the track illustrate rising and setting, and the spina lies between them like a great ocean, and the top of the obelisk is at the mid-point of the centre. The race for victory also concludes with seven circuits, which is the number of planetary orbits that ring the heavens in like manner. A two-horse chariot is always dedicated to the Moon, a four-horse to the Sun, and single horses are traditionally dedicated to the Castors. Our races are founded on matters divine, and their esteem has grown great by their honour of the gods.

The final epigram of the collection, one of the longest and most interesting, presents an allegorical interpretation of the layout of the circus and the process of chariot racing in astronomical, cosmological and other terms. Thus the number of starting gates mirrors the number of months in the year and the number of signs of the zodiac, the number of horses in a *quadriga* mirrors the seasons, the four factional colours stand for the elements, the seven laps of a race represent the orbits of the seven planets, the spina of the circus is the ocean, and so on. This type of interpretation was popular in late Antiquity, and extended examples similar to this poem occur in Corippus (*Laud. Just.* 1.314-44), Cassiodorus (*Var.* 3.51), Isidore (*Or.* 18.36 f.), John Malalas (7.4-5, p. 135 Thurn) and John Lydus (*De Mens.* 4.30), with examples of similar thinking in Dracontius, Martianus Capella and others. To a limited extent the origins of such interpretations can be found in earlier authors (in some fragments of Charax of Pergamum (cos. AD 147), for example, which are collected at *FGH* 103 F32 f. Jacoby and are a source for John Malalas' account of circus cosmology; and also at Tert. *De Spect.* 8-9, which may in turn borrow from or derive from an earlier account by Suetonius in a lost work, the fragments of which (almost entirely from Tertullian) are collected at Reifferscheid, p. 332 f.), but the elaboration into this type of fully-worked allegory is probably much later, all such extant treatments being from the sixth century onwards. Interdependence between the authors of the various accounts is difficult to prove with any degree of certainty, not least because much of the symbolism is so obvious that it would occur to anyone writing on the subject, and many of the individual topics are common (as will be clear from the following notes).

Hanfmann's comment (*Season Sarcophagus*, 163) summarises the intellectual climate in which these allegorical accounts were written: 'That this interpretation of the universe was attempted in spite of all logical contradictions is indicative of the transcendental trend in the

Commentary

mentality of the late Empire; the political, social or historical explanation of Roman customs does not satisfy the late Roman scholars, for whom the phenomena of their world have meaning and value only as reflections of a higher divine universe'. In this connection it is notable that the author of the present epigram is content to couch his allegory in, and sum it up with, wholly pagan sentiments: 'divinis constant nostra spectacula rebus, / gratia magna quibus crevit honore deum' (lines 19-20). Other authors could find a Christian interpretation (e.g. Coripp. *Laud. Just.* 1.341 f.) or warn readers of the pagan evils of the circus (Tert. *De Spect.* 8-9; Isid. *Or.* 18.41.

The popularity of the circus and chariot racing in North Africa at a late date is well attested: there is further evidence in this collection (e.g. 180.7; 181.5); Luxorius has many epigrams about charioteers and the circus (*AL* 288; 301; 307; 308; 315; 319; 322; 323); monumental stone-built circuses are known from remains at Carthage, Utica, Cherchel, Sousse and Lepcis Magna; and Carthaginian enthusiasm for racing was often remarked (e.g. Tert. *De Spect.* 16; Aug. *Conf.* 6.7; Salv. *De Gub. Dei* 6.12 etc.), and produced more extant mosaics on the subject than anywhere else (Dunbabin, *North Africa*, ch. 6). The circus at Carthage was probably in use until well into the sixth, if not seventh, century (see Humphrey, *Circus at Carthage*, 31; 57).

Further on circus arenas see Humphrey, *Circuses*; for the allegorical interpretations see esp. Averil Cameron's commentary on Coripp. *Laud. Just.* 1.314 f.; E. Castorina's introduction to his commentary on Tert. *De Spect.*, lxxxiv f. (where he analyses, arguably over-analyses, the individual allegorising topics in all the various accounts listed above: he catalogues forty-five such topics, with Isidore displaying the most at twenty-eight, Corippus the least at nine, and this epigram being in the middle with fifteen); P. Wuilleumier, 'Cirque et astrologie', *MEFR* 44.1927.184 f. (dealing with astrological texts, which are only tangentially considered in the following notes); E.B. Lyle, 'The Circus as Cosmos', *Latomus* 43.1984.827 f.; and S.T. Stevens, 'The Circus Poems in the Latin Anthology' in Humphrey, *Circus at Carthage*, 1.172 f.

To assist with understanding of the following notes a schematic plan of a circus for chariot-racing, showing the main features of what was a standardised layout and design, will be helpful:

Commentary

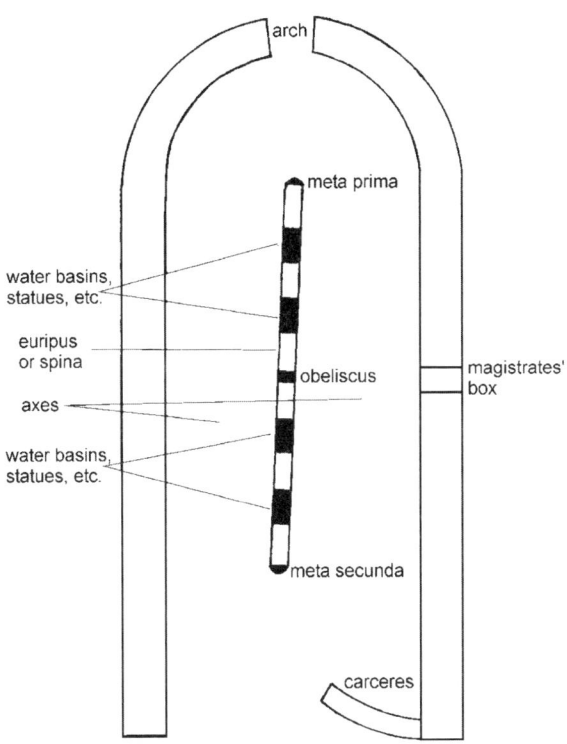

1. docta vetustas: i.e. 'docti viri vetustatis', a phrase similar to 'antiquitas docta' at Cass. *Var.* 1.10.5; Corippus says at the beginning of his allegorical digression on the circus 'solis honore novi grati spectacula circi / antiqui sanxere patres ...' (*Laud. Just.* 1.314 f.).

2. condidit ad (Barth; et (codd.)) numeros: the first question to consider is whose is the 'forma' which 'docta vetustas condidit', because the pronoun 'cui' in line 1 could depend on either 'circus' or 'poli' (or indeed 'imago'). This is bound up with the particular meaning here of 'condidit', which could be either 'set up', 'founded' or 'described in writing' (*OLD* condo 10 and 14(b)). If, however, men of old founded the shape of the circus (when 'cui' picks up 'circus'), they obviously cannot be said also ('et') to have founded the 'numeri limitis aetherii', but it is precisely the author's point in all that follows that the form of the circus reflects astronomical and astrological phenomena, and it would well accord with this that men of old designed the shape of the circus on astronomical / astrological principles; Barth's correction of 'ad' for 'et' would then be necessary. The alternative interpretation of this opening couplet, that men of old set down in writing the form of the 'polus' and the 'numeri limitis aetherii' (when 'cui' picks up 'poli' or 'imago poli'), is much inferior,

Commentary

because a connection between the forms of the circus and the heavens ('circus imago poli') is then not effectively made. Barth's conjecture should therefore be accepted.

numeros limitis aetherii: much that follows is quite literally concerned with numbers, beginning with the twelve 'ostia' which mirror the twelve months of the year. The noun 'numeros' should be understood accordingly, rather than taking the whole phrase as a more abstract 'clockwork of the heavens'. 'limes aetherius' is synonymous with the 'polus' of line 1, 'the heavens as defined by their *limes*', that is 'the region of the heavens'; cf. Stat. *Theb.* 1.156 f. 'quid si peteretur crimine tanto / limes uterque poli …'.

3. duodenigenas (Heinsius); duodecim annis genas (codd.); duodena anni (Shackleton Bailey); duodena vagos (Heinsius): although SB (app. crit.) comments '*forma vix probabili*' of Heinsius' generally accepted conjecture 'duodenigenas', because the formation of a distributive numeral with a '-genas' suffix is unparalleled and presumably a humorous coinage ('born by the twelve'; cf. *unigena*), it gives good sense and since it is a ἅπαξ λεγόμενον would explain the muddle in the mss. This author is also demonstrably partial to unusual *-genus* and *-gena* compounds (cf. 83.1; 106.3*; 109.8; 125.4*; 167.3*; 178.2: those marked with an asterisk are ἅπαξ). While SB's conjecture would give the required sense, it does not account for mss 'genas' and is also open to the objection that it introduces the metrical irregularity of hiatus at the main hexameter caesura (although there are examples of the phenomenon elsewhere in the collection, it is questionable practice to add to them by emendation (see p. 23 f.)).

ostendunt ostia menses: the jingle 'ostendunt ostia' is no doubt intentional. The 'ostia' here are the openings of the starting pens or *carceres* from which the chariots issued on the commencement of a race (see also 'cardinibus propriis' at line 7 below, with note); *ostium* is found with this meaning also at Stat. *Theb.* 6.617; Aus. 27.10.11; Cass. *Var.* 3.51.4; 7 (see 4 n. below). Twelve was the usual number of *carceres* in the circus layout (first at Jul. Obseq. *Prod.* 70 (42 BC); also e.g. Aus. 27.10.11; Sid. *Carm.* 23.317 f.; with Humphrey, *Circuses*, 136 f.). This is, surprisingly (since their writers like the obvious), the only instance in the extant allegories of the parallel drawn between the *carceres* and the twelve months of the year.

4. quaeque … astra: for the twelve signs of the zodiac being termed *astra*, cf. Manil. 1.540 f. 'quantis bis sena ferantur / finibus astra'. This same parallel is drawn at Cass. *Var.* 3.51.4 'bis sena quippe ostia ad duodecim signa posuerunt' and John Malalas 7.4 'τὰς δὲ δεκαδύο θύρας τοὺς δώδεκα οἴκους ἱστόρησεν τοῦ ζωδιακοῦ κύκλου τοῦ διοικοῦντος τὴν γῆν' ('he explained that the twelve gates were the twelve houses of the circle of the zodiac which goes round the earth'; 'he' is Charax of Pergamum, Malalas' source, on whom see intro. above).

Commentary

meat (BW; mea (A)); ineat (Riese): SB (*Towards a Text*, 26) rightly defends 'meat' against Riese's emendation, on the grounds that an indicative verb is desirable and that *meare* (or its compound forms) takes an object on other occasions also: e.g. Hor. *Sat.* 1.6.94 'aevum remeare peractum'; *ML* 70.5 Courtney (= *CE* 434.5 f., with p. 855) 'dogmata Pythagorae sensusque meavi sophorum / et lyricos legi'.

cursim: here 'at the gallop' (cf. the derivation from *currere*, often used of horses galloping), as at Plaut. *Poen.* 567 'hoc cito et cursim est agendum'; the swift passage of the sun is mirrored by the swift laps of the chariots.

aureus ... iubar: *iubar* is usually neuter, though in the nominative singular only it can be masculine, as here (see Enn. *Ann.* 571 Skutsch, with his note; *Aetna* 333).

5. tempora cornipedes referunt, elementa colores: this is one of the most frequent topics of circus symbolism, that the four horses of the *quadriga* or the four colours of the circus factions mirror the seasons and / or the elements. It goes back as far as Tertullian's account (*De Spect.* 9): 'albus hiemi ob nives candidas, russeus aestati ob solis ruborem voti erant. Sed postea ... consecraverunt prasinum ... Terrae matri vel verno, venetum Caelo et Mari vel autumno'. Cf. Coripp. *Laud. Just.* 1.317 f. 'tempora continui signantes quattuor anni / in quorum speciem signis numerisque modisque / aurigas totidem, totidem posuere colores ...', with Cameron's note on 317; Isid. *Or.* 18. 41 'circa causas quoque elementorum idem gentiles etiam colores equorum iunxerunt, russeos enim soli, id est igni, albos aeri, prasinos terrae, venetos mari adsimilantes'; ibid. 18.36; Cass. *Var.* 3.51.5; John Malalas 7.5 (p. 135 Thurn); John Lydus *De Mens.* 4.30 (p. 89 Wünsch). The gods of the four seasons were also depicted in the visual arts as racing charioteers (see Hanfmann, *Season Sarcophagus*, 159 f.).

The symbolism occurs in other contexts, as at e.g. Mart. Cap. 2.189 f. and Drac. *Laud. Dei* 2.7 f., where Dracontius draws a parallel between the colours of the circus factions, the four horses of the Sun's chariot, and the four elements and seasons:

> non quia vectus equis est quattuor axe rotato
> sed quia praefectus sol quattuor est elementis,
> quattuor alternat sollers auriga colores;
> permutat iussus sol tempora quattuor anni.

The linking of the sun's four horses to the seasons is however symbolism which pre-dates circus racing (e.g. Eur. frag. 937 Nauck 2).

6. auriga, ut Phoebus: see 5 n. above for the equation of the four horses of a *quadriga* with the four horses of the sun's chariot. The sun usually

Commentary

drove a *quadriga* (Ovid *Met.* 2.153 f.; Tert. *De Spect.* 9; Hyg. *Fab.* 183; Fulg. *Myth.* 1.12), though Martial apparently puts him in a *biga* at 8.21.7 f.). See also 17 n. below.

aptat (Heinsius); aptet (B); urget (W); habet (A): all variant verbs give possible sense here, with Heinsius' necessary correction to indicative mood for B's subjunctive. But the opening eight lines of the poem deal with race preliminaries and offer general comments before the race has started (cf. the change at 'ast ubi panduntur ...' in line 9). Therefore 'aptat' should be read; it alludes to the attachment of the horses to the chariot (cf. *AL* 873.1R 'te cuperet Phoebus roseis aptare quadrigis').

7-16: cardinibus propriis ... sorte pari: this section moves away from the basic numerical parallels between the circus and the heavens to deal, not at all convincingly, with the way in which races are run at the circus, a description which introduces some more details of its layout. The general point is that as chariots are seen by spectators to circuit the race track, so are heavenly bodies seen by observers to circuit the sky, with the two long axes of the race track representing their rising and setting (it becomes evident that the poet refers principally to planets, because, as viewed from the earth, they are the bodies that change their positional relationship to each other in regular orbits of the heavens). But this gives him problems. These surface most apparently with the obelisk at the centre of the whole arena, because it is already laden with its own sun symbolism and ought to lend itself to allegorical treatment (see 14 n.). But when he mentions it the poet is in the middle of developing the allegory of the circuits of racing chariots being like the orbits of the planets. Since his universe is geocentric, and the sun is a planet, the obelisk cannot represent a central sun as it logically should: therefore an excellent allegorical opportunity has to be foregone, and all that can be made of the obelisk is a lame, unallegorical reference to its central siting. The next difficulty he has is the equation between racing chariots and planetary orbits, because chariots exist to overtake one another in a race to the end of a course, but that is the last thing required in the predictable and eternal motions of the planets. Therefore some loose wording is employed (line 10), which suits neither chariots nor planets but is a compromise between them; for the same reason the details about the start of a chariot race also seem disconnected from the allegory (7-8). Finally, if his allegory in this section were taken to its logical conclusion, he ought to be able to say that there are seven chariots in a race, the number of planets which orbit the heavens. But there are usually twelve chariots in a race (line 3); he therefore again fudges the issue by appending a couplet to the effect that there are seven laps in a race (15 f.). Corippus was sensible to treat this area in his similar allegory much more concisely (*Laud. Just.* 1.330-3).

Commentary

7. cardinibus (codd.); carceribus (Schrader): this is the only occasion on which *cardo* is used in connection with the *carceres*, and it probably refers *pars pro toto* to the doors of them (see also 'ostia' at line 3 above, with note). Although Schrader's conjecture 'carceribus' might seem attractive, the noun would be otiose with the ensuing 'saepta', which is synonymous with 'carceres'. There are detailed depictions in the visual arts of the *carceres*, showing the double-leafed doors which fronted them, the opening of which began the race (see Humphrey, *Circuses*, 138 f., with figs 60; 64). *Cardo* also has both astronomical (*OLD* cardo 3(a): 'either of the pivots or poles on which the universe was supposed to rotate about the earth') and astrological (ibid. 4(a): 'any of the four "cardinal" points, also the four corresponding points on the ecliptic') meanings; whilst there appears to be no intended or precise ambiguity here, it may be that such overtones influenced the poet's choice of word in the context.

8. Ianus vexillum ... levans: 'Janus' is not found in this race-starter's role elsewhere, and what or who he or it might be is obscure. The signal for the race to begin was usually given by the presiding magistrate, for example the consul or city praetor, who would raise and lower a *mappa* (similar to a handkerchief): cf. Enn. *Ann.* 79 Sk.; Varro *Ling. Lat.* 5.153; Ovid *Am.* 3.2.65 f.; Mart. 12.28(29).9 f.; Suet. *Nero* 22.2; Juv. 11.193; Tert. *De Spect.* 16; Cass. *Var.* 3.51.9. The starter usually occupied a box above the central entrance to the arena (though he may sometimes have been positioned above the *carceres*: see Enn. loc. cit.), as is evidenced by a mosaic from Piazza Armerina and a heavily restored relief in the Vatican (see Humphrey, *Circuses*, 146 figs 66; 67). On this line Humphrey comments 'There must be a connection here between the central entrance ('Janus, ianua') and the official located in the box directly above that entrance, while the *vexillum* may be simply a synonym for the *mappa* which was of course raised before it was dropped' (ibid., 136 f.). Courtney (*MH* 45.1988.57) suggests that the poet here had in mind representations in calendars for January which showed a consul holding aloft his *mappa* (see also 106.1 n.); and as with 'cardinibus' (line 7 n.), the poet's choice of the noun 'Ianus' may have been influenced by its easy association with the start of the year, and the astronomical and astrological significance that carries (the starter sets the chariots off on their circular courses, which represent the revolutions of heavenly bodies round the earth). However, it is difficult to believe that the person starting a race was generally known as 'Janus', and the term does not feature elsewhere. Perhaps there was some kind of mechanism or figure which in some way resembled Janus, and which served to indicate clearly to the whole arena (since some of those present might not have been able to view the starter himself) that the signal for the race to begin had been given; the 'vexillum' might thus suggest a flag larger than a 'mappa'.

Commentary

9. repagula: the doors of the starting pens were closed with 'repagula' (Ovid *Met.* 2.155; Sil. It. 16.317; Lucan 1.294 f.); the verb *reserare* is used of the removal of these bars and the opening of the doors (Ovid. *Am.* 3.2.77; *Ars* 3.595; Sil.It. 16.315 etc.). Ensuring that all the *repagula* were removed simultaneously for a fair start must have involved considerable mechanical ingenuity (see Humphrey, *Circuses*, 157 f.); the *carceres* were sometimes built on a slight curve for the same reason.

10. cogitur ire prius (codd.); cernitur ire prius (Watt); cogitat ire prius (Schrader): Schrader's emendation has generally been preferred to the mss text by editors, but SB reverts to the mss on the grounds that all or most of the chariots, not a single one, would have wanted to be first and win the race; yet 'cogitur' is open to almost the same objection, because it implies an unwillingness of chariots to lead the race (and it might have intruded from the similar 'cogitur ire ferus' at 186.6). Nevertheless, the mss text is probably correct, because the poet needs to mask an unsoundness in his allegory of racing chariots as planets (see 7-16 n. above): he has to equate a chariot race which has no fixed outcome with the orderly orbits of the planets, which, although they appear to move around relative to each other when seen from the earth, clearly cannot be alleged to race against each other as chariots do. So he fudges the issue by saying that both a chariot and a planet have got to be at the front of their respective packs (at any given time). If emendation is nevertheless thought desirable, Schrader's conjecture is no improvement on the mss; Watt's 'cernitur' (*HSCPh* 101.2003.453) is preferable.

11. metarum ... cursibus: the *metae*, of which there were two, were the turning points of the race track situated at the ends of the central spina; they usually consisted of a high platform surmounted by three vertical cones (Humphrey, *Circuses*, 255 f., with figs 80-1). Here they stand allegorically for the east and west of the heavens, since in the following line the 'axes gemini' of the track represent 'rising' and 'setting': cf. Cass. *Var.* 3.51.8 'Eoae Orientis et Occidentis terminos designant'; Isid. *Or.* 18.30; John Malalas 7.4.

circumdare ... orbes: 'to go round in orbit', as the planets (were thought to) go round the earth.

12. axes gemini: on the race track these 'axes' are the course taken by the chariots on either side of the spina, turning at the *metae*; the laps run by the chariots resemble the rising and setting of the heavenly bodies as viewed from earth.

docent: '*i.e. significant*', as Riese says (app. crit.): cf. Ovid *Ars* 3.643 'nomine cum doceat, quid agamus, adultera clavis', with *TLL* 5.1.1714.69 f.

Commentary

13. atque (de Saumaise); namque (codd.); iamque (Pithou): mss 'namque' has intruded from the preceding line; Pithou's conjecture is palaeographically close and preferred by most editors, but it is less convincing than de Saumaise's conjecture of the simple connective 'atque'.

his ... aequor: 'his' refers to the 'axes gemini' of the preceding line, and the point is simply that the euripus (or spina), like the ocean, lies between the rising and setting sun and other heavenly bodies (thus, essentially, Courtney, *MH* 45.1988.57).

euripus: geographically the Euripus was the strait which separates Euboea from Boeotia (cf. Cic. *De Nat. Deor.* 3.24), but the noun was then applied to artificial channels like canals and aqueducts (as at e.g. Sen. *Ep.* 55.6; Petr. 36.3) and specifically to a section of the Aqua Virgo (Ovid *Pont.* 1.8.38; Sen. *Ep.* 83.5). It was also the word in general use for reference to the spina in circus arenas (as at e.g. Tert. *De Spect.* 8; Sid. *Carm.* 23.360; Cass. *Var.* 3.51.8; *AL* 3.6R, with *TLL* 5.2.1078.6 f.); only Cassiodorus (*Var.* 3.51.8) uses the term 'spina'. It must have acquired this specific reference to circus architecture from the idea of something separating two stretches of land (equivalent to the two axes of the track); it often housed a large number of water basins and other features for decorative purposes, and these would have contributed to the aptness of its marine name (cf. *SHA* Heliog. 23.1; Cass. *Var.* 3.51.8; Humphrey, *Circuses*, 275 f.). In the allegorical interpretation of the circus layout the equation of the euripus / spina with the ocean is therefore easy (as also at Cass. *Var.* 3.51.8; John Malalas 7.4).

14. et medius centri summus obliscus adest (Riese; adit (codd.)); et medium centri summus obliscus obit (Shackleton Bailey); *alii alia*: the obelisk which was a standard feature of the spina is often said to represent the sun at its zenith in the allegorical interpretations, since it is the highest point of the racing arena and situated at its very centre: cf. Isid. *Or.* 18.31.2 'medio autem spatio ab utraque meta constitutus oboliscus fastigium summitatemque caeli significat, quum sol ab utroque spatio medio horarum discrimine transcendit'; Cass. *Var.* 3.51.8; and Tert. *De Spect.* 8. Its connection with the sun goes further. Augustus had been the first to set up an obelisk in a circus arena, namely the Circus Maximus, and he set a fashion with other examples being known at e.g. Tyre, Caesarea, Antioch, Arles, Vienne and Constantinople. His obelisk was nearly 25 m. high and weighed 400 tons (it now resides in the Piazza del Popolo); it was dedicated to the sun (*CIL* 6.701), and the subsequent association of such obelisks with the sun became commonplace (e.g. Cass. *Var.* 3.51.8; Isid. *Or.* 18.31.2 'summo obolisco superpositum est quoddam auratum in modum flammae formatum'; Tert. *De Spect.* 8; and see further Humphrey, *Circuses*, 269 f.; 661 n. 217). It is however notable that the poet here attempts no explicit allegory, and indeed avoids any reference

Commentary

to the sun; he states a simple fact about the location of an object (on the reason for this see 7-16 n. above).

As for the text of this line, mss 'medius centri' with 'summus' gives an accurate description of the topmost point of the obelisk, which was positioned on the middle of the spina, itself the middle of the track, so no emendation there appears necessary. But mss 'adit' makes no sense, and Riese's 'adest' is the simplest emendation.

For the syncopated form of the noun 'obliscus' compare 'tablistis' at 187.7, with note.

15. septem ... gyris (guiris (AB); giris (W); gyri (Riese)): seven laps was the usual duration of a chariot race (see my note on Aus. *Epig.* 7.2); on the orthography of *gyrus* see 92.5 n. Riese's conjecture 'gyri' is worth consideration, but 'claudere' can have an absolute sense ('come to an end') like *concludere*: e.g. Sen. *Suas.* 2.16 'Potamon ... sic novissime clausit'; *TLL* 3.1309.77 f.; L. Feltenius, *Intransitivizations in Latin*, Uppsala 1977, 77 f.

16. quot (W; quod (AB)) caelum stringunt cingula: the reference is to the orbits of the seven planets (Saturn, Jupiter, Mars, Mercury, Venus, Sun and Moon) around the earth, though *cingulum* does not seem to be used with this sense elsewhere. For the thought cf. Isid. *Or.* 18.37 'septem spatia quadrigae currunt referentes hoc ad cursum septem stellarum, quibus mundum regi dicunt, sive ad cursum septem dierum praesentium'; Cassiodorus opts for the parallel with the seven days of the week (*Var.* 3.51.7), and Malalas for the courses of the seven stars of Ursa Major (7.4).

17. Lunae biga: whilst the racing of two-horse chariots is not as well attested as that of four-horse ones, the economies of cost and scale it offered, as well as the variety it afforded, suggest it could have been frequently staged. There are some tantalising bits of evidence: for instance a charioteer's epitaph from Spain (*CIL* 2.4314) says that he was only qualified to race *bigae*, not *quadrigae*; at a track in Spain, Santiago do Cacém, the *carceres* are so narrow it is unlikely anything larger than *bigae* could have been accommodated; and various mosaics show *bigae* races (see Humphrey, *Circuses*, 378; 422 etc.). For the linking of the *biga* with the moon, and the *quadriga* with the sun, a common topic in the cosmological circus treatments and elsewhere, cf. Tert. *De Spect.* 9 'seiugas vero Iovi, quadrigas Soli, bigas Lunae sanxerunt'; Cass. *Var.* 3.51.6; Isid. *Or.* 18.36; Coripp. *Laud. Just.* 1.315 f.; and Sen. *Agam.* 818 with Tarrant's note for non-circus references.

Solique quadriga: see above and 5n.; 6n.

18. Castoribus simpli ... equi: H.A. Harris (*Sport in Greece and Rome*,

Commentary

London 1972, 179) comments that ridden-horse racing aroused far less interest in the ancient world than chariot racing 'and was omitted by the Romans altogether from their programme'. That, on the grounds of probability if nothing else, may be too sweeping a statement, and ridden-horse racing is attested in the Greek tradition up to the third century AD (evidence, largely inscriptional, can be found in J. Ebert, 'Griechische Epigramme auf Sieger an gymnischen und hippischen Agonen', *Abh. der sächs. Akad. der Wiss. Leipzig* 63.2.1972 nos 5-7; 17; 49; 80 etc.). As regards the present reference Isidore in his treatment of circuses and horses, after mentioning that *bigae* are dedicated to the moon and so forth, says 'desultores Lucifero et Hespero sacraverunt' (*Or.* 18.36.1); this is helpfully amplified at Cass. *Var.* 3.51.6 'biga quasi Lunae, quadriga Solis imitatione reperta est. Equi desultorii, per quos circensium ministri missus denuntiant exituros, Luciferi praecursorias velocitates imitantur' (i.e. *equi desultorii* or *desultores*, which I take to be equivalent to the 'simpli equi' of this epigram, did not race in the circus, but were an entertainment beforehand, precursors of the chariots, and a signal that a race would shortly begin). It may therefore be that ridden-horses were a usual feature in chariot race meetings, but their function was more entertainment and ceremonial than racing (see further *RE* 5.255 f.).

For Castor and Pollux together referred to as 'Castores' cf. Serv. ap. Verg. *Georg.* 3.89 'certe ideo Pollucem pro Castore posuit, quia ambo licenter et Polluces et Castores vocantur; nam et ludi et templum et stellae Castorum nominantur'; the earliest such usage seems to be Plin. *Nat. Hist.* 1.2.37 'de stellis quae Castores vocantur'; cf. Tert. *De Spect.* 8; with *TLL* Onom. C. 244.55 f. and Nisbet-Rudd on Hor. *Carm.* 3.29.63-4. For this so-termed 'elliptical plural', cf. also 'Quirinos' (Romulus and Remus) at Juv. 11.105 (with Courtney's note), and Löfstedt, *Syntactica*, 1.67 f. The dedication of horses to the Dioscuri, horsemen par excellence, is self-explanatory.

simpli: *simplus* is strictly a proportional numeral, like *duplus*, *triplus*, *quadruplus* etc, its usual reference being to finance (*simplum*, 'the sum itself', 'the principal'). The extension of meaning here, stressing singularity (= 'singuli'), is easy enough in the series *biga, quadriga* etc.; compare Prud. *Peristeph.* 10.878 f. 'ne morte simpla criminosus multiplex / cadat vel una perfidus caede oppetat: / quot membra gestat, tot modis pereat volo'.

19-20. divinis ... honore deum: the concluding *sententia* sums up the allegory of the whole poem: the demonstration that the circus and its races symbolise and reflect the workings of heaven, the planets, and time, and specifically honour deities such as the Sun, the Moon and the Dioscuri, proves that they are based on 'res divinae' and have gained a high reputation through proper respect of the divine ('honore deum').

Index of Names and Places

Achilles, 172, 285 f., 313
Acis, 262 f.
Aegyptius, 326, 328
Aethiops, 325, 326
Alpheus, 134 f.
Amphion, 150
Aprilis, 165
Arethusa (fountain of), 131, 134 f.
Arzuges, 212
Atalanta, 222
Augustus, 168

Bacchus (human), 195
Bacchus, 336 f.
Baiae, 130, 186, 188
Barbatus, 273
Belisarius, 8, 94
Bellator, 132
Bellerophon, 86 f.
Briseis/Briseida, 225 f.
Bromius (human), 197
Bumbulus, 342 f., 346 f.

Caballina, 207 f.
Carthage, 5 f., 7 f., 94 f., 132
Castores, 375
Chalybes, 153
Chimaira, 86 f., 88 f.
Chintila, 69
Cinyps, 164
Cressida, 226
Cumae, 185, 188
Cypris (human), 196
Cyrila, 9

Daedalus, 145
Daphne, 299 f.
Dione, 165
Dioscuri, 242 f.
Discordia, 225

Epeos, 312

Euripus, 373
Europa, 243

Februus, 163 f.
Filager, 249
Filocalus, 177 f.
Filocalus, Furius Dionysius, 159, 179, 184
Fortuna, 181

Galatea, 262 f., 265 f.
Garamantes, 326
Genitor, 240
Graeculus, 197

Hadrumetum, 331
Hector, 285 f.
Hecuba, 113 f.
Hesperides, 224
Hippomenes, 296
Hyacinthus, 291

Ianus, 162, 371
Iason, 103
Ithacus, 113
Iulius Caesar, 168
Iulius, 168
Iunius, 167
Iuventa, 167

Laocoon / Laucon, 90 f.
Leda, 239 f., 241 f.
Lenaeus, 337
Liber, 339
Libra, 169
Luna, 374

Maius, 165 f.
Manlius, M., 117
Marsyas / Marsya, 301 f., 303
Martius, 205
Matius, Cn., 221

Index of Names and Places

Medea, 100 f.
Melania, 177 f.
Memnon, 340
Mucius Scaevola, 271, 354, 357

Narcissus, 246 f.

Oedipus/Idippus, 321
Orcus, 112
Orpheus, 150

Palamedes, 357
Parca, 279
Paris, 222, 288 f.
Pasiphae, 216, 254
Philoctetes, 304 f.
Pierus, 66 f.
Polyxena, 313
Pyrrhus, 313

Quintilis, 167

Salautensis, 275
Scyros, 333 f.
Solomon, 76 f.
Sphinx, 319 f.

Telephus, 332
Tethys, 135
Thermae Alianae, 129 f.
Thetis, 172
Timomachus Byz., 101 f.
Titan (=Phoebus), 189
Troia, 287

Vandal kings, 6, 7 f.
Varitinna, 273 f.
Venus (and Mars), 206
Venus (temple of), 94 f., 152
Vita (person), 316
Vita (place), 255

Index of Authors and Works

Aegritudo Perdicae, 10
AL poets, 9

Cassius Felix, 10, 280 f.
Cato (Vandal poet), 9
Catullus, 13, 282
Christian Latin writers, Vandal, 10 f. post-Vandal, 11 f.
Corippus, 11, 365 f.
Coronatus, 9

Damasus, 82
Dracontius, 7, 10, 103 (*Orest.* 431), 105 (*Rom.* 10.530 f.), 363 (*Laud. Dei* 1.580)

Ennius, 13, 287 (*op. incert.* vi Sk.)
Ennodius, 98

Felix, Flavius, 6, 9, 129 f. (*AL* 201), 173 (*AL* 201 f.)
Fulgentius, 10

Hilasius, 278 f.
Hildebert of Lavardin, 284
Hippocrates, 281 f.
Homer, 88
Horace, 13, 150 (*Carm.* 1.12.11 f.), 212 f. (*Carm.* 1.1.1)

Juvenal, 13, 125 (6.O.29 f.), 317 (1.79), 324 (1.140 f.), 344 (13.167 f.)

Lucretius, 13, 88 (5.904 f.), 163 (2.40 f.)
Luxorius, 2, 6, 9, 65 f. (*AL* 282-5), 73, 211 (*AL* 311), 230 (*AL* 322), 322 (*AL* 370), 325 (*AL* 288)

Martial, 13, 65 f., 67, 79, 120 (7.25), 200 (3.24.14), 220 (13.37), 251 (1.90.8)
Martianus Capella, 10 f.
Mico of St. Riquier, 323

Ovid, 13, 113 f. (*Met.* 13.489 f.), 218, 246 (*Met.* 3.339 f.)

Palladas, 193
Paulinus of Nola, 70 f., 76 f., 81

Reposianus, 10

Seneca, 13, 290 (*Agam.* 920 f.; *Tro.* 204 f.)
Sofocles (Vandal poet), 323

Theodorus Priscianus, 280 f.

Vatican Mythographers, 243
Vergil, 12 f., 83 (*Georg.* 4.197 f.), 89 (*Aen.* 3.426 f.), 90 (*Aen.* 2.203 f.), 93 (*Aen.* 1.8 f.), 96 (*Aen.* 4.88 f.), 104 (*Aen.* 5.783), 109 (*Aen.* 4.401 f.), 113 (*Aen.* 2.362), 116 (*Aen.* 8.655 f.), 134 (*Aen.* 3.694 f.), 150 (*Aen.* 6.542 f.), 165 (*Aen.* 3.19); 167 (*Ecl.* 6.22), 215 (*Georg.* 4.145), 252 (*Aen.* 8.387 f.), 277 f., 295 (*Georg.* 2.126 f.), 297 (*Georg.* 2.131), 298 (*Georg.* 2.134 f.), 305 (*Aen.* 6.848), 306 (*Aen.* 2.354), 330 (*Aen.* 1.327 f.), 337 (*Georg.* 3.509 f.), 338 (*Georg.* 2.380)
Victor of Vita, 9, 10

Wandalbert of Prüm, 157, 168

Index of Latin Words

actor, 184
addictus + dat., 235
adductor, 198, 202
admissarius, 256
adorare, 138
adstruere, 145
adulter, 216
aerius, 302
alterna (adv.), 154
alumnus, 243 f.
alveolus, 354
antrum, 185
arbos, 297
arbutus, 213
argenteus, 116
arma (agric.), 162
articulus, 122
artus, 303
ascea, 214
astra (of zodiac), 368
athla, 255
atramentare, 331 f.
auctor, 183, 347
aureus, 98
auritus, 150

bacchigena, 162
baiae, 130 f.
barbula, 275
barrus, 361
basterna, 97, 98
biga, 374
boletar, 268
buda, 83
burdo, 100
buxeus, 154

caballa, 253
caballus, 91
camera, 133
campus (of execution), 235
candens, 108

canticum, 139
cantor, 139 f.
caper, 200
captare, 307
carcer, 368, 372
cardo, 371
cassare, 339
castrator, 128
catadromus, 142, 143
cattus, 322
cauculo/calculo, 84
cauculus/calculus, 353
caulae, 257
causidicus, 249
cautus, 125 f.
cavea, 110
cereus, 79
chalybs, 153
cicindelum, 335 f.
cingulum, 374
citare, 211
citrum/-us, 295 f., 298
classis, 153
claudere, 98
clunis, 127
cognatum numen, 196
collis et ima, 358
comitiacus, 201
condens, 182 f.
confirmare, 172
congruus, 267
congustus, 316
conubium, 289
conventus, 343
cor (=mens), 67 f., 214
cornipes, 250
cornutus, 360
cortex, 298
cottidianus, 204
crotalum, 165
cupedia, 308
cycnus, 241

381

Index of Latin Words

dare + double acc., 123
declinare, 137 f.
deliciae, 185
dicare, 166, 194 f.
dicere quod, 334 f.
diffundere, 241, 267
dis- (prefix), 241
discolor, 353
discruciare, 324 f.
dispendium, 252
distinguere, 219 f.
distractor, 286
docta manus, 305
dogma, 281
domare, 260
dona (of Nature), 164, 214
ducere (= facere), 312
ducere nomen, 205
duellum, 164
dulcis (of water), 135
dulcisonus, 116
duodenigenas, 368
dux, 346

edomare, 361
edurus, 215
elementa ('creation'), 264
ephebus, 75
-erna (suffix), 98
esca, 121
esitiatus/-um, 309 f.
esse (ellipse of), 117, 132, 140
euripus, 373
excipere, 362 f.
excussus, 209
extare, 125, 131

fabrica, 313
fabula, 145, 206 f.
facere (= sufficere), 121
facere + inf., 140 f.
factum, 112 f.
faex, 328 f.
famulare, 251
fax, 89
fel, 120
fides, 261
fiscus, 203, 232
flabellum, 169
flagrans/fraglans, 247
flamma, 254

fluenta, 176
fremere, 209
fricare, 250, 346
fundus, 182
furere, 209
furtum, 246
fututor, 253

gamba, 257 f.
geminus, 99
-genus/-a (suffix), 162, 368
gignere, 242
gillo, 227 f.
gravidus, 312
gryllus, 230
gurges, 135, 175
gyrus, 107, 374

hebes, 253 f.
heniochus, 345
hic ... ubi, 130, 195 f.
hospes, 182

iam (metrical padding), 93, 112
ignis, 246
imbrigenus, 229
immaculatus, 74
impius, 150
-ina (suffix), 208
incepto (adv.), 282
infamis, 274
inflammare, 267
insons, 73
intrare, 347 f.
isiciatus, see esitiatus
iucundus, 200
iustus, 74
iuventa (= iuvenis), 143

labor, 288
labrum, 324
lacerare, 92
lacteus, 164, 270
laeta (of goddesses), 196
laguna, 231
larva, 330 f.
lascivare, 312
latrare, 115
latus, 99
lea/leo, 320
lector, 67

Index of Latin Words

legeris (pf. subj.), 327
lenare, 198
leno maritus, 197
lentus, 79
levare, 105 f.
lex (of poetry), 214
libidinare, 257
libido, 267 f.
linea, 259 f.
linguatus, 149
litterulae, 85
loci urbani, 318
lucubrare, 249
ludere, 214, 215 f., 261
ludi magister, 86
lumina tendere, 269
luxus, 256
lympha, 269 f.

machina, 239
magis + adv., 192
magis an, 128
magister (mahout), 361
malum Matianum, 220
malum, 290
malus (tree), 295
massa, 270
meare + acc., 369
meatus, 256
medella, 297
medium (subst.), 298
melo, 169
mensuum (gen. pl.), 161
mentiri + acc., 245
merx (= lucrum), 127
meta, 372
metere, 104
micare, 210, 295
militiae utriusque comes, 204
mille, 333, 340
minae, 96
miraculum, 95, 135
moles, 131, 233
monstrifer, 256
mors pretiosa, 363
morum, 167
moveri, 127
multifidus, 148
mulus (of humans), 211
munus, 108
mutare, 133, 362

nam, 192
nigellus, 111
nivescere, 229
nocte silente, 117
non (postponed), 340
numerus, 367 f.
nunc, 112
nymphigena, 314

-o/-onis (suffix), 84
obliscus, 373
olor, 241
orbis, 239
organum, 155
ostium, 368

pactio, 314
paludigenus, 79
pannus, 201 f.
parvula aetas, 66
pastus, 203
patina, 266 f.
pecus/-oris (single animal), 254
pellere (= impellere), 290
pennifer, 310
phasianus, 217 f.
pica, 323
pictura, 300
pietas, 78
pignus, 78, 103, 289
pistor, 108
pius, 82
pluteus, 236 f., 277 f.
poena, 306, 324
pomum, 296
pontivagus, 185
populus (military), 203
posse, 221
postumus, 288
potius, 121
praedo, 244
praefulgere (third conj.), 218
praesul, 182
premere, 105
pretium, 222
procax, 198
prodere, 304 f.
prolixus, 281
proprius, 198
prurire, 206
pubes, 124

383

Index of Latin Words

pygmaeus, 343 f.
pyrgus, 354
pyrrhica, 152

quadra, 108
quidem, 172

rames/-ex, 233
rastrum, 95
re- (prefix), 71 f.
regna caelestia, 74
relaxare, 176
remeare, 293
repagulum, 372
reparator, 150
rigor, 277 f.
rogare + subj., 256
rostrum, 360

sacer, 151, 239, 255
saeptum, 100
saginare, 311
sal Pierius, 66
salus, 319
sceptrum, 363
scriptum, 353
scrutare/-ari, 248
se (reciprocal), 153, 154, 358
sellifer, 281
sentum (= senticetum), 166
sepia, 119
servare (= observare), 300
sessor, 252
sexus, 127, 138
similis, 260 f.
simplus, 375
simul (reciprocal), 353
simulacra duelli, 163
sinus, 245
soccus, 274
sollers, 111
sorex, 323
sors externa, 333
spina, 373
stamen, 146
sternere, 276
strepitus, 116
struere, 216
stuppeus, 142
subare, 257

subducere, 279
summus (= ultimus), 185
super- (prefix), 143
superaerius, 143
sus (= aper), 285
suspirare + acc., 248
syringa, 234

tabella, 259
tablista, 364
tabula/tabla, 348 f., 352 f.
talio, 338
talus (= tessera), 356
techna, 313
tectus (weapons), 153
templum, 82, 195
tener, 124
tenso pede, 203
tepidus, 307
testis, 126
thermae, 192
titillare, 251
titulus, 70 f., 327 f.
-tor/-toris (suffix), 84
truncus, 213
turdus (= cunnus), 253

unusquisque, 298 f.
urbani loci, 318

vaporus, 190
varius, 319
vectrix, 256
vel (= et), 216
velum, 69 f.
venire (= esse), 363
venter solutus, 309
venus, 204, 206, 251, 276
verna, 329
verum, 140, 261
vexillum, 371
vibrare, 210
vicus, 114
vidua, 103
vindicta, 339
vir (= is), 246 f.
vires, 124
vispillo, 235
voluptas, 126

General Index

acrostichs, 117 f., 180 f., 183
adjectives: black/white juxtaposed, 119, 326, 362
   diminutives of, 111
adverb: compar. for superl., 121
advertising, 97, 119, 179, 220 f., 294
alliteration, 73, 102 f., 123, 153, 198, 322, 327, 332
animals and epigram, 109
animals as familiars, 112
ants: proverbial qualities, 109 f.
apples/apples in myth, 220 f., 223 f. 224 f.
armillary sphere, 237 f.
'art restoring life', 279

backgammon, 348 f.
baths, 129 f., 173, 177 f., 315
   circulation of people through, 191
   decoration in, 174
   euergetism and, 132 f., 180
   health from, 319
   heating of, 187
   hot springs, 174, 185, 187 f
   inscriptional epigrams in, 4, 129, 174, 179
   land for: see under 'land'
   lighting in, 188
   'more urbico' claim, 318
   nudity, 189
   paintings in, 174
   relaxation from, 176, 182
   solar power, 187, 190
   spas, 174, 185
   steam and, 190 f., 307
   water supply of, 131, 188, 191, 192, 306 f.
beard-pulling, 275
beauty, indicators of, 218
bees, Christian symbolism and, 83 f.
Bellerophon Christianus, 87
bestiality, 248 f., 255 f.

black people, 325, 328, 340
black people, demons portrayed as, 330 f.
black people/black as ill-omened, 112, 328 f., 341
board games, 348 f.
burglars, 117

calendar, 168
Calendar of 354, 160 f.
candles, 79 f., 80 f.
   Christian symbolism and, 80 f.
   religious uses of, 80 f.
caricatures, 230
celestial globe, 237 f.
chariot-racing, 365 f.
Christian iconography, 330 f.
church fabrics, 69 f.
circus, 345, 365 f.
   allegory of, 365 f.
   circus factions, 347
   layout of, 367 f.
citharodes, 146 f. 148 f.
citrons, 294 f.
cockerel, 217 f.
collection, this:
   architecture of, 3
   author of, 7
   Christianity and, 4
   date of composition of, 5 f., 94 f., 177 f., 185
   external knowledge of, 97 f., 157
   genres used in, 2 f.
   length of, 2
   literary influences on, 6 f., 12 f.
   metres used in, 22
   pairs/groupings/cycles of epigrams in, 3, 68, 110, 146, 173, 233, 269
   place of composition of, 5 f., 94 f., 132, 177 f., 181
   subject matter of epigrams in, 2
   see also 'separation' and

'superscriptions'
concluding sententiae, 92 f., 272, 317, 348, 364
consuls, 161
consuls' sceptres, 363
convivium, 275 f.
cooling of drinks, 227 f.
cuttlefish, 118 f.

death of animals, 322
death, picaresque, 322
demons/devils, 330 f.
doctors, training of, 280 f.
'double benefit', 117, 120, 176, 316
dwarfs, 342

ecphrastic epigrams (describing works of art), 101, 156 f., 171 f., 236, 240, 243, 262 f., 265 f., 270, 291, 299 f.
elements, 264
elephants, 360 f.
enjambement, 67
entrapment rackets, 198, 199
environment and land use, 132
epic phraseology used obscenely, 245, 252
epigrams: see 'collection'
epitaphs, Christian, 72 f.
  pagan themes in Christian, 72 f., 75 f.
equinox, 169
Ethiopians, 325 f.
eunuchs, 122 f., 126 f.
everyday objects, 2 f., 97

false ancestry, 272
familiars of gods etc., 112
Floralia, 85
funambulism, 141 f.

gambling, 171, 357
geese, 115 f.
gender, play on, 128, 137, 205
geocentric universe, 370, 372, 373
goats and Bacchus, 336 f.
goatskins for wine, 337
Greek and medicine, 280 f.
Greeks, 197, 345
guards, faithful, 125 f.

hapax legomena, 162, 185, 229, 310, 314, 368
hernia, 229 f.
historiola, 283 f.
homosexuality, 205
  effeminate gait and, 127
horses, colour of, 209
  men likened to, 256
  women likened to, 207 f.
hyacinth, 292

icons, 259
incomplete epigrams, 285 f.
ink, 120
inscriptional/epigraphic poems, 4, 68 f., 179
  see also under 'baths'
ivory, 358, 363 f.

judgement of Paris, 288 f.
judgement of Solomon, 76 f.

lamps, 335
land, proper use of, 132, 315
lawyers, 249
lex talionis, 338
libraries, 193 f.
'love conquers all', 264
ludus duodecim scriptorum, 350
lyres, 148 f.

man beaten by wife, 272 f.
manuscript illumination, 277
manuscripts, 13 f.
  Codex Salmasianus, 1, 2, 13 f., 16 f., 176
  Codex Thuaneus, 14 f.
  Schedae Divionenses, 14
  sigla in commentary, 13 f.
marble, types of, 299 f., 302 f.
martyr cults, 82
medical language and terminology, 231 f., 234 f., 280 f.
medicine, 280 f.
metamorphosis, 94 (Hecuba), 240 (Jupiter), 291 f. (Hyacinth), 300 (Daphne)
metre, 22 f.
military life, 201 f.
milling as punishment, 106 f.
mills, grain mill, 106
  olive mill, 171

General Index

misers, 106
mock-modest pose of epigrammatist, 65 f.
months in art and literature, 158 f.

names, humour with and plays on, 181, 194-7, 205, 207 f., 270, 275, 282, 316, 342 f.
  see also 'nicknames'
nature, improved by man, 133 f., 317, 362
nicknames/sobriquets, 194, 196, 205, 206, 326
nouns, dative of (dis)advantage, 189, 203, 279
  elliptical plural, 375
  gender of animal nouns, 119
  generic plural, 222
  imprecision with synonyms, 75
  Latin nom. formed from Greek acc. sing., 226, 234, 320, 329
  plural for singular, 315
  voc. + nom. in address, 343

obscenity, 65, 252 f.
organ, 155

painting, see 'portraits', 'underdrawing', 'verisimilitude'
pantomime, 136 f.
papyrus wicks, 80, 82
paradox, 145, 205, 239, 247, 327
performing arts, epigrams on, 151 f.
personification of city, 287 f.
  of hand, 272
  of months, 159 f.
  of seasons, 156 f.
pheasants, 217
pimps, 197, 201
poets, lampoon of bad, 211 f.
portraits, 258 f., 277
prefatory poems, 1, 65 f.
prolepsis, 252, 304
prosody, 22 f.
prostitution, 196, 197, 201, 208, 345
punning/annominatio/wordplay, 86, 98, 99, 121 f., 126, 134, 138, 149, 150, 250, 251, 277, 282, 286, 290, 295, 315, 337, 339 etc.
pygmies and cranes, 343 f.

quotations used in epigrams, 200

racism, 325, 341
repetition of words, 89, 103, 205, 334
reversal of fortune, 114
rhyming words, 355
Rome (Capitol), 118
ropes, 142

seasons in art and literature, 155 f.
sententiae, see 'concluding sententiae'
separation of epigrams, 19, 288, 292 f., 307, 348
silver plate, 265 f.
souls travel to stars, 75
statues, 299 f., 301 f., 304 f.
stuffed food, 307
stupidity, comparators for, 213 f.
superscriptions, 18 f., 193
sympathetic magic, 334, 335
symposium, 275 f.
syringes, 234

Tablettes Albertini, 9
tableware, decorated silver, 265 f.
tabula/tabla, 348 f.
taverns, 193 f.
taxation, 232
teachers, 84
telestichs, see 'acrostichs'
Three Chapters dispute, 11 f.
tituli, 70 f., 76 f., 327

underdrawing, 260

Vandal Africa, 6, 7 f., 12 f.
Vandals, Christianity and, 9, 72
  coinage, 8
  culture, 8 f.
  external relations, 8
  Greek and, 12
  Latin and, 9, 11 f.
  literature, 9 f.
  pottery, 228, 232
  Romanophilia, 8 f.
  taxation, 232
verbs, conjugations varied, 218, 312
  inscriptional use of pf. subj., 327
  mixing of tenses, 67, 120, 214, 222, 241
  participial resumption, 334

simplex for compound, 290
Vergil, images of in art, 277 f.
verisimilitude in art, 260 f.

weapon dances, 152 f.
weapons of wood, 154
wineskins, 337